**Solutions Manual**

# Financial Accounting
## An Introduction to Concepts, Methods, and Uses
### Tenth Edition

## Clyde P. Stickney

Dartmouth College

## Roman L. Weil

University of Chicago

THOMSON
SOUTH-WESTERN

Australia · Canada · Mexico · Singapore · Spain · United Kingdom · United States

W9-BOO-306

THOMSON
─────✦─────
SOUTH-WESTERN

Solutions Manual for

**Financial Accounting: An Introduction to Concepts, Methods, and Uses, 10e**

Clyde P. Stickney, Roman L. Weil

**Editor-in-Chief:**
Jack W. Calhoun

**Team Leader:**
Melissa S. Acuña

**Acquisitions Editor:**
Julie Lindsay

**Developmental Editor:**
Craig Avery

**Marketing Manager:**
Keith Chasse

**Production Editor:**
Heather Mann, Sam Versetto

**Manufacturing Coordinator:**
Doug Wilke

**Printer:**
Globus Printing, Inc.
Minster, OH

**Cover Design:**
Rik Moore

COPYRIGHT © 2003
by South-Western, a division of
Thomson Learning. Thomson
Learning™ is a trademark used herein
under license.

Printed in the United States of America
  2  3  4  5    05  04  03

For more information
contact South-Western,
5191 Natorp Boulevard,
Mason, Ohio 45040.
Or you can visit our Internet site at:
http://www.swcollege.com

ALL RIGHTS RESERVED.
No part of this work covered by the
copyright hereon may be reproduced or
used in any form or by any means—
graphic, electronic, or mechanical,
including photocopying, recording,
taping, Web distribution or information
storage and retrieval systems—without
the written permission of the publisher.

For permission to use material from this
text or product, contact us by
Tel (800) 730-2214
Fax (800) 730-2215
http://www.thomsonrights.com

ISBN: 0-324-18486-7

# CONTENTS

# PREFACE

This book presents answers and solutions for the questions, exercises, problems and cases contained in each chapter of the textbook *Financial Accounting:   An Introduction to Concepts, Methods and Uses* Tenth Edition.

If you have any suggestions as to how this book might be improved in subsequent editions, please feel free to bring them to our attention.


C.P.S.

R.L.W.

# CHAPTER 1

## INTRODUCTION TO BUSINESS ACTIVITIES AND OVERVIEW OF FINANCIAL STATEMENTS AND THE REPORTING PROCESS

*Questions, Exercises, Problems, and Cases: Answers and Solutions*

1.1     The first question at the end of each chapter requires the student to review the important concepts or terms discussed in the chapter. In addition to the definitions or descriptions in the chapter, a glossary appears at the end of the book.

1.2     *Setting Goals and Strategies*: A charitable organization would not pursue profit or increasing wealth as goals. Instead, it would direct its efforts at providing some type of service to particular constituencies.

*Financing*: Charitable organizations generally obtain the majority of their financing from contributions, although they may engage in borrowing in some situations. Charitable organizations do not issue common stock or other forms of owners' equity. Because they do not operate for a profit, charitable organizations do not have retained earnings.

*Investing*: Charitable organizations may acquire supplies, buildings, equipment and other assets to carry out their charitable activities.

*Operations*: A charitable organization might prepare a financial statement each period that compares contributions received with operating expenses. Although such a financial statement might resemble an income statement, the organization would probably not label the difference between contributions received and operating expenses as net income or net loss.

1.3     A balance sheet reports the assets, liabilities, and shareholders' equity of a firm at a moment in time (similar to a snapshot), whereas the income statement and statement of cash flows report amounts for a period of time (similar to a motion picture).

1.4     Revenues measure the increase in net assets (assets minus liabilities) and expenses measure the decrease in net assets from selling goods and providing services. An asset such as inventory generally appears on the balance sheet at acquisition cost while it is held. Thus, the asset valuation remains the same and the firm recognizes no revenue. When the firm sells the inventory, the inventory item leaves the firm and cash or a receivable from a customer comes in. If more assets flow in than flow out, total assets increase and the firm recognizes income (revenue minus expense).

1.5     As Chapter 3 makes clear, firms do not necessarily recognize revenues when they receive cash or recognize expenses when they disburse cash. Thus, net income will not necessarily equal cash flow from operations each period. Furthermore, firms disburse cash to acquire property, plant and equipment, repay debt, and pay dividends. Thus, net income and cash flows usually differ. A profitable firm will likely borrow funds in order to remain in business, but eventually operations must generate cash to repay the borrowing.

1.6     No. The unqualified opinion of the CPA indicates that the presentation is a fair reflection of the financial position and operating results of the firm. Because the accountant bases this opinion on an audit of only a portion of the transactions occurring during the year, the CPA does not vouch for the absolute accuracy of every item in the financial statements. The unqualified opinion has evolved to mean, however, that the firm has made sufficient disclosures in the statements so they are not misleading. This interpretation of the unqualified opinion suggests that the statements are free of gross misrepresentations. In court suits against the independent accountants, where courts have found gross misrepresentation to exist, the principal issue is whether the CPA had reasonable grounds (based on audit tests) to believe that the statements were fairly presented at the time the accountant issued the unqualified opinion.

1.7     A wide range of individuals and entities (creditors, investors, security analysts, governmental agencies) use financial accounting reports for a broad range of purposes. If each firm selected whatever format and content of financial reports it deemed best, the resulting reporting process would probably be incomprehensible to many users. Accounting reports generated for internal management purposes, on the other hand, satisfy the information needs of a more limited set of users. Standardization is, therefore, not as necessary.

1.8     **Advantages**

1.  Government authorities can enforce their pronouncements by law.

2.  Firms need maintain only one set of accounting records that serves the needs of both financial and tax reporting.

1.8 continued.

3. Greater uniformity in accounting methods across firms likely results because firms either use the methods prescribed for tax purposes or, where there is a choice of several alternative methods for a particular item, use the method that minimizes the present value of tax payments.

### *Disadvantages*

1. The objectives in setting accounting methods for tax purposes (raising tax revenues) may differ from the objectives for financial reporting (measuring financial position and results of operations).

2. Individuals in the government responsible for setting accounting methods may not have the necessary technical expertise or financial statement user perspective.

3. Political lobbying could dominate the standard-setting process.

1.9 The accounting method would be uniform but the resulting information in the financial statements may not provide uniform measures of financial position or results of operations. If the economic characteristics of firms' activities differ, then different accounting methods may be needed to reflect these differences.

1.10 Accounting standards set in the public sector (that is, by a government agency) become subject to political pressures inherent in a democratic system. Accounting standards set in the private sector become subject to political pressures of various preparer and user groups. Because accounting standards set in the private sector have no enforcement power on their own, private-sector standard-setting bodies must respond to these political pressures by gaining acceptance for their standards.

1.11 We would disagree. Within capital market settings, someone must analyze and interpret financial accounting reports if market prices are to incorporate information from those reports. The principal message of efficient market research is that digestion of such information occurs very quickly. In addition, there are many users and uses of financial accounting reports outside of a capital market setting (lending, antitrust regulation, competitor analysis).

1.12 (Preparing a personal balance sheet.)

There is no distinction between contributed capital and retained earnings, because an individual does not issue common stock. The excess of assets over liabilities is called an individual's *net worth*. The methods used in valuing an individual's assets and liabilities are critical variables in determining net worth. Possibilities include acquisition cost, current replacement cost, current selling price, and others.

1.13    (Classifying financial statement accounts.)

    a.  NA.

    b.  NI (revenue).

    c.  CC.

    d.  X.

    e.  NA.

    f.  CA.

    g.  X (a footnote to the balance sheet would probably disclose the lawsuit).

    h.  NI (expense).

    i.  CA.

    j.  CL.

    k.  X (not recognized as a gain until the firm sells the land).

    l.  RE.

    m.  CL.

    n.  NL.

1.14    (Sports Authority; balance sheet relations.)

    a.  The **given** (boldface) and missing items appear below (amounts in millions).

|  | Year 8 | Year 9 | Year 10 | Year 11 |
|---|---|---|---|---|
| Current Assets | $ **306** | $ 312 | $ 445 | $ 389[b] |
| Noncurrent Assets | **157** | **212** | **309** | **423** |
| Total Assets | $ **463** | $ **524** | $ **754** | $ 812 |
| Current Liabilities | $ **197** | $ **228** | $ 269[a] | $ 290 |
| Noncurrent Liabilities | **14** | 18 | 175 | **188** |
| Shareholders' Equity | 252 | **278** | 310 | 334 |
| Total Liabilities and Share-   holders' Equity | $ **463** | $ **524** | $ **754** | $ **812** |

[a]$269 = $445 − $176.
[b]$389 = $290 + $99.

**1.14 continued.**

    b.  Noncurrent assets increased as a proportion of total assets, suggesting major new investments in property, plant, and equipment or the acquisition of a firm with heavy investments in property, plant and equipment.

    c.  The proportion of liabilities (both current and noncurrent) increased while the proportion of shareholders' equity decreased. Sports Authority used debt to finance the acquisition of property, plant and equipment.

**1.15**    (TJX Cos., Inc.; balance sheet relations.)

    a.  The **given** (boldface) and missing items appear below (amounts in millions).

| | Year 8 | Year 9 | Year 10 | Year 11 |
|---|---|---|---|---|
| Current Assets | **$ 1,008** | $ 1,615 | **$ 1,662** | **$ 1,683** |
| Noncurrent Assets | 592 | **1,059** | 899 | 927 |
| Total Assets | **$ 1,600** | $ 2,674 | **$ 2,561** | **$ 2,610** |
| Current Liabilities | **$ 720** | $ 1,206 | **$ 1,182** | **$ 1,218** |
| Noncurrent Liabilities | **273** | **703** | 252 | **228** |
| Shareholders' Equity | 607 | **765** | **1,127** | 1,164 |
| Total Liabilities and Shareholders' Equity | $ 1,600 | **$ 2,674** | $ 2,561 | $ 2,610 |

    b.  Noncurrent assets increased as a percentage of total assets, suggesting investments in property, plant and equipment. TJX Cos., Inc. may have also acquired other firms which had higher proportions of noncurrent assets than TJX Cos., Inc.

    c.  Total liabilities, particularly noncurrent liabilities, increased as a percentage of total financing, suggesting the use of debt to finance the growth in noncurrent assets.

    d.  Noncurrent assets decreased as a percentage of total assets, probably because TJX Cos., Inc. sold off some of the noncurrent assets acquired during Year 9.

    e.  Total liabilities, particularly noncurrent liabilities, decreased as a percentage of total financing, suggesting that TJX Cos., Inc. used some of the cash proceeds from selling noncurrent assets to repay noncurrent liabilities.

1.16    (Procter & Gamble; balance sheet relations.)

a. The **given** (boldface) and missing items appear below (amounts in millions).

|  | Year 6 | Year 7 | Year 8 | Year 9 |
|---|---|---|---|---|
| Current Assets | $ **8,435** | $ 9,366[a] | $ **9,975** | $ **9,988** |
| Noncurrent Assets | 12,033 | 14,659 | **14,960** | 15,547 |
| Total Assets | $ 20,468 | $ **24,025** | $24,935 | $ 25,535 |
| Current Liabilities | $ **6,733** | $ **7,642** | $ **8,287** | $ 8,040[c] |
| Noncurrent Liabilities | **5,999** | 7,312 | **9,207** | 8,663 |
| Contributed Capital | 1,017 | **1,149** | 1,292 | **1,399** |
| Retained Earnings | **6,719** | **7,922** | 6,149[b] | 7,433[d] |
| Total Liabilities and Shareholders' Equity | $ **20,468** | $ 24,025 | $24,935 | $ **25,535** |

[a] $7,642 + $1,724 = $9,366.
[b] $7,922 − $656 − $1,117 = $6,149.
[c] $9,988 − $1,948 = $8,040.
[d] $6,149 + $2,524 − $1,240 = $7,433.

b. Procter & Gamble likely acquired another firm. The acquired firm probably has a slightly higher percentage of noncurrent assets than Procter & Gamble. Because the mix of short- versus long-term financing and debt versus equity financing did not change substantially between the two years, either Procter & Gamble used a mix of these types of financing or the acquired firm had a capital structure similar to Procter & Gamble's. The acquisition target in this case was the cosmetics and fragrance business of Revlon.

c. Noncurrent liabilities increased in an amount approximately equal to the decrease in retained earnings. Procter & Gamble operated at a net loss during Year 8. One possible explanation is that the net loss reduced cash, requiring Procter & Gamble to obtain additional financing. The actual explanation in this case is that Procter & Gamble adopted the provisions of Financial Accounting Standards Board *Statement No. 106* and *Statement 109*. The adoptions resulted in a charge against earnings and an increase in noncurrent liabilities.

d. Procter & Gamble was profitable during Year 9. It used a portion of the cash generated by profitable operations to repay short- and long-term financing.

**1.17** (Anheuser-Busch; balance sheet relations.)

a. The **given** (boldface) and missing items appear below (amounts in millions).

| | Year 6 | Year 7 | Year 8 | Year 9 |
|---|---|---|---|---|
| Current Assets | $ **1,546** | $ 1,511 | $ **1,466** | $ 1,584 |
| Noncurrent Assets | 9,001 | **9,080** | **8,998** | **10,143** |
| Total Assets | $ **10,547** | $ 10,591 | $10,464 | $11,727 |
| Current Liabilities | $ **1,489** | $ 1,242 | $ **1,432** | $ **1,501** |
| Noncurrent Liabilities | **4,643** | **4,915** | 5,003 | 6,184 |
| Shareholders' Equity | 4,415 | **4,434** | **4,029** | **4,042** |
| Total Liabilities and Shareholders' Equity | $ **10,547** | $ **10,591** | $10,464 | $11,727 |
| Current Assets/Current Liabilities | 1.038 | 1.217 | **1.024** | **1.055** |

b. The proportion of total assets comprising noncurrent assets increased during the four years, suggesting either additional beer-brewing capacity or additional investments in theme parks. Anheuser-Busch increased the proportion of noncurrent liabilities in the capital structure. It likely used the additional noncurrent liabilities to finance the growth in noncurrent assets.

**1.18** (Texas Instruments; balance sheet relations.)

a. The **given** (boldface) and missing items appear below (amounts in millions).

| | Year 5 | Year 6 | Year 7 | Year 8 |
|---|---|---|---|---|
| Current Assets | $ 2,381 | $ **2,626** | $ **3,314** | $ **4,024** |
| Noncurrent Assets | **2,628** | 2,559 | **2,679** | 2,965 |
| Total Assets | $ 5,009 | $ **5,185** | $ **5,993** | $ **6,989** |
| Current Liabilities | $ **1,568** | $ **1,662** | $ **2,001** | $ **2,199** |
| Noncurrent Liabilities | **1,486** | 1,576 | **1,677** | **1,751** |
| Contributed Capital | 1,189 | **1,031** | 1,008 | **1,127** |
| Retained Earnings | **766** | **916** | 1,307[a] | 1,912[b] |
| Total Liabilities and Shareholders' Equity | $ **5,009** | $ **5,185** | $ **5,993** | $ **6,989** |
| Current Assets/Current Liabilities | 1.52 | **1.58** | 1.66 | **1.83** |

[a]$916 + $472 − $81 = $1,307.
[b]$1,307 + $691 − $86 = $1,912.

1.18 continued.

b.  Although current assets and noncurrent assets increased during the four years, current assets increased faster than noncurrent assets. One possible explanation is that Texas Instruments had unused manufacturing capacity at the beginning of Year 6 which it increasingly used in later years to manufacture inventory and to generate increased sales. Thus, inventories and accounts receivable grew faster than property, plant and equipment. The proportion of noncurrent liabilities and contributed capital in the capital structure declined over the four years while the proportion from retained earnings increased. Texas Instruments experienced rapidly increased earnings during the three-year period. It used the assets generated by these earnings to finance the growth in assets. The growth in assets was also financed in part with additional noncurrent liabilities and contributed capital.

1.19    (Olin Corporation, retained earnings relations.)

a.  The **given** (boldface) and missing items appear below (amounts in millions).

|  | **Year 6** | **Year 7** | **Year 8** | **Year 9** |
|---|---|---|---|---|
| Retained Earnings, Beginning of Year | **$ 499** | **$ 435** | **$ 388** | **$ 238** |
| Net Income | (13) | **9** | (92) | **91** |
| Dividends Declared and Paid | **(51)** | **(56)** | **(58)** | **(60)** |
| Retained Earnings, End of Year | **$ 435** | **$ 388** | **$ 238** | **$ 269** |

b.  The sales of Olin Corporation are cyclical. The economy was apparently in a recession during Year 6, Year 7 and Year 8 and began pulling out of the recession in Year 9.

c.  A slowly growing but continuous dividend sends a signal to common shareholders that the firm expects to grow and return to profitable operations when the economy pulls out of the recession. Also, shareholders who rely on dividends for their living expenses will probably prefer steady dividends instead of distributions that vary with net income each year.

1.20    (Volvo Group; retained earnings relations.)

a.  The changes in retained earnings appear below. **Given** amounts appear in boldface (amounts in millions of Swedish Krona).

|  | **Year 3** | **Year 4** | **Year 5** | **Year 6** |
|---|---|---|---|---|
| Retained Earnings, January 1...... | **25,634** | 30,484 | 34,338 | **37,922** |
| Net Income...................................... | **5,665** | **4,940** | 4,787 | (1,050)* |
| Dividends........................................ | (815) | (1,086) | **(1,203)** | **(1,203)** |
| Retained Earnings, December 31 ............................................... | 30,484 | **34,338** | **37,922** | **35,669** |

*Net loss.

b.  Volvo Group experienced decreasing amounts of net income over the four years, even operating at a net loss in Year 6. The firm, however, increased or at least maintained its dividends during this period of declining profitability. Thus, retained earnings grew at a declining rate (Year 3 to Year 5) or decreased (Year 6).

1.21    (Home Depot; relating net income to balance sheet changes.)

a.

|  (Amount in Millions) | **Year 3** | **Year 4** |
|---|---|---|
| Retained Earnings, Beginning of Year....................... | $ 2,579 | $ 3,407 |
| Plus Net Income................................................. | 938 | 1,162 |
| Less Dividends Declared and Paid............................. | (110) | (139) |
| Retained Earnings, End of Year ................ ............... | $ 3,407 | $ 4,430 |

b.

$$\text{Net Income} = \text{Increase in Assets} - \text{Increase in Liabilities} - \text{Increase in Contributed Capital} + \text{Dividends}$$

**Year 3**

$$\$938 = \$1,988 - \$999 - \$161 + \$110$$

**Year 4**

$$\$1,162 = \$1,887 - \$726 - \$138 + \$139$$

**1.22** (Nestle Group; relating net income to balance sheet changes.)

a.

| (Amount in Millions) | Year 5 | Year 6 |
|---|---|---|
| Retained Earnings, Beginning of Year................... | SF17,096 | SF18,439 |
| Plus Net Income................................................ | 1,960 | 1,896 |
| Less Dividends Declared and Paid....................... | (617) | (740) |
| Retained Earnings, End of Year .......................... | SF18,439 | SF19,595 |

b.

$$\text{Net Income} = \frac{\text{Increase}}{\text{in Assets}} - \frac{\text{Increase}}{\text{in Liabilities}} - \frac{\text{Increase in}}{\text{Contributed Capital}} + \text{Dividends}$$

**Year 5**

| SF1,960 | = SF1,996 | − | SF635 | − | SF18 | + | SF617 |
|---|---|---|---|---|---|---|---|

**Year 6**

| SF1,896 | = SF231 | − | SF(−925) − | | SF0 | + | SF740 |
|---|---|---|---|---|---|---|---|

**1.23** (Dell Computer; income statement relations.)

a. The **given** (boldface) and missing items appear below (amounts are in millions).

| | Year 4 | Year 5 | Year 6 |
|---|---|---|---|
| Sales.............................................................. | **$ 5,296** | **$ 7,759** | **$ 12,327** |
| Interest Revenue........................................... | **6** | **33** | **52** |
| Cost of Goods Sold........................................ | **(4,229)** | **(6,093)** | **(9,605)** |
| Research and Development Expenses...... | **(95)** | **(126)** | **(204)** |
| Marketing and Administrative Expenses ............................................ | **(595)** | **(826)** | **(1,202)** |
| Income Tax Expense .................................... | **(111)** | **(216)** | **(424)** |
| Net Income................................................... | $ 272 | $ 531 | $ 944 |

b. The common size income statement appears below:

| | Year 4 | Year 5 | Year 6 |
|---|---|---|---|
| Sales.............................................................. | 100.0% | 100.0% | 100.0% |
| Interest Revenue........................................... | .1 | .4 | .4 |
| Cost of Goods Sold........................................ | (79.9) | (78.5) | (77.9) |
| Research and Development Expenses....... | (1.8) | (1.6) | (1.6) |
| Marketing and Administrative Expenses.. | (11.2) | (10.7) | (9.8) |
| Income Tax Expense .................................... | (2.1) | (2.8) | (3.4) |
| Net Income................................................... | 5.1% | 6.8% | 7.7% |

The ratio of net income to sales increased steadily during the three years. The cost of goods sold to sales percentage and the marketing and administrative expense to sales percentage both decreased steadily. One possible explanation is that excess demand in computer products

**1.23 b. continued.**

permitted Dell to raise its selling prices. Another possible explanation is that the increased sales were spread over certain relatively fixed manufacturing, marketing, or administrative expenses, lowering the expense percentages.

**1.24**   (Circuit City Stores; income statement relations.)

a.   The **given** (boldface) and missing items appear below (amounts in millions).

|  | Year 6 | Year 7 | Year 8 |
|---|---|---|---|
| Sales | **$ 7,029** | **$ 7,664** | **$ 8,871** |
| Cost of Goods Sold | **(5,394)** | **(5,903)** | **(6,827)** |
| Marketing and Administrative Expenses | **(1,322)** | **(1,511)** | **(1,849)** |
| Interest Expense | **(25)** | **(30)** | **(27)** |
| Income Tax Expense | (108) | (84) | (64) |
| Net Income | **$    180** | **$    136** | **$    104** |

b.   The common size income statement appears below.

|  | Year 6 | Year 7 | Year 8 |
|---|---|---|---|
| Sales | 100.0% | 100.0% | 100.0% |
| Cost of Goods Sold | (76.7) | (77.0) | (77.0) |
| Marketing and Administrative Expenses | (18.8) | (19.7) | (20.8) |
| Interest Expense | (.4) | (.4) | (.3) |
| Income Tax Expense | (1.5) | (1.1) | (.7) |
| Net Income | 2.6% | 1.8% | 1.2% |

Circuit City Stores experienced a declining net income to sales percentage during the three-year period. The principal contributing factor was an increase in the marketing and administrative expense to sales percentage. Increased competition may have increased marketing expenditures. Growth in new stores may have increased administrative expenses.

**1.25** (Delta Airlines; statement of cash flows relations.)

a.
### DELTA AIRLINES
### Statement of Cash Flows
### (Amounts in Millions)

|  | Year 2 | Year 3 | Year 4 |
|---|---|---|---|
| Operations: |  |  |  |
| Revenues Increasing Cash...................... | $10,519 | $12,196 | $ 12,528 |
| Expenses Decreasing Cash .................... | (10,369) | (11,519) | (11,204) |
| Cash Flow from Operations ........................ | $    150 | $    677 | $  1,324 |
| Investing: |  |  |  |
| Sale of Property and Equipment ........... | $     43 | $     87 | $     103 |
| Acquisition of Property and |  |  |  |
| Equipment ......................................... | (3,082) | (1,414) | (1,613) |
| Cash Flow from Investing ......................... | $ (3,039) | $ (1,327) | $ (1,510) |
| Financing: |  |  |  |
| Increase (Decrease) in Short-term |  |  |  |
| Debt........................................................ | $    746 | $   (801) | $       0 |
| Increase in Long-term Debt .................. | 2,313 | 2,111 | 975 |
| Increase in Common Stock .................... | 0 | 1,127 | 0 |
| Decrease in Long-term Debt .................. | (794) | (519) | (547) |
| Dividends .............................................. | (89) | (138) | (120) |
| Cash Flow from Financing........................ | $ 2,176 | $ 1,780 | $     308 |
| Change in Cash........................................... | $   (713) | $ 1,130 | $     122 |

b. Although cash flow from operations increased during the three years, its amount was not sufficient to finance acquisition of property and equipment. Delta financed these acquisitions with long-term debt in all three years and with common stock in Year 3.

1.26    (Nike; statement of cash flows relations.)

a.
**NIKE, INC.**
**Statement of Cash Flows**
**(Amounts in Millions)**

|  | Year 8 | Year 9 | Year 10 |
|---|---|---|---|
| Operations: |  |  |  |
| Revenues Increasing Cash...................... | $ 6,184 | $ 6,087 | $ 9,633 |
| Expenses Decreasing Cash .................... | (5,844) | (5,764) | (9,115) |
| Cash Flow from Operations ........................ | $ 340 | $ 323 | $ 518 |
| Investing: |  |  |  |
| Acquisition of Property, Plant and |  |  |  |
| Equipment .............................................. | $ (240) | $ (496) | $ (595) |
| Cash Flow from Investing ........................... | $ (240) | $ (496) | $ (595) |
| Financing: |  |  |  |
| Proceeds of Bank Borrowing.................... | $ 23 | $ 388 | $ 26 |
| Issue of Common Stock ........................... | 2 | 69 | 12 |
| Repurchase of Common Stock ............... | -- | -- | (170) |
| Dividends .................................................... | (79) | (101) | (127) |
| Cash Flow from Financing........................... | $ (54) | $ 356 | $ (259) |
| Change in Cash............................................. | $ 46 | $ 183 | $ (336) |

b.  Nike made a larger amount of sales on account during Year 8 and Year 9 than it collected from customers from sales on account (that is, accounts receivable increased). Likewise, Nike manufactured more products than it sold in order to meet growing demand. Thus, cash inflows were less than sales revenues and cash outflows for operations exceeded expenses. The net result was that net income exceeded cash flow from operations. Net income declined significantly between Year 9 and Year 10, suggesting the likelihood of decreased sales. Nike collected more receivables than sales on account and reduced production levels. Thus, cash flow from operations exceeded net income.

1.27    (Relations between financial statements.)

a.  $630 + $3,290 − $2,780 = a; a = $1,140.

b.  $1,240 + b − $8,290 = $1,410; b = $8,460.

c.  $89,000 − c + $17,600 = $102,150; c = $4,450.

d.  $76,200 + $14,200 − d = $83,300; d = $7,100.

1.28    (America Online; preparing a balance sheet and income statement.)

a.
### AMERICA ONLINE
### Income Statement
### For the Year Ended June 30, Year 8

| | |
|---|---:|
| Revenues: | |
| Sales | $2,600,000 |
| Interest Revenue | 21,000 |
| Total Revenues | $2,621,000 |
| Less Expenses: | |
| Cost of Goods Sold | $1,678,000 |
| Research and Development Expense | 175,000 |
| Selling and Administrative Expense | 604,000 |
| Depreciation Expense | 14,000 |
| Interest Expense | 58,000 |
| Total Expenses | 2,529,000 |
| Net Income | $    92,000 |

b.
### AMERICA ONLINE
### Comparative Balance Sheet
### (Amounts in Thousands)

| | June 30, Year 7 | June 30, Year 8 |
|---|---:|---:|
| *Assets* | | |
| Current Assets: | | |
| Cash | $124,000 | $   631,000 |
| Accounts Receivable | 65,000 | 104,000 |
| Other Current Assets | 134,000 | 195,000 |
| Total Current Assets | $323,000 | $   930,000 |
| Noncurrent Assets: | | |
| Investments in Securities | $277,000 | $   921,000 |
| Property, Plant and Equipment—Net of Depreciation | 233,000 | 363,000 |
| Total Noncurrent Assets | $510,000 | $1,284,000 |
| Total Assets | $833,000 | $2,214,000 |
| *Liabilities and Shareholders' Equity* | | |
| Current Liabilities: | | |
| Accounts Payable to Suppliers | $ 68,000 | $    87,000 |
| Other Current Liabilities | 485,000 | 807,000 |
| Total Current Liabilities | $553,000 | $   894,000 |
| Long-Term Debt | 140,000 | 722,000 |
| Total Liabilities | $693,000 | $1,616,000 |
| Shareholders' Equity: | | |
| Common Stock | $647,000 | $1,013,000 |
| Retained Earnings (Deficit) | (507,000) | (415,000) |
| Total Shareholders' Equity | $140,000 | $   598,000 |
| Total Liabilities and Shareholders' Equity | $833,000 | $2,214,000 |

1.28 continued.

c.
| | |
|---|---:|
| Retained Earnings, (Deficit) June 30, Year 7 ..................... | $ (507,000) |
| Plus Net Income for Year Ending June 30, Year 8 ................ | 92,000 |
| Subtract Dividends for Year Ending June 30, Year 8 ........... | 0 |
| Retained Earnings (Deficit), June 30, Year 8 ........................ | $ (415,000) |

1.29    (The GAP; preparing a balance sheet and an income statement.)  (Amounts in Thousands)

a.
### THE GAP
### Balance Sheet

| | Jan. 31, Year 9 | Jan. 31, Year 10 |
|---|---:|---:|
| *Assets* | | |
| Cash............................................................... | $ 565,253 | $ 450,352 |
| Merchandise Inventory................................... | 1,056,444 | 1,462,045 |
| Other Current Assets..................................... | 250,127 | 285,393 |
| Total Current Assets.................................. | $1,871,824 | $2,197,790 |
| Property, Plant and Equipment (Net).......... | 1,876,370 | 2,715,315 |
| Other Noncurrent Assets............................... | 215,725 | 275,651 |
| Total Assets............................................... | $3,963,919 | $5,188,756 |
| *Liabilities and Shareholders' Equity* | | |
| Accounts Payable ........................................... | $ 684,130 | $ 805,945 |
| Notes Payable to Banks................................. | 90,690 | 168,961 |
| Other Current Liabilities .............................. | 778,283 | 777,973 |
| Total Current Liabilities............................ | $1,553,103 | $1,752,879 |
| Long-Term Debt .............................................. | 496,455 | 784,925 |
| Other Noncurrent Liabilities......................... | 340,682 | 417,907 |
| Total Liabilities ........................................ | $2,390,240 | $2,955,711 |
| Common Stock ................................................ | $ 354,719 | $ 135,034 |
| Retained Earnings.......................................... | 1,218,960 | 2,098,011 |
| Total Shareholders' Equity ....................... | $1,573,679 | $2,233,045 |
| Total Liabilities and Shareholders' Equity ........................................................ | $3,963,919 | $5,188,756 |

1.29 continued.

b.

**THE GAP**
**Income Statement**
**(Amounts in Thousands)**

| For the Year Ended : | Jan. 31, Year 10 |
|---|---|
| Sales | $ 11,635,398 |
| Cost of Goods Sold | (6,775,262) |
| Selling Expenses | (2,239,437) |
| Administrative Expenses | (803,995) |
| Interest Expense | (31,755) |
| Income Taxes | (657,884) |
| Net Income | $ 1,127,065 |

c.

| | |
|---|---|
| Retained Earnings, January 31, Year 9 | $ 1,218,960 |
| Plus Net Income for Year 10 | 1,127,065 |
| Less Dividends Declared and Paid during Year 10 | (248,014) |
| Retained Earnings, January 31, Year 10 | $ 2,098,011 |

d. The Gap increased its inventories and property, plant and equipment significantly during Year 10, most likely the result of opening new stores. It financed the growth with an increase in accounts payable, short-term bank borrowing, and long-term debt. It also repurchased shares of its common stock. Despite the reduction in common stock, total shareholders' equity increased due to the retention of earnings.

1.30    (Southwest Airlines; preparing a balance sheet and an income statement.)

a.

**SOUTHWEST AIRLINES**
**Balance Sheet**
**(Amounts in Thousands)**

| | Dec. 31, Year 8 | Dec. 31, Year 9 |
|---|---|---|
| *Assets* | | |
| Cash | $ 378,511 | $ 418,819 |
| Accounts Receivable | 88,799 | 73,448 |
| Inventories | 50,035 | 65,152 |
| Other Current Assets | 56,810 | 73,586 |
| Total Current Assets | $ 574,155 | $ 631,005 |
| Property, Plant and Equipment (Net) | 4,137,610 | 5,008,166 |
| Other Noncurrent Assets | 4,231 | 12,942 |
| Total Assets | $4,715,996 | $5,652,113 |
| | | |
| *Liabilities and Shareholders' Equity* | | |
| Accounts Payable | $ 157,415 | $ 156,755 |
| Current Maturities of Long-Term Debt | 11,996 | 7,873 |
| Other Current Liabilities | 681,242 | 795,838 |
| Total Current Liabilities | $ 850,653 | $ 960,466 |
| Long-Term Debt | 623,309 | 871,717 |
| Other Noncurrent Liabilities | 844,116 | 984,142 |
| Total Liabilities | $2,318,078 | $2,816,325 |
| Common Stock | $ 352,943 | $ 449,934 |
| Retained Earnings | 2,044,975 | 2,385,854 |
| Total Shareholders' Equity | $2,397,918 | $2,835,788 |
| Total Liabilities and Shareholders' Equity | $4,715,996 | $5,652,113 |

1.30 continued.

b.

**SOUTHWEST AIRLINES**
**Income Statement**
**(Amounts in Thousands)**

| For the Year Ended: | Dec. 31, Year 9 |
|---|---|
| Sales.......................................................................... | $4,735,587 |
| Interest Revenue...................................................... | 14,918 |
| Total Revenues................................................... | $4,750,505 |
| Salaries and Benefits Expense............................... | (1,455,237) |
| Fuel Expense............................................................. | (492,415) |
| Maintenance Expense............................................... | (367,606) |
| Other Operating Expenses....................................... | (1,638,753) |
| Interest Expense....................................................... | (22,883) |
| Income Tax Expense................................................ | (299,233) |
| Net Income................................................................ | $ 474,378 |

| c. | |
|---|---|
| Retained Earnings, December 31, Year 8 ................. | $2,044,975 |
| Plus Net Income for Year 9...................................... | 474,378 |
| Less Dividends Declared and Paid during Year 9 ...... | (133,499) |
| Retained Earnings, December 31, Year 9 ................. | $2,385,854 |

d.  Southwest Airlines made substantial investments in property, plant and equipment during Year 9. It financed these expenditures with additional long-term debt, additional common stock, and the retention of earnings.

1.31   (ABC Company; relation between net income and cash flows.)

a.

| Month | Cash Balance at Beginning of Month | + Cash Receipts from Customers | − Cash Disbursements for Production Costs | = Cash Balance at End of the Month |
|---|---|---|---|---|
| January | $ 875 | $1,000 | $ 750 | $ 1,125 |
| February | 1,125 | 1,000 | 1,500 | 625 |
| March | 625 | 1,500 | 1,875 | 250 |
| April | 250 | 2,000 | 2,250 | 0 |

b.  The cash flow problem arises because of a lag between cash expenditures incurred in producing goods and cash collections from customers once the firm sells those goods. For example, cash expenditures during February ($1,500) are for goods produced during February and sold during March. Cash is not collected from customers on these sales, however, until April ($2,000). A growing firm must gen-

1.31 b. continued.

erally produce more units than it sells during a period if it is to have sufficient quantities of inventory on hand for future sales. The cash needed for this higher level of production may well exceed the cash received from the prior period's sales. Thus, a cash shortage develops.

The difference between the selling price of goods sold and the cost of those goods equals net income for the period. As long as selling prices exceed the cost of the goods, a positive net income results. As the number of units sold increases, net income increases. A firm does not necessarily recognize revenues and expenses in the same period as the related cash receipts and expenditures. Thus, cash decreases, even though net income increases.

c. The income statement and statement of cash flows provide information about the profitability and liquidity respectively of a firm during a period. The fact that net income and cash flows can move in opposite directions highlights the need for information from both statements. A firm without sufficient cash will not survive, even if it operates profitably. The balance sheet indicates a firm's asset and equity position at a moment in time. The deteriorating cash position is evident from the listing of assets at the beginning of each month. Examining the cash receipts and disbursements during each month, however, identifies the reasons for the deterioration.

d. Strategies for dealing with the cash flow problem center around (a) reducing the lag between cash outflows to produce widgets and cash inflows from their sale, and (b) increasing the margin between selling prices and production costs.

To reduce the lag on collection of accounts receivable, ABC might:

(1) Provide to customers an incentive to pay faster than 30 days, such as offering a discount if customers pay more quickly or charge interest if customers delay payment.

(2) Use the accounts receivable as a basis for external financing, such as borrowing from a bank and using the receivables as collateral or selling (factoring) the receivables for immediate cash

(3) Sell only for cash, although competition may preclude this alternative.

To delay the payment for widgets, ABC might:

(1) Delay paying its suppliers (increases accounts payable) or borrow from a bank using the inventory as collateral (increases bank loan payable).

1.31 d. continued.

(2) Reduce the holding period for inventories by instituting a just-in-time inventory system. This alternative requires ordering raw materials only when needed in production and manufacturing widgets only to customer orders. Demand appears to be sufficiently predictable so that opportunities for a just-in-time inventory system seem attractive.

To increase the margin between selling price and manufacturing cost, ABC might:

(1) Negotiate a lower purchase price with suppliers of raw materials.

(2) Substitute more efficient manufacturing equipment for work now done by employees.

(3) Increase selling prices.

The cash flow problem is short-term because it will neutralize itself by June. This neutralization occurs because the growth rate in sales is declining (500 additional units sold on top of an ever-increasing sales base). Thus, the firm needs a short-term solution to the cash flow problem. If the growth rate were steady or increasing, ABC might consider obtaining a more permanent source of cash, such as issuing long-term debt or common stock.

1.32    (Balance sheet and income statement relations.)

a. Bushels of wheat are the most convenient in this case with the given information. This question emphasizes the need for a common measuring unit.

1.32 continued.

b.

**IVAN AND IGOR**
**Comparative Balance Sheets**
**(Amounts in Bushels of Wheat)**

| | IVAN | | IGOR | |
|---|---|---|---|---|
| *Assets* | Beginning of Period | End of Period | Beginning of Period | End of Period |
| Wheat............................. | 20 | 223 | 10 | 105 |
| Fertilizer...................... | 2 | -- | 1 | -- |
| Ox.................................. | 40 | 36 | 40 | 36 |
| Plow.............................. | -- | -- | -- | 2 |
| Land.............................. | 100 | 100 | 50 | 50 |
|    Total Assets........... | 162 | 359 | 101 | 193 |
| *Liabilities and Owners' Equity* | | | | |
| Accounts Payable..... | -- | 3 | -- | -- |
| Owners' Equity........... | 162 | 356 | 101 | 193 |
|    Total Liabilities and Owners' Equity.................. | 162 | 359 | 101 | 193 |

Questions will likely arise as to the accounting entity. One view is that there are two accounting entities (Ivan and Igor) to whom the Red Bearded Baron has entrusted assets and required a periodic reporting on stewardship. The "owner" in owners' equity in this case is the Red Bearded Baron. Another view is that the Red Bearded Baron is the accounting entity, in which case financial statements that combine the financial statements for Ivan and Igor are appropriate. Identifying the accounting entity depends on the intended use of the financial statements. For purposes of evaluating the performance of Ivan and Igor, the accounting entities are separate—Ivan and Igor. To assess the change in wealth of the Red Bearded Baron during the period, the combined financial statements reflect the accounting entity.

1.32 continued.

c.
## IVAN AND IGOR
### Comparative Income Statement
### (Amounts in Bushels of Wheat)

|  | IVAN | IGOR |
|---|---|---|
| Revenues | 243 | 138 |
| Expenses: |  |  |
| Seed | 20 | 10 |
| Fertilizer | 2 | 1 |
| Depreciation on Ox | 4 | 4 |
| Plow | 3 | 1 |
| Total Expenses | 29 | 16 |
| Net Income | 214 | 122 |

Chapter 1 does not expose students to the concept of depreciation. Most students, however, grasp the need to record some amount of expense for the ox and the plow.

d.

| (Amounts in Bushels of Wheat) | IVAN | IGOR |
|---|---|---|
| Owners' Equity, Beginning of Period | 162 | 101 |
| Plus Net Income | 214 | 122 |
| Less Distributions to Owner | (20) | (30) |
| Owners' Equity, End of Period | 356 | 193 |

e. We cannot simply compare the amounts of net income for Ivan and Igor because the Red Bearded Baron entrusted them with different amounts of resources. We must relate the net income amounts to some base. Several possibilities include:

|  | IVAN | IGOR |
|---|---|---|
| Net Income/Average Total Assets | 82.2% | 83.0% |
| Net Income/Beginning Total Assets | 132.1% | 120.8% |
| Net Income/Average Noncurrent Assets | 155.1% | 137.1% |
| Net Income/Beginning Noncurrent Assets | 152.9% | 135.6% |
| Net Income/Average Owners' Equity | 82.6% | 82.0% |
| Net Income/Beginning Owners' Equity | 132.1% | 120.8% |
| Net Income/Acre | $10.70 | $12.20 |

This question has no definitive answer. Its purpose is to get students to think about performance measurement. The instructor may or may not wish to devote class time at this point discussing which base is more appropriate.

# CHAPTER 2

## BALANCE SHEET: PRESENTING THE INVESTMENTS AND FINANCING OF A FIRM

*Questions, Exercises, Problems, and Cases: Answers and Solutions*

2.1     See the text or the glossary at the end of the book.

2.2     Based on the conservatively reported earnings, a shareholder might sell shares of stock based on the assessment that the firm is not performing well. If the economic or "true" earnings of the firm are larger, the shareholder's assessment would result in a poor decision. Or, shareholders might dismiss the management of a firm because they feel the firm is not performing well. It should be emphasized here that the principal objective of accounting reports as currently prepared is to present *fairly* the results of operations and the financial condition of the firm. When doubt exists as to the treatment of a particular item or transaction, accountants tend to select the procedure resulting in the more conservative measurement of earnings.

2.3     The justification relates to the need for a reasonably high degree of objectivity in the preparation of the financial statements. When there is an exchange between a firm and some other entity, there is market evidence of the economic effects of the transaction. The independent auditor verifies these economic effects by referring to contracts, cancelled checks and other documents underlying the transaction. If accounting recognized events without such a market exchange (for example, the increase in market value of a firm's assets), increased subjectivity would enter into the preparation of the financial statements.

2.4     The justification relates to the uncertainty as to the ultimate economic effects of the contracts. One party or the other may pull out of the contract. The accountant may not know the benefits and costs of the contract at the time of signing. Until one party or the other begins to perform under the contract, accounting gives no recognition. Accountants often disclose significant contracts of this nature in the notes to the financial statements.

2.5     Accountants record assets at acquisition cost. Cash discounts reduce acquisition cost and, therefore, the amount recorded for merchandise or equipment.

2.6　a.　The contract between the investors and the construction company as well as cancelled checks provide evidence as to the acquisition cost.

　　b.　Adjusted acquisition cost differs from the amount in Part *a.* by the portion of acquisition cost applicable to the services of the asset consumed during the first five years. There are several generally accepted methods of computing this amount (discussed in Chapter 8). A review of the accounting records for the office building should indicate how the firm calculated this amount.

　　c.　There are at least two possibilities for ascertaining current replacement cost. One alternative is to consult a construction company to determine the cost of constructing a similar office building (that is, with respect to location, materials, size). The accountant would then adjust the current cost of constructing a new building downward to reflect the used condition of the five-year old office building. The current replacement cost amount could be reduced by 12.5 percent (= 5/40) if the asset's service potential decreases evenly with age. The actual economic decline in the value of the building during the first five years is likely to differ from 12.5 percent and, therefore, some other rate is probably appropriate. A second alternative for ascertaining current replacement cost is to consult a real estate dealer to determine the cost of acquiring a used office building providing services similar to the building that the investors own. The accountant might encounter difficulties in locating such a similar building.

　　d.　The accountant might consult a local real estate dealer to ascertain the current market price, net of transactions cost, at which the investors might sell the building. There is always the question as to whether an interested buyer could be found at the quoted price. The accountant might also use any recent offers to purchase the building received by the investors.

　　e.　The accountant measures the present value of the future net cash flows using estimated rental receipts and operating expenses (excluding depreciation) for the building's remaining 35-year life. These cash flows are then discounted to the present using an appropriate rate of interest.

2.7　a.　Liability—Receivable from Supplier or Prepaid Merchandise Orders.

　　b.　Liability—Investment in Bonds.

　　c.　Asset—Interest Payable.

　　d.　Asset—Insurance Premiums Received in Advance.

　　e.　Liability—Prepaid Rent.

2.8    (Eli Lilly and Company; asset recognition and valuation.)

a.   Prepaid Insurance, $12,000,000.

b.   Deposit on Equipment, $500,000.

c.   Investment in Securities, $325,000.

d.   Raw Materials Inventory, $784,000 (= .98 × $800,000).

e.   Accounting does not recognize the employment contract, a mutually unexecuted contract, as an asset.

f.   Marketable Securities, $3,200,000.

g.   Accounting does not recognize the customer's order, a mutually unexecuted contract, as an asset because no exchange between the buyer and the seller has occurred.

h.   Raw Materials Inventory, $200,000.  Legal rights to use the raw materials have passed to Eli Lilly, creating a legal obligation to make payment.

2.9    (Delta Airlines; asset recognition and valuation.)

a.   The placing of an order does not give rise to an asset.

b.   Deposit on Aircraft, $5 million.

c.   Landing Rights, $4 million.

d.   Equipment, $10 million.

e.   Accounting does not recognize the employment contract, a mutually unexecuted contract, as an asset.

f.   Equipment, $60 million.  The book value of the aircraft on the seller's books is not relevant to Delta Airlines' recording of the purchase.

g.   Accounting does not recognize prepayments for advertising as an asset because of the difficulty of measuring any future benefits with reasonable precision.

h.   Investment in Bond, $4 million.  Delta Airlines should record the purchase of the bond at its acquisition cost, not the amount ultimately received at maturity.

2.10    (General Mills, Inc.; asset recognition and valuation.)

    a.   Accounting does not recognize as assets, under generally accepted accounting principles, expenditures firms make internally to develop new products. Too much uncertainty exists as to the existence and valuation of future benefits to justify recognition of an asset.

    b.   Contractual Rights to Food Products (or similar creative account title), $2,800,000. In contrast to Part *a.*, the exchange between buyer and seller of presumably a commercially feasible product permits the identification and valuation of future benefits to justify recognition of an asset. A thin line appears to distinguish the situation in Part *a.* and Part *b.*

    c.   Purchase Options on Land, $1,800,000.

    d.   Accounting does not recognize an asset because of the difficulty of identifying and measuring any future benefits from these advertising expenditures.

    e.   Investment in Securities, $3,500,000. The market value of the shares of General Mills given in exchange is probably a more reliable indicator of value than independent appraisals.

    f.   Land, $2,188,000. Acquisition cost includes all expenditures made to prepare an asset for its intended use.

2.11    (Office Depot; asset recognition and valuation.)

    a.   Prepaid Rent, $125,000; Security Deposit, $130,000.

    b.   Leasehold Improvements, $36,500 (= $10,000 + $6,500 + $20,000). These expenditures prepare the rented facility for its intended use as a retail store.

    c.   Equipment or Fixtures, $31,400 [= .98 X $30,000) + $1,200 + $800]. The latter two expenditures prepare the display counters for their intended use.

    d.   Accounting does not recognize an asset for the future services of employees.

    e.   Accounting does not recognize any portion of expenditures on advertising as assets because any future benefits of the advertising are too uncertain.

2.11 continued.

    f.   Merchandise Inventory $145,600 [= (.98 X $120,000) + $40,000 − $12,000]. One might argue that Office Depot should reduce the acquisition cost of the $28,000 (= $40,000 − $12,000) of merchandise that it has not yet paid for by the 2 percent discount. It is possible, however, that cash discounts are not available on this merchandise. If Office Depot takes advantage of any discounts when it pays for this merchandise, it will reduce the acquisition cost at that time.

2.12    (Asset recognition and valuation.)

    a.

| | |
|---|---:|
| Automobile, List Price | $ 20,000 |
| Less Cash Discount | (1,600) |
| Dealer Preparation Charges | 350 |
| Sales Tax (.06 X $18,750) | 1,125 |
| Name Painted on Truck | 190 |
| Total Cost of Delivery Truck (a noncurrent asset) | $ 20,065 |
| Prepaid Insurance (current asset) | $ 500 |
| Prepaid License Fees (current asset) | $ 125 |

    b.   This part and the next are designed to stimulate discussion. There is no right answer, although our reading of APB *Opinion No. 29* and the facts of the situation lead us to use $5,200,000, the apparent value of the Microsoft shares. (We recall once a student who answered this question in no uncertain terms that the appraiser's figure was correct. When pressed as to why he picked this answer and why he was so certain, he admitted that he was the son of a real estate appraiser and that appraisers never make mistakes!)

    c.   Here we are more inclined to believe the appraiser rather than the stock market, but we are not unanimous in agreeing on the right answer. Historical cost accounting is not as objective and verifiable as is sometimes thought.

2.13    (Travelers Insurance Company; liability recognition and valuation.)

    a.   Insurance Premiums Received in Advance or Advances from Customers, $6,500,000.

    b.   Accounting normally does not recognize a liability for mutually unexecuted contracts. When the president renders services, a liability arises.

    c.   Legal Fees Payable, $1,200,000.

    d.   Common stock does not meet the definition of a liability because the firm need not repay the funds in a particular amount at a particular time.

2.13 continued.

    e.    Salaries and Commissions Payable, $950,000; Payroll Taxes Payable, $76,000 (= .08 × $950,000).

    f.    The treatment of this item depends on the probability of having to make a cash payment in the future, whose amount and timing of payment the Company can estimate with reasonable accuracy. Most firms do not recognize unsettled lawsuits as liabilities because it is not clear (1) that the firm received benefits in the past, and (2) that the lawsuit will require a future cash payment.

2.14    (Kansas City Royals, Inc.; liability recognition and valuation.)

    a.    Accounting normally does not recognize a liability for mutually unexecuted contracts. When the player renders services, a liability arises.

    b.    Advances from Customers, $2,700,000.

    c.    Bonds Payable, $8,400,000.

    d.    Utilities Payable, $3,400.

    e.    The treatment of this item depends on the probability of having to make a cash payment in the future, whose amount and timing of payment the firm can estimate with reasonable accuracy. Most firms do not recognize unsettled lawsuits as liabilities because it is not clear (1) that the firm has received benefits in the past, and (2) that the lawsuit will require a future cash payment.

    f.    The firm does not recognize a liability for the uniforms until the supplier makes delivery. The $10,000 deposit appears as a Deposit on Uniforms, an asset, on the firm's balance sheet and an Advance from Customers, a liability, on the balance sheet of the supplier.

2.15    (Liability recognition and valuation.)

    a.    Bonds Payable, $10,000,000.

    b.    Accounting normally does not recognize a liability for unexecuted contracts. The $2,000,000 deposit appears as an asset, Deposit on Building, on the college's balance sheet and as a liability, Advance from Customers, on the balance sheet of the construction company.

    c.    Advances from Customers, $1,800,000.

    d.    Accounts Payable, $170,000.

2.15 continued.

    e.   Compensation Payable, $280,000; Payroll Taxes Payable $16,800 (.06 × $280,000).

    f.   The college does not recognize a liability for the grant. Although it receives the benefits of the funds, it incurs no obligation to repay the amount of the grant in the future.

2.16    (Chicago Symphony Orchestra; liability recognition and valuation.)

    a.   Advances from Customers, $340,000.

    b.   Chicago Symphony Orchestra does not recognize a liability because it has not yet received benefits obligating it to pay.

    c.   Accounts Payable, $85,000.

    d.   Chicago Symphony Orchestra would not normally recognize a liability for an unsettled lawsuit unless payment is probable. Because the suit has not yet come to trial, it is unclear whether any liability exists.

    e.   Chicago Symphony Orchestra would not recognize a liability for this mutually unexecuted contract.

    f.   The issue of common stock increases shareholders' equity, not a liability.

    g.   Loan Payable, $40,000. Chicago Symphony Orchestra records the loan at the amount received, not the amount ultimately repaid, which includes interest.

2.17    (Balance sheet classification.)

| | | | | | |
|---|---|---|---|---|---|
| a. | 2 | f. | 2 | k. | 1 |
| b. | 3 | g. | 1 | l. | 1 (if purchased from another firm) |
| c. | 1 | h. | 2 | | 4 (if created by the firm) |
| d. | 4 | i. | 4 | m. | 4 |
| e. | 1 | j. | 2 | n. | 3 |

2.18    (Balance sheet classification.)

| | | | | |
|---|---|---|---|---|
| a. | 3 | | h. | 2 |
| b. | 1 | | i. | 1 |
| c. | 4 | | j. | 2 |
| d. | 1 | | k. | 2 |
| e. | 3 | | l. | 1 |
| f. | 1 | | m. | 2 |
| g. | 1 | (if purchased from another firm) | n. | 3 |
| | 4 | (if created by the firm) | | |

2.19    (Brackin Corporation; journal entries for various transactions.)

(1) **October 2**
Cash.......................................................................... 9,600,000
    Common Stock..................................................        6,000,000
    Additional Paid-in Capital .............................        3,600,000
Issue of 600,000 shares of $10 par value
common stock at $16 per share.

(2) **October 3**
Building..................................................................... 3,000,000
    Cash .................................................................          300,000
    Note Payable....................................................        2,700,000
Acquisition of building for cash and
issuance of a note.

(3) **October 8**
Equipment .............................................................. 40,000
    Cash .................................................................            40,000
Acquisition of equipment for cash.

(4) **October 15**
Merchandise Inventory...................................... 130,000
    Accounts Payable............................................         130,000
Acquisition of merchandise inventory on
account.

(5) **October 18**
Prepaid Insurance............................................... 800
    Cash .................................................................              800
Prepayment of insurance premium for cover-
age beginning November 1.

(6) **October 20**
Cash.......................................................................... 2,200
    Advances from Customers...........................           2,200
Advance from customers on merchandise to
be delivered on November 5.

(7) **October 26**
Accounts Payable ............................................. 90,000
    Cash .................................................................          88,200
    Merchandise Inventory ................................           1,800
Payment of invoices totaling $90,000 but
subject to a 2 percent discount for prompt
payment.

2.19 continued.

(8) **October 30**

| | | |
|---|---|---|
| Accounts Payable | 40,000 | |
| Cash | | 40,000 |

Payment of invoices totaling $40,000.

*Note*: Some students treat the lost discounts of $800 (= .02 × $40,000) as an expense and reduce the book value of merchandise inventory accordingly. We allow this answer as well.

2.20 (Kirkland Corporation; journal entries for various transactions.)

| | | |
|---|---|---|
| (1) Inventories | 30,000 | |
| Land | 15,000 | |
| Buildings | 125,000 | |
| Equipment | 60,000 | |
| Goodwill | 20,000 | |
| Common Stock | | 100,000 |
| Additional Paid-in Capital | | 150,000 |
| | | |
| (2) Advance to Supplier | 5,000 | |
| Cash | | 5,000 |
| | | |
| (3) Merchandise Inventories | 36,000 | |
| Advance to Supplier | | 5,000 |
| Accounts Payable | | 31,000 |
| | | |
| (4) Accounts Payable | 3,500 | |
| Merchandise Inventories | | 3,500 |
| | | |
| (5) Accounts Payable ($31,000 − $3,500) | 27,500 | |
| Cash {[.98($36,000 − $3,500)] − $5,000} | | 26,850 |
| Merchandise Inventories [.02($36,000 − $3,500)] | | 650 |
| | | |
| (6) Cash | 800 | |
| Advance from Customers | | 800 |
| | | |
| (7) Automobile | 18,000 | |
| Cash | | 2,000 |
| Note Payable | | 16,000 |
| | | |
| (8) Prepaid Insurance | 24,000 | |
| Cash | | 24,000 |

2.21    (Winkle Grocery Store; journal entries for various transactions.)

(1)  Cash............................................................................... 30,000
     Common Stock .......................................................... 30,000

(2)  Cash............................................................................... 5,000
     Notes Payable.......................................................... 5,000

(3)  Prepaid Rent................................................................. 12,000
     Cash........................................................................... 12,000

(4)  Equipment..................................................................... 8,000
     Cash........................................................................... 8,000

(5)  Merchandise Inventory .............................................. 25,000
     Cash........................................................................... 12,000
     Accounts Payable .................................................... 13,000

(6)  Cash............................................................................... 4,000
     Advances from Customers...................................... 4,000

(7)  Prepaid Insurance ....................................................... 1,200
     Cash........................................................................... 1,200

(8)  Prepaid Advertising..................................................... 600
     Cash........................................................................... 600

(9)  The placing of an order does not give rise to a journal entry because it represents a mutually unexecuted contract.

2.22    (Journal entries for various transactions.)

(1)  Investment in Bonds.................................................... 103,500
     Cash........................................................................... 103,500

(2)  Cash .............................................................................. 6,390
     Insurance Premiums Received in
       Advance................................................................ 6,390

(3)  Land............................................................................... 15,000
     Building ........................................................................ 105,000
     Equipment.................................................................... 60,000
     Common Stock—Par Value..................................... 144,000
     Additional Paid-in Capital ...................................... 36,000

(4)  Accounting makes no entry because an exchange between the buyer and seller has not yet occurred to warrant recognition of either an asset or a liability.

2.22 continued.

    (5)  Patent ............................................................................. 7,500
             Preferred Stock—Par Value............................... 6,000
             Additional Paid-in Capital ................................ 1,500

    (6)  Cash .............................................................................. 650
             Admission Fees Received in Advance ................ 650

    (7)  No entry is made until accountants establish the amount and timing of payment.

    (8)  Accounts Payable........................................................ 4,000
             Merchandise Inventory........................................ 4,000

2.23    (Wendy's International, Inc.; journal entries for various transactions.)

    (1)  The firm does not make an entry for the supplies until it receives them.

    (2)  Supplies Inventory...................................................... 1,600,000
             Accounts Payable ............................................... 1,600,000

    (3)  Accounts Payable........................................................ 40,000
             Supplies Inventory.............................................. 40,000

    (4)  Accounts Payable........................................................ 1,400,000
             Cash (.98 × $1,400,000)..................................... 1,372,000
             Supplies Inventory.............................................. 28,000

    (5)  Accounts Payable........................................................ 160,000
             Cash....................................................................... 160,000

*Note*:   Some students treat the lost discounts of $3,200 (= .02 × $160,000) as an expense and reduce Supplies Inventory accordingly. We allow this answer as well.

    (6)  Deposit on Equipment ............................................... 200,000
             Cash....................................................................... 200,000

    (7)  Equipment.................................................................... 900,000
             Deposit on Equipment......................................... 200,000
             Cash....................................................................... 700,000

    (8)  Equipment.................................................................... 27,000
             Cash....................................................................... 27,000

    (9)  Receivable from Supplier .......................................... 22,000
             Equipment ............................................................ 22,000

   (10)  Cash .............................................................................. 22,000
             Receivable from Supplier.................................... 22,000

2.24    (Effect of transactions on balance sheet equation.)

| Transaction Number | | Assets | = | Liabilities | + | Shareholders' Equity |
|---|---|---|---|---|---|---|
| (1) | | +$30,000 | | | | + $30,000 |
| | Subtotal | $30,000 | = | | | $30,000 |
| (2) | | + 18,900 | | + $18,900 | | |
| | Subtotal | $48,900 | = | $18,900 | + | $30,000 |
| (3) | | + 12,700 | | | | |
| | | − 2,000 | | + 10,700 | | |
| | Subtotal | $59,600 | = | $29,600 | + | $30,000 |
| (4) | | + 1,800 | | | | |
| | | − 1,800 | | | | |
| | Subtotal | $59,600 | = | $29,600 | + | $30,000 |
| (5) | | | | − 10,700 | | + 10,700 |
| | Subtotal | $59,600 | = | $18,900 | + | $40,700 |
| (6) | | − 18,900 | | − 18,900 | | |
| | Total | $40,700 | = | -0- | + | $40,700 |

2.25    (Regaldo Department Stores; effect of transactions on balance sheet equation.)

a.

| Transaction Number | Cash | + Inventories | + Other Assets | = Liabilities | + Common Stock | + Retained Earnings |
|---|---|---|---|---|---|---|
| (1) | +Ps 500,000 | | | | +Ps 500,000 | |
| (2) | −Ps 24,000 | | +Ps 24,000 | | | |
| (3)[a] | | | | | | |
| (4) | −Ps 60,000 | | +Ps 60,000 | | | |
| (5) | | +Ps 200,000 | | +Ps 200,000 | | |
| (6) | | −Ps 8,000 | | −Ps 8,000 | | |
| (7) | −Ps 156,800 | −Ps 3,200 | | −Ps 160,000 | | |
| (8) | −Ps 12,000 | | +Ps 12,000 | | | |
| | Ps 247,200 | + Ps 188,800 | + Ps 96,000 | = Ps 32,000 | + Ps 500,000 | + Ps 0 |

[a]Accounting views the ordering of merchandise as a mutually unexecuted contract and, therefore, makes no entry at this time.

2.25 continued.

b.
### REGALDO DEPARTMENT STORES
### Balance Sheet
### January 31, Year 8

*Assets*

Current Assets:

| | |
|---|---:|
| Cash | Ps247,200 |
| Merchandise Inventories | 188,800 |
| Prepaid Rent | 60,000 |
| Prepaid Insurance | 12,000 |
| Total Current Assets | Ps508,000 |
| Patent | 24,000 |
| Total Assets | Ps532,000 |

*Liabilities and Shareholders' Equity*

Current Liabilities:

| | |
|---|---:|
| Accounts Payable | Ps 32,000 |
| Total Current Liabilities | Ps 32,000 |

Shareholders' Equity:

| | |
|---|---:|
| Common Stock | Ps500,000 |
| Retained Earnings | 0 |
| Total Shareholders' Equity | Ps500,000 |
| Total Liabilities and Shareholders' Equity | Ps532,000 |

2.26    (T-account entries for various transactions.)

| Cash (A) | | | |
|---|---|---|---|
| (1) 240,000 | 80,000 | (2) | |
| (5) 20,000 | 3,000 | (4) | |
| (7) 600 | 22,000 | (6) | |
| 155,600 | | | |

| Merchandise Inventory (A) | |
|---|---|
| (3) 35,000 | |
| 35,000 | |

| Prepaid Insurance (A) | |
|---|---|
| (4) 3,000 | |
| 3,000 | |

| Building (A) | |
|---|---|
| (2) 500,000 | |
| 500,000 | |

| Equipment (A) | |
|---|---|
| (3) 20,000 | |
| 20,000 | |

| Accounts Payable (L) | | |
|---|---|---|
| (6) 22,000 | 55,000 | (3) |
| | 33,000 | |

| Note Payable (L) | | |
|---|---|---|
| | 20,000 | (5) |
| | 20,000 | |

| Advances from Customers (L) | | |
|---|---|---|
| | 600 | (7) |
| | 600 | |

| Mortgage Payable (L) | | |
|---|---|---|
| | 420,000 | (2) |
| | 420,000 | |

| Common Stock— Par Value (SE) | | |
|---|---|---|
| | 100,000 | (1) |
| | 100,000 | |

| Additional Paid-in Capital (SE) | | |
|---|---|---|
| | 140,000 | (1) |
| | 140,000 | |

**2.27** (Patterson Manufacturing Corporation; T-account entries and balance sheet preparation.)

a.

| Cash (A) | | | |
|---|---|---|---|
| (1) 210,000 | 5,400 | (5) |
| (11) 4,500 | 350 | (6) |
| | 1,400 | (8) |
| | 58,200 | (9) |
| | 7,000 | (12) |
| | 95,000 | (14) |
| 47,150 | | |

| Marketable Securities (A) | |
|---|---|
| (14) 95,000 | |
| 95,000 | |

| Receivable from Supplier (A) | |
|---|---|
| (13) 1,455 | |
| 1,455 | |

| Raw Materials Inventory (A) | | | |
|---|---|---|---|
| (4) 75,000 | 800 | (7) |
| | 1,800 | (9) |
| | 1,455 | (13) |
| 70,945 | | |

| Prepaid Rent (A) | | |
|---|---|---|
| (8) 1,400 | |
| 1,400 | |

| Land (A) | | |
|---|---|---|
| (2) 80,000 | |
| 80,000 | |

| Buildings (A) | |
|---|---|
| (2) 220,000 | |
| (12) 60,000 | |
| 280,000 | |

| Equipment (A) | | |
|---|---|---|
| (2) 92,000 | |
| (5) 5,400 | |
| (6) 350 | |
| 97,750 | |

| Patent (A) | |
|---|---|
| (3) 28,000 | |
| 28,000 | |

| Accounts Payable (L) | | | |
|---|---|---|---|
| (7) 800 | 75,000 | (4) |
| (9) 60,000 | | |
| | 14,200 | |

| Advances from Customers (L) | | |
|---|---|---|
| | 4,500 | (11) |
| | 4,500 | |

| Mortgage Payable (L) | | |
|---|---|---|
| | 53,000 | (12) |
| | 53,000 | |

| Common Stock Par Value (SE) | | |
|---|---|---|
| | 150,000 | (1) |
| | 280,000 | (2) |
| | 20,000 | (3) |
| | 450,000 | |

| Additional Paid-in Capital (SE) | | |
|---|---|---|
| | 60,000 | (1) |
| | 112,000 | (2) |
| | 8,000 | (3) |
| | 180,000 | |

(10) Because no insurance coverage has yet been provided and no cash has changed hands, the principle of mutual exchange suggests that no asset and no liability be recorded.

2.27 continued.

b.
## PATTERSON MANUFACTURING CORPORATION
### Balance Sheet
### January 31

*Assets*

Current Assets:

| | | |
|---|---:|---:|
| Cash .......................................................... | $ 47,150 | |
| Marketable Securities ............................... | 95,000 | |
| Receivable from Supplier............................ | 1,455 | |
| Raw Materials Inventory.......................... | 70,945 | |
| Prepaid Rent[a].......................................... | 1,400 | |
| Total Current Assets................................ | | $ 215,950 |
| Property, Plant, and Equipment (at Acquisition Cost): | | |
| Land........................................................... | $ 80,000 | |
| Buildings .................................................. | 280,000 | |
| Equipment.................................................. | 97,750 | |
| Total Property, Plant, and Equipment... | | 457,750 |
| Intangibles: | | |
| Patent ........................................................ | | 28,000 |
| Total Assets ............................................. | | $ 701,700 |

*Liabilities and Shareholders' Equity*

Current Liabilities:

| | | |
|---|---:|---:|
| Accounts Payable[a] ..................................... | $ 14,200 | |
| Advances from Customers.......................... | 4,500 | |
| Total Current Liabilities .......................... | | $ 18,700 |
| Long-Term Debt: | | |
| Mortgage Payable....................................... | | 53,000 |
| Total Liabilities........................................ | | $ 71,700 |
| Shareholders' Equity: | | |
| Common Stock—$10 Par Value ................. | $ 450,000 | |
| Additional Paid-in Capital .......................... | 180,000 | |
| Total Shareholders' Equity...................... | | 630,000 |
| Total Liabilities and Shareholders' Equity................................................. | | $ 701,700 |

[a]See discussion of transaction (10) on the preceding page. It is not wrong to show a current asset, Prepaid Insurance, of $400 and an additional $400 in the current liability, Accounts Payable. If that amount is shown, then, of course, the various subtotals and totals will increase by $400.

**2.28** (Whitley Products Corporation; T-account entries and balance sheet preparation.)

a.

| Cash (A) | | | |
|---|---|---|---|
| (1) 375,000 | 50,000 | (2) |
| (7) 1,500 | 125,000 | (3) |
| | 2,800 | (4) |
| | 3,200 | (5) |
| | 12,000 | (6) |
| | 50,960 | (12) |
| **132,540** | | |

| Merchandise Inventory (A) | | |
|---|---|---|
| (10) 60,000 | 8,000 | (11) |
| | 1,040 | (12) |
| **50,960** | | |

| Prepaid Insurance (A) | |
|---|---|
| (6) 12,000 | |
| **12,000** | |

| Land (A) | |
|---|---|
| (2) 25,000 | |
| **25,000** | |

| Buildings (A) | |
|---|---|
| (2) 275,000 | |
| **275,000** | |

| Equipment (A) | |
|---|---|
| (3) 125,000 | |
| (4) 2,800 | |
| (5) 3,200 | |
| **131,000** | |

| Note Payable (L) | |
|---|---|
| | 250,000 (2) |
| | **250,000** |

| Accounts Payable (L) | |
|---|---|
| (11) 8,000 | 60,000 (10) |
| (12) 52,000 | |
| | **0** |

| Advances from Customers (L) | |
|---|---|
| | 1,500 (7) |
| | **1,500** |

| Common Stock (SE) | |
|---|---|
| | 250,000 (1) |
| | **250,000** |

| Additional Paid-in Capital (SE) | |
|---|---|
| | 125,000 (1) |
| | **125,000** |

2.28 continued.

b.

## WHITLEY PRODUCTS CORPORATION
### Balance Sheet
### April 30

*Assets*

Current Assets:
Cash.................................................................. $ 132,540
Merchandise Inventory............................... 50,960
Prepaid Insurance....................................... 12,000
    Total Current Assets.............................. $ 195,500
Property, Plant, and Equipment:
Land.............................................................. $ 25,000
Buildings...................................................... 275,000
Equipment.................................................... 131,000
    Total Property, Plant, and Equipment... 431,000
    Total Assets............................................. $ 626,500

*Liabilities and Shareholders' Equity*

Current Liabilities:
Note Payable................................................ $ 250,000
Advances from Customers.......................... 1,500
    Total Current Liabilities....................... $ 251,500
Shareholders' Equity:
Common Stock—$10 Par Value................. 250,000
Additional Paid-in Capital......................... 125,000
    Total Shareholders' Equity.................... 375,000
    Total Liabilities and Shareholders'
        Equity.................................................. $ 626,500

**2.29** (Soybel Corporation; T-account entries and balance sheet preparation.)

a.

| Cash (A) | | Merchandise Inventory (A) | | Prepaid Insurance (A) | |
|---|---|---|---|---|---|
| (1) 150,000 | 220,000 (3) | (5) 75,000 | 8,000 (6) | (7) 3,200 | |
| (2) 250,000 | 88,200 (4) | | | | |
| (8) 900 | 3,200 (7) | | | | |
| | 64,000 (9) | | | | |
| 25,500 | | 67,000 | | 3,200 | |

| Land (A) | | Buildings (A) | | Equipment (A) | |
|---|---|---|---|---|---|
| (3) 60,000 | | (3) 240,000 | | (4) 88,200 | |
| 60,000 | | 240,000 | | 88,200 | |

| Accounts Payable (L) | | Advances from Customers (L) | | Mortgage Payable (L) | |
|---|---|---|---|---|---|
| (6) 8,000 | 75,000 (5) | | 900 (8) | | 80,000 (3) |
| (9) 64,000 | | | | | |
| | 3,000 | | 900 | | 80,000 |

| Bonds Payable (L) | | Common Stock (SE) | | Additional Paid-in Capital (SE) | |
|---|---|---|---|---|---|
| | 250,000 (2) | | 100,000 (1) | | 50,000 (1) |
| | 250,000 | | 100,000 | | 50,000 |

b.

**SOYBEL CORPORATION**
**Balance Sheet**
**January 31**

*Assets*

| | | |
|---|---|---|
| Current Assets: | | |
| Cash | $ 25,500 | |
| Merchandise Inventory | 67,000 | |
| Prepaid Insurance | 3,200 | |
| Total Current Assets | | $ 95,700 |
| Property, Plant and Equipment: | | |
| Land | $ 60,000 | |
| Buildings | 240,000 | |
| Equipment | 88,200 | |
| Total Property, Plant and Equipment | | 388,200 |
| Total Assets | | $483,900 |

2.29 b. continued.

*Liabilities and Shareholders' Equity*

Current Liabilities:
Accounts Payable............................................. $    3,000
Advances from Customers............................         900
   Total Current Liabilities ...........................                          $      3,900
Long-Term Debt:
Mortgage Payable............................................ $  80,000
Bonds Payable................................................    250,000
   Total Long-Term Debt................................                             330,000
   Total Liabilities...........................................                          $333,900
Shareholders' Equity:
Common Stock.................................................. $ 100,000
Additional Paid-in Capital .............................      50,000
   Total Shareholders' Equity........................                             150,000
   Total Liabilities and Shareholders'
     Equity........................................................                          $483,900

2.30  (Computer Graphics, Inc.; T-account entries and balance sheet preparation.)

a.

| Cash (A) | | Supplies Inventory (A) | | Prepaid Rent (A) | |
|---|---|---|---|---|---|
| (1) 150,000 | 18,000 (4) | (8) 4,900 | 98 (10) | (4) 18,000 | |
| (7) 1,500 | 12,000 (5) | (9) 900 | | | |
| | 900 (9) | | | | |
| | 4,802 (10) | | | | |
| 115,798 | | 5,702 | | 18,000 | |

| Equipment (A) | | Software (A) | | Patent (A) | |
|---|---|---|---|---|---|
| (5) 12,000 | | (2) 90,000 | | (3) 1,500 | |
| 12,000 | | 90,000 | | 1,500 | |

| Accounts Payable (L) | | Advances from Customers (L) | | Common Stock (SE) | |
|---|---|---|---|---|---|
| (10) 4,900 | 4,900 (8) | | 1,500 (7) | | 100,000 (1) |
| | | | | | 60,000 (2) |
| | | | | | 1,000 (3) |
| -- | -- | | 1,500 | | 161,000 |

2.30 a. continued.

Additional Paid-In
Capital (SE)
|  | 50,000 (1) |
|  | 30,000 (2) |
|  | 500 (3) |
| | |
|  | <u>80,500</u> |

b.

**COMPUTER GRAPHICS, INC.**
**Balance Sheet**
**May 30**

*Assets*

| Current Assets: | | |
|---|---|---|
| Cash | $ 115,798 | |
| Supplies Inventory | 5,702 | |
| Prepaid Rent | <u>18,000</u> | |
| Total Current Assets | | $ 139,500 |
| Noncurrent Assets: | | |
| Equipment | $ 12,000 | |
| Computer Software | 90,000 | |
| Patent | <u>1,500</u> | |
| Total Noncurrent Assets | | <u>103,500</u> |
| Total Assets | | <u>$ 243,000</u> |

*Liabilities and Shareholders' Equity*

| Current Liabilities: | | |
|---|---|---|
| Advances from Customers | | $ 1,500 |
| Shareholders' Equity: | | |
| Common Stock | $ 161,000 | |
| Additional Paid-in Capital | <u>80,500</u> | |
| Total Shareholders' Equity | | <u>241,500</u> |
| Total Liabilities and Shareholders' Equity | | <u>$ 243,000</u> |

2.31    (Blacksmith's Bakery, Inc.; T-account entries and balance sheet preparation.)

a.

| Cash (A) | | | | Supplies Inventory (A) | | | | Prepayments (A) | |
|---|---|---|---|---|---|---|---|---|---|
| (1) 2,000 | 450 (4) | | (7) 390 | | | | (6) 800 | |
| (2) 220 | 580 (5) | | (9) 240 | | | | (8) 120 | |
| (3) 500 | 800 (6) | | | | | | | |
| | 390 (7) | | | | | | | |
| | 120 (8) | | | | | | | |
| __380__ | | | __630__ | | | | __920__ | |

| Equipment (A) | | | Accounts Payable (L) | | | Advances from Customers (L) | |
|---|---|---|---|---|---|---|---|
| (4) 450 | | | | 240 (9) | | | 220 (2) |
| (5) 580 | | | | 750 (10) | | | |
| (10) 750 | | | | | | | |
| __1,780__ | | | | __990__ | | | __220__ |

| Common Stock (SE) | | | Additional Paid-in Capital (SE) | |
|---|---|---|---|---|
| | 2,000 (1) | | | 500 (3)* |
| | __2,000__ | | | __500__ |

*Note:* *The chapter does not discuss the correct credit entry for transaction (3). Students should realize that the absence of a repayment obligation precludes recognition of a liability. The principal issue is the appropriate shareholders' equity account. We tend to allow various account titles.

2.31 continued.

b.

**BLACKSMITH'S BAKERY, INC.,**
**Balance Sheet**
**August 31**

*Assets*

Current Assets:
| | | |
|---|---|---|
| Cash .......................................................... | $ 380 | |
| Supplies Inventory ..................................... | 630 | |
| Prepaid Rent .............................................. | 920 | |
| Total Current Assets ................................ | | $ 1,930 |

Noncurrent Assets:
| | | |
|---|---|---|
| Equipment ................................................... | | 1,780 |
| Total Assets ............................................ | | $ 3,710 |

*Liabilities and Shareholders' Equity*

Current Liabilities:
| | | |
|---|---|---|
| Accounts Payable ....................................... | $ 990 | |
| Advances from Customers ......................... | 220 | |
| Total Current Liabilities ........................ | | $ 1,210 |

Shareholders' Equity:
| | | |
|---|---|---|
| Common Stock .............................................. | $ 2,000 | |
| Additional Paid-in Capital ....................... | 500 | |
| Total Shareholders' Equity .................... | | 2,500 |
| Total Liabilities and Shareholders' Equity ..................................................... | | $ 3,710 |

2.32    (Effect of recording errors on balance sheet equation.)

| Transaction Number | Assets | = | Liabilities | + | Shareholders' Equity |
|---|---|---|---|---|---|
| (1) | No | | No | | No |
| (2) | O/S $ 9,000 | | O/S $ 9,000 | | No |
| (3) | U/S $16,000 | | U/S $16,000 | | No |
| (4) | No | | No | | No |
| (5) | U/S $ 1,500 | | U/S $ 1,500 | | No |
| (6) | U/S $12,000 | | No | | U/S $12,000 |
| (7) | No | | No | | No |

2.33    (Effect of recording errors on balance sheet equation.)

| Transaction Number | Assets | = | Liabilities | + | Shareholders' Equity |
|---|---|---|---|---|---|
| (1) | U/S $760,000 | | U/S $760,000 | | No |
| (2) | O/S $ 800[a] | | No | | No |
| | U/S $ 800[a] | | | | No |
| (3) | No | | No | | No |
| (4) | No | | O/S $ 10,000 | | U/S $10,000 |
| (5) | U/S $ 900[a] | | | | |
| | O/S $ 900[a] | | | | |
| (6) | No | | No | | No |
| (7) | O/S $ 2,000 | | No | | O/S $ 2,000 |
| (8) | O/S $ 3,000[b] | | O/S $ 3,000 | | No |

[a]The response "No" is also acceptable here.

[b]Cash is overstated $2,940 and inventory is overstated $60.

2.34    (Effect of recording errors on balance sheet equation.)

| Transaction Number | Assets | = | Liabilities | + | Shareholders' Equity |
|---|---|---|---|---|---|
| (1) | U/S $ 8,000 | | U/S $ 8,000 | | No |
| (2) | O/S $ 3,000 | | O/S $ 3,000 | | No |
| (3) | U/S $ 800 | | U/S $ 800 | | No |
| (4) | O/S $ 1,000 | | O/S $ 1,000 | | No |
| (5) | U/S $ 2,500 | | No | | U/S $2,500 |
| (6) | O/S $ 4,900[a] | | No | | No |
| | U/S $ 4,900[a] | | | | |

[a]The response "No" is also acceptable here.

**2.35** (Marks and Spenser; balance sheet format, terminology, and accounting methods.)

a.
**MARKS AND SPENCER, PLC**
**Balance Sheet**
**(In Millions of Pounds)**

| | March 30 Year 4 | March 30 Year 5 |
|---|---|---|
| *Assets* | | |
| Current Assets: | | |
| Cash | £ 266 | £ 293 |
| Marketable Securities | 28 | 29 |
| Accounts Receivable | 192 | 212 |
| Inventories | 374 | 351 |
| Prepayments | 134 | 142 |
| Total Current Assets | £ 994 | £ 1,027 |
| Property, Plant and Equipment: | | |
| Land and Buildings | £ 1,636[a] | £ 1,733[b] |
| Equipment | 375 | 419 |
| Total Property, Plant and Equipment | £ 2,011 | £ 2,152 |
| Other Noncurrent Assets | £ 212 | £ 264 |
| Total Assets | £ 3,217 | £ 3,443 |
| *Liabilities and Shareholders' Equity* | | |
| Current Liabilities: | | |
| Accounts Payable | £ 187 | £ 168 |
| Bank Loans | 100 | 107 |
| Other Current Liabilities | 638 | 622 |
| Total Current Liabilities | £ 925 | £ 897 |
| Noncurrent Liabilities: | | |
| Bonds Payable | £ 565 | £ 550 |
| Other Noncurrent Liabilities | 4 | 19 |
| Total Noncurrent Liabilities | £ 569 | £ 569 |
| Total Liabilities | £ 1,494 | £ 1,466 |
| Shareholders' Equity: | | |
| Common Stock | £ 675 | £ 680 |
| Additional Paid-in Capital | 50 | 69 |
| Retained Earnings | 998 | 1,228 |
| Total Shareholders' Equity | £ 1,723 | £ 1,977 |
| Total Liabilities and Shareholders' Equity | £ 3,217 | £ 3,443 |

[a]£2,094 − £458 = £1,636.

[b]£2,193 − £460 = £1,733.

b. A close relation exists between the amount of current assets and current liabilities and between noncurrent assets and noncurrent liabilities plus shareholders' equity.

2.36    (United Breweries Group; balance sheet format, terminology, and accounting methods.)

a.

## UNITED BREWERIES GROUP
### Balance Sheet
### (In Millions of Kronor)

|  | September 30 Year 8 | September 30 Year 9 |
|---|---|---|
| *Assets* | | |
| **Current Assets:** | | |
| Cash | Kr 810 | Kr 1,224 |
| Marketable Securities | 3,018 | 3,460 |
| Accounts Receivable | 1,413 | 1,444 |
| Inventories | 1,290 | 1,393 |
| Prepayments | 317 | 285 |
| Total Current Assets | Kr 6,848 | Kr 7,806 |
| Investments in Securities | 422 | 573 |
| Property, Plant and Equipment[a] | 3,518 | 3,545 |
| Total Assets | Kr 10,788 | Kr 11,924 |
| *Liabilities and Shareholders' Equity* | | |
| **Current Liabilities:** | | |
| Accounts Payable | Kr 913 | Kr 902 |
| Bank Debt | 619 | 986 |
| Other Current Liabilities | 2,157 | 2,240 |
| Total Current Liabilities | Kr 3,689 | Kr 4,128 |
| Bonds Payable | 1,805 | 1,723 |
| Other Noncurrent Liabilities | 1,149 | 1,425 |
| Total Liabilities | Kr 6,643 | Kr 7,276 |
| **Shareholders' Equity:** | | |
| Common Stock | Kr 976 | Kr 976 |
| Retained Earnings | 3,169 | 3,672 |
| Total Shareholders' Equity | Kr 4,145 | Kr 4,648 |
| Total Liabilities and Shareholders' Equity | Kr 10,788 | Kr 11,924 |

[a]The amounts for this account reflect historical costs instead of current market values as follows:

| | As Reported By Company | – Revaluation Reserve | + As Restated |
|---|---|---|---|
| Property, Plant and Equipment: | | | |
| September 30, Year 8 | Kr3,934 | – Kr416 | + Kr3,518 |
| September 30, Year 9 | Kr4,106 | – Kr561 | + Kr3,545 |

b.   Current assets significantly exceed current liabilities, primarily because of the high proportion of current assets that comprises cash and marketable securities. United Breweries has apparently generated substantial cash flow from operations which it has not reinvested in operating assets.

2.37    (Staples, Inc.; interpreting balance sheet changes.)

    a.   The principal assets of a retail chain are inventories and retail stores. Merchandise inventories dominate the balance sheet of Staples, in part because some of its retail space is leased from other entities and does not appear in property, plant and equipment. Accounts payable to suppliers of merchandise is the largest current liability. Thus, Staples uses short-term financing to finance short-term assets. The common size percentage for long-term debt is approximately the same as the percentage for property, plant and equipment. Staples, therefore, appears to use long-term financing for long-term assets. The relatively large common size percentage for total shareholders' equity suggests that Staples uses long-term financing to finance both current and noncurrent assets. Such a financing strategy permits Staples to grow both its current and noncurrent assets without needing to repay borrowing in the near term, possibly constraining its ability to grow.

    b.   The common size percentage for cash increased significantly between Year 6 and Year 7. The decreased common size percentage for accounts receivable may suggest more stringent credit policies that permitted Staples to collect more quickly from customers. The increased common size percentage for accounts payable may suggest that Staples delayed paying its suppliers, thereby conserving cash.

    c.   The percentages in the common size balance sheet are not independent of each other. A decrease in the dollar amount of property, plant and equipment may result in an increasing, decreasing, or stable proportion for this balance sheet item, depending on the changes in other assets.

2.38    (Pacific Gas and Electric Company; interpreting balance sheet changes.)

    a.   The largest asset is property, plant, and equipment, which represents the generating and distribution capacity of the utility. Long-term financing dominates the financing side of the balance sheet, with the largest proportion coming from long-term debt. The historically predictable cash flows of utilities from their regulated monopoly status permit them to take on a large portion of long-term debt financing.

    b.   Pacific Gas and Electric operated at a net loss during Year 10 as evidenced by the change from a positive to a negative balance in retained earnings. The decreased percentages for property, plant, and equipment and for other noncurrent assets suggest that the firm wrote down these assets during the year, leading to the net loss. The mix of financing in the capital structure changed from shareholders' equity to liabilities and from noncurrent liabilities to current liabilities. The firm likely took on additional short-term financing to pay off long-term debt.

2.39    (Relating market value to book value of shareholders' equity.)

a.  (1)  **Coke**—One important asset missing from the balance sheet of Coke is the value of its brand names. Coke follows generally accepted accounting principles (GAAP) in expensing the cost of developing and maintaining its brand names each year (for example, product development, quality control, advertising). The future benefits of these expenditures are too difficult to identify and measure with sufficient precision to justify recognizing an asset. Coke also reports its property, plant and equipment at acquisition cost (adjusted downward for depreciation) instead of current market values. Acquisition cost valuations are more objective and easier to audit than current market valuations.

(2)  **Bristol**—Bristol engages in research and development to discover new drugs. GAAP requires firms to expense research and development expenditures immediately. The future benefits of these expenditures are too uncertain to justify recognizing an asset. Thus, the value of patents and technologies developed by Bristol, as well as the value of the research scientists employed by Bristol, do not appear on its balance sheet.

(3)  **Bankers Trust**—The market-to-book ratio for Bankers is 1.0. Most of the assets and liabilities of Bankers are monetary items and turn over frequently. Thus, the market values and book values closely conform.

(4)  **International Paper (IP)**—IP reports its forest lands on the balance sheet at acquisition cost. IP likely acquired the land many years ago. The acquisition cost of the land is considerably less than its current market value. Also, IP follows general industry practice and expenses the annual cost of maintaining its forest lands. Thus, the value of forest lands increases each year as trees grow. The market incorporates this value increase into its price of the common stock of IP even though GAAP does not reflect the value increase on the balance sheet. The value increase is too difficult to measure objectively to justify substituting market values for acquisition cost.

(5)  **Disney**—Disney depreciates the cost of film inventory over its expected useful life. Fortunately for Disney and other film production companies, the value of old films has increased in recent years with the growth of cable networks. Thus, the market value of some of Disney's films exceeds their book values. The market-to-book ratio reflects this under valuation. Also, Disney reports its property, plant and equipment at acquisition cost (adjusted downward for depreciation) instead of current market values. The land underlying its theme parks has likely increased in value since

**2.39 a. continued.**

the date of acquisition, but the accounting records do not reflect the value increase under GAAP.

b. (1) **Coke**—Coke's current assets are less than its current liabilities. This relation indicates short-term liquidity risk. The high market-to-book ratio suggests that the market value (selling price) of its inventory exceeds the book value, so current assets probably equal or exceed current liabilities at market value. Shareholders' equity represents a higher proportion of long-term financing than long-term debt. One explanation for the relatively low proportion of long-term debt is that Coke is very profitable (suggested by the high market-to-book ratio) and therefore generates most of its needed cash from operations. Further support for the internal generation of cash is the high proportion of retained earnings and significant treasury stock purchases. Another explanation for the relatively low proportion of long-term debt relates to the investments in its bottlers. Chapter 11 discusses the accounting for intercorporate investments. Because Coke owns less than 50 percent of the outstanding common stock of these bottlers, it does not consolidate them. Thus, the assets and the financing of the bottlers are "off balance sheet." These bottlers may carry significantly more long-term debt than Coke.

(2) **Bristol**—The interesting insight from studying Bristol's capital structure is the relatively small proportion of long-term debt. The products of Bristol are subject to technological obsolescence. Competitors could develop technologically superior drugs that would replace those of Bristol in the market. Given this product risk, Bristol probably does not want to add the financial risk that fixed interest and principal payments on debt create.

(3) **Bankers Trust**—Bankers relies heavily on short-term sources for financing, principally deposits and short-term borrowing. Customers can withdraw their funds on no, or very short, notice. Thus, Bankers must maintain a relatively liquid balance sheet. Most of its assets are in cash, short-term marketable securities, and loans. The loans are less liquid than cash and marketable securities but tend to have predictable cash flows. Note that shareholders' equity makes up approximately 5 percent of liabilities plus shareholders' equities. Such a low percentage is common for commercial banks. Banks carry high proportions of liabilities because of the high liquidity of their assets.

2.39 b. continued.

(4) **International Paper (IP)**—IP carries a high proportion of noncurrent assets and matches this with a high proportion of long-term financing. IP uses approximately equal proportions of long-term liabilities and shareholders' equity to finance its noncurrent assets. The sales of paper products vary with movements through economic cycles. During recessionary periods, demand slackens and firms reduce prices in order to utilize capital-intensive manufacturing facilities. Paper companies do not want too much debt in their capital structures that could force them into bankruptcy during these times. On the other hand, when the economy is booming, the profits and cash flows of paper companies increase significantly. Firms spread the cost of their capital-intensive plants over larger volumes of output. In these cases, shareholders benefit from debt in the capital structure (a phenomenon known as *financial leverage*, discussed in Chapter 5). Thus, the approximately equal proportions of long-term debt and shareholders' equity reflect these opposing considerations.

(5) **Disney**—Disney reports a significant excess of current assets over current liabilities. Interpreting this excess involves two opposing considerations. Some of Disney's films continue to generate revenues and cash flows, even though the films carry a zero book value on Disney's books. On the other hand, Disney accumulates the cost of films in process in the inventory account without knowing whether or not the films will be a commercial success. Disney uses a higher proportion of shareholders' equity than long-term debt in its long-term financing structure. Its property, plant and equipment can serve as collateral for long-term borrowing. Its predictable revenue and cash flows from theme parks also argues for a high proportion of long-term debt relative to shareholders' equity. Perhaps Disney did not want to use up its borrowing capacity in case it had the opportunity to make an acquisition (such as Capital Cities/ABC) and needed to borrow to finance the transaction.

2.40    (Relating market value to book value of shareholders' equity.)

a. (1) **Pfizer**—Pharmaceutical firms make ongoing expenditures on research and development (R&D) to develop new products. Some of these expenditures result in profitable new products, while other expenditures do not provide any future benefit. The difficulty encountered in trying to identify whether or not a particular R&D expenditure results in a future benefit has led accounting standard setters to require the immediate expensing of R&D costs in the year incurred. Thus, the valuable patents for pharmaceutical products and the value of potential products in the research pipeline do not appear on the balance sheet of Pfizer. The market does place a value on these technologies in deciding on an appropriate market price for the firm's stock.

Students might suggest approaches that technology firms could follow to measure the value of their technology resources. One approach might be to study the past success record of discovering new technologies For example, if 20 percent of expenditures in the past resulted in valuable technologies, the firm might report 20 percent of the expenditures on R&D each period as an asset. If these new technologies provided benefits for, say, seven years on average, then the firm would amortize the amount recognized as an asset over seven years. An alternative approach would be to use the prices paid recently when acquiring firms purchase target firms that have similar technologies. Each of these approaches involves a degree of subjectivity that has led standard setters to require the immediate expensing of R&D expenditures in the year incurred.

(2) **Nestle**—The products of Nestle carry a high degree of brand recognition, which leads loyal customers to purchase Nestle products on a regular basis and new customers to try its products. The value of the Nestle and its other brand names is created through advertising, quality control, and new product introductions. Nestle follows GAAP in expensing these expenditures each year. Thus, the value of the brand name does not appear on the balance sheet as an asset. If the brand name did appear on the balance sheet, assets and shareholders' equity would be larger and the market-to-book ratio would be closer to 1.0.

One might ask how Nestle might value its brand names if it were permitted to recognize these valuable resources as assets. One approach might be to determine the profit margin (that is, net income divided by sales) that Nestle realizes on sales of its products relative to the profit margin of competitors. Nestle would then multiply the excess profit margin times the number of units expected to be sold in future years to measure its excess profitability. It would then discount the future excess earnings to a present value. An alternative approach is to identify the prices paid recently by firms acquiring other branded consumer products companies to ascertain the approximate price paid for identifiable assets and the portion paid for brand names. Each of these approaches involves a degree of subjectivity and opens the door for firms to cast their balance sheets in the most favorable light possible. Accounting standard setters in most countries recognize this potential source of bias and require firms to expense brand development costs in the year expenditures are made.

(3) **Promodes**—Promodes is the largest grocery store chain in France and likely has some brand name recognition that does not appear on its balance sheet. In addition, the stores of Promodes are valued at

2.40 a. continued.

acquisition cost adjusted downward for depreciation to date. The land and perhaps the store buildings probably have market values that exceed their book values. Standard setters in most countries require firms to account for land and buildings using acquisition costs instead of current market values because of the subjectivity in the latter valuations. This real estate is probably easier to value than brand names and technological know how because of active real estate markets. Thus, the market-to-book ratio probably reflects brand recognition and undervalued fixed assets.

(4) **Deutsche Bank**—Most of the assets of a commercial bank are reported on the balance sheet at current market values. Marketable securities are revalued to market value at each balance sheet date. Loans receivable are stated net of estimated uncollectibles and should therefore reflect cash-equivalent values. Deposits and short-term borrowing on the liability side of the balance sheet appear at current cash-equivalent values. Thus, the market-to-book ratio should be approximately 1.0. The ratio of 1.7 for Deutsche Bank suggests the presence of intangibles that do not appear on the balance sheet. Possibilities include the size and dominant influence of Deutsche Bank in the German economy, technologically sophisticated information systems, and superior work force. The financial consulting capabilities of its investment banking employees are a valuable resource that does not appear on the balance sheet as an asset.

(5) **British Airways**—The aircraft and ground facilities of British Airways appear at acquisition cost net of depreciation to date. The market values of these fixed assets likely exceed their book values. In addition, British Airways has landing and gateway rights that appear on the balance sheet only to the extent that the firm has paid amounts up front. In most cases, British Airways pays fees periodically as it uses these facilities. Thus, no asset appears on the balance sheet.

(6) **New Oji Paper Co.**—The balance sheet of New Oji Paper Co. includes a high proportion of intercorporate investments in securities and property, plant, and equipment. GAAP in Japan reports these assets at acquisition cost, with plant and equipment adjusted downward for depreciation to date. The market value of land probably exceeds its book value. The market values of securities in Japan have decreased significantly in recent years but may still exceed their book values if the investments were made many years ago. Note that the market-to-book ratio does not exceed 1.0 by as much as the consumer products and pharmaceutical companies with brand recognition.

2.40 continued.

b. (1) **Pfizer**—One question related to Pfizer is why it would use such a small percentage of long-term debt financing. Pharmaceutical firms face product obsolescence and legal liability risks. They tend not to add financial risk from having a high proportion of long-term debt on the balance sheet. Although this exercise does not provide the needed information, Pfizer is very profitable and generates sufficient cash flow from operations that it does not need much external financing.

A second question related to Pfizer is the large percentage for other noncurrent liabilities on the balance sheet. This amount includes its healthcare benefit obligation to employees and deferred income taxes. Students generally have not studied these two items sufficiently to generate much discussion.

A third question related to Pfizer is its high proportion of treasury stock. Economic theory would suggest that if the market fairly values a firm prior to a stock buyback, then the market price of the stock should not change. The economic value of the firm should decrease by the amount of cash paid out. The number of shares of common stock outstanding should decline proportionally and the stock price should remain the same. However, the effect of stock buybacks generally is to increase the market price of the stock. One possible explanation for the market price increase is that the market views the buyback as a positive signal by management about the firm's future prospects. Management knows about the firm's future plans and might feel that the market is underpricing the firm, given these future plans. The buyback signals this positive information and the market price increases.

(2) **Nestle**—Nestle, like Pfizer, has highly predictable cash flows from its brand name products and generates sufficient cash flows in the long term to reduce the need for long-term debt financing. Nestle, however, extends credit to customers and must carry inventory for some period of time before sale. It uses suppliers and short-term borrowing to finance this working capital.

(3) **Promodes**—The majority of the assets of Promodes is short-term receivables and inventories. The majority of its financing is likewise short-term. Thus, firms attempt to match the term structure of their financing to the term structure of their assets.

(4) **Deutsche Bank**—Deutsche Bank obtains the vast majority of its funds from depositors and short-term borrowing. Such a high proportion of short-term financing might appear risky. However, a large portion of its assets is in highly liquid cash and short-term investments. A large portion is also in loans to businesses and consumers. Although loans are generally not as liquid as cash and investments, they do have predictable cash flows. The large num-

2.40 b. continued.

ber of borrowers also diversifies the risk of Deutsche Bank on these loans. The low level of risk on the asset side of the balance sheet and the stability of the deposit base means that banks need only a small proportion of shareholders' equity.

(5) **British Airways**—The majority of the assets of British Airways is in flight and ground support equipment. British Airways matches these long-term assets with long-term financing, either in the form of long-term debt or shareholders' equity. The heavier use of debt financing stems from its lower cost and the availability of the equipment to serve as collateral for the borrowing. Lenders generally prefer that firms have more current assets than current liabilities. The excess current liabilities of British Airways stem from advance sales of airline tickets (appears in Other Current Liabilities). British Airways will satisfy this liability by providing transportation services rather than paying cash. Thus, the net current liability position is not of particular concern.

(6) **New Oji Paper Co.**—The balance sheet of Oji portrays some relationships that are typical of Japanese companies. First, note the high proportion of investments in securities. Many Japanese companies are part of corporate groups (called "Kieretsus"). The investments in firms in the corporate groups tend to represent 20 percent to 30 percent of these other companies and appear as intercorporate investments on the balance sheet. Secondly, note the relatively high proportion of short-term bank borrowing. Most corporate groups have a commercial bank as a member. This commercial bank is not likely to force a member of the group into bankruptcy if it is unable to repay a loan at maturity. The bank will more likely simply extend the term of the loan. Short-term borrowing is usually less costly than long-term borrowing and helps explain the high proportion of short-term borrowing on the balance sheet.

2.41    (Identifying industries using common size balance sheet percentages).

Firm (1) has a high percentage of receivables among its assets and substantial borrowing in its capital structure. This mix of assets and financing is typical of the finance company, Household International. We ask students why the capital markets allow a finance company to have such a high proportion of borrowing in its capital structure. The answer is threefold: (1) finance companies have contractual rights to receive cash flows in the future from borrowers; the cash flow tends to be highly predictable, (2) finance companies lend to many different individuals, which diversifies their risk, and (3) borrowers often pledge collateral to back up the loan, which provides the finance companies with an alternative for collecting cash if borrowers default on their loans. The relative mix of current liabilities and long-term debt suggests that loans with maturities longer than

2.41 continued.

one year exceed loans maturing within the next year, since companies attempt to match the maturities of their debt with the maturities of their assets.

Firms (2) and (3) have a high proportion of their assets in property, plant, and equipment. Commonwealth Edison and Newmont Mining are both capital intensive. These firms differ primarily with respect to their financing. Firm (2) has a higher proportion of long-term debt and Firm (3) has a higher proportion of financing from shareholders' equity. Commonwealth Edison has essentially a monopoly position in its market area and is subject to regulation with respect to rates charged. The reasonably assured cash flows permit it to take on more debt than Newmont Mining. Newmont Mining faces uncertainties with respect to the amount of gold and other minerals that it will discover and the price it will obtain for gold and minerals sold. Its high proportion of fixed costs in its cost structure means that its earnings can vary significantly as revenues increase and decrease over time. This larger business risk for Newmont Mining suggest that it should take on less long-term debt than Commonwealth Edison. Thus, Firm (2) is Commonwealth Edison and Firm (3) is Newmont Mining.

This leaves Hewlett Packard and May Department Stores and Firms (4) and (5). Firms (4) and (5) both have substantial receivables and inventories, which we would expect for both firms. Firm (4) has a lower proportion of property, plant, and equipment than Firm (5). Hewlett-Packard outsources the manufacturing of components and then assembles the components in its factories. The outsourcing reduces somewhat its need for fixed assets. May Department Stores, on the other hand, has fixed assets from its retail stores. This suggests that Firm (4) is Hewlett-Packard and Firm (5) is May Department Stores. The financing provides additional evidence for this pairing. Technological change reduces the product life cycles of computers and printers. Long-term lenders are reluctant to lend when substantial uncertainty exists about the long-term sales potential of a firm's products. The land and buildings of department stores serve as collateral for borrowing and permit a higher level of long-term debt in the capital structure. Firm (4) has a lower proportion of long-term debt than Firm (5), consistent with Firm (4) being Hewlett-Packard and Firm (5) being May Department Stores.

# CHAPTER 3

## INCOME STATEMENT: REPORTING THE RESULTS OF OPERATING ACTIVITIES

*Questions, Exercises, Problems, and Cases: Answers and Solutions*

3.1     See the text or the glossary at the end of the book.

3.2     Net income equals cash inflows minus cash outflows from operating, investing, and non-owner financing activities. If the period were long enough, then sales of goods and services (revenue under the accrual basis) and cash receipts from customers (revenue under the cash basis) would both occur in the same long-enough time period. Revenues would therefore not differ between the cash and accrual basis. Likewise, costs incurred to generated revenues (expenses under the accrual basis) and cash expenditures for goods and services consumed (expenses under the cash basis) would both occur in the same period. Expenses would also not differ between the cash and accrual basis. With the same amounts of revenues and expenses, net income on an accrual basis would equal net income on a cash basis.

3.3     The amount of revenue recognized equals the amount of cash the firm expects to collect from customers. The firm does not necessarily recognize the revenue, however, at the time it receives the cash. It typically recognizes revenue at the time of sale even though it has not yet collected cash from customers. Likewise, the amount of expense recognized equals the cash disbursement made for equipment, materials, labor, and so forth. However, the firm recognizes the expense when it consumes the services of these factor inputs, not when it makes the cash expenditure.

3.4     Revenues measure the inflow of net assets from operating activities and expenses measure the outflow of net assets consumed in the process of generating revenues. Thus, recognizing revenues and expenses always involves a simultaneous entry in an asset and/or liability account. Likewise, adjusting entries almost always involve an entry in at least one income statement and one balance sheet account.

3.5     Revenues and expenses measure the inflows and outflows of net assets from selling goods and providing services for a particular period of time. If the accountant did not close revenue and expense accounts at the end of each period, the revenue and expense amounts of one period would mingle with similar amounts of subsequent periods.

3.6    Before the books are closed, both balance sheet (permanent) and income statement (temporary) accounts have nonzero balances. After the closing of income statement accounts, only the balance sheet accounts have nonzero balances.

3.7    Some events occur that affect the net income and financial position of a firm but for which an external transaction does not occur by the end of a period that signals the need for an entry in the accounting records. For example, a firm uses depreciable assets during the year. Because no external exchange occurs, the use of such depreciable assets is not recorded until the accountant makes adjusting entries. Likewise, workers earn salaries during the last several days of the year but are not paid until early next year. Here, again, no external exchange occurs before year end to trigger recognition of the cost of the labor services in the accounts. The adjusting entry accomplishes this.

3.8    Contra accounts provide disaggregated information concerning the net amount of an asset, liability, or shareholders' equity item. For example, the account, Accounts Receivable Net of Estimated Uncollectible Accounts, does not indicate separately the gross amount of receivables from customers and the estimated amount of the gross receivables that the firm expects to collect. If the firm used a contra account, it would have such information. The alternative to using contra accounts is to debit or credit directly the principal account involved (for example, Buildings and Equipment). This alternative procedure, however, does not permit computation of disaggregated information about the net balance in the account. Note that the use of contra accounts does not affect the total of assets, liabilities, shareholders' equity, revenues, or expenses.

3.9    (Neiman Marcus; revenue recognition.)

|     | February | March | April |
| --- | --- | --- | --- |
| a. | -- | -- | $   800 |
| b. | -- | $  2,160 | -- |
| c. | $39,200 | -- | -- |
| d. | -- | $ 59,400 | -- |
| e. | -- | $  9,000 | $ 9,000 |
| f. | -- | $  9,000 | $ 9,000 |

3.10    (Revenue recognition.)

a.   No (Magnavox has not yet delivered the goods).

b.   Yes.

3.10 continued.

    c.   No (this is a financing, not an operating, transaction).

    d.   No (NIKE has not identified a customer, set a price, or shipped the goods).

    e.   No (the concert will not take place for two weeks).

    f.   Yes (the agent has provided the services); the revenue amount is only the commission, however.

    g.   Yes (on an accrual basis, accounting recognizes interest as time passes).

    h.   No (accounting usually recognizes revenue when a firm sells goods or services).

    i.   Yes.

3.11    (Sun Microsystems; expense recognition.)

| | June | July | August |
|---|---|---|---|
| a. | -- | $ 15,000 | $ 15,000 |
| b. | $ 4,560 | -- | -- |
| c. | -- | $ 5,800 | $ 6,300 |
| d. | $ 600 | $ 600 | $ 600 |
| e. | -- | -- | -- |
| f. | -- | -- | $ 4,500 |
| g. | $ 6,600 | -- | -- |

3.12    (Kroger Stores; expense recognition.)

    a.   None (this is a September expense).

    b.   $200 (= $12,000/60).

    c.   $2,000 (= $24,000/12).

    d.   $12,300 (= $2,900 + $12,900 − $3,500).

    e.   $1,200 (the repair does not extend the life beyond that originally expected).

3.12 continued.

    f.  None (the firm will include the deposit in the acquisition cost of the land).

    g.  $10,000 (the firm includes the remaining $10,000 in prepaid rent).

3.13    (Demski Company; income recognition.)

    a.

| | | |
|---|---:|---:|
| Cash Equivalent Value of Consideration Received at Time of Sale | | $ 147,000 |
| Less Expenses: | | |
| Cost of Trucks | $ 125,000 | |
| Preparation Costs | 8,000 | |
| Delivery Costs | 6,000 | |
| Total Expenses | | 139,000 |
| Profit on Sale | | $ 8,000 |

    b.  Same as *a.* above.

    c.  Same as *a.* above.

3.14    (Identifying missing half of journal entries.)

    a.  Merchandise Inventory or Finished Goods Inventory decreases because the firm has sold goods.

    b.  Sales Revenue increases because of sales.

    c.  Cash increases because of collections from customers.

    d.  Cash decreases because of payments to creditors.

    e.  Either an inventory account or an expense account increases because of receipts of goods or services.

    f.  Depreciation Expense increases because an adjusting entry recognizes the expense.

    g.  Dividends Payable increases because of the dividend; or closing entry for an expense or income summary account showing a loss.

    h.  Either Insurance Expense increases (period expense) or Work-in-Process Inventory increases (product cost) as a result of an adjusting entry.

    i.  Cash decreases because a firm pays property taxes.

    j.  Either Accounts Payable increases or Cash decreases because of acquisition of Inventory.

3.14 continued.

    k. Revenue increases because a firm provides goods or services to customers.

    l. Assets increase for the amount of the cash or goods received from supplier.

3.15    (Restaurant Supply Company/Wendy's; journal entries for notes receivable and notes payable.)

    a.  **Year 6**
        **Dec. 1**

| | | |
|---|---:|---:|
| Notes Receivable | 60,000 | |
|     Accounts Receivable | | 60,000 |

        **Dec. 31**

| | | |
|---|---:|---:|
| Interest Receivable | 400 | |
|     Interest Revenue | | 400 |

$60,000 \times .08 \times 30/360$.

        **Dec. 31**

| | | |
|---|---:|---:|
| Interest Revenue | 400 | |
|     Retained Earnings (or Income Summary) | | 400 |

Entry assumes this note is the only one giving rise to interest revenue during the period.

        **Year 7**
        **March 1**

| | | |
|---|---:|---:|
| Cash | 61,200 | |
|     Interest Receivable | | 400 |
|     Interest Revenue | | 800 |
|     Notes Receivable | | 60,000 |

    b.  **Year 6**
        **Dec. 1**

| | | |
|---|---:|---:|
| Accounts Payable | 60,000 | |
|     Notes Payable | | 60,000 |

        **Dec. 31**

| | | |
|---|---:|---:|
| Interest Expense | 400 | |
|     Interest Payable | | 400 |

        **Dec. 31**

| | | |
|---|---:|---:|
| Retained Earnings (or Income Summary) | 400 | |
|     Interest Expense | | 400 |

Entry assumes this note is the only one giving rise to interest expense during the period.

3.15 b. continued.

**Year 7**
**March 1**

| | | |
|---|---|---|
| Interest Payable | 400 | |
| Interest Expense | 800 | |
| Notes Payable | 60,000 | |
|     Cash | | 61,200 |

3.16    (Kelly Services; journal entries for office supply inventories.)

a.  **1/1–3/31**

| | | |
|---|---|---|
| Office Supplies Inventory | 137,900 | |
|     Accounts Payable | | 137,900 |

**March 31**

| | | |
|---|---|---|
| Office Supplies Expense | 149,200 | |
|     Office Supplies Inventory | | 149,200 |

$149,200 = \$48,700 + \$137,900 - \$37,400$.

b.  **1/1–3/31**

| | | |
|---|---|---|
| Office Supplies Expense | 137,900 | |
|     Accounts Payable | | 137,900 |

**March 31**

| | | |
|---|---|---|
| Office Supplies Expense | 11,300 | |
|     Office Supplies Inventory | | 11,300 |

$11,300 = \$48,700 - \$37,400$.

3.17    (Arizona Realty Company; journal entries for rental receipts and payments.)

**(Arizona Realty Company)**
**May 1**

| | | |
|---|---|---|
| Cash | 900 | |
|     Advances from Tenant | | 900 |

**May 30**

| | | |
|---|---|---|
| Advances from Tenant | 900 | |
|     Rent Revenue | | 900 |

**May 30**

| | | |
|---|---|---|
| Rent Revenue | 900 | |
|     Income Summary | | 900 |

**June 1**

| | | |
|---|---|---|
| Cash | 1,800 | |
|     Advances from Tenant | | 1,800 |

3.17 continued.

**June 30**

| | | |
|---|---|---|
| Advances from Tenant | 900 | |
|     Rent Revenue | | 900 |

**June 30**

| | | |
|---|---|---|
| Rent Revenue | 900 | |
|     Income Summary | | 900 |

**July 31**

| | | |
|---|---|---|
| Advances from Tenant | 900 | |
|     Rent Revenue | | 900 |

**July 31**

| | | |
|---|---|---|
| Rent Revenue | 900 | |
|     Income Summary | | 900 |

**Aug. 1**

| | | |
|---|---|---|
| Cash | 2,700 | |
|     Advances from Tenant | | 2,700 |

**Aug. 31**

| | | |
|---|---|---|
| Advances from Tenant | 900 | |
|     Rent Revenue | | 900 |

**Aug. 31**

| | | |
|---|---|---|
| Rent Revenue | 900 | |
|     Income Summary | | 900 |

*Note:* An alternative set of journal entries credits Rent Revenue instead of Advances from Tenant when the firm receives amounts on the first of any month covering rental fees for that month.

**(Hagen Consultants)**
**May 1**

| | | |
|---|---|---|
| Prepaid Rent | 900 | |
|     Cash | | 900 |

**May 30**

| | | |
|---|---|---|
| Rent Expense | 900 | |
|     Prepaid Rent | | 900 |

**May 30**

| | | |
|---|---|---|
| Income Summary | 900 | |
|     Rent Expense | | 900 |

3.17 continued.

**June 1**

| | | |
|---|---|---|
| Prepaid Rent ............................................................ | 1,800 | |
| Cash ................................................................... | | 1,800 |

**June 30**

| | | |
|---|---|---|
| Rent Expense ......................................................... | 900 | |
| Prepaid Rent ...................................................... | | 900 |

**June 30**

| | | |
|---|---|---|
| Income Summary .................................................... | 900 | |
| Rent Expense ...................................................... | | 900 |

**July 31**

| | | |
|---|---|---|
| Rent Expense ......................................................... | 900 | |
| Prepaid Rent ...................................................... | | 900 |

**July 31**

| | | |
|---|---|---|
| Income Summary .................................................... | 900 | |
| Rent Expense ...................................................... | | 900 |

**Aug. 1**

| | | |
|---|---|---|
| Prepaid Rent ......................................................... | 2,700 | |
| Cash ................................................................... | | 2,700 |

**Aug. 31**

| | | |
|---|---|---|
| Rent Expense ......................................................... | 900 | |
| Prepaid Rent ...................................................... | | 900 |

**Aug. 31**

| | | |
|---|---|---|
| Income Summary .................................................... | 900 | |
| Rent Expense ...................................................... | | 900 |

*Note:* An alternative set of journal entries debits Rent Expense instead of Prepaid Rent when the firm pays amounts on the first of any month covering rental fees for that month.

3.18 (Effect of errors on financial statements.)

| | Assets | Liabilities | Shareholders' Equity |
|---|---|---|---|
| a. | U/S $ 6,000 | -- | U/S $ 6,000 |
| b. | -- | U/S $ 1,200 | O/S $ 1,200 |
| c. | U/S $ 4,600 | -- | U/S $ 4,600 |
| d. | O/S $   250 | -- | O/S $   250 |
| e. | -- | U/S $ 1,500 | O/S $ 1,500 |
| f. | -- | O/S $11,600 | U/S $11,600 |

3.19    (Forgetful Corporation; effect of recording errors on financial statements.)

a.  **Actual Entry:**

| | | |
|---|---|---|
| Cash | 1,400 | |
|    Sales Revenue | | 1,400 |

**Correct Entry:**

| | | |
|---|---|---|
| Cash | 1,400 | |
|    Advance from Customer | | 1,400 |

Liabilities understated by $1,400 and shareholders' equity overstated by $1,400.

b.  **Actual Entry:**

| | | |
|---|---|---|
| Cost of Goods Sold | 5,000 | |
|    Cash | | 5,000 |

**Correct Entries:**

| | | |
|---|---|---|
| Machine | 5,000 | |
|    Cash | | 5,000 |
| Depreciation Expense | 500 | |
|    Accumulated Depreciation | | 500 |

Assets understated by $4,500 and shareholders' equity understated by $4,500.

c.  **Actual Entry:**
None for accrued interest.

**Correct Entry:**

| | | |
|---|---|---|
| Interest Receivable ($2,000 \times .12 \times 60/360$) | 40 | |
|    Interest Revenue | | 40 |

Assets understated by $40 and shareholders' equity understated by $40.

d.  The entry is correct as recorded.

e.  **Actual Entry:**
None for declared dividend.

**Correct Entry:**

| | | |
|---|---|---|
| Retained Earnings | 1,500 | |
|    Dividend Payable | | 1,500 |

Liabilities understated by $1,500 and shareholders' equity overstated by $1,500.

3.19 continued.

f. **Actual Entries:**

| | | |
|---|---:|---:|
| Machinery | 50,000 | |
|     Accounts Payable | | 50,000 |
| | | |
| Accounts Payable | 50,000 | |
|     Cash | | 49,000 |
|     Miscellaneous Revenue | | 1,000 |
| | | |
| Maintenance Expense | 4,000 | |
|     Cash | | 4,000 |

**Correct Entries:**

| | | |
|---|---:|---:|
| Machinery | 50,000 | |
|     Accounts Payable | | 50,000 |
| | | |
| Accounts Payable | 50,000 | |
|     Cash | | 49,000 |
|     Machinery | | 1,000 |
| | | |
| Machinery | 4,000 | |
|     Cash | | 4,000 |

Assets understated by $3,000 and shareholders' equity understated by $3,000.

3.20 (Ailawadi Corporation; cash versus accrual basis of accounting.)

**a. and b.**

|  | a. Accrual Basis | b. Cash Basis |
|---|---|---|
| Sales Revenue | $ 69,500 | $ 61,200[a] |
| Less Expenses: | | |
| Cost of Merchandise Sold | $ 43,200[b] | -- |
| Payments on Merchandise Purchased | -- | $ 44,800 |
| Depreciation Expense | 1,000[c] | -- |
| Payments on Equipment Purchased | -- | 36,000 |
| Utilities Expense | 1,010[d] | 750 |
| Salaries Expense | 4,760[e] | 3,500 |
| Rent Expense | 3,000 | 6,000 |
| Insurance Expense | 100 | 1,200 |
| Interest Expense | 200[f] | -- |
| Total Expenses | $(53,270) | $ (92,250) |
| Net Income (Loss) | $ 16,230 | $ (31,050) |

[a]$61,200 = $60,000 + $1,200.
[b]$43,200 = $44,800 + $3,900 − $5,500.
[c]$1,000 = ($36,000/3)/12.
[d]$1,010 = $750 + $260.
[e]$4,760 = $3,500 + $1,260.
[f]$200 = (.06 × $40,000) × 30/360.

c. The accrual basis of accounting provides superior measures of operating performance because it matches revenues generated from selling activities during January with the costs incurred in generating that revenue. Note that the capital contribution and bank loan do not give rise to revenue under either basis of accounting because they represent financing, not operating, activities.

**3.21**     (McKindly Consultants, Inc.; cash versus accrual basis of accounting.)

**a. and b.**

| | a. Accrual Basis | b. Cash Basis |
|---|---|---|
| Consulting Revenue | $135,000 | $109,000 |
| Less Expenses: | | |
| Rental Expense | $ 7,500 | $ 7,500 |
| Depreciation Expense | 2,000[a] | -- |
| Payments on Equipment Purchased | -- | 24,000 |
| Utilities Expense | 4,040[b] | 3,460 |
| Salaries Expense | 109,800[c] | 98,500 |
| Supplies Expense | 3,630[d] | 2,790 |
| Interest Expense | 2,000[e] | -- |
| Total Expenses | $128,970 | $136,250 |
| Net Income (Loss) | $ 6,030 | $ (27,250) |

[a]$2,000 = ($24,000/5) \times 5/12$.

[b]$4,040 = $3,460 + $580$.

[c]$109,800 = $98,500 + $11,300$.

[d]$3,630 = $2,790 + $840$.

[e]$2,000 = ($60,000 \times .08) \times 5/12$.

c.   See the answer for Problem 3.20, Part *c*. above.

**3.22**     (Hansen Retail Store; preparing income statement and balance sheet using accrual basis.)

a.
**HANSEN RETAIL STORE**
**Income Statement**
**For the Year Ended December 31, Year 8**

| | |
|---|---|
| Sales ($52,900 + $116,100) | $ 169,000 |
| Cost of Goods Sold ($125,000 − $15,400) | (109,600) |
| Salary Expense ($34,200 + $2,400) | (36,600) |
| Utility Expense ($2,600 + $180) | (2,780) |
| Depreciation Expense ($60,000/30) | (2,000) |
| Interest Expense (.10 × $40,000) | (4,000) |
| Net Income before Income Taxes | $ 14,020 |
| Income Taxes at 40 Percent | (5,608) |
| Net Income | $ 8,412 |

3.22 continued.

b.

**HANSEN RETAIL STORE**
**Balance Sheet**
**December 31, Year 8**

*Assets*

| | |
|---|---:|
| Cash ($50,000 + $40,000 − $60,000 − $97,400 + $52,900 + $54,800 − $34,200 − $2,600) | $ 3,500 |
| Accounts Receivable ($116,100 − $54,800) | 61,300 |
| Inventories | 15,400 |
| Total Current Assets | $ 80,200 |
| Building ($60,000 − $2,000) | 58,000 |
| Total Assets | $ 138,200 |

*Liabilities and Shareholders' Equity*

| | |
|---|---:|
| Accounts Payable ($125,000 − $97,400) | $ 27,600 |
| Salaries Payable | 2,400 |
| Utilities Payable | 180 |
| Income Taxes Payable | 5,608 |
| Interest Payable | 4,000 |
| Loan Payable | 40,000 |
| Total Current Liabilities | $ 79,788 |
| Common Stock | $ 50,000 |
| Retained Earnings | 8,412 |
| Total Shareholders' Equity | $ 58,412 |
| Total Liabilities and Shareholders' Equity | $ 138,200 |

3.23 (Regaldo Department Stores; work sheet preparation of income statement and balance sheet.)

a. and b.

**Cash**
Ps 247,200
+ Ps  62,900 (3)
− Ps  32,400 (4)
− Ps   2,700 (5)
+ Ps  84,600 (6)
+ Ps 234,800 (7)
− Ps 124,800

**Accounts Receivable**
+ Ps194,600 (3)
−        84,600 (6)
Ps110,000

**Inventories**
Ps188,800
+ Ps217,900 (2)
− Ps162,400 (3)
− Ps   4,200 (7)
Ps240,100

**Prepaid Rent**
Ps 60,000
− Ps30,000 (11)
Ps30,000

**Prepaid Insurance**
Ps 12,000
− Ps 1,000 (12)
Ps11,000

**Equipment**
+ Ps 90,000 (1)
− Ps  1,500 (10)
Ps 88,500

**Patent**
Ps 24,000
− Ps    400
Ps 23,600

**Accounts Payable**
Ps 32,000
+ Ps 217,900 (2)
− Ps 239,000 (7)
Ps  10,900

**Salaries Payable**
+ Ps 6,700 (8)
Ps 6,700

**Utilities Payable**
+ Ps 800 (9)
Ps 800

**Interest Payable**
− Ps 900 (14)
Ps 900

**Income Tax Payable**
+ Ps 5,610 (15)
Ps 5,610

**Loan Payable**
+ Ps 90,000 (1)
Ps 90,000

**Common Stock**
Ps 50,000
Ps 50,000

**Revenues**
+ Ps 257,500 (3) Sales Revenue
Ps 257,500

**Expenses**
− Ps162,400 (3) Cost of Goods Sold
− Ps 32,400 (4) Compensation Expense
− Ps  2,700 (5) Utilities Expense
− Ps  6,700 (8) Compensation Expense
− Ps    800 (9) Utilities Expense
− Ps  1,500 (10) Depreciation Expense
− Ps 30,000 (11) Rent Expense
− Ps  1,000 (12) Insurance Expense
− Ps    400 (13) Amortization Expense
− Ps    900 (14) Interest Expense
− Ps  5,610 (15) Income Tax Expense
Ps244,410

3.23 continued.

c.
**REGALDO DEPARTMENT STORES**
**Income Statement**
**For the Month of February Year 8**

| | |
|---|---:|
| Sales Revenue | Ps257,500 |
| Expenses: | |
|     Cost of Goods Sold | Ps162,400 |
|     Compensation (Ps32,400 + Ps6,700) | 39,100 |
|     Utilities (Ps2,700 + Ps800) | 3,500 |
|     Depreciation | 1,500 |
|     Rent | 30,000 |
|     Insurance | 1,000 |
|     Patent Amortization | 400 |
|     Interest | 900 |
|       Total Expenses | Ps238,800 |
| Net Income before Income Taxes | Ps 18,700 |
| Income Tax Expense at 30 Percent | (5,610) |
| Net Income | Ps 13,090 |

d.
**REGALDO DEPARTMENT STORES**
**Balance Sheet**
**February 28, Year 8**

*Assets*

| | |
|---|---:|
| Cash | Ps124,800 |
| Accounts Receivable | 110,000 |
| Inventories | 240,100 |
| Prepaid Rent | 30,000 |
| Prepaid Insurance | 11,000 |
|     Total Current Assets | Ps515,900 |
| Equipment | 88,500 |
| Patent | 23,600 |
|     Total Assets | Ps628,000 |

*Liabilities and Shareholders' Equity*

| | |
|---|---:|
| Accounts Payable | Ps 10,900 |
| Salaries Payable | 6,700 |
| Utilities Payable | 800 |
| Interest Payable | 900 |
| Income Tax Payable | 5,610 |
| Loan Payable | 90,000 |
|     Total Liabilities | Ps114,910 |
| Common Stock | Ps500,000 |
| Retained Earnings | 13,090 |
|     Total Shareholders' Equity | Ps513,090 |
|     Total Liabilities and Shareholders' Equity | Ps628,000 |

3.24    (Miscellaneous transactions and adjusting entries.)

a. (1) Accounts Payable (L)..................................... 6,000
            Notes Payable (L)................................... 6,000

   (2) Interest Expense (SE).................................. 50
            Interest Payable (L)............................... 50
       [$6,000 × .10 × (30/360)] = $50.

b. (1) Cash (A)..................................................... 18,000
            Advances from Customers (L)................ 18,000

   (2) Advances from Customers (L)......................... 3,000
            Insurance Revenue (SE)............................ 3,000
       ($18,000 × 4/24) = $3,000.

c. (1) Equipment (A)............................................. 40,000
            Cash (A)................................................. 40,000

   (2) Depreciation Expense (SE)............................ 2,250
            Accumulated Depreciation (XA).................. 2,250
       [.25($40,000 − $4,000)/4].

d. (1) Automobile (A)............................................ 24,000
            Cash (A)................................................. 24,000

   (2) Depreciation Expense (SE)............................ 3,500
            Accumulated Depreciation (XA).................. 3,500
       .5 × [($24,000 − $3,000)/3] = $3,500.

e. (1) Prepaid Rent (A)......................................... 12,000
            Cash (A)................................................. 12,000

   (2) Rent Expense (SE)...................................... 4,000
            Prepaid Rent (A)..................................... 4,000

f. (1) Office Supplies Inventory (A)......................... 7,000
            Accounts Payable (L)................................ 7,000

   (2) Accounts Payable (L)................................... 5,000
            Cash (A)................................................. 5,000

   (3) Office Supplies Expense (SE)......................... 5,500
            Office Supplies Inventory (A).................... 5,500
       ($7,000 − $1,500) = $5,500.

3.25    (Miscellaneous transactions and adjusting entries.)

a.  (1)  Cash ..................................................................  48,000
              Rental Fees Received in Advance ................                48,000

    (2)  Rental Fees Received in Advance .....................  12,000
              Rent Revenue ................................................                12,000

b.  (1)  Notes Receivable ...........................................  10,000
              Accounts Receivable ..................................                10,000

    (2)  Interest Receivable ........................................      50
              Interest Revenue ........................................                     50
         $10,000 × .06 × 30/360 = $50.

c.  (1)  Prepaid Insurance .........................................   6,600
              Cash ............................................................                 6,600

    (2)  Insurance Expense ..........................................   3,250
              Prepaid Insurance ......................................                 3,250
         $500 + ($6,600 × 10/24) = $3,250.

Alternate entries for Part c. are:

    (1)  Insurance Expense ..........................................     500
         Prepaid Insurance ($6,600 − $500) ..................   6,100
              Cash ............................................................                 6,600

    (2)  Insurance Expense ..........................................   2,750
              Prepaid Insurance ......................................                 2,750
         $6,600 × 10/24 = $2,750.

d.  (1)  Repair Expense ..............................................  14,900
              Cash ............................................................                14,900

    (2)  Repair Expense ................................................     200
              Repair Parts Inventory .............................                   200

e.  (1)  Equipment ......................................................  200,000
              Cash ............................................................               200,000

    (2)  Depreciation Expense .....................................   9,000
              Accumulated Depreciation ..........................                 9,000
         ($200,000 − $20,000) × .5/10.

f.  (1)  Property Tax Expense .....................................  12,000
              Cash ............................................................                12,000

    (2)  No adjusting entry required because the full amount paid is an
         expense for Year 3.

3.26    (Miscellaneous adjusting entries.)

a.  The Wages Payable account should have a credit balance of $4,000 at the end of April, but it has a balance of $5,000 carried over from the end of March. The adjusting entry must reduce the balance by $1,000, which requires a debit to the Wages Payable account.

Wages Payable................................................................. 1,000
    Wage Expense ..........................................................                1,000
To reduce the balance in the Wages Payable account, reducing the amount in the Wage Expense account.

Wage Expense is $29,000 (= $30,000 – $1,000).

b.  The Prepaid Insurance account balance of $3,000 represents four months of coverage. Thus, the cost of insurance is $750 (= $3,000/4) per month. The adjusting entry for a single month is as follows:

Insurance Expense......................................................... 750
    Prepaid Insurance...................................................                750
To recognize cost of one month's insurance cost as expense of the month.

c.  The Advances from Tenants account has a balance of $25,000 carried over from the start of the year. At the end of Year 3, it should have a balance of $30,000. Thus the adjusting entry must increase the balance by $5,000, which requires a credit to the liability account.

Rent Revenue................................................................. 5,000
    Advances from Tenants ...........................................                5,000
To increase the balance in the Advances from Tenants account, reducing the amount in the Rent Revenue account.

Rent Revenue for Year 3 is $245,000 (= $250,000 – $5,000).

d.  The Depreciation Expense for the year should be $2,000 (= $10,000/5). The balance in the Accumulated Depreciation account should also be $2,000; thus, the firm must reduce (credit) the Depreciation Expense account by $8,000 (= $10,000 – $2,000). The adjusting entry not only reduces recorded Depreciation Expense but also sets up the asset account and its accumulated depreciation contra account.

Equipment....................................................................... 10,000
    Accumulated Depreciation.....................................                2,000
    Depreciation Expense .............................................                8,000
To reduce Depreciation Expense, setting up the asset and its contra account.

**3.27** (Bosworth Computer Repair Services; preparation of T-account entries, adjusted trial balance, income statement, and balance sheet.)

**a., b., and d.**

| Cash | | | |
|---|---|---|---|
| Bal. 4,800 | 1,000 | (3) | |
| (1) 2,250 | 240 | (4) | |
| (8) 250 | 150 | (5) | |
| | 325 | (6) | |
| | 90 | (7) | |
| | 1,100 | (9) | |
| Bal. 4,395 | | | |

| Repair Parts Inventory | | |
|---|---|---|
| Bal. 1,500 | 450 | (11) |
| Bal. 1,050 | | |

| Office Supplies Inventory | | |
|---|---|---|
| Bal. 200 | 100 | (12) |
| Bal. 100 | | |

| Equipment | |
|---|---|
| Bal. 5,500 | |
| Bal. 5,500 | |

| Accumulated Depreciation | |
|---|---|
| | 750 Bal. |
| | 75 (13) |
| | 825 Bal. |

| Accounts Payable | | |
|---|---|---|
| (3) 1,000 | 6,250 | Bal. |
| | 5,250 | Bal. |

| Common Stock | |
|---|---|
| | 1,250 Bal. |
| | 1,250 Bal. |

| Retained Earnings | |
|---|---|
| | 3,750 Bal. |
| | 440 (23) |
| | 1,100 Bal. |

| Repair Revenue | | |
|---|---|---|
| (14) 2,750 | 2,250 | (1) |
| | 500 | (2) |
| | 2,750 | |

| Accounts Receivable | | |
|---|---|---|
| (2) 500 | 250 | (8) |
| Bal. 250 | | |

| Prepaid Insurance | | |
|---|---|---|
| (4) 240 | 20 | (10) |
| Bal. 220 | | |

| Advertising Expense | | |
|---|---|---|
| (5) 150 | 150 | (15) |

| Rent Expense | | |
|---|---|---|
| (6) 325 | 325 | (16) |

| Telephone Expense | | |
|---|---|---|
| (7) 90 | 90 | (17) |

| Salary Expense | | |
|---|---|---|
| (9) 1,100 | 1,100 | (18) |

3.27 a., b., and d. continued.

| Insurance Expense | | | | Repair Parts Expense | | | | Office Supplies Expense | | |
|---|---|---|---|---|---|---|---|---|---|---|
| (10) | 20 | 20 | (19) | (11) | 450 | 450 | (20) | (12) | 100 | 100 (21) |

| Depreciation Expense | | | | Income Summary | | | |
|---|---|---|---|---|---|---|---|
| (13) | 75 | 75 (22) | | (15) | 150 | 2,750 | (14) |
| | | | | (16) | 325 | | |
| | | | | (17) | 90 | | |
| | | | | (18) | 1,100 | | |
| | | | | (19) | 20 | | |
| | | | | (20) | 450 | | |
| | | | | (21) | 100 | | |
| | | | | (22) | 75 | | |
| | | | | (23) | 440 | | |
| | | | | | 2,750 | | |

*Note:* T-account entries (1) through (13) respond to Part *b.*, after which students can perform Part *c.* requirements. T-account entries (14) through (22) respond to Part *d.*, after which students can perform Part *e.* requirements.

c.
### BOSWORTH COMPUTER REPAIR SERVICES
### Adjusted Preclosing Trial Balance
### July 31, Year 8

| | | |
|---|---:|---:|
| Cash | $ 4,395 | |
| Repair Parts Inventory | 1,050 | |
| Office Supplies Inventory | 100 | |
| Equipment | 5,500 | |
| Accumulated Depreciation | | $ 825 |
| Accounts Payable | | 5,250 |
| Common Stock | | 1,250 |
| Retained Earnings | | 3,750 |
| Repair Revenue | | 2,750 |
| Accounts Receivable | 250 | |
| Prepaid Insurance | 220 | |
| Advertising Expense | 150 | |
| Rent Expense | 325 | |
| Telephone Expense | 90 | |
| Salary Expense | 1,100 | |
| Insurance Expense | 20 | |
| Repair Parts Expense | 450 | |
| Office Supplies Expense | 100 | |
| Depreciation Expense | 75 | |
| Totals | $13,825 | $13,825 |

3.27 c. continued.

## BOSWORTH COMPUTER REPAIR SERVICES
### Income Statement
### For the Month of July, Year 8

| | | |
|---|---:|---:|
| Repair Revenue............................................. | | $ 2,750 |
| Expenses: | | |
| Advertising Expense................................. | $    150 | |
| Rent Expense............................................. | 325 | |
| Telephone Expense.................................... | 90 | |
| Salary Expense ......................................... | 1,100 | |
| Insurance Expense.................................... | 20 | |
| Repair Parts Expense............................... | 450 | |
| Office Supplies Expense ........................... | 100 | |
| Depreciation Expense .............................. | 75 | |
| Total Expenses.................................... | | 2,310 |
| Net Income ................................................. | | $    440 |

e.
## BOSWORTH COMPUTER REPAIR SERVICES
### Balance Sheet
### July 31, Year 8

*Assets*

| | | |
|---|---:|---:|
| Current Assets: | | |
| Cash......................................................... | $ 4,395 | |
| Accounts Receivable............................... | 250 | |
| Repair Parts Inventory ........................... | 1,050 | |
| Office Supplies Inventory........................ | 100 | |
| Prepaid Insurance.................................... | 220 | |
| Total Current Assets............................ | | $  6,015 |
| Property, Plant, and Equipment: | | |
| Equipment................................................ | $ 5,500 | |
| Less Accumulated Depreciation................ | (825) | |
| Total Property, Plant, and Equipment.. | | 4,675 |
| Total Assets.......................................... | | $10,690 |

*Liabilities and Shareholders' Equity*

| | | |
|---|---:|---:|
| Current Liabilities: | | |
| Accounts Payable..................................... | | $ 5,250 |
| Shareholders' Equity: | | |
| Common Stock.......................................... | $ 1,250 | |
| Retained Earnings ................................... | 4,190 | |
| Total Shareholders' Equity ..................... | | 5,440 |
| Total Liabilities and Shareholders' | | |
| Equity................................................. | | $10,690 |

**3.28** (Jones Shoe Repair Shop, Inc.; preparation of T-account entries, adjusted trial balance, income statement, and balance sheet.)

**a., b., and d.**

| | Cash | | | | Accounts Receivable | | | | Supplies Inventory | |
|---|---|---|---|---|---|---|---|---|---|---|
| Bal. | 6,060 | 5,800 | (5) | Bal. 15,200 | 18,200 | (2) | Bal. | 4,800 | 6,820 | (8) |
| (1) | 22,000 | 1,000 | (6) | (1) 14,900 | | | (4) | 3,700 | | |
| (2) | 18,200 | 11,900 | (7) | | | | | | | |
| Bal. | 27,560 | | | Bal. 11,900 | | | Bal. | 1,680 | | |

| | Prepaid Insurance | | | Equipment | | | Accumulated Depreciation | |
|---|---|---|---|---|---|---|---|---|
| Bal. | 900 | 400 (11) | Bal. 65,000 | | | | 11,460 | Bal. |
| | | | | | | | 2,820 | (9) |
| Bal. | 500 | | Bal. 65,000 | | | | 14,280 | Bal. |

| | Accounts Payable | | | Common Stock | | Retained Earnings | |
|---|---|---|---|---|---|---|---|
| (5) | 5,800 | 6,120 Bal. | | 15,000 Bal. | | 47,360 | Bal. |
| | | 1,200 (3) | | | | 23,860 | (14) |
| | | 3,700 (4) | | | | | |
| | | 920 (10) | | | | | |
| | | 6,140 Bal. | | 15,000 Bal. | | 71,220 | Bal. |

| | Sales Revenue | | | Salaries and Wages Expense | | | Cost of Outside Work | |
|---|---|---|---|---|---|---|---|---|
| (12) 82,960 | 46,060 Bal. | | Bal. 26,600 | 38,500 (13) | | Bal. | 2,040 | 3,240 (13) |
| | 22,000 (1) | | (7) 11,900 | | | (3) | 1,200 | |
| | 14,900 (1) | | | | | | | |
| 82,960 | 82,960 | | 38,500 | 38,500 | | | 3,240 | 3,240 |

| | Advertising Expense | | | Rent Expense | | | Power, Gas, and Water Expense | |
|---|---|---|---|---|---|---|---|---|
| Bal. | 900 | 1,300 (13) | Bal. | 1,200 | 2,200 (13) | Bal. | 880 | 1,400 (13) |
| (10) | 400 | | (6) | 1,000 | | (10) | 520 | |
| | 1,300 | 1,300 | | 2,200 | 2,200 | | 1,400 | 1,400 |

| | Supplies Expense | | | Depreciation Expense | | | Insurance Expense | |
|---|---|---|---|---|---|---|---|---|
| (8) | 6,820 | 6,820 (13) | (9) | 2,820 | 2,820 (13) | (11) | 400 | 400 (13) |
| | 6,820 | 6,820 | | 2,820 | 2,820 | | 400 | 400 |

3.28 a., b., and d. continued.

| | Miscellaneous Expense | | | | Income Summary | | |
|---|---|---|---|---|---|---|---|
| Bal. | 2,420 | 2,420 | (13) | (13) | 59,100 | 82,960 | (12) |
| | | | | (14) | 23,860 | | |
| | 2,420 | 2,420 | | | 82,960 | 82,960 | |

*Note:* T-account entries (1) through (11) respond to Part *b.*, after which students can perform Part *c.* requirements. T-account entries (12) through (14) respond to Part *d.*, after which students can perform Part *e.* requirements.

c.
## JONES SHOE REPAIR SHOP, INC.
### Adjusted Preclosing Trial Balance
### March 31, Year 2

| | | |
|---|---:|---:|
| Cash | $ 27,560 | |
| Accounts Receivable | 11,900 | |
| Supplies Inventory | 1,680 | |
| Prepaid Insurance | 500 | |
| Equipment | 65,000 | |
| Accumulated Depreciation | | $ 14,280 |
| Accounts Payable | | 6,140 |
| Common Stock | | 15,000 |
| Retained Earnings | | 47,360 |
| Sales Revenue | | 82,960 |
| Salaries and Wages Expense | 38,500 | |
| Cost of Outside Work | 3,240 | |
| Advertising Expense | 1,300 | |
| Rent Expense | 2,200 | |
| Power, Gas, and Water Expense | 1,400 | |
| Supplies Expense | 6,820 | |
| Depreciation Expense | 2,820 | |
| Insurance Expense | 400 | |
| Miscellaneous Expense | 2,420 | |
| Totals | $ 165,740 | $ 165,740 |

3.28 c. continued.

**JONES SHOE REPAIR SHOP, INC.**
**Income Statement**
**For the Three Months Ending March 31, Year 2**

| | | |
|---|---:|---:|
| Sales Revenue | | $82,960 |
| Expenses: | | |
| Salaries and Wages Expense | $38,500 | |
| Cost of Outside Work | 3,240 | |
| Advertising Expense | 1,300 | |
| Rent Expense | 2,200 | |
| Power, Gas, and Water Expense | 1,400 | |
| Supplies Expense | 6,820 | |
| Depreciation Expense | 2,820 | |
| Insurance Expense | 400 | |
| Miscellaneous Expense | 2,420 | |
| Total Expenses | | 59,100 |
| Net Income for the Quarter | | $23,860 |

e.

**JONES SHOE REPAIR SHOP, INC.**
**Balance Sheet**
**March 31, Year 2**

*Assets*

| | | |
|---|---:|---:|
| Current Assets: | | |
| Cash | $27,560 | |
| Accounts Receivable | 11,900 | |
| Supplies Inventory | 1,680 | |
| Prepaid Insurance | 500 | |
| Total Current Assets | | $41,640 |
| Property, Plant, and Equipment: | | |
| Equipment | $65,000 | |
| Less Accumulated Depreciation | (14,280) | |
| Total Property, Plant, and Equipment | | 50,720 |
| Total Assets | | $92,360 |

*Liabilities and Shareholders' Equity*

| | | |
|---|---:|---:|
| Current Liabilities: | | |
| Accounts Payable | $ 6,140 | |
| Total Current Liabilities | | $ 6,140 |
| Shareholders' Equity: | | |
| Common Stock | $15,000 | |
| Retained Earnings | 71,220 | |
| Total Shareholders' Equity | | 86,220 |
| Total Liabilities and Shareholders' Equity | | $92,360 |

3.29    (Zealock Bookstore; preparation of T-accounts, income statement, and balance sheet.)

**a. and c.**

| Cash | | | |
|---|---|---|---|
| (1) | 25,000 | 20,000 | (3) |
| (2) | 30,000 | 4,000 | (4) |
| (8) | 24,600 | 10,000 | (5) |
| (10) | 142,400 | 8,000 | (6) |
| (13) | 850 | 16,700 | (11) |
| | | 139,800 | (12) |
| | 24,350 | | |

| Accounts Receivable (A) | | | |
|---|---|---|---|
| (8) | 148,200 | 142,400 | (10) |
| | 5,800 | | |

| Merchandise Inventories (A) | | | |
|---|---|---|---|
| (7) | 160,000 | 140,000 | (8) |
| | | 14,600 | (9) |
| | 5,400 | | |

| Prepaid Rent (A) | | | |
|---|---|---|---|
| (3) | 20,000 | 10,000 | (15) |
| | 10,000 | | |

| Security Deposit | |
|---|---|
| (6) | 8,000 |
| | 8,000 |

| Equipment (A) | |
|---|---|
| (4) | 4,000 |
| (5) | 10,000 |
| | 14,000 |

| Accumulated Depreciation (XA) | | |
|---|---|---|
| | 400 | (16) |
| | 1,500 | (17) |
| | 1,900 | |

| Bank Loan Payable (L) | | |
|---|---|---|
| | 30,000 | (2) |
| | 30,000 | |

| Accounts Payable (L) | | | |
|---|---|---|---|
| (9) | 14,600 | 160,000 | (7) |
| (12) | 139,800 | | |
| | | 5,600 | |

| Advances from Customers (L) | | |
|---|---|---|
| | 850 | (13) |
| | 850 | |

| Interest Payable (L) | | |
|---|---|---|
| | 900 | (14) |
| | 900 | |

| Income Tax Payable (L) | | |
|---|---|---|
| | 1,320 | (19) |
| | 1,320 | |

| Common Stock (SE) | | |
|---|---|---|
| | 10,000 | (1) |
| | 10,000 | |

| Additional Paid-In Capital (SE) | | |
|---|---|---|
| | 15,000 | (1) |
| | 15,000 | |

3.29 a. and c. continued.

| Retained Earnings (SE) | |
|---|---|
| | 1,980 (20) |
| | 1,980 |

| Sales Revenue (SE) | |
|---|---|
| (20) 172,800 | 172,800 (8) |

| Cost of Goods Sold (SE) | |
|---|---|
| (8) 140,000 | 140,000 (20) |

| Compensation Expense (SE) | |
|---|---|
| (11) 16,700 | 16,700 (20) |

| Interest Expense (SE) | |
|---|---|
| (14) 900 | 900 (20) |

| Rent Expense (SE) | |
|---|---|
| (15) 10,000 | 10,000 (20) |

| Depreciation Expense (SE) | |
|---|---|
| (16) 400 | 1,900 (20) |
| (17) 1,500 | |

| Income Tax Expense (SE) | |
|---|---|
| (19) 1,320 | 1,320 (20) |

b.

**ZEALOCK BOOKSTORE**
**Income Statement**
**For the Six Months Ending December 31, Year 10**

| | |
|---|---|
| Sales Revenue.......................................................................... | $172,800 |
| Less Expenses: | |
|    Cost of Goods Sold................................................................ | $140,000 |
|    Compensation Expense......................................................... | 16,700 |
|    Interest Expense.................................................................... | 900 |
|    Rent Expense......................................................................... | 10,000 |
|    Depreciation Expense .......................................................... | 1,900 |
|    Income Tax Expense.............................................................. | 1,320 |
|      Total Expenses................................................................ | $170,820 |
| Net Income ............................................................................... | $   1,980 |

3-26

3.29 continued.

d.

**ZEALOCK BOOKSTORE**
**Balance Sheet**
**December 31, Year 10**

*Assets*

Current Assets:
| | |
|---|---:|
| Cash | $ 24,350 |
| Accounts Receivable | 5,800 |
| Merchandise Inventories | 5,400 |
| Prepaid Rent | 10,000 |
| Security Deposit | 8,000 |
| Total Current Assets | $ 53,550 |
| Equipment | $ 14,000 |
| Less Accumulated Depreciation | (1,900) |
| Equipment (Net) | $ 12,100 |
| Total Assets | $ 65,650 |

*Liabilities and Shareholders' Equity*

Current Liabilities:
| | |
|---|---:|
| Bank Loan Payable | $ 30,000 |
| Accounts Payable | 5,600 |
| Advances from Customers | 850 |
| Interest Payable | 900 |
| Income Tax Payable | 1,320 |
| Total Current Liabilities | $ 38,670 |
| Shareholders' Equity: | |
| Common Stock | $ 10,000 |
| Additional Paid-In Capital | 15,000 |
| Retained Earnings | 1,980 |
| Total Shareholders' Equity | $ 26,980 |
| Total Liabilities and Shareholders' Equity | $ 65,650 |

e. Net income was positive, which is unusual for a new business in its first year. The profit margin, however, is only 1.1 percent (= $1,980/$172,800). This small margin does not leave much room for unexpected events. Current Assets exceed Current Liabilities by a comfortable margin. The firm sells its inventory quickly and collects its accounts receivable soon after sale. It must also pay its suppliers quickly.

3.30 (Zealock Bookstore; preparation of T-accounts, comparative income statement, and comparative balance sheet.)

**a., b., and c.**

| | Cash | | |
|---|---|---|---|
| √ | 24,350 | | |
| (3) | 75,000 | 1,320 | (1) |
| (4) | 8,000 | 31,800 | (2) |
| (7) | 24,900 | 20,000 | (5) |
| (9) | 320,600 | 29,400 | (10) |
| | | 281,100 | (11) |
| | | 4,000 | (12) |
| √ | 82,230 | | |

| | Accounts Receivable (A) | | |
|---|---|---|---|
| √ | 5,800 | | |
| (7) | 327,950 | 320,600 | (9) |
| √ | 13,150 | | |

| | Merchandise Inventories (A) | | |
|---|---|---|---|
| √ | 5,400 | | |
| (6) | 310,000 | 286,400 | (7) |
| | | 22,700 | (8) |
| √ | 6,300 | | |

| | Prepaid Rent (A) | | |
|---|---|---|---|
| √ | 10,000 | | |
| (5) | 20,000 | 20,000 | (13) |
| √ | 10,000 | | |

| | Security Deposit | | |
|---|---|---|---|
| √ | 8,000 | | |
| | | 8,000 | (4) |
| √ | 0 | | |

| | Equipment (A) | | |
|---|---|---|---|
| √ | 14,000 | | |
| √ | 14,000 | | |

| Accumulated Depreciation (XA) | | |
|---|---|---|
| | 1,900 | √ |
| | 800 | (14) |
| | 3,000 | (15) |
| | 5,700 | √ |

| | Bank Loan Payable (L) | | |
|---|---|---|---|
| | | 30,000 | √ |
| (2) | 30,000 | 75,000 | (3) |
| | | 75,000 | √ |

| | Accounts Payable (L) | | |
|---|---|---|---|
| | | 5,600 | √ |
| (8) | 22,700 | 310,000 | (6) |
| (12) | 281,100 | | |
| | | 11,800 | √ |

| | Advances from Customers (L) | | |
|---|---|---|---|
| | | 850 | √ |
| (7) | 850 | | |
| | | 0 | √ |

| | Interest Payable (L) | | |
|---|---|---|---|
| | | 900 | √ |
| (2) | 900 | 3,000 | (16) |
| | | 3,000 | √ |

| | Income Tax Payable (L) | | |
|---|---|---|---|
| | | 1,320 | √ |
| (1) | 1,320 | 4,080 | (17) |
| | | 4,080 | √ |

3.30 a., b., and c. continued.

| Common Stock (SE) | | |
|---|---|---|
| | 10,000 | √ |
| | 10,000 | √ |

| Additional Paid-In Capital (SE) | | |
|---|---|---|
| | 15,000 | √ |
| | 15,000 | √ |

| Retained Earnings (SE) | | | |
|---|---|---|---|
| | | 1,980 | √ |
| (12) | 4,000 | 6,120 | (18) |
| | | 4,100 | √ |

| Sales Revenue (SE) | | | |
|---|---|---|---|
| (18) | 353,700 | 353,700 | (7) |

| Cost of Goods Sold (SE) | | | |
|---|---|---|---|
| (7) | 286,400 | 286,400 | (18) |

| Compensation Expense (SE) | | | |
|---|---|---|---|
| (10) | 29,400 | 29,400 | (18) |

| Interest Expense (SE) | | | |
|---|---|---|---|
| (2) | 900 | | |
| (16) | 3,000 | 3,900 | (18) |

| Rent Expense (SE) | | | |
|---|---|---|---|
| (13) | 20,000 | 20,000 | (18) |

| Depreciation Expense (SE) | | | |
|---|---|---|---|
| (14) | 800 | | |
| (15) | 3,000 | 3,800 | (18) |

| Income Tax Expense (SE) | | | |
|---|---|---|---|
| (17) | 4,080 | 4,080 | (18) |

d.
**ZEALOCK BOOKSTORE**
**Comparative Income Statement**
**For Year 10 and Year 11**

| | Year 10 | Year 11 |
|---|---|---|
| Sales Revenue | $172,800 | $353,700 |
| Less Expenses: | | |
| Cost of Goods Sold | $140,000 | $286,400 |
| Compensation Expense | 16,700 | 29,400 |
| Interest Expense | 900 | 3,900 |
| Rent Expense | 10,000 | 20,000 |
| Depreciation Expense | 1,900 | 3,800 |
| Income Tax Expense | 1,320 | 4,080 |
| Total Expenses | $170,820 | $347,580 |
| Net Income | $ 1,980 | $ 6,120 |

3.30 continued.

e.

**ZEALOCK BOOKSTORE**
**Comparative Balance Sheet**
**December 31, Year 10 and Year 11**

| | Year 10 | Year 11 |
|---|---|---|
| *Assets* | | |
| Current Assets: | | |
| Cash | $ 24,350 | $ 85,230 |
| Accounts Receivable | 5,800 | 13,150 |
| Merchandise Inventories | 5,400 | 6,300 |
| Prepaid Rent | 10,000 | 10,000 |
| Security Deposit | 8,000 | -- |
| Total Current Assets | $ 53,550 | $ 114,680 |
| Noncurrent Assets: | | |
| Equipment | $ 14,000 | $ 14,000 |
| Less Accumulated Depreciation | (1,900) | (5,700) |
| Equipment (Net) | $ 12,100 | $ 8,300 |
| Total Assets | $ 65,650 | $ 122,980 |

*Liabilities and Shareholders' Equity*

| | Year 10 | Year 11 |
|---|---|---|
| Current Liabilities: | | |
| Bank Loan Payable | $ 30,000 | $ 75,000 |
| Accounts Payable | 5,600 | 11,800 |
| Advances from Customers | 850 | -- |
| Interest Payable | 900 | 3,000 |
| Income Tax Payable | 1,320 | 4,080 |
| Total Current Liabilities | $ 38,670 | $ 93,880 |
| Shareholders' Equity: | | |
| Common Stock | $ 10,000 | $ 10,000 |
| Additional Paid-In Capital | 15,000 | 15,000 |
| Retained Earnings | 1,980 | 4,100 |
| Total Shareholders' Equity | $ 26,980 | $ 29,100 |
| Total Liabilities and Shareholders' Equity | $ 65,650 | $ 122,980 |

3.30 continued.

f.  Schedule 1 of this solution presents selected financial ratios for Zealock Bookstore. The profit margin percentage increased slightly. The principal driver was a decrease in the compensation expense to sales percentage. The bookstore must have employees operating the store regardless of the number of books sold. Sales more than doubled between the six-month period in Year 10 and the 12-month period in Year 11. Compensation did not increase proportionally, suggesting the benefits of spreading relatively fixed costs over a larger sales base. The interest expense to revenues percentage increased because of the larger amount of debt and larger interest rate. The income tax expense to sales percentage increased because of higher pre-tax profitability. The income tax rate was 40 percent in both years.

The current ratio declined, although it is still at a healthy level. The proportion of liabilities in the capital structure increased significantly. It appears that Zealock Bookstore may have taken on more short-term borrowing than it needed. Inventories did not increase as fast as sales. Thus, the firm collected cash more quickly in Year 11 than in Year 10 and may not have needed as much financing as it obtained.

## SCHEDULE 1
## Financial Ratios for Zealock Bookstore

|  | 2000 | 2001 |
|---|---|---|
| Sales | 100.0% | 100.0% |
| Cost of Goods Sold | (81.0) | (81.0) |
| Compensation Expense | (9.7) | (8.3) |
| Interest Expense | (.5) | (1.1) |
| Rent Expense | (5.8) | (5.7) |
| Depreciation Expense | (1.1) | (1.1) |
| Income Tax Expense | (.8) | (1.1) |
| Net Income | 1.1% | 1.7% |
|  |  |  |
| Current Assets/Current Liabilities | 1.4 | 1.2 |
| Liabilities/Liabilities + Shareholders' Equity | 58.9% | 76.3% |

3.31    (Rybowiak's Building Supplies; preparation of journal entries, T-accounts, adjusted trial balance, income statement, and balance sheet.)

a.   (T): Transaction Entry        (A):  Adjusting Entry

(1)  Accounts Receivable............................................  85,000
(T)      Sales Revenue .................................................          85,000

(2)  Merchandise Inventory .....................................  46,300
(T)      Accounts Payable..........................................          46,300

(3)  Rent Expense .......................................................  11,750
(T)      Cash..................................................................          11,750

(4)  Salaries Payable..................................................   1,250
(T)  Salaries Expense ...............................................  19,350
         Cash..................................................................          20,600

(5)  Cash ......................................................................  34,150
(T)      Accounts Receivable....................................          34,150

(6)  Accounts Payable...............................................  38,950
(T)      Cash..................................................................          38,950

(7)  Miscellaneous Expenses....................................   3,200
(T)      Cash..................................................................           3,200

(8)  Insurance Expense..............................................      50
(A)      Prepaid Insurance.........................................              50
     $400/8 months.

(9)  Depreciation Expense ........................................   1,750
(A)      Accumulated Depreciation...........................           1,750
     1/12 × $210,000/10.

(10) Salaries Expense ...............................................   1,600
(A)      Salaries Payable ...........................................           1,600

(11) Interest Expense ...............................................      50
(A)      Interest Payable ...........................................              50
     $5,000 × .12 × 30/360.

(12) Cost of Goods Sold ...........................................  36,500
(A)      Merchandise Inventory.................................          36,500
     $68,150 + $46,300 − $77,950.

3.31 continued.

**b. and e.**

| | Cash | | |
|---|---|---|---|
| Bal. | 44,200 | 11,750 | (3) |
| (5) | 34,150 | 20,600 | (4) |
| | | 38,950 | (6) |
| | | 3,200 | (7) |
| Bal. | 3,850 | | |

| | Accounts Receivable | | |
|---|---|---|---|
| Bal. | 27,250 | 34,150 | (5) |
| (1) | 85,000 | | |
| Bal. | 78,100 | | |

| | Merchandise Inventory | | |
|---|---|---|---|
| Bal. | 68,150 | 36,500 | (12) |
| (2) | 46,300 | | |
| Bal. | 77,950 | | |

| | Prepaid Insurance | | |
|---|---|---|---|
| Bal. | 400 | 50 | (8) |
| Bal. | 350 | | |

| | Equipment | | |
|---|---|---|---|
| Bal. | 210,000 | | |
| Bal. | 210,000 | | |

| Accumulated Depreciation | | |
|---|---|---|
| | 84,000 | Bal. |
| | 1,750 | (9) |
| | 85,750 | Bal. |

| | Accounts Payable | | |
|---|---|---|---|
| | | 33,100 | Bal. |
| (6) | 38,950 | 46,300 | (2) |
| | | 40,450 | Bal. |

| Note Payable | | |
|---|---|---|
| | 5,000 | Bal. |
| | 5,000 | Bal. |

| | Salaries Payable | | |
|---|---|---|---|
| (4) | 1,250 | 1,250 | Bal. |
| | | 1,600 | (10) |
| | | 1,600 | Bal. |

| Common Stock | | |
|---|---|---|
| | 150,000 | Bal. |
| | 150,000 | Bal. |

| | Retained Earnings | | |
|---|---|---|---|
| | | 76,650 | Bal. |
| | | 10,750 | (15) |
| | | 87,400 | Bal. |

| | Sales Revenue | | |
|---|---|---|---|
| (13) | 85,000 | 85,000 | (1) |

| | Rent Expense | | |
|---|---|---|---|
| (3) | 11,750 | 11,750 | (14) |

| | Salaries Expense | | |
|---|---|---|---|
| (4) | 19,350 | | |
| (10) | 1,600 | 20,950 | (14) |
| | 20,950 | | |

3.31 b. and e. continued.

| Miscellaneous Expenses | | | | Insurance Expense | | |
|---|---|---|---|---|---|---|
| (7) | 3,200 | 3,200 | (14) | (8) | 50 | 50 | (14) |

| Depreciation Expense | | | | Interest Expense | | |
|---|---|---|---|---|---|---|
| (9) | 1,750 | 1,750 | (14) | (11) | 50 | 50 | (14) |

| Interest Payable | | | | Cost of Goods Sold | | |
|---|---|---|---|---|---|---|
| | | 50 | (11) | (12) | 36,500 | 36,500 | (14) |
| | | 50 | Bal. | | | | |

| Income Summary | | | |
|---|---|---|---|
| (14) | 74,250 | 85,000 | (13) |
| (15) | 10,750 | | |
| | 85,000 | | |

c.

## RYBOWIAK'S BUILDING SUPPLIES
### Adjusted Preclosing Trial Balance
### July 31, Year 9

| | | |
|---|---|---|
| Cash | $ 3,850 | |
| Accounts Receivable | 78,100 | |
| Merchandise Inventory | 77,950 | |
| Prepaid Insurance | 350 | |
| Equipment | 210,000 | |
| Accumulated Depreciation | | $ 85,750 |
| Accounts Payable | | 40,450 |
| Note Payable | | 5,000 |
| Salaries Payable | | 1,600 |
| Common Stock | | 150,000 |
| Retained Earnings (June 30) | | 76,650 |
| Sales Revenue | | 85,000 |
| Rent Expense | 11,750 | |
| Salaries Expense | 20,950 | |
| Miscellaneous Expenses | 3,200 | |
| Insurance Expense | 50 | |
| Depreciation Expense | 1,750 | |
| Interest Expense | 50 | |
| Interest Payable | | 50 |
| Cost of Goods Sold | 36,500 | |
| Totals | $444,500 | $444,500 |

3.31 continued.

d.
### RYBOWIAK'S BUILDING SUPPLIES
### Income Statement
### For the Month of July, Year 9

| | | |
|---|---:|---:|
| Sales Revenue................................................ | | $ 85,000 |
| Less Expenses: | | |
| Cost of Goods Sold.................................... | $ 36,500 | |
| Salaries Expense........................................ | 20,950 | |
| Rent Expense............................................. | 11,750 | |
| Depreciation Expense ............................... | 1,750 | |
| Insurance Expense..................................... | 50 | |
| Interest Expense........................................ | 50 | |
| Miscellaneous Expenses............................ | 3,200 | (74,250) |
| Net Income ................................................... | | $ 10,750 |

f.
### RYBOWIAK'S BUILDING SUPPLIES
### Balance Sheet
### July 31, Year 9

*Assets*

| | | |
|---|---:|---:|
| Current Assets: | | |
| Cash........................................................ | | $ 3,850 |
| Accounts Receivable............................... | | 78,100 |
| Merchandise Inventory............................ | | 77,950 |
| Prepaid Insurance................................... | | 350 |
| Total Current Assets............................ | | $ 160,250 |
| Noncurrent Assets: | | |
| Equipment—at Cost ................................ | $ 210,000 | |
| Less Accumulated Depreciation................. | (85,750) | |
| Total Noncurrent Assets ....................... | | 124,250 |
| Total Assets......................................... | | $ 284,500 |

*Liabilities and Shareholders' Equity*

| | | |
|---|---:|---:|
| Current Liabilities: | | |
| Accounts Payable..................................... | | $ 40,450 |
| Note Payable .......................................... | | 5,000 |
| Salaries Payable ..................................... | | 1,600 |
| Interest Payable ..................................... | | 50 |
| Total Current Liabilities....................... | | $ 47,100 |
| Shareholders' Equity: | | |
| Common Stock......................................... | | $ 150,000 |
| Retained Earnings .................................. | | 87,400 |
| Total Shareholders' Equity ................... | | $ 237,400 |
| Total Liabilities and Shareholders' | | |
| Equity................................................. | | $ 284,500 |

3.32      (Reliable Appliance Company; preparation of adjusting entries.)

| | | | |
|---|---|--:|--:|
| (1) | Depreciation Expense............................................. | 88 | |
| | Accumulated Depreciation................................. | | 88 |
| | 1/12 X ($5,280/5). | | |
| | | | |
| (2) | Depreciation Expense............................................. | 500 | |
| | Accumulated Depreciation................................. | | 500 |
| | 1/12 X ($24,000/4). | | |
| | | | |
| (3) | Rent Expense ........................................................ | 1,800 | |
| | Leasehold.......................................................... | | 1,800 |
| | | | |
| (4) | Accounts Payable.................................................. | 360 | |
| | Merchandise Inventory..................................... | | 360 |
| | | | |
| (5) | Salaries and Commissions Expense........................ | 210 | |
| | Salaries and Commissions Payable..................... | | 210 |
| | | | |
| (6) | Advances by Customers......................................... | 490 | |
| | Accounts Receivable........................................... | | 490 |
| | | | |
| (7) | Insurance Expense................................................. | 50 | |
| | Prepaid Insurance............................................. | | 50 |
| | $900/18 = $50. | | |
| | | | |
| (8) | Retained Earnings................................................. | 2,500 | |
| | Dividends Payable.............................................. | | 2,500 |
| | | | |
| (9) | Merchandise Cost of Goods Sold............................. | 37,440 | |
| | Merchandise Inventory....................................... | | 37,440 |
| | $99,000 − $360 − $61,200 = $37,440. | | |

3.33    (Williamson Corporation; preparation of adjusting entries.)

(1) Depreciation Expense.................................................... 6,250
       Accumulated Depreciation..................................... 6,250
    ($50,000/8) = $6,250.

(2) Advances from Customers........................................ 290
       Sales Revenue ........................................................ 290

(3) Accounts Payable...................................................... 860
       Accounts Receivable............................................. 860

(4) Prepaid Rent............................................................. 200
       Marketing and Administrative Expenses ............ 200
    ($1,400 − $1,200) = $200.

(5) Marketing and Administrative Expenses................. 450
       Salaries Payable ................................................... 450
    ($2,250 − $1,800) = $450.

(6) Merchandise Cost of Goods Sold............................... 94,800
       Merchandise Inventory......................................... 94,800
    ($110,000 − $15,200) = $94,800.

(7) Income Tax Expense.................................................. 1,017
       Income Tax Payable.............................................. 1,017
    .30[($150,000 + $290) − ($94,800 + $45,000 +
    $6,250 − $200 + $450)] = $1,017.

3.34    (Creative Photographers, Inc.; preparation of closing entries.)

a.   Revenue—Commercial Photography..........................   54,270
     Revenue—Printing Service.......................................   14,040
          Advertising Expense.........................................                 4,500
          Depreciation Expense—Cameras and Equip-
               ment......................................................................                   540
          Depreciation Expense—Furniture and Fix-
               tures......................................................................                   315
          Electricity Expense..........................................                   900
          Equipment Repairs Expense............................                   540
          Insurance Expense...........................................                   990
          Photographic Supplies Expense......................                 5,850
          Rent Expense...................................................                 4,275
          Salaries Expense..............................................                32,400
          Telephone Expense..........................................                   360
          Retained Earnings...........................................                17,640

b.

| Revenue—<br>Commercial<br>Photography | Revenue—<br>Printing Service | Advertising Expense |
|---|---|---|
| (1) 54,270 \| 54,270 Bal. | (1) 14,040 \| 14,040 Bal. | Bal. 4,500 \| 4,500 (1) |

| Depreciation<br>Expense—Cameras<br>and Equipment | Depreciation<br>Expense—Furniture<br>and Fixtures | Electricity Expense |
|---|---|---|
| Bal. 540 \| 540 (1) | Bal. 315 \| 315 (1) | Bal. 900 \| 900 (1) |

| Equipment Repairs<br>Expense | Insurance Expense | Photographic<br>Supplies Expense |
|---|---|---|
| Bal. 540 \| 540 (1) | Bal. 990 \| 990 (1) | Bal. 5,850 \| 5,850 (1) |

| Rent Expense | Salaries Expense | Telephone Expense |
|---|---|---|
| Bal. 4,275 \| 4,275 (1) | Bal. 32,400 \| 32,400 (1) | Bal. 360 \| 360 (1) |

| Retained Earnings |
|---|
| 42,414 Bal. |
| 17,640 (1) |

3.35 (Prima Company; working backwards to balance sheet at beginning of period.)

**PRIMA COMPANY**
**Balance Sheet**
**As of January 1, Year 2**

*Assets*

| | | |
|---|---:|---:|
| Cash............................................................................ | | $ 11,700 |
| Marketable Securities................................................ | | 12,000 |
| Accounts Receivable.................................................. | | 22,000 |
| Merchandise Inventory.............................................. | | 33,000 |
| Prepayments ............................................................. | | 1,700 |
| Land, Buildings, and Equipment ............................. | $ 40,000 | |
| Less Accumulated Depreciation............................... | (12,000) | 28,000 |
| Total Assets......................................................... | | $ 108,400 |

*Equities*

| | | |
|---|---:|---:|
| Accounts Payable....................................................... | | $ 26,000 |
| Interest Payable ........................................................ | | 300 |
| Taxes Payable ............................................................ | | 3,500 |
| Notes Payable (6 Percent)......................................... | | 20,000 |
| Capital Stock.............................................................. | | 50,000 |
| Retained Earnings ..................................................... | | 8,600 |
| Total Equities...................................................... | | $ 108,400 |

A T account method for deriving the solution appears below and on the following page. The end-of-year balance appears at the bottom of the T-account. The derived starting balance appears at the top. "p" indicates plug; "c," closing entry.

| | Cash | | | | | Marketable Securities | | |
|---|---:|---:|---|---|---|---:|---:|---|
| (p) | 11,700 | | | | (p) | 12,000 | | |
| (1) | 47,000 | 128,000 | (3) | | (8) | 8,000 | | |
| (2) | 150,000 | 49,000 | (4) | | | | | |
| | | 7,500 | (5) | | | | | |
| | | 1,200 | (6) | | | | | |
| | | 5,000 | (7) | | | | | |
| | | 8,000 | (8) | | | | | |
| Bal. | 10,000 | | | | Bal. | 20,000 | | |

| | Accounts Receivable | | | | | Merchandise Inventory | | |
|---|---:|---:|---|---|---|---:|---:|---|
| (p) | 22,000 | | | | (p) | 33,000 | | |
| (10) | 153,000 | 150,000 | (2) | | (9) | 127,000 | 130,000 | (11) |
| Bal. | 25,000 | | | | Bal. | 30,000 | | |

3.35 continued.

### Prepayments for Miscellaneous Services

| | | | |
|---|---|---|---|
| (p) | 1,700 | | |
| (4) | 49,000 | 47,700 | (14) |
| Bal. | 3,000 | | |

### Land, Buildings, and Equipment

| | | | |
|---|---|---|---|
| (p) | 40,000 | | |
| Bal. | 40,000 | | |

### Accounts Payable (for Merchandise)

| | | | |
|---|---|---|---|
| | | 26,000 | (p) |
| (3) | 128,000 | 127,000 | (9) |
| | | 25,000 | Bal. |

### Interest Payable

| | | | |
|---|---|---|---|
| | | 300 | (p) |
| (6) | 1,200 | 1,200 | (15) |
| | | 300 | Bal. |

### Taxes Payable

| | | | |
|---|---|---|---|
| | | 3,500 | (p) |
| (5) | 7,500 | 8,000 | (13) |
| | | 4,000 | Bal. |

### Notes Payable

| | | | |
|---|---|---|---|
| | | 20,000 | (p) |
| | | 20,000 | Bal. |

### Accumulated Depreciation

| | | | |
|---|---|---|---|
| | | 12,000 | (p) |
| | | 4,000 | (12) |
| | | 16,000 | Bal. |

### Capital Stock

| | | | |
|---|---|---|---|
| | | 50,000 | (p) |
| | | 50,000 | Bal. |

### Retained Earnings

| | | | |
|---|---|---|---|
| | | 8,600 | (p) |
| (7) | 5,000 | 9,100 | (22) |
| | | 12,700 | Bal. |

### Sales

| | | | |
|---|---|---|---|
| | | 47,000 | (1) |
| (16c) | 200,000 | 153,000 | (10) |

### Cost of Goods Sold

| | | | |
|---|---|---|---|
| (11) | 130,000 | 130,000 | (17c) |

### Depreciation Expense

| | | | |
|---|---|---|---|
| (12) | 4,000 | 4,000 | (18c) |

### Taxes Expense

| | | | |
|---|---|---|---|
| (13) | 8,000 | 8,000 | (19c) |

### Other Operating Expense

| | | | |
|---|---|---|---|
| (14) | 47,700 | 47,700 | (20c) |

### Interest Expense

| | | | |
|---|---|---|---|
| (15) | 1,200 | 1,200 | (21c) |

### Income Summary

| | | | |
|---|---|---|---|
| (17) | 130,000 | 200,000 | (16) |
| (18) | 4,000 | | |
| (19) | 8,000 | | |
| (20) | 47,700 | | |
| (21) | 1,200 | | |
| (22c) | 9,100 | | |

**3.36** (Secunda Company; working backwards to the balance sheet at the beginning of the period.)

## SECUNDA COMPANY
### Cash Receipts and Disbursements Schedule

| | | |
|---|---:|---:|
| Receipts: | | |
|    Collections from Customers............................ | | $85,000 |
| Disbursements: | | |
|    Suppliers of Merchandise and Other Services...................................................... | $81,000 | |
|    Mortgage........................................................ | 3,000 | |
|    Dividends ...................................................... | 10,000 | |
|    Interest.......................................................... | 2,000 | |
|      Total Disbursements.................................. | | 96,000 |
| Decrease in Cash ............................................ | | $11,000 |
| Cash Balance, January 1.................................. | | 20,000 |
| Cash Balance, December 31 ............................. | | $ 9,000 |

A T-account method for deriving the solution appears below and on the following page. After Entry (6), we have explained all revenue and expense account changes. Plugging for the unknown amounts determines the remaining, unexplained changes in balance sheet accounts. A "p" next to the entry number designates these entries. Note that the revenue and expense accounts are not yet closed to retained earnings, so dividends account for the decrease in the Retained Earnings account during the year of $10,000.

| Cash | | | | | Accounts Receivable | | | |
|---|---|---|---|---|---|---|---|---|
| Bal. | 20,000 | | | | Bal. | 36,000 | | |
| (7) | 85,000 | | | | (1) | 100,000 | 85,000 | (7p) |
| | | 2,000 | (9) | | | | | |
| | | 81,000 | (10) | | | | | |
| | | 3,000 | (11) | | | | | |
| | | 10,000 | (12) | | | | | |
| Bal. | 9,000 | | | | Bal. | 51,000 | | |

| Merchandise Inventory | | | | | Prepayments | | | |
|---|---|---|---|---|---|---|---|---|
| Bal. | 45,000 | | | | Bal. | 2,000 | | |
| (8p) | 65,000 | 50,000 | (2) | | | | 1,000 | (5) |
| Bal. | 60,000 | | | | Bal. | 1,000 | | |

| Land, Buildings and Equipment | | | | Cost of Goods Sold | | |
|---|---|---|---|---|---|---|
| Bal. | 40,000 | | | Bal. | 0 | |
| | | | | (2) | 50,000 | |
| Bal. | 40,000 | | | Bal. | 50,000 | |

3.36 continued.

| Interest Expense | | |
|---|---|---|
| Bal. | 0 | |
| (3) | 3,000 | |
| Bal. | 3,000 | |

| Other Operating Expenses | | |
|---|---|---|
| Bal. | 0 | |
| (4) | 2,000 | |
| (5) | 1,000 | |
| (6p) | 26,000 | |
| Bal. | 29,000 | |

| Accumulated Depreciation | | |
|---|---|---|
| | 16,000 | Bal. |
| | 2,000 | (4) |
| | 18,000 | Bal. |

| Interest Payable | | |
|---|---|---|
| | 1,000 | Bal. |
| (9p) 2,000 | 3,000 | (3) |
| | 2,000 | Bal. |

| Accounts Payable | | |
|---|---|---|
| | 30,000 | Bal. |
| (10p) 81,000 | 26,000 | (6) |
| | 65,000 | (8) |
| | 40,000 | Bal. |

| Mortgage Payable | | |
|---|---|---|
| | 20,000 | Bal. |
| (11p) 3,000 | | |
| | 17,000 | Bal. |

| Capital Stock | | |
|---|---|---|
| | 50,000 | Bal. |
| | 50,000 | Bal. |

| Retained Earnings | | |
|---|---|---|
| | 26,000 | Bal. |
| (12p) 10,000 | | |
| | 16,000 | Bal. |

| Sales | | |
|---|---|---|
| | 0 | Bal. |
| | 100,000 | (1) |
| | 100,000 | Bal. |

**3.37** (Tertia Company; working backwards to income statement.)

## TERTIA COMPANY
### Statement of Income and Retained Earnings

Revenues:

| | | |
|---|---|---|
| Sales...................................................................... | $212,000 | |
| Interest Revenue.................................................. | 700 | |
| Total Revenues................................................. | | $212,700 |

Expenses:

| | | |
|---|---|---|
| Cost of Goods Sold ............................................. | $126,500 | |
| Property Tax Expense......................................... | 1,700 | |
| Depreciation Expense.......................................... | 2,000 | |
| Interest Expense ................................................. | 500 | |
| Miscellaneous Expenses...................................... | 56,800 | |
| Total Expenses................................................. | | 187,500 |
| Net Income............................................................ | | $ 25,200 |
| Less Dividends..................................................... | | (2,000) |
| Increase in Retained Earnings........................... | | $ 23,200 |
| Retained Earnings, Beginning of Year ............... | | 76,000 |
| Retained Earnings, End of Year.......................... | | $ 99,200 |

A T-account method for deriving the solution appears below and on the following pages. Transactions (1) – (9) correspond to the numbered cash transactions information. In transactions (10) – (25), "p" indicates that the figure was derived by a "plug" and "c" indicates a closing entry. The final check is that the debit to close Income Summary in (25) matches the plug in the Retained Earnings account.

| | Cash | | | | | Accounts and Notes Receivable | | |
|---|---|---|---|---|---|---|---|---|
| Bal. | (a) | | | | Bal. | 36,000 | | |
| (1) | 144,000 | 114,000 | (4) | | (10p) | 149,000 | 144,000 | (1) |
| (2) | 63,000 | 5,000 | (5) | | | | | |
| (3) | 1,000 | 500 | (6) | | | | | |
| | | 57,500 | (7) | | | | | |
| | | 1,200 | (8) | | | | | |
| | | 2,000 | (9) | | | | | |
| Bal. | (b) | | | | Bal. | 41,000 | | |

(a) Total debits, $183,000, less specific, known debits, $143,000, equal beginning balance in Cash account of $40,000.

(b) Beginning balance of $40,000 plus increase in cash balance for the year of $27,800 equals ending balance in Cash account of $67,800.

3.37 continued.

| Merchandise Inventory | | | |
|---|---|---|---|
| Bal. | 55,000 | | |
| (14) | 121,000 | 126,500 | (15p) |
| Bal. | 49,500 | | |

| Interest Receivable | | | |
|---|---|---|---|
| Bal. | 1,000 | | |
| (11p) | 700 | 1,000 | (3) |
| Bal. | 700 | | |

| Prepaid Miscellaneous Services | | | |
|---|---|---|---|
| Bal. | 4,000 | | |
| (7) | 57,500 | 56,300 | (12p) |
| Bal. | 5,200 | | |

| Building, Machinery, and Equipment | | |
|---|---|---|
| Bal. | 47,000 | |
| Bal. | 47,000 | |

| Accounts Payable (Miscellaneous Services) | | | |
|---|---|---|---|
| | | 2,000 | Bal. |
| | | 500 | (13p) |
| | | 2,500 | Bal. |

| Accounts Payable (Merchandise) | | | |
|---|---|---|---|
| | | 34,000 | Bal. |
| (4) | 114,000 | 121,000 | (14p) |
| | | 41,000 | Bal. |

| Property Taxes Payable | | | |
|---|---|---|---|
| | | 1,000 | Bal. |
| (8) | 1,200 | 1,700 | (16p) |
| | | 1,500 | Bal. |

| Accumulated Depreciation | | | |
|---|---|---|---|
| | | 10,000 | Bal. |
| | | 2,000 | (17p) |
| | | 12,000 | Bal. |

| Mortgage Payable | | | |
|---|---|---|---|
| | | 35,000 | Bal. |
| (5) | 5,000 | | |
| | | 30,000 | Bal. |

| Capital Stock | | | |
|---|---|---|---|
| | | 25,000 | Bal. |
| | | 25,000 | Bal. |

| Retained Earnings | | | |
|---|---|---|---|
| | | 76,000 | Bal. |
| (9) | 2,000 | 25,200 | (25p) |
| | | 99,200 | Bal. |

| Sales | | | |
|---|---|---|---|
| | | 63,000 | (2) |
| | | 149,000 | (10) |
| (18c) | 212,000 | 212,000 | |

| Cost of Goods Sold | | | |
|---|---|---|---|
| (15) | 126,500 | 126,500 | (20c) |

| Interest Expense | | | |
|---|---|---|---|
| (6) | 500 | 500 | (21c) |

3.37 continued.

| | Interest Revenue | | | | Miscellaneous Expenses | | |
|---|---|---|---|---|---|---|---|
| (19c) | 700 | 700 | (11) | (12) | 56,300 | | |
| | | | | (13) | 500 | | |
| | | | | | 56,800 | 56,800 | (22c) |

| | Property Tax Expense | | | | Depreciation Expense | | |
|---|---|---|---|---|---|---|---|
| (16) | 1,700 | 1,700 | (23c) | (17) | 2,000 | 2,000 | (24c) |

| | Income Summary | | |
|---|---|---|---|
| (20) | 126,500 | 212,000 | (18) |
| (21) | 500 | 700 | (19) |
| (22) | 56,800 | | |
| (23) | 1,700 | | |
| (24) | 2,000 | | |
| (25c) | 25,200 | | |

3.38    (Portobello Co.; reconstructing the income statement and balance sheet.)

**PORTOBELLO CO.**
**Income Statement**
**For the Year Ended December 31, Year 10**

| | |
|---|---|
| Revenues: | |
| Sales | $ 227,200 |
| Interest | 300 |
| Total Revenues | $ 227,500 |
| Expenses: | |
| Cost of Goods Sold | $ 88,000 |
| Depreciation | 17,500 |
| Salaries | 75,800 |
| Taxes | 18,000 |
| Insurance | 3,000 |
| Consulting | 4,800 |
| Interest | 5,000 |
| Total Expenses | $ 212,100 |
| Net Income | $ 15,400 |

3.38 continued.

**PORTOBELLO CO.**
**Balance Sheet**
**December 31, Year 10**

*Assets*

Current Assets:
| | | |
|---|---|---|
| Cash........................................................ | | $ 4,700 |
| Accounts Receivable.............................. | | 51,000 |
| Merchandise Inventories........................ | | 40,000 |
| Prepaid Insurance.................................. | | 1,500 |
| Prepaid Salaries ..................................... | | 4,000 |
| Prepaid Taxes ......................................... | | 3,000 |
|     Total Current Assets............................. | | $ 104,200 |

Noncurrent Assets:
| | | |
|---|---|---|
| Computer System—at Cost...................... | $ 78,000 | |
| Less Accumulated Depreciation............... | (39,000) | $ 39,000 |
| Delivery Trucks....................................... | $ 60,000 | |
| Less Accumulated Depreciation............... | (4,500) | 55,500 |
|     Total Noncurrent Assets ...................... | | $ 94,500 |
|     Total Assets........................................ | | $ 198,700 |

*Liabilities and Shareholders' Equity*

Current Liabilities:
| | |
|---|---|
| Accounts Payable.................................... | $ 16,000 |
| Interest Payable ..................................... | 2,000 |
| Dividend Payable.................................... | 3,000 |
| Salaries Payable ..................................... | 1,300 |
| Taxes Payable ......................................... | 4,000 |
| Consulting Fee Payable............................ | 4,800 |
| Advances from Customers ....................... | 1,400 |
|     Total Current Liabilities........................ | $ 32,500 |
| Note Payable ........................................... | 60,000 |
|     Total Liabilities .................................. | $ 92,500 |

Shareholders' Equity:
| | |
|---|---|
| Common Stock......................................... | $ 51,000 |
| Retained Earnings .................................. | 55,200 |
|     Total Shareholders' Equity ................... | $ 106,200 |
| Total Liabilities and Shareholders' | |
|     Equity............................................... | $ 198,700 |

T-accounts to derive the amounts in the income statement and balance sheet appear on the following pages.

| | Cash | | | | | Accounts Receivable | | |
|---|---|---|---|---|---|---|---|---|
| √ | 18,600 | | | | √ | 33,000 | | |
| (4) | 10,900 | 4,800 | (3) | | (15) | 228,000 | 210,000 | (14) |
| (14) | 210,000 | 115,000 | (5) | | | | | |
| | | 3,000 | (10) | | | | | |
| | | 85,000 | (17) | | | | | |
| | | 27,000 | (19) | | | | | |
| √ | 4,700 | | | | √ | 51,000 | | |

| | Notes Receivable | | | | | Interest Receivable | | |
|---|---|---|---|---|---|---|---|---|
| √ | 10,000 | | | | √ | 600 | | |
| | | 10,000 | (4) | | | | 600 | (4) |
| √ | 0 | | | | √ | 0 | | |

| | Merchandise Inventories | | | | | Prepaid Insurance | | |
|---|---|---|---|---|---|---|---|---|
| √ | 22,000 | | | | √ | 4,500 | | |
| (6) | 95,000 | 88,000 | (8) | | | | 3,000 | (1) |
| (7) | 11,000 | | | | | | | |
| √ | 40,000 | | | | √ | 1,500 | | |

| | Prepaid Salaries | | | | Prepaid Taxes | |
|---|---|---|---|---|---|---|
| √ | 0 | | | √ | 0 | |
| (17) | 4,000 | | (19) | 3,000 | |
| √ | 4,000 | | √ | 3,000 | |

| | Computer System (at Cost) | | | Accumulated Depreciation—Computer System | | |
|---|---|---|---|---|---|---|
| √ | 78,000 | | | | 26,000 | √ |
| | | | | | 13,000 | (13) |
| √ | 78,000 | | | | 39,000 | √ |

| | Delivery Trucks | | | Accumulated Depreciation—Delivery Trucks | | |
|---|---|---|---|---|---|---|
| √ | 0 | | | | 0 | √ |
| (9) | 60,000 | | | | 4,500 | (12) |
| √ | 60,000 | | | | 4,500 | √ |

3.38 continued.

### Accounts Payable

|  |  |  |  |
|---|---|---|---|
|  |  | 36,000 | √ |
| (5) | 115,000 | 95,000 | (6) |
|  |  | 16,000 | √ |

### Notes Payable

|  |  |  |  |
|---|---|---|---|
|  |  | 0 | √ |
|  |  | 60,000 | (9) |
|  |  | 60,000 | √ |

### Interest Payable

|  |  |  |  |
|---|---|---|---|
|  |  | 0 | √ |
|  |  | 2,000 | (11) |
|  |  | 2,000 | √ |

### Dividend Payable

|  |  |  |  |
|---|---|---|---|
|  |  | 1,800 | √ |
| (3) | 4,800 | 6,000 | (2) |
|  |  | 3,000 | √ |

### Salaries Payable

|  |  |  |  |
|---|---|---|---|
|  |  | 6,500 | √ |
| (17) | 6,500 |  |  |
|  |  | 1,300 | (18) |
|  |  | 1,300 | √ |

### Taxes Payable

|  |  |  |  |
|---|---|---|---|
|  |  | 10,000 | √ |
| (19) | 10,000 | 4,000 | (20) |
|  |  | 4,000 | √ |

### Consulting Fee Payable

|  |  |  |  |
|---|---|---|---|
|  |  | 0 | √ |
|  |  | 4,800 | (21) |
|  |  | 4,800 | √ |

### Advances from Customers

|  |  |  |  |
|---|---|---|---|
|  |  | 600 | √ |
| (16) | 600 | 1,400 | (15) |
|  |  | 1,400 | √ |

### Common Stock

|  |  |  |  |
|---|---|---|---|
|  |  | 40,000 | √ |
|  |  | 11,000 | (7) |
|  |  | 51,000 | √ |

### Retained Earnings

|  |  |  |  |
|---|---|---|---|
|  |  | 45,800 | √ |
| (2) | 6,000 | 15,400 | (31) |
|  |  | 55,200 | √ |

### Sales Revenue

|  |  |  |  |
|---|---|---|---|
|  |  | 226,600 | (15) |
| (22) | 227,200 | 600 | (16) |

### Interest Revenue

|  |  |  |  |
|---|---|---|---|
| (23) | 300 | 300 | (4) |

### Cost of Goods Sold

|  |  |  |  |
|---|---|---|---|
| (8) | 88,000 | 88,000 | (24) |

### Depreciation Expense

|  |  |  |  |
|---|---|---|---|
| (12) | 4,500 |  |  |
| (13) | 13,000 | 17,500 | (25) |

### Salary Expense

|  |  |  |  |
|---|---|---|---|
| (17) | 74,500 |  |  |
| (18) | 1,300 | 75,800 | (26) |

### Tax Expense

|  |  |  |  |
|---|---|---|---|
| (19) | 14,000 |  |  |
| (20) | 4,000 | 18,000 | (27) |

3.38 continued.

| Insurance Expense | | | | Consulting Expense | | | |
|---|---|---|---|---|---|---|---|
| (1) | 3,000 | 3,000 | (28) | (21) | 4,800 | 4,800 | (29) |

| Interest Expense | | | | Income Summary | | | |
|---|---|---|---|---|---|---|---|
| (10) | 3,000 | | | (24) | 88,000 | 227,200 | (22) |
| (11) | 2,000 | 5,000 | (30) | (25) | 17,500 | 300 | (23) |
| | | | | (26) | 75,800 | | |
| | | | | (27) | 18,000 | | |
| | | | | (28) | 3,000 | | |
| | | | | (29) | 4,800 | | |
| | | | | (30) | 5,000 | | |
| | | | | (31) | 15,400 | | |

3.39    (Computer Needs, Inc.; reconstructing the income statement and balance sheet.)

a.

| Cash | | | | Accounts Receivable | | | |
|---|---|---|---|---|---|---|---|
| √ | 15,600 | | | √ | 32,100 | | |
| (A) | 37,500 | 164,600 | (D) | (C) | 159,700 | 151,500 | (B) |
| (B) | 151,500 | 21,000 | (G) | | | | |
| | | 3,390 | (H) | | | | |
| | | 4,800 | (I) | | | | |
| | | 6,000 | (J) | | | | |
| √ | 4,810 | | | √ | 40,300 | | |

| Inventories | | | | Prepayments | | |
|---|---|---|---|---|---|---|
| √ | 46,700 | | | √ | 1,500 | |
| (E) | 172,100 | 158,100 | (F) | (G) | 300 | |
| √ | 60,700 | | | √ | 1,800 | |

| Property, Plant and Equipment | | | Accumulated Depreciation | | |
|---|---|---|---|---|---|
| √ | 59,700 | | | 2,800 | √ |
| (J) | 6,000 | | | 3,300 | (K) |
| √ | 65,700 | | | 6,100 | √ |

| Accounts Payable—Merchandise | | | Income Tax Payable | | |
|---|---|---|---|---|---|
| | | 37,800 | √ | | 3,390 | √ |
| (D) | 164,600 | 172,100 | (E) | (H) | 3,390 | 3,584 | (L) |
| | | 45,300 | √ | | | 3,584 | √ |

3-49

3.39 a. continued.

| Other Current Liabilities | | |
|---|---|---|
| | 2,900 | √ |
| (G) 1,700 | | |
| | 1,200 | √ |

| Mortgage Payable | | |
|---|---|---|
| | 50,000 | √ |
| (I) 800 | | |
| | 49,200 | √ |

| Common Stock | | |
|---|---|---|
| | 50,000 | √ |
| | 50,000 | √ |

| Retained Earnings | | |
|---|---|---|
| | 8,710 | √ |
| | 9,216 | (M) |
| | 17,926 | √ |

| Sales | | |
|---|---|---|
| | 37,500 | (A) |
| (M) 197,200 | 159,700 | (B) |

| Cost of Goods Sold | | |
|---|---|---|
| (F) 158,100 | 158,100 | (M) |

| Selling & Admin. Expense | | |
|---|---|---|
| (G) 19,000 | 19,000 | (M) |

| Depreciation Expense | | |
|---|---|---|
| (K) 3,300 | 3,300 | (M) |

| Interest Expense | | |
|---|---|---|
| (I) 4,000 | 4,000 | (M) |

| Income Tax Expense | | |
|---|---|---|
| (L) 3,584 | 3,584 | (M) |

## COMPUTER NEEDS, INC.
### Income Statement
### For the Years Ended December 31

| | Year 8 | | Year 9 | |
|---|---|---|---|---|
| | Amounts | Percentages | Amounts | Percentages |
| Sales | $152,700 | 100.0% | $197,200 | 100.0% |
| Cost of Goods Sold | (116,400) | (76.2) | (158,100) | (80.2) |
| Selling and Administration Expenses | (17,400) | (11.4) | (19,000) | (9.6) |
| Depreciation | (2,800) | (1.9) | (3,300) | (1.7) |
| Interest | (4,000) | (2.6) | (4,000) | (2.0) |
| Income Taxes | (3,390) | (2.2) | (3,584) | (1.8) |
| Net Income | $ 8,710 | 5.7% | $ 9,216 | 4.7% |

3.39 a. continued.

## COMPUTER NEEDS, INC.
### Balance Sheet
### December 31

| | Year 8 | | Year 9 | |
|---|---|---|---|---|
| | Amounts | Percentages | Amounts | Percentages |
| *Assets* | | | | |
| Cash.................................... | $ 15,600 | 10.2% | $ 4,810 | 2.9% |
| Accounts Receivable.......... | 32,100 | 21.0 | 40,300 | 24.1 |
| Inventories.......................... | 46,700 | 30.6 | 60,700 | 36.3 |
| Prepayments...................... | 1,500 | 1.0 | 1,800 | 1.1 |
| Total Current Assets..... | $ 95,900 | 62.8% | $107,610 | 64.4% |
| Property, Plant and Equipment: | | | | |
| At Cost.......................... | $ 59,700 | 39.0% | $ 65,700 | 39.3% |
| Less Accumulated Depreciation............... | (2,800) | (1.8) | (6,100) | (3.7) |
| Net.................................. | $ 56,900 | 37.2% | $ 59,600 | 35.6% |
| Total Assets.................... | $152,800 | 100.0% | $167,210 | 100.0% |
| | | | | |
| *Liabilities and Share-holders' Equity* | | | | |
| Accounts Payable— Merchandise..................... | $ 37,800 | 24.8% | $ 45,300 | 27.1% |
| Income Tax Payable........... | 3,390 | 2.2 | 3,584 | 2.2 |
| Other Current Liabilities... | 2,900 | 1.9 | 1,200 | .7 |
| Total Current Liabilities................................. | $ 44,090 | 28.9% | $ 50,084 | 30.0% |
| Mortgage Payable............... | 50,000 | 32.7 | 49,200 | 29.4 |
| Total Liabilities............... | $ 94,090 | 61.6% | $ 99,284 | 59.4% |
| Common Stock................... | $ 50,000 | 32.7% | $ 50,000 | 29.9% |
| Retained Earnings.............. | 8,710 | 5.7 | 17,926 | 10.7 |
| Total Shareholders' Equity........................... | $ 58,710 | 38.4% | $ 67,926 | 40.6% |
| Total Liabilities and Shareholders' Equity... | $152,800 | 100.0% | $167,210 | 100.0% |

3.39 continued.

b. Although sales increased between Year 8 and Year 9, net income as a percentage of sales declined from 5.7% to 4.7%. The decline occurs primarily as a result of an increase in the cost of goods sold to sales percentage. The increased percentage might suggest (1) increased competition, which forced Computer Needs, Inc. to lower its prices, (2) increased cost of merchandise, which Computer Needs, Inc. could not or chose not to pass on to customers, or (3) a shift in product mix to lower margin products. The percentage is also affected by the estimates made for the December 31, Year 9 balances in Accounts Receivable, Inventories, and Accounts Payable. The following summarizes the effects of an overstatement or understatement of each of these three accounts, assuming the other two accounts are correctly stated, on the cost of goods sold to sales percentage.

| December 31, Year 9 Balance Is: | Effect of Cost of Goods Sold to Sales Percentage | | |
|---|---|---|---|
| | Numerator | Denominator | Net Effect |
| Accounts Receivable Overstated.... | O | O/S | U/S |
| Accounts Receivable Understated . | O | U/S | O/S |
| Inventories Overstated...................... | U/S | O | U/S |
| Inventories Understated................... | O/S | O | O/S |
| Accounts Payable Overstated......... | O/S | O | O/S |
| Accounts Payable Understated ...... | U/S | O | U/S |

Of course, there could be compounding or offsetting errors in each of these three accounts.

The selling and administrative expense to sales percentage declined. Compensation of employees is largely a fixed cost, so the increased sales should permit Computer Needs, Inc. to spread this cost over the larger sales base. The estimate of Accounts Receivable and Other Current Liabilities on December 31, Year 9 also can affect this percentage.

The reduced expense percentage for depreciation reflects the spreading of this fixed cost over a larger sales base. Although depreciation expense increased between Year 8 and Year 9, sales increased by a higher percentage.

The reduced expense percentage for interest likewise results from spreading this fixed cost of a larger sales base. Note that interest expense was the same amount in Year 8 and Year 9. Given that the amount of the loan outstanding decreased, the interest rate on the loan must have increased.

The decreased income tax percentage results from a lower income before taxes to sales percentage. The income tax rate was 28 percent in both years.

3.39 b. continued.

|  | Year 8 | | Year 9 | |
|---|---|---|---|---|
|  | Amounts | Percentages | Amounts | Percentages |
| Net Income before Taxes .. | $ 12,100 | 100.0% | $ 12,800 | 100.0% |
| Income Tax Expense.......... | (3,390) | (28.0) | (3,584) | (28.0) |
| Net Income.......................... | $ 8,710 | 72.0% | $ 9,216 | 72.0% |

The balance sheet shows a significant decline in cash and a buildup of accounts receivable, inventories, and accounts payable. It is possible that each of these accounts is overstated. The decline in cash, however, is consistent with the buildup of accounts receivable. The buildup of accounts payable is consistent with a buildup in inventories.

3.40 (The GAP and The Limited; interpreting common-size income statements.)

a. The decreasing cost of goods sold to sales percentages for both firms suggest a common explanation. One possibility is that the economy was doing well and both firms were able to increase selling prices and thereby their profit margins. Another possibility is that the firms were able to purchase merchandise in larger quantities or pay more quickly to take advantage of discounts. A third possibility is that the firms implemented more effective inventory control systems, thereby reducing obsolescence and the need to reduce selling prices to move their merchandise. Another possibility is that sales grew rapidly and the firms were able to spread their relatively fixed occupancy costs over a larger sales base.

b. The Limited relies more heavily on in-store promotions, which tend to increase its cost of goods sold to sales percentages, whereas The GAP relies more on advertising to stimulate sales, which The GAP includes in selling and administrative expenses.

c. The increasing selling and administrative expenses to sales percentages for both firms suggest a common explanation. One possibility is that the specialty retailing industry became more competitive over this period (from new entrants and from the Internet) and the firms had to increase marketing expenses to compete. This explanation, however, is inconsistent with a more attractive pricing environment suggested in Part a. above. Another possibility is that both firms experienced increased administrative expenses as they introduced new store concepts and opened new stores.

d. The explanation in Part b. applies here as well. The GAP includes its promotion costs in selling and administrative expenses, whereas more of those of The Limited appear in cost of goods sold.

e.  The interest expense to sales percentage decreased for The GAP and increased for The Limited. One possible explanation is The GAP reduced the amount of debt outstanding or grew it at a slower pace than that of The Limited. Another possibility is that the market viewed The GAP as increasingly less risky, permitting it to borrow at lower interest rates. On the other hand, the market viewed The Limited as more risky and required it to pay a higher interest rate. These two possibilities are not independent. Perhaps The GAP was able to borrow at a lower rate because it reduced the amount of debt in its capital structure. The higher interest rate for The Limited may reflect increased risk from an increased proportion of debt in its capital structure.

f.  Both firms experienced increased net income relative to sales. Both firms should therefore experience increased income tax expense relative to sales. A more meaningful way to interpret income taxes is to relate income tax expense to income before income taxes. The latter is the base on which governments impose income taxes. Consider the following:

|  | The GAP | | | The Limited | | |
|---|---|---|---|---|---|---|
|  | Year 8 | Year 9 | Year 10 | Year 8 | Year 9 | Year 10 |
| (1) Income before Income Taxes (plug)............... | 12.4% | 14.6% | 16.3% | 5.8% | 6.5% | 6.9% |
| (2) Income Tax Expense........... | (4.2) | (5.5) | (6.6) | (2.0) | (2.3) | (2.4) |
| (3) Net Income ...... | 8.2% | 9.1% | 9.7% | 3.8% | 4.2% | 4.5% |
| (2)/(1)...................... | 33.9% | 37.7% | 40.5% | 34.5% | 35.4% | 34.8% |

The income tax expense to income before income taxes percentages for The GAP continually increased while those of The Limited remained relatively stable. One possible explanation is that The GAP expanded its operations into other countries and perhaps experienced higher income tax rates in those countries than it experiences in the United States.

g.  The profit margins of The Limited are just slightly larger than that for Wal-Mart in Exhibit 3.12. One would expect specialty retailers to differentiate their products and services more than Wal-Mart and achieve a higher profit margin percentage. The question is: How much higher? The GAP achieves profit margins similar to those for General Mills (branded foods) and Interpublic Group (creative marketing services). Extensive competition characterizes specialty apparel retailing, which dampens profit margins. However, new fashions and trends stimulate demand and permit higher profit margins. One might therefore expect an average profit margin for specialty retailers some-

3.40 g. continued.

> where between that of The Limited and The GAP. The Limited appears to have performed worse during this period than one might expect and The GAP performed better.

3.41 (Nokia; interpreting common size income statements.)

The improved profit margin results primarily from decreases in the cost of goods sold to sales percentage and in the selling and administrative expense to sales percentage. One possible explanation for these decreased percentages is that either Nokia's market dominance or the rapid growth in industry sales gave it pricing flexibility and Nokia was able to price its products favorably relative to its costs. Another possibility is that the rapid sales growth permitted Nokia to spread fixed manufacturing, selling, and administrative expenses over a much larger sales base. The decreasing interest expense to sales percentage also favorably affected the profit margin. Nokia may have reduced the amount of debt in its capital structure or replaced debt with a higher interest rate with debt carrying a lower interest rate. It is also possible that Nokia grew its debt but at a less rapid pace than the growth in sales, permitting the interest expense to sales percentage to decline.

Offsetting these favorable effects on the profit margin percentage is a reduction in the other revenues percentage. We have no information to interpret this change. The income tax expense to sales percentage increased, the result in part of an increase in net income before income taxes. The average income tax rate also increased, as the following analysis shows.

| | Year 7 | Year 8 | Year 9 |
|---|---|---|---|
| (1) Income before Income Taxes (plug) | 15.7% | 18.3% | 18.9% |
| (2) Income Tax Expense | (4.0) | (5.7) | (6.1) |
| (3) Net Income | 11.7% | 12.6% | 12.8% |
| (2)/(1) | 25.5% | 31.1% | 32.3% |

3.42 (Identifying industries using common-size income statement percentages.)

Exhibit 3.30 indicates that two firms have relatively low profit margins, two firms have medium profit margins, and two firms have relatively large profit margins. Low barriers to entry, extensive competition, and commodity products characterize firms with low profit margins. The likely candidates for Firms (1) and (2) are Kelly Services and Kroger Stores. The office services offered by Kelly Services are clerical in nature and not particularly unique. Kelly Services serves essentially as an intermediary between the employee and the customer, offering relatively little value added. Grocery products are commodities, with little, if any, differentiation between grocery stores. Firms (1) and (2) differ primarily with respect to depreciation and interest expense. Grocery stores require retail and warehouse space. Kelly Services should require relatively little space, since its employees work on the customers' premises. Thus, Firm (1) is Kroger Stores and Firm (2) is Kelly Services.

Firms with the highest profit margin should operate in industries with high barriers to entry, relatively little competition, and differentiated products. Electric utilities have operated until recently as regulated utilities and require extensive amounts of capital to build capital-intensive plants. Regulation and capital serve as barriers to entry. Gillette offers brand name products. The brand names serve as an entry barrier. Customers also perceive its products to be differentiated. Thus, Firm (5) and Firm (6) are likely to be Commonwealth Edison and Gillette in some order. Firm (5) has considerably more depreciation and interest expense than Firm (6) and Firm (6) has considerably more selling and administrative expenses than Firm (5). Thus, Firm (5) is Commonwealth Edison and Firm (6) is Gillette.

This leaves Hewlett-Packard and Delta Airlines with medium profit margins. Hewlett-Packard offers products that are somewhat differentiated and with some brand name appeal. However, competition in the computer industry and rapid technological change drive down profit margins. Delta Airlines offers a commodity product, but the need for capital to acquire airplanes serves as a barrier to entry. Thus, these two firms have some characteristics of firms with relatively low profit margins and some characteristics of firms with relatively high profit margins. Firm (3) appears to have considerably more debt in its capital structure than Firm (4). The short product life cycles in the computer industry tend to drive down their use of debt. The aircraft of Delta Airlines can serve as collateral for borrowing. Thus, one would expect Delta Airlines to have a higher amount of borrowing. This clue suggests that Firm (3) is Delta Airlines and Firm (4) is Hewlett-Packard.

# CHAPTER 4

## STATEMENT OF CASH FLOWS: REPORTING THE EFFECTS OF OPERATING, INVESTING, AND FINANCING ACTIVITIES ON CASH FLOWS

*Questions, Exercises, Problems, and Cases: Answers and Solutions*

4.1    See the text or the glossary at the end of the book.

4.2    One can criticize a single income statement using a cash basis of accounting from two standpoints: (1) it provides a poor measure of operating performance each period because of the inaccurate matching of revenues and expenses (see discussion in Chapter 3), and (2) it excludes important investing (acquisitions and sales of long-lived assets) activities and financing (issuance or redemption of bonds or capital stock) activities of a firm that affect cash flow.

4.3    Accrual accounting attempts to provide a measure of operating performance that relates inputs to output without regard to when a firm receives or disburses cash. Accrual accounting also attempts to portray the resources of a firm and the claims on those resources without regard to whether the firm holds the resource in the form of cash. Although accrual accounting may satisfy user's needs for information about operating performance and financial position, it does not provide sufficient information about the cash flow effects of a firm's operating, investing, and financing activities. The latter is the objective of the statement of cash flows.

4.4    The statement of cash flows reports changes in the investing and financing activities of a firm. Significant changes in property, plant, and equipment affect the maturity structure of assets on the balance sheet. Significant changes in long-term debt or capital stock affect both the maturity structure of equities as well as the mix of debt versus shareholder financing.

4.5    The indirect method reconciles net income, the primary measure of a firm's profitability, with cash flow from operations. Some would argue that the relation between net income and cash flow from operations is less evident when a firm reports using the direct method. The frequent use of the indirect method prior to the issuance of FASB *Statement No. 95* also probably explains its continuing popularity.

4.6    The classification in the statement of cash flows parallels that in the income statement, where interest on debt is an expense but payments on the principal amount of the debt are not an expense but a reduction in a liability.

4.7    The classification in the statement of cash flows parallels that in the income statement, where interest on debt is an expense but dividends are a distribution of earnings, not an expense.

4.8    Firms generally use accounts payable directly in financing purchases of inventory and other operating costs. Firms might use short-term bank financing indirectly in financing accounts receivable, inventories, or operating costs or use it to finance acquisitions of noncurrent assets or reductions in long-term financing. Thus, the link between short-term bank financing and operations is less direct and may not even relate to operating activities. To achieve consistency in classification, the FASB stipulates that changes in short-term bank loans are financing activities.

4.9    This is an investing and financing transaction whose disclosure helps the statement user understand why property, plant and equipment and long-term debt changed during the period. Because the transaction does not affect cash directly, however, firms must distinguish it from investing and financing transactions that do affect cash flow.

4.10   Both are correct, but the writer's point is not expressed clearly. Depreciation expense is a charge to operations, but does not require cash. If revenues precisely equal total expenses, there will be a retention of net funds in the business equal to the amount of the depreciation. As long as replacement of the depreciating assets is not necessary, it is possible to finance considerable expansion without resorting to borrowing or the issuance of additional stock.

       The "reader" is correct in saying that depreciation in itself is not a source of cash and that the total cash available would not have increased by adding larger amounts to the depreciation accounts. The source of cash is sales to customers.

       When one considers income tax effects, however, depreciation expenses do save cash because taxable income and, hence, income tax expense using cash are lower than they would be in the absence of depreciation charges.

4.11   The firm must have increased substantially its investment in accounts receivable or inventories or decreased substantially its current liabilities.

4.12   The firm might be capital intensive and, therefore, subtracted substantial amounts of depreciation expense in computing net income. This depreciation expense is added back to net income in computing cash flow from operations. In addition, the firm might have decreased significantly its investment in accounts receivable or inventories or increased its current liabilities.

4.13 The accountant classifies the entire cash proceeds from the equipment sale as an investing activity. Because the calculation of cash flow from operations starts with net income (which includes the gain on sale of equipment), the accountant must subtract the gain to avoid counting cash flow equal to the gain twice, once as an operating activity and once as an investing activity.

4.14 (Amazon.com; calculating and interpreting cash flows.) (Amounts in Thousands)

a. **Year 4**

| | Balance Sheet Changes | Operations | Investing | Financing |
|---|---|---|---|---|
| **(Increases) Decreases in Assets** | | | | |
| Marketable Securities............. | — | | | |
| Inventories................................. | $ (554) | $ (554) | | |
| Prepayments ............................ | (307) | (307) | | |
| Property, Plant and Equipment (at Cost) ...................... | (1,360) | | $ (1,360) | |
| Accumulated Depreciation..... | 286 | 286 | | |
| **Increases (Decreases) in Liabilities and Shareholders' Equity** | | | | |
| Accounts Payable—Merchandise Suppliers.............. | 2,759 | 2,759 | | |
| Other Current Liabilities....... | 2,010 | 2,010 | | |
| Long-Term Debt...................... | — | | | |
| Common Stock.......................... | 8,201 | | | $ 8,201 |
| Retained Earnings................... | (5,777) | (5,777) | | |
| Increase (Decrease) in Cash...................................... | $ 5,252 | $ (1,589) | $ (1,360) | $ 8,201 |

4.14 a. continued.

**Year 5**

| | Balance Sheet Changes | Operations | Investing | Financing |
|---|---|---|---|---|
| **(Increases) Decreases in Assets** | | | | |
| Marketable Securities....... | $ (15,256) | | $ (15,256) | |
| Inventories........................... | (8,400) | $ (8,400) | | |
| Prepayments ....................... | (2,977) | (2,977) | | |
| Property, Plant and Equipment (at Cost) ..... | (15,283) | | (15,283) | |
| Accumulated Depreciation................................ | 4,742 | 4,742 | | |
| **Increases (Decreases) in Liabilities and Shareholders' Equity** | | | | |
| Accounts Payable—Merchandise Suppliers........ | 29,845 | 29,845 | | |
| Other Current Liabilities ................................ | 7,603 | 7,603 | | |
| Long-Term Debt................. | 78,202 | | | $ 78,202 |
| Common Stock.................... | 52,675 | | | 52,675 |
| Retained Earnings............. | (27,590) | (27,590) | | |
| Increase (Decrease) in Cash................................ | $ 103,561 | $ 3,223 | $ (30,539) | $ 130,877 |

4.14 continued.

b.
## AMAZON.COM
### Statement of Cash Flows
### For Year 4 and Year 5

|  | Year 4 | Year 5 |
|---|---|---|
| Operations: |  |  |
| Net Income (Loss)............................................. | $ (5,777) | $ (27,590) |
| Depreciation .................................................... | 286 | 4,742 |
| (Increase) Decrease in Inventories................... | (554) | (8,400) |
| (Increase) Decrease in Prepayments ............... | (307) | (2,977) |
| Increase (Decrease) in Accounts Payable— |  |  |
| Merchandise Suppliers.................................... | 2,753 | 29,845 |
| Increase (Decrease) in Other Current Lia- |  |  |
| bilities.............................................................. | 2,010 | 7,603 |
| Cash Flow from Operations................................. | $ (1,589) | $ 3,223 |
| Investing: |  |  |
| Acquisition of Property, Plant, Equipment, |  |  |
| and Marketable Securities............................ | $ (1,360) | $ (30,539) |
| Financing: |  |  |
| Increase in Long-Term Debt.............................. |  | $ 78,202 |
| Issue of Common Stock...................................... | $ 8,201 | 52,675 |
| Cash Flow from Financing.................................... | $ 8,201 | $ 130,877 |
| Increase (Decrease) in Cash .............................. | $ 5,252 | $ 103,561 |
| Cash, Beginning of Year...................................... | 996 | 6,248 |
| Cash, End of Year................................................. | $ 6,248 | $ 109,809 |

c. Amazon.com operated at a net loss each year. Its cash flow from operations was not as negative as the net loss, and even turned positive in Year 5, because the firm delayed paying its creditors. Note that the increase in accounts payable to merchandise suppliers exceeds the increase in merchandise inventories each year. Cash flow from operations was not sufficient in Year 5 to finance the substantial growth in capital expenditures. Amazon.com used a mixture of long-term debt and common stock to finance these long-term assets.

**4.15** (Yahoo, Inc.; calculating and interpreting cash flows.)

a. **Year 8**

| | Balance Sheet Changes | Operations | Investing | Financing |
|---|---|---|---|---|
| **(Increases) Decreases in Assets** | | | | |
| Marketable Securities....... | $ (60,689) | | $ (60,689) | |
| Accounts Receivable.......... | (4,267) | $ (4,267) | | |
| Prepayments...................... | (384) | (384) | | |
| Property, Plant and Equipment (at Cost)..... | (3,155) | | (3,155) | |
| Accumulated Depreciation............................... | 552 | 552 | | |
| Investment in Securities.. | (10,477) | | (10,477) | |
| **Increases (Decreases) in Liabilities and Shareholders' Equity** | | | | |
| Accounts Payable............... | 1,086 | 1,086 | | |
| Other Current Liabilities ................................. | 6,447 | 6,447 | | |
| Common Stock.................... | 103,796 | | | $ 103,796 |
| Retained Earnings............. | (4,659) | (4,659) | | |
| Increase (Decrease) in Cash................................. | $ 28,250 | $ (1,225) | $ (74,321) | $ 103,796 |

**Year 9**

| | Balance Sheet Changes | Operations | Investing | Financing |
|---|---|---|---|---|
| **(Increases) Decreases in Assets** | | | | |
| Marketable Securities....... | $ 32,917 | | $ 32,917 | |
| Accounts Receivable.......... | (5,904) | $ (5,904) | | |
| Prepayments...................... | (5,509) | (5,509) | | |
| Property, Plant and Equipment (at Cost)..... | (14,930) | | (14,930) | |
| Accumulated Depreciation............................... | 2,554 | 2,554 | | |
| Investment in Securities.. | (9,053) | | (9,053) | |
| **Increases (Decreases) in Liabilities and Shareholders' Equity** | | | | |
| Accounts Payable............... | 3,605 | 3,605 | | |
| Other Current Liabilities ................................. | 11,598 | 11,598 | | |
| Common Stock.................... | 36,980 | | | $ 36,980 |
| Retained Earnings............. | (23,267) | (23,267) | | |
| Increase (Decrease) in Cash................................. | $ 28,991 | $ (16,923) | $ 8,934 | $ 36,980 |

4.15 continued.

b.
**YAHOO, INC.**
**Statement of Cash Flows**
**For Year 8 and Year 9**

| | Year 8 | Year 9 |
|---|---|---|
| Operations: | | |
| Net Income (Loss)............................................ | $ (4,659) | $ (23,267) |
| Depreciation .................................................... | 552 | 2,554 |
| (Increase) Decrease in Accounts Receivable...................................................... | (4,267) | (5,904) |
| (Increase) Decrease in Prepayments .............. | (384) | (5,509) |
| Increase (Decrease) in Accounts Payable....... | 1,086 | 3,605 |
| Increase (Decrease) in Other Current Liabilities.......................................................... | 6,447 | 11,598 |
| Cash Flow from Operations............................. | $ (1,225) | $ (16,923) |
| Investing: | | |
| Acquisition of Property, Plant and Equipment.................................................................. | $ (3,155) | $ (14,930) |
| Sale of Marketable Securities ......................... | -- | 32,917 |
| Acquisition of Marketable Securities.............. | (60,689) | -- |
| Acquisition of Investment in Securities.......... | (10,477) | (9,053) |
| Cash Flow from Investing................................. | $ (74,321) | $ 8,934 |
| Financing: | | |
| Issue of Common Stock.................................... | $103,796 | $ 36,980 |
| Increase (Decrease) in Cash............................ | $ 28,250 | $ 28,991 |
| Cash, Beginning of Year.................................. | 5,297 | 33,547 |
| Cash, End of Year............................................ | $ 33,547 | $ 62,538 |

c. Yahoo, Inc. operated at a loss and generated negative cash flow from operations each year. Such operating results are not unusual for a startup company. Although its expenditures on property, plant and equipment increased significantly between the two years, Yahoo, Inc. is not heavily capital intensive. The firm used common stock to finance its growth during the startup phase. The main resources of an internet service provider are its software and customer list, neither of which serves as safe collateral for borrowing. Yahoo, Inc., therefore, did not use long-term borrowing to finance itself. The firm did not need all of the cash immediately to finance operations and capital expenditures. It invested the excess cash in marketable securities and investments in securities. Yahoo, Inc. sold some of its marketable securities during Year 9 to provide cash for conducting its operations.

4.16    (Green Mountain Coffee Roasters; preparing a columnar work sheet for a statement of cash flows from changes in balance sheet accounts.) (Amounts in Thousands.)

a.

| | Balance Sheet Changes | Operations | Investing | Financing |
|---|---|---|---|---|
| **(Increases) Decreases in Assets** | | | | |
| Accounts Receivable................. | $(2,231) | $ (2,231) | | |
| Inventories................................ | 59 | 59 | | |
| Prepayments............................. | 475 | 475 | | |
| Property, Plant and Equipment (at Cost) ...................... | (2,129) | | $ 2,468[a] (4,597) | |
| Accumulated Depreciation..... | 1,038 | 2,968 | (1,930)[a] | |
| Other Noncurrent Assets ....... | (434) | (434) | | |
| **Increases (Decreases) in Liabilities and Shareholders' Equity** | | | | |
| Accounts Payable...................... | 1,574 | 1,574 | | |
| Other Current Liabilities....... | 560 | 560 | | |
| Bonds Payable .......................... | 2,827 | | | $ 5,567 (2,740) |
| Common Stock........................... | (5,878) | | | (5,878) |
| Retained Earnings.................... | 4,213 | 4,213 | | |
| Increase (Decrease) in Cash...................................... | $   74 | $ 7,184 | $ (4,059) | $ (3,051) |

[a]Cash proceeds of sale are $538 thousand (= $2,468 – $1,930).

b.  Cash flow from operations approximately equaled net income plus depreciation. Accounts receivable increased during the year. The firm appeared to increase accounts payable to finance the buildup in accounts receivable. Cash flow from operations was more than sufficient to finance capital expenditures. The firm used the excess cash flow and the proceeds of additional long-term borrowing to repay long-term debt and reacquire common stock.

**4.17** (Southwest Airlines; preparing a statement of cash flows from changes in balance sheet accounts.)

a.

**SOUTHWEST AIRLINES**
**Statement of Cash Flows**
**For the Year**
**(Amounts in Thousands)**

| | | |
|---|---|---:|
| Operations: | | |
| Net Income | $ | 474,378 |
| Additions: | | |
| Depreciation Expense | | 264,088 |
| Decrease in Accounts Receivable | | 15,351 |
| Increase in Other Current Liabilities | | 114,596 |
| Subtractions: | | |
| Increase in Inventories | | (15,117) |
| Increase in Prepayments | | (16,776) |
| Decrease in Accounts Payable | | (660) |
| Cash Flow from Operations | $ | 835,860 |
| Investing: | | |
| Acquisition of Property, Plant and Equipment | $ | (1,134,644) |
| Decrease in Other Non-operating Assets | | (8,711) |
| Cash Flow from Investing | $ | (1,143,355) |
| Financing: | | |
| Increase in Long-term Debt | $ | 244,285 |
| Increase in Common Stock | | 96,991 |
| Payment of Dividends | | (133,499) |
| Increase in Non-operating Liabilities | | 140,026 |
| Cash Flow from Financing | $ | 347,803 |
| Net Change in Cash | $ | 40,308 |
| Cash, Beginning of Year | | 378,511 |
| Cash, End of Year | $ | 418,819 |

b. Cash flow from operations exceeds net income primarily because of the addback for depreciation expense and increases in other current liabilities. Cash flow from operations was insufficient to finance acquisitions of property, plant and equipment, so Southwest Airlines relied on long-term debt and common stock.

4.18   (Information Technologies; calculating and interpreting cash flow from operations.)

a.  Net Income .................................................................................... $   312[a]
    Additions:
        Depreciation Expense.................................................................   114
        Decrease in Accounts Receivable..............................................   778
        Decrease In Inventories.............................................................   76
        Decrease in Prepayments..........................................................   102
        Increase in Accounts Payable...................................................   90
    Subtraction:
        Decrease in Other Current Liabilities......................................   (242)
    Cash Flow from Operations...........................................................   $ 1,230

[a]$312 = $14,508 – $114 – $210 – $13,872.

b.  Information Technologies decreased its noncash current assets, particularly accounts receivable, generating positive cash flows. Although it repaid other current liabilities, the reduction in accounts receivable dominated and caused cash flow from operations to exceed net income.

4.19   (Nokia; calculating and interpreting cash flow from operations.)

a.

|  | Year 8 | Year 9 | Year 10 | Year 11 |
|---|---|---|---|---|
| Net Income ..................... | € 1,032 | € 1,689 | € 2,542 | € 3,847 |
| Depreciation Expense ...................... | 465 | 509 | 665 | 1,009 |
| (Inc.) Dec. in Accounts Receivable ................ | (272) | (1,573) | (982) | (2,304) |
| (Inc.) Dec. in Inventories...................... | (121) | (103) | (362) | (422) |
| (Inc.) Dec. in Prepayments.................... | 77 | (17) | (33) | 49 |
| Inc. (Dec.) in Accounts Payable ...................... | 90 | 140 | 312 | 458 |
| Inc. (Dec.) in Other Current Liabilities .. | 450 | 1,049 | 867 | 923 |
| Cash Flow from Operations ................ | € 1,721 | € 1,694 | € 3,009 | € 3,560 |

b.  The addback for depreciation, a noncash expense, causes cash flow from operations to exceed net income each year. Inventories increased in line with increases in net income. Nokia increases its accounts payable to finance the increased inventories. The firm also increased other current liabilities to finance growing operations. Variations in the relation between net income and cash flow from operations result from variations in accounts receivable. Unusually large increases in

4.19 b. continued.

accounts receivable in Year 9 and Year 11 cause cash flow from operations to approximately equal net income in Year 9 and to be less than net income in Year 11. The variations in accounts receivable might result from a conscious effort by Nokia to vary credit terms to stimulate sales. It may also reflect conditions in the economy that cause its customers to delay payments in some years.

4.20    (Omnicom Group; calculating and interpreting cash flows.)

a.

### OMNICOM GROUP
### Comparative Statement of Cash Flows
### (Amounts in Thousands)

|  | Year 3 | Year 4 | Year 5 |
|---|---|---|---|
| Operations |  |  |  |
| Net Income............................... | $     279 | $    363 | $     499 |
| Depreciation and Amortization.... | 164 | 196 | 226 |
| (Inc.) Dec. in Accounts Receivable.................................... | (238) | (648) | (514) |
| (Inc.) Dec. in Inventories............... | (35) | (13) | (98) |
| (Inc.) Dec. in Prepayments............ | (64) | 10 | (125) |
| Inc. (Dec.) in Accounts Payable.... | 330 | 786 | 277 |
| Inc. (Dec.) in Other Current Liabilities.................................... | 70 | 278 | 420 |
| Cash Flow from Operations...... | $    506 | $    972 | $     685 |
| Investing |  |  |  |
| Acquisition of Property, Plant and Equipment........................... | $   (115) | $  (130) | $    (150) |
| Acquisition of Investments in Securities.................................... | (469) | (643) | (885) |
| Cash Flow from Investing......... | $   (584) | $  (773) | $  (1,035) |
| Financing |  |  |  |
| Long-term Debt Issued.................. | $     208 | $      83 | $     599 |
| Common Stock Issued (Reacquired)............................................. | 42 | (252) | (187) |
| Dividends Paid............................... | (88) | (104) | (122) |
| Cash Flow from Financing........ | $     162 | $  (273) | $     290 |
| Change in Cash............................... | $      84 | $    (74) | $      (60) |

b.    Interpreting cash flow from operations for a marketing services firm requires a comparison of the change in accounts receivable from clients and accounts payable to various media. Marketing services firms act as agents between these two constituents. In Year 3 and Year 4, the increase in accounts payable slightly exceeded the increase in accounts receivable, indicating that Omnicom Group used the media to finance its accounts receivable. In Year 5, however, accounts payable did not increase nearly as much as accounts receivable. It is

4-11

4.20 b. continued.

unclear whether the media demanded earlier payment, whether the media offered incentives to pay more quickly, or some other reason. As a consequence, cash flow from operations decreased in Year 5. Cash flow from operations continually exceeds expenditures on property, plant, and equipment. This relation is not surprising, given that marketing services firms are not capital intensive. Omnicom Group invested significantly in other entities during the three years. The classification of these investments as noncurrent suggests that they were not made with temporarily excess cash but as a more permanent investment. Cash flow from operations was not sufficient to finance both capital expenditures and these investments. The firm relied on long-term debt to finance the difference. Given the marketing service firms are labor-intensive, one might question the use of debt instead of equity financing for these investments. In fact, Omnicom Group repurchased share of its common stock in Year 4 and Year 5. Thus, the capital structure of the firm became more risky during the three years.

4.21 (American Airlines; working backwards from changes in buildings and equipment account.)

| Buildings and Equipment (Original Cost) | | Accumulated Depreciation | |
|---|---|---|---|
| Balance, 12/31/Year 3 | $16,825 | Balance, 12/31/Year 3 | $ 4,914 |
| Outlays in Year 4 | 1,314 | Depreciation in Year 4 | 1,253 |
| | $18,139 | | $ 6,167 |
| Balance, 12/31/Year 4 | 17,369 | Balance, 12/31/Year 4 | 5,465 |
| Retirements in Year 4 | $ 770 | Retirements in Year 4 | $ 702 |

Proceeds = Book Value
= $770 – $702
= $68.

4.22    (Largay Corporation; effects of gains and losses from sales of equipment
        on cash flows.) (Amounts in Thousands)

|  | a. | b. | c. |
|---|---|---|---|
| Operations: | | | |
| Net Income...................................................... | $ 100 | $ 102 | $ 98 |
| Depreciation Expense.................................. | 15 | 15 | 15 |
| Gain on Sale of Equipment........................ | -- | (2) | -- |
| Loss on Sale of Equipment ....................... | -- | -- | 2 |
| Changes in Working Capital Accounts .... | (40) | (40) | (40) |
| Cash Flow from Operations.......................... | $ 75 | $ 75 | $ 75 |
| Investing: | | | |
| Sale of Equipment ....................................... | $ 10 | $ 12 | $ 8 |
| Acquisition of Buildings and Equip- | | | |
| ment ............................................................. | (30) | (30) | (30) |
| Cash Flow from Investing.............................. | $ (20) | $ (18) | $ (22) |
| Financing: | | | |
| Repayment of Long-term Debt................... | $ (40) | $ (40) | $ (40) |
| Change in Cash............................................... | $ 15 | $ 17 | $ 13 |
| Cash, Beginning of Year................................ | 27 | 27 | 27 |
| Cash, End of Year ........................................... | $ 42 | $ 44 | $ 40 |

4.23    (Effect of various transactions on statement of cash flows.)

If you use transparencies in class, it is effective to flash onto the screen
the answer transparency for some problem showing a comprehensive
statoment of cash flows. Then you can point to the lines affooted as the
students attempt to answer the question. It helps them by letting them
see the possibilities. We use this question for in-class discussion. We
seldom assign it for actual homework. A favorite form of question for
examinations is to present a schematic statement of cash flows and to ask
which lines certain transactions affect and how much. When we use this
problem in class, we invariably tell students that it makes a good
examination question; this serves to strengthen their interest in the
discussion.

a.  (1)  Decreases by $600; reduces net income through amortization
         expense.
    (2)  Increases by $600; amount of expense is added back to net income
         in deriving cash flow from operations.
    No effect on net cash flow from operations.

b.  The transaction does not appear in the statement of cash flows
    because it does not affect cash. The firm must disclose information
    about the transaction in a supplemental schedule or note.

c.  (2)  Increases by $7,500; operating increase in cash from increase in
         Accounts Payable.

4.23 c. continued.

        (3) Increases by $7,500; operating decrease in cash for increase in inventory.

        The net effect of these two transactions is to leave cash from operations unchanged, because the amounts added and subtracted change in such a way as to cancel out each other.

d. (1) Decreases by $1,500; net income goes down.
    (2) Increases by $1,500; additions go up because inventory, not cash, was destroyed.

e. (2) Increases by $1,450; operating increase in cash reflected by decrease in the amount of Accounts Receivable.
    (9) Increases by $1,450.

f. (6) Increases by $10,000; increase in cash from security issue.
    (9) Increases by $10,000.

g. (4) Increases by $4,500; increase in cash from sale of noncurrent asset.
    (9) Increases by $4,500.

4.24    (The GAP; preparing and interpreting the statement of cash flows using a columnar work sheet.) (Amounts in Millions)

a. **Year 6**

| | Balance Sheet Changes | Operations | Investing | Financing |
|---|---|---|---|---|
| **(Increases) Decreases in Assets** | | | | |
| Marketable Securities.............. | $ (46) | | $ (46) | |
| Merchandise Inventories........ | (96) | $ (96) | | |
| Prepayments...................... | (1) | (1) | | |
| Property, Plant and Equipment (at Cost)...................... | (372) | | (372) | |
| Accumulated Depreciation..... | 215 | 215 | | |
| Other Noncurrent Assets....... | (51) | | (51) | |
| **Increases (Decreases) in Liabilities and Shareholders' Equity** | | | | |
| Accounts Payable—Merchandise Suppliers.............. | 114 | 114 | | |
| Notes Payable to Banks.......... | 18 | | | $ 18 |
| Income Taxes Payable ........... | 26 | 26 | | |
| Other Current Liabilities....... | 90 | 90 | | |
| Common Stock......................... | (360) | | | (360) |
| Retained Earnings.................. | 369 | 453 | | (84) |
| Increase (Decrease) in Cash...................................... | $ (94) | $ 801 | $ (469) | $ (426) |

4.24 a. continued.

**Year 7**

| (Increases) Decreases in Assets | Balance Sheet Changes | Operations | Investing | Financing |
|---|---|---|---|---|
| Marketable Securities............. | $ 46 | | $ 46 | |
| Merchandise Inventories........ | (154) | $ (154) | | |
| Prepayments............................ | (56) | (56) | | |
| Property, Plant and Equipment (at Cost)...................... | (466) | | (466) | |
| Accumulated Depreciation..... | 270 | 270 | | |
| Other Noncurrent Assets....... | (15) | | (15) | |
| **Increases (Decreases) in Liabilities and Shareholders' Equity** | | | | |
| Accounts Payable—Merchandise Suppliers.............. | 134 | 134 | | |
| Notes Payable to Banks.......... | 45 | | | $ 45 |
| Income Taxes Payable ............ | (7) | (7) | | |
| Other Current Liabilities....... | 123 | 123 | | |
| Bonds Payable ......................... | 577 | | | 577 |
| Common Stock......................... | (524) | | | (524) |
| Retained Earnings................... | 455 | 534 | | (79) |
| Increase (Decrease) in Cash...................................... | $ 428 | $ 844 | $ (435) | $ 19 |

4.24 continued.

b.

## THE GAP
## Statement of Cash Flows
## For Year 6 and Year 7

|  | Year 6 | Year 7 |
|---|---|---|
| Operations: | | |
| Net Income | $ 453 | $ 534 |
| Depreciation | 215 | 270 |
| (Increase) Decrease in Merchandise Inventories | (96) | (154) |
| (Increase) Decrease in Prepayments | (1) | (56) |
| Increase (Decrease) in Accounts Payable—Merchandise Suppliers | 114 | 134 |
| Increase (Decrease) in Income Taxes Payable | 26 | (7) |
| Increase (Decrease) in Other Current Liabilities | 90 | 123 |
| Cash Flow from Operations | $ 801 | $ 844 |
| Investing: | | |
| Acquisition of Property, Plant and Equipment | $ (372) | $ (466) |
| Sale of Marketable Securities | -- | 46 |
| Acquisition of Marketable Securities | (46) | -- |
| Acquisition of Other Noncurrent Assets | (51) | (15) |
| Cash Flow from Investing | $ (469) | $ (435) |
| Financing: | | |
| Increase in Short-Term Borrowing | $ 18 | $ 45 |
| Increase in Long-Term Borrowing | -- | 577 |
| Decrease in Common Stock | (360) | (524) |
| Dividends | (84) | (79) |
| Cash Flow from Financing | $ (426) | $ 19 |
| Increase (Decrease) in Cash | $ (94) | $ 428 |
| Cash, Beginning of Year | 580 | 486 |
| Cash, End of Year | $ 486 | $ 914 |

**4.24 continued.**

c. **Year 6**

| | Income Statement Account | + | Operating Balance Sheet Changes | = | Cash Receipts | – | Cash Disburse-ments | = | Cash Flow from Operations |
|---|---|---|---|---|---|---|---|---|---|
| Sales.................................. | $ 5,284 | | | | $ 5,284 | | | | |
| Cost of Goods Sold ........ | (3,285) | | $ (96) | | | | $(3,267) | | |
| | | | 114 | | | | | | |
| Selling and Adminis-trative Expenses......... | (1,250) | | (1) | | | | (946) | | |
| | | | 215 | | | | | | |
| | | | 90 | | | | | | |
| Income Tax Expense .... | (296) | | 26 | | | | (270) | | |
| Net Income .................... | $ 453 | + | $ 348 | = | $ 5,284 | – | $(4,483) | = | $ 801 |

**Year 7**

| | Income Statement Account | + | Operating Balance Sheet Changes | = | Cash Receipts | – | Cash Disburse-ments | = | Cash Flow from Operations |
|---|---|---|---|---|---|---|---|---|---|
| Sales.................................. | $ 6,508 | | | | $ 6,508 | | | | |
| Cost of Goods Sold ........ | (4,022) | | $(154) | | | | $(4,042) | | |
| | | | 134 | | | | | | |
| Selling and Adminis-trative Expenses......... | (1,632) | | (56) | | | | (1,295) | | |
| | | | 270 | | | | | | |
| | | | 123 | | | | | | |
| Income Tax Expense .... | (320) | | (7) | | | | (327) | | |
| Net Income .................... | $ 534 | + | $ 310 | = | $ 6,508 | – | $(5,664) | = | $ 844 |

d. Cash flow from operations exceeded net income each year primarily because of the addback for depreciation and the delay in paying Other Current Liabilities. Cash flow from operations was more than sufficient to finance acquisition of property, plant and equipment. The Gap used its excess cash flow during each year to repurchase shares of its common stock. The firm increased its long-term borrowing in Year 7, thereby increasing the balance in its cash account.

**4.25** (Circuit City; preparing and interpreting the statement of cash flows using a columnar work sheet.) (Amounts in Millions)

a. **Year 7**

| | Balance Sheet Changes | Operations | Investing | Financing |
|---|---|---|---|---|
| **(Increases) Decreases in Assets** | | | | |
| Accounts Receivable................ | $(208) | $ (208) | | |
| Merchandise Inventories........ | (69) | (69) | | |
| Prepayments........................... | 8 | 8 | | |
| Property, Plant and Equipment (at Cost)...................... | (209) | | $ (209) | |
| Accumulated Depreciation..... | 99 | 99 | | |
| **Increases (Decreases) in Liabilities and Shareholders' Equity** | | | | |
| Accounts Payable—Merchandise Suppliers.............. | 117 | 117 | | |
| Notes Payable to Banks.......... | (92) | | | $ (92) |
| Other Current Liabilities....... | (71) | (71) | | |
| Bonds Payable ......................... | 31 | | | 31 |
| Common Stock.......................... | 428 | | | 428 |
| Retained Earnings................... | 125 | 136 | | (11) |
| Increase (Decrease) in Cash.. | $ 159 | $ 12 | $ (209) | $ 356 |

**Year 8**

| | Balance Sheet Changes | Operations | Investing | Financing |
|---|---|---|---|---|
| **(Increases) Decreases in Assets** | | | | |
| Accounts Receivable................ | $ (66) | $ (66) | | |
| Merchandise Inventories........ | (19) | (19) | | |
| Prepayments........................... | 15 | 15 | | |
| Property, Plant and Equipment (at Cost)...................... | (291) | | $ (291) | |
| Accumulated Depreciation..... | 116 | 116 | | |
| **Increases (Decreases) in Liabilities and Shareholders' Equity** | | | | |
| Accounts Payable—Merchandise Suppliers.............. | 44 | 44 | | |
| Notes Payable to Banks.......... | 27 | | | $ 27 |
| Other Current Liabilities....... | (9) | (9) | | |
| Bonds Payable ......................... | (19) | | | (19) |
| Common Stock.......................... | 25 | | | 25 |
| Retained Earnings................... | 91 | 104 | | (13) |
| Increase (Decrease) in Cash.. | $ (86) | $ 185 | $ (291) | $ 20 |

4.25 continued.

b.
## CIRCUIT CITY
### Statement of Cash Flows
### For Year 7 and Year 8

| | Year 7 | Year 8 |
|---|---|---|
| Operations: | | |
| Net Income.................................................. | $ 136 | $ 104 |
| Depreciation ............................................... | 99 | 116 |
| (Increase) Decrease in Accounts Receivable ........... | (208) | (66) |
| (Increase) Decrease in Merchandise Inventories... | (69) | (19) |
| (Increase) Decrease in Prepayments ..................... | 8 | 15 |
| Increase (Decrease) in Accounts Payable— | | |
| Merchandise Suppliers.................................... | 117 | 44 |
| Increase (Decrease) in Other Current Liabil- | | |
| ities................................................................ | (71) | (9) |
| Cash Flow from Operations................................ | $ 12 | $ 185 |
| Investing: | | |
| Acquisition of Property, Plant and Equipment...... | $ (209) | $ (291) |
| Financing: | | |
| Increase (Decrease) in Short-Term Borrowing....... | $ (92) | $ 27 |
| Increase (Decrease) in Long-Term Borrowing........ | 31 | (19) |
| Increase (Decrease) in Common Stock.................... | 428 | 25 |
| Dividends .................................................... | (11) | (13) |
| Cash Flow from Financing................................... | $ 356 | $ 20 |
| Increase (Decrease) in Cash | $ 159 | $ (86) |
| Cash, Beginning of Year...................................... | 44 | 203 |
| Cash, End of Year................................................ | $ 203 | $ 117 |

| c. | Year 7 | Year 8 |
|---|---|---|
| Sales Revenue.................................................. | $ 7,664 | $ 8,871 |
| Less Increase in Accounts Receivable..................... | (208) | (66) |
| Cash Collected from Customers ............................ | $ 7,456 | $ 8,805 |

| d. | Year 7 | Year 8 |
|---|---|---|
| Cost of Goods Sold ......................................... | $ (5,903) | $ (6,827) |
| Plus Increase in Inventories................................. | (69) | (19) |
| Less Increase in Accounts Payable—Merchan- | | |
| dise Suppliers................................................. | 117 | 44 |
| Cash Payments to Suppliers ............................... | $ (5,855) | $ (6,802) |

| e. | Year 7 | Year 8 |
|---|---|---|
| Selling and Administrative Expenses..................... | $ (1,511) | $ (1,849) |
| Plus Decrease in Prepayments ............................. | 8 | 15 |
| Less Decrease in Other Current Liabilities........... | (71) | (9) |
| Plus Depreciation............................................. | 99 | 116 |
| Cash Paid to Suppliers of Selling and Adminis- | | |
| trative Services............................................... | $ (1,475) | $ (1,727) |

4.25 continued.

    f.   Cash flow from operations was significantly less than net income during Year 7, primarily because of a buildup of accounts receivable from customers. Circuit City financed its acquisitions of property, plant and equipment by issuing common stock. Cash flow from operations exceeded net income during Year 8 because of the addback for depreciation and a smaller increase in accounts receivable. Cash flow from operations was not sufficient to finance capital expenditures. Circuit City used cash on hand at the beginning of the year to finance the shortfall.

4.26    (Swan Corporation; preparing and interpreting a statement of cash flows using a columnar work sheet.)

a.

| | Balance Sheet Changes | Operations | Investing | Financing |
|---|---|---|---|---|
| **(Increases) Decreases in Assets** | | | | |
| Accounts Receivable........... | $(12,000) | $(12,000) | | |
| Merchandise Inventories... | (20,000) | (20,000) | | |
| Property, Plant and Equipment ...................... | (75,000) | | $(75,000) | |
| Accumulated Depreciation............................... | 79,000 | 79,000 | | |
| **Increases (Decreases) in Liabilities and Shareholders' Equity** | | | | |
| Accounts Payable............... | (25,000) | (25,000) | | |
| Income Taxes Payable ....... | 5,000 | 5,000 | | |
| Bonds Payable .................... | (4,000) | | | $ (4,000) |
| Common Stock..................... | 5,000 | | | 5,000 |
| Retained Earnings.............. | 50,000 | 50,000 | | |
| Increase (Decrease) in Cash................................ | $ 3,000 | $ 77,000 | $(75,000) | $ 1,000 |

4.26 continued.

b.

**SWAN CORPORATION**
**Statement of Cash Flows**
**For the Current Year**

Operations:

| | | |
|---|---|---|
| Net Income | $50,000 | |
| Additions: | | |
| Depreciation Expense | 79,000 | |
| Increase in Income Taxes Payable | 5,000 | |
| Subtractions: | | |
| Increase in Accounts Receivable | (12,000) | |
| Increase in Merchandise Inventories | (20,000) | |
| Decrease in Accounts Payable | (25,000) | |
| Cash Flow from Operations | | $77,000 |
| Investing: | | |
| Acquisition of Property, Plant, and Equipment | | (75,000) |
| Financing: | | |
| Issue of Common Stock | $ 5,000 | |
| Retirement of Bonds | (4,000) | |
| Cash Flow from Financing | | 1,000 |
| Net Change in Cash | | $ 3,000 |
| | | |
| Cash, January 1 | | 12,000 |
| Cash, December 31 | | $ 15,000 |

c.  Cash flow from operations was positive and sufficient to finance acquisitions of property, plant and equipment. The firm issued common stock to finance the retirement of long-term debt.

4.27   (Hale Company; preparing and interpreting a statement of cash flows using a T-account work sheet.)

a.

**HALE COMPANY**
**Statement of Cash Flows**
**For the Year**

Operations:
  Net Income ............................................................... $ 44,000
  Additions:
    Depreciation Expense............................................. 54,000
    Increase in Accounts Payable............................. 5,000
  Subtractions:
    Increase in Accounts Receivable........................ (13,000)
    Increase in Inventory ........................................... (11,000)
    Decrease in Interest Payable.............................. (2,000)
  Cash Flow from Operations....................................... $77,000
Investing:
  Sale of Equipment ................................................... $ 5,000
  Acquisition of Equipment ....................................... (55,000)
  Cash Flow from Investing........................................ (50,000)
Financing:
  Dividends.................................................................. $(10,000)
  Retirement of Portion of Mortgage Payable .......... (11,000)
  Cash Flow from Financing....................................... (21,000)
Net Change in Cash...................................................... $ 6,000
Cash, January 1........................................................... 52,000
Cash, December 31 ...................................................... $58,000

4.27 a. continued.

The amounts in the T-account work sheet below are in thousands.

## Cash

| | | | | | |
|---|---|---|---|---|---|
| √ | 52 | | | | |

### Operations

| | | | | | |
|---|---|---|---|---|---|
| Net Income | (1) | 44 | 13 | (5) | Increase in Accounts Receivable |
| Depreciation | (3) | 54 | | | |
| Increase in Accounts Payable | (8) | 5 | 11 | (6) | Increase in Inventory |
| | | | 2 | (9) | Decrease in Interest Payable |

### Investing

| | | | | | |
|---|---|---|---|---|---|
| Sale of Equipment | (4) | 5 | 55 | (7) | Acquisition of Equipment |

### Financing

| | | | | | |
|---|---|---|---|---|---|
| | | | 10 | (2) | Dividends |
| | | | 11 | (10) | Payment of Mortgage Payable |

| | | |
|---|---|---|
| √ | 58 | |

| Accounts Receivable | |
|---|---|
| √ 93 | |
| (5) 13 | |
| √ 106 | |

| Inventory | |
|---|---|
| √ 151 | |
| (6) 11 | |
| √ 162 | |

| Land | |
|---|---|
| √ 30 | |
| | |
| √ 30 | |

| Buildings and Equipment (Cost) | |
|---|---|
| √ 790 | |
| (7) 55 | 15 (4) |
| √ 830 | |

| Accumulated Depreciation | |
|---|---|
| | 460 √ |
| (4) 10 | 54 (3) |
| | 504 √ |

| Accounts Payable | |
|---|---|
| | 136 √ |
| | 5 (8) |
| | 141 √ |

| Interest Payable | |
|---|---|
| | 10 √ |
| (9) 2 | |
| | 8 √ |

| Mortgage Payable | |
|---|---|
| | 120 √ |
| (10) 11 | |
| | 109 √ |

| Common Stock | |
|---|---|
| | 250 √ |
| | |
| | 250 √ |

4.27 a. continued.

```
        Retained Earnings
                    │   140   √
   (2)        10   │    44  (1)
                    │   174   √
                    │
```

b.  Sales Revenue............................................................... $ 1,200,000
    Less Increase in Accounts Receivable ($106,000 –
       $93,000)................................................................ (13,000)
    Cash Collected from Customers during the Year.............. $ 1,187,000

c.  Cost of Goods Sold ......................................................... $ (788,000)
    Less Increase in Inventories ($162,000 – $151,000)......... (11,000)
    Plus Increase in Accounts Payable for Inventory
       ($141,000 – $136,000)............................................... 5,000
    Cash Paid to Suppliers of Inventory during the Year...... $ (794,000)

d.  Interest Expense............................................................. $ (12,000)
    Less Decrease in Interest Payable ($8,000 – $10,000)..... (2,000)
    Cash Paid for Interest during the Year.............................. $ (14,000)

e.  Cash flow from operations was sufficient to finance acquisitions of
    equipment during the year. The firm used the excess cash flow to pay
    dividends and retire long-term debt.

4.28    (Dickerson Manufacturing Company; preparing and interpreting a statement of cash flows using a T-account work sheet.)

a.
## DICKERSON MANUFACTURING COMPANY
### Statement of Cash Flows
### For the Year

| | | |
|---|---:|---:|
| Operations: | | |
| Net Income | $ 568,000 | |
| Additions: | | |
| Depreciation | 510,000 | |
| Loss on Sale of Machinery | 5,000 | |
| Increase in Accounts Payable | 146,000 | |
| Increase in Taxes Payable | 16,000 | |
| Increase in Short-Term Payables | 138,000 | |
| Subtractions: | | |
| Increase in Accounts Receivable | (106,000) | |
| Increase in Inventory | (204,000) | |
| Cash Flow from Operations | | $ 1,073,000 |
| Investing: | | |
| Sale of Machinery | $ 25,000 | |
| Acquisition of Land | (36,000) | |
| Acquisition of Buildings and Machinery | (1,018,000) | |
| Cash Flow from Investing | | (1,029,000) |
| Financing: | | |
| Issue of Common Stock | $ 32,000 | |
| Dividends Paid | (60,000) | |
| Bonds Retired | (50,000) | |
| Cash Flow from Financing | | (78,000) |
| Net Change in Cash | | $ (34,000) |
| Cash, January 1 | | 358,000 |
| Cash, December 31 | | $ 324,000 |

4.28 a. continued.

The amounts in the T-account work sheet below are in thousands.

### Cash

| | | | | | | | |
|---|---|---|---|---|---|---|---|
| √ | | | 358 | | | | |

#### Operations

| | | | | | |
|---|---|---|---|---|---|
| Net Income | (1) | 568 | 106 | (5) | Increase in Accounts Receivable |
| Depreciation Expense | (3) | 510 | | | |
| Loss on Sale of Equipment | (4) | 5 | 204 | (6) | Increase in Inventory |
| Increase in Accounts Payable | (9) | 146 | | | |
| Increase in Taxes Payable | (10) | 16 | | | |
| Increase in Other Short-Term Payables | (11) | 138 | | | |

#### Investing

| | | | | | |
|---|---|---|---|---|---|
| Sale of Machinery | (4) | 25 | 1,018 | (7) | Acquisition of Buildings and Machinery |
| | | | 36 | (8) | Acquisition of Land |

#### Financing

| | | | | | |
|---|---|---|---|---|---|
| Issue of Common Stock | (13) | 32 | 60 | (2) | Dividends |
| | | | 50 | (12) | Retirement of Bonds |
| √ | | 324 | | | |

| Accounts Receivable | | |
|---|---|---|
| √ | 946 | |
| (5) | 106 | |
| √ | 1,052 | |

| Inventory | | |
|---|---|---|
| √ | 1,004 | |
| (6) | 204 | |
| √ | 1,208 | |

| Buildings and Machinery | | | |
|---|---|---|---|
| √ | 8,678 | | |
| (7) | 1,018 | 150 | (4) |
| √ | 9,546 | | |

| Accumulated Depreciation— Buildings and Machinery | | | |
|---|---|---|---|
| | | 3,974 | √ |
| (4) | 120 | 510 | (3) |
| | | 4,364 | √ |

4.28 a. continued.

| Land | | | |
|---|---|---|---|
| √ | 594 | | |
| (8) | 36 | | |
| √ | 630 | | |

| | | Accounts Payable | |
|---|---|---|---|
| | | 412 | √ |
| | | 146 | (9) |
| | | 558 | √ |

| Taxes Payable | | | |
|---|---|---|---|
| | | 274 | √ |
| | | 16 | (10) |
| | | 290 | √ |

| | | Other Short-Term Payables | |
|---|---|---|---|
| | | 588 | √ |
| | | 138 | (11) |
| | | 726 | √ |

| Bonds Payable | | | |
|---|---|---|---|
| | | 1,984 | √ |
| (12) | 50 | | |
| | | 1,934 | √ |

| | | Common Stock | |
|---|---|---|---|
| | | 1,672 | √ |
| | | 32 | (13) |
| | | 1,704 | √ |

| Retained Earnings | | | |
|---|---|---|---|
| | | 2,676 | √ |
| (2) | 60 | 568 | (1) |
| | | 3,184 | √ |

b.  Dickerson Manufacturing Company is heavily capital intensive.  Its cash flow from operations exceeds net income because of the depreciation expense addback.  Cash flow from operations appears substantial, but so are its expenditures for building and equipment. The firm's relatively low dividend payout rate suggests that it expects large capital expenditures to continue.

4.29    (GTI, Inc.; preparing and interpreting a statement of cash flows using a T-account work sheet.)

a.

## T-Account Work Sheet for Year 8

### Cash

| | | | | | |
|---|---|---|---|---|---|
| √ | 430 | | | | |

**Operations**

| | | | | | |
|---|---|---|---|---|---|
| Net Income | (1) | 417 | 168 | (3) | Increase in Accounts Receivable |
| Depreciation Expense | (6) | 641 | 632 | (4) | Increase in Inventories |
| Amortization Expense | (8) | 25 | 154 | (5) | Increase in Prepayments |
| | | | 769 | (10) | Decrease in Accounts Payable |
| | | | 299 | (12) | Decrease in Other Current Liabilities |
| | | | 37 | (14) | Decrease in Other Noncurrent Liabilities |

**Investing**

| | | | | | |
|---|---|---|---|---|---|
| | | | 1,433 | (7) | Acquisition of Property, Plant, and Equipment |
| | | | 391 | (9) | Acquisition of Patent |

**Financing**

| | | | | | |
|---|---|---|---|---|---|
| Issue of Notes Payable | (11) | 220 | 12 | (2) | Dividends Paid |
| Increase in Long-term Debt | (13) | 2,339 | | | |
| Increase in Preferred Stock | (15) | 289 | | | |
| Increase in Common Stock | (16) | 9 | | | |

| | | | | | |
|---|---|---|---|---|---|
| √ | 475 | | | | |

4.29 a. continued.

**Accounts Receivable**

| Debit | | Credit | |
|---|---|---|---|
| √ | 3,768 | | |
| (3) | 168 | | |
| √ | 3,936 | | |

**Inventories**

| Debit | | Credit | |
|---|---|---|---|
| √ | 2,334 | | |
| (4) | 632 | | |
| √ | 2,966 | | |

**Prepayments**

| Debit | | Credit | |
|---|---|---|---|
| √ | 116 | | |
| (5) | 154 | | |
| √ | 270 | | |

**Property, Plant and Equipment (Net)**

| Debit | | Credit | |
|---|---|---|---|
| √ | 3,806 | | |
| (7) | 1,433 | 641 | (6) |
| √ | 4,598 | | |

**Other Noncurrent Assets**

| Debit | | Credit | |
|---|---|---|---|
| √ | 193 | | |
| (9) | 391 | 25 | (8) |
| √ | 559 | | |

**Accounts Payable**

| Debit | | Credit | |
|---|---|---|---|
| | | 1,578 | √ |
| (10) | 769 | | |
| | | 809 | √ |

**Notes Payable to Banks**

| Debit | | Credit | |
|---|---|---|---|
| | | 11 | √ |
| | | 220 | (11) |
| | | 231 | √ |

**Other Current Liabilities**

| Debit | | Credit | |
|---|---|---|---|
| | | 1,076 | √ |
| (12) | 299 | | |
| | | 777 | √ |

**Long Term Debt**

| Debit | | Credit | |
|---|---|---|---|
| | | 2,353 | √ |
| | | 2,339 | (13) |
| | | 4,692 | √ |

**Other Noncurrent Liabilities**

| Debit | | Credit | |
|---|---|---|---|
| | | 126 | √ |
| (14) | 37 | | |
| | | 89 | √ |

**Preferred Stock**

| Debit | | Credit | |
|---|---|---|---|
| | | 0 | √ |
| | | 289 | (15) |
| | | 289 | √ |

**Common Stock**

| Debit | | Credit | |
|---|---|---|---|
| | | 83 | √ |
| | | 2 | (16) |
| | | 85 | √ |

**Additional Paid-in Capital**

| Debit | | Credit | |
|---|---|---|---|
| | | 4,385 | √ |
| | | 7 | (16) |
| | | 4,392 | √ |

**Retained Earnings**

| Debit | | Credit | |
|---|---|---|---|
| | | 1,035 | √ |
| (2) | 12 | 417 | (1) |
| | | 1,440 | √ |

4.29 a. continued.

## T-Account Work Sheet for Year 9

|  |  | Cash |  |  |  |
|---|---|---|---|---|---|
|  | √ | 475 |  |  |  |
|  |  | **Operations** |  |  |  |
|  |  |  | 2,691 | (1) | Net Loss |
| Decrease in Accounts Receivable | (3) | 1,391 | 13 | (10) | Decrease in Accounts Payable |
| Decrease in Inventories | (4) | 872 |  |  |  |
| Decrease in Prepayments | (5) | 148 | 82 | (12) | Decrease in Other Current Liabilities |
| Depreciation Expense | (6) | 625 |  |  |  |
| Amortization Expense | (8) | 40 |  |  |  |
| Increase in Other Non-current Liabilities | (14) | 24 |  |  |  |
|  |  | **Investing** |  |  |  |
| Sale of Patents | (9) | 63 | 54 | (7) | Acquisition of Property, Plant, and Equipment |
|  |  | **Financing** |  |  |  |
|  |  |  | 8 | (2) | Dividends Paid |
| Issue of Notes Payable to Banks | (11) | 2,182 | 2,608 | (13) | Decrease in Long-Term Debt |
| Increase in Common Stock | (15) | 3 |  |  |  |
|  | √ | 367 |  |  |  |

4.29 a. continued.

| Accounts Receivable | | |
|---|---|---|
| √ 3,936 | | |
| | 1,391 | (3) |
| √ 2,545 | | |

| Inventories | | |
|---|---|---|
| √ 2,966 | | |
| | 872 | (4) |
| √ 2,094 | | |

| Prepayments | | |
|---|---|---|
| √ 270 | | |
| | 148 | (5) |
| √ 122 | | |

| Property, Plant and Equipment (Net) | | | |
|---|---|---|---|
| √ 4,598 | | | |
| (7) 54 | | 625 | (6) |
| √ 4,027 | | | |

| Other Noncurrent Assets | | |
|---|---|---|
| √ 559 | | |
| | 40 | (8) |
| | 63 | (9) |
| √ 456 | | |

| Accounts Payable | | |
|---|---|---|
| | 809 | √ |
| (10) 13 | | |
| | 796 | √ |

| Notes Payable to Banks | | |
|---|---|---|
| | 231 | √ |
| | 2,182 | (11) |
| | 2,413 | √ |

| Other Current Liabilities | | |
|---|---|---|
| | 777 | √ |
| (12) 82 | | |
| | 695 | √ |

| Long-Term Debt | | |
|---|---|---|
| | 4,692 | √ |
| (13) 2,608 | | |
| | 2,084 | √ |

| Other Noncurrent Liabilities | | |
|---|---|---|
| | 89 | √ |
| | 24 | (14) |
| | 113 | √ |

| Preferred Stock | | |
|---|---|---|
| | 289 | √ |
| | 289 | √ |

| Common Stock | | |
|---|---|---|
| | 85 | √ |
| | 85 | √ |

| Additional Paid-in Capital | | |
|---|---|---|
| | 4,392 | √ |
| | 3 | (15) |
| | 4,395 | √ |

| Retained Earnings | | |
|---|---|---|
| | 1,440 | √ |
| (1) 2,691 | | |
| (2) 8 | | |
| √ 1,259 | | |

4.29 continued.

b.
## GTI, INC.
### Statement of Cash Flows
### For Year 8 and Year 9

|  | Year 8 | Year 9 |
|---|---|---|
| Operations: |  |  |
| Net Income (Loss)..................................................... | $ 417 | $ (2,691) |
| Depreciation Expense............................................. | 641 | 625 |
| Amortization Expense............................................ | 25 | 40 |
| Inc. (Dec.) in Other Noncurrent Liabilities.... | (37) | 24 |
| (Inc.) Dec. in Accounts Receivable.................... | (168) | 1,391 |
| (Inc.) Dec. in Inventories .................................... | (632) | 872 |
| (Inc.) Dec. in Prepayments................................. | (154) | 148 |
| Inc. (Dec.) in Accounts Payable........................ | (769) | (13) |
| Inc. (Dec.) in Other Current Liabilities........... | (299) | (82) |
| Cash Flow from Operations.................................. | $ (976) | $ 314 |
| Investing: |  |  |
| Sale of Patents........................................................ | $ -- | $ 63 |
| Acquisition of Property, Plant and Equip- |  |  |
| ment........................................................................ | (1,433) | (54) |
| Acquisition of Patents .......................................... | (391) | -- |
| Cash Flow from Investing...................................... | $ (1,824) | $ 9 |
| Financing: |  |  |
| Inc. (Dec.) in Notes Payable to Banks ............. | $ 220 | $ 2,182 |
| Inc. (Dec.) in Long-Term Debt........................... | 2,339 | (2,608) |
| Increase in Preferred Stock ................................ | 289 | -- |
| Increase in Common Stock.................................. | 9 | 3 |
| Dividends Paid........................................................ | (12) | (8) |
| Cash Flow from Financing.................................... | $ 2,845 | $ (431) |
| Net Change in Cash ................................................. | $ 45 | $ (108) |
| Cash, Beginning of Year......................................... | 430 | 475 |
| Cash, End of Year ..................................................... | $ 475 | $ 367 |

c.  Cash flow from operations was negative during Year 8, despite positive net income, primarily because GTI reduced accounts payable and other current liabilities. The increases in receivables, inventories, and prepayments suggest that GTI grew during Year 8 relative to Year 7. One usually finds in these cases that current operating liabilities increase as well. The reduction in these current liabilities occurred either because GTI chose to use cash to liquidate these obligations or because creditors forced the firm to repay. GTI obtained the cash needed to finance the operating cash flow shortfall and capital expenditures by increasing short- and long-term debt and issuing preferred stock.

**4.29 c. continued.**

GTI experienced a net loss in Year 9 but its cash flow from operations turned positive. The firm reduced receivables, inventories and prepayments with only minor reductions in current operating liabilities. The small reductions in current operating liabilities relative to the declines in current operating assets reflect either a stretching of short-term creditors or a return to a normal level of current operating liabilities after the repayment made in Year 8. GTI dramatically decreased capital expenditures in Year 9 and replaced long-term debt with short-term borrowing.

4.30 (Flight Training Corporation; preparing and interpreting a statement of cash flows using a T-account work sheet.)

a.

## T-Account Work Sheet for Year 2

| | | | | | |
|---|---|---|---|---|---|
| **Cash** | | | | | |
| √ | 142 | | | | |
| | | | | | |
| **Operations** | | | | | |
| Net Income | (1) | 739 | 185 | (2) | Increase in Accounts Receivable |
| Depreciation Expense | (6) | 1,425 | | | |
| Increase in Accounts Payable | (8) | 54 | 950 | (3) | Increase in Inventories |
| Increase in Other Current Liabilities | (12) | 1,113 | 412 | (4) | Increase in Prepayments |
| Increase in Other Noncurrent Liabilities | (13) | 1,029 | | | |
| | | | | | |
| **Investing** | | | | | |
| Sale of Noncurrent Assets | (7) | 471 | 6,230 | (5) | Acquisition of Property, Plant, and Equipment |
| | | | | | |
| **Financing** | | | | | |
| Increase in Long-Term Debt | (11) | 3,751 | 881 | (9) | Decrease in Notes Payable |
| Increase in Common Stock | (14) | 247 | | | |
| | | | | | |
| √ | 313 | | | | |

4.30 a. continued.

| Accounts Receivable | | | | Inventories | |
|---|---|---|---|---|---|
| √ | 2,490 | | √ | 602 | |
| (2) | 185 | | (3) | 950 | |
| √ | 2,675 | | √ | 1,552 | |

| Prepayments | | | | Property, Plant and Equipment | |
|---|---|---|---|---|---|
| √ | 57 | | √ | 17,809 | |
| (4) | 412 | | (5) | 6,230 | |
| √ | 469 | | √ | 24,039 | |

| Accumulated Depreciation | | | | Other Noncurrent Assets | |
|---|---|---|---|---|---|
| | 4,288 | √ | √ | 1,112 | |
| | 1,425 | (6) | | | 471 | (7) |
| | 5,713 | √ | √ | 641 | |

| Accounts Payable | | | | Notes Payable | |
|---|---|---|---|---|---|
| | 939 | √ | | | 1,021 | √ |
| | 54 | (8) | (9) | 881 | |
| | 993 | √ | | | 140 | √ |

| Current Portion— Long-Term Debt | | | | Other Current Liabilities | |
|---|---|---|---|---|---|
| | 1,104 | √ | | | 1,310 | √ |
| | 685 | (10) | | | 1,113 | (12) |
| | 1,789 | √ | | | 2,423 | √ |

| Long-Term Debt | | | | Other Noncurrent Liabilities | |
|---|---|---|---|---|---|
| | 6,738 | √ | | | -- | √ |
| (10) | 685 | 3,751 | (11) | | 1,029 | (13) |
| | 9,804 | √ | | | 1,029 | √ |

| Common Stock | | | | Additional Paid-In Capital | |
|---|---|---|---|---|---|
| | 20 | √ | | | 4,323 | √ |
| | 1 | (14) | | | 246 | (14) |
| | 21 | √ | | | 4,569 | √ |

| Retained Earnings | | |
|---|---|---|
| | 2,469 | √ |
| | 739 | (1) |
| | 3,208 | √ |

4.30 a. continued.

**T-Account Work Sheet for Year 3**

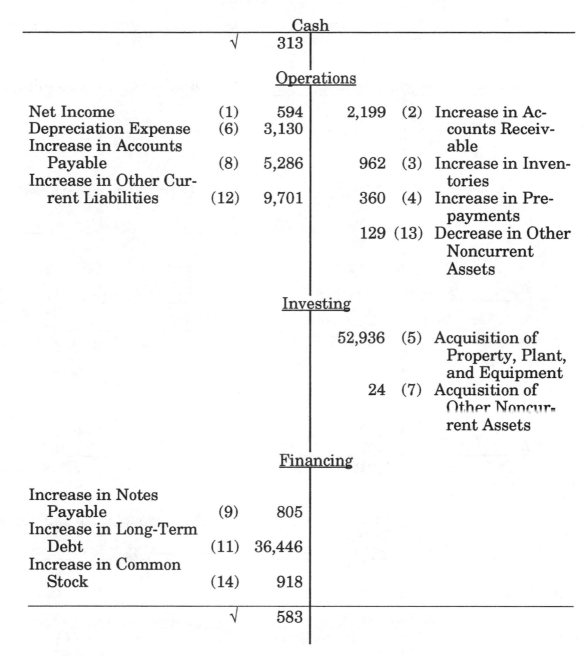

|  | | Cash | | |
|---|---|---|---|---|
| | √ | 313 | | |

**Operations**

| Net Income | (1) | 594 | 2,199 | (2) | Increase in Accounts Receivable |
| Depreciation Expense | (6) | 3,130 | | | |
| Increase in Accounts Payable | (8) | 5,286 | 962 | (3) | Increase in Inventories |
| Increase in Other Current Liabilities | (12) | 9,701 | 360 | (4) | Increase in Prepayments |
| | | | 129 | (13) | Decrease in Other Noncurrent Assets |

**Investing**

| | | | 52,936 | (5) | Acquisition of Property, Plant, and Equipment |
| | | | 24 | (7) | Acquisition of Other Noncurrent Assets |

**Financing**

| Increase in Notes Payable | (9) | 805 | | | |
| Increase in Long-Term Debt | (11) | 36,446 | | | |
| Increase in Common Stock | (14) | 918 | | | |
| | √ | 583 | | | |

4.30 a. continued.

| Accounts Receivable | | |
|---|---|---|
| √ | 2,675 | |
| (2) | 2,199 | |
| √ | 4,874 | |

| Inventories | | |
|---|---|---|
| √ | 1,552 | |
| (3) | 962 | |
| √ | 2,514 | |

| Prepayments | | |
|---|---|---|
| √ | 469 | |
| (4) | 360 | |
| √ | 829 | |

| Property, Plant and Equipment | | |
|---|---|---|
| √ | 24,039 | |
| (5) | 52,936 | |
| √ | 76,975 | |

| Accumulated Depreciation | | |
|---|---|---|
| | 5,713 | √ |
| | 3,130 | (6) |
| | 8,843 | √ |

| Other Noncurrent Assets | | |
|---|---|---|
| √ | 641 | |
| (7) | 24 | |
| √ | 665 | |

| Accounts Payable | | |
|---|---|---|
| | 993 | √ |
| | 5,286 | (8) |
| | 6,279 | √ |

| Notes Payable | | |
|---|---|---|
| | 140 | √ |
| | 805 | (9) |
| | 945 | √ |

| Current Portion—Long-Term Debt | | |
|---|---|---|
| | 1,789 | √ |
| | 5,229 | (10) |
| | 7,018 | √ |

| Other Current Liabilities | | |
|---|---|---|
| | 2,423 | √ |
| | 9,701 | (12) |
| | 12,124 | √ |

| Long-Term Debt | | | |
|---|---|---|---|
| | | 9,804 | √ |
| (10) | 5,229 | 36,446 | (11) |
| | | 41,021 | √ |

| Other Noncurrent Liabilities | | | |
|---|---|---|---|
| | | 1,029 | √ |
| (13) | 129 | | |
| | | 900 | √ |

| Common Stock | | |
|---|---|---|
| | 21 | √ |
| | 1 | (14) |
| | 22 | √ |

| Additional Paid-In Capital | | |
|---|---|---|
| | 4,569 | √ |
| | 917 | (14) |
| | 5,486 | √ |

| Retained Earnings | | |
|---|---|---|
| | 3,208 | √ |
| | 594 | (1) |
| | 3,802 | √ |

4.30 a. continued.

## T-Account Work Sheet for Year 4

### Cash

| | | √ | 583 | |
|---|---|---|---|---|

#### Operations

| | | | | | | |
|---|---|---|---|---|---|---|
| | | | 3,831 | (1) | Net Loss |
| Decrease in Prepayments | (4) | 164 | 1,671 | (2) | Increase in Accounts Receivable |
| Depreciation Expense | (6) | 8,388 | | | |
| Increase in Accounts Payable | (8) | 6,149 | 2,592 | (3) | Increase in Inventories |
| Increase in Other Current Liabilities | (12) | 779 | 900 | (13) | Decrease in Other Noncurrent Liabilities |

#### Investing

| | | | | | | |
|---|---|---|---|---|---|---|
| | | | 29,554 | (5) | Acquisition of Property, Plant, and Equipment |
| Sale of Noncurrent Assets | (7) | 195 | | | |

#### Financing

| | | | | | | |
|---|---|---|---|---|---|---|
| | | | 945 | (9) | Decrease in Notes Payable |
| Increase in Long-Term Debt | (11) | 12,551 | | | |
| Increase in Common Stock | (14) | 10,843 | | | |

| | | √ | 159 | |
|---|---|---|---|---|

**4.30 a. continued.**

| Accounts Receivable | | |
|---|---|---|
| √ | 4,874 | |
| (2) | 1,671 | |
| √ | 6,545 | |

| Inventories | | |
|---|---|---|
| √ | 2,514 | |
| (3) | 2,592 | |
| √ | 5,106 | |

| Prepayments | | |
|---|---|---|
| √ | 829 | |
| | | 164 (4) |
| √ | 665 | |

| Property, Plant and Equipment | | |
|---|---|---|
| √ | 76,975 | |
| (5) | 29,554 | |
| √ | 106,529 | |

| Accumulated Depreciation | | |
|---|---|---|
| | 8,843 | √ |
| | 8,388 | (6) |
| | 17,231 | √ |

| Other Noncurrent Assets | | |
|---|---|---|
| √ | 665 | |
| | | 195 (7) |
| √ | 470 | |

| Accounts Payable | | |
|---|---|---|
| | 6,279 | √ |
| | 6,149 | (8) |
| | 12,428 | √ |

| Notes Payable | | |
|---|---|---|
| | | 945 √ |
| (9) | 945 | |
| | | 0 √ |

| Current Portion—Long-Term Debt | | |
|---|---|---|
| | 7,018 | √ |
| | 53,572 | (10) |
| | 60,590 | √ |

| Other Current Liabilities | | |
|---|---|---|
| | | 12,124 √ |
| | | 779 (12) |
| | | 12,903 √ |

| Long-Term Debt | | | |
|---|---|---|---|
| | | 41,021 | √ |
| (10) | 53,572 | 12,551 | (11) |
| | | 0 | √ |

| Other Noncurrent Liabilities | | |
|---|---|---|
| | | 900 √ |
| (13) | 900 | |
| | | 0 √ |

| Common Stock | | |
|---|---|---|
| | 22 | √ |
| | 12 | (14) |
| | 34 | √ |

| Additional Paid-In Capital | | |
|---|---|---|
| | | 5,486 √ |
| | | 10,831 (14) |
| | | 16,317 √ |

| Retained Earnings | | |
|---|---|---|
| | | 3,802 √ |
| (1) | 3,831 | |
| √ | 29 | |

4.30 continued.

b.

# FLIGHT TRAINING CORPORATION
## Statement of Cash Flows
### (Amounts in Thousands)

| | Year Ended December 31 | | |
| --- | --- | --- | --- |
| | Year 2 | Year 3 | Year 4 |
| Operations: | | | |
| Net Income (Loss) | $ 739 | $ 594 | $ (3,831) |
| Depreciation | 1,425 | 3,130 | 8,388 |
| Increase (Decrease) in Other Non-current Liabilities | 1,029 | (129) | (900) |
| (Increase) Decrease in Accounts Receivable | (185) | (2,199) | (1,671) |
| (Increase) Decrease in Inventories. | (950) | (962) | (2,592) |
| (Increase) Decrease in Prepayments | (412) | (360) | 164 |
| Increase (Decrease) in Accounts Payable | 54 | 5,286 | 6,149 |
| Increase (Decrease) in Other Current Liabilities | 1,113 | 9,701 | 779 |
| Cash Flow from Operations | $ 2,813 | $ 15,061 | $ 6,486 |
| Investing: | | | |
| Acquisition of Property, Plant, and Equipment | $ (6,230) | $ (52,936) | $ (29,554) |
| Sale (Acquisition) of Other Non-current Assets | 471 | (24) | 195 |
| Cash Flow from Investing | $ (5,759) | $ (52,960) | $ (29,359) |
| Financing: | | | |
| Increase (Decrease) in Notes Payable | $ (881) | $ 805 | $ (945) |
| Increase (Decrease) in Long-Term Debt | 3,751 | 36,446 | 12,551 |
| Increase in Common Stock | 247 | 918 | 10,843 |
| Cash Flow from Financing | $ 3,117 | $ 38,169 | $ 22,449 |
| Change in Cash | $ 171 | $ 270 | $ (424) |
| Cash, Beginning of Year | 142 | 313 | 583 |
| Cash, End of Year | $ 313 | $ 583 | $ 159 |

4.30 continued.

c.  Cash flow from operations exceeded net income during Year 2 because of the addbacks for depreciation and other noncurrent liabilities. Changes in current assets just slightly exceeded changes in current liabilities, suggesting effective working capital management. Cash flow from operations was insufficient to fund expenditures on property, plant, and equipment. The firm primarily used long-term debt to finance the shortfall from operating cash flows in acquiring these fixed assets.

Net income declined between Year 2 and Year 3 but cash flow from operations increased significantly. The increased cash flow from operations, however, results primarily from increases in accounts payable and other current liabilities. The firm had insufficient cash to pay its suppliers and therefore stretched the payment time. The firm increased substantially its purchase of property, plant, and equipment during Year 3, financing its purchases with cash flow from operations and additional long-term debt. The use of operating cash flows to finance purchases of fixed assets is generally undesirable if it occurs as it does in this case from stretching short-term suppliers.

Net income turns negative in Year 4, primarily because of a substantial increase in depreciation expense from purchases of depreciable assets in the current and prior years. Cash flow from operations is positive because of the addback for depreciation expense and the continued stretching of accounts payable suppliers. Flight Training Corporation again spent significant amounts on property, plant, and equipment, financing the purchases in part with additional long-term debt and in part with issuances of common stock.

d.  The cash flow problems of Flight Training Corporation trace to expanding fixed assets too rapidly, relative to increases in sales, and to using cash flow from operations in part to finance the purchases. Sales increased 76.3 percent [= ($36,597/$20,758) − 1] between Year 2 and Year 3 while fixed assets increased 220.2 percent [= ($76,975/$24,039) − 1] between those years. Sales increased 50.3 percent [= ($54,988/$36,597) − 1] between Year 3 and Year 4 while fixed assets increased 38.4 percent [= ($106,529/$76,975) − 1]. For the two years as a whole, sales increased 164.9 percent [= ($54,988/$20,758) − 1] while depreciable assets increased 343.2 percent [= ($106,529/$24,039) − 1]. Although these sales increases are substantial, they are significantly less than the increase in fixed assets. Stretching creditors to purchase these fixed assets could jeopardize the availability of goods (for example, jet fuel) and services (pilots' services) needed to remain in business.

4.31    (Quebec Company; preparing a statement of cash flows over a 2-year period using a T-account work sheet.)

a.
### QUEBEC COMPANY
### Statement of Cash Flows
### For Year 2

Operations:
| | | |
|---|---|---|
| Net Income......................................................... | $ 166,000 | |
| Additions: | | |
|   Depreciation Expense ................................. | 174,000 | |
|   Decrease in Merchandise | | |
|     Inventories.............................................. | 20,000 | |
| Subtractions: | | |
|   Increase in Accounts Receivable ............... | (20,000) | |
|   Decrease in Accounts Payable ................... | (2,000) | |
| Cash Flow from Operations............................... | | $ 338,000 |
| Investing: | | |
|   Sale of Property, Plant, and Equipment...... | $  88,000 | |
|   Acquisition of Property, Plant, and | | |
|     Equipment...................................................... | (342,000) | |
| Cash Flow from Investing.................................. | | (254,000) |
| Financing: | | |
|   Issue of Common Stock.................................... | $  92,000 | |
|   Dividends Paid.................................................. | (80,000) | |
|   Retirement of Bonds........................................ | (32,000) | |
| Cash Flow from Financing................................. | | (20,000) |
| Net Change In Cash ........................................... | | $   64,000 |
| Cash, January 1, Year 2..................................... | | 110,000 |
| Cash, December 31, Year 2................................. | | $ 174,000 |

4.31 a. continued.

### Cash

|  |  |  |  |  |  |
|---|---|---|---|---|---|
| √ | 110 |  |  |  |  |

**Operations**

| | | | | | |
|---|---|---|---|---|---|
| Net Income | (1) | 166[a] | 20 | (6) | Increase in Accounts Receivable |
| Depreciation | (3) | 174 | | | |
| Decrease in Merchandise Inventories | (7) | 20 | 2 | (8) | Decrease in Accounts Payable |

**Investing**

| | | | | | |
|---|---|---|---|---|---|
| | | | 342 | (5) | Acquisition of Property, Plant, and Equipment |
| Sale of Property, Plant, and Equipment | (4) | 88[b] | | | |

**Financing**

| | | | | | |
|---|---|---|---|---|---|
| | | | 80 | (2) | Dividends |
| Issue of Common Stock | (10) | 92 | 32 | (9) | Retirement of Bonds |

| | |
|---|---|
| √ | 174 |

[a]See footnote *a* on following page.
[b]See footnote *b* on following page.

| Accounts Receivable | | | Merchandise Inventories | | | Property, Plant, and Equipment | | |
|---|---|---|---|---|---|---|---|---|
| √ | 220 | | √ | 250 | | √ | 3,232 | |
| (6) | 20 | | | | 20 (7) | (5) | 342 | 216[b](4) |
| √ | 240 | | √ | 230 | | √ | 3,358 | |

| Accounts Payable | | | Accumulated Depreciation | | | Bonds Payable | | |
|---|---|---|---|---|---|---|---|---|
| | | 162 √ | | | 1,394 √ | | | 212 √ |
| (8) | 2 | | (4) | 128 | 174 (3) | (9) | 32 | |
| | | 160 √ | | | 1,440 √ | | | 180 √ |

4.31 a. continued.

| Common Stock | | | Retained Earnings | | |
|---|---|---|---|---|---|
| | 754 √ | | | 1,290 √ | |
| | 92 (10) | (2) | 80 | 166[a] (1) | |
| | 846 √ | | | 1,376 √ | |

[a]$166 = $1,820 + $10 − $740 − $640 − $174 − $110.

[b]Journal entry made at time of sale:

| | | |
|---|---|---|
| Cash (Plug)......................................................... | 88 | |
| Accumulated Depreciation............................. | 128 | |
|    Property, Plant, and Equipment.............. | | 216 |

b.
## QUEBEC COMPANY
### Statement of Cash Flows
### For Year 3

| | | |
|---|---|---|
| Operations: | | |
| Net Income........................................................ | $ 198,000 | |
| Additions: | | |
|   Depreciation Expense................................. | 192,000 | |
|   Loss on Sale of Equipment ......................... | 4,000 | |
|   Decrease in Accounts Receivable .............. | 30,000 | |
|   Increase in Accounts Payable .................... | 6,000 | |
| Subtractions: | | |
|   Increase in Merchandise Inventories....... | (50,000) | |
| Cash Flow from Operations.............................. | | $ 380,000 |
| Investing: | | |
| Sale of Property, Plant, and Equipment...... | $ 98,000 | |
| Acquisition of Property, Plant, and | | |
|   Equipment................................................. | (636,000) | |
| Cash Flow from Investing................................. | | (538,000) |
| Financing: | | |
| Issue of Bonds................................................. | $ 90,000 | |
| Issue of Common Stock.................................. | 182,000 | |
| Dividends Paid................................................. | (94,000) | |
| Cash Flow from Financing................................ | | 178,000 |
| Net Change in Cash ......................................... | | $ 20,000 |
| Cash, January 1, Year 3.................................... | | 174,000 |
| Cash, December 31, Year 3................................ | | $ 194,000 |

**4.31 b. continued.**

|  |  | Cash |  |  |
|---|---|---|---|---|
| | √ | 174 | | |

**Operations**

| | | | | | |
|---|---|---|---|---|---|
| Net Income | (1) | 198[a] | 50 | (7) | Increase in Mer-chandise Inven-tories |
| Depreciation | (3) | 192 | | | |
| Loss on Sale of Equipment | (5) | 4 | | | |
| Decrease in Ac-counts Receiv-able | (6) | 30 | | | |
| Increase in Ac-counts Payable | (8) | 6 | | | |

**Investing**

| | | | | | |
|---|---|---|---|---|---|
| Sale of Property, Plant, and Equipment | (5) | 98[b] | 636 | (4) | Acquisition of Property, Plant, and Equipment |

**Financing**

| | | | | | |
|---|---|---|---|---|---|
| Issue of Bonds Payable | (9) | 90 | 94 | (2) | Dividends |
| Issue of Common Stock | (10) | 182 | | | |
| | √ | 194 | | | |

[a]See footnote *a* on following page.

[b]See footnote *b* on following page.

| Accounts Receivable | | | | Merchandise Inventories | | | | Property, Plant, and Equipment | | | |
|---|---|---|---|---|---|---|---|---|---|---|---|
| √ | 240 | | | √ | 230 | | | √ | 3,358 | | |
| | | 30 | (6) | (7) | 50 | | | (4) | 636 | 244[b] | (5) |
| √ | 210 | | | √ | 280 | | | √ | 3,750 | | |

4.31 b. continued.

| Accounts Payable | | | Accumulated Depreciation | | | Bonds Payable | |
|---|---|---|---|---|---|---|---|
| | 160  √ | | | 1,440  √ | | | 180  √ |
| | 6  (8) | (5) | 142b | 192  (3) | | | 90  (9) |
| | 166  √ | | | 1,490  √ | | | 270  √ |

| Common Stock | | | Retained Earnings | |
|---|---|---|---|---|
| | 846  √ | | | 1,376  √ |
| | 182  (10) | (2) | 94 | 198a  (1) |
| | 1,028  √ | | | 1,480  √ |

a$198 = $1,940 + $14 − $826 − $602 − $192 − $4 − $132.

bJournal entry made at time of sale:

| | | |
|---|---|---|
| Cash (Plug)..................................................... | 98 | |
| Accumulated Depreciation.......................... | 142 | |
| Loss on Sale of Equipment ......................... | 4 | |
| Property, Plant, and Equipment .......... | | 244 |

c.  During Year 2, cash flow from operations was more than sufficient to fund capital expenditures and pay dividends. The firm issued common stock and used the proceeds to retire debt and increase the amount of cash on hand. During Year 3, expenditures on property, plant and equipment increased significantly. Operating cash flows were insufficient to fund these capital expenditures and pay dividends, so the firm issued additional bonds and common stock.

**4.32** (Quinta Company; working backwards through the statement of cash flows.)

### QUINTA COMPANY
### Balance Sheet
### January 1, Year 5
### ($ in 000's)

*Assets*

| | | |
|---|---:|---:|
| Current Assets: | | |
| Cash ........................................................................ | $ 20 | |
| Accounts Receivable............................................... | 190 | |
| Merchandise Inventories........................................ | 280 | |
| Total Current Assets ......................................... | | $ 490 |
| Land ......................................................................... | | 50 |
| Buildings and Equipment ....................................... | $ 405 | |
| Less Accumulated Depreciation............................. | (160) | 245 |
| Investments............................................................. | | 140 |
| Total Assets ........................................................ | | $ 925 |

*Liabilities and Shareholders' Equity*

| | | |
|---|---:|---:|
| Current Liabilities: | | |
| Accounts Payable.................................................... | $ 255 | |
| Other Current Liabilities....................................... | 130 | |
| Total Current Liabilities .................................. | | $ 385 |
| Bonds Payable......................................................... | | 60 |
| Common Stock ......................................................... | | 140 |
| Retained Earnings.................................................. | | 340 |
| Total Liabilities and Shareholders' Equity........ | | $ 925 |

Shown below are T-accounts for deriving the solution. Entries (1)—(13) are reconstructed from the statement of cash flows. Changes for the year are appropriately debited or credited to end-of-year balances to get beginning-of-year balances. T-account amounts are shown in thousands.

| | Cash | | | | Accounts Receivable | | | | Merchandise Inventories | |
|---|---:|---:|---:|---|---:|---|---|---|---:|---|
| | 20 | | | | 190 | | | | 280 | |
| (1) | 200 | 30 | (4) | (4) | 30 | | | (5) | 40 | |
| (2) | 60 | 40 | (5) | | | | | | | |
| (3) | 25 | 45 | (6) | | | | | | | |
| (7) | 40 | 130 | (10) | | | | | | | |
| (8) | 15 | 200 | (13) | | | | | | | |
| (9) | 10 | | | | | | | | | |
| (11) | 60 | | | | | | | | | |
| (12) | 40 | | | | | | | | | |
| √ | 25 | | | √ | 220 | | | √ | 320 | |

4-46

4.32 continued.

| | Land | | | Buildings and Equipment | | | | Investments | |
|---|---|---|---|---|---|---|---|---|---|
| | 50 | | | 405 | | | | 140 | |
| | | 10 (9) | (10) | 130 | 35 (8) | | | | 40 (7) |
| √ | 40 | | √ | 500 | | | √ | 100 | |

| | Accumulated Depreciation | | | Accounts Payable | | | | Other Current Liabilities | |
|---|---|---|---|---|---|---|---|---|---|
| | | 160 | | | 255 | | | | 130 |
| (8) | 20 | 60 (2) | | | 25 (3) | (6) | 45 | | |
| | | 200 √ | | | 280 √ | | | | 85 √ |

| | Bonds Payable | | | Common Stock | | | | Retained Earnings | |
|---|---|---|---|---|---|---|---|---|---|
| | | 60 | | | 140 | | | | 340 |
| | | 40 (12) | | | 60 (11) | (13) | 200 | | 200 (1) |
| | | 100 √ | | | 200 √ | | | | 340 √ |

4.33 (RV Suppliers, Inc.; preparing and interpreting the statement of cash flows using the indirect method.)

This problem was adapted from financial statement data of Winnebago Industries for its 1973 and 1974 fiscal years. A statement of cash flows, and T-account work sheets for Year 5 and Year 6, follow.

The Year 5 period for RV Suppliers, Inc., shows results that are typical of those for a growing firm. Although net income is $34,600, cash flow from operations is only $4,000, due primarily to an increase in accounts receivable and inventories. To finance acquisitions of property, plant, and equipment, the firm relied on short-term bank borrowing. Sound financial policy usually dictates the financing of noncurrent assets with long-term debt or capital stock. The market prospects for recreational vehicles were sufficiently poor during this period that the firm was probably unable to tap the long-term credit and equity markets and had to use short-term bank financing.

The Year 6 period shows results that are typical of those for a firm experiencing a business contraction. Because of decreased sales, accounts receivable decreased and the level of inventories decreased. Cash flow generated from the decrease in receivables and inventories was used to pay off accounts payable. Operations was a net user of cash. The firm again financed acquisitions of property, plant, and equipment with short-term bank borrowing. The firm reduced drastically its rate of capital expenditures, however, during Year 6.

4.33 continued.

### RV SUPPLIERS, INC.
### Statement of Cash Flows
### For Year 5 and Year 6

|  | Year 5 | Year 6 |
|---|---|---|
| Operations: |  |  |
| Net Income (Loss) | $ 34.6 | $ (13.4) |
| Plus Additions: |  |  |
| Depreciation Expense | 4.8 | 8.0 |
| Decrease in Accounts Receivable | -- | 31.4 |
| Decrease in Inventories | -- | 4.6 |
| Decrease in Prepayments | -- | 1.8 |
| Increase in Accounts Payable | 21.8 | -- |
| Increase in Income Taxes Payable | 1.2 | -- |
| Increase in Other Current Liabilities | 2.6 | -- |
| Less Subtractions: |  |  |
| Increase in Accounts Receivable | (26.8) | -- |
| Increase in Inventories | (31.6) | -- |
| Increase in Tax Refund Receivable | -- | (5.0) |
| Increase in Prepayments | (2.6) | -- |
| Decrease in Accounts Payable | -- | (36.0) |
| Decrease in Income Taxes Payable | -- | (7.0) |
| Decrease in Other Current Liabilities | -- | (2.4) |
| Cash Flow from Operations | $ 4.0 | $ (18.0) |
| Investing: |  |  |
| Sale of Property, Plant, and Equipment | $ .4 | $ 5.4 |
| Acquisition of Property, Plant, and Equipment | (48.4) | (12.2) |
| Cash Flow from Investing | $ (48.0) | $ (6.8) |
| Financing: |  |  |
| Bank Borrowing (Net) | $ 42.0 | $ 18.0 |
| Net Change in Cash | $ (2.0) | $ (6.8) |

4.33 continued.

## RV SUPPLIERS, INC.—YEAR 5

### Cash

| | | | |
|---|---|---|---|
| √ | 14.0 | | |

#### Operations

| | | | |
|---|---|---|---|
| (1) | 34.6 | 26.8 | (5) |
| (2) | 4.8 | 31.6 | (6) |
| (9) | 21.8 | 2.6 | (7) |
| (10) | 1.2 | | |
| (11) | 2.6 | | |

#### Investing

| | | | |
|---|---|---|---|
| (4) | .4 | 48.4 | (3) |

#### Financing

| | | | |
|---|---|---|---|
| (8) | 42.0 | | |
| √ | 12.0 | | |

| Accounts Receivable | | Inventories | | Prepayments | |
|---|---|---|---|---|---|
| √ | 28.8 | √ | 54.0 | √ | 4.8 |
| (5) | 26.8 | (6) | 31.6 | (7) | 2.6 |
| √ | 55.6 | √ | 85.6 | √ | 7.4 |

| Property, Plant, and Equipment (Net) | | | | Bank Note Payable | | Accounts Payable | |
|---|---|---|---|---|---|---|---|
| √ | 30.2 | | | | 10.0 √ | | 31.6 √ |
| (3) | 48.4 | 4.8 | (2) | | 42.0 (8) | | 21.8 (9) |
| | | .4 | (4) | | | | |
| √ | 73.4 | | | | 52.0 √ | | 53.4 √ |

| Income Taxes Payable | | Other Current Liabilities | | Capital Stock | |
|---|---|---|---|---|---|
| | 5.8 √ | | 4.2 √ | | 44.6 √ |
| | 1.2 (10) | | 2.6 (11) | | |
| | 7.0 √ | | 6.8 √ | | 44.6 √ |

| Retained Earnings | |
|---|---|
| | 35.6 √ |
| | 34.6 (1) |
| | 70.2 √ |

4.33 continued.

## RV SUPPLIERS, INC.—YEAR 6

### Cash

| | | | |
|---|---|---|---|
| √ | 12.0 | | |

**Operations**

| | | | |
|---|---|---|---|
| (2) | 8.0 | 13.4 | (1) |
| (5) | 31.4 | 5.0 | (7) |
| (6) | 4.6 | 36.0 | (10) |
| (8) | 1.8 | 7.0 | (11) |
| | | 2.4 | (12) |

**Investing**

| | | | |
|---|---|---|---|
| (4) | 5.4 | 12.2 | (3) |

**Financing**

| | | | |
|---|---|---|---|
| (9) | 18.0 | | |
| √ | 5.2 | | |

### Accounts Receivable

| | | | |
|---|---|---|---|
| √ | 55.6 | | |
| | | 31.4 | (5) |
| √ | 24.2 | | |

### Inventories

| | | | |
|---|---|---|---|
| √ | 85.6 | | |
| | | 4.6 | (6) |
| √ | 81.0 | | |

### Tax Refund Receivable

| | | | |
|---|---|---|---|
| √ | .0 | | |
| (7) | 5.0 | | |
| √ | 5.0 | | |

### Prepayments

| | | | |
|---|---|---|---|
| √ | 7.4 | | |
| | | 1.8 | (8) |
| √ | 5.6 | | |

### Property, Plant, and Equipment (Net)

| | | | |
|---|---|---|---|
| √ | 73.4 | | |
| (3) | 12.2 | 8.0 | (2) |
| | | 5.4 | (4) |
| √ | 72.2 | | |

### Bank Note Payable

| | | | |
|---|---|---|---|
| | | 52.0 | √ |
| | | 18.0 | (9) |
| | | 70.0 | √ |

### Accounts Payable

| | | | |
|---|---|---|---|
| | | 53.4 | √ |
| (10) | 36.0 | | |
| | | 17.4 | √ |

### Income Taxes Payable

| | | | |
|---|---|---|---|
| | | 7.0 | √ |
| (11) | 7.0 | | |
| | | 0.0 | √ |

### Other Current Liabilities

| | | | |
|---|---|---|---|
| | | 6.8 | √ |
| (12) | 2.4 | | |
| | | 4.4 | √ |

### Capital Stock

| | | | |
|---|---|---|---|
| | | 44.6 | √ |
| | | 44.6 | √ |

### Retained Earnings

| | | | |
|---|---|---|---|
| | | 70.2 | √ |
| (1) | 13.4 | | |
| | | 56.8 | √ |

4.34    (Heidi's Hide-Out; inferring cash flows from trial balance data.)

a.  Sales Revenue from Retail Customers............................................ $ 120,000
    Less Increase in Accounts Receivable from Retail Cus-
        tomers ($8,900 – $8,000)........................................................ (900)
    Plus Increase in Advances from Retail Customers
        ($10,000 – $9,000)................................................................... 1,000
    Cash Collected from Retail Customers.................................... $ 120,100

b.  Rent Expense.................................................................................. $ (33,000)
    Less Increase in Advances to Landlords ($5,600 –
        $5,000).......................................................................................... (600)
    Less Decrease in Rent Payable to Landlords ($5,300 –
        $6,000)........................................................................................... (700)
    Cash Paid to Landlords................................................................. $ (34,300)

c.  Wage Expense................................................................................... $ (20,000)
    Less Increase in Advances to Employees ($1,500 –
        $1,000)........................................................................................... (500)
    Less Decrease in Wages Payable to Employees ($1,800 –
        $2,000)........................................................................................... (200)
    Cash Paid to Employees................................................................ $ (20,700)

d.  Cost of Retail Merchandise Sold ............................................... $ (90,000)
    Plus Decrease in Inventory of Retail Merchandise
        ($10,000 – $11,000)................................................................. 1,000
    Less Increase in Advances to Suppliers of Retail Merchan
        dise ($10,500 – $10,000) ....................................................... (500)
    Less Increase in Accounts Payable to Suppliers of Retail
        Merchandise ($7,700 – $8,000) ........................................... (300)
    Cash Paid to Suppliers of Retail Merchandise...................... $ (89,800)

4.35    (Digit Retail Enterprises, Inc.; inferring cash flows from balance sheet and
        income statement data.)

a.  Sales Revenue................................................................................. $ 270,000
    Less Increase in Accounts Receivable ($38,000 –
        $23,000)........................................................................................ (15,000)
    Less Decrease in Advances from Customers ($6,100 –
        $8,500) .......................................................................................... (2,400)
    Cash Received from Customers during the Year .................. $ 252,600

b.  Cost of Goods Sold ........................................................................ $ (145,000)
    Less Increase in Merchandise Inventory ($65,000 –
        $48,000)......................................................................................... (17,000)
    Acquisition Cost of Merchandise Purchased during the
        Year ............................................................................................... $ (162,000)

4.35 continued.

c.  Acquisition Cost of Merchandise Purchased during the
Year (from Part b.)................................................................. $ (162,000)
Plus Increase in Accounts Payable—Merchandise Sup-
pliers ($20,000 – $18,000) ................................................ 2,000
Cash Paid for Acquisitions of Merchandise during the
Year .......................................................................................... $ (160,000)

d.  Salaries Expense.................................................................... $ (68,000)
Plus Increase in Salaries Payable ($2,800 – $2,100)............ 700
Cash Paid to Salaried Employees during the Year............... $ (67,300)

e.  Insurance Expense ................................................................ $ (5,000)
Less Increase in Prepaid Insurance ($12,000 – $9,000) ....... (3,000)
Cash Paid to Insurance Companies during the Year ........... $ (8,000)

f.  Rent Expense.......................................................................... $ (12,000)
Plus Decrease in Prepaid Rent ($0 – $2,000) ........................ 2,000
Plus Increase in Rent Payable ($3,000 – $0)........................ 3,000
Cash Paid to Landlords for Rental of Space during the
Year .......................................................................................... $ (7,000)

g.  Increase in Retained Earnings ($11,800 – $11,500).............. $ 300
Less Net Income...................................................................... (9,600)
Dividend Declared .................................................................. $ (9,300)
Plus Decrease in Dividend Payable ($2,600 – $4,200)......... (1,600)
Cash Paid for Dividends during the Year ............................ $ (10,900)

h.  Depreciation Expense ........................................................... $ (20,000)
Plus Increase in Accumulated Depreciation ($35,000 –
$20,000)................................................................................... 15,000
Accumulated Depreciation of Property, Plant and Equip-
ment Sold ................................................................................ $ (5,000)
Cost of Property, Plant and Equipment Sold ($100,000 –
$90,000)................................................................................... 10,000
Book Value of Property, Plant and Equipment Sold............ $ 5,000
Plus Gain on Sale of Property, Plant and Equipment........... 3,200
Cash Received from Sale of Property, Plant and Equip-
ment .......................................................................................... $ 8,200

4.36    (NIKE, Inc.; interpreting the statement of cash flows.)

   a.   NIKE's growth in sales and net income led to increases of account receivable and inventories. NIKE, however, did not increase its accounts payable and other current operating liabilities to help finance the buildup in current assets. Thus, its cash flow from operations decreased.

   b.   NIKE increased its acquisitions of property, plant and equipment to provide the firm with operating capacity to sustain its rapid growth. NIKE also acquired investments in securities of other firms. It is not clear from the statement of cash flows whether the investments represented short-term investments of temporarily excess cash (a current asset) or long-term investments made to develop an operating relation with another firm (noncurrent asset).

   c.   NIKE used cash flow from operations during Year 7 and Year 8 to finance its investing activities. The excess cash flow after investing activities served to repay short- and long-term debt and pay dividends. Cash flow from operations during Year 9 was insufficient to finance investing activities. NIKE engaged in short-term borrowing to make up the shortfall and finance the payment of dividends.

   d.   Operating cash flows should generally finance the payment of dividends. Either operating cash flows or long-term sources of capital should generally finance acquisitions of property, plant and equipment. Thus, NIKE's use of short-term borrowing seems inappropriate. One might justify such an action if NIKE (1) expected cash flow from operations during Year 10 to return to its historical levels, (2) expected cash outflows for property, plant and equipment to decrease during Year 10, or (3) took advantage of comparatively low short-term borrowing rates during Year 9 and planned to refinance this debt with long-term borrowing during Year 10.

4.37    (Boise Cascade; interpreting the statement of cash flows.)

   a.   Forest products companies are capital intensive. Depreciation is therefore a substantial non-cash expense each year. The addback for depreciation converts a net loss each year into positive cash flow from operations. Note that cash flow from operations increased each year as the net loss decreased.

   b.   Boise Cascade had substantial changes in its property, plant and equipment during the three years. It likely built new, more efficient production facilities and sold off older, less efficient facilities.

4.37 continued.

    c.  For the three years combined, Boise Cascade reduced its long-term debt and replaced it with preferred stock. The sales of forest products are cyclical. When the economy is in a recession, as apparently occurred during the three years, the high fixed cost of capital-intensive manufacturing facilities can result in net losses. If Boise Cascade is unable to repay debt on schedule during such years, it causes expensive financial distress or even bankruptcy. Firms have more latitude with respect to dividends on preferred stock than interest on debt. Thus, a shift toward preferred stock and away from long-term debt reduces the bankruptcy risk of Boise Cascade. Note that Boise Cascade continued to pay, and even increase, dividends despite operating at a net loss. Most shareholders prefer less rather than more fluctuation in their dividends over the business cycle.

4.38    (Interpreting the statement of cash flow relations.)

**American Airlines**—Property, plant and equipment comprises a large proportion of the total assets of American Airlines. Depreciation expense is a major expense for the airline. The firm operated at a net loss for the year, but the addback for depreciation resulted in a positive cash flow from operations. Cash flow from operations was not sufficient to fund capital expenditures on new property, plant and equipment. American Airlines is apparently growing since its capital expenditures exceed depreciation expense for the year. The firm financed its capital expenditures in part with cash flow from operations and in part with the issuance of additional long-term debt and capital stock. The net effect of the cash flow from financing is a reduction in liabilities and an increase in capital stock (actually preferred stock). Operating at a net loss increases the risk of bankruptcy. Perhaps American Airlines reduced the amount of debt in its capital structure to reduce fixed payment claims and substituted preferred stock that generally requires dividend payments only when declared by the board of directors.

**American Home Products**—Because of patent protection, pharmaceutical companies tend to generate relatively high profit margins and significant cash flows from operations. Although the manufacturing process for pharmaceutical products is capital intensive, cash flow from operations is usually sufficient to fund capital expenditures. American Home Products used the excess cash flow to pay dividends and repurchase capital stock. The firm also borrowed short-term funds and invested the proceeds in the acquisition of another business. Borrowing short term to finance investments in long-term assets is usually undesirable, because the firm must repay the debt before the long-term assets generate sufficient cash flow. Perhaps American Home Products needed to borrow short term to consummate the acquisition, with the expectation of refinancing the short-term debt with long-term borrowing soon after the acquisition. Alternatively, American Home Products might have anticipated a decline in long-term rates in the near future and borrowed short term until long-term rates actually declined.

4.38 continued.

**Interpublic Group**—An advertising agency serves as a link between clients desiring advertising time and space and various media with advertising time and space to sell. Thus, the principal asset of an advertising agency is accounts receivable from clients and the principal liability is accounts payable to various media. Interpublic Group reports an increase in accounts receivable of $66 million and an increase in accounts payable of $59 million. Thus, the firm appeared to manage its receivables/payables position well. Advertising agencies lease most of the physical facilities used in their operations. They purchase equipment for use in designing and producing advertising copy. Thus, they must make some capital expenditures. Cash flow from operations, however, is more than sufficient to finance acquisitions of equipment. Interpublic Group used the excess cash flow plus the proceeds of additional short- and long-term borrowing to pay dividends, repurchase capital stock, and increase cash on the balance sheet.

**Procter & Gamble**—Procter & Gamble's brand names create high profit margins and cash flows from operations. Cash flow from operations is more than adequate to finance capital expenditures. Note that capital expenditures significantly exceed depreciation, suggesting that the firm is still in a growth mode. The firm used the excess cash flow to repay short- and long-term debt and to pay dividends.

**Reebok**—Cash flow from operations for Reebok is less than net income plus depreciation, a somewhat unusual relationship for a seasoned firm. Reebok increased its accounts receivable and inventories during the year but did not stretch its accounts payable commensurably. The financing section of the statement of cash flows suggests that Reebok might have used short-term debt to finance some of its working capital needs. Cash flow from operations was still more than sufficient to fund capital expenditures. One explanation for the sufficiency of cash flow from operations to cover capital expenditures is that Reebok is not very capital intensive. The relation between depreciation expense and net income supports this explanation. Reebok outsources virtually all of its manufacturing. Reebok used the excess cash flows from operating and investing activities to pay dividends and repurchase its capital stock.

**Texas Instruments**—Like American Home Products and Upjohn (discussed later), Texas Instruments invests heavily in technology to create a competitive advantage. Patents and copyrights on computer hardware, software, and other products serve as a barrier to entry by competitors and provide Texas Instruments with an attractive profit margin. Texas Instruments differs from the two pharmaceutical companies with respect to the amount of depreciation relative to net income. Despite generating less than one-half of the net income of American Home Products, Texas Instruments has more than twice the amount of depreciation expense and capital expenditures. Thus, Texas Instruments is likely more capital intensive than the other two technology-

4.38 continued.

based companies. Note that the changes in individual working capital accounts are relatively large, compared to the amount of net income. These relations suggest, although do not prove, that the operations of Texas Instruments grew significantly during the year. Cash flow from operations was sufficient to fund capital expenditures and increase the balance of cash on the balance sheet. Note that Texas Instruments issued capital stock during the year and repaid long-term debt. The amounts involved, however, are small.

**The Limited**—Current assets and current liabilities dominate the balance sheets of retailers. Thus, working capital management is of particular importance. The Limited increased its current liabilities in line with increases in accounts receivable and inventories. Thus, cash flow from operations approximately equals net income plus depreciation. The Limited invested most of the cash flow from operations in additional property, plant and equipment, the acquisition of other businesses, the repayment of short-term debt, and the payment of dividends.

**Upjohn**—This problem includes Upjohn primarily to compare and contrast it with American Home Products, also a pharmaceutical company. Both companies generated sufficient cash flow from operations to fund capital expenditures and pay dividends. Upjohn sold a portion of its business during the year and invested the proceeds in marketable securities.

# CHAPTER 5

## INTRODUCTION TO FINANCIAL STATEMENT ANALYSIS

*Questions, Exercises, Problems, and Cases: Answers and Solutions*

5.1     See the text or the glossary at the end of the book.

5.2     1.   The firm may have changed its methods of accounting over time.

        2.   The firm may have changed its product lines, production techniques, investment or financing strategies, or even its managerial personnel.

5.3     1.   The firms may use different methods of accounting.

        2.   The firms may pursue different operating, investing, or financing strategies, so that they have different technologies, production techniques, and selling strategies.

5.4     The adjustment in the numerator of rate of return on assets is for the *incremental* effect on *net* income of having versus not having interest expense. Because interest expense reduces taxable income and, therefore, income taxes otherwise payable, the tax savings from interest expense incrementally affect net income. The computation of the numerator must, therefore, incorporate this tax effect.

5.5     The first company apparently has a relatively small profit margin and must rely on turnover to generate a satisfactory rate of return. A discount department store is an example. The second company, on the other hand, has a larger profit margin and does not need as much turnover as the first company to generate a satisfactory rate of return.

5.6     Management strives to keep its inventories at a level that is neither too low so that it loses sales nor too high so that it incurs high storage costs. Thus, there is an optimal level of inventory for a particular firm in a particular period and an optimal inventory turnover ratio.

5.7     The rate of return on common shareholders' equity exceeds the rate of return on assets when the latter rate exceeds the return required by creditors and preferred shareholders (net of tax effects). In this situation, leverage is working to the benefit of the common shareholders. The rate of return on common shareholders' equity will be less than the return on assets when the latter rate is less than the return required by creditors and preferred shareholders. This situation generally occurs during periods of very poor earnings performance.

5.8    This statement suggests that the difference between the rate of return on assets and the aftertax cost of debt is positive but small. Increasing the amount of debt will require a higher interest rate that will eliminate this positive difference and leverage will work to the disadvantage of the common shareholders.

5.9    Financial leverage involves using debt capital that has a smaller aftertax cost than the return a firm can generate from investing the capital in various assets. The excess return belongs to the common shareholders. A firm cannot continually increase the amount of debt in the capital structure without limit. Increasing the debt level increases the risk to the common shareholders. These shareholders will not tolerate risk levels that they consider too high. Also, the cost of borrowing increases as a firm assumes larger proportions of debt. Sooner or later, the excess of the rate of return on assets over the aftertax cost of borrowing approaches zero or even becomes negative. Leverage then works to the disadvantage of the common shareholders.

5.10

|  | Dec. 31, Year 1 | Dec. 31, Year 2 |
|---|---|---|
| Current Assets | $ 800,000 | $ 600,000 |
| Current Liabilities | (400,000) | (240,000) |
| Working Capital | $ 400,000 | $ 360,000 |
| Current Ratio | 2:1 | 2.5:1 |

5.11   (Cracker Barrel Old Country Store and Outback Steakhouse; calculating and disaggregating rate of return on assets.)

a.  **Cracker Barrel:** $\dfrac{\$104,136 + (1 - .35)(\$3,026)}{\$910,407} = 11.7$ percent.

   **Outback:** $\dfrac{\$91,273 + (1 - .35)(\$2,489)}{\$531,312} = 17.5$ percent.

b.

| Rate of Return on Assets | = | Profit Margin Ratio | X Total Asset Turnover Ratio |
|---|---|---|---|

**Cracker Barrel:**

$\dfrac{\$104,136 + (1 - .35)(\$3,026)}{\$910,407} = \dfrac{\$104,136 + (1 - .35)(\$3,026)}{\$1,317,104} \times \dfrac{\$1,317,104}{\$910,407}$

| 11.7 percent | = | 8.1 percent | X | 1.45 |

**Outback:**

$\dfrac{\$91,273 + (1 - .35)(\$2,489)}{\$531,312} = \dfrac{\$91,273 + (1 - .35)(\$2,489)}{\$1,151,637} \times \dfrac{\$1,151,637}{\$531,312}$

| 17.5 percent | = | 8.1 percent | X | 2.17 |

5.11 continued.

c. The analyst might expect Cracker Barrel to have a lower profit margin and a higher asset turnover, given its value pricing policy and the serving of meals all day. Cracker Barrel's profit margin on its restaurants is probably lower than that of Outback. The similar overall profit margins probably result from the ability of Cracker Barrel to generate a higher profit margin on craft items than on its restaurants. The higher asset turnover of Outback may result from locating its restaurants in buildings that were formerly restaurants, perhaps purchasing the properties for lower costs and bypassing zoning and other regulatory costs. Another possible explanation for the faster assets turnover of Outback is that it just serves meals, whereas Cracker Barrel must maintain an inventory of craft items that turn over less rapidly than food.

5.12 (TJX and The GAP; profitability analysis for two types of retailers.)

Company A is the specialty retailer (The GAP) because of its higher profit margin and lower total assets turnover, relative to Company B (TJX).

| | Rate of Return On Assets | = | Profit Margin Ratio | X | Total Assets Turnover Ratio |
|---|---|---|---|---|---|
| Company A | $\dfrac{\$533,901 + (1-.35)(\$0)}{\$2,982,215}$ | = | $\dfrac{\$533,901 + (1-.35)(\$0)}{\$6,507,825}$ | X | $\dfrac{\$6,507,825}{\$2,982,215}$ |
| | 17.9 percent | = | 8.2 percent | X | 2.18 |
| Company B: | $\dfrac{\$306,592 + (1-.35)(\$4,502)}{\$2,585,422}$ | = | $\dfrac{\$306,592 + (1-.35)(\$4,502)}{\$7,389,069}$ | X | $\dfrac{\$7,389,069}{\$2,585,422}$ |
| | 12.0 percent | = | 4.2 percent | X | 2.86 |

5.13 (Gateway 2000 and Sun Microsystems; analyzing accounts receivable for two companies.)

a.

**Gateway 2000**

$$\frac{\$7,866,656}{.5(\$562,154 + \$638,349)}$$

= 13.1 Times per Year.

**Sun Microsystems**

$$\frac{\$9,790,840}{.5(\$1,666,523 + \$1,845,765)}$$

= 5.6 Times per Year.

b. $\dfrac{365}{13.1}$ = 27.9 days.

$\dfrac{365}{5.6}$ = 65.2 days.

5.13 continued.

   c.   Gateway 2000 sells primarily to individuals who pay with credit cards. Gateway 2000 collects these accounts receivable quickly. Sun Microsystems sells to businesses. Customers may require Sun Microsystems to finance their purchases. Customers may also delay paying Sun Microsystems until their computers are set up and working properly. Sun Microsystems may also offer liberal credit terms as an inducement to businesses to purchase its computers.

5.14    (Kellogg; analyzing inventories over three years.)

a.

| Year | Numerator | Denominator | Inventory Turnover |
|---|---|---|---|
| 6 | $ 3,178 | $ 387 | 8.21 |
| 7 | 3,123 | 401 | 7.79 |
| 8 | 3,270 | 430 | 7.60 |

b.

| Year | Numerator | Denominator | Days Inventory Held |
|---|---|---|---|
| 6 | 365 | 8.21 | 44.5 |
| 7 | 365 | 7.79 | 46.9 |
| 8 | 365 | 7.60 | 48.0 |

c.

| Year | Numerator | Denominator | Cost of Goods Sold Percentage |
|---|---|---|---|
| 6 | $ 3,178 | $ 7,004 | 45.4% |
| 7 | 3,123 | 6,677 | 46.8% |
| 8 | 3,270 | 6,830 | 47.9% |

   d.   Kellogg experienced a decreasing inventory turnover and an increasing cost of goods sold to sales percentage. Sales declined between Year 6 and Year 7 and increased only 2.3 percent [= ($6,830/$6,677) − 1] between Year 7 and Year 8. Kellogg experienced difficulty moving its products during this period. It might have lowered prices in an effort to sell cereals, leading to an increasing cost of goods sold percentage. The decreasing inventory turnover suggests either that Kellogg did not obtain the increased volume of sales it anticipated from the lower prices or that Kellogg continued to produce cereals at its usual rate to keep its factories open and workers hired, or some combination of the two.

**5.15** (Anheuser Busch; analyzing fixed asset turnover over three years.)

a.

| Year | Numerator | Denominator | Plant Asset Turnover |
|------|-----------|-------------|----------------------|
| 3 | $10,345 | $ 6,629 | 1.56 |
| 4 | 10,884 | 6,986 | 1.56 |
| 5 | 11,066 | 7,479 | 1.48 |

b. The fixed asset turnover was flat between Year 3 and Year 4, suggesting that sales of Anheuser Busch increased in line with additions to property, plant and equipment. Anheuser Busch increased its capital expenditures significantly in Year 5 and the fixed asset turnover declined. Firms seldom experience increases in sales immediately when they purchase new fixed assets. Thus, the decline in the fixed asset turnover in Year 5 is not a cause for concern.

**5.16** (Circuit City; calculating and disaggregating rate of return on common shareholders' equity.)

a.

| Year | Numerator | Denominator | Rate of Return on Common Shareholders' Equity |
|------|-----------|-------------|-----------------------------------------------|
| 4 | $ 179 | $ 971 | 18.4% |
| 5 | 136 | 1,339 | 10.2% |
| 6 | 104 | 1,672 | 6.2% |

b. **Profit margin**

| Year | Numerator | Denominator | Profit Margin |
|------|-----------|-------------|---------------|
| 4 | $ 179 | $ 7,029 | 2.5% |
| 5 | 136 | 7,664 | 1.8% |
| 6 | 104 | 8,871 | 1.2% |

**Total Asset Turnover**

| Year | Numerator | Denominator | Total Asset Turnover |
|------|-----------|-------------|----------------------|
| 4 | $ 7,029 | $ 2,265 | 3.10 |
| 5 | 7,664 | 2,804 | 2.73 |
| 6 | 8,871 | 3,156 | 2.81 |

**Leverage Ratio**

| Year | Numerator | Denominator | Leverage Ratio |
|------|-----------|-------------|----------------|
| 4 | $ 2,265 | $ 971 | 2.33 |
| 5 | 2,804 | 1,339 | 2.09 |
| 6 | 3,156 | 1,672 | 1.89 |

5.16 continued.

    c.   The rate of return on common shareholders' equity declined steadily during the three-year period. Although Circuit City experienced increased sales, its profit margin probably declined because of increased competition from other superstores (for example, Best Buy) and purchases over the Internet. The total assets turnover declined between Year 4 and Year 5 and increased slightly in Year 6. Circuit City may have opened new stores expecting more growth in sales than it realized. The decreased financial leverage might have resulted from reductions in debt, to increases in common stock, or the retention of earnings. An examination of the financial statements for Circuit City indicates that most of the decreased leverage ratio results from issuing additional common stock.

5.17    (Profitability analysis for three companies.)

a.

| | **Rate of Return on Assets** | = | **Profit Margin** | X | **Total Asset Turnover** |
|---|---|---|---|---|---|
| **Company A:** | $\dfrac{\$69}{\$925}$ | = | $\dfrac{\$69}{\$1,308}$ | X | $\dfrac{\$1,308}{\$925}$ |
| | 7.5 percent | = | 5.3 percent | X | 1.41 |
| **Company B:** | $\dfrac{\$174}{\$1,449}$ | = | $\dfrac{\$174}{\$1,763}$ | X | $\dfrac{\$1,763}{\$1,449}$ |
| | 12.0 percent | = | 9.9 percent | X | 1.22 |
| **Company C:** | $\dfrac{\$359}{\$3,985}$ | = | $\dfrac{\$359}{\$3,817}$ | X | $\dfrac{\$3,817}{\$3,985}$ |
| | 9.0 percent | = | 9.4 percent | X | .96 |

5.17 continued.

b.

| | Rate of Return on Common Shareholders' Equity | = | Profit Margin | X | Total Assets Turnover | X | Leverage Ratio |
|---|---|---|---|---|---|---|---|
| Company A: | $\frac{\$68}{\$664}$ | = | $\frac{\$68}{\$1,308}$ | X | $\frac{\$1,308}{\$925}$ | X | $\frac{\$925}{\$664}$ |
| | 10.2 percent | = | 5.2 percent | X | 1.41 | X | 1.39 |
| Company B: | $\frac{\$174}{\$745}$ | = | $\frac{\$174}{\$1,763}$ | X | $\frac{\$1,763}{\$1,449}$ | X | $\frac{\$1,449}{\$745}$ |
| | 23.4 percent | = | 9.9 percent | X | 1.22 | X | 1.94 |
| Company C: | $\frac{\$318}{\$1,829}$ | = | $\frac{\$318}{\$3,817}$ | X | $\frac{\$3,817}{\$3,985}$ | X | $\frac{\$3,985}{\$1,829}$ |
| | 17.4 percent | = | 8.3 percent | X | .96 | X | 2.18 |

c. Company A is Starbucks, Company B is Harley Davidson, and Company C is Southwest Airlines. Starbucks typically leases the space for its restaurants and, therefore, has few fixed assets. It sells for cash and, therefore, has few accounts receivable. It will maintain some inventory, but the need for freshness of its foods suggests a rapid turnover. Thus, we would expect Starbucks to have the fastest total assets turnover. Harley Davidson needs fixed assets to manufacture its motor cycles and Southwest Airlines needs aircraft and ground facilities to operate its airline. The smaller profit margin for Starbucks is somewhat of a surprise. Competition from other coffee shops and supermarkets with fresh ground coffees probably dampens its profit margin. Starbuck's low leverage ratio reflects its lack of assets to use as collateral for borrowing. The manufacturing of motor cycles is essentially an assembly operation. Thus, Harley Davidson likely needs fewer fixed assets than Southwest Airlines. The larger proportion of fixed assets for Southwest Airlines permits it to have a higher proportion of debt in its capital structure. The slightly higher profit margin of Harley Davidson probably reflects its brand name. Southwest Airlines achieves a relatively high profit margin by spreading its fixed costs over a high volume of business.

5.18    (Profitability analysis for three companies.)

a.

| | Rate of Return on Assets | = | Profit Margin | X | Total Asset Turnover |
|---|---|---|---|---|---|
| Company A: | $\dfrac{\$2,213}{\$15,002}$ | = | $\dfrac{\$2,213}{\$12,504}$ | X | $\dfrac{\$12,504}{\$15,002}$ |
| | 14.8 percent | = | 17.7 percent | X | .83 |
| Company B: | $\dfrac{\$449}{\$8,209}$ | = | $\dfrac{\$449}{\$19,139}$ | X | $\dfrac{\$19,139}{\$8,209}$ |
| | 5.5 percent | = | 2.3 percent | X | 2.33 |
| Company C: | $\dfrac{\$2,254}{\$39,938}$ | = | $\dfrac{\$2,254}{\$22,976}$ | X | $\dfrac{\$22,976}{\$39,938}$ |
| | 5.6 percent | = | 9.8 percent | X | .58 |

b.

| | Rate of Return on Common Shareholders' Equity | = | Profit Margin | X | Total Assets Turnover | X | Leverage Ratio |
|---|---|---|---|---|---|---|---|
| Company A: | $\dfrac{\$2,213}{\$7,444}$ | = | $\dfrac{\$2,213}{\$12,504}$ | X | $\dfrac{\$12,504}{\$15,002}$ | X | $\dfrac{\$15,002}{\$7,444}$ |
| | 29.7 percent | = | 17.7 percent | X | .83 | X | 2.02 |
| Company B: | $\dfrac{\$299}{\$2,422}$ | = | $\dfrac{\$299}{\$19,139}$ | X | $\dfrac{\$19,139}{\$8,209}$ | X | $\dfrac{\$8,209}{\$2,422}$ |
| | 12.3 percent | = | 1.6 percent | X | 2.33 | X | 3.39 |
| Company C: | $\dfrac{\$1,850}{\$18,337}$ | = | $\dfrac{\$1,850}{\$22,976}$ | X | $\dfrac{\$22,976}{\$39,938}$ | X | $\dfrac{\$39,938}{\$18,337}$ |
| | 10.1 percent | = | 8.1 percent | X | .58 | X | 2.18 |

c.    Company B is American Stores. Grocery products are commodities. Competition among many grocery store chains for nondifferentiated products drives the profit margin down. Grocery stores compensate for the low profit margin by a high asset turnover. Many grocery products are perishable and firms must turn them over rapidly. The high leverage ratio for Company B might appear strange for a grocery store chain. American Stores uses long-term debt to finance its buildings and supplier financing for its inventories.

5.18 c. continued.

The principal difference between Company A and Company C is the profit margin percentages. Disney has brand name recognition which might provide a high profit margin. Pfizer has patents to limit competition for its drugs and drive up its profit margin. Company A is somewhat less asset intensive and carries slightly less debt. Company A is Pfizer and Company C is Disney. Disney's theme parks require heavy investments in fixed assets, which Disney can use for long-term borrowing. Technology risk for Pfizer tends to dampen its desire to take on much long-term debt.

5.19    (Relating profitability to financial leverage.)

a.

| Case | Net Income Plus Aftertax Interest Expense[a] | Aftertax Interest Expense[b] | Net Income[c] | Rate of Return on Common Shareholders' Equity |
|------|------|------|------|------|
| A | $12 | $6.0 | $ 6 | $  6/$100  =  6% |
| B | $16 | $6.0 | $10 | $ 10/$100  = 10% |
| C | $16 | $7.2 | $ 8.8 | $  8.8/$80  = 11% |
| D | $ 8 | $6.0 | $ 2 | $  2/$100  =  2% |
| E | $12 | $3.0 | $ 9 | $  9/$100  =  9% |
| F | $10 | $3.0 | $ 7 | $  7/$100  =  7% |

[a]Numerator of the rate of return on assets. In Case A, $12 = .06 \times \$200$.

[b]After tax cost of borrowing times interest-bearing debt. In Case A, $6.0 = .06 \times \$100$.

[c]Net income plus after tax interest expense minus after tax interest expense. In Case A, $6 = \$12 - \$6$.

b.   Leverage works successfully in Cases B, C, E, and F with respect to total debt. With respect to interest-bearing debt, leverage works successfully in Cases B and C.

5.20    (Company A/Company B; interpreting changes in earnings per share.)

a.    **Company A Earnings
        per Share:**

Year 1................    $\dfrac{\$100,000}{100,000\ \text{Shares}} = \$1$ per Share.

Year 2................    $\dfrac{\$100,000}{100,000\ \text{Shares}} = \$1$ per Share.

**Company B Earnings
    per Share:**

Year 1................    $\dfrac{\$100,000}{100,000\ \text{Shares}} = \$1$ per Share.

Year 2................    $\dfrac{.10 \times (\$1,000,000 + \$100,000)}{100,000\ \text{Shares}} = \$1.10$ per Share.

b.    Company A:  No growth.
      Company B:  10 percent annual growth.

c.    Company B:  This result is misleading.  Comparisons of growth in earnings per share are valid only if firms employ equal amounts of assets in the business.  Both the rate of return on assets and on shareholders' equity are better measures of growth performance.  Earnings per share results do not, in general (as in this problem), take earnings retention into account.

5.21    (NIKE; calculating and interpreting short-term liquidity ratios.)

a.  **Current Ratio**

| Year End | Numerator | Denominator | Current Ratio |
|---|---|---|---|
| 5 | $ 2,046 | $ 1,107 | 1.85 |
| 6 | 2,727 | 1,467 | 1.86 |
| 7 | 3,831 | 1,867 | 2.05 |
| 8 | 3,533 | 1,704 | 2.07 |

**Quick Ratio**

| Year End | Numerator | Denominator | Quick Ratio |
|---|---|---|---|
| 5 | $ 1,269 | $ 1,107 | 1.15 |
| 6 | 1,608 | 1,467 | 1.10 |
| 7 | 2,199 | 1,867 | 1.18 |
| 8 | 1,783 | 1,704 | 1.05 |

b.  **Cash Flow from Operations to Current Liabilities Ratio**

| Year | Numerator | Denominator | Cash Flow from Operations to Current Liabilities Ratio |
|---|---|---|---|
| 6 | $ 340 | $ 1,287.0[a] | 26.4% |
| 7 | 323 | 1,667.0[b] | 19.4% |
| 8 | 518 | 1,785.5[c] | 29.0% |

[a].5($1,107 + $1,467) = $1,287.0.
[b].5($1,467 + $1,867) = $1,667.0.
[c].5($1,867 + $1,704) = $1,785.5.

**Accounts Receivable Turnover Ratio**

| Year | Numerator | Denominator | Accounts Receivable Turnover Ratio |
|---|---|---|---|
| 6 | $ 6,471 | $ 1,199.5[a] | 5.39 |
| 7 | 9,187 | 1,550.0[b] | 5.93 |
| 8 | 9,153 | 1,714.0[c] | 5.34 |

[a].5($1,053 + $1,346) = $1,199.5.
[b].5($1,346 + $1,754) = $1,550.0.
[c].5($1,754 + $1,674) = $1,714.0.

5.21 b. continued.

### Inventory Turnover Ratio

| Year | Numerator | Denominator | Inventory Turnover Ratio |
|------|-----------|-------------|--------------------------|
| 6 | $ 3,907 | $ 780.5[a] | 5.01 |
| 7 | 5,503 | 1,135.0[b] | 4.85 |
| 8 | 6,066 | 1,368.0[c] | 4.43 |

[a].5($630 + $931) = $780.5.
[b].5($931 + $1,339) = $1,135.0.
[c].5($1,339 + $1,397) = $1,368.0.

### Accounts Payable Turnover Ratio

| Year | Numerator | Denominator | Accounts Payable Turnover Ratio |
|------|-----------|-------------|---------------------------------|
| 6 | $ 4,208[a] | $ 376.5[d] | 11.18 |
| 7 | 5,911[b] | 571.0[e] | 10.35 |
| 8 | 6,124[c] | 636.0[f] | 9.63 |

[a]$3,907 + $931 − $630 = $4,208.     [d].5($298 + $455) = $376.5.
[b]$5,503 + $1,339 − $931 = $5,911.     [e].5($455 + $687) = $571.0.
[c]$6,066 + $1,397 − $1,339 = $6,124.     [f].5($687 + $585) = $636.0.

c.  Sales increased 42.0 percent [= ($9,187/$6,471) − 1] between Year 6 and Year 7 but decreased between Year 7 and Year 8. The large increase in sales during Year 7 led NIKE to increase inventories in expectation of still higher sales in the future, causing its inventory turnover to decline. To finance the buildup of inventories, NIKE stretched its creditors, slowing the accounts payable turnover. Cash flow from operations to average current liabilities declined between Year 6 and Year 7, because of the need to finance the inventory buildup. The accounts receivable turnover increased between these years, which increased cash flow from operations. The decline in sales between Year 7 and Year 8 permitted NIKE to collect accounts receivable from Year 7 sales, increasing cash flow from operations. The inventory turnover declined still further, suggesting that the decreased sales caught NIKE by surprise. NIKE again stretched its creditors to help finance the inventories. The cash flow from operations to average current liabilities ratio is consistently below the 40 percent level usually found for healthy companies. The current and quick ratios for NIKE, however, are well above 1.0, suggesting little short-term liquidity risk. The principal short-term liquidity concerns for NIKE are its inventory buildup and the continued stretching of creditors.

**5.22**    (Nokia; calculating and interpreting short-term liquidity ratios.)

a. **Current Ratio**

| Year End | Numerator | Denominator | Current Ratio |
|---|---|---|---|
| 2 | EUR 5,431 | EUR 3,091 | 1.76 |
| 3 | 7,814 | 4,453 | 1.75 |
| 4 | 10,792 | 6,372 | 1.69 |
| 5 | 13,560 | 8,594 | 1.58 |

**Quick Ratio**

| Year End | Numerator | Denominator | Quick Ratio |
|---|---|---|---|
| 2 | EUR 3,700 | EUR 3,091 | 1.20 |
| 3 | 5,697 | 4,453 | 1.28 |
| 4 | 7,986 | 6,372 | 1.25 |
| 5 | 9,835 | 8,594 | 1.14 |

b. **Cash Flow from Operations to Current Liabilities Ratio**

| Year | Numerator | Denominator | Cash Flow from Operations to Current Liabilities Ratio |
|---|---|---|---|
| 3 | EUR 1,694 | EUR 3,772.0[a] | 44.9% |
| 4 | 3,009 | 5,412.5[b] | 55.6% |
| 5 | 3,560 | 7,483.0[c] | 47.5% |

[a].5(EUR3,091 + EUR4,453) = EUR3,772.0.
[b].5(EUR4,453 + EUR6,372) = EUR5,412.5.
[c].5(EUR6,372 + EUR8,594) = EUR7,483.0.

**Accounts Receivable Turnover Ratio**

| Year | Numerator | Denominator | Accounts Receivable Turnover Ratio |
|---|---|---|---|
| 3 | EUR13,326 | EUR 2,223.0[a] | 5.99 |
| 4 | 19,772 | 3,316.5[b] | 5.96 |
| 5 | 30,376 | 4,710.5[c] | 6.45 |

[a].5(EUR1,640 + EUR2,806) = EUR2,223.0.
[b].5(EUR2,806 + EUR3,827) = EUR3,316.5.
[c].5(EUR3,827 + EUR5,594) = EUR4,710.5.

5.22 b. continued.

### Inventory Turnover Ratio

| Year | Numerator | Denominator | Inventory Turnover Ratio |
|---|---|---|---|
| 3 | EUR 8,299 | EUR 1,261.0[a] | 6.58 |
| 4 | 12,227 | 1,532.0[b] | 7.98 |
| 5 | 19,072 | 2,017.5[c] | 9.45 |

[a].5(EUR1,230 + EUR1,292) = EUR1,261.0.
[b].5(EUR1,292 + EUR1,772) = EUR1,532.0.
[c].5(EUR1,772 + EUR2,263) = EUR2,017.5.

### Accounts Payable Turnover Ratio

| Year | Numerator | Denominator | Accounts Payable Turnover Ratio |
|---|---|---|---|
| 3 | EUR 8,361[a] | EUR 1,087.5[d] | 7.69 |
| 4 | 12,707[b] | 1,779.5[e] | 7.14 |
| 5 | 19,563[c] | 2,508.0[f] | 7.80 |

[a]EUR8,299 + EUR1,292 − EUR1,230 = EUR8,361.
[b]EUR12,227 + EUR1,772 − EUR1,292 = EUR12,707.
[c]EUR19,072 + EUR2,263 − EUR1,772 = EUR19,563.
[d].5(EUR818 + EUR1,357) = EUR1,087.5.
[e].5(EUR1,357 + EUR2,202) = EUR1,779.5.
[f].5(EUR2,202 + EUR2,814) = EUR2,508.0.

c.   The current and quick ratios both declined during the last four years. The decline occurs primarily because of the increase in the accounts receivable and inventory turnovers. Although the amount of accounts receivable and inventory increased, they did not increase as rapidly as the level of sales and operations. The levels of the current and quick ratios are still quite healthy. The cash flow from operations to average current liabilities ratio increased in Year 4, primarily as a result of reducing the accounts payable turnover (that is, stretching accounts payable) and increasing other current liabilities. The cash flow ratio declined again in Year 4 as Nokia increased its accounts payable turnover. The cash flow ratio still exceeds the 40 percent level commonly found for healthy firms. Thus, the short-term liquidity risk was healthy in all three years and did not change significantly.

5.23    (Ericsson; calculating and interpreting long-term liquidity ratios.)

a.  **Long-Term Debt Ratio**

| Year End | Numerator | Denominator | | Long-Term Debt Ratio |
|---|---|---|---|---|
| 1 | SEK 14,407 | SEK 14,407 + | SEK 57,364 | 20.1% |
| 2 | 19,667 | 19,667 + | 70,320 | 21.9% |
| 3 | 32,298 | 32,298 + | 85,616 | 27.4% |
| 4 | 35,247 | 35,247 + | 109,217 | 24.4% |

**Debt-Equity Ratio**

| Year End | Numerator | Denominator | | Debt-Equity Ratio |
|---|---|---|---|---|
| 1 | SEK 103,483 | SEK 103,483 + | SEK 57,364 | 64.3% |
| 2 | 115,152 | 115,152 + | 70,320 | 62.1% |
| 3 | 148,895 | 148,895 + | 85,616 | 63.5% |
| 4 | 180,208 | 180,208 + | 109,217 | 62.3% |

b.  **Cash Flow from Operations to Total Liabilities Ratio**

| Year | Numerator | Denominator | Cash Flow from Operations to Total Liabilities Ratio |
|---|---|---|---|
| 2 | SEK 7,394 | .5(SEK 103,483 + SEK 115,152) | 6.8% |
| 3 | 12,925 | .5(SEK 115,152 + SEK 148,895) | 9.8% |
| 4 | (10,848) | .5(SEK 148,895 + SEK 180,208) | (6.6)% |

**Interest Coverage Ratio**

| Year | Numerator | Denominator | Times Interest Charges Earned |
|---|---|---|---|
| 2 | SEK 25,020 | SEK 2,532 | 9.9 |
| 3 | 24,293 | 3,041 | 8.0 |
| 4 | 17,191 | 5,166 | 3.3 |

c.  The proportion of debt in the capital structure changed relatively little during the three-year period. There was a slight shift from short-term to long-term debt. The cash flow from operations to average total liabilities ratio is low, relative to the 20 percent level commonly found for healthy firms. The cash flow ratio declined sharply during Year 4. Earnings declined in Year 4 and cash flow from operations turned negative. The interest coverage ratio, while at healthy levels in Year 2 and Year 3, dropped to a worrisome level in Year 4. Thus, the long-term liquidity risk appeared to increase during the three years.

5.24    (American Airlines; calculating and interpreting long-term liquidity ratios.)

a.  **Long-Term Debt Ratio**

| Year End | Numerator | Denominator | Long-Term Debt Ratio |
|---|---|---|---|
| 4 | $ 3,482 | $ 3,482 + $3,233 | 51.9% |
| 5 | 3,095 | 3,095 + 3,646 | 45.9% |
| 6 | 2,503 | 2,503 + 4,528 | 35.6% |
| 7 | 2,319 | 2,319 + 5,354 | 30.2% |

**Debt-Equity Ratio**

| Year End | Numerator | Denominator | Debt-Equity Ratio |
|---|---|---|---|
| 4 | $14,090 | $14,090 + $3,233 | 81.3% |
| 5 | 13,983 | 13,983 + 3,646 | 79.3% |
| 6 | 13,034 | 13,034 + 4,528 | 74.2% |
| 7 | 12,399 | 12,399 + 5,354 | 69.8% |

b.  **Cash Flow from Operations to Total Liabilities Ratio**

| Year | Numerator | Denominator | Cash Flow from Operations to Total Liabilities Ratio |
|---|---|---|---|
| 5 | $ 1,996 | .5($14,090 + $13,983) | 14.2% |
| 6 | 2,139 | .5($13,983 + $13,034) | 15.8% |
| 7 | 2,266 | .5($13,034 + $12,399) | 17.8% |

**Interest Coverage Ratio**

| Year | Numerator | Denominator | Times Interest Charges Earned |
|---|---|---|---|
| 5 | $ 1,086 | $ 273 | 3.98 |
| 6 | 1,331 | 203 | 6.56 |
| 7 | 1,447 | 194 | 7.46 |

c.  The debt ratios of American Airlines steadily declined and the cash flow from operations to average total liabilities ratio and the interest coverage ratio steadily increased, suggesting decreasing long-term solvency risk. American Airlines actually decreased the amount of debt during this period. This exercise offers an opportunity to point out that the numbers in the financial statements can give a misleading picture in some cases. During these years American Airlines replaced capital leases on old aircraft with operating leases on new aircraft. If these operating leases were capitalized, the debt ratios would have increased instead of decreased.

5.25    (Effect of various transactions on financial statement ratios.)

| Transaction | Rate of Return on Common Shareholders' Equity | Current Ratio | Debt-Equity Ratio |
|---|---|---|---|
| a. | No Effect | (1) | Increase |
| b. | Increase | Increase | Decrease |
| c. | No Effect | No Effect | No Effect |
| d. | No Effect | (2) | Decrease |
| e. | No Effect | Increase | No Effect |
| f. | Increase | Decrease | Increase |
| g. | Decrease | Increase | Decrease |
| h. | No Effect | Decrease | Increase |

(1) The current ratio remains the same if it was one to one prior to the transaction, decreases if it was greater than one, and increases if it was less than one.

(2) The current ratio remains the same if it was equal to one prior to the transaction, increases if it was greater than one, and decreases if it was less than one.

5.26    (Effect of various transactions on financial statement ratios.)

| Transaction | Earnings per Common Share | Working Capital | Quick Ratio |
|---|---|---|---|
| a. | Increase | Increase | Increase |
| b. | No Effect | Decrease | Decrease |
| c. | No Effect | No Effect | Decrease |
| d. | No Effect | Increase | Increase |
| e. | No Effect | No Effect | Increase |
| f. | Decrease | Increase | Decrease |

5.27    (Wal-Mart Stores, Inc.; calculating and interpreting profitability and risk ratios.)

a.  1.  Rate of Return on Assets $= \dfrac{\$6{,}295 + (1 - .35)(\$1{,}374)}{.5(\$73{,}381 + \$82{,}613)} = 9.2$ percent.

2.  Profit Margin for Rate of Return on Assets $= \dfrac{\$6{,}295 + (1 - .35)(\$1{,}374)}{\$191{,}329}) = 3.8$ percent.

3.  Total Assets Turnover $= \dfrac{\$191{,}329}{.5(\$73{,}381 + \$82{,}613)} = 2.45$ times.

4.  Cost of Goods Sold/Sales $= \dfrac{\$150{,}255}{\$191{,}329} = 78.5$ percent.

5.  Marketing and Administrative Expense/Sales $= \dfrac{\$31{,}679}{\$191{,}329} = 16.6$ percent.

6.  Interest Expense/Sales $= \dfrac{\$1{,}374}{\$191{,}329} = .7$ percent.

7.  Income Tax Expense/Sales $= \dfrac{\$3{,}692}{\$191{,}329} = 1.9$ percent.

8.  Accounts Receivable Turnover Ratio $= \dfrac{\$191{,}329}{.5(\$1{,}341 + \$1{,}768)} = 123.1$ times.

9.  Inventory Turnover Ratio $= \dfrac{\$150{,}255}{.5(\$19{,}793 + \$21{,}442)} = 7.3$ times.

10.  Fixed Asset Turnover $= \dfrac{\$191{,}329}{.5(\$39{,}001 + \$45{,}413)} = 4.5$ times.

11.  Rate of Return on Common Shareholders' Equity $= \dfrac{\$6{,}295}{.5(\$25{,}834 + \$31{,}343)} = 22.0$ percent.

12.  Profit Margin for Return on Common Shareholders' Equity $= \dfrac{\$6{,}295}{\$191{,}329} = 3.3$ percent.

5.27 a. continued.

13.  Leverage Ratio $= \dfrac{.5(\$73,381 + \$82,613)}{.5(\$25,834 + \$31,343)} = 2.73.$

14.  Current Ratio $= \dfrac{\$26,555}{\$28,949} = .92.$

15.  Quick Ratio $= \dfrac{\$2,054 + \$1,768}{\$28,949} = .13.$

16.  Accounts Payable Turnover $= \dfrac{(\$150,255 + \$21,442 - \$19,793)}{.5(\$13,105 + \$15,092)} = 10.8$ times.

17.  Cash Flow from Operations to Current Liabilities Ratio $= \dfrac{\$10,055}{.5(\$25,803 + \$28,949)} = 36.7$ percent.

18.  Long-Term Debt Ratio $= \dfrac{\$20,138}{(\$20,138 + \$31,343)} = 39.1$ percent.

19.  Total Liabilities to Total Assets Ratio $= \dfrac{\$51,270}{\$82,613} = 62.1$ percent.

20.  Cash Flow from Operations to Total Liabilities Ratio $= \dfrac{\$10,055}{.5(\$47,547 + \$51,270)} = 20.4$ percent.

21.  Interest Coverage Ratio $= \dfrac{(\$6,295 + \$3,692 + \$1,374)}{\$1,374} = 8.3$ times.

5.27 continued.

   b.  **Rate of Return on Assets (ROA)**
       The ROA of Wal-Mart increased slightly between Year 8 and Year 9 and
       then decreased more significantly between Year 9 and Year 10. The
       improved ROA between Year 8 and Year 9 results from an increased
       profit margin offset by a decreased total assets turnover. The
       decreased ROA between Year 9 and Year 10 results from a decreased
       total assets turnover.

       **Profit Margin for ROA**  The increase in the profit margin for ROA
       results from the net effect of a decrease in the cost of goods sold to sales
       percentage and an increase in the selling and administrative expense to
       sales percentage. Most of the change in the overall profit margin
       occurred between Year 8 and Year 9. The profit margin was relatively
       stable between Year 9 and Year 10.

       **Cost of Goods Sold/Sales**  The cost of goods sold to sales percentage
       steadily declined during the three years, while the inventory turnover
       steadily increased. Possible explanations include the following:

       • Improved inventory control systems, which reduced the need for
         inventory markdowns and lowered inventory carrying costs. This
         explanation in particular might relate to incorporation of Wal-Mart's
         inventory control systems in units acquired internationally.

       • Increased influence over suppliers because of Wal-Mart's buying
         power.

       **Selling and Administrative Expense to Sales**  The selling and
       administrative expense to sales percentage steadily increased during
       the three years. Possible explanations include the following:

       • Administrative costs were incurred to identify international
         acquisition candidates, consummate the acquisitions, and then
         digest the acquisitions when completed.

       • Increased costs to promote the supercenter concept and establish
         new stores.

       **Segment Data**  The segment profitability ratios in Exhibit 5.19 in the
       text provide additional insight into the changes in the profit margin
       ratio. Segment data aggregate all operating expenses, so we cannot
       identify what portion of the change in the profitability of a segment is
       due to changes in the cost of goods sold to sales percentage and what
       portion is due to changes in the selling and administrative expense to
       sales percentage.

5.27 b. continued.

- **Increased profit margin in Wal-Mart discount stores and Supercenters between Year 8 and Year 9.** Given that the overall profit margin for the firm increased between Year 8 and Year 9 and was stable between Year 9 and Year 10, we want to look to these first two years to understand the changes in profitability. Given that the expense item that caused the increased profit margin between Year 8 and Year 9 was a reduced cost of goods sold to sales percentage, we look to this expense to understand the higher overall profit margin. The segment data show that the one segment with the largest change in its profit margin between Year 8 and Year 9 was discount stores and supercenters, the explanation for the increased overall profit margin must lie in the cost of goods sold to sales percentage for the discount and supercenter segment. In its annual report, Wal-Mart attributes the lower cost of goods sold to sales percentage in part to "a favorable sales mix of higher margin categories, improvements in shrinkage and markdowns…" One would have expected the shift to grocery products to increase the cost of goods sold to sales percentage. The decreased cost of goods sold to sales percentage for the total company may reflect Wal-Mart's larger size and thereby its ability to exert more control over its suppliers. The sales mix shifted away from the discount stores and supercenter segment, Wal-Mart's most profitable segment, and shifted to its international segment, which has a lower profit margin. This mix shift by itself should have lowered the overall profit margin. The increased profit margin in the discount stores and supercenter segment more than offset the mix shift toward the lower margin international segment and resulted in an increased profit margin overall between Year 8 and Year 9.

- **Decreased percentage of sales from the lower margin Sam's Clubs.** Wal-Mart lists this as part of the reason for the decreased cost of goods sold to sales percentage between Year 8 and Year 9.

- **The percentage of sales from the international segment increased during the three years.** The international segment has a lower profit margin than Wal-Mart's discount stores and supercenters and its profit margin steadily decreased. Thus, one would expect a decline in the overall profit margin from the sale mix shift toward international operations. The fact that this did not occur is attributable to the increased profitability of Wal-Mart's still dominant segment, discount stores and supercenters. Wal-Mart attributes the decreased profit margin in its international segment to markdowns to eliminate obsolete inventory, store remodeling costs, and costs to establish new distribution systems.

- **Decreased losses in Wal-Mart's Distribution segment.** Although Wal-Mart operates its distribution activity as a separate business and therefore must report it separately in its segment data

5.27 b. continued.

its obvious that Wal-Mart does not operate this unit at a profit. The decline over the three years in the size of the negative profit margin should help Wal-Mart's overall profitability. This segment contributes such a small part to the sales mix, however, that its influence is minimal.

**Income Taxes.** Income tax expense as a percentage of sales was relatively steady at 1.9 to 2.0 percent each year. Because income taxes are a tax on income and not sales, we obtain better insight by expressing income taxes as a percentage of income before income taxes. The average income tax rate each year is as follows:

**Year 8:** $2,740/($4,430 + $2,740) = 38.2%
**Year 9:** $3,338/($5,575 + $3,338) = 37.5%
**Year 10:** $3,692/($6,295 + $3,692) = 37.0%

Thus, the average income tax rate declined slightly during the three years. The decrease probably results from the shift in the sales mix to other countries where the tax rate is likely to be lower.

**Total Assets Turnover** The total assets turnover steadily declined during the last three years. We obtain additional insight into the change in the total assets turnover by examining turnover ratios for accounts receivable, inventories, and fixed assets.

**Accounts Receivable Turnover** The increase in the accounts receivable turnover in Year 9 and the decrease in Year 10 are not particularly significant. Wal-Mart makes most of its sales for cash or using a third-party credit card. Thus, it obtains its cash almost immediately (3 days). Accounts receivable represent only 2 percent of total assets. Thus, the increased accounts receivable turnover has little effect on the overall assets turnover.

**Inventory Turnover** Inventories comprise approximately one-third of total assets. The increasing inventory turnover does therefore have a large influence on the total assets turnover. The discussion of the cost of goods sold to sales percentage indicates likely reasons for the increasing inventory turnover. The increasing inventory turnover runs counter to the trend in the total assets turnover.

**Fixed Assets Turnover** The decreased fixed asset turnover results from fixed assets growing faster than sales. The growth in fixed assets relates to both the building of supercenters and the acquisition of retail stores in other countries. Supercenters enter into the denominator of the fixed asset turnover when the capital investment is made, although a full year of sales does not enter the numerator of the ratio for at least a year. Growing the supercenters will therefore have a dampening ef-

5.27 b. continued.

fect on the fixed asset turnover. A part of Wal-Mart's strategy in acquiring retail chains abroad is to install Wal-Mart information systems and policies and thereby improve the profitability of these chains. The decreasing fixed asset turnover suggests that these improvements in productivity have not yet played themselves out for Wal-Mart.

Another factor dampening the total assets turnover in Year 9 is an increase in Other Assets, probably goodwill related to an acquisition.

c. **Rate of Return on Common Shareholders' Equity**
The ROCE increased between Year 8 and Year 9 and then decreased in Year 10. The increase in ROCE between Year 8 and Year 9 results from slightly improved operating profitability (ROA and its components) and increased financial leverage. The decrease in ROCE between Year 9 and Year 10 results from decreased operating profitability offset by increased financial leverage. The increased financial leverage between Year 8 and Year 9 results from increased short- and long-term borrowing related to corporate acquisitions. Because the leverage ratio uses average assets and average shareholders' equity in its computation, financing acquisitions in Year 9 also impacted the leverage ratio for Year 10 and caused it to increase still further.

d. **Short-Term Liquidity Risk**
Wal-Mart's short-term liquidity ratios suggest somewhat increased risk over the three-year period. The deterioration in Year 9 is due primarily to increased short-term borrowing in connection with acquisitions. A current ratio less than 1.0 and a quick ratio of only .13 would appear troublesome. However, Wal-Mart is essentially a cash business. It turns its inventory over quickly (every 50 days on average during Year 10). Thus, its inventory is almost as liquid as the receivables of most other businesses. Its cash flow from operations to average current liabilities ratio is just slightly below the 40 percent benchmark for a healthy firm. The decline below this benchmark at the end of Year 9 is due to the short-term borrowing for corporate acquisitions. Thus, short-term liquidity risk is low for Wal-Mart.

e. **Long-Term Solvency Risk**
Wal-Mart's debt ratios increased in Year 9, primarily to finance corporate acquisitions. Its cash flow from operations to average current liabilities ratio is right around the 20 percent benchmark for a healthy firm. Although the interest coverage ratio declined (related to the increased borrowing related to corporate acquisitions), its interest coverage ratio is still very high. Thus, long-term solvency risk is low for Wal-Mart.

5.28   (The GAP and The Limited; calculating and interpreting profitability and risk ratios.)

The financial statement ratios on pages 5-25, 5-26, and 5-27 form the basis for the responses to the questions raised.

a.   The GAP is more profitable in Year 2, the result of a significantly higher profit margin and slightly higher total assets turnover. The higher profit margin results primarily from a lower cost of goods sold to sales percentage. The clothes of The GAP are more standardized than those of The Limited, perhaps permitting lower manufacturing costs (for example, from quantity discounts on materials, fewer machine setups, less training of employees). The GAP probably also incurs fewer inventory writedowns from obsolescence because its clothing line is less fashion oriented. The faster total asset turnover of The GAP is not due to either inventories or fixed assets, because The Limited has faster turnover ratios for these assets. Accounts receivable comprises such a small proportion of the total assets of both companies that the differences in the accounts receivable turnover ratios exert very little influence on the total assets turnover. The difference in total assets turnover related to the proportion of cash on the balance sheet of each company. Cash averages 6.9 percent of total assets for The GAP for the two years, whereas it averages 11.5 percent of total assets for The Limited. Cash does not generate sales revenue and therefore reduces the total assets turnover of The Limited. The larger rate of return on assets of The GAP carries over to the rate of return on common shareholders' equity. In addition to larger operating profitability, The GAP carries more financial leverage, enhancing its profitability advantage over The Limited even more.

b.   The current and quick ratios suggest that The GAP has more short-term liquidity risk than The Limited. The Limited also pays its suppliers more quickly than The GAP. We have already noted that The Limited has a higher percentage of its assets in cash. On the other hand, the cash flow from operations to average total liabilities ratio for The GAP is much larger than that of The Limited. The GAP's advantage on the cash flow ratio likely results from its superiority profitability. Thus, neither firms displays high short-term liquidity risk.

c.   The GAP has somewhat higher levels of debt than The Limited. However, the superior profitability of The GAP provides it with significantly higher cash flow from operations to average total liabilities and interest coverage ratios. The latter two ratios for The Limited are at such low levels as to suggest considerable long-term solvency risk.

5.28 continued.

|  |  | The GAP | The Limited |
|---|---|---|---|
| 1. | Rate of Return on Assets | $= \dfrac{\$1,127 + (1 - .35)(\$254)}{.5(\$6,613 + \$8,525)} = 17.1$ percent. | $\dfrac{\$439 + (1 - .35)(\$335)}{.5(\$7,765 + \$6,910)} = 9.0$ percent. |
| 2. | Profit Margin for Return on Assets | $= \dfrac{\$1,127 + (1 - .35)(\$254)}{\$11,635} = 11.1$ percent. | $\dfrac{\$439 + (1 - .35)(\$335)}{\$9,723} = 6.8$ percent. |
| 3. | Total Assets Turnover | $= \dfrac{\$11,635}{.5(\$6,613 + \$8,525)} = 1.5$ times per year. | $\dfrac{\$9,723}{.5(\$7,765 + \$6,910)} = 1.3$ times per year. |
| 4. | Cost of Goods Sold to Sales | $= \dfrac{\$6,575}{\$11,635} = 56.5$ percent. | $\dfrac{\$6,109}{\$9,723} = 62.8$ percent. |
| 5. | Selling and Administration Expenses to Sales | $= \dfrac{\$3,043}{\$11,635} = 26.2$ percent. | $\dfrac{\$2,533}{\$9,723} = 26.1$ percent. |
| 6. | Interest Expenses to Sales | $= \dfrac{\$254}{\$11,635} = 2.2$ percent. | $\dfrac{\$335}{\$9,723} = 3.4$ percent. |
| 7. | Income Tax Expenses to Sales | $= \dfrac{\$658}{\$11,635} = 5.7$ percent. | $\dfrac{\$358}{\$9,723} = 3.7$ percent. |
| 8. | Accounts Receivable Turnover | $= \dfrac{\$11,635}{.5(\$30 + \$33)} = 369.4$ times per year. | $\dfrac{\$9,723}{.5(\$78 + \$109)} = 104.0$ times per year. |
| 9. | Inventory Turnover | $= \dfrac{\$6,575}{.5(\$1,056 + \$1,462)} = 5.2$ times per year. | $\dfrac{\$6,109}{.5(\$1,120 + \$1,051)} = 5.6$ times per year. |
| 10. | Fixed Asset Turnover | $= \dfrac{\$11,635}{.5(\$4,525 + \$6,051)} = 2.2$ times per year. | $\dfrac{\$9,723}{.5(\$4,577 + \$4,052)} = 2.3$ times per year. |

5.28 continued

11. Rate of Return on Common Shareholders' Equity

$$= \frac{\$1,127}{.5(\$1,574 + \$2,233)} = 59.2 \text{ percent.}$$

$$\frac{\$439}{.5(\$2,233 + \$2,147)} = 20.0 \text{ percent.}$$

12. Profit Margin for Return on Common Shareholders' Equity

$$= \frac{\$1,127}{\$11,635} = 9.7 \text{ percent.}$$

$$\frac{\$439}{\$9,723} = 4.5 \text{ percent.}$$

13. Leverage Ratio

$$= \frac{.5(\$6,613 + \$8,525)}{.5(\$1,574 + \$2,233)} = 4.0.$$

$$\frac{.5(\$7,765 + \$6,910)}{.5(\$2,233 + \$2,147)} = 3.4.$$

14. Current Ratio: Beginning of Year

$$= \frac{\$1,872}{\$1,553} = 1.2.$$

$$\frac{\$2,318}{\$1,248} = 1.9.$$

End of Year

$$= \frac{\$2,198}{\$1,753} = 1.3.$$

$$\frac{\$2,246}{\$1,238} = 1.8.$$

15. Quick Ratio: Beginning of Year

$$= \frac{\$595}{\$1,553} = .4.$$

$$\frac{\$948}{\$1,246} = .8.$$

End of Year

$$= \frac{\$483}{\$1,753} = .3.$$

$$\frac{\$926}{\$1,238} = .7.$$

16. Cash Flow from Operations to Current Liabilities

$$= \frac{\$1,478}{.5(\$1,553 + \$1,753)} = 89.4 \text{ percent.}$$

$$\frac{\$586}{.5(\$1,248 + \$1,238)} = 47.1 \text{ percent.}$$

17. Accounts Payable Turnover

$$= \frac{\$6,575 + \$1,462 - \$1,056}{.5(\$684 + \$806)} = 9.4 \text{ times per year.}$$

$$\frac{\$6,109 + \$1,051 - \$1,120}{.5(\$290 + \$256)} = 22.1 \text{ times per year.}$$

5.28 continued.

18. Long-Term Debt Ratio:

Beginning of Year:
$$= \frac{\$3,145}{(\$3,145 + \$1,574)} = 66.6 \text{ percent.} \qquad = \frac{\$4,117}{(\$4,117 + \$2,233)} = 64.8 \text{ percent.}$$

End of Year:
$$= \frac{\$4,121}{(\$4,121 + \$2,233)} = 64.9 \text{ percent.} \qquad = \frac{\$3,222}{(\$3,222 + \$2,147)} = 60.0 \text{ percent.}$$

19. Debt-Equity Ratio:

Beginning of Year:
$$= \frac{\$5,039}{\$6,613} = 76.2 \text{ percent.} \qquad \frac{\$5,532}{\$7,765} = 71.2 \text{ percent.}$$

End of Year:
$$= \frac{\$6,292}{\$8,525} = 73.8 \text{ percent.} \qquad \frac{\$4,763}{\$6,910} = 68.9 \text{ percent.}$$

20. Cash Flow from Operations to Total Liabilities:
$$= \frac{\$,478}{.5(\$5,039 + \$6,292)} = 26.1 \text{ percent.} \qquad \frac{\$586}{.5(\$5,532 + \$4,763)} = 11.4 \text{ percent.}$$

21. Interest Coverage Ratio:
$$= \frac{\$1,127 - \$658 + \$254}{\$254} = 8.0 \text{ times.} \qquad \frac{\$439 + \$358 + \$338}{\$335} = 3.4 \text{ times.}$$

5.29    (International Paper Company; interpreting profitability and risk ratios.)

a.  The main reason for the decrease in the cost of goods sold to sales percentage from 80.0 percent in Year 8 to 75.4 percent in Year 9 is the increase in sales volume of 32.3 percent. This is a very capital-intensive company, with significant fixed manufacturing costs. With the greater volume, fixed costs are spread over more units, lowering the unit cost. We also may presume from the increased demand that IPC enjoyed a more favorable marketing climate, enabling price increases, a more profitable sales mix, etc. Finally, the faster inventory turnover should be noted. This typically results in lower carrying costs and obsolescence costs.

b.  Two interacting factors explain the decrease in fixed asset turnover from 1.67 in Year 9 to 1.33 in Year 10. On the one hand, the rate of sales growth slows from 32.3 percent to 1.7 percent. Thus, the numerator essentially is flat. On the other hand, the denominator continues to increase, as International Paper Company expands its productive capacity. Capital expenditures' growth drops from 69.2 percent to 16.7 percent but still is substantially greater than sales growth.

c.  Financial leverage was favorable in Year 10 as evidenced by the fact that the rate of return on common equity of 5.1 percent exceeded the rate of return on assets of 3.6 percent. International Paper Company earns more on its non-common capital (liabilities and preferred stock, if any) than the cost of that capital; the excess goes to the benefit of the common equity.

d.  The reason for the decrease in the current ratio from 1.21 in Year 9 to 1.02 in Year 10 must be that current liabilities have grown relatively more than current assets. The evidence points toward a growth in current assets—cash continues to grow and the turnover of both receivables and inventory slows. The days accounts payable that are outstanding have increased, which increases current liabilities. Also suggestive of an increase in current liabilities is the decrease in the quick ratio.

e.  The decrease in cash flow from operations to total liabilities from 16.3 percent in Year 9 to 9.9 percent in Year 10 is very substantial and is explained primarily by a significant slowing of cash flow from operations. Sales growth has declined from 32.3 percent to 1.7 percent, and the profit margin is down from 8.2 percent to 4.7 percent. Also slowing the cash flow from operations is that the turnover of both receivables and inventory has slowed, resulting in added investment of operating cash flows in these current assets.

5.30    (Marks & Spencer; interpreting profitability and risk ratios.)

   a. Sales grew only 4.7 percent between Year 5 and Year 6 and then decreased in Year 7 and Year 8. Marks & Spencer probably had to mark down its merchandise in order to move it. It may also have had to write down merchandise that it could not sell.

   b. Marks & Spencer likely increased advertising and other marketing expenditures in an effort to stimulate sales. It may have experienced diseconomies of scale as it spread increased administrative expenses over a declining sales base.

   c. The decrease in the income tax expense percentage occurs because of decreased operating profitability. The average income tax rate (income tax expense as a percentage of income before income taxes) actually increased during the period.

   > Year 6:  4.5%/(10.8% +  4.5%) = 29.4%
   > Year 7:  2.5%/(5.3% +  2.5 %) = 32.1%
   > Year 8:  2.5%/(4.2% +  2.5%) = 37.3%

   d. Mark & Spencer increased its capital expenditures significantly in Year 6 and Year 7, yet sales increased only slightly in Year 6 and decreased in Year 7.

   e. Mark & Spencer increased the proportion of debt in the capital structure, particularly long-term debt. Yet, sales declined in Year 7 and Year 8, causing the interest expense to sales percentage to increase.

   f. Financial leverage worked to the advantage of the common shareholders in each year because the rate of return on common shareholders' equity exceeds the rate of return on assets. Financial leverage worked less effectively each year relative to the previous year, however, as decreasing operating profitability narrowed the gap between the return on assets and the after-tax cost of borrowing.

5.31    (Detective analysis; identify company.)

   There are various approaches to this exercise. One approach begins with a particular company, identifies unique financial characteristics (for example, steel companies have a high proportion of property, plant, and equipment among their assets), and then searches the common size financial data to identify the company with that unique characteristic. Another approach begins with the common size data, identifies unusual financial statement relationships (for example, Firm (12) has a high proportion of cash, marketable securities, and receivables among its assets), and then looks over the list of companies to identify the one most likely to have that unusual financial statement relationship. This teaching note employs both approaches.

5.31 continued.

**Firm 12**—The high proportions of cash, marketable securities, and receivables for Firm (12) suggest that it is Fortis, the Dutch insurance and banking company. Insurance companies receive cash from premiums each year and invest the funds in various investment vehicles until needed to pay insurance claims. They recognize premium revenue from the cash received and investment income from investments each year. They must match against this revenue an appropriate portion of the expected cost of insurance claims from policies in force during the year. Fortis includes this amount on the line labeled Operating Expenses in Exhibit 5.28. Operating revenues also includes interest revenue on loans made. One might ask: Why does Fortis have such a high proportion of financing in the form of current liabilities? This balance sheet category includes the estimated cost of claims not yet paid from insurance in force. It also includes deposits by customers to its banks. One might also ask: What types of quality of earnings issues arise for a company like Fortis? One issue relates to the measurement of insurance claims expense each period. The ultimate cost of claims will not be known with certainty until customers make claims and the firm makes settlements. Prior to that time, Fortis must estimate what that cost will be. The need to make such estimates creates the opportunity to manage earnings and lowers the quality of earnings. Another issue relates to estimated uncollectible loans. Fortis recognizes interest revenue from loans each year and must match against this revenue the cost of any loans that will not be repaid. The need to make such estimates also provides management with an opportunity to manage earnings and therefore lowers the quality of earnings.

**Firms (2), (3), (5), and (9)**—There are four firms with research and development (R&D) expenses, (2), (3), (5) and (9). These are likely to be Nestle, Roche Holding, Sun Microsystems, and Toyota Motor in some combination.

Roche Holding and Sun Microsystems are more technology oriented and therefore likely to have a higher percentage of R&D to sales. This suggests that they are Firms (2) and (9) in some combination. The inventories of Firm (9) turn over more slowly at 1.4 times per year (= 27.2/20) than those of Firm (2) at 16.1 times per year (= 45.2/2.8). Firm (9) is also more capital intensive than firm (2). This suggests that Firm (2) is Sun Microsystems and Firm (9) is Roche Holdings. Sun uses only 11.8 cents in fixed assets for each dollar of sales generated. These ratios are consistent with Sun's strategy of outsourcing most of its manufacturing operations. The inventory turnover of Roche is consistent with the making of fewer production runs for each pharmaceutical product to gain production efficiencies. The manufacture of pharmaceuticals is highly automated, consistent with the slower fixed asset turnover of Roche. These two firms have the highest profit margins of the twelve firms studied. Sun is a technology leader in engineering workstations and servers. Roche sells products protected by patents. These advantages permit the firms to achieve high profit margins. Roche has a very high proportion of its assets

**5.31 continued.**

in cash and marketable securities. It generates interest revenue from these investments, which it includes in other revenues. It is interesting to observe the relatively small cost of goods sold to sales percentage for Roche. The manufacturing cost of pharmaceutical products primarily includes the cost of the chemical raw materials, which machines combine into various drugs. Pharmaceutical firms must price their products significantly above manufacturing costs to recoup their investments in R&D. Note also that Sun has very little long-term debt in its capital structure. Computer products have short product life cycles. Lenders are reluctant to lend for a long period because of the concern for technological obsolescence. Computer companies that outsource their production also have few assets that can serve as collateral for long-term borrowing.

This leaves Firms (3) and (5) as Nestle and Toyota Motor in some combination. Firm (5) has a larger amount of receivables relative to sales than Firm (3), consistent with Toyota Motor providing financing for its customers' purchases of automobiles. Nestle will have receivables from wholesalers and distributors of its food products as well, but not to the extent of the multi-year financing of automobiles. The inventory turnover of Firm (3) is 4.5 times a year (= 44.5%/9.9%), whereas the inventory turnover of Firm (5) is 10.6 times a year (= 68%/6.4%). One might at first expect a food processor to have a much higher inventory turnover than an automobile manufacturer, suggesting that Firm (3) is Toyota Motor and Firm (5) is Nestle. Toyota Motor, however, has implemented just-in-time inventory systems, which speed its inventory turnover. Nestle tends to manufacture chocolates to meet seasonal demands, and therefore carries inventory somewhat longer than one might expect. Firm (3) has a much higher percentage of selling and administrative expense to sales than Firm (5). Both of these firms advertise their products heavily. It is difficult to know why one would have a substantially different percentage than the other. The profit margin of Firm (3) is substantially higher than that of Firm (5). The auto industry is more competitive than at least the chocolate side of the food industry. However, other food products encounter extensive competition. Firm (5) has a high proportion of intercorporate investments. Japanese companies tend to operate within groups, called *kieretsu*. The members of the group make investments in the securities of other firms within the group. This would suggest that Firm (5) is Toyota Motor. Another characteristic of Japanese companies is their heavier use of debt in their capital structures. One of the members of these Japanese corporate groups is typically a bank, which lends to group members as needed. With this more-or-less assured source of funds, Japanese firms tend to take on more debt. Although the ratios give somewhat confusing signals, Firm (3) is Nestle and Firm (5) is Toyota Motor.

5.31 continued.

**Firms 10 and 11**—Firms (10) and (11) are unique in that they are both very fixed-asset intensive. Electric utilities and telecommunication firms both utilize fixed assets in the delivery of their services. Firm (11) is the most fixed-asset intensive of the two firms and carries a higher proportion of long-term debt. Electric-generating plants are more fixed-asset intensive than the infrastructure needed for distribution of telecommunication services. This would suggest that Firm (10) is Deutsche Telekon and Firm (11) is Tokyo Electric Power. The telecommunication industry is going through deregulation whereas Tokyo Electric Power still has a monopoly position in Japan. Thus, the selling and administrative expense to operating revenues percentage for Deutsche Telekon is substantially higher than for Tokyo Electric Power.

**Firms (6) and (8)**—Two of the remaining industries are also capital intensive, but not to the extent of Deutsche Telekon and Tokyo Electric Power. These firms are Accor, a hotel group, and Arbed-Acier, a steel manufacturer. Firms (6) and (8) require the next highest fixed assets per dollar of sales after Firms (10 and (11). Thus, Firms (6) and (8) are Accor and Arbed-Acier in some combination. Firm (8) has virtually no inventories, whereas Firm (6) has substantial inventories. This suggests that Firm (6) is Arbed-Acier, the steel company, and Firm (8) is Accor, the hotel group. Accor has grown in recent years by acquiring established hotel chains. Accor allocates a portion of the purchase price to goodwill in its acquisitions, which accounts for its higher percentage for Other Assets. Steel products are commodities, whereas hotels have some brand recognition appeal. These factors may explain the higher profit margin for Firm (6) than for Firm (8).

**Firm (7)**—Firm (7) has an unusually high proportion of its assets in receivables and in current liabilities. Although this pattern would be typical for a commercial bank, we identified Firm (12) earlier as the financial institution. The pattern is also typical for an advertising agency, which creates and sells advertising copy for clients (for which it has a current receivable) and purchasing time and space on various media to display it (for which it has a current liability). Additional evidence that Firm (7) is Interpublic Group is the high percentage for Other Assets, representing goodwill from acquisitions. Firm (7) also has a relatively high profit margin percentage, reflective of its ability to differentiate its creative services.

**Firm (1)**—Firm (1) is distinguished by its high cost of goods sold to sales and small profit margin percentages. This pattern suggests commodity products with low value added. Of the remaining firms, this characterizes a grocery business. Firm (1) is Carrefour. Its combination of a rapid receivables turnover of 11.8 times per year (= 100/8.5) and rapid inventory turnover of 8.9 times per year (= 87.8/9.9) are also consistent with a grocery business. Current liabilities comprise more than half of its financing. Current assets make up a similarly high proportion of its current assets.

5.31 continued.

> **Firm (4)**—The remaining firm is Firm (4), which is Marks & Spencer the department store chain. Firm (4) has substantial receivables, consistent with having a credit card.

5.32 (Wal-Mart Stores, Inc.; preparing pro forma financial statements requires Appendix 5.1.)

> a. See attached pro forma financial statements and related financial ratios.
>
> b. The statement of cash flows suggests several explanations for the deficit in cash. First, note that cash flow from operations is insufficient to finance capital expenditures and other investing activities. Capital expenditures and other investing activities are projected to grow 16.1 percent per year, whereas sales are projected to grow only 15.9 percent per year. The rationale for the different growth rates is that Wal-Mart will continue to grow the number of superstores and engage in international acquisitions. Slowing down the growth rate in capital expenditures will solve the cash flow problem, but one must ask if this is reasonable. The growth rate in property, plant and equipment has exceeded the growth rate in sales during the preceding three years. A second possibility is that the projections do not assume a fast enough growth in long-term debt. Although we assume that long-term debt will grow at the growth rate in property, plant and equipment, long-term debt at the end of fiscal Year 10 of $20,138 is much less than property, plant and equipment of $45,417. Growing both amounts at 16.1 percent will result in an increasing gap between the two amounts. One possibility is to grow long-term debt faster than property, plant and equipment. Growing long-term debt at 1.4 times the growth rate in property, plant and equipment will solve the cash deficit problem. Another possibility is to grow common stock sufficiently to solve the cash flow problem. This approach, however, requires a very large increase in common stock. Still another possibility is to reduce the assumed growth rate in dividends. However, a growth rate in dividends of just 10 percent will not solve the cash flow problem.

5.32 a. continued.

The following pro forma financial statements were generated by a spreadsheet program that rounds to many decimal places. Rounding causes some of the sub-totals and totals to differ from the sum of the amounts that comprise them.

## WAL-MART STORES, INC.
## PRO FORMA INCOME STATEMENT
## YEAR ENDED JANUARY 31

|  | Year 10 | Year 11 | Year 12 | Year 13 | Year 14 |
|---|---|---|---|---|---|
| Sales Revenue.............. | $ 191,329 | $ 221,750 | $ 257,009 | $ 297,873 | $ 345,235 |
| Other Revenues............ | 1,966 | 2,218 | 2,570 | 2,979 | 3,452 |
| Total Revenues......... | $ 193,295 | $ 223,968 | $ 259,579 | $ 300,852 | $ 348,687 |
| Expenses: |  |  |  |  |  |
| Cost of Goods Sold.... | $ 150,255 | $ 173,852 | $ 201,495 | $ 233,532 | $ 270,664 |
| Selling and Admin-istration.................. | 31,679 | 37,254 | 43,177 | 50,043 | 57,999 |
| Interest ...................... | 1,374 | 1,315 | 1,352 | 1,495 | 1,646 |
| Income Taxes............ | 3,692 | 4,318 | 5,069 | 5,902 | 6,873 |
| Total Expenses...... | $ 187,000 | $ 216,740 | $ 251,093 | $ 290,973 | $ 337,183 |
| Net Income.................... | $ 6,295 | $ 7,228 | $ 8,485 | $ 9,879 | $ 11,504 |
| Dividends...................... | (1,070) | (1,327) | (1,645) | (2,040) | (2,530) |
| Increase in Retained Earnings.................... | $ 5,225 | $ 5,901 | $ 6,840 | $ 7,839 | $ 8,975 |

## Assumptions:

| | | |
|---|---|---|
| Growth Rate of Sales.... | 15.9% | |
| Other Revenues............ | 1.0% | of sales |
| Cost of Goods Sold......... | 78.4% | of sales |
| Selling and Administra-tion ............................... | 16.8% | of sales |
| Interest Expense........... | 5.0% | of interest bearing debt |
| Income Tax Rate........... | 37.4% | of income before income taxes |
| Dividends........................ | 24.0% | growth rate |

5.32 a. continued.

## WAL-MART STORES, INC.
## PRO FORMA BALANCE SHEET
## JANUARY 31

| | Year 10 | Year 11 | Year 12 | Year 13 | Year 14 |
|---|---|---|---|---|---|
| Cash | $ 2,054 | $ (1,816) | $ (3,220) | $ (4,004) | $ (6,633) |
| Accounts Receivable | 1,768 | 2,049 | 2,375 | 2,753 | 3,190 |
| Inventories | 21,442 | 24,851 | 28,803 | 33,382 | 38,690 |
| Prepayments | 1,291 | 1,496 | 1,734 | 2,010 | 2,329 |
| Total Current Assets | $ 26,555 | $ 26,580 | $ 29,692 | $ 34,141 | $ 37,577 |
| Property, Plant and Equipment | 45,417 | 30,032 | 34,237 | 39,030 | 44,494 |
| Other Assets | 10,641 | 2,717 | 3,043 | 3,408 | 3,817 |
| Total Assets | $ 82,613 | $ 53,452 | $ 59,402 | $ 66,305 | $ 72,771 |
| Accounts Payable | $ 15,092 | $ 17,734 | $ 20,311 | $ 23,783 | $ 27,322 |
| Notes Payable | 2,286 | 2,654 | 3,081 | 3,577 | 4,153 |
| Current Portion— Long Term Debt | 4,375 | 1,362 | 809 | 1,926 | 750 |
| Other Current Liabilities | 7,196 | 8,340 | 9,666 | 11,203 | 12,984 |
| Total Current Liabilities | $ 28,949 | $ 30,090 | $ 33,868 | $ 40,490 | $ 45,210 |
| Long-Term Debt | 20,138 | 21,799 | 24,369 | 26,057 | 29,381 |
| Other Noncurrent Liabilities | 2,183 | 2,530 | 2,932 | 3,399 | 3,939 |
| Total Liabilities | $ 51,270 | $ 54,419 | $ 61,170 | $ 69,945 | $ 78,530 |
| Common Stock | $ 447 | $ 447 | $ 447 | $ 447 | $ 447 |
| Additional Paid-in Capital | 1,411 | 1,411 | 1,411 | 1,411 | 1,411 |
| Retained Earnings | 29,485 | 35,386 | 42,226 | 50,065 | 59,040 |
| Total Shareholders' Equity | $ 31,343 | $ 37,244 | $ 44,084 | $ 51,923 | $ 60,898 |
| Total Liabilities and Shareholders' Equity | $ 82,613 | $ 91,664 | $ 105,254 | $ 121,868 | $ 139,428 |

**(See Following Page for Assumptions)**

5.32 a. continued.

## (Assumptions for Pro Forma Balance Sheet)

**Assumptions:**

| | |
|---|---|
| Cash............................... | PLUG |
| Accounts Receivable .... | Sales Growth Rate |
| Inventory ....................... | Sales Growth Rate |
| Prepayments.................. | Sales Growth Rate |
| Property, Plant and Equipment.................. | 16.1% Growth Rate |
| Other Assets ................. | 16.1% Growth Rate |
| Accounts Payable Turnover ..................... | 10.8 |

| | | | | |
|---|---|---|---|---|
| Merchandise Pur-chases.......................... | 177,262 | 205,446 | 238,112 | 275,972 |
| Average Payables ......... | 16,413 | 19,023 | 22,047 | 25,553 |

| | |
|---|---|
| Notes Payable............... | Property, Plant and Equipment Growth Rate |
| Other Current Liabilities .................... | Sales Growth Rate |
| Long-Term Debt ............ | Property, Plant and Equipment Growth Rate |
| Other Noncurrent Liabilities ................... | Sales Growth Rate |
| Common Stock, APIC............................ | 0.0% Growth Rate |

5.32 a. continued.

**WAL-MART STORES, INC.**
**PRO FORMA STATEMENT OF CASH FLOWS**
**FOR THE YEAR ENDED JANUARY 31**

| Cash Flow Statement | Year 10 | Year 11 | Year 12 | Year 13 | Year 14 |
|---|---|---|---|---|---|
| Operations: | | | | | |
| Net Income.................. | $ 6,295 | $ 7,228 | $ 8,485 | $ 9,879 | $ 11,504 |
| Depreciation and Amortization.................. | 2,868 | 3,330 | 3,866 | 4,488 | 5,211 |
| Other........................... | 0 | 347 | 402 | 466 | 540 |
| (Inc.)/Dec. in Accounts Receivable........................... | (422) | (281) | (326) | (378) | (438) |
| (Inc.)/Dec. in Inventory........................... | (1,795) | (3,409) | (3,951) | (4,580) | (5,308) |
| (Inc.)/Dec. in Prepayments................. | 75 | (205) | (238) | (276) | (320) |
| Inc./(Dec.) in Accounts Payable....... | 2,061 | 2,642 | 2,577 | 3,472 | 3,539 |
| Inc./(Dec.) in Other Current Liabilities........................... | 522 | 1,144 | 1,326 | 1,537 | 1,781 |
| Cash Flow from Operations................... | $ 9,604 | $ 10,795 | $ 12,141 | $ 14,610 | $ 16,511 |
| Investing: | | | | | |
| Acquisition of Property, Plant and Equipment....... | $ (8,042) | $(10,475) | $(12,162) | $(14,120) | $(16,393) |
| Other Investing........... | (672) | (1,880) | (2,182) | (2,534) | (2,942) |
| Cash Flow from Investing...................... | $ (8,714) | $(12,355) | $(14,344) | $(16,654) | $(19,335) |
| Financing: | | | | | |
| Inc./(Dec.) in Short-Term Borrowing...... | $ (2,022) | $ 368 | $ 427 | $ 496 | $ 576 |
| Inc./(Dec.) in Long-Term Borrowing...... | 2,086 | (1,352) | 2,017 | 2,804 | 2,148 |
| Inc./(Dec.) in Common Stock................ | 388 | 0 | 0 | 0 | 0 |
| Dividends...................... | (1,070) | (1,327) | (1,645) | (2,040) | (2,530) |
| Other Financing.......... | (74) | 0 | 0 | 0 | 0 |
| Cash Flow from Financing..................... | $ (692) | $ (2,311) | $ 799 | $ 1,260 | $ 195 |
| Change in Cash............. | $ 198 | $ (3,870) | $ (1,403) | $ (784) | $ (2,629) |
| Cash, Beginning of Year............................. | 1,856 | 2,054 | (1,816) | (3,220) | (4,004) |
| Cash, End of Year.......... | $ 2,054 | $ (1,816) | $ (3,220) | $ (4,004) | $ (6,633) |

**(See Following Page for Assumptions)**

5.32 a. continued.

## (Assumptions for Pro Forma Statement of Cash Flows)

**Assumptions:**

| | |
|---|---|
| Depreciation and Amortization Growth Rate .......................... | Same as Property, Plant, and Equipment |
| Other Operating Add-backs .......................... | Change in Noncurrent Liabilities |
| Other Investing Cash Flows.......................... | Change in Other Noncurrent Assets |

## WAL-MART STORES, INC.
## PRO FORMA FINANCIAL RATIOS

| | Year 10 | Year 11 | Year 12 | Year 13 | Year 14 |
|---|---|---|---|---|---|
| Rate of Return on Assets...... | 9.22% | 9.24% | 9.48% | 9.52% | 9.59% |
| Profit Margin for ROA............ | 3.8% | 3.6% | 3.6% | 3.6% | 3.6% |
| Total Assets Turnover........... | 2.45 | 2.54 | 2.61 | 2.62 | 2.64 |
| Cost of Goods Sold/Sales ....... | 78.5% | 78.4% | 78.4% | 78.4% | 78.4% |
| Selling and Administrative Expenses/Sales............ | 16.6% | 16.8% | 16.8% | 16.8% | 16.8% |
| Interest Expense/Sales ......... | 0.7% | 0.6% | 0.5% | 0.5% | 0.5% |
| Income Tax Expense/Sales... | 1.9% | 1.9% | 2.0% | 2.0% | 2.0% |
| Accounts Receivable Turnover Ratio............................. | 123.1 | 116.2 | 116.2 | 116.2 | 116.2 |
| Inventory Turnover Ratio..... | 7.3 | 7.5 | 7.5 | 7.5 | 7.5 |
| Fixed Assets Turnover Ratio.................................... | 4.5 | 4.5 | 4.5 | 4.5 | 4.5 |
| Rate of Return on Common Equity.................................. | 22.0% | 21.1% | 20.9% | 20.6% | 20.4% |
| Profit Margin for ROCE......... | 3.3% | 3.3% | 3.3% | 3.3% | 3.3% |
| Leverage Ratio........................ | 2.7 | 2.5 | 2.4 | 2.4 | 2.3 |
| Current Ratio .......................... | 0.92 | 0.88 | 0.88 | 0.84 | 0.83 |
| Quick Ratio ............................. | 0.13 | 0.01 | −0.02 | −0.03 | −0.08 |
| Cash Flow from Operations/ Current Liabilities.............. | 35.1% | 36.6% | 38.0% | 39.3% | 38.5% |
| Accounts Payable Turnover Ratio...................................... | 10.8 | 10.8 | 10.8 | 10.8 | 10.8 |
| Long-Term Debt Ratio........... | 39.1% | 36.9% | 35.6% | 33.4% | 32.5% |
| Debt-Equity Ratio .................. | 62.1% | 59.4% | 58.1% | 57.4% | 56.3% |
| Cash Flow from Operations/ Total Liabilities.................... | 19.4% | 20.4% | 21.0% | 22.3% | 22.2% |
| Interest Coverage Ratio........ | 8.3 | 9.8 | 11.0 | 11.6 | 12.2 |

# CHAPTER 6

## RECEIVABLES AND REVENUE RECOGNITION

*Questions, Exercises, Problems, and Cases: Answers and Solutions*

6.1     See the text or the glossary at the end of the book.

6.2     The allowance method, because it reports bad debt expense during the period of the sale, not during the later period(s) when the specific accounts become uncollectible.

6.3     The direct write-off method matches the loss from an uncollectible account with revenue of the period when a particular account becomes uncollectible. The allowance method matches the loss from an uncollectible account with revenue of the period of the sale instead of the later period when a particular account becomes uncollectible.

6.4     a.  A firm with stable sales (both volume and price) and a constant proportion of uncollectible accounts will likely report similar amounts for bad debt expense each period.

        b.  The direct write-off method should always result in larger amounts for accounts receivable-net on the balance sheet than the allowance method.

6.5     a.  This statement is valid. Most businesses ought not to set credit policies so stringent that they have no uncollectible accounts. To do so would require extremely careful screening of customers, which is costly, and the probable loss of many customers who will take their business elsewhere. So long as the revenues collected from credit sales exceed the sum of both selling costs and the cost of goods sold on credit, then the firm should not be concerned if some percentage of its accounts receivable are uncollectible.

        b.  If a business liberalizes its credit policy by granting to a group of customers, who were not previously granted this privilege, the right to buy on account, it can find that its net revenues from the new credit customers exceed the cost of goods sold to them and the selling expenses of executing the sales. The extension of credit to new customers can increase net income even though it results in more uncollectible accounts.

6.5 continued

    c.   When the net present value of the receipts from selling to new customers is larger than the net present value of the costs of putting goods into their hands.

6.6    If a firm computes the Bad Debt Expense figure at the end of the accounting period but writes off specific accounts receivable during the period as information about uncollectible accounts becomes available, then the Allowance for Uncollectibles will have a debit balance whenever the amount of accounts written off during the period exceeds the opening credit balance in the Allowance account. Firms prepare balance sheets only after making adjusting entries. Both the Bad Debt Expense and the Allowance for Uncollectibles accounts must be made current with appropriate adjusting entries before preparing the balance sheet. Because the Allowance for Uncollectibles account is an asset contra, it will always show a credit (or perhaps a zero) balance after making adjusting entries.

6.7    Manufacturing firms typically do not identify a customer or establish a firm selling price until they sell products. Thus, these firms do not satisfy the criteria for revenue recognition while production is taking place. In contrast, construction companies usually identify a customer and establish a contract price before construction begins. In addition, the production process for a manufacturing firm is usually much shorter than for a construction firm. The recognition of revenue at the time of production or at the time of sale does not result in a significantly different pattern of income for a manufacturing firm. For a construction company, the pattern of income could differ significantly.

6.8    Under the installment method, accountants recognize proportionate parts of the costs incurred as expenses each period as they recognize proportionate parts of the selling price as revenues. Under the cost-recovery-first method, costs match dollar-for-dollar with revenues until revenues equal total costs. Thus, the income patterns differ because of the *expense* recognition pattern, not the revenue recognition pattern.

6.9    Under both the installment method and the cash basis of accounting, accountants recognize revenue when the firm receives cash. The installment method recognizes expenses in the same period as the associated revenues. The cash basis recognizes expenses when the firm makes cash expenditures.

6.10    Application of the installment method requires a reasonably accurate estimate of the total amount of cash the firm expects to receive from customers. The cost-recovery-first method does not require such an estimate.

6.11 Accountants are more concerned with the objectivity or reliability of income data than are economists. Accountants are responsible for measuring and auditing income amounts and, therefore, require objective measures of wealth changes. Such evidence usually takes the form of market transactions.

6.12 The user of the financial statements must identify the reason for the decline in the quality of earnings. Does the measurement of revenues and expenses for a particular business require numerous estimates? Is there evidence that the firm has used the inherent flexibility in the measurement of revenues and expenses to its advantage? Is the declining quality of earnings due to unusual or nonrecurring items which the financial statement user can exclude when assessing operating profitability? In some cases the financial statement user can adjust net income to eliminate the source of the decreasing earnings quality; in other cases, such adjustments are not possible.

6.13 (Kesler Company; journal entries for the allowance method.)

a. **Year 6**

| | | |
|---|---|---|
| Bad Debt Expense.................................................... | 8,400 | |
|    Allowance for Uncollectible Accounts ................. | | 8,400 |
| .02 × $420,000 = $8,400. | | |

| | | |
|---|---|---|
| Allowance for Uncollectible Accounts....................... | 1,200 | |
|    Accounts Receivable............................................. | | 1,200 |

**Year 7**

| | | |
|---|---|---|
| Bad Debt Expense.................................................... | 9,600 | |
|    Allowance for Uncollectible Accounts ................. | | 9,600 |
| .02 × $480,000 = $9,600. | | |

| | | |
|---|---|---|
| Allowance for Uncollectible Accounts....................... | 7,000 | |
|    Accounts Receivable............................................. | | 7,000 |

**Year 8**

| | | |
|---|---|---|
| Bad Debt Expense.................................................... | 11,000 | |
|    Allowance for Uncollectible Accounts ................. | | 11,000 |
| .02 × $550,000 = $11,000. | | |

| | | |
|---|---|---|
| Allowance for Uncollectible Accounts....................... | 9,700 | |
|    Accounts Receivable............................................. | | 9,700 |

b. Yes. Uncollectible accounts arising from sales of Years 6, 7 and 8 total $28,800, which equals 1.99 percent (= $28,800/$1,450,000) of total sales on account during the three year period.

6.14    (Emmons Corporation; journal entries for the allowance method.)

a.  **Dec. 31**
    Bad Debt Expense......................................................  45,000
        Allowance for Uncollectible Accounts .................          45,000
    .03 × $1,500,000 = $45,000.

    Allowance for Uncollectible Accounts......................  2,300
        Accounts Receivable.............................................          2,300

    **Year 2**
    Bad Debt Expense......................................................  54,000
        Allowance for Uncollectible Accounts .................          54,000
    .03 × $1,800,000 = $54,000.

    Allowance for Uncollectible Accounts......................  22,100
        Accounts Receivable.............................................          22,100

    **Year 3**
    Bad Debt Expense......................................................  72,000
        Allowance for Uncollectible Accounts .................          72,000
    .03 × $2,400,000 = $72,000.

    Allowance for Uncollectible Accounts......................  38,000
        Accounts Receivable.............................................          38,000

b.  No. The actual loss experience is 2 percent (= $113,800/$5,700,000) of
    sales on account for sales during Years 1 through 3.

6.15    (Pandora and Milton; Allowance method: reconstructing journal entry from
        events.)

a.  **Pandora**
    Bad Debt Expense......................................................  3,700
        Allowance for Uncollectibles.................................          3,700
    Write-off of $2,200 + Ending Balance of Allow-
    ance of $5,000 − Beginning Balance of $3,500 =
    $3,700.

6.15 continued.

b.

| Accounts Receivable | | | Allowance for Uncollectible Accounts | |
|---|---|---|---|---|
| √ 15,200,000 | | | | 1,400,000  √ |
| (see below) | | | | (see below) |
| √ 17,600,000 | | | | 1,550,000  √ |

Accounts Receivable................................................ 75,000,000
   Sales....................................................................                 75,000,000
$750,000 is 1 percent of sales; sales = $750,000/.01.

Bad Debt Expense....................................................     750,000
   Allowance for Uncollectible Accounts .....................              750,000

Allowance for Uncollectible Accounts .........................     600,000
   Accounts Receivable...............................................              600,000
$1,400,000 + $750,000 − $1,550,000 = $600,000.

Cash ..................................................................... 72,000,000
   Accounts Receivable...............................................              72,000,000
$15,200,000 + $75,000,000 − $600,000 −
$17,600,000 = $72,000,000.

6.16    (Seward Corporation; reconstructing events when using the allowance method.)

| Cash | | Accounts Receivable | | Allowance for Uncollectible Accounts | |
|---|---|---|---|---|---|
| | | √  82,900 | | | 8,700  √ |
| (4) 231,200 | | (1) 240,000 | 4,400 (3) | (3)  4,400 | 4,800  (2) |
| | | | 231,200 (4) | | |
| | | √  87,300 | | | 9,100  √ |

| Bad Debt Expense | | Sales | |
|---|---|---|---|
| -- | | | -- |
| (2)  4,800 | | | 240,000 (1) |
| √  4,800 | | | 240,000 |

(1)  Sales on account.
(2)  Provision for estimated uncollectible accounts.
(3)  Write off of actual uncollectible accounts.
(4)  Collection of cash from customers for sales on account.

6.17    (Logue Corporation; reconstructing events when using the allowance method.)

| Cash | | Accounts Receivable | | Allowance for Uncollectible Accounts | |
|---|---|---|---|---|---|
| | | √ 115,900 | | | 18,200 √ |
| (3) 422,100 | | (1) 450,000 | 21,100 (2) | (2) 21,100 | |
| | | | 422,100 (3) | | |
| | | √ 122,700 | | √ 2,900 | |
| | | | | | 27,000 (4) |
| | | | | | 24,100 √ |

| Bad Debt Expense | | Sales | |
|---|---|---|---|
| -- | | -- | |
| (4) 27,000 | | | 450,000 (1) |
| √ 27,000 | | | 450,000 √ |

(1) Sales on account.
(2) Write off of actual uncollectible accounts during year.
(3) Collection of cash from customers for sales on account.
(4) Provision for estimated uncollectible accounts on December 31.
.06 X $450,000 = $27,000.

6.18    (Dove Company; aging accounts receivable.)

Bad Debt Expense............................................................  3,700
    Allowance for Uncollectible Accounts ....................           3,700
To adopt auditor's suggestion that total allowance
now be $20,900 [(= .005 X $400,000) + (.01 X $90,000)
+ (.10 X $40,000) + (.70 X $20,000)].  $20,900 –
$17,200 = $3,700.

6.19    (Rorke Company; aging accounts receivable.)

Allowance for Uncollectible Accounts .........................  6,250
    Bad Debt Expense.......................................................           6,250

The Allowance account requires a balance of $29,750 = (.005 X $700,000) + (.01 X $225,000) + (.10 X $90,000) + (.30 X $50,000).  The adjusting entry *reduces* the Allowance account by $6,250 (= $36,000 – $29,750) and reduces Bad Debt Expense for the period by the same amount.

6.20   (Reconstructing events from journal entries.)

a.  Estimated bad debt expense for the period is $2,300 using the allowance method.

b.  A firm writes off specific customers' accounts totaling $450 as uncollectible under the allowance method.

c.  A firm writes off specific customers' accounts totaling $495 as uncollectible under the direct write-off method.

6.21   (Home and Office Depot; effects of transactions involving suppliers and customers on cash flows.)

a.  $127,450 = $130,000 − ($8,600 − $8,000) + ($750 − $700) − $2,000
           = $130,000 − $600 + $50 − $2,000

b.  $85,100 = $85,000 − ($7,500 − $7,000) + ($10,400 − $10,000) +
              ($11,200 − $11,000)
           = $85,000 − $500 + $400 + $200

6.22   (Bechtel Construction Company; percentage-of-completion and completed contract methods of income recognition.)

**Percentage-of-Completion Method**

| Year | Degree of Completion | | Revenue | Expense | Income |
|---|---|---|---|---|---|
| 1 | $ 800,000/$3,200,000 | = 25.0% | $1,000,000 | $ 800,000 | $ 200,000 |
| 2 | $1,920,000/$3,200,000 | = 60.0% | 2,400,000 | 1,920,000 | 480,000 |
| 3 | $ 480,000/$3,200,000 | = 15.0% | 600,000 | 480,000 | 120,000 |
| | | | $4,000,000 | $3,200,000 | $800,000 |

**Completed Contract Method**

| Year | Revenue | Expense | Income |
|---|---|---|---|
| 1 | -- | -- | -- |
| 2 | -- | -- | -- |
| 3 | $4,000,000 | $3,200,000 | $800,000 |
| | $4,000,000 | $3,200,000 | $800,000 |

6.23 (JMB Realty Partners; installment and cost-recovery-first methods of income recognition.)

**Installment Method**

| Year | Revenue | Percentage of Selling Price | Expense | Income |
|------|---------|------------------------------|---------|--------|
| 1 | $ 25,000 | 25% | $15,000 | $10,000 |
| 2 | 25,000 | 25% | 15,000 | 10,000 |
| 3 | 25,000 | 25% | 15,000 | 10,000 |
| 4 | 25,000 | 25% | 15,000 | 10,000 |
| | $100,000 | | $60,000 | $40,000 |

**Cost-Recovery-First Method**

| Year | Revenue | Expense | Income |
|------|---------|---------|--------|
| 1 | $ 25,000 | $ 25,000 | $ -0- |
| 2 | 25,000 | 25,000 | -0- |
| 3 | 25,000 | 10,000 | 15,000 |
| 4 | 25,000 | -0- | 25,000 |
| | $100,000 | $ 60,000 | $40,000 |

6.24 (Revenue recognition for various types of businesses.)

We have found this question to be an excellent one for class discussion because it forces the student to think about both revenue *and* expense timing and measurement questions. It also generates active student interest. We have found it helpful to begin consideration of each item by drawing a time line similar to that in Figure 6.1 and appropriately labeling it. Some of the items are relatively obvious while others require more discussion.

a. Time of sale.

b. Probably as work progresses using the percentage-of-completion method. Students normally assume the sale is to the United States Government. We ask them if it would make any difference if the sale was to a relatively weak government in Africa or South America. This question gets at the issue of whether the amount of cash the firm will receive is subject to reasonably accurate estimation.

c. Probably as the firm collects cash using the installment method.

d. At the time of sale.

6.24 continued.

e. At the time the firm picks citrus products and delivers them to customers. We ask students if their response would change if the citrus firm had a five-year contract at a set price to supply a particular quantity of citrus products to a citrus processor. The issue here is whether, given uncertainties about future weather conditions, the citrus grower will be able to make delivery on the contract.

f. AICPA *Statement of Position 79-4* stipulates that the firm should not recognize revenue until it meets all of the following conditions:

1. The firm knows the sales price.

2. The firm knows the cost of the film or can reasonably estimate the loss.

3. The firm is reasonably assured as to the collectibility of the selling price.

4. A licensee has accepted the film in accordance with the license agreement.

5. The film is available (that is, the licensee can exercise the right to use the film and all conflicting licenses have expired).

Revenue recognition from the sale of rights to the television network is appropriate as soon as the firm meets these conditions even though the license period is three years. The firm cannot recognize revenues from the sale of subsequent rights to others until the three-year licensing period has expired. An important question in this example is when to recognize the production costs as an expense. Should the firm recognize all of the costs as an expense on the initial sale to the television network? Or, should it treat some portion of the costs as an asset, matched against future sales of license rights? Most accountants would probably match all of the costs against revenue from the television network license agreement, unless the firm has signed other license agreements for periods beginning after the initial three-year period at the same time as the television license agreement.

g. At the time of sale of each house to a specific buyer.

h. At the time of sale to a specific buyer at a set price. This will vary, depending on who owns the whiskey during the aging process. We pose the following situation: Suppose a particular whiskey producer has an on-going supplier relationship with a whiskey distributor. The quantity purchased by the distributor and the price set depend on supply and de-

6.24 h. continued.

mand conditions at the time aged whiskey is brought to the market. The supplier always purchases some minimum quantity. When should the firm recognize revenue? This question gets at the issue of measuring revenue in a reasonably objective manner. You may also want to discuss the following other wrinkle. Suppose the whiskey producer doubles capacity. The firm cannot sell any of the whiskey produced from this new capacity for six years. What should the firm do with the costs of this new capacity?

i. As time passes and the firm lets borrowers use funds.

j. The alternatives here are (1) as customers make reservations, (2) as customers make some formal commitments to confirm their reservations, or (3) as the agency receives cash from commissions. The second alternative is probably best. However, past experience may provide sufficient evidence as to the proportion of reservations that customers ultimately confirm to justify earlier recognition.

k. At the completion of the printing activity.

l. The issue here is whether to recognize revenue when the firm sells stamps to food stores or when customers turn in the stamps for redemption. One might argue for revenue recognition at the time of sale of the stamps, since the seller must have some estimate of the redemption rate in setting the price for the sale of the stamps.

m. At the time the wholesaler delivers food products to stores.

n. The issue here is whether to recognize revenue while the livestock is growing. A grower of timber faces a similar issue. For the reasons Part $h$. above discusses, it is probably best to await the time of delivery to a specific customer at an agreed upon price.

o. Probably during each period in a manner similar to the percentage-of-completion method. In practice firms use several methods.

6.25   (Income recognition for various businesses.)

a. Company A is selling software and access to data and other software. Recognizing all of the revenue at the time of initial delivery of the software appears premature because ongoing access to data and other software is a significant part of the product. If the firm can reasonably disaggregate the initial selling price into the portion applicable to the software and the portion applicable to the later services, then it could recognize the software sales as revenues at the time of delivery and then recognize the remaining selling price over the two year period as customers use the web-accessed services. If not, then recognizing the revenue ratably over the two-year period seems more appropriate.

b.    The issue in this case for Company B is the ability of the SAPs to pay for the software. Their ability to pay depends on the number of customers they sign up and the collection of cash from these customers. Recognizing revenue using either the installment or the cost-recovery-first methods seems most appropriate in this case.

c.    The issue with Company C is whether it satisfies the "substantial performance" criterion at the beginning of the two-year period (collectibility of cash is not an issue). Most accountants would argue that Company D should recognize the revenue ratably over the two-year period. It will likely add new software to the web site during the two-year period which initial subscribers will be able to access. Recognizing all of the revenue at the beginning of the two-year contract would theoretically require Company C to estimate the cost of developing the new software and match it against any revenue initially recognized.

d.    Assuming that Company D can collect the up-front fee with a high degree of certainty, it should be able to recognize this fee at the time of initial listing. It should recognize the transaction fee no earlier than the time of the transaction. The timing of its recognition depends on the predictability of buyers backing out on the purchase. If the probability of buyers backing out is either low or highly predictable, then recognizing the transaction fee at the time of the transaction is appropriate. Otherwise, delaying the recognition of the transaction fee until the transaction is completed is appropriate.

e.    Company E should recognize only the fee as revenue, not the selling price of the product as revenue and the cost of the good as cost of goods sold. Company E bears none of the risk of purchasing and holding the product in this case. Although it might desire to inflate its revenues to obtain a higher pricing multiple from the market for its common stock, GAAP would not permit this.

f.    Company F assumes more product risk in this case than in Part *e.* and could probably justify recognizing revenue for the specified minimum number of units each month and expense for the cost of those units.

g.    The issue for Company G is its ability to estimate at the time of the initial sale of the computer the cost of any rebates that will have to be paid to the Internet service provider after the time of the sale. If this amount is highly predictable, then Company G can justify recognizing the full selling price as revenue at the time of sale and the initial 10 percent cost of the rebate and any additional later cost of reallocated rebates as an expense. The difficulty here is that linked computer/Internet sales are a new arrangement and Company G may have difficulty estimating the cost of reallocated rebates. The $400 re-

6.25 g. continued.

bate appears to be a substantial amount relative to the selling price of the personal computer so the issue is not trivial. The arrangement seems to be more to stimulate sales of the Internet service provider than those of Company G, given the .90/.10 cost-sharing percentages. If predictability of the reallocated rebate cost is highly uncertain, than recognizing the selling price minus $360 (= .9 X $400) as revenue at the time of sale of the computer and the remaining $360 ratably over the three-year period seems appropriate. Actual costs of any reallocated rebates would be recognized as incurred each year.

h.  Most accountants would likely argue that Company H should recognize one-twelfth of the annual fee each month, as time passes and the contract provisions are satisfied. Company H might argue that the likelihood of not meeting the minimums is very low because it could simply instruct its employees to call up the site a sufficient number of times each month to meet the minimum. Following this line of reasoning, Company H might argue for up-front recognition of the full year's fee.

i.  The issue for Company I is the ability to measure the cash-equivalent value of the common stock. Company I would need to obtain sufficient information from Upstart Company to value the common stock received in order to justify recognizing revenue at the time of providing the advertising services.

j.  This is a classic barter transaction. To justify recognizing revenue from advertising space sold and expense for advertising space purchased, these companies would need to demonstrate the price that they would charge for a cash sale of the advertising space to other customers. Note that this transaction has zero effect on earnings, because the amount of expense for space purchased equals the amount of revenue for space sold.

**6.26** (American Express; analyzing changes in accounts receivable.)

a.

| | Year 5 | Year 6 | Year 7 |
|---|---|---|---|
| **(1) Sales on Account** | | | |
| Accounts Receivable ... | 19,132 | 21,278 | 23,675 |
| Sales Revenue .......... | 19,132 | 21,278 | 23,675 |
| **(2) Provision for Estimated Uncollectible Accounts** | | | |
| Bad Debt Expense........ | 2,187 | 2,212 | 2,439 |
| Allowance for Uncollectible Accounts................. | 2,187 | 2,212 | 2,439 |
| **(3) Write Off of Actual Bad Debts** | | | |
| Allowance for Uncollectible Accounts .... | 2,195[a] | 2,064[b] | 2,270[c] |
| Accounts Receivable ................... | 2,195 | 2,064 | 2,270 |

[a]$1,419 + $2,187 − $1,411 = $2,195.
[b]$1,411 + $2,212 − $1,559 = $2,064.
[c]$1,559 + $2,439 − $1,728 = $2,270.

| | Year 5 | Year 6 | Year 7 |
|---|---|---|---|
| **(4) Collection of Cash from Customers** | | | |
| Cash........................... | 15,550[d] | 12,295[e] | 14,654[f] |
| Accounts Receivable ................... | 15,550 | 12,295 | 14,654 |

[d]$41,883 + $19,132 − $2,187 − $43,278 = $15,550.
[e]$43,278 + $21,278 − $2,212 − $50,049 = $12,295.
[f]$50,049 + $23,675 − $2,439 − $56,631 = $14,654.

b.

| | Year 5 | Year 6 | Year 7 |
|---|---|---|---|
| **(1) Accounts Receivable Turnover** | | | |
| Year 5: $19,132/.5($41,883 + $43,278)... | .45 | | |
| Year 6: $21,278/.5($43,278 + $50,049)... | | .46 | |
| Year 7: $23,675/.5($50,049 + $56,631)... | | | .44 |
| **(2) Provision for Uncollectible Accounts/ Revenues** | | | |
| Year 5: $2,187/$19,132.............................. | 11.4% | | |
| Year 6: $2,212/$21,278............................. | | 10.4% | |
| Year 7: $2,439/$23,675............................. | | | 10.3% |

6.26 b. continued.

<table>
<tr><td></td><td>Year 5</td><td>Year 6</td><td>Year 7</td></tr>
<tr><td>(3) Allowance for Uncollectible Accounts/<br>Gross Accounts Receivable at End of Year<br>Year 5: $1,411/($43,278 + $1,411)...........</td><td>3.2%</td><td></td><td></td></tr>
<tr><td>Year 6: $1,559/($50,049 + $1,559)...........</td><td></td><td>3.0%</td><td></td></tr>
<tr><td>Year 7: $1,728/($56,631 + $1,728)...........</td><td></td><td></td><td>3.0%</td></tr>
<tr><td>(4) Accounts Written Off/Average Gross<br>Accounts Receivable<br>Year 5: $2,195/.5($41,883 + $1,419 +<br>$43,278 + $1,411)...................</td><td>5.0%</td><td></td><td></td></tr>
<tr><td>Year 6: $2,064/.5($43,278 + $1,411 +<br>$50,049 + $1,559)...................</td><td></td><td>4.3%</td><td></td></tr>
<tr><td>Year 7: $2,270/.5($50,049 + $1,559 +<br>$56,631 + $1,728)...................</td><td></td><td></td><td>4.1%</td></tr>
</table>

c. The accounts receivable turnover was relatively steady during the three-year period. Write-offs as a percentage of average gross accounts receivable declined, suggesting fewer bad debts. Because of the improved collection experience, American Express reduced its provision for uncollectible accounts as a percentage of revenues and the balance in the allowance account as a percentage of gross accounts receivable.

6.27 (May Department Stores; analyzing changes in accounts receivable.)

a.

| (Amounts in Millions) | Year 9 | Year 10 | Year11 | Year 12 |
|---|---|---|---|---|
| Allowance for Uncollectable Accounts, Beginning of Year............. | $ 47 | $ 61 | $ 66 | $ 84 |
| Plus Bad Debt Expense......................... | 57 | 64 | 82 | 96 |
| Less Accounts Written Off (Plug)........ | (43) | (59) | (64) | (81) |
| Allowance for Uncollectable Accounts, End of Year ...................... | $ 61 | $ 66 | $ 84 | $ 99 |

b.

| | Year 9 | Year 10 | Year11 | Year 12 |
|---|---|---|---|---|
| Accounts Receivable, Gross at Beginning of Year............................. | $ 1,592 | $ 2,099 | $ 2,223 | $ 2,456 |
| Plus Sales on Account[a]....................... | 5,181 | 6,137 | 6,713 | 7,293 |
| Less Accounts Written Off................ | (43) | (59) | (64) | (81) |
| Less Cash Collections from Credit Customers (Plug)............................ | (4,631) | (5,954) | (6,416) | (7,061) |
| Accounts Receivable, Gross at End of Year............................................. | $ 2,099 | $ 2,223 | $ 2,456 | $ 2,607 |

[a]Total Sales × (Credit Sales ÷ Total Sales Percentage).

6.27 continued.

c. Total Sales/Average Accounts Receivable, Net:

| | Year 9 | Year 10 | Year11 | Year 12 |
|---|---|---|---|---|
| $8,330/.5($1,545 + $2,038).......... | 4.65 | | | |
| $9,456/.5($2,038 + $2,157).......... | | 4.51 | | |
| $10,035/.5($2,157 + $2,372)........ | | | 4.43 | |
| $10,615/.5($2,372 + $2,508)........ | | | | 4.35 |

d. Credit Sales/Average Accounts Receivable, Net:

| | Year 9 | Year 10 | Year11 | Year 12 |
|---|---|---|---|---|
| $5,181/.5($1,545 + $2,038).......... | 2.89 | | | |
| $6,137/.5($2,038 + $2,157).......... | | 2.93 | | |
| $6,713/.5($2,157 + $2,372).......... | | | 2.96 | |
| $7,293/.5($2,372 + $2,508).......... | | | | 2.99 |

e. The accounts receivable turnover ratio based on total sales decreases because of the increasing proportion of credit sales in total sales. The increasing accounts receivable turnover ratio based on credit sales results from actions that cause customers to pay more quickly. Examples include increased finance charges on unpaid balances, reduced repayment period on credit sales, and more stringent controls on the granting of credit.

6.28 (Sears; analyzing changes in accounts receivable.)

a.

| | Year 7 | | Year 8 | | Year 9 | |
|---|---|---|---|---|---|---|
| **(1) Sales on Account** | | | | | | |
| Accounts Receivable ... | 39,953 | | 39,484 | | 40,937 | |
| Sales Revenue .......... | | 39,953 | | 39,484 | | 40,937 |
| **(2) Provision for Estimated Uncollectible Accounts** | | | | | | |
| Bad Debt Expense........ | 1,287 | | 871 | | 884 | |
| Allowance for Uncollectible Accounts................. | | 1,287 | | 871 | | 884 |
| **(3) Write Off of Actual Bad Debts** | | | | | | |
| Allowance for Uncollectible Accounts .... | 1,426[a] | | 1,085[b] | | 958[c] | |
| Accounts Receivable ................... | | 1,426 | | 1,085 | | 958 |

[a]$1,113 + $1,287 − $974 = $1,426.
[b]$974 + $871 − $760 = $1,085.
[c]$760 + $884 − $686 = $958.

6.28 a. continued.

|  | Year 7 | Year 8 | Year 9 |
|---|---|---|---|
| **(4) Collection of Cash from Customers** | | | |
| Cash............................ | 40,537[d] | 38,552[e] | 40,769[f] |
| Accounts Receivable......................... | 40,537 | 38,552 | 40,769 |

[d]$19,843 + $39,953 − $1,287 − $17,972 = $40,537.
[e]$17,972 + $39,484 − $871 − $18,033 = $38,552.
[f]$18,033 + $40,937 − $884 − $17,317 = $40,769.

b.

|  | Year 7 | Year 8 | Year 9 |
|---|---|---|---|
| (1) Accounts Receivable Turnover | | | |
| Year 7: $39,953/.5($19,843 + $17,972)... | 2.11 | | |
| Year 8: $39,484/.5($17,972 + $18,033)... | | 2.19 | |
| Year 9: $40,937/.5($18,033 + $17,317)... | | | 2.32 |
| (2) Provision for Uncollectible Accounts/ Revenues | | | |
| Year 7: $1,287/$39,953.............................. | 3.2% | | |
| Year 8: $871/$39,484 ................................. | | 2.2% | |
| Year 9: $884/$40,937 ................................. | | | 2.2% |
| (3) Allowance for Uncollectible Accounts/ Gross Accounts Receivable at End of Year | | | |
| Year 7: $974/($17,972 + $974).................. | 5.1% | | |
| Year 8: $760/($18,033 + $760).................. | | 4.0% | |
| Year 9: $686/($17,317 + $686).................. | | | 3.8% |
| (4) Accounts Written Off/Average Gross Accounts Receivable | | | |
| Year 7: $1,426/.5($19,843 + $1,113 + $17,972 + $974)........................ | 7.1% | | |
| Year 8: $1,085/.5($17,972 + $974 + $18,033 + $760)........................ | | 5.8% | |
| Year 9: $958/.5($18,033 + $760 + $17,317 + $686)........................ | | | 5.2% |

c. The accounts receivable turnover increased during the three-year period, indicating that Sears collected its accounts receivable more quickly. Its write-offs of uncollectible accounts as a percentage of gross accounts receivable declined during the three-year period, suggesting improved credit experience. Consistent with this improved credit experience is a decline in the provision for uncollectible accounts as a percentage of revenues and the balance in the Allowance for Uncollectible Accounts account as a percentage of gross accounts receivable.

6.29    (Pins Company; reconstructing transactions affecting accounts receivable and uncollectible accounts.)

   a.   $192,000 Dr. = $700,000 − $500,000 − $8,000.

   b.   $6,000 Cr. = (.02 × $700,000) − $8,000.

   c.   $21,000 = $10,000 + $11,000.

   d.   $16,000 = $6,000 + $10,000.

   e.   $676,000 = $192,000 + $800,000 − $16,000 − $300,000.

   f.   $289,000 = $300,000 − $11,000.

6.30    (Nordstrom; decision to extend credit to a new class of customers.)

| Gross Margin on New Sales: | a. | b. |
|---|---|---|
| **a.** .30 × $10,000;  **b.** .30 × $7,000............................ | $3,000 | $2,100 |
| Less: Uncollectibles (.07 × $10,000)........................... | (700) | (800) |
| All Other Costs.................................................. | (1,100) | (750) |
| Contribution to Profits ............................................. | $1,200 | $ 550 |

   a.   Nordstrom will be $1,200 better off.

   b.   Nordstrom will be $550 better off.

6.31    (Hanrahan Company; decision to extend credit: working backwards to uncollectible rate.)

| | | |
|---|---|---|
| Margin on New Sales Before Charge for Uncollectible Accounts (.20 × $20,000)..................................... | | $ 4,000 |
| Less: Uncollectibles on Total Sales (.03 × $270,000)................................................. | $ 8,100 | |
| Previous Amount of Uncollectibles (.02 × $250,000)................................................. | (5,000) | |
| Increase in Uncollectibles......................................... | | (3,100) |
| Less Other Expenses ............................................... | | (300) |
| Incremental Contribution to Profits........................ | | $ 600 |

Percentage Uncollectible:  $3,100/$20,000 = 15.5 percent.

6.32 (Effect of errors involving accounts receivable on financial statement ratios.)

| Journal Entry | | Rate of Return on Assets | Accounts Receivable Turnover Ratio | Debt Equity Ratio |
|---|---|---|---|---|
| a. | Bad Debt Expense ............... X | $\dfrac{O/S}{O/S} = O/S$ | $\dfrac{NO}{O/S} = U/S$ | $\dfrac{NO}{O/S} = U/S$ |
| | Allowance for Uncollectible Accounts ...... X | | | |
| b. | Allowance for Uncollectible Accounts ...... X | $\dfrac{NO}{NO} = NO$ | $\dfrac{NO}{NO} = NO$ | $\dfrac{NO}{NO} = NO$ |
| | Accounts Receivable ............... X | | | |
| c. | Advances from Customers ............ X | $\dfrac{NO}{O/S} = U/S$ | $\dfrac{NO}{O/S} = U/S$ | $\dfrac{O/S}{O/S} = O/S$ |
| | Accounts Receivable ............... X | | | |
| d. | Sales Revenue ............... X | $\dfrac{O/S}{O/S} = O/S$ | $\dfrac{O/S}{O/S} = O/S$ | $\dfrac{NO}{O/S} = U/S$ |
| | Accounts Receivable ............... X | | | |
| | Inventory ............... X | | | |
| | Cost of Goods Sold ............... X | | | |
| e. | Sales Returns ............... X | $\dfrac{O/S}{O/S} = O/S$ | $\dfrac{O/S}{O/S} = O/S$ | $\dfrac{NO}{O/S} = U/S$ |
| | Accounts Receivable ............... X | | | |
| | Inventory ............... X | | | |
| | Cost of Goods Sold ............... X | | | |

*Note*: This problem asks only for the net effect of each error on the three financial ratios. The journal entries and the numerator and denominator effects appear to show the reason for the net effect.

6.33    (General Electric Company; income recognition for nuclear generator manufacturer.)

a.1.  Percentage-of-Completion Method

| Year | Incremental Percentage Complete | | Revenue Recognized | Expenses Recognized | Net Income |
|------|-----------------|-------|-----------------|-----------------|-----------------|
| 2 | 42/120 | (.35) | $ 70,000,000 | $ 42,000,000 | $ 28,000,000 |
| 3 | 54/120 | (.45) | 90,000,000 | 54,000,000 | 36,000,000 |
| 4 | 24/120 | (.20) | 40,000,000 | 24,000,000 | 16,000,000 |
| Total..... | 120/120 | (1.00) | $200,000,000 | $120,000,000 | $ 80,000,000 |

2.  Completed Contract Method

| Year | Revenue Recognized | Expenses Recognized | Net Income |
|------|-----------------|-----------------|-----------------|
| 2 | -0- | -0- | -0- |
| 3 | -0- | -0- | -0- |
| 4 | $200,000,000 | $120,000,000 | $80,000,000 |
| Total.... | $200,000,000 | $120,000,000 | $80,000,000 |

3.  Installment Method

| Year | Cash Collected (= Revenue) | Fraction of Cash Collected | Expenses (= Fraction X Total Cost) | Net Income |
|------|-----------------|-----------------|-----------------|-----------------|
| 2 | $ 20,000,000 | 1/10 | $ 12,000,000 | $ 8,000,000 |
| 3 | 100,000,000 | 5/10 | 60,000,000 | 40,000,000 |
| 4 | 80,000,000 | 4/10 | 48,000,000 | 32,000,000 |
| Total...... | $ 200,000,000 | 1.00 | $120,000,000 | $ 80,000,000 |

4.  Cost-Recovery-First Method

| Year | Cash Collected (= Revenue) | Expenses Recognized | Net Income |
|------|-----------------|-----------------|-----------------|
| 2 | $ 20,000,000 | $ 20,000,000 | -0- |
| 3 | 100,000,000 | 100,000,000 | -0- |
| 4 | 80,000,000 | -0- | $80,000,000 |
| Total..... | $200,000,000 | $120,000,000 | $80,000,000 |

b.  The percentage-of-completion method probably provides a better measure of performance over the life of the contract because each period receives a portion of the net income from the contract. General Electric's original estimates of the cost of the contract were correct. Also, the periodic payments from Consolidated Edison suggest that General Electric will probably collect cash in the amount of the contract price.

6.34    (Bush Construction Company; income recognition for a contractor.)

a.1.  Percentage-of-Completion Method

| Year | Incremental Percentage Complete | Revenue Recognized | Expenses Recognized | Net Income |
|------|------|------|------|------|
| 1 | 20/100 (.20) | $ 24,000,000 | $ 20,000,000 | $ 4,000,000 |
| 2 | 30/100 (.30) | 36,000,000 | 30,000,000 | 6,000,000 |
| 3 | 35/100 (.35) | 42,000,000 | 35,000,000 | 7,000,000 |
| 4 | 15/100 (.15) | 18,000,000 | 15,000,000 | 3,000,000 |
| Total....... | 100/100 (1.00) | $120,000,000 | $100,000,000 | $20,000,000 |

2.  Completed Contract Method

| Year | Revenue Recognized | Expenses Recognized | Net Income |
|------|------|------|------|
| 1 | -0- | -0- | -0- |
| 2 | -0- | -0- | -0- |
| 3 | -0- | -0- | -0- |
| 4 | $120,000,000 | $100,000,000 | $20,000,000 |
| Total.... | $120,000,000 | $100,000,000 | $20,000,000 |

3.  Installment Method

| Year | Cash Collected (= Revenue) | Percentage of Cash Collected | Expenses (= Percentage × Total Cost) | Net Income |
|------|------|------|------|------|
| 1 | $ 24,000,000 | .20 | $ 20,000,000 | $ 4,000,000 |
| 2 | 30,000,000 | .25 | 25,000,000 | 5,000,000 |
| 3 | 30,000,000 | .25 | 25,000,000 | 5,000,000 |
| 4 | 36,000,000 | .30 | 30,000,000 | 6,000,000 |
| Total...... | $120,000,000 | 1.00 | $100,000,000 | $ 20,000,000 |

4.  Cost-Recovery-First Method

| Year | Cash Collected (= Revenue) | Expense Recognized | Net Income |
|------|------|------|------|
| 1 | $ 24,000,000 | $ 24,000,000 | -0- |
| 2 | 30,000,000 | 30,000,000 | -0- |
| 3 | 30,000,000 | 30,000,000 | -0- |
| 4 | 36,000,000 | 16,000,000 | $20,000,000 |
| Total..... | $120,000,000 | $100,000,000 | $20,000,000 |

b.  The percentage-of-completion method probably gives the best measure of Bush's performance each year under the contract. The original estimates of costs on the contract turned out to be correct. Also, the periodic cash collections suggest that the firm will probably collect cash in the amount of the contract price.

6.35    (J. C. Spangle; point-of-sale versus installment method of income recognition.)

a.

| | Year 8 | Year 9 |
|---|---|---|
| Sales...................................................... | $ 200,000 | $ 300,000 |
| Expenses: | | |
|   Cost of Goods Sold*............................... | $ 120,000 | $ 186,000 |
|   All Other Expenses............................... | 32,000 | 44,000 |
|     Total Expenses ................................. | $ 152,000 | $ 230,000 |
| Net Income.............................................. | $ 48,000 | $ 70,000 |
| | | |
|   *Beginning Inventory ............................. | $ 0 | $ 60,000 |
|    Purchases.......................................... | 180,000 | 240,000 |
|    Goods Available................................. | $ 180,000 | $ 300,000 |
|    Ending Inventory............................... | (60,000) | (114,000) |
|    Cost of Goods Sold ............................ | $ 120,000 | $ 186,000 |

Cost of Goods Sold/Sales:
   Year 8--$120,000/$200,000 = 60 percent.
   Year 9--$186,000/$300,000 = 62 percent.

b.

| | Year 8 | Year 9 |
|---|---|---|
| Collections from Customers........................... | $ 90,000 | $ 230,000 |
| Expenses:............................................... | | |
|   Merchandise Cost of Collections*.............. | $ 54,000 | $ 140,400 |
|   All Other Expenses............................... | 32,000 | 44,000 |
|     Total Expenses ................................. | $ 86,000 | $ 184,400 |
| Net Income.............................................. | $ 4,000 | $ 45,600 |

| *Calculation: | Year 8 | Year 9 |
|---|---|---|
| Merchandise Cost of Collections: | | |
|   Of Goods Sold: | | |
|     In Year 8, 60 percent of $90,000........ | $ 54,000 | |
|     In Year 9, 60 percent of $110,000...... | | $ 66,000 |
|   Of Goods Sold in Year 9: | | |
|     62 percent of $120,000........................ | | 74,400 |
| | $ 54,000 | $ 140,400 |

| An Alternative Presentation Would Be: | Year 8 | Year 9 |
|---|---|---|
| Realized Gross Margin............................ | $ 36,000 | $ 89,600 |
| All Other Expenses ................................ | 32,000 | 44,000 |
| Net Income ......................................... | $ 4,000 | $ 45,600 |

6.36    (Pickin Chicken; revenue recognition for a franchise.)

a.

| Year | Pickin Chicken, Inc. | Country Delight, Inc. |
|------|---------------------|----------------------|
| 2 | $ 400,000 (= $50,000 X 8) | $ 160,000 (= $20,000 X 8) |
| 3 | 250,000 (= $50,000 X 5) | 148,000 (= $20,000 X 5 + $6,000 X 8) |
| 4 | 0 | 78,000 (= $6,000 X 13) |
| 5 | 0 | 78,000 (= $6,000 X 13) |
| 6 | 0 | 78,000 (= $6,000 X 13) |
| 7 | 0 | 78,000 (= $6,000 X 13) |
| 8 | 0 | 30,000 (= $6,000 X 5) |
| Total.. | $650,000 | $650,000 |

b.  The issue here is whether sufficient uncertainty exists regarding the amount the firm will ultimately collect to justify postponing revenue recognition until the time of collection. The casualty rate among franchisees has been very high and has led some accountants to argue that the installment method is the appropriate basis for revenue recognition.

6.37    (Income recognition for various types of businesses.)

a.  **Amgen**—The principal income recognition issue for Amgen is the significant lag between the incurrence of research and development expenditures and the realization of sales from any resulting products. Biotechnology firms are a relatively new industry and therefore have few commercially feasible products. Thus, research and development expenditures will likely represent a significant percentage of revenues, as is the case for Amgen. More established technology firms, such as pharmaceuticals, have established products as well as products in the pipeline and therefore research and development expenditures represent both a smaller and a more stable percentage of revenues. GAAP requires biotechnology firms to expense research and development expenditures in the year incurred.

**Brown Forman**—The principal revenue recognition issue for Brown Forman is whether it should recognize the increase in value of hard liquors while they are aging (that is, revalue the liquors to market value each year) or wait until the liquors are sold at the end of the aging process. Most accountants would argue that the market values of aging liquors are too uncertain prior to sale to justify periodic revaluations and revenue recognition. Brown Forman should include in the cost of the liquor inventory not only the initial production costs but also the cost incurred during the aging process. In this way, the firm can match total incurred costs with revenues generated at the time of sale.

**Deere**—Deere faces issues of revenue recognition with respect to both the sale of farm equipment to dealers and the provision of financing services. The concern with respect to the sale of farm equipment to dealers is the right of dealers to return any unsold equipment. If dealers have no right of return, then recognition of revenue at the time of sale is appropriate. If dealers can return any equipment discovered to be faulty prior to sale and the amount of such returns is reasonably predictable, then Deere can reduce the amount of revenue recognized each year for estimated returns. If dealers can return any unsold equipment, then delaying recognition of revenue until the dealer sells the equipment is appropriate. Deere should match the cost of manufacturing the equipment against the sales revenue. Deere reports research and development expense in its income statement. Given the farm equipment industry, one wonders about what proportions of these expenditures Deere makes to enhance existing products versus to develop new products. Although contrary to GAAP, one can make the case that Deere should capitalize and amortize expenditures on new products.

Deere should accrue revenue from financing (interest) and insurance (premiums) services over time. To achieve matching, Deere should capitalize and amortize any initial administrative costs to check customer credit quality and prepare legal documents.

**Fluor**—The appropriate timing of revenue recognition for Fluor depends on the basis for pricing its services. If the fee is fixed for any particular construction project, then Fluor should recognize the fee in relation to the degree of completion of the construction project. If the fee is a percentage of total construction costs incurred on the project, then Fluor should recognize revenue in relation to costs incurred. If the fee is a percentage of the costs incurred by Fluor (salaries of their employees working on the project), then it should recognize revenue in relation to the incurrence of these costs. It seems clear that a percentage of completion method of revenue recognition is more appropriate than the completed contract method.

**Golden West**—Golden West should recognize interest revenue from home mortgage loans as time passes. It should provide for estimated uncollectible accounts each year. The uncollectible amount should reflect the resale value of homes repossessed. The more difficult question relates to recognition of revenue from points. One possibility is to recognize the full amount in the initial year of the loan. The rationale for such a procedure is that the points cover administrative costs of setting up the loan. Both the points and the administrative costs would be recognized in full in the initial year of the loan. An alternative view is that the points effectively reduce the amount lent by the savings and loan company and increase its yield beyond the stated interest rate. This view suggests that Golden West amortize

6.37 a. continued.

the points over the term of the loan and match against this revenue amortization of the initial administrative costs to set up the loan. Golden West should recognize interest expense on deposits as time passes. There is no direct relation between interest expense on deposits and interest revenue from loans so Golden West matches interest expense to the period it is incurred.

**Merrill Lynch**—The principal income recognition issue for Merrill Lynch is whether it should report financial instruments held as assets and liabilities at their acquisition cost or their current market value. These assets and liabilities generally have easily measured market values. They are typically held for short periods of time (days or weeks). Thus, one can argue that use of current market values is appropriate. However, we are still left with the question as to whether the unrealized gain or loss should flow through to the income statement immediately or wait until realization at the time of sale. The argument for immediate recognition is that Merrill Lynch takes short-term financing and investing positions for short-term returns. Its income statement should reflect its operating performance during this period. The case for not recognizing the unrealized gains and losses is that they could reverse prior to realization and, in any case, will be realized very soon. Merrill Lynch should recognize revenue from fee-based services as it provides the services.

**Rockwell**—The absence of research and development expense from the income statement suggests that Rockwell charges all such costs to specific contracts. These costs become expenses as Rockwell recognizes revenue from the contracts. The multi-year nature of its contracts and the credit quality of the U.S. government suggest use of the percentage-of-completion method of income recognition. One difficulty encountered in applying the percentage-of-completion method is that Rockwell's contracts for projects such as the space shuttle get continually renewed. This procedure makes it difficult to identify a single contract price and accumulate costs for a single contract, which the percentage-of-completion method envisions.

b. **Amgen**—Amgen realized the highest profit margin of the seven companies. Its biotechnology products are protected by patents. It therefore maintains a monopoly position. Note that the cost of manufacturing its products is a small percent of revenues. Amgen's major cost is for research and development. Sales of its existing products are not only sufficient to cover its high, on-going research work but to provide a substantial profit margin as well. Its relatively low revenue to assets percentage is somewhat unexpected, given that its major "assets" are patents and research scientists. The reason for this low percentage (reason not provided in the case) is that cash and marketable securities comprise approximately 25 percent of its assets.

6.37 b. continued.

These assets generated a return of approximately 3 percent during the year. This rate of return decreased the overall ratio of revenues to assets for Amgen.

**Brown Forman**—Brown Forman realized the third highest profit margin among the seven companies. If one views the excise taxes as a reduction in revenues rather than as an expense, its profit margin is 10.4 percent [= 8.8%/(100.0% − 15.4%)]. Concerns about excess alcoholic drinking in recent years have resulted in some exodus of companies from the industry, leaving the remaining companies with a larger share of a smaller market. The products of Brown Forman carry brand name recognition, permitting the firm to obtain attractive prices.

**Deere**—Deere's relatively low profit margin reflects (1) weaknesses in the farming industry in recent years, which puts downward pressure on margins, and (2) decreased interest rates, which lowers profit margins. The revenue-to-assets percentage of Deere reflects its capital-intensive manufacturing operations and the low interest rate on outstanding loans to dealers and customers.

**Fluor**—The low profit margin of Fluor reflects the relatively low value added of construction services. It may also reflect recessionary conditions when construction activity is weak and profit margins are thin.

**Golden West**—The 12 percent profit margin seems high, relative to interest rates in recent years. Recall though that Golden West pays short-term interest rates on its deposits but obtains long-term interest rates on its loans. An upward-sloping yield curve provides a positive differential. Also, the existence of shareholders' equity funds in the capital structure means that Golden West has assets earning returns for which it recognizes no expense in its income statement (that is, firms do not recognize an expense for the implicit cost of shareholders' funds). Note also that the ratio of revenue to assets is only .1. Thus, the assets of Golden West earned a return of only 1.2 percent (= 12.0% × .1) during the year.

**Merrill Lynch**—The lower profit margin for Merrill Lynch relative to Golden West reflects in part the fact that both the investments and financing of Merrill Lynch are short term. Merrill Lynch, however, realizes revenue from fee-based services. Firms like Merrill Lynch can differentiate these services somewhat and realize attractive profit margins. However, such services have been quickly copied by competitors in recent years, reducing the profit margins accordingly.

6.37 b. continued.

**Rockwell**—Rockwell's profit margin is in the middle of the seven companies. Factors arguing for a high profit margin include Rockwell's technological know-how and its role in long-term contracts with the U.S. government. Factors arguing for a lower profit margin include cutbacks in defense expenditures and excess capacity in the aerospace industry.

# CHAPTER 7

## INVENTORIES: THE SOURCE OF OPERATING PROFITS

*Questions, Exercises, Problems, and Cases: Answers and Solutions*

7.1 See the text or the glossary at the end of the book.

7.2 The underlying principle is that acquisition cost includes all costs required to prepare an asset for its intended use. Assets provide future services. Costs that a firm must incur to obtain those expected services add value to the asset. Accountants therefore include such costs in the acquisition cost valuation of the asset.

7.3 Depreciation on manufacturing equipment is a product cost and remains in inventory accounts until the firm sells the manufactured goods. Depreciation on selling and administrative equipment is a period expense, because the use of such equipment does not create an asset with future service potential.

7.4 Both the Merchandise Inventory and Finished Goods Inventory accounts include the cost of completed units ready for sale. A merchandising firm acquires the units in finished form and debits Merchandise Inventory for their acquisition cost. A manufacturing firm incurs direct material, direct labor, and manufacturing overhead costs in transforming the units to a finished, salable condition. The Raw Materials Inventory and Work-in-Process Inventory accounts include such costs until the completion of manufacturing operations. Thus, the accountant debits the Finished Goods Inventory account for the cost of producing completed units. The accountant credits both the Merchandise Inventory and Finished Goods Inventory accounts for the cost of units sold and reports them as current assets on the balance sheet.

7.5 The accountant allocates the total income (cash inflow minus cash outflow) over the periods between purchase and sale. The inventory valuation method dictates this allocation. The acquisition cost valuation method allocates all of the income to the period of sale. A current cost valuation method allocates holding gains and losses to the periods when a firm holds inventory and an operating margin (sales minus replacement cost of goods sold) to the period of sale. A lower-of-cost-or-market valuation allocates holding losses to the periods when a firm holds inventory and holding gains plus operating margins to the period of sale.

7.6    Income increases in the year of change because of the recognition of the unrealized holding gains. Cost of goods sold in the next year will increase by the same amount, so that income in the second year will be less by the same amount as it was greater in the year of change. Over long enough time spans, accounting income equals cash inflows minus cash outflows; the valuation method affects the timing of income recognition, not its amount.

7.7    Accounting reports cost flows, not flows of physical quantities. Cost flow assumptions trace costs, not physical flows of goods. With specific identification, management manipulates cost flows by controlling goods flows.

7.8    Rising Purchase Prices:
       Higher Inventory Amount:    FIFO
       Lower Inventory Amount:     LIFO

       Falling Purchase Prices:
       Higher Inventory Amount:    LIFO; LIFO results in a constant inventory amount so long as quantities do not change.
       Lower Inventory Amount:     FIFO; FIFO results in an even lower inventory than does the weighted-average assumption.

7.9    a.  Higher cost of goods sold amount:   LIFO
           Lower cost of goods sold amount:    FIFO

       b.  Higher cost of goods sold amount:   FIFO
           Lower cost of goods sold amount:    LIFO

7.10   LIFO provides cost of goods sold closer to current costs than does FIFO so long as inventory quantities do not decrease and a firm does not liquidate old LIFO layers. Some would say, then, that LIFO does provide more meaningful income data when quantities do not decrease. The LIFO balance sheet always reflects older costs than does the FIFO balance sheet.

7.11   a.  FIFO typically uses older acquisition costs for cost of goods sold than LIFO (except during a period of dipping into a LIFO layer), whereas LIFO uses older acquisition costs for ending inventory than FIFO. The larger the rate of change in the acquisition cost of inventory items, the more the older costs will differ from current costs and the larger will be the difference in cost of goods sold and ending inventory values between FIFO and LIFO.

       b.  As the rate of inventory turnover increases, purchases during a period comprise an increasing proportion of cost of goods sold for that period under both FIFO and LIFO and differences in the beginning or ending inventory values under FIFO and LIFO play a decreasing role. Because

7.11 b. continued.

      purchases are the same regardless of the cost flow assumption, cost of goods sold under FIFO and LIFO should not differ significantly (unless the firm experienced dips into old LIFO layers).

    c.  The inventory turnover ratio relates cost of goods sold to average inventories. A faster inventory turnover means a smaller level of inventories in the denominator relative to cost of goods sold in the numerator. The difference between FIFO and LIFO amounts in the denominator depends on the age of a firm's LIFO layers and the rate of change in the cost of inventory items since the firm adopted LIFO. These latter items relate to the passage of time rather than to the rate of turnover within a period of time.

7.12    Dipping into an old LIFO layer may not be within a firm's control, such as when shortages prevent the firm from replacing a particular raw material. A dip may be partially within a firm's control, such as when a labor strike by employees forces the firm to reduce its finished goods inventory. A dip may be fully within a firm's control, such as when it delays purchases toward the end of the period in an effort to decrease cost of goods sold and increase net income.

7.13    Firms that maintain a relatively constant relation between the replacement cost of inventory items and selling prices will show a constant operating margin percentage (that is, operating margin/sales) each period. The operating margin will be the same under FIFO and LIFO. Both firms also include a realized holding gain or loss in their gross margins. The realized holding gain or loss reflects the change in the replacement cost of inventory items between the time of acquisition and the time of sale. The assumed holding period for FIFO is longer than for LIFO. Thus, FIFO likely includes more price changes (both increases and decreases) in the realized holding gain or loss than LIFO. If prices change at a constant rate and in a constant direction, then both FIFO and LIFO produce a smooth gross margin trend over time. If either the rate or direction of price change varies over time, FIFO more fully reflects these variations in the gross margin than LIFO.

7.14    Assuming a period of rising purchase prices, the firm might prefer to report higher earnings to shareholders and give up the tax savings that LIFO provides. Management's compensation often uses reported earnings as a base in its computation. Management obtains higher compensation by reporting higher earnings under FIFO. The firm might be experiencing operating difficulties and need to report higher earnings to keep shareholders happy. We question the rationality of such thinking but don't doubt that such reasoning occurs.

      The firm might be experiencing decreasing prices (costs) for its inventory items and obtain the maximum tax benefits by using FIFO. Note, however, that the Internal Revenue Code does not preclude a firm from using FIFO for tax purposes and LIFO for financial reporting. This

7.14 continued.

combination minimizes taxes but maximizes earnings reported to shareholders.

If prices are not changing much or if inventory turns over rapidly, then FIFO and LIFO do not differ significantly in terms of their effects on earnings or balance sheet amounts. The record keeping costs and fears of dipping into very old LIFO layers might lead a firm to use FIFO under these circumstances.

7.15 The firm saved taxes in earlier years when it created its LIFO layers and must pay the taxes in the year that it dips. It has at least delayed paying the taxes relative to FIFO, even if it must pay the same amount of taxes over time under both cost flow assumptions. Thus, the present value of the taxes saved under LIFO exceeds the present value under FIFO.

If tax rates were to rise dramatically during the period of the dip, the higher tax rate might overwhelm the effect of interest rates. Suppose the interest rate is 10 percent per period. Assume LIFO defers $100 at the end of Period 1, which the firm repays at the end of Period 3. The tax deferral is worth $21 [= (1.10 X 1.10 X $100) − $100]. If the income tax rate has increased by more than 21 percent between the end of Period 1 and the end of Period 3, then the deferral will not have saved present value dollars.

7.16 (Trembly Department Store; identifying inventory cost inclusions.)

| | | |
|---|---|---:|
| a. | Purchase Price | $ 300,000 |
| b. | Freight Cost | 13,800 |
| c. | Salary of Purchasing Manager | 3,000 |
| d. | Depreciation, taxes, Insurance and Utilities on Warehouse | 27,300 |
| e. | Salary of Warehouse Manager | 2,200 |
| f. | Merchandise Returns | (18,500) |
| g. | Cash Discounts Taken | (4,900) |
| | Acquisition Cost | $ 322,900 |

The underlying principle is that inventories should include all costs required to get the inventory ready for sale. The purchase of the inventory items (items a., c., f., and g.) provides the physical goods to be sold, the freight cost (item b.) puts the inventory items in the place most convenient for sale, and the storage costs (items d. and e.) keep the inventory items until the time of sale. Economists characterize these costs as providing form, place, and time utility, or benefits. Although accounting theory suggests the inclusion of each of these items in the valuation of inventory, some firms might exclude items c., d., e., and g. on the basis of lack of materiality.

7.17    (Identifying product costs and period expenses.)

|     |                    |     |     |     |     |
|-----|--------------------|-----|-----|-----|-----|
| a.  | 1 (Product Cost)   | g.  | 1   | m.  | 2   |
| b.  | 2 (Period Expense) | h.  | 1   | n.  | 2   |
| c.  | 1                  | i.  | 1   | o.  | 1   |
| d.  | 1                  | j.  | 1   | p.  | 2   |
| e.  | 1                  | k.  | 2   | q.  | 2   |
| f.  | 2                  | l.  | 2   |     |     |

7.18    (Identifying product costs, period expenses, and assets.)

|     |                          |     |     |
|-----|--------------------------|-----|-----|
| a.  | 1 (Period Expense)       | g.  | 3   |
| b.  | 2 (Product Cost)         | h.  | 2   |
| c.  | 3 (Other Balance Sheet)  | i.  | 1   |
| d.  | 1                        | j.  | 1   |
| e.  | 2                        | k.  | 2   |
| f.  | 1                        |     |     |

7.19    (General Mills; income computation for a manufacturing firm.)

| | |
|---|---:|
| Sales........................................................................................ | $ 6,700.2 |
| Less Cost of Goods Sold........................................................ | (2,697.6) |
| Less Selling and Administrative Expenses ............................. | (2,903.7) |
| Less Interest Expense............................................................ | (151.9) |
| Income before Income Taxes ................................................. | $   947.0 |
| Income Tax Expense at 35%.................................................. | (331.5) |
| Net Income ............................................................................ | $   615.5 |
| | |
| Work-in-Process Inventory, June 1....................................... | $   100.8 |
| Plus Manufacturing Costs Incurred during Year ................... | 2,752.0 |
| Less Work-in-Process Inventory, May 30............................... | (119.1) |
| Cost of Goods Completed during Year ................................... | $ 2,733.7 |
| Plus Finished Goods Inventory, June 1.................................. | 286.2 |
| Less Finished Goods Inventory, May 30................................. | (322.3) |
| Cost of Goods Sold ................................................................ | $ 2,697.6 |

7.20     (Rockwell International Corporation; income computation for a manufacturing firm.)

| | |
|---|---:|
| Sales | $11,123 |
| Less Cost of Goods Sold | (8,675) |
| Less Marketing and Administrative Expenses | (1,409) |
| Less Interest Expense | (100) |
| Income before Income Taxes | $ 939 |
| Income Tax Expense at 35% | (329) |
| Net Income | $ 610 |
| | |
| Work-in-Process Inventory, October 1 | $ 850 |
| Plus Manufacturing Costs Incurred during Year | 8,771 |
| Less Work-in-Process Inventory, September 30 | (920) |
| Cost of Goods Completed during Year | $ 8,701 |
| Plus Finished Goods Inventory, October 1 | 330 |
| Less Finished Goods Inventory, September 30 | (356) |
| Cost of Goods Sold | $ 8,675 |

7.21     (Colt Real Estate Development Corporation; effect of inventory valuation basis on net income.)

a.

| | Parcel A | Parcel B |
|---|---:|---:|
| **(1) Acquisition Cost** | | |
| Year 6: | -- | -- |
| Year 7: ($24,600 – $9,000) | $ 15,600 | -- |
| Year 8: ($19,700 – $9,000) | -- | $ 10,700 |
| Total | $ 15,600 | $ 10,700 |
| | | |
| **(2) Market Value** | | |
| Year 6: ($16,700 – $9,000); | | |
| ($8,500 – $9,000) | $ 7,700 | $ (500) |
| Year 7: ($24,600 – $16,700); | | |
| ($14,400 – $8,500) | 7,900 | 5,900 |
| Year 8: ($19,700 – $14,400) | -- | 5,300 |
| Total | $ 15,600 | $ 10,700 |
| | | |
| **(3) Lower of Cost or Market** | | |
| Year 6: ($8,500 – $9,000) | -- | $ (500) |
| Year 7: ($24,600 – $9,000) | $ 15,600 | -- |
| Year 8: ($19,700 – $8,500) | -- | $ 11,200 |
| Total | $ 15,600 | $ 10,700 |

7.21 continued.

b.  The three inventory valuation methods report the same total income for the three years combined, equal to cash inflows minus cash outflows for each parcel. The acquisition cost basis allocates all of the income to the year of sale. The market value basis allocates a portion of the income to each period while the firm holds the land. The lower-of-cost-or-market method allocates holding gains to the period of sale but unrealized holding losses to the period when inventory values decline.

7.22    (Duggan Company; over sufficiently long spans, income is cash in less cash out; cost basis for inventory.)

a. **Lower of Cost or Market:**

| | Year 1 | Year 2 | Year 3 |
|---|---|---|---|
| Sales............................................. | $200,000 | $300,000 | $400,000 |
| Inventories, January 1............. | -- | $ 50,000 | $ 65,000 |
| Purchases .................................. | $210,000 | 271,000 | 352,000 |
| Goods Available for Sale ......... | $210,000 | $321,000 | $417,000 |
| Less Inventories, December 31 .............................. | (50,000) | (65,000) | (115,000) |
| Cost of Goods Sold.................... | $160,000 | $256,000 | $302,000 |
| Gross Profit on Sales ............... | $ 40,000 | $ 44,000 | $ 98,000 |

b. **Acquisition Cost:**

| | Year 1 | Year 2 | Year 3 |
|---|---|---|---|
| Sales............................................. | $200,000 | $300,000 | $400,000 |
| Inventory, January 1............... | -- | $ 60,000 | $ 80,000 |
| Purchases .................................. | $210,000 | 271,000 | 352,000 |
| Gain Available from Sale......... | $210,000 | $331,000 | $432,000 |
| Less Inventory, December 31 .............................. | (60,000) | (80,000) | (115,000) |
| Cost of Goods Sold.................... | $150,000 | $251,000 | $317,000 |
| Gross Profit on Sales ............... | $ 50,000 | $ 49,000 | $ 83,000 |

c.  The lower-of-cost-or-market basis recognizes lower income in years when prices are falling. However, when that trend is reversed, it produces higher reported income figures than the acquisition cost basis. Over long enough time periods, income is constant, equal to cash inflows minus cash outflows. Compare the total gross profit over all three years, a constant $182,000.

7.23　(Cypres; When goods available for sale exceed sales, firms can manipulate income even when they use specific identification.)

| | Revenue | − Cost of Goods Sold | = Gross Margin |
|---|---|---|---|
| a. FIFO Cost Flow: | 200 × \$600 = \$120,000 | 100 × \$300 + 100 × \$400 = \$70,000 | \$50,000 |
| b. Minimum Income: | 200 × \$600 = \$120,000 | 100 × \$400 + 100 × \$350 = \$75,000 | \$45,000 |
| c. Maximum Income: | 200 × \$600 = \$120,000 | 100 × \$300 + 100 × \$350 = \$65,000 | \$55,000 |

7.24　(Harris Company; computations involving different cost flow assumptions.)

| | Pounds | a. FIFO | b. Weighted Average | c. LIFO |
|---|---|---|---|---|
| Goods Available for Sale | 13,500 | \$65,925 | \$65,925 | \$ 65,925 |
| Less Ending Inventory | (2,500) | (13,075)[a] | (12,208)[c] | (11,350)[e] |
| Goods Sold | 11,000 | \$52,850[b] | \$53,717[d] | \$ 54,575[f] |

[a](2,000 × \$5.25) + (500 × \$5.15) = \$13,075.

[b](1,500 × \$4.50) + (4,000 × \$4.60) + (2,500 × \$4.90) + (3,000 × \$5.15) = \$52,850.

[c](\$65,925/13,500) × 2,500 = \$12,208.

[d](\$65,925/13,500) × 11,000 = \$53,717.

[e](1,500 × \$4.50) + (1,000 × \$4.60) = \$11,350.

[f](2,000 × \$5.25) + (3,500 × \$5.15) + (2,500 × \$4.90) + (3,000 × \$4.60) = \$54,575.

7.25　(Sun Health Foods; computations involving different cost flow assumptions.)

| | Units | a. FIFO | b. Weighted Average | c. LIFO |
|---|---|---|---|---|
| Goods Available for Sale | 2,500 | \$10,439 | \$10,439 | \$10,439 |
| Less Ending Inventory | (420) | (1,722)[a] | (1,754)[c] | (1,806)[e] |
| Goods Sold | 2,080 | \$ 8,717[b] | \$ 8,685[d] | \$ 8,633[f] |

[a](420 × \$4.10) = \$1,722.

[b](460 × \$4.30) + (670 × \$4.20) + (500 × \$4.16) + (450 × \$4.10) = \$8,717.

[c](\$10,439/2,500) × 420 = \$1,754.

[d](\$10,439/2,500) × 2,080 = \$8,685.

[e](420 × \$4.30) = \$1,806.

[f](870 × \$4.10) + (500 × \$4.16) + (670 × \$4.20) + (40 × \$4.30) = \$8,633.

7.26    (Howell Corporation; effect of LIFO on financial statements over several periods.)

a.  **Year**                    **Ending Inventory**

    7              8,000 × $10.00......................................    $  80,000

    8              (8,000 × $10.00) + (2,000 × $10.50).............    $101,000

    9              7,000 × $10.00......................................    $  70,000

    10             (7,000 × $10.00) + (1,000 × $12.40).............    $  82,400

b. **Year        Sales              –    Cost of Goods Sold      =  Income**
   7   28,000 × $12.00 = $336,000  28,000 × $10.00 = $280,000   $56,000
   8   38,000 × $12.60 = $478,800  38,000 × $10.50 = $399,000   $79,800
   9   48,000 × $13.23 = $635,040  45,000 × $11.30 +
                                   2,000 × $10.50 +
                                   1,000 × $10.00 = $539,500    $95,540
   10  52,000 × $13.89 = $722,280  52,000 × $12.40 = $644,800   $77,480

c.

| Year | Income | Sales | Rate of Income to Sales |
|------|--------|-------|-------------------------|
| 7 | $56,000 | $336,000 | 16.67% |
| 8 | 79,800 | 478,800 | 16.67% |
| 9 | 95,540 | 635,040 | 15.00% |
| 10 | 77,480 | 722,280 | 10.73% |

d.  Howell Corporation increased selling prices 5 percent [= ($12.60/$12.00) – 1] between Year 7 and Year 8 in line with the 5 percent [= ($10.50/$10.00) – 1] increase in acquisition costs. During Year 9, acquisition costs increased 7.6 percent [= ($11.30/$10.50) – 1] but the firm again increased selling prices only 5 percent [= ($13.23/$12.60) – 1]. Thus, the income to sales percentage declined. During Year 10, acquisition costs increased 9.7 percent [= ($12.40/$11.30) – 1] but the firm again increased selling prices only 5 percent [= $13.89/$13.23) – 1]. The income to sales percentage decreased even further.

7.27    (Barnard Corporation; effect of LIFO on financial statements over several periods.)

a.  **Year**                 **Ending Inventory**

3               2,000 × $4.00.............................................. **$ 8,000**

4               (2,000 × $4.00) + (2,800 × $4.40)................. **$20,320**

5               (2,000 × $4.00) + (2,800 × $4.40) +
                    (1,200 × $4.75)........................................... **$26,020**

6               (2,000 × $4.00) + (1,800 × $4.40)................. **$15,920**

7               (2,000 × $4.00) + (1,800 × $4.40) +
                    (1,700 × $5.85).......................................... **$25,865**

b. **Year**     **Sales**          –      **Cost of Goods Sold**    = **Income**

| Year | Sales | | | Cost of Goods Sold | | = Income |
|---|---|---|---|---|---|---|
| 3 | 6,000 × $5.00 = | $ 30,000 | 6,000 × $4.00 = | $ 24,000 | | $ 6,000 |
| 4 | 8,200 × 5.50 = | 45,100 | 8,200 × $4.40 = | $ 36,080 | | 9,020 |
| 5 | 10,800 × 5.94 = | 64,152 | 10,800 × $4.75 = | $ 51,300 | | 12,852 |
| 6 | 17,200 × 6.65 = | 114,380 | 15,000 × $5.32 = | $ 79,800 | | |
| | | | 1,200 × $4.75 = | 5,700 | | |
| | | | 1,000 × $4.40 = | 4,400 | | |
| | | | | $ 89,900 | | 24,480 |
| 7 | 18,300 × $7.32 = | 133,956 | 18,300 × $5.85 = | $ 107,055 | | 26,901 |
| Totals | | $ 387,588 | | $ 308,335 | | $ 79,253 |

c.

| Year | Income | Sales | Rate of Income to Sales |
|---|---|---|---|
| 3 | $ 6,000 | $ 30,000 | 20.0% |
| 4 | 9,020 | 45,100 | 20.0% |
| 5 | 12,852 | 64,152 | 20.0% |
| 6 | 24,480 | 114,380 | 21.4% |
| 7 | 26,901 | 133,956 | 20.0% |

d.  Barnard Corporation attempts to maintain a constant relation between replacement costs and selling prices. This relation held for each year. The income to sales percentage increased during Year 6, however, because the firm dipped into LIFO layers of earlier years. The firm matched selling prices during Year 6 with acquisition costs of Year 5 and Year 4, inflating the income to sales percentage.

7.28    (Chan Company; reconstructing financial statement data from information on effects of liquidations of LIFO layers.)

a.   $8. Cost of goods sold was $900,000 lower than it would have been had the firm maintained inventories at 200,000 units. The average cost of the 50,000 units removed from the beginning inventory was $18 (= $900,000/50,000 units) less than current cost: $26 − $18 = $8.

b.   $1,000,000. Derived as follows: $8 × 50,000 units = $400,000 decline in inventory during the year. Beginning inventory must have been $400,000 + $600,000 (ending inventory) = $1,000,000.

7.29    (EKG Company; LIFO provides opportunity for income manipulation.)

a.   Largest cost of goods sold results from producing 70,000 (or more) additional units at a cost of $22 each, giving cost of goods sold of $1,540,000.

b.   Smallest cost of goods sold results from producing no additional units, giving cost of goods sold of $980,000 [= ($8 × 10,000) + ($15 × 60,000)].

c.

|  | Income Reported | |
|---|---|---|
|  | **Minimum** | **Maximum** |
| Revenues ($30 × 70,000)............................... | $2,100,000 | $2,100,000 |
| Less Cost of Goods Sold ................................ | (1,540,000) | (980,000) |
| Gross Margin................................................. | $  560,000 | $1,120,000 |

7.30    (Sears; analysis of annual report, usage of LIFO.)

a.   Reported pretax income would have been higher by $230 million (= $670 million − $440 million).

b.   After taxes, net income would increase $230 million × .66 = $151.8 million. $151.8/$606.0 = .25; so net income would be 25 percent larger than shown, or $757.8 million.

7.31 (Giles Computer Store; separating operating margin from holding gains.)

| | FIFO | LIFO |
|---|---|---|
| **a.** | | |
| Beginning Inventory (200 × $300)............. | $ 60,000 | $ 60,000 |
| Purchases (2,500 × $400)..................... | 1,000,000 | 1,000,000 |
| Goods Available for Sale..................... | $1,060,000 | $1,060,000 |
| Less Ending Inventory: | | |
| (400 × $400).............................. | (160,000) | |
| (200 × $300) + (200 × $400)............... | | (140,000) |
| Cost of Goods Sold........................ | $ 900,000 | $ 920,000 |
| **b.** | | |
| Revenues (2,300 × $800)...................... | $1,840,000 | $1,840,000 |
| Less Cost of Goods Sold...................... | (900,000) | (920,000) |
| Gross Margin on Sales........................ | $ 940,000 | $ 920,000 |
| **c.** | | |
| Revenues..................................... | $1,840,000 | $1,840,000 |
| Less Replacement Cost of Goods Sold (2,300 × $400)... | (920,000) | (920,000) |
| Operating Margin............................. | $ 920,000 | $ 920,000 |
| Realized Holding Gains: | | |
| Replacement Cost of Goods Sold............ | $ 920,000 | $ 920,000 |
| Less Historical Cost of Goods Sold........ | (900,000) | (920,000) |
| Realized Holding Gain..................... | $ 20,000 | $ -0- |
| Gross Margin on Sales..................... | $ 940,000 | $ 920,000 |
| **d.** | | |
| Unrealized Holding Gains: | | |
| Replacement Cost of Ending Inventory (400 × $500)... | $ 200,000 | $ 200,000 |
| Less Historical Cost of Ending Inventory: | | |
| (400 × $400).............................. | (160,000) | |
| (200 × $300) + (200 × $400)............... | | (140,000) |
| Unrealized Holding Gains.................. | $ 40,000 | 60,000 |
| Total Realized Gross Margin and Unrealized Holding Gains...... | $ 980,000 | $ 980,000 |

7.32    (Warren Company; effect of inventory errors.)

a.  None.                                   f.  Understatement by $1,000.
b.  None.                                   g.  Understatement by $1,000.
c.  Understatement by $1,000.     h.  None.
d.  Overstatement by $1,000.       i.  None.
e.  Overstatement by $1,000.

7.33    (Soft-Touch, Inc.; preparation of journal entries and income statement for a manufacturing firm.)

a.  (1)  Raw Materials Inventory ..................................    66,700
             Accounts Payable............................................             66,700

     (2)  Work-in-Process Inventory..............................    63,900
             Raw Materials Inventory...............................              63,900

     (3)  Work-in-Process Inventory............................  175,770
             Selling Expenses............................................    19,200
             Administrative Expenses ...............................    22,500
             Cash ...............................................................           217,470

     (4)  Work-in-Process Inventory..............................    16,200
             Selling Expenses.............................................      3,100
             Administrative Expenses ...............................      2,200
             Accumulated Depreciation ...........................             21,500

     (5)  Work in Process Inventory..............................    18,300
             Selling Expenses.............................................      5,600
             Administrative Expenses ...............................      4,100
             Cash................................................................             28,000

     (6)  Finished Goods Inventory................................  270,870
             Work-in-Process Inventory .........................           270,870

     (7)  Accounts Receivable ......................................  350,000
             Sales................................................................           350,000

     (8)  Cost of Goods Sold.............................................  268,670
             Finished Goods Inventory ...........................           268,670
             $38,000 + $270,870 − $40,200 = $268,670.

7.33 continued.

b.
**SOFT-TOUCH, INC.**
**Income Statement**
**For the Month of January**

| | | |
|---|---:|---:|
| Sales................................................. | | $ 350,000 |
| Less Expenses: | | |
| Cost of Goods Sold ......................... | $ 268,670 | |
| Selling................................................ | 27,900 | |
| Administrative .................................. | 28,800 | (325,370) |
| Net Income........................................ | | $ 24,630 |

*Note:* Instead of using a functional classification of expenses (that is, selling, administrative), classification by their nature (salary, depreciation, other operating) is acceptable.

7.34 (Famous Horse Garment Factory; preparation of journal entries and income statement for a manufacturing firm.)

a. (1)

| | | |
|---|---:|---:|
| Raw Materials Inventory ................................... | 245,400 | |
| Accounts Payable.......................................... | | 245,400 |

(2)

| | | |
|---|---:|---:|
| Work-in-Process Inventory............................... | 238,400 | |
| Raw Materials Inventory............................... | | 238,400 |

(3)

| | | |
|---|---:|---:|
| Work-in-Process Inventory............................... | 175,200 | |
| Selling Expenses.............................................. | 37,800 | |
| Administrative Expenses ............................... | 54,800 | |
| Cash ................................................................. | | 267,800 |

(4)

| | | |
|---|---:|---:|
| Work-in-Process Inventory............................... | 29,400 | |
| Selling Expenses.............................................. | 4,800 | |
| Administrative Expenses ............................... | 5,800 | |
| Accumulated Depreciation ........................ | | 40,000 |

(5)

| | | |
|---|---:|---:|
| Work-in-Process Inventory............................... | 36,400 | |
| Selling Expenses.............................................. | 14,600 | |
| Administrative Expenses ............................... | 8,800 | |
| Cash ................................................................. | | 59,800 |

(6)

| | | |
|---|---:|---:|
| Finished Goods Inventory................................. | 468,000 | |
| Work-in-Process Inventory ......................... | | 468,000 |

(7)

| | | |
|---|---:|---:|
| Accounts Receivable ........................................ | 650,000 | |
| Sales............................................................... | | 650,000 |

7.34 a. continued.

        (8)   Cost of Goods Sold............................................... 474,000
                 Finished Goods Inventory ............................         474,000
           $146,000 + $468,000 − $140,000 = $474,000.

b.
### FAMOUS HORSE GARMENT FACTORY
#### Income Statement
#### For the Month of January
#### (In Hong Kong Dollars)

| | | |
|---|---:|---:|
| Sales.................................................................. | | $ 650,000 |
| Less Expenses: | | |
|   Cost of Goods Sold......................................... | $ 474,000 | |
|   Selling............................................................. | 57,200 | |
|   Administrative ................................................ | 69,400 | (600,600) |
| Net Income....................................................... | | $ 49,400 |

*Note:*  Instead of using a functional classification of expenses (that is, selling, administrative), classification by their nature (salary, depreciation, other operating) is acceptable.

7.35    (Cornell Company; flow of manufacturing costs through the accounts.)

    a.  Raw Materials Used: $432,300.
        Supplies Used: $22,200.

    b.  Cost of Units Completed: $867,300.

    c.  Cost of Goods Sold: $872,600.

    d.  Net Income: $110,220 [= (1 − .40)($1,350,000 − $872,300 − $246,900 − $47,100)].

T-accounts to support the amounts for Parts *a.*, *b.*, and *c.* above appear below.

| Raw Materials Inventory | | | | Factory Supplies Inventory | | |
|---|---:|---:|---|---|---:|---:|
| √ | 46,900 | | | √ | 7,600 | |
| (1) | 429,000 | 432,300   (2) | | (3) | 22,300 | 22,200   (4) |
| √ | 43,600 | | | √ | 7,700 | |

7.35 continued.

| Work-in-Process Inventory | | | Finished Goods Inventory | | |
|---|---|---|---|---|---|
| √ | 110,900 | | √ | 76,700 | |
| (2) | 432,300 | | (10) | 867,300 | 872,600 (11) |
| (4) | 22,200 | | | | |
| (5) | 362,100 | | | | |
| (6) | 10,300 | | | | |
| (7) | 4,200 | | | | |
| (8) | 36,900 | | | | |
| (9) | 3,600 | 867,300 (10) | | | |
| √ | 115,200 | | √ | 71,400 | |

| Cost of Goods Sold | | | Other Balance Sheet Accounts | | |
|---|---|---|---|---|---|
| (11) | 872,600 | | | 429,000 | (1) |
| | | | | 22,300 | (3) |
| | | | | 362,100 | (5) |
| | | | | 10,300 | (6) |
| | | | | 4,200 | (7) |
| | | | | 36,900 | (8) |
| | | | | 3,600 | (9) |

7.36    (Oak Ridge Industries; flow of manufacturing costs through the accounts.)

a.    The cost of raw materials used is $89,400.

b.    The cost of units completed and transferred to the finished goods storeroom is $183,700.

c.    Net income is $26,300 (= $250,000 – $182,400 – $41,300).

The derivation of the amounts in Parts a., b., and c. above appear in the T-accounts following.

| Raw Materials Inventory | | | Work-in-Process Inventory | | |
|---|---|---|---|---|---|
| | 25,300 | | | 78,100 | |
| (1) | 91,300 | 89,400 (2)* | (2) | 89,400 | |
| | | | (3) | 72,400 | 183,700 (6)* |
| | | | (4) | 3,100 | |
| | | | (5) | 17,600 | |
| | 27,200 | | | 76,900 | |

7.36 c. continued.

| Finished Goods Inventory | | | | | Cost of Goods Sold | | |
|---|---|---|---|---|---|---|---|
| | 38,400 | | | (7) | 182,400 | | |
| (6) | 183,700 | 182,400 | (7)* | | | | |
| | 39,700 | | | | | | |

| Accumulated Depreciation | | | | Sales | | |
|---|---|---|---|---|---|---|
| | | 17,600 | (5) | | 250,000 | (8) |

| Selling and Administrative Expenses | | | | Other Accounts | | |
|---|---|---|---|---|---|---|
| (9) | 41,300 | | (8) | 250,000 | 91,300 | (1) |
| | | | | | 72,400 | (3) |
| | | | | | 3,100 | (4) |
| | | | | | 41,300 | (9) |

*Amount derived by plugging.

7.37 (Wilmington Chemical Company; preparing T-account entries, income statement, and balance sheet for a manufacturing firm.)

a., b., and c.

| Cash | | | | | Accounts Receivable | | |
|---|---|---|---|---|---|---|---|
| Bal. | 580,800 | 60,000 | (4) | (10) | 510,900 | 495,000 | (11) |
| (11) | 495,000 | 446,010 | (5) | | | | |
| | | 105,570 | (13) | | | | |
| Bal. | 464,220 | | | Bal. | 15,900 | | |

| Raw Materials Inventory | | | | | Work-in-Process Inventory | | |
|---|---|---|---|---|---|---|---|
| Bal. | 28,800 | 253,200 | (3) | (2) | 222,000 | 422,625 | (9) |
| (1) | 242,400 | | | (3) | 253,200 | | |
| | | | | (5) | 9,000 | | |
| | | | | (5) | 4,380 | | |
| | | | | (5) | 39,600 | | |
| | | | | (6) | 180 | | |
| | | | | (7) | 1,800 | | |
| | | | | (8) | 1,200 | | |
| Bal. | 18,000 | | | Bal. | 108,735 | | |

7.37 a., b., and c. continued.

| Finished Goods Inventory | | |
|---|---|---|
| (9) 422,625 | 334,125 | (15) |
| Bal. 88,500 | | |

| Office Supplies Inventory | | |
|---|---|---|
| (13) 2,400 | 1,200 | (14) |
| Bal. 1,200 | | |

| Prepaid Insurance | | |
|---|---|---|
| (5) 14,400 | 1,200 | (8) |
| Bal. 13,200 | | |

| Factory Equipment | |
|---|---|
| Bal. 204,000 | |
| (4) 168,000 | |
| (6) 3,600 | |
| Bal. 375,600 | |

| Accumulated Depreciation | | |
|---|---|---|
| | 1,800 | (7) |
| | 1,800 | Bal. |

| Accounts Payable | | |
|---|---|---|
| (5) 210,000 | 33,600 | Bal. |
| | 242,400 | (1) |
| | 3,780 | (6) |
| | 69,780 | Bal. |

| Equipment Contract Payable | | |
|---|---|---|
| | 108,000 | (4) |
| | 108,000 | Bal. |

| Wages and Salaries Payable | | |
|---|---|---|
| (5) 168,630 | 222,000 | (2) |
| (13) 41,445 | 93,000 | (12) |
| (13) 41,325 | | |
| | 63,600 | Bal. |

| Capital Stock | | |
|---|---|---|
| | 780,000 | Bal. |
| | 780,000 | Bal. |

| Retained Earnings | | |
|---|---|---|
| | 62,175 | (18) |
| | 62,175 | Bal. |

| Sales Revenue | | |
|---|---|---|
| (17) 510,900 | 510,900 | (10) |

| Cost of Goods Sold | | |
|---|---|---|
| (15) 334,125 | 334,125 | (16) |

| Sales Salaries Expense | | |
|---|---|---|
| (12) 46,200 | 46,200 | (16) |

| Office Salaries Expense | | |
|---|---|---|
| (12) 46,800 | 46,800 | (16) |

| Advertising Expense | | |
|---|---|---|
| (13) 10,800 | 10,800 | (16) |

| Office Rent Expense | | |
|---|---|---|
| (13) 3,300 | 3,300 | (16) |

7.37 a., b., and c. continued.

| Miscellaneous Office Expenses | | | | Miscellaneous Selling Expenses | | |
|---|---|---|---|---|---|---|
| (13) | 2,100 | 2,100 | (16) | (13) | 4,200 | 4,200 | (16) |

| Office Supplies Expense | | | | Income Summary | | |
|---|---|---|---|---|---|---|
| (14) | 1,200 | 1,200 | (16) | (16) | 448,725 | 510,900 | (17) |
| | | | | (18) | 62,175 | | |
| | | | | | 510,900 | | |

d.

**WILMINGTON CHEMICAL COMPANY**
**Statement of Income and Retained Earnings**
**For the Month of October**

| | | |
|---|---|---|
| Sales................................................... | | $510,900 |
| Less Operating Expenses: | | |
| Cost of Goods Sold............................ | $334,125 | |
| Sales Salaries Expense..................... | 46,200 | |
| Office Salaries Expense..................... | 46,800 | |
| Advertising Expense ......................... | 10,800 | |
| Office Rent Expense........................... | 3,300 | |
| Miscellaneous Office Expenses......... | 2,100 | |
| Miscellaneous Selling Expenses....... | 4,200 | |
| Office Supplies Expense .................... | 1,200 | |
| Total Operating Expenses........... | | (448,725) |
| Net Income....................................... | | $ 62,175 |
| Retained Earnings, October 1............ | | -0- |
| Retained Earnings, October 31........ | | $ 62,175 |

7.37 continued.

e.

**WILMINGTON CHEMICAL COMPANY**
**Balance Sheet**
**October 31**

*Assets*

Current Assets:
Cash ............................................................. $ 464,220
Accounts Receivable .................................... 15,900
Raw Materials Inventory ............................ 18,000
Work-in-Process Inventory ......................... 108,735
Finished Goods Inventory ........................... 88,500
Office Supplies Inventory ........................... 1,200
Prepaid Insurance ....................................... 13,200
Total Current Assets .............................. $ 709,755
Noncurrent Assets:
Factory Equipment ...................................... $ 375,600
Less Accumulated Depreciation .................. (1,800)
Total Noncurrent Assets ........................ 373,800
Total Assets ............................................. $1,083,555

*Liabilities and Shareholders' Equity*

Liabilities:
Accounts Payable ......................................... $ 69,780
Equipment Contract Payable ...................... 108,000
Wages and Salaries Payable ....................... 63,600
Total Liabilities ...................................... $ 241,380
Shareholders' Equity:
Capital Stock ............................................... $ 780,000
Retained Earnings ....................................... 62,175
Total Shareholders' Equity .................... 842,175
Total Liabilities and Shareholders'
Equity ...................................................... $1,083,555

7.38     (Hartison Corporation; detailed comparison of various choices for inventory accounting.)

| | FIFO | LIFO | Weighted Average |
|---|---|---|---|
| Inventory, 1/1/Year 1 | $ 0 | $ 0 | $ 0 |
| Purchases for Year 1 | 25,600 | 25,600 | 25,600 |
| Goods Available for Sale During Year 1 | $25,600 | $25,600 | $ 25,600 |
| Less Inventory, 12/31/Year 1 | (6,400)[1] | (5,000)[2] | (5,565)[3] |
| Cost of Goods Sold for Year 1 | $19,200 | $20,600 | $ 20,035 |
| Inventory, 1/1/Year 2 | $ 6,400 [1] | $ 5,000 [2] | $ 5,565 [3] |
| Purchases for Year 2 | 42,600 | 42,600 | 42,600 |
| Goods Available for Sale During Year 2 | $49,000 | $47,600 | $ 48,165 |
| Less Inventory, 12/31/Year 2 | (5,400)[4] | (3,000)[5] | (4,661)[6] |
| Cost of Goods Sold for Year 2 | $43,600 | $44,600 | $ 43,504 |

[1] $(400 \times \$13) + (100 \times \$12) = \$6,400$.
[2] $500 \times \$10 = \$5,000$.
[3] $(\$25,600/2,300) \times 500 = \$5,565$.
[4] $300 \times \$18 = \$5,400$.
[5] $300 \times \$10 = \$3,000$.
[6] $(\$48,165/3,100) \times 300 = \$4,661$.

a. $19,200.
b. $20,600.
c. $20,035.

d. $43,600.
e. $44,600.
f. $43,504.

g.

| | Cost of Goods Sold for Two Years |
|---|---|
| FIFO | $62,800 |
| LIFO | 65,200 |

The FIFO cost flow assumption results in reported pretax income which is higher by $2,400 (= $65,200 − $62,800) over the two-year period. After taxes, the difference is reduced to .60 × $2,400 = $1,440.

h. Management might prefer to report the higher net income from FIFO of $1,440. To do so, however, requires $960 (= .40 × $2,400) of extra income tax payments currently that could be postponed until Hartison Corporation dips further into its January Year 1 purchases. We think management should use LIFO for tax purposes and, because financial reports must conform to tax reporting, in this case the firm should use LIFO for financial reporting.

**7.39** (Hartison Corporation; continuation of preceding problem introducing current cost concepts.)

a.

|  | FIFO | LIFO | Weighted Average |
|---|---|---|---|
| Sales (1,800 × $18)................... | $32,400 | $32,400 | $ 32,400 |
| Less Cost of Goods Sold at Average Current Replacement Cost (1,800 × $12)..... | (21,600) | (21,600) | (21,600) |
| Operating Margin...................... | $10,800 | $10,800 | $ 10,800 |
| Realized Holding Gain: | | | |
| Cost of Goods Sold at Current Replacement Cost.. | $21,600 | $21,600 | $ 21,600 |
| Less Cost of Goods Sold at Acquisition Cost............... | (19,200) | (20,600) | (20,035) |
| Total Realized Holding Gain...................... | $ 2,400 | $ 1,000 | $ 1,565 |
| Conventional Gross Margin.... | $13,200 | $11,800 | $ 12,365 |
| Unrealized Holding Gain: | | | |
| Ending Inventory at Current Replacement Cost (500 × $14)...................... | $ 7,000 | $ 7,000 | $ 7,000 |
| Less Ending Inventory at Acquisition Cost............... | (6,400) | (5,000) | (5,565) |
| Total Unrealized Holding Gain.............. | $ 600 | $ 2,000 | $ 1,435 |
| Less Unrealized Holding Gain at Beginning of Period............................... | -- | -- | -- |
| Total Profit Including Holding Gain[a]............................... | $13,800 | $13,800 | $ 13,800 |

[a]Total of operating margin, realized holding gain, and unrealized holding gain.

7.39 continued.

b.

| | FIFO | LIFO | Weighted Average |
|---|---|---|---|
| Sales (2,800 × $24) | $67,200 | $67,200 | $ 67,200 |
| Less Cost of Goods Sold at Average Current Replacement Cost (2,800 × $16) | (44,800) | (44,800) | (44,800) |
| Operating Margin | $22,400 | $22,400 | $ 22,400 |
| Realized Holding Gain: | | | |
| Cost of Goods Sold at Current Replacement Cost | $44,800 | $44,800 | $ 44,800 |
| Less Cost of Goods Sold at Acquisition Cost | (43,600) | (44,600) | (43,504) |
| Total Realized Holding Gain | $ 1,200 | $ 200 | $ 1,296 |
| Conventional Gross Margin | $23,600 | $22,600 | $ 23,696 |
| Unrealized Holding Gain: | | | |
| Ending Inventory at Current Replacement Cost (300 × $18) | $ 5,400 | $ 5,400 | $ 5,400 |
| Less Ending Inventory at Acquisition Cost | (5,400) | (3,000) | (4,661) |
| Total Unrealized Holding Gain | $ 0 | $ 2,400 | $ 739 |
| Less Unrealized Holding Gain at Beginning of Period (see Part a.) | (600) | (2,000) | $ (1,435) |
| Increase (Decrease) in Unrealized Holding Gain during Year 2 | $ (600) | $ 400 | $ (696) |
| Total Profit Including Holding Gain | $23,000 | $23,000 | $ 23,000 |

c.

| | FIFO | LIFO | Weighted Average |
|---|---|---|---|
| Operating Margin—Year 1 | $10,800 | $10,800 | $10,800 |
| —Year 2 | 22,400 | 22,400 | 22,400 |
| Realized Holding Gain— | | | |
| Year 1 | 2,400 | 1,000 | 1,565 |
| Year 2 | 1,200 | 200 | 1,296 |
| Unrealized Holding Gain at the End of Year 2 | 0 | 2,400 | 739 |
| Total Profit Including Holding Gain | $36,800 | $36,800 | $36,800 |

7.40    (Burton Corporation; detailed comparison of various choices for inventory accounting.)

| | FIFO | LIFO | Weighted Average |
|---|---|---|---|
| Inventory, 1/1/Year 1...................... | $ 0 | $ 0 | $ 0 |
| Purchases for Year 1...................... | 14,400 | 14,400 | 14,400 |
| Goods Available for Sale During Year 1 ......................................... | $14,400 | $14,400 | $ 14,400 |
| Less Inventory, 12/31/Year 1........ | (3,000)[1] | (2,000)[2] | (2,400)[3] |
| Cost of Goods Sold for Year 1 ........ | $11,400 | $12,400 | $ 12,000 |
| Inventory, 1/1/Year 2...................... | $ 3,000 [1] | $ 2,000 [2] | $ 2,400 [3] |
| Purchases for Year 2...................... | 21,000 | 21,000 | 21,000 |
| Goods Available for Sale During Year 2 ......................................... | $24,000 | $23,000 | $ 23,400 |
| Less Inventory, 12/31/Year 2........ | (5,000)[4] | (6,200)[5] | (5,850)[6] |
| Cost of Goods Sold for Year 2 ........ | $19,000 | $16,800 | $ 17,550 |

[1] $200 \times \$15 = \$3,000$.
[2] $200 \times \$10 = \$2,000$.
[3] $(\$14,400/1,200) \times 200 = \$2,400$.
[4] $500 \times \$10 = \$5,000$.
[5] $(200 \times \$10) + (300 \times \$14) = \$6,200$.
[6] $(\$23,400/2,000) \times 500 = \$5,850$.

| | | | |
|---|---|---|---|
| a. | $11,400. | d. | $19,000. |
| b. | $12,400. | e. | $16,800. |
| c. | $12,000. | f. | $17,550. |

g.    FIFO results in higher net income for Year 1. Purchase prices for inventory items increased during Year 1. FIFO uses older, lower purchase prices to measure cost of goods sold, whereas LIFO uses more recent, higher prices.

h.    LIFO results in higher net income for Year 2. Purchase prices for inventory items decreased during Year 2. LIFO uses more recent, lower prices to measure cost of goods sold, whereas FIFO uses older, higher prices.

7.41    (Burton Corporation; continuation of preceding problem introducing current cost concepts.)

a.

|  | FIFO | LIFO | Weighted Average |
|---|---|---|---|
| Sales (1,000 X $25)..................... | $25,000 | $25,000 | $ 25,000 |
| Less Cost of Goods Sold at Average Current Replacement Cost (1,000 X $14)..... | (14,000) | (14,000) | (14,000) |
| Operating Margin ...................... | $11,000 | $11,000 | $ 11,000 |
| Realized Holding Gain: | | | |
| Cost of Goods Sold at Current Replacement Cost.. | $14,000 | $14,000 | $ 14,000 |
| Less Cost of Goods Sold at Acquisition Cost............... | (11,400) | (12,400) | (12,000) |
| Total Realized Holding Gain.......................... | $ 2,600 | $ 1,600 | $ 2,000 |
| Conventional Gross Margin.... | $13,600 | $12,600 | $ 13,000 |
| Unrealized Holding Gain: | | | |
| Ending Inventory at Current Replacement Cost (200 X $16)....................... | $ 3,200 | $ 3,200 | $ 3,200 |
| Less Ending Inventory at Acquisition Cost............... | (3,000) | (2,000) | (2,400) |
| Total Unrealized Holding Gain ............ | $ 200 | $ 1,200 | $ 800 |
| Total Profit Including Holding Gain[a]..................................... | $13,800 | $13,800 | $ 13,800 |

[a]Total of operating margin, realized holding gain, and unrealized holding gain.

7.41 continued.

b.

| | FIFO | LIFO | Weighted Average |
|---|---|---|---|
| Sales (1,500 X $22)................... | $33,000 | $33,000 | $ 33,000 |
| Less Cost of Goods Sold at Average Current Replacement Cost (1,500 X $12)..... | (18,000) | (18,000) | (18,000) |
| Operating Margin ..................... | $15,000 | $15,000 | $ 15,000 |
| Realized Holding Gain: | | | |
| Cost of Goods Sold at Current Replacement Cost.. | $18,000 | $18,000 | $ 18,000 |
| Less Cost of Goods Sold at Acquisition Cost............... | (19,000) | (16,800) | (17,550) |
| Total Realized Holding Gain (Loss)............... | $ (1,000) | $ 1,200 | $ 450 |
| Conventional Gross Margin.... | $14,000 | $16,200 | $ 15,450 |
| Unrealized Holding Gain: | | | |
| Ending Inventory at Current Replacement Cost (500 X $10)...................... | $ 5,000 | $ 5,000 | $ 5,000 |
| Less Ending Inventory at Acquisition Cost.............. | (5,000) | (6,200) | (5,850) |
| Total Unrealized Holding Gain (Loss)..................... | $ 0 | $ (1,200) | $ (850) |
| Less Unrealized Holding Gain at Beginning of Period (see Part a.)............................. | (200) | (1,200) | (800) |
| Increase (Decrease) in Unrealized Holding Gain during Year 2............................ | $ (200) | $ (2,400) | $ (1,650) |
| Total Profit Including Holding Gain ................................... | $13,800 | $13,800 | $ 13,800 |

c.

| | FIFO | LIFO | Weighted Average |
|---|---|---|---|
| Operating Margin—Year 1 ...... | $11,000 | $11,000 | $11,000 |
| —Year 2...... | 15,000 | 15,000 | 15,000 |
| Realized Holding Gain (Loss) | | | |
| Year 1..................................... | 2,600 | 1,600 | 2,000 |
| Year 2..................................... | (1,000) | 1,200 | 450 |
| Unrealized Holding Gain at the End of Year 2 ................... | 0 | (1,200) | (850) |
| Total Profit Including Holding Gain (Loss) ..... | $27,600 | $27,600 | $27,600 |

7.42    (Hanover Oil Products; effect of FIFO and LIFO on income statement and balance sheet.)

a.

|  | FIFO | LIFO |
|---|---|---|
| Beginning Inventory | $       0 | $       0 |
| Purchases: | | |
| 1/1:   4,000 @ $1.40 | $   5,600 | $   5,600 |
| 1/13: 6,000 @ $1.46 | 8,760 | 8,760 |
| 1/28: 5,000 @ $1.50 | 7,500 | 7,500 |
| Total Purchases | $ 21,860 | $ 21,860 |
| Available for Sale | $ 21,860 | $ 21,860 |
| Less Ending Inventory: | | |
| FIFO:  2,000 × $1.50 | (3,000) | |
| LIFO:  2,000 × $1.40 | | (2,800) |
| Cost of Goods Sold | $ 18,860 | $ 19,060 |

b.

|  | FIFO | LIFO |
|---|---|---|
| Beginning Inventory | $   3,000 | $   2,800 |
| Purchases: | | |
| 2/5:    7,000 @ $1.53 | $ 10,710 | $ 10,710 |
| 2/14:   6,000 @ $1.47 | 8,820 | 8,820 |
| 2/21: 10,000 @ $1.42 | 14,200 | 14,200 |
| Total Purchases | $ 33,730 | $ 33,730 |
| Available for Sale | $ 36,730 | $ 36,530 |
| Less Ending Inventory: | | |
| FIFO:  3,000 × $1.42 | (4,260) | |
| LIFO:  (2,000 × $1.40) + (1,000 × $1.53) | | (4,330) |
| Cost of Goods Sold | $ 32,470 | $ 32,200 |

c.

|  | FIFO | LIFO |
|---|---|---|
| Beginning Inventory | $   4,260 | $   4,330 |
| Purchases: | | |
| 3/2:   6,000 @ $1.48 | $   8,880 | $   8,880 |
| 3/15: 5,000 @ $1.54 | 7,700 | 7,700 |
| 3/26: 4,000 @ $1.60 | 6,400 | 6,400 |
| Total Purchases | $ 22,980 | $ 22,980 |
| Available for Sale | $ 27,240 | $ 27,310 |
| Less Ending Inventory: | | |
| FIFO:  1,000 × $1.60 | (1,600) | |
| LIFO:  1,000 × $1.40 | | (1,400) |
| Cost of Goods Sold | $ 25,640 | $ 25,910 |

d.  Acquisition costs increased during January.  During such periods, LIFO generally provides larger cost of goods sold amounts than FIFO because LIFO uses the most recent higher cost.  Acquisition costs decreased during February.  Under these circumstances, FIFO generally results in higher cost of goods sold because it uses the higher older cost.  During March, acquisition costs increased.  There was a liquidation of LIFO

7.42 d. continued.

layers, however, which makes it more difficult to generalize about which cost flow assumption results in the higher cost of goods sold. LIFO results in the higher cost of goods sold in this case because the effect of increasing purchase costs dominated the effect of the LIFO liquidation.

e.

|  | January FIFO | January LIFO | February FIFO | February LIFO | March FIFO | March LIFO |
|---|---|---|---|---|---|---|
| (1) Sales.......... | $20,840 | $20,840 | $35,490 | $35,490 | $28,648 | $28,648 |
| (2) Cost of Goods Sold ... | 18,860 | 19,060 | 32,470 | 32,200 | 25,640 | 25,910 |
| (2)/(1)............... | 90.5% | 91.5% | 91.5% | 90.7% | 89.5% | 90.4% |

f. LIFO provides the most stable cost of goods sold to sales percentage because LIFO cost of goods sold amounts reflect current replacement cost more fully than FIFO. The firm prices its gasoline at a 10 percent markup on current replacement cost, so the cost of goods sold to sales percentage under LIFO will be closer to 90.9 percent (= 1/1.1) than FIFO.

g.

| | | |
|---|---|---|
| Available for Sale (from Part c.)...................... | $ 27,240 | $ 27,310 |
| Plus Additional Purchases: 2,000 x $1.60..... | 3,200 | 3,200 |
| Less Ending Inventory: | | |
| FIFO: 3,000 x $1.60................................... | (4,800) | |
| LIFO: (2,000 x $1.40) + (1,000 x $1.53)..... | | (4,330) |
| Cost of Goods Sold............................................ | $ 25,640 | $ 26,180 |

Costs of goods sold will not change under FIFO because the additional purchases simply increase both the quantity and valuation of the ending inventory. Cost of goods sold increases under LIFO because the additional purchases increase the quantity of ending inventory but the purchase price paid substitutes for the LIFO layers liquidated in measuring cost of goods sold.

7.43　(The Back Store; dealing with LIFO inventory layers.)

a.　200,000 units purchased in Year 30 – 10,000 units purchased in Year 30 included in the 12/31/Year 30 inventory = 190,000 units.

b.
| | |
|---|---|
| Revenue (300,000 Units @ $15) | $4,500,000 |
| Replacement Cost of Goods Sold (300,000 Units @ $10) | 3,000,000 |
| Operating Margin on Sales | $1,500,000 |

c.
| | | |
|---|---|---|
| Replacement Cost of Goods Sold (Average) | | $3,000,000 |
| Less Acquisition Cost: | | |
| 250,000 × $10 | $2,500,000 | |
| 10,000 × $9 | 90,000 | |
| 20,000 × $6 | 120,000 | |
| 20,000 × $3 | 60,000 | 2,770,000 |
| Realized Holding Gain | | $ 230,000 |

Thus:　$1,500,000 + $230,000 = $1,730,000 (conventional gross margin).

d.
| | | |
|---|---|---|
| Conventional Gross Margin | | $1,730,000 |
| Unrealized Holding Gain: | | |
| Replacement Cost at Period-End: 40,000 × $11 | $ 440,000 | |
| Acquisition Cost: 40,000 × $3 | (120,000) | 320,000 |
| Less: Unrealized Holding Gain in Beginning Inventory: | | |
| Replacement Cost on 12/31/Year 30: 90,000 × $8 | $ 720,000 | |
| Inventory Cost on 12/31/Year 30 | 390,000 | (330,000) |
| Economic Profit | | $1,720,000 |

e.
| | | |
|---|---|---|
| Sales (300,000 × $15) | | $4,500,000 |
| Less Acquisition Cost of Goods Sold: | | |
| 90,000 × $9 | $ 810,000 | |
| 210,000 × $10 | 2,100,000 | (2,910,000) |
| Conventional Gross Margin (FIFO) | | $1,590,000 |

This equals the operating margin on sales of $1,500,000 (see Part b. above) plus the realized holding gain of $90,000 which is the replacement cost of goods sold of $3,000,000 less the acquisition cost of goods sold of $2,910,000.

7.44    (Burch Corporation; reconstructing underlying events from ending inventory amounts [adapted from CPA examination].)

a.  Down. Notice that lower of cost or market is lower than acquisition cost (FIFO); current market price is less than cost.

b.  Up. FIFO means last-in, still-here. The last purchases (FIFO = LISH) cost $44,000 and the earlier purchases (LIFO = FISH) cost $41,800. Also, lower-of-cost-or-market basis shows acquisition costs which are greater than or equal to current cost.

c.  LIFO Cost. Other things being equal, the largest income results from the method that shows the largest *increase* in inventory during the year.

Margin  = Revenues – Cost of Goods Sold
        = Revenues – Beginning Inventory – Purchases + Ending Inventory
        = Revenues – Purchases + Increase in Inventory.

Because the beginning inventory in Year 1 is zero, the method with the largest closing inventory amount implies the largest increase and hence the largest income.

d.  Lower of Cost or Market. The method with the "largest increase in inventory" during the year in this case is the method with the smallest decrease, because all methods show declines in inventory during Year 2. Lower of cost or market shows a decrease in inventory of only $3,000 during Year 2—the other methods show larger decreases ($3,800; $4,000).

e.  Lower of Cost or Market. The method with the largest increase in inventory: $10,000. LIFO shows a $5,400 increase while FIFO shows $8,000.

f.  LIFO Cost. The lower income for all three years results from the method that shows the smallest increase in inventory over the three years. Because all beginning inventories were zero under all methods, we need merely find the method with the smallest ending inventory at Year 3 year-end.

g.  FIFO lower by $2,000. Under FIFO, inventories increased $8,000 during Year 3. Under lower of cost or market, inventories increased $10,000 during Year 3. Lower of cost or market has a bigger increase—$2,000—and therefore lower of cost or market shows a $2,000 larger income than FIFO for Year 3.

7.45 (Wilson Company; LIFO layers influence purchasing behavior and provide opportunity for income manipulation.)

| | Cost per Pound | Layer | Beginning Inventory Cost ($000) | + Purchases Cost ($000) | – Ending Inventory Pounds | – Ending Inventory Cost ($000) | = Cost of Goods Sold ($000) |
|---|---|---|---|---|---|---|---|
| a. | (Controller) | Year 1 | $ 60.0 | --- | 2,000 | $ 60.0 | --- |
| | | Year 6 | 9.2 | --- | 200 | 9.2 | --- |
| | | Year 7 | 19.2 | --- | 400 | 19.2 | --- |
| | 7,000 @ | Year 10 | 72.8 | --- | 1,400 | 72.8 | --- |
| | $62/lb. | Year 11 | --- | $ 434.0 | --- | --- | 434.0 |
| | | | $ 161.2 | $ 434.0 | 4,000 | $ 161.2 | $ 434.0 |
| | | | | | | | |
| b. | (Purchasing | Year 1 | $ 60.0 | --- | 600 | $ 18.0 | $ 42.0 |
| | Agent) | Year 6 | 9.2 | --- | --- | --- | 9.2 |
| | | Year 7 | 19.2 | --- | --- | --- | 19.2 |
| | 3,600 @ | Year 10 | 72.8 | --- | --- | --- | 72.8 |
| | $62/lb. | Year 11 | --- | $ 223.2 | --- | --- | 223.2 |
| | | | $ 161.2 | $ 223.2 | 600 | $ 18.0 | $ 366.4 |

c. Controller's Policy COGS $62/lb...........................................  $ 434.00
Less Purchasing Agent's COGS...........................................  (366.40)
Controller's Extra Deductions............................................  $ 67.60
Tax Rate: 40 Percent......................................................  X .40
Controller's Tax Savings..................................................  $ 27.04
Controller's Extra Cash Costs for Inventory; 3,400 @
  $10/lb. .................................................................  $ 34.00

d. Follow the purchasing agent's advice. The controller's policy does save taxes but not as much in taxes as the extra inventory costs.

e. Not a coincidence. Total increase in wealth includes both realized and unrealized holding gains and the sum of those two does not depend on cost flow assumption. Cost flow assumption determines split of total holding gain between realized and unrealized, not their total.

© 2003 Thomson Learning, Inc.
Solutions

7.45 continued.

e. To maximize income for Year 11, liquidate all our LIFO inventory layers, 4,000 lbs. with total cost $161,200, and purchase only 3,000 lbs. at $62 each during Year 11. To minimize income, acquire 7,000 lbs. at $62 each.

| Policy | Cost of Goods Sold for Year 11 |
|---|---|
| Minimum Income: | |
| 7,000 lbs. × $62 | $434,000 |
| Maximum Income: | |
| 4,000 lbs. of Old Layer | (161,200) |
| 3,000 lbs. at $62 | (186,000) |
| Income Spread before Taxes | $ 86,800 |
| Taxes at 40 Percent | (34,720) |
| Income Spread after Taxes | $ 52,080 |

By manipulating purchases of expensium, Wilson Company reports aftertax income anywhere in the range from $50,000 (by following the controller's policy) up to $102,080 (= $50,000 + $52,080) by acquiring only 3,000 lbs. and liquidating all LIFO layers.

7.46 (Bethlehem Steel; assessing the effect of LIFO versus FIFO on financial statements.) (Amounts in Millions)

a.

| | Year 9 | Year 10 | Year 11 |
|---|---|---|---|
| Cost of Goods Sold: LIFO | $4,399.1 | $4,327.2 | $4,059.7 |
| Plus Excess of FIFO Cost over LIFO Values, Beginning of Year | 530.1 | 562.5 | 499.1 |
| Less Excess of FIFO Cost over LIFO Values, End of Year | (562.5) | (499.1) | (504.9) |
| Cost of Goods Sold: FIFO | $4,366.7 | $4,390.6 | $4,053.9 |

b.

| Cost of Goods Sold/Sales | Year 9 | Year 10 | Year 11 |
|---|---|---|---|
| LIFO: $4,399.1/$5,250.9 | 83.8% | | |
| $4,327.2/$4,899.2 | | 88.3% | |
| $4,059.7/$4,317.9 | | | 94.0% |
| | | | |
| FIFO: $4,366.7/$5,250.9 | 83.2% | | |
| $4,390.6/$4,899.2 | | 89.6% | |
| $4,053.9/$4,317.9 | | | 93.9% |

7.46 continued.

 c. Inventory quantities increased during Year 9 (LIFO ending inventory exceeds LIFO beginning inventory) but it is difficult to conclude for sure the direction of the change in manufacturing costs. It appears, however, that manufacturing costs increased during the year because cost of goods sold using LIFO exceeds cost of goods sold using FIFO. Inventory quantities increased again during Year 10 but it appears that manufacturing costs decreased, resulting in a higher cost of goods sold using FIFO than using LIFO. Clues that manufacturing costs decreased include (1) the excess of FIFO cost over LIFO values declined during Year 10, despite an increase in inventory quantities, and (2) ending inventory using FIFO is less that beginning inventory using FIFO, despite an increase in inventory quantities. Inventory quantities decreased during Year 11 but it appears that manufacturing costs increased. The principal clue for the latter conclusion is that the excess of FIFO cost over LIFO values increased during the year, despite a decrease in inventory quantities. The slightly higher cost of goods sold percentage using LIFO results from using higher manufacturing costs toward the end of Year 11 as well as dipping into the Year 10 LIFO layer priced at the higher manufacturing cost at the beginning of Year 10.

| d. **Inventory Turnover Ratio** | **Year 9** | **Year 10** | **Year 11** |
|---|---|---|---|
| LIFO: $4,399.1/.5($369.0 + $410.3)... | 11.3 | | |
| $4,327.2/.5($410.3 + $468.3)... | | 9.9 | |
| $4,059.7/.5($468.3 + $453.4)... | | | 8.8 |
| | | | |
| FIFO: $4,366.7/.5($899.1 + $972.8)... | 4.7 | | |
| $4,390.6/.5($972.8 + $967.4)... | | 4.5 | |
| $4,053.9/.5($967.4 + $958.3)... | | | 4.2 |

 e. The inventory turnover ratio for LIFO includes current cost data in the numerator and old cost data in the denominator, whereas this ratio under FIFO includes somewhat out-of-date cost data in the numerator and a mixture of out-of-date and current cost data in the denominator. The mismatching of cost data is less severe for FIFO than for LIFO because of the very old LIFO layers. Thus, the inventory turnover ratio using FIFO probably more accurately measures the actual rate of inventory turnover.

**Solutions**

7.46 continued.

f. 
| Current Ratio | Year 8 | Year 9 | Year 10 | Year 11 |
|---|---|---|---|---|
| LIFO: $1,439.8/$870.1........ | 1.65 | | | |
| $1,435.2/$838.0........ | | 1.71 | | |
| $1,203.2/$831.4........ | | | 1.45 | |
| $957.8/$931.0.......... | | | | 1.03 |
| | | | | |
| FIFO: $1,439.8 + (.66 X $530.1)/$870.1........ | 2.06 | | | |
| $1,435.2 + (.66 X $562.5)/$838.0........ | | 2.16 | | |
| $1,203.2 + (.66 X $499.1/)/$831.4....... | | | 1.84 | |
| $957.8 + (.66 X $504.9)/$931.0........ | | | | 1.39 |

g. The current ratio decreased between Year 9 and Year 11, suggesting increased short-term liquidity risk. The current ratio using a FIFO cost-flow assumption for inventories probably reflects better the potential of current assets to cover current liabilities because the FIFO inventory values use more recent cost data. The current ratio using FIFO inventory values still exceeds 1.0 at the end of Year 11, suggesting that short-term liquidity risk is not yet at a serious level. However, the sharp decrease during the three-year period coupled with a slower inventory turnover (see Part *d.* above) raise doubts about the future.

*Note:* The annual report indicates that the decreased current ratio occurs primarily because of reductions in cash that Bethlehem Steel Company needed to help finance its deteriorating operating position.

7.47 (British Petroleum Company; calculating operating margins and realized holding gains.)

a. (Amounts in Millions of British Pounds)

| | Year 8 | Year 9 | Year 10 | Year 11 |
|---|---|---|---|---|
| Sales...................................... | £ 25,922 | £29,641 | £ 33,039 | £ 32,613 |
| Replacement Cost of Goods Sold......................... | (19,330) | (22,095) | (24,655) | (25,117) |
| Operating Margin............... | £ 6,592 | £ 7,546 | £ 8,384 | £ 7,496 |
| Realized Holding Gain: Replacement Cost of Goods Sold...................... | £ 19,330 | £22,095 | £ 24,655 | £ 25,117 |
| Acquisition Cost of Goods Sold...................... | (19,562) | (21,705) | (24,178) | (25,746) |
| Total............................. | £ (232) | £ 390 | £ 477 | £ (629) |
| Gross Margin....................... | £ 6,360 | £ 7,936 | £ 8,861 | £ 6,867 |

7.47 continued.

    b.  **Operating Margin/Sales**

| | | | |
|---|---|---|---|
| £6,592/£25,922................... | 25.4% | | |
| £7,546/£29,641................... | | 25.5% | |
| £8,384/£33,039................... | | | 25.4% |
| £7,496/£32,613................... | | | 23.0% |

       **Gross Margin/Sales**

| | | | |
|---|---|---|---|
| £6,360/£25,922................... | 24.5% | | |
| £7,936/£29,641................... | | 26.8% | |
| £8,861/£33,039................... | | | 26.8% |
| £6,867/£32,613................... | | | 21.1% |

    c.  BP's operating margin to sales percentage fluctuates less than its gross margin to sales percentage. Perhaps BP provides the replacement cost of goods sold data to show the financial community that it prices its products at a relatively constant markup on replacement cost (except for Year 11). Variations in the gross margin percentage result from varying rates of change in oil prices over which BP has little, if any, control. The effects of these variations appear in realized holding gains and losses. Although BP's operating margin to sales percentage decreased in Year 11, the rate of decrease is not as large as the decrease in the gross margin to sales percentage. BP was able to almost maintain its historical operating margin percentage, despite decreases in petroleum costs.

         In years when significant increases in oil prices occur because of problems in the Middle East, these disclosures permit BP to show that most of the increase in its gross margin results from realized holding gains instead of increased operating margin. By including these disclosures each year, even when oil prices do not change much, BP educates the financial community regarding the effect of factors outside of its control on profitability.

7.48    (Olin Corporation; interpreting inventory disclosures.)

    a.  $2,161 + ($501 − $320) − ($474 − $329) = $2,197.

    b.  The quantities of inventory items increased since Olin Corporation added a new LIFO layer during the year (that is, the ending inventory under LIFO exceeds the beginning inventory under LIFO).

    c.  The cost of inventory items decreased during the year. One clue is that the cost of goods sold under FIFO exceeds that under LIFO. A second clue is that the excess of FIFO over LIFO inventory at the end of the year is less than at the beginning of the year despite an increase in quantities.

7.48 continued.

    d.   LIFO:  $2,161/.5($320 + $329) = 6.7.
         FIFO:  $2,197/.5($501 + $474) = 4.5.

    e.   The difference in the rate of inventory turnover occurs because LIFO uses old costs in computing inventory amounts whereas FIFO uses more up-to-date costs.  Both cost flow assumptions use relatively recent costs in the numerator of the ratio, although those for LIFO are more up-to-date.

    f.   The amount for purchases in the numerator of the accounts payable turnover ratio should not differ between LIFO and FIFO, unless the firm accelerates purchases or production at the end of a year to avoid dipping into its LIFO layers. The average balance for accounts payable in the denominator of the ratio should not differ between LIFO and FIFO, unless the extra income taxes paid under FIFO (rising prices) or LIFO (falling prices) constrains a firm's ability to repay its suppliers.

7.49    (Eli Lilly; analyzing inventory disclosures.)

    a.

|  | Year 8 | Year 9 | Year 10 |
|---|---|---|---|
| Cost of Goods Sold using LIFO | $2,015.1 | $2,098.0 | $2,055.7 |
| Plus (Minus) Excess of FIFO (LIFO) over LIFO (FIFO) Beginning Inventory | 11.7 | (2.7) | (7.1) |
| Less (Minus) Excess of FIFO (LIFO) over LIFO (FIFO) Ending Inventory | 2.7 | 7.1 | (11.9) |
| Cost of Goods Sold using FIFO | $2,029.5 | $2,102.4 | $2,036.7 |

    b.   The inventory at the end of Year 8 under LIFO exceeded the inventory at the end of Year 9, suggesting that Eli Lilly dipped into LIFO layers during Year 9. Likewise, the inventory at the end of Year 9 under LIFO exceeded the inventory at the end of Year 10, suggesting that Eli Lilly dipped into LIFO layers during Year 10.

    c.   Manufacturing likely increased during some years and decreased in other years. Manufacturing costs likely decreased during Year 8.  Cost of goods sold under FIFO exceeded cost of goods sold under LIFO during Year 8. Eli Lilly did not appear to dip into LIFO layers during Year 8 since its ending inventory exceeded its beginning inventory. The ending inventory under LIFO exceeds the ending inventory under FIFO, providing further evidence that manufacturing costs decreased during the year.

7.49 c. continued.

       Manufacturing costs likely decreased further during Year 9. Cost of goods sold under FIFO again exceeds cost of goods sold under LIFO. However, it appears that Eli Lilly dipped into LIFO layers of earlier years. If these layers had a lower cost than the manufacturing costs incurred during Year 9, then part of the reason for the lower LIFO cost of goods sold could relate to the LIFO liquidations. The ending inventory under LIFO exceeds the ending inventory under FIFO, despite lower inventory levels at the end of Year 9 than at the end of Year 8. The excess of LIFO ending inventory over FIFO ending inventory increased during Year 9, lending further support to the conclusion that manufacturing costs decreased during Year 9.

       Manufacturing costs likely increased during Year 10. Cost of goods sold under LIFO exceeds cost of goods sold under FIFO. This occurred despite Eli Lilly dipping into LIFO layers during the year. The ending inventory under FIFO exceeds that under LIFO, lending further support for an increase in manufacturing costs during Year 10.

d.

| | LIFO | FIFO |
|---|---|---|
| **Year 8** | $2,015.1/$9,236.8 = 21.8% | $2,029.5/$9,236.8 = 22.0% |
| **Year 9** | $2,098.0/$10,002.6 = 21.0% | $2,102.4/$10,002.6 = 21.0% |
| **Year 10** | $2,055.7/$10,862.2 = 18.9% | $2,036.7/$10,862.2 = 18.8% |

e.

| | LIFO | FIFO |
|---|---|---|
| **Year 8** | $2,015.1/.5($900.7 + $999.9) = 2.1 | $2,029.5/.5($912.4 + $997.2) = 2.1 |
| **Year 9** | $2,098.0/.5($999.9 + $899.6) = 2.2 | $2,102.4/.5($997.2 + $892.5) = 2.2 |
| **Year 10** | $2,055.7/.5($899.6 + $883.1) = 2.3 | $2,036.7/.5($892.5 + $895.0) = 2.3 |

f.

| | Year 8 | Year 9 | Year 10 |
|---|---|---|---|
| Cost of Goods Sold.................. | $ 2,029.5 | $ 2,102.4 | $ 2,036.7 |
| Plus Ending Finished Goods Inventory............................ | 236.3 | 224.7 | 284.3 |
| Less Beginning Finished Goods Inventory................ | (191.0) | (236.3) | (224.7) |
| Cost of Goods Manufactured during the Year................ | $ 2,074.8 | $ 2,090.8 | $ 2,096.3 |

g.   **Year 8:**  $2,029.5/.5($191.0 + $236.3) = 9.5
    **Year 9:**  $2,102.4/.5($236.3 + $224.7) = 9.1
    **Year 10:** $2,036.7/.5($224.7 + $284.3) = 8.0

h.   **Year 8:**  $2,074.8/.5($459.4 + $435.8) = 4.6
    **Year 9:**  $2,090.8/.5($435.8 + $372.7) = 5.2
    **Year 10:** $2,096.3/.5($372.7 + $380.6) = 5.6

7.49 continued.

i. The decrease in the cost of goods sold to sales percentage between Year 8 and Year 9 relates in part to lower manufacturing costs. Sales increased 8.3 percent [= ($10,002.6/$9,236.8) − 1]. Perhaps the firm spread the relatively fixed costs of its manufacturing facilities over a larger sales base, reducing its average per unit costs. The firm may also have raised its prices, thereby reducing its cost of goods sold to sales percentage. Note that the percentage decreased on both a LIFO and a FIFO basis, so the cost flow assumption and the dipping into LIFO layers does not change this trend. The decrease in the cost of goods sold to sales percentage between Year 9 and Year 10 likely results from increased selling prices. Manufacturing costs increased during the year.

The increase in the inventory turnover ratio suggests more effective inventory control. The analysis in Parts *g.* and *h.* suggests that the improvement relates to an increase in the work-in-process inventory turnover, offset by a decrease in the finished goods inventory turnover.

# CHAPTER 8

## PLANT, EQUIPMENT, AND INTANGIBLE ASSETS: THE SOURCE OF OPERATING CAPACITY

*Questions, Exercises, Problems, and Cases: Answers and Solutions*

8.1     See the text or the glossary at the end of the book.

8.2     Maintenance services provided for selling and administrative activities appear as expenses of the current period. Maintenance services provided for manufacturing activities accumulate in Work-in-Process and Finished Goods Inventory accounts. These costs become expenses in the period of sale. Expenditures from any of these activities that increase the service life or service potential of assets beyond that originally expected increase the assets' depreciable base. Such expenditures become expenses as the firm recognizes depreciation during future years.

8.3     Generally accepted accounting principles use acquisition costs in the valuation of most assets. Accounting gives no recognition to the fact that some firms can acquire a particular asset for a lower price than other firms can acquire it. Part of the explanation relates to measuring the relevant cost savings. There is seldom a single, unique alternative price. Additionally, accounting views firms as generating income from using assets in operations, not from simply purchasing them.

The income effect of both recording procedures is a net expense of $250,000, the cash outflow to self-construct the warehouse. The generally accepted procedure recognizes $250,000 as depreciation expense over the life of the warehouse. The unacceptable procedure recognizes revenue of $50,000 upon completion of the warehouse and depreciation expense of $300,000 over the life of the warehouse.

8.4     a.  Over the life of the project, income is cash-in less cash-out. Capitalizing and then amortizing interest versus expensing it affects the timing but not the total amount of income. Capitalizing interest defers expense from the construction period to the periods of use, increasing income in the early years of construction and decreasing it in the periods of use, when depreciation charges are larger.

        b.  The "catch-up" described in the preceding part is indefinitely delayed. Reported income in each year increases by the policy of capitalizing interest. When the self-construction activity declines, then the reported income declines as a result of reduced capitalization of interest, but not before.

8.5     a.   If the life of an asset is shorter than the accounting period (or that portion of the period remaining after the purchase of the asset), depreciation, as an accounting measurement problem, disappears. The difficulties increase as it becomes necessary to spread the cost of an asset over a number of periods of time. If the accounting period were ten years, fewer items would have to be spread, or "depreciated." If no asset lasted more than a year or two, accountants could make even annual depreciation calculations with considerable accuracy.

          b.   Depreciation accounting allocates the cost of long-lived assets to the periods of use in an orderly, reasonable manner. Charging depreciation does not "provide funds" for the firm. Selling the firm's products to customers provides funds.

8.6     a.   Depreciation life is: $100,000/$10,000 per year = 10 years.

             Age of the asset is: $60,000 accumulated depreciation charge divided by $10,000 depreciation per year = 6 years.

          b.   Age of the asset in years = accumulated depreciation at the end of a year divided by depreciation charge for the year.

8.7     Depreciation for years prior to the change in estimate is larger or smaller than it would have been if the firm had originally used the revised estimate. Depreciation for the current and future years is also smaller or larger than it would be if the firm corrected for the original misestimate retroactively. Thus, depreciation in no year of the assets' service life will show the appropriate depreciation for the actual depreciable life of assets.

8.8     The small amounts of certain expenditures often do not justify the record keeping cost of capitalization and amortization. Firms therefore expense all expenditures below a certain threshold amount.

8.9     The relevant question to apply generally accepted accounting principles is whether the expenditure maintained the originally expected useful life or extended that useful life. Firms should expense, as maintenance or repairs, expenditures that maintain the originally expected five-year life. In this case, the expenditure both maintains and extends the useful life. A portion of the expenditure should appear as an expense immediately (perhaps two-thirds) and a portion (perhaps one-third) should increase the depreciable base for the asset.

8.10    Accounting views sales of plant assets as peripheral to a firm's principal business activities. Revenues and expenses from a firm's principal business activities appear as sales revenue and cost of goods sold. Accounting nets the revenues and expenses from peripheral activities to show only the gain or loss.

8.11    Generally accepted accounting principles compares the undiscounted cash flows from an asset to its book value to determine if an impairment loss has occurred. The rationale is that an impairment loss has not occurred if a firm will receive cash flows in the future at least equal to the book value of the asset. Receiving such cash flows will permit the firm to recover the book value. This criterion ignores the time value of money. Cash received earlier has more economic value than cash received later, but this criterion ignores such differences.

8.12    Some critics of the required expensing of research and development (R & D) costs argue that there is little difference to justify the different accounting treatments. One possible explanation for the different treatment is the greater tangible nature of mineral resources relative to most R & D expenditures. Yet, some R & D expenditures result in tangible prototypes or products. Another possible explanation for the difference is the established market for most mineral resources versus the more unknown market potential for R & D expenditures.

8.13    Critics of the required expensing of research and development (R & D) costs argue that there is little rationale to justify the different accounting. One difference between the two cases is that firms make R & D expenditures for an uncertain future result (that is, the possibility of a patent), whereas less uncertainty exists for the purchase of a completed patent. A market transaction between an independent buyer and seller establish the existence and value of future benefits in the case of a purchased patent. Similar expenditures for R & D simply establish that a firm has made an expenditure.

8.14    (Classifying expenditure as asset or expense.)

    a.  Expense.

    b.  Expense.

    c.  Expense.

    d.  Noncurrent asset (machine).

    e.  Expense.

    f.  Expense.

    g.  Current asset Product Cost (inventory).

    h.  Noncurrent asset (equipment).

    i.  Expense.

    j.  Noncurrent asset (ore deposit).

8.14 continued.

        k.  Current asset (prepayment).

        l.  Current asset (marketable securities).

        m.  Current asset product cost (inventories).

        n.  Noncurrent asset (trademark).

        o.  Noncurrent asset (copyright).

        p.  Noncurrent asset (computer software).

        q.  Expense.

8.15    (Bolton Company; cost of self-constructed assets.)

| Land | | | Factory Building | | | |
|---|---|---|---|---|---|---|
| 70,000 | | (1) | 200,000 | 7,000 | (7) | |
| (14) 2,000 | | (2) | 12,000 | | | |
| √ 72,000 | | (3) | 140,000 | | | |
| | | (5) | 6,000 | | | |
| | | (8) | 10,000 | | | |
| | | (9) | 8,000 | | | |
| **Office Building** | | (10) | 3,000[a] | | | |
| 20,000 | | (11) | 8,000[b] | | | |
| (4) 13,000 | | (13) | 4,000 | | | |
| √ 33,000 | | (15) | 1,000[a] | | | |
| | | √ | 385,000 | | | |
| **Site Improvements** | | | | | | |
| (12) 5,000 | | | | | | |
| √ 5,000 | | | | | | |

[a]The firm might expense these items. It depends on the rationality of the firm's "self-insurance" policy.

[b]The firm might prorate these items in part to the remodeling of the office building.

Item (6) is omitted because of *SFAS No. 34*.

Item (16) is omitted because no arm's length transaction occurred in which the firm earned a profit.

8.16    (New Hampshire Wood Stove Company; cost of self-developed product.)

The first four items qualify as research and development costs which the firm must expense in the year incurred. It might appear that the firm should capitalize the cost of the prototype because it acquires the prototype from an external contractor. However, completion of a prototype does not signify a viable product. Purchasing the prototype externally versus constructing it internally does not change the accounting.

The firm should capitalize the legal fees to register and establish the patent as part of the cost of the patent. The firm might consider this cost as sufficiently immaterial to warrant treatment as an asset and expense it immediately.

The firm should capitalize the cost of the castings and amortize them over the expected useful life of the wood stove product.

8.17    (Samson Chemical Company; amount of interest capitalized during construction.)

a.    Average Construction = ($40,000,000 + $60,000,000)/2 = $50,000,000.

| Relevant Loans | Interest Anticipated |
|---|---|
| $ 30,000,000 at .10 | $3,000,000 |
| 20,000,000 at .08 | 1,600,000 |
| $ 50,000,000 | $4,600,000 |

b.  Interest Expense ............................................... 8,600,000
        Interest Payable ............................................ 8,600,000
      ($30,000,000 X .10) + ($70,000,000 X .08).

    Construction in Process ....................................... 4,600,000
        Interest Expense ........................................... 4,600,000

c.  Interest Expense ............................................... 8,600,000
        Interest Payable ............................................ 8,600,000
      ($30,000,000 X .10) + ($70,000,000 X .08).

    Construction in Process ....................................... 8,600,000
        Interest Expense ........................................... 8,600,000
      ($30,000,000 X .10) + ($70,000,000 X .08).

Note: Although the average balance in the Construction in Process account was $110 million during Year 7, the firm cannot capitalize more interest than the actual interest expense for the year.

8.18    (Nebok Company; capitalizing interest during construction.)  (Amounts in Thousands)

   a.  Weighted average interest rate:  $5,480/.5($51,500 + $49,700) = 10.83 percent.

       Weighted average balance in Construction in Process:  .5($23,186 + $68,797) = $45,992.

       Interest Capitalized:  .1083 × $45,992 = $4,981.

   b.  Interest Expense.............................................................  5,480
           Interest Payable.....................................................         5,480

       Construction in Process..............................................  4,981
           Interest Expense ....................................................         4,981

   c.  Income before Interest Expense and Income
          Taxes...................................................................  $16,300
       Interest Expense ($5,480 – $4,981)...............................      (499)
       Income before Income Taxes....................................... $15,801
       Income Tax Expense at 35 Percent .............................   (5,530)
       Net Income................................................................ $10,271

   d.  $16,300/$499 = 32.67 times.

   e.  $16,300/$5,480 = 2.97 times.

   f.  The interest coverage ratio in Part e. indicates the interest that the firm must pay and therefore provides a better measure for assessing risk.

8.19    (Galeway Motors; calculations for various depreciation methods.)

| | Year 1 | Year 2 | Year 3 |
|---|---|---|---|
| a.  Straight-Line Method .............  ($29,600 – $2,600)/6 = $4,500. | $4,500 | $4,500 | $4,500 |
| b.  Sum-of-the-Years'-Digits Method....................................  (6 × 7)/2 = 21 sum-of-the-years'-digits. | $7,714 | $6,429 | $5,143 |
| c.  Declining-Balance Method......  33 percent rate. | $9,768 | $6,545 | $4,385 |
| d.  Production Method ..................  $27,000/30,000 = $.90 per hour. | $4,050 | $4,500 | $4,950 |

8.20    (Luck Delivery Company; calculations for various depreciation methods.)

a.

**Depreciation Charge (Straight-Line)**

| | | |
|---|---|---|
| Year 8 | $ 6,000 | (30,000/5) |
| Year 9 | 6,000 | |
| Year 10 | 6,000 | |
| Year 11 | 6,000 | |
| Year 12 | 6,000 | |
| | $30,000 | |

b.

**Depreciation Charge (Double-Declining-Balance)**

| | | |
|---|---|---|
| Year 8 | $12,000 | ($30,000 × .40) |
| Year 9 | 7,200 | ($18,000 × .40) |
| Year 10 | 4,320 | ($10,800 × .40) |
| Year 11 | 3,240 | ($6,480/2) |
| Year 12 | 3,240 | (balance) |
| | $30,000 | |

c.

**Depreciation Charge (Sum-of-the-Years'-Digits)**

| | | |
|---|---|---|
| Year 8 | $10,000 | ($30,000 × 5/15) |
| Year 9 | 8,000 | ($30,000 × 4/15) |
| Year 10 | 6,000 | ($30,000 × 3/15) |
| Year 11 | 4,000 | ($30,000 × 2/15) |
| Year 12 | 2,000 | ($30,000 × 1/15) |
| | $30,000 | |

d.

**ACRS (5-Year Class)**

| | | |
|---|---|---|
| Year 8 | $ 6,000 | (= $30,000 × .20) |
| Year 9 | 9,600 | (= $30,000 × .32) |
| Year 10 | 5,760 | (= $30,000 × .192) |
| Year 11 | 3,450 | (= $30,000 × .115) |
| Year 12 | 3,450 | (= $30,000 × .115) |
| Year 13 | 1,740 | (= $30,000 × .058) |
| | $30,000 | |

e.

**Depreciation Charge (Sum-of-the-Years'-Digits)**

| | | | | |
|---|---|---|---|---|
| Year 8 | 3/4 × $10,000 | | = | $ 7,500 |
| Year 9 | 3/4 × $ 8,000 + | 1/4 × $10,000 = | | 8,500 |
| Year 10 | 3/4 × $ 6,000 + | 1/4 × $ 8,000 = | | 6,500 |
| Year 11 | 3/4 × $ 4,000 + | 1/4 × $ 6,000 = | | 4,500 |
| Year 12 | 3/4 × $ 2,000 + | 1/4 × $ 4,000 = | | 2,500 |
| Year 13 | | 1/4 × $ 2,000 = | | 500 |
| | | | | $ 30,000 |

8.21    (Calculations for various depreciation and amortization methods.)

|     | Year 1 | Year 2 | |
| --- | --- | --- | --- |
| a. | $10,000 | $10,000 | ($450,000 − $50,000)/40 = $10,000. |
| b. | $22,000 | $19,800 | ($220,000 × 2/20) = $22,000;<br>($198,000 × 2/20) = $19,800. |
| c. | $20,000 | $16,000 | ($80,000 − $20,000) × 5/15 = $20,000;<br>($80,000 − $20,000) × 4/15 = $16,000. |
| d. | $18,750 | $15,937.50 | $125,000 × 1.5/10 = $18,750;<br>$106,250 × 1.5/10 = $15,937.50. |
| e. | $ 3,333 | $ 3,333 | ($24,000 − $4,000)/6 = $3,333. |
| f. | $ 9,600 | $ 9,600 | ($48,000 − 0)/5 = $9,600. |

8.22    (United Express; production or use depreciation.)

a.    ($22,600 − $2,600)/100,000 miles = $.20 per mile.

|  | Miles at $.20 Each | Depreciation Charge |
| --- | --- | --- |
| Year 6............................ | 14,000 Miles | $ 2,800 |
| Year 7............................ | 34,000 Miles | 6,800 |
| Year 8............................ | 32,000 Miles | 6,400 |
|  | 80,000 Miles | $16,000 |

b.    **June 16, Year 9**

| | | |
| --- | --- | --- |
| Depreciation Expense................................................... | 3,600 | |
|    Accumulated Depreciation ..................................... | | 3,600 |

18,000 (= 98,000 − 80,000) miles at $.20 per mile
= $3,600.  Accumulated Depreciation is now
$19,600 (= $.20 × 98,000 miles).

| | | |
| --- | --- | --- |
| Cash........................................................................ | 2,600 | |
| Accumulated Depreciation......................................... | 19,600 | |
| Loss on Sale of Truck ................................................ | 400 | |
|    Truck................................................................... | | 22,600 |

8.23    (Fast Pace Shipping Company; revision of estimated service life changes depreciation schedule.)

Summary of the depreciation charges under the two methods:

| | a. Straight-Line | b. Sum-of-the-Years'-Digits |
|---|---|---|
| Year 7 | $ 3,600[a] | $ 6,545[c] |
| Year 8 | 3,600[a] | 5,891[d] |
| Year 9 | 4,800[b] | 6,733[e] |
| Year 10 | 4,800[b] | 5,610[f] |
| | $16,800 | $24,779 |

[a]($40,000 − $4,000)/10 = $3,600.
[b]($40,000 − $3,600 − $3,600 − $4,000)/6 = $4,800.
[c][($40,000 − $4,000) × 10/55] = $6,545.
[d][($40,000 − $4,000) × 9/55] = $5,891.
[e]($40,000 − $6,545 − $5,891 − $4,000) × 6/21 = $6,733.
[f]($40,000 − $6,545 − $5,891 − $4,000) × 5/21 = $5,610.

8.24    (Fort Manufacturing Corporation; journal entries for revising estimate of life.)

a.  Work-in-Process Inventory ......................................... 600
        Accumulated Depreciation ..................................... 600
    ($45,000 − $1,800)/144 = $300 per month.

b.  Work-in-Process Inventory ......................................... 3,600
        Accumulated Depreciation ..................................... 3,600
    12 × $300 = $3,600.

c.  Depreciation to 1/1/Year 15 = 62 × $300 = $18,600.
    Remaining depreciation = $45,000 − $18,600 − $960 = $25,440.
    Remaining life = 168 months − 62 months = 106 months as of
        1/1/Year 15.
    Depreciation charge per month = $25,440/106 = $240.

    Work-in-Process Inventory ......................................... 2,880
        Accumulated Depreciation ..................................... 2,880
    12 × $240 = $2,880.

d.  By March 31, Year 20, the machine has been on the new depreciation schedule for Year 15 through Year 19 plus 3 months or 63 months altogether.  Accumulated depreciation is $18,600 + (63 × $240) = $18,600 + $15,120 = $33,720.

    Book value is $45,000 − $33,720 = $11,280; loss is $1,280.

**8.24 d. continued.**

Journal entries are:

| | | |
|---|---|---|
| Work-in-Process Inventory........................................ | 720 | |
|    Accumulated Depreciation .................................. | | 720 |

$3 \times \$240 = \$720$; to bring depreciation up to date
as of 3/31/Year 20.

| | | |
|---|---|---|
| Cash........................................................................ | 10,000 | |
| Accumulated Depreciation....................................... | 33,720 | |
| Loss on Disposal of Machinery............................... | 1,280 | |
|    Machinery ...................................................... | | 45,000 |

**8.25** (Neptune Equipment Corporation; retirement of plant assets.)

a.

| | Depreciation Charge For the Year | Accumulated Depreciation at July 1 |
|---|---|---|
| Year 4—Year 5............ | $ 2,000 | $ 2,000 |
| Year 5—Year 6............ | 2,000 | 4,000 |
| Year 6—Year 7............ | 2,000 | 6,000 |
| | $ 6,000 | |

b. **9/30/Year 7**

| | | |
|---|---|---|
| Work-in-Process Inventory........................................ | 500 | |
|    Accumulated Depreciation .................................. | | 500 |

3 months' depreciation since 6/30/Year 7:
$\$2,000/4 = \$500$.

**9/30/Year 7**

| | | |
|---|---|---|
| Cash........................................................................ | 2,700 | |
| Accumulated Depreciation....................................... | 6,500 | |
| Loss on Sale of Machinery...................................... | 400 | |
|    Machinery ...................................................... | | 9,600 |

$\$6,000 + \$500 = \$6,500$.

c. **12/31/Year 7**

| | | |
|---|---|---|
| Work-in-Process Inventory........................................ | 1,000 | |
|    Accumulated Depreciation .................................. | | 1,000 |

6 months' depreciation since 6/30/Year 7:
$\$2,000/2 = \$1,000$.

**12/31/Year 7**

| | | |
|---|---|---|
| Cash........................................................................ | 2,700 | |
| Accumulated Depreciation....................................... | 7,000 | |
|    Machinery ...................................................... | | 9,600 |
|    Gain on Sale of Machinery................................. | | 100 |

$\$6,000 + \$1,000 = \$7,000$.

**8.26**  (Wilcox Corporation; working backwards to derive proceeds from disposition of plant assets.)

| | |
|---|---|
| Cost of Equipment Sold: | $400,000 + $230,000 − $550,000 = $80,000. |
| Accumulated Depreciation on Equipment Sold: | $180,000 + $50,000 − $160,000 = $70,000. |
| Book Value of Equipment Sold: | $80,000 − $70,000 = $10,000. |
| Proceeds of Sale: | $10,000 + $4,000 = $14,000. |

**8.27**  (Kieran Corporation; comparing the amount of impairment loss.)

| | Book Value | Undis- counted Cash Flows | Impair- ment Loss Recog- nized | Market Value | Amount of Loss |
|---|---|---|---|---|---|
| Accounts Receivable.......................... | $  550,000 | $ 750,000 | No | $  520,000 | $         0 |
| Inventories................. | 750,000 | 600,000 | Yes | 580,000 | 170,000 |
| Property, Plant and Equipment............ | 1,200,000 | 950,000 | Yes | 800,000 | 400,000 |
| Goodwill...................... | 500,000 | -- | Yes | 300,000 | 200,000 |
| Total...................... | $3,000,000 | | | $2,200,000 | $770,000 |

Goodwill of Kieran Corporation on January 1, Year 6 is $500,000 (= $2,400,000 − $400,000 − $600,000 − $900,000).

**8.28**  (Journal entries to correct accounting errors.)

a.  
| | | |
|---|---|---|
| Depreciation Expense................................................. | 375 | |
|    Accumulated Depreciation ...................................... | | 375 |

$3,000 × .25 × 6/12 = $375.

| | | |
|---|---|---|
| Accumulated Depreciation......................................... | 1,875 | |
| Loss on Disposal of Equipment ............................... | 325 | |
|    Equipment........................................................... | | 2,200 |

$3,000 × .25 × 2.5 = $1,875.  $3,200 + $3000 − $4,000 = $2,200.

b.  
| | | |
|---|---|---|
| Accumulated Depreciation......................................... | 5,000 | |
|    Truck................................................................. | | 5,000 |

8.28 continued.

    c.  Depreciation Expense.............................................. 60
          Accumulated Depreciation ................................ 60
        $1,200 × .10 × 6/12 = $60.

        Accumulated Depreciation...................................... 270
          Theft Loss ........................................................ 270
        $1,200 × .10 × 27/12 = $270.

8.29    (Boston Can Corporation; journal entries for depreciable asset transactions.)

**3/31/Year 6**
Depreciation Expense.......................................................... 350
    Accumulated Depreciation .......................................... 350
($12,000 − $800)/8 = $1,400 per year; 3/12 × $1,400 = $350.

**3/31/Year 6**
Cash ...................................................................................... 4,000
Accumulated Depreciation ................................................. 7,350
Loss on Sale......................................................................... 650
    Machinery (Old)............................................................ 12,000
($1,400 × 5) + $350 = $7,350.

Machinery (New) ................................................................. 16,000
    Notes Payable................................................................ 6,000
    Cash ................................................................................ 10,000

**12/31/Year 6**
Interest Expense ................................................................. 450
    Interest Payable............................................................ 450
$6,000 × .10 × 9/12 = $450.

Depreciation Expense.......................................................... 1,125
    Accumulated Depreciation .......................................... 1,125
($16,000 − $1,000)/10 = $1,500 per year; 9/12 × $1,500 = $1,125.

8.30     (Effects of transactions on statement of cash flows.)

a.   The journal entry to record this transaction is as follows:

| | | |
|---|---|---|
| Cash........................................................................... | 3,000 | |
| Accumulated Depreciation........................................... | 6,000 | |
| Loss on Sale of Machine............................................. | 1,000 | |
|    Machine ............................................................... | | 10,000 |

The debit to the Cash account means that Line (9) increases by $3,000. Sales of plant assets are investing transactions, so Line (4) increases by $3,000. The loss on the sale reduces net income, so Line (1) decreases by $1,000. Because we show the full cash proceeds of $3,000 on Line (4), we must offset the effect of the $1,000 reduction on Line (1). Thus, Line (2) increases by $1,000. The net effect of the entries on Lines (1) and (2) is zero.

b.   The journal entry to record this transaction is as follows:

| | | |
|---|---|---|
| Cash............................................................................ | 5,000 | |
| Accumulated Depreciation........................................... | 6,000 | |
|    Machine ............................................................... | | 10,000 |
|    Gain on Sale of Machine....................................... | | 1,000 |

The debit to the Cash account means that Line (9) increases by $5,000. Sales of plant assets are investing transactions, so Line (4) increases by $5,000. The gain on the sale increases net income, so Line (1) increases by $1,000. Because we show the full cash proceeds of $5,000 on Line (4), we must offset the effect of the $1,000 increase on Line (1). Thus, Line (3) increases by $1,000. The net effect of the entries on Lines (1) and (3) is zero.

c.   The journal entry to record this transaction is as follows:

| | | |
|---|---|---|
| Machine (New)........................................................... | 8,000 | |
| Accumulated Depreciation (Old) ............................... | 6,000 | |
|    Machine (Old)....................................................... | | 10,000 |
|    Cash ..................................................................... | | 4,000 |

The credit to the Cash account reduces Line (9) by $4,000. Acquisitions of plant assets are investing transactions, so Line (5) increases by $4,000. Because this entry does not involve an income statement account, there is no effect on the Operating section of the statement of cash flows.

d.   The journal entry to record this transaction is as follows:

| | | |
|---|---|---|
| Loss from Fire............................................................ | 50,000 | |
| Accumulated Depreciation........................................... | 40,000 | |
|    Warehouse ........................................................... | | 90,000 |

8.30 d. continued.

Because this entry does not involve an entry to the Cash account there is no effect on Line (9). The loss from the fire reduces net income, so Line (1) decreases by $50,000. We must offset this loss if the net effect on Line (9) is to be zero. Thus, Line (2) increases by $50,000 for the loss that does not use cash.

e.   The journal entry to record this transaction is as follows:

| | | |
|---|---|---|
| Loss from Fire | 60,000 | |
|    Inventory | | 60,000 |

This entry does not involve a debit or credit to the Cash account so Line (9) is not affected. The loss from the fire reduces net income, so Line (1) decreases by $60,000. We must offset this loss if the net effect on Line (9) is to be zero. Thus, Line (2) increases by $60,000 for the decrease in inventories.

8.31   (May Department Stores; improvements versus repairs or maintenance.)

a.   **January 2**

| | | |
|---|---|---|
| Building (or Entrances) | 28,000 | |
|    Cash | | 28,000 |

To record cost of new entrances.

**December 31**

| | | |
|---|---|---|
| Depreciation Expense | 24,000 | |
|    Accumulated Depreciation on Building | | 24,000 |

$24,000 = 1/7 \times [(\$800,000 - \$660,000 + \$28,000)] = 1/40 \times \$800,000 + 1/7 \times \$28,000$.

b.   **January 2**

| | | |
|---|---|---|
| Loss | 28,000 | |
|    Building (or Accumulated Depreciation on Building) | | 28,000 |

Recognize loss from destruction.

| | | |
|---|---|---|
| Building (or Accumulated Depreciation on Building) | 28,000 | |
|    Cash | | 28,000 |

To recognize cost of new entrance facilities.

These two entries are equivalent to, and could be replaced by:

| | | |
|---|---|---|
| Loss | 28,000 | |
|    Cash | | 28,000 |

8.31 b. continued.

**December 31**

| | | |
|---|---|---|
| Depreciation Expense................................................ | 20,000 | |
| Accumulated Depreciation ..................................... | | 20,000 |

Depreciation for year on remaining $140,000
over 7 years = $800,000/40 years.

c. Same as *b.* above.

d. Opinions differ on this one. Some favor the treatment in Part *a.* (capitalize and amortize), while others favor the treatment in Part *b.* or Part *c.* (immediate loss). Those favoring Part *a.* point to the voluntary nature of the decision to replace the entrances rather than to close down. Presumably, society as a whole benefits from use of handicapped-accessible entrances or else regulations would not require them. If future benefits to society as a whole result and the firm decides to make the expenditure, an asset results which the firm will depreciate over its estimated service life. It would be improper, some say, to charge the entire cost of making future operations possible to this year. They cite the enormous expenditures for antipollution equipment as being similar.

Those favoring the treatment in Part *b.* argue that regulators require this expenditure to maintain the service potential of the building assets at the same level as before passage of the law. They see no essential difference between the economic effects of destruction by natural disaster (Part *b.*), human disaster (Part *c.*), and another form of human "disaster" (Part *d.*). It may seem antisocial to say that the passage of a law results in damage no different from vandalism, but the economic consequences to the owner of the business are the same as in Parts *c.* and *d.*, and so they urge immediate expensing. They agree that the enormous expenditures for antipollution equipment are also a loss (at least to the degree that costs exceed firm-specific benefits) even though most firms do not expense such items.

The holders of the opposing (capitalize) view see a significant difference between natural (or human) disasters and democratic social decisions, which they view as not being " human disasters."

e. If you believe that Part *d.* is like Part *a.*, then so is Part *e.* like Part *a.*. If you believe that Part *d.* is like Parts *b.* and *c.*, then the loss here should be only $21,000 (= $28,000 − $7,000). Depreciation expense for each of the last seven years is $21,000 [= ($140,000 + $7,000)/7 years].

8.32    (Capitalizing versus expensing; if capitalized, what amortization period?)

a.  If the firm makes this expenditure to secure future benefits, then there is an argument for capitalizing it. The entries would be:

Building (or Fire Escapes)............................................ 28,000
    Cash ...................................................................        28,000
To capitalize improvements.

Depreciation Expense................................................. 4,000
    Accumulated Depreciation ....................................        4,000
One year's amortization of improvements based
on a seven-year life.

A somewhat more logical view is that the firm made the expenditure to maintain the service potential that it had planned previously. It obtains no additional benefits beyond those planned. See the discussion in Part *d.* of Problem 8.31 above. The expenditure is a result of new legislation, so this view results in the following entry at the time the law is passed:

Loss from New Legislation......................................... 28,000
    Building (or Accumulated Depreciation).............        28,000
To recognize loss.

When the expenditure is made, the entry is:

Building (or Fire Escapes)............................................ 28,000
    Cash ...................................................................        28,000
To capitalize expenditure for fire escapes.

This second treatment results in immediate recognition of the loss, and subsequent depreciation of the building improvements and fire escapes is the same as before the law was passed.

b.  Building.................................................................... 1,050,000
        Investment in General Electric Stock..................        100,000
        Gain on Disposal of Investment ...........................        950,000

In the case of widely traded stock, the stock market valuation is probably a better guide than is the appraisal value of a single building.

c.  Building.................................................................... 1,000,000
        Investment in Small Timers Stock.......................        100,000
        Gain on Disposal of Investment ...........................        900,000

For thinly traded issues, the appraisal value of the building may be a more reliable guide. Many people think that investors cannot sell large blocks of such stock at once, except at a discount from the quoted price per share. We would not argue with the same answer as Part *b.* above.

d. Garages ................................................................. 18,000
   Cash .................................................................. 18,000
To capitalize improvements to garages.

Depreciation Expense................................................. 900
   Accumulated Depreciation ................................. 900
$18,000/20 years = $900 per year.

The useful life of the improvements in this case is likely to be as long as the useful lives of the garages. A case can be made, however, for amortization over five or ten years.

e. Advertising Expense.................................................. 400,000
   Cash .................................................................. 400,000

Firms generally immediately expense expenditures on advertising. Theoretically, the firm should capitalize some portion of the expenditures as an asset because the company probably would not spend on advertising unless it expected future benefits. However, firms seldom follow the more theoretically sound procedure in practice due to the difficulty of identifying and measuring the future benefits.

f. Research Expense..................................................... 1,500,000
   Cash .................................................................. 1,500,000

This is the treatment required by FASB *Statement No. 2*, although we criticize it. The company has a proven record of success with its research and it would not continue the research expenditures unless it expected future benefits. Capitalization of these benefits on the balance sheet and subsequent amortization is at least a theoretically superior treatment.

g. Charitable Contribution (Expense).......................... 250,000
   Cash .................................................................. 250,000

Although some indirect future benefit may come to the company, it is too indefinite to justify recognition. We wonder, though, if companies give away money without some expectation of future benefit.

h. Machine Tools .......................................................... 6,000,000
   Cash .................................................................. 6,000,000
To set up asset account.

8.32 h. continued.

Depreciation of Machine Tools (a production
   cost).............................................................................. 2,000,000
      Machine Tools .......................................................          2,000,000
Amortize over 3 years, the life of the automobile
model. An alternative entry debits the Inventory
account.

The tools will be obsolete in three years; their physical life of six years is
irrelevant. For some reason, automobile manufacturers do not show
accumulated depreciation on special tools in published statements;
credits appear to go directly to the asset account.

i.   (Dollar Amounts in Millions)

**Start of Year**
Plant Assets (Airplanes)..............................................          100
   Cash ......................................................................................          100
To record purchase of airplanes.

Plant Assets (Spare Parts)........................................          20
   Cash ......................................................................................          20
To record spare parts as plant assets, not as
inventory. This is the point of the question.
Because the spare parts are giving up their future
benefits as the firm uses the airplanes, we treat
their cost as plant assets. At the end of the useful
life of the airplanes, the spare parts will be
worthless. We think they should be depreciated
over the life of the airplanes, not accounted for like
an inventory of parts which the firm can use in
various alternative ways. Nothing in the chapter
alerts the student to this treatment and many, if
not most, will set up the asset as inventory.

(Dollar Amounts in Millions)

**End of Year**
Depreciation Expense.................................................          12
   Accumulated Depreciation ...................................          12
Depreciation on plant assets for 1/10 of useful life
costing $120 (= $100 + $20) in total. This
treatment is consistent with that described in the
preceding entry.

8.32 i. continued.

Whether or not the instructor or students agree with us, the point is worth discussing. Is the cost of spare parts acquired solely for use with a plant asset and therefore treated like plant assets or like inventory?

j.   (Dollar Amounts in Millions)

**End of Year**

| | | |
|---|---|---|
| Depreciation Expense......................................................... | 12 | |
|    Accumulated Depreciation ...................................... | | 12 |

The entry made for the same reason as in the preceding question. We think the following entries, which result from treating the spare parts as inventory, are wrong:

| | | |
|---|---|---|
| Depreciation Expense......................................................... | 10 | |
|    Accumulated Depreciation ...................................... | | 10 |
| | | |
| Repair Expense.................................................................. | 1 | |
|    Spare Parts Inventory .......................................... | | 1 |

8.33    (Epstein Company; accounting for intangibles.)

a.   The issue here is the length of the amortization period. In spite of the fact that the company plans to make and sell indefinitely, the fair market value of $100,000 attached to the property right is allocable only to the next three years of use. After that, anyone can use the patent. Thus, we would amortize this patent over three years.

b.   The same problem and reasoning above leads us to use a five-year life.

c.   The amortization period here is theoretically indefinite, so FASB *Statement No. 142* does not require amortization.

d.   In Year 2, we should debit expense and credit asset for the diminution in the value of the trade secret. This amount will be hard to estimate. The auditor may argue that the secret has lost all of its value and will require the write off of the remaining book value.

e.   The firm should capitalize the film as an asset and write it off over its economic life. This is an easy statement to make, but the estimate of life might be as short as three years or as long as the firm sells thyristors, which appears to be the indefinite future. The firm will pick a number and be prepared to give in to the auditor who asks for a shorter life. Management will lack any sound arguments as to what the life should be. We would argue only with the immediate expensing of the film's cost.

8.33 continued.

Sheldon L. Epstein, former patent counsel of Brunswick Corporation, suggested this question to us. His reaction to the above answers is as follows:

a. The trademark registration is simple proof of ownership in the United States which the company could renew again and again for twenty-year periods. Because trademark rights will continue to exist as long as the company properly uses the mark, the amortization period is theoretically indefinite. FASB *Statement No. 142* requires no amortization. In the event that the company discontinues the use of the mark or loses the exclusive right to use the mark, the firm should write off the unamortized amount in the year in which the event occurs as an impairment loss. Where the company owns a foreign trademark, the right to exclusive use may be dependent on a valid registration, and loss or expiration of the registration could require complete write off in the year when such an event occurs. Note that trademarks receive a different accounting treatment from that given patents because trademarks can have an indefinite life while patents expire on a known date.

b. The design patent grants the company the right to exclude others from manufacturing, using or selling the same or similar containers for 5 years. After that, anyone is free to copy the design. Therefore, the privilege of exclusivity diminishes with time and the value should be amortized over the remaining life of the patent.

c. I agree with your answer.

d. I agree with your answer but with the caveat that its value depends on what the competitor does with its knowledge of the trade secret. If it does nothing, then there is little or no loss of value. If it uses it for the purpose of competition, then its value diminishes by the present value of anticipated lost profits and the accountant should recognize the value lost in the year the event occurs. If a competitor publishes the trade secret, then all of its value is lost.

e. The answer is generally correct; however, note that the accounting treatment for copyrights lies somewhere between that used for patents and that used for trademarks. Under the copyright law, it is possible for the copyright to extend for periods well beyond 40 years or for a substantially shorter period (as would be the case for an old work). The important point is to ask what the remaining life of the exclusive privilege is and, in the case of a work licensed by the company from an individual, when the right reverts to the author (35 years). For example, copyrights in new works last for the life of the author plus 50 years except for anonymous or pseudonymous works for which the period is the first of 75 years from publication or 100 years from creation. For older works, many will expire on December 31, 2002; however, there are a number of exceptions.

8.34    (The Mead Corporation; interpreting disclosures regarding property, plant and equipment.)

a.    Property, Plant and Equipment ...................................... 315.6
            Cash .................................................................................        315.6

      Depreciation Expense.......................................................... 188.1
            Accumulated Depreciation ........................................        188.1

      Cash (Given)......................................................................... 38.7
      Loss on Sale of Property, Plant and Equipment
            (Plug) .............................................................................. 19.9
      Accumulated Depreciation ($1,803.7 + $188.1 – x
            = $1,849.3; x = $142.5)............................................. 142.5
                  Property, Plant and Equipment ($3,824.0 +
                        $315.6 – x = $3,938.5; x = $201.1)...............        201.1

b.    .5($3,824.0 + $3,938.5)/$188.1 = 20.6 years.

c.    .5($1,803.7 + $1,849.3)/$188.1 = 9.7 years.

d.    $4,557.5/.5($2,020.3 + $2,089.2) = 2.2.

e.    $4,557.5/.5($1,013.8[a] + $1,108.0[b]) = 4.3.

      [a]$3,824.0 – $2,810.2 = $1,013.8.
      [b]$3,938.5 – $2,830.5 = $1,108.0.

8.35    (PepsiCo; interpreting disclosures regarding property, plant and equipment.)

a.    Property, Plant and Equipment .................................... 2,253.2
            Cash ................................................................................        2,253.2

      Depreciation Expense.......................................................... 1,200.0
            Accumulated Depreciation ........................................        1,200.0

      Cash......................................................................................... 55.3
      Accumulated Depreciation ($5,394.4 + $1,200.0
            – x = $6,247.3; x = $347.1).................................... 347.1
                  Property, Plant and Equipment ($14,250.0 +
                        $2,253.2 – y = $16,130.1; y = 373.1)...........        373.1
                  Gain on Sale of Property, Plant and Equip-
                        ment (Plug)......................................................        29.3

b.    .5($14,250.0 + $16,130.1)/$1,200.0 = 12.7 years.

c.    .5($5,394.4 + $6,247.3)/$1,200.0 = 4.9 years.

d.    $28,472.4/.5($8,855.6 + $9,882.8) = 3.0.

8.35 continued.

    e.   $\$28,472.4/.5(\$7,231.2^{a} + \$8,393.4^{b}) = 3.6.$

          $^{a}\$14,250.0 - \$7,018.8 = \$7,231.2.$
          $^{b}\$16,130.1 - \$7,736.7 = \$8,393.4.$

8.36    (American Airlines; effect on net income of changes in estimates for depreciable assets.)

Income has been about $180 million (= .06 X $3 billion) per year.

**Reconciliation of Plant Data:**

| | |
|---|---:|
| Airplanes Cost | $ 2,500,000,000 |
|     Less Salvage Value (10%) | 250,000,000 |
|     Depreciable Basis | $ 2,250,000,000 |
| Divided by 10-Year Life Equals Yearly Depreciation Charges | $ 225,000,000 |
| Times 4 Years Equals Accumulated Depreciation | $ 900,000,000 |
| Plus Net Book Value | 1,600,000,000 |
| Airplanes Cost | $ 2,500,000,000 |

**New Depreciation Charge:**

| | |
|---|---:|
| Net Book Value | $ 1,600,000,000 |
|     Less Salvage Value (12% of Cost) | 300,000,000 |
|     Depreciation Basis | $ 1,300,000,000 |
| Divided by 10 (= 14 − 4) Years Equals Revised Yearly Depreciation Charge | $ 130,000,000 |

**Increase in Pretax Income:**

| | |
|---|---:|
| Old Depreciation Charges | $ 225,000,000 |
| New Depreciation Charges | 130,000,000 |
| | $ 95,000,000 |
| Multiplied by (1 − tax rate) = 1 − .35 = .65 | X .65 |
| Increase in Aftertax Income | $ 61,750,000 |

Income will rise by about 34.3 percent (= $61.75/$180.0).

8.37    (Moon Macrosystems; recording transactions involving tangible and intangible assets.)

    a.

| | | |
|---|---:|---:|
| Machinery | 400,000 | |
| Computer Software | 40,000 | |
|     Cash | | 440,000 |

8.37 continued.

b.

| | | |
|---|---|---|
| Machinery................................................................. | 20,000 | |
| Computer Software ................................................ | 10,000 | |
|    Cash................................................................ | | 30,000 |

c. **Year 6 and Year 7**

| | | |
|---|---|---|
| Depreciation Expense ($400,000 + $20,000 – | | |
|   $40,000)/10................................................... | 38,000 | |
| Amortization Expense ($40,000 + $10,000)/4 ........ | 12,500 | |
|    Accumulated Depreciation .................................... | | 38,000 |
|    Computer Software................................................. | | 12,500 |

d.

| | | |
|---|---|---|
| Impairment Loss of Computer Software ($40,000 | | |
|   + $10,000 – $12,500 – $12,500)............................ | 25,000 | |
|    Computer Software ............................................. | | 25,000 |

e.

| | | |
|---|---|---|
| Depreciation Expense ($400,000 + $20,000 – | | |
|   $38,000 – $38,000 – $56,000)/12 ......................... | 24,000 | |
|    Accumulated Depreciation.................................... | | 24,000 |

f.

| | | |
|---|---|---|
| Depreciation Expense......................................... | 24,000 | |
|    Accumulated Depreciation ................................. | | 24,000 |

| | | |
|---|---|---|
| Cash...................................................................... | 260,000 | |
| Accumulated Depreciation ($38,000 + $38,000 + | | |
|   $24,000 + $24,000)....... ............................... | 124,000 | |
| Loss on Sale of Machinery................................... | 36,000 | |
|    Machinery .......................................................... | | 420,000 |

8.38    (Recognizing and measuring impairment losses.)

a.    The loss occurs because of an adverse action by a governmental entity.
The undiscounted cash flows of $50 million are less than the book value
of the building of $60 million. An impairment loss has therefore
occurred. The market value of the building of $32 million is less than
the book value of $60 million. Thus, the amount of the impairment loss
is $28 million (= $60 million – $32 million). The journal entry to record
the impairment loss is (in millions):

| | | |
|---|---|---|
| Loss from Impairment............................................ | 28 | |
| Accumulated Depreciation......................................... | 20 | |
|    Building ............................................................. | | 48 |

This entry records the impairment loss, eliminates the accumulated
depreciation, and writes down the building to its market value of $32
million (= $80 – $48).

8.38 continued.

b. The undiscounted cash flows of $70 exceed the book value of the building of $60 million. Thus, no impairment loss occurs according to the definition in FASB *Statement No. 121*. An ***economic*** loss occurred but GAAP do not permit it to be recognized.

c. The loss arises because the accumulated costs significantly exceed the amount originally anticipated. The book value of the building of $25 million exceeds the undiscounted future cash flows of $22 million. Thus, an impairment loss has occurred. The impairment loss recognized equals $9 million (= $25 million – $16 million). The journal entry is (in millions):

| | | |
|---|---|---|
| Loss from Impairment................................................. | 9 | |
|    Construction in Process ............................................ | | 9 |

d. The loss occurs because of a significant decline in the market value of the patent. FASB *Statement No. 142* requires calculation of the impairment loss on the patent before computing the value loss on goodwill. The undiscounted future cash flows of $18 million are less than the book value of the patent of $20 million. Thus, an impairment loss occurred. The amount of the loss is $8 million (= $20 million – $12 million). The journal entry to record the loss is:

| | | |
|---|---|---|
| Loss from Impairment................................................. | 8 | |
|   Patent ......................................................................... | | 8 |

The second step is to determine if an impairment loss on the goodwill occurred. The market value of the entity is $25 million. The book value after writing down the patent is $27 million (= $12 million for patent and $15 million for goodwill). Thus, a goodwill impairment loss occurred. If the market value of the patent is $12 million, the market value of the goodwill is $13 million. The impairment loss on goodwill is therefore $2 million (= $15 million – $13 million). The journal entry is:

| | | |
|---|---|---|
| Loss from Impairment................................................. | 2 | |
|   Goodwill....................................................................... | | 2 |

e. The loss occurs because of a significant change in the business climate for Chicken Franchisees. One might question whether this loss is temporary or permanent. Evidence from previous similar events (for example, Tylenol) suggests that consumers soon forget or at least forgive the offending company. The FASB reporting standard discusses but rejects the use of a permanency criterion in identifying impairment losses. Thus, an impairment loss occurs in this case because the future undiscounted cash flows of $6 million from the franchise rights are less than the book value of the franchise rights of $10 million. Note that Chicken Franchisees must separate the cash flows associated with the prepar-

© 2003 Thomson Learning, Inc.

8.38 e. continued.

ing and selling of chicken in its physical facilities from the cash flows associated with the Chicken Delight franchise name. The amount of the impairment loss is $7 million (= $10 million − $3 million). The journal entry is (in millions):

| | | |
|---|---|---|
| Impairment Loss............................................................... | 7 | |
|     Franchise Rights......................................................... | | 7 |

This entry assumes that Chicken Franchisees does not use an Accumulated Amortization account.

8.39    (Grand Met; accounting for plant asset revaluations.)

a. **December 31, Year 3 to Year 5**

| | | |
|---|---|---|
| Depreciation Expense................................................ | 10,000 | |
|     Accumulated Depreciation .................................. | | 10,000 |

£10,000 = £50,000/5.

b. **January 1, Year 6**

| | | |
|---|---|---|
| Equipment ................................................................ | 5,000 | |
|     Revaluation Allowance........................................... | | 5,000 |

| | |
|---|---|
| Current Market Value.................................................. | £ 25,000 |
| Book Value:  £50,000 − (£10,000 × 3)......................... | (20,000) |
| | £  5,000 |

c. **December 31, Year 6 and Year 7**

| | | |
|---|---|---|
| Depreciation Expense................................................ | 10,000 | |
| Revaluation Allowance.............................................. | 2,500 | |
|     Accumulated Depreciation .................................. | | 12,500 |

£2,500 = £5,000/2.

d.  The revaluation and subsequent depreciation of the revaluation had no effect on net income. At the end of Year 7 just prior to removing the equipment from the books, the accounts appear as follows:

| | |
|---|---|
| Equipment (£50,000 + £5,000)...................................... | £ 55,000 |
| Accumulated Depreciation (£10,000 × 5) + (£2,500 × 2)......... | 55,000 |
| Revaluation Allowance [£5,000 − (£2,500 × 2)]...................... | -0- |

8.40    (Pfizer; expensing versus capitalizing research and development costs.) (Amounts in Millions)

a. **Expense Costs as Incurred**

| | Year 1 | Year 2 | Year 3 | Year 4 |
|---|---|---|---|---|
| Other Income........................ | $ 30 | $ 30 | $ 30 | $ 30 |
| Additional Income from R&D: | | | | |
| First Year's R&D ........ | 36 | 36 | 36 | |
| Second Year's R&D .... | | 36 | 36 | 36 |
| Third Year's R&D........ | | | 36 | 36 |
| Fourth Year's R&D..... | | | | 36 |
| R&D Expense...................... | (90) | (90) | (90) | (90) |
| Net Income (Loss).............. | $ (24) | $ 12 | $ 48 | $ 48 |

b. **Capitalize and Amortize Over 3 Years (Including Year of Occurrence)**

| | Year 1 | Year 2 | Year 3 | Year 4 |
|---|---|---|---|---|
| Other Income........................ | $ 30 | $ 30 | $ 30 | $ 30 |
| Additional Income from R&D: | | | | |
| First Year's R&D ........ | 36 | 36 | 36 | |
| Second Year's R&D .... | | 36 | 36 | 36 |
| Third Year's R&D........ | | | 36 | 36 |
| Fourth Year's R&D..... | | | | 36 |
| R&D Amortization Expense: | | | | |
| First Year's R&D ........ | (30) | (30) | (30) | |
| Second Year's R&D .... | | (30) | (30) | (30) |
| Third Year's R&D........ | | | (30) | (30) |
| Fourth Year's R&D..... | | | | (30) |
| Net Income ......................... | $ 36 | $ 42 | $ 48 | $ 48 |
| Deferred R&D Asset on Balance Sheet: | | | | |
| First Year's R&D ........ | $ 60 | $ 30 | | |
| Second Year's R&D .... | | 60 | $ 30 | |
| Third Year's R&D........ | | | 60 | $ 30 |
| Fourth Year's R&D..... | | | | 60 |
| Total ..................................... | $ 60 | $ 90 | $ 90 | $ 90 |

8.40 continued.

    c.   The expensing policy leads to higher expenses, lower income, and lower asset totals in the first two years. After that, the two policies are the same. When the firm ceases to spend on R&D, the policy of expensing will show higher income in the two years when the benefits of prior R&D continue, but there are no matching expenses. There are no expenses under Policy (1), but Policy (2) continues to show amortization expense.

    d.   The income under the two policies will continue to be the same if there is no growth or change in policy. Policy (2) will show a lower rate of return on total assets and a lower rate of return on stockholders' equity than will Policy (1) because the asset and equity totals are larger under Policy (2) than under Policy (1). When there is growth in R&D amounts over time and corresponding growth in income, Policy (2) will always appear worse than will Policy (1).

8.41    (Ross Laboratories; valuation of brand name.) (Dollar amounts in millions.)

|  | Part a. | Part b. |
|---|---|---|
| (1) Operating Margin | $ 600.0 | $ 600.0 |
| Employed Physical Capital $500.0 | | |
| Subtract Pretax Profit on Physical Capital Required at 10 (Part a.) or 20 (Part b.) | (50.0) | (100.0) |
| (2) Profit Generated by Brand | $ 550.0 | $ 500.0 |
| Subtract Income Taxes at 40 Percent | (220.0) | (200.0) |
| (3) Net Brand Profits | $ 330.0 | $ 300.0 |
| Multiply by Aftertax Capitalization Factor | 17.0 | 8.0 |
| (4) Estimate of Brand Value | $5,610.0 | $2,400.0 |

8.42  (Ormes Company; preparing statement of cash flows.) A T-account work sheet for Ormes Company for Year 2 appears after the statement of cash flows.

## ORMES COMPANY
## Statement of Cash Flows
## For Year 2

| | | |
|---|---:|---:|
| Operations: | | |
| Net Income | $ 60,000 | |
| Addbacks and Additions: | | |
| Bad Debt Expense | 20,000 | |
| Depreciation Expense | 39,000 | |
| Loss on Sale of Equipment | 8,000 | |
| Amortization Expense | 15,000 | |
| Increase in Accounts Payable | 27,000 | |
| Subtractions: | | |
| Gain on Sale of Patent | (125,000) | |
| Increase in Accounts Receivable | (29,200) | |
| Increase in Inventories | (25,000) | |
| Cash Flow from Operations | | $ (10,200) |
| Investing: | | |
| Sale of Patents | $125,000 | |
| Sale of Property, Plant and Equipment | 10,000 | |
| Acquisition of Patent | (75,000) | |
| Acquisition of Property, Plant and Equipment | (62,900) | |
| Cash Flow from Investing | | (2,900) |
| Financing: | | |
| Common Stock Issued | $ 43,900 | |
| Dividends | (25,000) | |
| Cash Flow from Financing | | 18,900 |
| Change in Cash | | $ 5,800 |
| Cash, Beginning of Year 2 | | 25,700 |
| Cash, End of Year 2 | | $ 31,500 |

### Supplementary Information

Ormes Company issued $30,000 of its common stock in the acquisition of property, plant and equipment during Year 2.

8.42 continued.

## Cash

√ 25,700

### Operations

| | | | |
|---|---|---|---|
| (1) | 60,000 | 125,000 | (5) |
| (7) | 20,000 | 29,200 | (9) |
| (11) | 39,000 | 25,000 | (10) |
| (12) | 8,000 | | |
| (13) | 15,000 | | |
| (14) | 27,000 | | |

### Investing

| | | | |
|---|---|---|---|
| (5) | 125,000 | 62,900 | (3) |
| (12) | 10,000 | 75,000 | (6) |

### Financing

| | | | |
|---|---|---|---|
| (15) | 43,900 | 25,000 | (2) |

√ 31,500

| Accounts Receivable | | | | Allowance for Uncollectable Accounts | | | |
|---|---|---|---|---|---|---|---|
| √ | 120,000 | | | | | 2,400 | √ |
| (9) | 29,200 | 19,200 | (8) | (8) | 19,200 | 20,000 | (7) |
| √ | 130,000 | | | | | 3,200 | √ |

| Inventory | | | Property, Plant and Equipment | | | |
|---|---|---|---|---|---|---|
| √ | 175,000 | | √ | 247,300 | | |
| (10) | 25,000 | | (3) | 62,900 | 40,000 | (12) |
| | | | (4) | 30,000 | | |
| √ | 200,000 | | √ | 300,200 | | |

| Accumulated Depreciation | | | | Patents | | |
|---|---|---|---|---|---|---|
| | | 78,000 | √ | | | |
| (12) | 22,000 | 39,000 | (11) | (6) | 75,000 | |
| | | 95,000 | √ | √ | 75,000 | |

8.42 continued.

| Accumulated Amortization | | | |
|---|---|---|---|
| | -- | | |
| | 15,000 | (13) | |
| | 15,000 | √ | |

| Accounts Payable | | | |
|---|---|---|---|
| | 155,000 | √ | |
| | 27,000 | (14) | |
| | 182,000 | √ | |

| Common Stock | | | |
|---|---|---|---|
| | 100,000 | √ | |
| | 30,000 | (4) | |
| | 43,900 | (15) | |
| | 173,900 | √ | |

| Retained Earnings | | | | |
|---|---|---|---|---|
| (2) | 25,000 | 232,600 | √ | |
| | | 60,000 | (1) | |
| | | 267,600 | √ | |

# CHAPTER 9

## LIABILITIES: INTRODUCTION

*Questions, Exercises, Problems, and Cases: Answers and Solutions*

9.1    See the text or the glossary at the end of the book.

9.2    a.  Yes; amount of accrued interest payable.

   b.  Yes.  In spite of the indefiniteness of the time of delivery of the goods or services and the amount, the balance sheet reports a liability in the amount of the cash received.

   c.  No; accounting does not record executory promises.

   d.  Yes; at the present value, calculated using the yield rate at the time of issue, of the remaining coupon and principal payments.

   e.  Yes; at the expected, undiscounted value of future service costs arising from all sales made prior to the balance sheet date.  The income statement includes warranty expense because of a desire to match all expenses of a sale with the sale; presumably one reason the firm sold the product was the promise of free repairs.  When recognizing the expense, the accountant credits a liability account to recognize the need for the future expenditures.

   f.  No.  If the firm expected to lose a reasonably estimable amount in the suit, then it would show an estimated liability.

   g.  Yes, assuming statutes or contracts require the restoration.  The present value of an estimate of the costs is the theoretically correct answer, but many accountants would use the full amount undiscounted.

   h.  No; viewed as executory.

   i.  Airlines recognize an expense and a liability for the estimated costs of providing the free flight during the periods when customers use flight services at regular fares.  The airlines accrue either the incremental cost of the free flight, which is a relatively small amount, or a portion of the average cost of a flight.  The incremental cost is small because customers use otherwise unused capacity.

9.3    The store should recognize the loss as soon as it is probable that it has incurred a liability and it can reasonably estimate the amount of the loss. Whether the store recognizes a loss at the time of the injury on July 5, Year 6, depends on the strength of the case the store feels it has against the customer's claims. If the floor was wet because a broken bottle had remained on the floor for several hours and was not cleaned up, then the store may feel it is probable that it has incurred a liability. If, on the other hand, the customer fell while running down a dry, uncluttered aisle while trying to shop quickly, then the store may feel that it is probable that it has not incurred a liability. Attorneys, not accountants, must make these probability assessments.

   If the store does not recognize a loss at the time of the injury, the next most likely time is June 15, Year 7, when the jury renders its verdict. Unless attorneys for the store feel that it is highly probable that the court will reverse the verdict on appeal, the store should recognize the loss at this time.

   If attorneys feel that the grounds for appeal are strong, then the next most likely time is on April 20, Year 8, when the jury in the lower court reaches the same verdict as previously. This is the latest time in this case at which the store should recognize the loss. If the store had recognized a loss on June 15, Year 7, it would recognize only the extra damage award in Year 8.

9.4    The expected value of the liability is $90,000 in both cases (.90 X $100,000 = $90,000; .09 X $1 X 1,000,000 = $90,000). Accounting would probably report the liability from the lawsuit as $100,000 and the liability for the coupons as $90,000. This inconsistency seems curious since the two situations differ only with respect to the number of possible outcomes (that is, all or nothing with respect to the lawsuit, whereas the coupon redemption rate conceivably ranges from one to one million).

9.5    Suppliers often grant a discount if customers pay within a certain number of days after the invoice date, in which case this source of funds has an explicit interest cost. Suppliers who do not offer discounts for prompt payment often include an implicit interest change in the selling price of the product. Customers in this second category should delay payment as long as possible because they are paying for the use of the funds. Firms should not delay payment to such an extent that it hurts their credit rating and raises their cost of financing.

9.6    The school should accrue the salary in ten monthly installments of $36,000 each at the end of each month, September through June. It will have paid $30,000 at the end of each of these months, so that by the end of the reporting year, it reports a current liability of $60,000 [= $360,000 − (10 X $30,000)].

9.7 There are two principal explanations. First, the obligation to customers in the event the firm does not publish the magazines is $45,000. Second, recognition of a liability of $32,000 requires a remaining credit of $13,000 to some other account. Recognizing the $13,000 as income is inappropriate because the publisher has not yet rendered the required services. Including the $13,000 is some type of Deferred Income account (a liability) has the same effect on total liabilities as reporting the Advance from Customers at $45,000.

9.8 It is cheaper (and, therefore, more profitable) to repair a few sets than to have such stringent quality control that the manufacturing process produces zero defectives. An allowance is justified when firms expect to have warranty costs. Manufacturers of TV sets for space travel or heart pacemakers should strive for zero defects.

9.9 **Similarities:** The accountant makes estimates of future events in both cases. The accountant charges the cost of estimated uncollectibles or warranties to income in the period of sale, not in the later period when specific items become uncollectible or break down. The income statement reports the charge against income as an expense in both cases, although some accountants report the charge for estimated uncollectibles as a revenue contra (and we prefer it that way).

**Differences:** The balance sheet account showing the expected costs of future uncollectibles reduces an asset account, while that for estimated warranties appears as a liability.

9.10 The coupon rate and par value of the bonds, the market rate of interest, and the market's opinion of the firm as a borrower. If the coupon rate is 8 percent, the market rate is 12 percent and the market views the firm as a relatively poor credit risk, the bonds will sell at a price to yield say, 15 percent. This means that the firm will receive less than the par value of the bonds it issues. We are told that when bonds are brought to the market, the investment banker attempts to set the coupon rate so the bonds will sell close to par.

9.11 a. Par value and face value are always synonymous.

b. Par value appears on the bond certificate and serves as the base for computing the periodic coupon interest payment. The book value is the same as the par value whenever the market-required interest rate on the date of issue equals the coupon interest rate. The book value will exceed the par value when the coupon rate exceeds the market rate at the time of issue. The par value will exceed the book value when the market rate exceeds the coupon rate at the time of issue.

9.11 continued.

    c.  Book value equals the present value of future cash flows on a bond discounted at the market-required interest rate at the time of issue. Current market value equals the present value of future cash flows on a bond discounted at the interest rate the market currently requires to induce purchase of the bond. The book value exceeds the current market value when the market interest rate at the time of issue was lower than the current market interest rate. The current market value will exceed the book value when the current market interest rate is lower than the market interest rate at the time of issue.

9.12    Accountants initially record assets at acquisition cost and then allocate this amount to future periods as an expense. Changes in the market value of most assets (except for use of the lower-of-cost-or-market method for inventories and the market value method for marketable securities and investments in securities) do not appear in the accounting records. Similarly, using the market interest rate at the time of issue to account for bonds results in an initial liability equal to the amount of cash received and a subsequent liability that reflects amortization of this initial amount. Changes in the market value of bonds do not appear in the accounting records.

9.13    $19,000. The aging analyses tell us the required ending balances in the balance sheet accounts. We plug for the expense required to achieve those balance sheet amounts. The percentage of sales method approximates the final number, but must yield to the analysis of the actual expected uncollectibles embedded in the current receivables and of the actual expected warranty costs embedded in the current obligations for warranties.

9.14    With bond financing, the firm borrows the entire principal, $1 million, for the entire term of the loan. With lease or mortgage financing, the firm repays part of the principal with each payment. Thus, the effective amount borrowed decreases over time and interest expenses should also decrease, even though the borrowings use the same rate.

9.15    Zero coupon bonds offer no cash payments to the investor until maturity. The issuer benefits by delaying cash payments. The issuer also gets a tax deduction for interest expense (that is, amortization of bond discount) during the period the bonds are outstanding even though it has no immediate cash outflow for interest. The investor locks in a yield at the time of purchase. The investor need not worry about having to invest periodic coupon payments during the life of the bonds. Thus, the investor avoids the risk of interest rate changes. The disadvantage to the investor is that the amortization of bond discount during the life of the bonds is taxable income even though the investor receives no cash. Most investors in zero coupon bonds do not pay taxes (for example, pension funds).

**9.16** The call premium, which typically declines as bonds approach maturity, compensates bondholders for the loss of interest payments when a firm calls, or buys back, some of its outstanding bonds before the maturity date. The call premium protects the bondholder from redemption by the issuer if interest rates in the market decline by reasonably small amounts.

**9.17** When market interest rates change, so do market values of bonds. When interest rates rise, bond prices decline, but book values of bonds remain unchanged. Firms can issue new bonds at current market rates and use the proceeds to retire outstanding bonds previously issued when rates were lower, and accountants record this transaction as a gain. The gain actually occurred as market rates rose and the burden of the debt fell. This is an unrealized holding gain in historical cost accounting. Because management can time bond retirements, management can time income recognition. This possibility explains in part the requirement that firms report gains and losses on bond retirements as extraordinary items in the income statement.

**9.18** (McGee Associates; journal entries for payroll.)

a.

| | | |
|---|---|---|
| Wage and Salary Expense | 700,000 | |
| U.S. Withholding Taxes Payable | | 126,000 |
| State Withholding Taxes Payable | | 35,000 |
| FICA Taxes Payable | | 42,000 |
| Wages and Salaries Payable | | 497,000 |

Amounts payable to and for employees.

| | | |
|---|---|---|
| Wage and Salary Expense | 107,800 | |
| FICA Taxes Payable | | 42,000 |
| FUTA Taxes Payable to U.S. Government | | 14,000 |
| FUTA Taxes Payable to State Government | | 7,000 |
| Payable to Profit Sharing Fund | | 28,000 |
| Vacation Liability | | 16,800 |

Employer's additional wage expense; estimated vacation liability is $16,800 (= 1.20 × $14,000).

b. $807,800 = $700,000 + $107,800.

**9.19** (Hurley Corporation; accounting for uncollectible accounts and warranties.)

a. **Allowance for Uncollectible Accounts**

| | | |
|---|---|---|
| Balance, December 31, Year 8 | $ | 355 |
| Plus Bad Debt Expense for Year 9: .02 × $18,000 | | 360 |
| Less Accounts Written Off (Plug) | | (310) |
| Balance, December 31, Year 9 | $ | 405 |
| Plus Bad Debt Expense for Year 10: .02 × $16,000 | | 320 |
| Less Accounts Written Off (Plug) | | (480) |
| Balance, December 31, Year 10 | $ | 245 |

9.19 continued.

    b. **Estimated Warranty Liability**

| | |
|---|---:|
| Balance, December 31, Year 8 | $ 1,325 |
| Plus Warranty Expense for Year 9: .06 × $18,000 | 1,080 |
| Less Actual Warranty Costs (Plug) | (870) |
| Balance, December 31, Year 9 | $ 1,535 |
| Plus Warranty Expense for Year 10: .06 × $16,000 | 960 |
| Less Actual Warranty Costs (Plug) | (775) |
| Balance, December 31, Year 10 | $ 1,720 |

9.20    (Morrison's Cafeteria; journal entries for coupons.)

    a. **January**

| | | |
|---|---:|---:|
| Cash | 50,100 | |
|     Sales Revenue | | 48,000 |
|     Coupon Liability | | 2,100 |
| | | |
| Coupon Liability | 1,600 | |
|     Sales Revenue | | 1,600 |

**February**

| | | |
|---|---:|---:|
| Cash | 50,700 | |
|     Sales Revenue | | 48,500 |
|     Coupon Liability | | 2,200 |
| | | |
| Coupon Liability | 2,300 | |
|     Sales Revenue | | 2,300 |

**March**

| | | |
|---|---:|---:|
| Cash | 52,400 | |
|     Sales Revenue | | 50,000 |
|     Coupon Liability | | 2,400 |
| | | |
| Coupon Liability | 2,100 | |
|     Sales Revenue | | 2,100 |

    b.  The Coupon Liability account has a balance of $4,700 (= $4,000 + $2,100 − $1,600 + $2,200 − $2,300 + $2,400 − $2,100) on March 31.

9.21    (Abson Corporation; journal entries for service contracts.)

    a. **1/31–3/31**

| | | |
|---|---:|---:|
| Cash | 180,000 | |
|     Service Contract Fees Received in Advance | | 180,000 |
| To record sale of 300 annual contracts. | | |

9.21 a. continued.

**3/31**

| | | |
|---|---|---|
| Service Contract Fees Received in Advance........... | 22,500 | |
|    Contract Revenues............................................ | | 22,500 |

To recognize revenue on 300 contracts sold during the first quarter; 1.5/12 × $180,000.

**1/01–3/31**

| | | |
|---|---|---|
| Service Expenses....................................................... | 32,000 | |
|    Cash (and Other Assets and Liabilities)............. | | 32,000 |

**4/01–6/30**

| | | |
|---|---|---|
| Cash............................................................................... | 300,000 | |
|    Service Contract Fees Received in Advance ...... | | 300,000 |

To record sale of 500 annual contracts.

**6/30**

| | | |
|---|---|---|
| Service Contract Fees Received in Advance........... | 82,500 | |
|    Contract Revenues ........................................... | | 82,500 |

To recognize revenue on 500 contracts sold and 300 contracts outstanding:
   First Quarter:
     3/12   × $180,000  = $45,000
   Second Quarter:
     1.5/12 × $300,000  =   37,500
                       $82,500

**4/01–6/30**

| | | |
|---|---|---|
| Service Expenses....................................................... | 71,000 | |
|    Cash (and Other Assets and Liabilities)............. | | 71,000 |

**7/01–9/30**

| | | |
|---|---|---|
| Cash............................................................................... | 240,000 | |
|    Service Contract Fees Received in Advance ...... | | 240,000 |

To record sale of 400 annual contracts.

**9/30**

| | | |
|---|---|---|
| Service Contract Fees Received in Advance........... | 150,000 | |
|    Contract Revenues ........................................... | | 150,000 |

To recognize revenue on 400 contracts sold and 800 contracts outstanding from prior sales.
   First Quarter Sales:
     3/12   × $180,000 = $  45,000
   Second Quarter Sales:
     3/12   × $300,000 =    75,000
   Third Quarter Sales:
     1.5/12 × $240,000 =    30,000
                   = $150,000

9.21 a. continued.

**7/01–9/30**
Service Expenses ....................................................... 105,000
   Cash (and Other Assets and Liabilities) ..............         105,000

b.  Balances in Service Contract Fees Received in Advance Account:

| | |
|---|---:|
| January 1 ................................................................................. | -- |
| Less First Quarter Expirations ............................................... | $ (22,500) |
| Plus First Quarter Sales ......................................................... | 180,000 |
| March 31 .................................................................................. | $ 157,500 |
| Less Second Quarter Expirations ........................................... | (82,500) |
| Plus Second Quarter Sales ..................................................... | 300,000 |
| June 30 .................................................................................... | $ 375,000 |
| Less Third Quarter Expirations ............................................. | (150,000) |
| Plus Third Quarter Sales ....................................................... | 240,000 |
| September 30 ........................................................................... | $ 465,000 |
| Less Fourth Quarter Expirations ........................................... | (195,000) |
| Plus Fourth Quarter Sales ..................................................... | 120,000 |
| December 31 ............................................................................ | $ 390,000 |

OR

| Contracts | X | **Balance Remaining** | X | $600 | = | Amount |
|---:|:---:|:---:|:---:|:---:|:---:|---:|
| 300 | X | 1.5/12 | X | $600 | = | $ 22,500 |
| 500 | X | 4.5/12 | X | $600 | = | 112,500 |
| 400 | X | 7.5/12 | X | $600 | = | 150,000 |
| 200 | X | 10.5/12 | X | $600 | = | 105,000 |
| | | | | | | $ 390,000 |

9.22    (Maypool Corporation; journal entries for estimated warranty liabilities and subsequent expenditures.)

a.  **Year 1**
Accounts Receivable ................................................... 1,200,000
   Sales ........................................................................       1,200,000

Estimated Warranty Liability .................................... 12,000
   Cash ........................................................................       12,000
Expenditures actually made.

Warranty Expense ........................................................ 48,000
   Estimated Warranty Liability .............................       48,000
.04 X $1,200,000.

9.22 a. continued.

**Year 2**

| Accounts Receivable | 1,500,000 | |
| Sales Revenue | | 1,500,000 |

| Estimated Warranty Liability | 50,000 | |
| Cash | | 50,000 |

Expenditures actually made.

| Warranty Expense | 60,000 | |
| Estimated Warranty Liability | | 60,000 |

.04 × $1,500,000.

b.   $46,000 = $48,000 − $12,000 + $60,000 − $50,000.

9.23   (Global Motors Corporation; journal entries for estimated warranty liabilities and subsequent expenditures.)

a.   **Year 1**

| Cash | 800,000 | |
| Sales Revenue | | 800,000 |

| Estimated Warranty Liability | 22,000 | |
| Cash | | 13,200 |
| Parts Inventory | | 8,800 |

| Warranty Expense | 48,000 | |
| Estimated Warranty Liability | | 48,000 |

.06 × $800,000 = $48,000.

**Year 2**

| Cash | 1,200,000 | |
| Sales Revenue | | 1,200,000 |

| Estimated Warranty Liability | 55,000 | |
| Cash | | 33,000 |
| Parts Inventory | | 22,000 |

| Warranty Expense | 72,000 | |
| Estimated Warranty Liability | | 72,000 |

.06 × $1,200,000 = $72,000.

9.23 a. continued.

**Year 3**

| | | |
|---|---|---|
| Cash........................................................................ | 900,000 | |
|    Sales Revenue....................................................... | | 900,000 |

| | | |
|---|---|---|
| Estimated Warranty Liability................................ | 52,000 | |
|    Cash ....................................................................... | | 31,200 |
|    Parts Inventory ..................................................... | | 20,800 |

| | | |
|---|---|---|
| Warranty Expense................................................. | 54,000 | |
|    Estimated Warranty Liability............................. | | 54,000 |

.06 X $900,000 = $54,000.

b. $48,000 − $22,000 + $72,000 − $55,000 + $54,000 − $52,000 = $45,000.

9.24 (Sung Company; journal entry for short-term note payable.)

a. **12/01**

| | | |
|---|---|---|
| Cash........................................................................ | 50,000 | |
|    Notes Payable........................................................ | | 50,000 |

**12/31**

| | | |
|---|---|---|
| Interest Expense................................................... | 250 | |
|    Interest Payable................................................... | | 250 |

$50,000 X .06 X 30/360 = $250.

**1/30**

| | | |
|---|---|---|
| Interest Expense................................................... | 250 | |
|    Interest Payable................................................... | | 250 |

**1/30**

| | | |
|---|---|---|
| Notes Payable (Original Note).................................. | 50,000 | |
| Interest Payable........................................................ | 500 | |
|    Notes Payable (New Note).................................... | | 50,000 |
|    Cash ....................................................................... | | 500 |

*Note:* Omitting the entries to the Notes Payable account above is also acceptable.

**3/2**

| | | |
|---|---|---|
| Notes Payable................................................................ | 50,000 | |
| Interest Expense......................................................... | 250 | |
|    Cash ....................................................................... | | 50,250 |

9.24 continued.

b. The entry to complete the accrual of interest (30 days) is the first entry under both alternatives. It is:

| | | |
|---|---:|---:|
| Interest Expense............................................... | 250 | |
|     Interest Payable......................................... | | 250 |

(1) **1/30**

| | | |
|---|---:|---:|
| Notes Payable (Original Note)......................... | 50,000 | |
| Interest Payable.............................................. | 500 | |
|     Cash ........................................................... | | 50,500 |

(2) **1/30**

| | | |
|---|---:|---:|
| Notes Payable (Original Note)......................... | 50,000 | |
| Interest Payable.............................................. | 500 | |
|     Notes Payable (New Note)............................. | | 50,500 |

9.25 (Blaydon Company; amortization schedule for note where explicit interest differs from market rate of interest.)

a. **Amortization Schedule for a Three-Year Note with a Maturity Value of $40,000, Calling for 8-Percent Annual Interest Payments, Yield of 12 Percent per Year**

| Year | Book Value Start of Year | Interest Expense for Period | Payment | Interest Added to (Subtracted from) Book Value | Book Value End of Year |
|---|---:|---:|---:|---:|---:|
| (1) | (2) | (3)a | (4) | (5) | (6) |
| 0 | | | | | $ 36,157 |
| 1 | $ 36,157 | $ 4,339 | $ 3,200 | $ 1,139 | 37,296 |
| 2 | 37,296 | 4,476 | 3,200 | 1,276 | 38,572 |
| 3 | 38,572 | 4,628 | 43,200 | (38,572) | -0- |

a(3) = (2) × .12, except in Year 3 where it is a plug.

b.

| | | |
|---|---:|---:|
| Computer....................................................................... | 36,157 | |
|     Note Payable.......................................................... | | 36,157 |
| To record purchase. | | |

**Annual Journal Entry for Interest and Principal**

| | | |
|---|---|---|
| Dr. Interest Expense.... | Amount in Col. (3) | |
|   Cr. Cash...................... | | Amount in Col. (4) |
|   Cr. Note Payable...... | | Amount in Col. (5)* |

*In third year, the firm debits Note Payable for $38,572.

9.26    (Computing the issue price of bonds.)

    a.  $1,000,000 × .09722[a]................................................................ $      97,220

        [a]Present value of $1 for 40 periods at 6%.

    b.  $50,000 × 23.11477[a]................................................................ $ 1,155,739

        [a]Present value of annuity for 40 periods at 3%.

    c.  $50,000 × 19.79277[a]................................................................ $    989,639
        $1,000,000 × .20829[b]................................................................     208,290
                                                  $ 1,197,929

        [a]Present value of annuity for 40 periods at 4%.
        [b]Present value of $1 for 40 periods at 4%.

    d.  $30,000 × 12.46221[a]................................................................ $    373,866
        $70,000 × 12.46221[a] × .37689[b] ...........................................     328,782
        $1,000,000 × .14205[c]................................................................     142,050
                                                    $    844,698

        [a]Present value of annuity for 20 periods at 5%.
        [b]Present value of $1 for 20 periods at 5%.
        [c]Present value of $1 for 40 periods at 5%.

9.27    (Huergo Dooley Corporation; accounting for bonds.)

    a.  $2,000,000 × .61391[a]................................................................ $ 1,227,820
        $80,000 × 7.72173[b]................................................................     617,738
                                                    $ 1,845,558

        [a]Present value of $1 for 10 periods at 5%.
        [b]Present value of an annuity for 10 periods at 5%.

    b.  Interest Expense (.05 × $1,845,558).........................  92,278
           Cash (.04 × $2,000,000)...........................................            80,000
           Bonds Payable (Plug)...............................................            12,278

    c.  Interest Expense [.05 × ($1,845,558 + $12,278)]...  92,892
           Cash (.04 × $2,000,000)...........................................            80,000
           Bonds Payable (Plug)...............................................            12,892

9.27 continued.

d. Bonds Payable [.20 × ($1,845,558 + $12,278 +
    $12,892)] ...................................................................... 374,146
   Loss on Repurchase of Bonds ................................... 53,933
    Cash ....................................................................... 428,079

$2,000,000 × .78941[a] ............................................... $ 1,578,820
$80,000 × 7.01969[b] .................................................. 561,575
                            $ 2,140,395
   Total ............................................................................ X .20
Purchase Price ................................................................ $ 428,079

[a]Present value of $1 for 8 periods at 3%.
[b]Present value of an annuity for 8 periods at 3%.

9.28    (O'Brien Corporation; computing the issue price of bonds and interest expense.)

a.  $8,000,000 × .30656[a] ............................................... $ 2,452,480
   $320,000 × 23.11477[b] ............................................... 7,396,726
    Issue Price ................................................................. $ 9,849,206

[a]Table 2, 3-percent column and 40-period row.
[b]Table 4, 3-percent column and 40-period row.

b.  .03 × $9,849,206 = $295,476.

c.  .03($9,849,206 + $295,476 − $320,000) = $294,740.

d.  Book Value: ($9,849,206 + $295,476 − $320,000 +
    $294,740 − $320,000) ................................................ $ 9,799,422

e.  $8,000,000 × .32523[a] ............................................... $ 2,601,840
   $320,000 × 22.49246[b] ............................................... 7,197,587
    Present Value ............................................................. $ 9,799,427

[a]Table 2, 3-percent column and 38-period row.
[b]Table 4 3-percent column and 38-period row.

The difference between the book value in Part d. and the present value in Part e. results from rounding present value factors.

9.29    (Robinson Company; computing the issue price of bonds and interest expense.)

   a.    $5,000,000 × .37689[a] ................................................................. $ 1,884,450
          $200,000 × 12.46221[b] ...............................................................   2,492,442
             Issue Price .............................................................................. $ 4,376,892

          [a]Table 2, 5-percent column and 20-period row.
          [b]Table 4, 5-percent column and 20-period row.

   b.    .05 × $4,376,892 = $218,845.

   c.    .05($4,376,892 + $218,845 − $200,000) = $219,787.

   d.    $4,376,892 + $218,845 − $200,000 + $219,787 − $200,000 = $4,415,524.

   e.    $5,000,000 × .41552[a] ................................................................. $ 2,077,600
          $200,000 × 11.68959[b] ...............................................................   2,337,918
             Present Value .......................................................................... $ 4,415,518

          [a]Table 2, 5-percent column and 18-period row.
          [b]Table 4, 5-percent column and 18-period row.

          The difference between the book value in Part *d.* and the present value in Part *e.* results from rounding present value factors.

9.30    (Florida Edison Company; using bond tables; computing interest expense.)

   a.    $885,301; see Table 5, 10-year row, 12-percent column.

   b.    $53,118 = .06 × $885,301.

   c.    $53,305 = .06 × $888,419; see Table 5, 9.5-year row, 12-percent column.

   d.    $926,399; see Table 5, 5-year row, 12-percent column.

   e.    $55,584 = .06 × $926,399.

9.31    (Centrix Company; using bond tables.)

        Refer to Table 6.

   a.    $1,084,658; 25-year row; 11-percent column.

   b.    $1,080,231; 20-year row; 11-percent column.

   c.    $1,072,669; 15-year row; 11-percent column.

9.31 continued.

    d. $1,072,669; same answer is *not* coincidental.

    e. ($1,000,000 × .06) − ($1,004,739 − $1,000,000) = $60,000 − $4,739 = $55,261; 0.5-year row; 11-percent column.

    f. $934,707; 15-year row; 13-percent column.

    g. 10 percent compounded semiannually; scan 10-year row to find 112.46.

9.32    (Mendoza Corporation; journal entries for bond coupon payments and retirements.)

    a. **7/1/Year 7**

| | | |
|---|---:|---:|
| Interest Expense (.05 × $1,124,622) | 56,231 | |
| Bonds Payable (plug) | 3,769 | |
|    Cash (.06 × $1,000,000) | | 60,000 |

       **12/31/Year 7**

| | | |
|---|---:|---:|
| Interest Expense[a] | 56,043 | |
| Bonds Payable (Plug) | 3,957 | |
|    Cash (as above) | | 60,000 |

       [a].05 × ($1,124,622 − $3,769) = $56,043.

    b.

| | | |
|---|---:|---:|
| Bonds Payable ($1,110,090/2) | 558,448 | |
|    Gain on Retirement (Plug) | | 108,743 |
|    Cash[a] | | 449,705 |

       [a]$500,000 × .899409 = $449,705 (value in a 14 percent market).

    c. It would appear as a gain on the income statement.

9.33    (Womack Company; amortization schedule for bonds.)

    a.

| | |
|---|---:|
| $100,000 × .67556[a] | $ 67,556 |
| $5,000 × 8.11090[b] | 40,555 |
|   Issue Price | $ 108,111[c] |

    [a]Table 2, 4-percent column and 10-period row.
    [b]Table 4, 4-percent column and 10-period row.
    [c]Also see Table 5.

9.33 continued.

b.

| Six-Month Period | Liability at Start of Period | Interest at 4 Percent for Period | Coupon at 5% of Par | Decrease in Book Value of Liability | Liability at End of Period |
|---|---|---|---|---|---|
| 0 | | | | | $ 108,111 |
| 1 | $ 108,111 | $ 4,324 | $ 5,000 | $ 676 | 107,435 |
| 2 | 107,435 | 4,297 | 5,000 | 703 | 106,732 |
| 3 | 106,732 | 4,269 | 5,000 | 731 | 106,001 |
| 4 | 106,001 | 4,240 | 5,000 | 760 | 105,241 |
| 5 | 105,241 | 4,210 | 5,000 | 790 | 104,451 |
| 6 | 104,451 | 4,178 | 5,000 | 822 | 103,629 |
| 7 | 103,629 | 4,145 | 5,000 | 855 | 102,774 |
| 8 | 102,774 | 4,111 | 5,000 | 889 | 101,885 |
| 9 | 101,885 | 4,075 | 5,000 | 925 | 100,960 |
| 10 | 100,960 | 4,040[a] | 5,000 | 960 | 100,000 |
| Total.................. | | $ 41,889 | $ 50,000 | $ 8,111 | |

[a]Does not equal .04 X $100,960 due to rounding.

c.   Book Value of Bonds: $10,363.

| | | |
|---|---|---|
| Bonds Payable................................................................... | 10,363 | |
|    Extraordinary Gain on Bond Retirement ........... | | 63 |
|    Cash.................................................................... | | 10,300 |

9.34   (Seward Corporation; amortization schedule for bonds.)

a.   $100,000 X .74622[a] ...................................................................... $ 74,622

    $4,000 X 5.07569[b].......................................................................... 20,303

      Issue Price........................................................................... $ 94,925

[a]Table 2, 5-percent column and 6-period row.
[b]Table 4, 5-percent column and 6-period row.

b.

| Six-Month Period | Liability at Start of Period | Interest at 5 Percent for Period | Coupon at 4% of Par | Increase in Book Value of Liability | Liability at End of Period |
|---|---|---|---|---|---|
| 0 | | | | | $ 94,925 |
| 1 | $ 94,925 | $ 4,746 | $ 4,000 | $ 746 | 95,671 |
| 2 | 95,671 | 4,784 | 4,000 | 784 | 96,455 |
| 3 | 96,455 | 4,823 | 4,000 | 823 | 97,278 |
| 4 | 97,278 | 4,864 | 4,000 | 864 | 98,142 |
| 5 | 98,142 | 4,907 | 4,000 | 907 | 99,049 |
| 6 | 99,049 | 4,951 | 4,000 | 951 | 100,000 |
| Total.................. | | $ 29,075 | $ 24,000 | $ 5,075 | |

9.34 continued.

c. **January 2, Year 1**

| | | |
|---|---|---|
| Cash | 94,925 | |
|     Bonds Payable | | 94,925 |

**June 30, Year 1**

| | | |
|---|---|---|
| Interest Expense | 4,746 | |
|     Interest Payable | | 4,000 |
|     Bonds Payable | | 746 |

**July 1, Year 1**

| | | |
|---|---|---|
| Interest Payable | 4,000 | |
|     Cash | | 4,000 |

**December 31, Year 1**

| | | |
|---|---|---|
| Interest Expense | 4,784 | |
|     Interest Payable | | 4,000 |
|     Bonds Payable | | 784 |

d. 

| | | |
|---|---|---|
| Bonds Payable (.20 X $98,142) | 19,628 | |
| Loss on Retirement of Bonds | 772 | |
|     Cash | | 20,400 |

9.35 (Brooks Corporation; journal entries to account for bonds.)

a.

| | |
|---|---|
| $100,000 X .55368[a] | $ 55,368 |
| $4,000 X 14.87747[b] | 59,510 |
| Issue Price | $ 114,878 |

[a]Table 2, 3-percent column and 20-period row.
[b]Table 4, 3-percent column and 20-period row.

b. **January 2, Year 2**

| | | |
|---|---|---|
| Cash | 114,878 | |
|     Bonds Payable | | 114,878 |

**June 30, Year 2**

| | | |
|---|---|---|
| Interest Expense (.03 X $114,878) | 3,446 | |
| Bonds Payable | 554 | |
|     Cash | | 4,000 |

**December 31, Year 2**

| | | |
|---|---|---|
| Interest Expense [.03 X ($114,878 − $554)] | 3,430 | |
| Bonds Payable | 570 | |
|     Cash | | 4,000 |

9.35 continued.

    c.   Book Value:  $114,878 – $554 – $570 = $113,754.
        Market Value:

| | |
|---|---:|
| $100,000 × .41552[a] | $ 41,552 |
| $4,000 × 11.68959[b] | 46,758 |
| Total Market Value | $ 88,310 |

[a]Table 2, 5-percent column and 18-period row.
[b]Table 4, 5-percent column and 18-period row.

| | | |
|---|---:|---:|
| Bonds Payable | 113,754 | |
| Cash | | 88,310 |
| Gain on Bond Retirement | | 25,444 |

9.36    (Central Appliance; allowance method for warranties; reconstructing transactions.)

    a.   $720,000 = $820,000 (Goods Available for Sale) – $100,000 (Beginning Inventory).

    b.   $700,000 = $820,000 (Goods Available for Sale) – $120,000 (Ending Inventory).

    c.   $21,000 = $6,000 (Cr. Balance) + $15,000 (Dr. Balance).

    d.   $20,000 = $5,000 (Required Cr. Balance) + $15,000 (Existing Dr. Balance).

    e.

| | | |
|---|---:|---:|
| Dr. Estimated Liability for Warranty Repairs | 21,000 | |
|   Cr. Various Assets Used for Repairs | | 21,000 |

Repairs made during Year 2.

| | | |
|---|---:|---:|
| Dr. Warranty Expense | 20,000 | |
|   Cr. Estimated Liability for Warranty Repairs | | 20,000 |

Expense recognition for Year 2.

| | | |
|---|---:|---:|
| Dr. Cost of Goods Sold | 700,000 | |
|   Cr. Merchandise Inventory | | 700,000 |

Cost of goods sold is goods available for sale less ending inventory.

9.37 (Time Warner, Inc.; accounting for zero-coupon debt; see *The Wall Street Journal* for December 8, 1992.)

a. $483 million = $1,550 million/3.20714; see table 1, 6-percent column, 20-period row.

b. 5.8 percent = $($1,550/$500)^{1/20} - 1 = 3.10^{1/20} - 1$. That is, for each dollar of the initial issue proceeds (of the $500 million), Time Warner must pay $3.10 (= $1,550/$500) at maturity of the notes. You can find the periodic interest rate to make $1.00 grow to $3.10 in 20 periods by trial and error or by using the exponential function on your computer or calculator. Note that you can state an equation to solve, as follows:

$$(1 + r)^{20} = 3.10; \text{ solve for } r.$$

You can see from Table 1 that 5.8 percent is approximately correct.

c. $28 million = .07 × $400 million.

d. $101.4 million. Ask, first, what must the book value of the notes be at the end of Year 19. Then, compute interest for the year on that amount. The book value of the loan at the end of Year 19 must be $1,448.6 (= $1,550/1.07) million. Interest for one year at 7 percent on $1,448.6 million is $101.4 (= .07 × $1,448.6 = $1,550.0 − $1,448.6) million. You can check this approach to finding the answer by noting that:

$$\$1,448.6 \times 1.07 = \$1,550.0.$$

9.38 (Aggarwal Corporation; accounting for long-term bonds.)

a. **Interest Expense**
First Six Months: .05 × $301,512 = $15,076.
Second Six Months: .05($301,512 + $15,076) = $15,829.
Book value of bonds on December 31, Year 4: $301,512 + $15,076 + $15,829 = $332,417.

b. **Book Value of Bonds on December 31, Year 3**
Interest:
   $35,000 × 8.11090 = $ 283,882    (Table 4, 10 periods and 4%)
Principal:
   $1,000,000 × .67556 = 675,560    (Table 2, 10 periods and 4%)
   Total.......................... $ 959,442

| | |
|---|---|
| Book Value of Bonds, December 31, Year 3............................ | $ 959,442 |
| Add Interest Expense for Year 4.................................... | X |
| Subtract Coupon Payments during Year 4............................ | (70,000) |
| Book Value of Bonds, December 31, Year 4............................ | $ 966,336 |

Interest expense for Year 4 is $76,894.

9.38 continued.

   c. **Book Value of Bonds on July 1, Year 4**

| | |
|---|---:|
| Book Value of Bonds, December 31, Year 3............................ | $ 1,305,832 |
| Plus Interest Expense for First Six Months of Year 4: .03 × $1,305,832................................................................ | 39,175 |
| Subtract Coupon Payment during First Six Months of Year 4.................................................................................... | (45,000) |
| Book Value of Bonds, July 1, Year 4.................................... | $ 1,300,007 |
| Book Value of One-Half of Bonds......................................... | $ 650,004 |

| | | |
|---|---:|---:|
| Bonds Payable............................................................... | 650,004 | |
| Cash ............................................................................... | | 526,720 |
| Gain on Bonds Retirement........................................... | | 123,284 |

   d. **Interest Expense for Second Six Months**
      .03 × $650,004 = $19,500.

9.39    (Wal-Mart Stores; accounting for long-term bonds.)

   a.

| | |
|---|---:|
| .06 × $83,758,595..................................................................... | $ 5,025,516 |
| .06($83,758,595 + $5,025,516 − $4,500,000) ...................... | 5,057,047 |
| | $ 10,082,563 |

   b.

| | |
|---|---:|
| Interest Expense...................................................................... | $ 10,082,563 |
| Interest Payable....................................................................... | 9,000,000 |
| Increase in Bonds Payable....................................................... | $ 1,082,563 |
| Book Value, January 31, Year 11............................................ | 83,758,595 |
| Book Value, January 31, Year 12............................................ | $ 84,841,158 |

   c.  Present Value = Maturity Value × Present Value Factors.
      $162,395,233 = Maturity Value × (4 percent, 11 periods).
      $175,646,684 = Maturity Value × (4 percent, 9 periods).
      Maturity Value = $250,000,000.

   d.  The book value equals the par value, so the initial market yield is the stated interest yield of 9.25 percent compounded semiannually.

9.40    (IBM Credit Corporation; comparison of straight-line and effective interest methods of amortizing bond discount.)

   a.  $58,173,000. See Table 2, 14-period column, 7-percent row, where the factor is .38782.

      .38782 × $150,000,000 = $58,173,000.

   b.  $4,072,110 = $58,173,000 × .07.

9.40 continued.

c.  $6,559,071 = ($150,000,000 − $58,173,000)/14.

$2,623,628 = .40 \times $6,559,071.

d.  $87,754,890 = $150,000,000 − $58,173,000 − $4,072,110
    = $150,000,000 − (1.07 \times $58,173,000).

e.  Issuers like not having to pay the cash for coupons during the life of the issue, but this fact is reflected in the original issue price of the bonds, so it is hard to justify this as being an economic advantage.

Some purchasers like zero coupon bonds, because there is no need to consider uncertainty about future interest rates and the reinvesting of interest coupons. If one wants a fixed sum some years in the future, then zero coupon notes may be a more useful instrument than coupon bonds. Investment advisors understand this advantage. Another advantage to the purchaser, but one not so well understood by the press, accountants, and even some investment bankers, is the extra call protection in a zero coupon note. Because the issuer can call the bonds at par value (and no other cash interest payments will occur over the entire life of the bond), it will never pay the issuer to call them unless interest rates drop to zero. Thus, the lender has more protection than in a callable coupon-bearing bond against interest rate declines. Of course, such protection has a price, and the lack of an "option" feature to the issuer may account for much of the apparently lower cost of borrowing via zero coupon notes.

As to the loophole, the Treasury might take offense that the tax rules, generally cash-based, allow the current deduction and current tax savings for an item whose cash flows occur seven years in the future. Note from the preceding part that the only cash effect of the interest and related tax transactions is IBMCC's saving $2,623,628 in income tax payments it would otherwise have made.

The Wall Street Journal story indicated, however, that the Treasury had in mind as a "loophole" the $2,486,961 difference between the $6,559,071 interest deduction resulting from using the straight-line method and the $4,072,110 interest computed "correctly" with the effective interest method. Using the straight-line method resulted in cash savings in taxes of $994,784 (= .40 \times $2,486,961) as compared to the effective interest method.

The Tax Equity and Fiscal Reform Act (TEFRA) of 1982 did indeed change the tax law so that issues must amortize original-issue discount for tax purposes using the effective interest method, not the straight-line method.

However, the Treasury position overlooks the symmetry in the tax treatment of zero coupon bonds to the issuer and the holder. While the issuer is entitled to deduct interest on a straight-line basis, the holder is taxable on a straight-line basis. The Treasury might respond to such

9.40 e. continued.

arguments by noting that the issuer is generally a taxable entity, while the holder of zero-coupon notes is often tax-exempt (a pension fund, for example).

If we choose to interpret the words "interest expense" in a precise mathematical fashion, the mathematics of compound interest seems to favor the effective interest method, as does Accounting Principles Board *Opinion No. 21*. The straight-line method is easier to compute, but the availability of low cost computing largely obviates this advantage. An alternative point of view, of course, is that the words "interest expense" mean whatever Congress and the courts define them to mean, insofar as taxes are concerned.

A more important economic issue is the symmetry of the tax laws. If both lender and borrower are taxed at the same rate, the total proceeds to the Treasury are the same under either method, so long as the lender and borrower are treated symmetrically. Of course, the *incidence* of the tax will be affected, holding all other things constant (i.e., in a partial equilibrium analysis). Switching to the effective interest method for both parties would shift taxes from the lender to the borrower. In a general equilibrium analysis, however, the subsequent readjustment of bond prices is much harder to compute. If, on the other hand, many of the lenders are tax exempt, revenues to the Treasury would be increased by the effective interest method, because it raises the present value of the borrower's tax liability. But again, the ultimate equilibrium that would be obtained after such a change is not readily apparent, at least to us.

9.41    (Quaker Oats Company; managing income and the debt-equity ratio through bond retirement.)

a.    $25,200,000 = .63 X $40,000,000 of cash must be raised to retire old issue.

|  | Dollars in Thousands | |
|---|---|---|
| Cash............................................................................. | 25,200 | |
| Bonds Payable—9 Percent.................................... | | 25,200 |
| Issue of new bonds. | | |
| | | |
| Bonds Payable—5 Percent.................................... | 40,000 | |
| Cash........................................................................ | | 25,200 |
| Gain on Bond Retirement (Extraordinary | | |
| Item) ................................................................ | | 14,800 |
| | | |
| Income Tax Expense................................................ | 5,920 | |
| Cash........................................................................ | | 5,920 |
| .40 X $14,800. | | |

9.41 continued.

b. Income increases by $8,880,000 [= (1 − .40) × $14,800,000], or by about 110 percent (= $8,880/$8,000) to about $17 million. Retained Earnings increases by $8,880,000.

c. Debt-equity ratio ($ in 000):

$$\frac{\$5,000 + \$25,200}{\$5,000 + \$25,200 + \$35,000 + \$8,880} = \frac{\$30,200}{\$74,080} = 40.8\%.$$

9.42 (FNB/OOPS; accounting for bonds in a troubled-debt restructuring.)

a. Present value of newly-promised cash flows at 20 percent, compounded semiannually = $2,563,903.

Present value of 50 semiannual payments of $1 discounted at 10 percent per period = 9.91481; see Table 4, 50-period row, 10-percent column.
9.91481 × $250,000 ................................................................. $2,478,703

Present value of $1 paid 50 periods hence, discounted at 10 percent per period = .00852; see Table 2, 50-period row, 10-percent column.
.00852 × $10,000,000 ................................................................. <u>85,200</u>
<u>$2,563,903</u>

b. Present value of newly-promised cash flows at 12 percent, compounded semiannually = $4,483,365.

Present value of 50 semiannual payments of $1 discounted at 6 percent per period = 15.76186; see Table 4, 50-period row, 6-percent column.
15.76186 × $250,000 ................................................................. $3,940,465

Present value of $1 paid 50 periods hence, discounted at 6 percent per period = .05429; see Table 2, 50-period row, 6-percent column.
.05429 × $10,000,000 ................................................................. <u>542,900</u>
<u>$4,483,365</u>

c. FNB would recognize a loss of $7,436,097 (= $10,000,000 − $2,563,903) under the first method. This would be followed by interest revenue of $12,500,000 (= 50 × $250,000) from cash receipts plus interest revenue from amortization of discount of $7,436,097. Total income under the first method would be $−7,436,097 for write down in 1990 plus $12,500,000 for cash receipts plus $7,436,097 for interest revenue from amortization; total income equal to $12,500,000.

9.42 c. continued.

Under the second method, FNB would recognize a loss of $5,516,635 (= $10,000,000 − $4,483,365). This would be followed by interest revenue of $12,500,000 (= 50 × $250,000) from cash receipts plus interest revenue from amortization of discount of $5,516,635. Total income under the second method would be $12,500,000 (= $−5,516,635 + $12,500,000 + $5,516,635).

Under the third method, income over the next twenty-five years would be $12,500,000 (= 50 × $250,000) for cash receipts.

Over long enough time spans, accounting income is equal to cash receipts. But note that the timing of income recognition varies drastically as a function of the treatment chosen.

d. We prefer the first method, because we think the troubled-debt restructuring results from an arm's length transaction. FASB *Statement No. 114*, however, requires the use of the second method.

9.43 (Discounting warranty obligations.)

a. **Year 1**
Warranty Expense.................................................... 2,000,000
    Estimated Warranty Liability............................         2,000,000

**Year 2**
Estimated Warranty Liability................................ 500,000
    Cash and Other Accounts.................................         500,000

**Year 3**
Estimated Warranty Liability................................ 600,000
    Cash and Other Accounts.................................         600,000

**Year 4**
Estimated Warranty Liability................................ 900,000
    Cash and Other Accounts.................................         900,000

b. The present value of the future cost amounts on December 31, Year 1, discounted as 10 percent, is $1,626,594, computed as follows:

| | | |
|---|---|---:|
| **Year 2**: | $500,000 × .90909 ................................................. | $ 454,545 |
| **Year 3**: | $600,000 × .82645 ................................................. | 495,870 |
| **Year 4**: | $900,000 × .75131 ................................................. | 676,179 |
| | Total................................................................. | $ 1,626,594 |

9.43 b. continued.

### Year 1

| | | |
|---|---|---|
| Warranty Expense | 1,626,594 | |
|    Estimated Warranty Liability | | 1,626,594 |

### Year 2

| | | |
|---|---|---|
| Interest Expense | 162,659 | |
|    Estimated Warranty Liability | | 162,659 |

.10 × $1,626,594 = $162,659.

### Year 2

| | | |
|---|---|---|
| Estimated Warranty Liability | 500,000 | |
|    Cash and Other Accounts | | 500,000 |

### Year 3

| | | |
|---|---|---|
| Interest Expense | 128,925 | |
|    Estimated Warranty Liability | | 128,925 |

.10($1,626,594 + $162,659 – $500,000) = $128,925.

### Year 3

| | | |
|---|---|---|
| Estimated Warranty Liability | 600,000 | |
|    Cash and Other Accounts | | 600,000 |

### Year 4

| | | |
|---|---|---|
| Interest Expense | 81,810 | |
|    Estimated Warranty Liability | | 81,818 |

.10($1,626,594 + $162,659 – $500,000 + $128,925 – $600,000) = .10 × $818,178 = $81,818.

### Year 4

| | | |
|---|---|---|
| Estimated Warranty Liability | 899,996 | |
| Interest Expense | 4 | |
|    Cash and Other Accounts | | 900,000 |

There is a rounding error of $4 in the Estimated Warranty Liability account at the end of Year 4. Interest expense for Year 4, therefore, increases by $4.

c. The firm must first acquire for cash the goods and services provided under the warranty plan. Thus, even though customers will receive goods and services, the firm must expend cash at some point. To be consistent with monetary liabilities, accounting would discount these amounts to their present value.

9.44    (Effects on statement of cash flows.)

a.  The journal entry to record this transaction is:

Cash...................................................................................... 100,000
    Bonds Payable.....................................................                              100,000

The debit to the Cash account results in an increase of $100,000 in Line (9). Issuing debit is a financing activity, so Line (6) increases by $100,000.

b.  The journal entry for this transaction is:

Building.................................................................................. 100,000
    Bonds Payable.....................................................                              100,000

The transaction does not affect the Cash account, so Line (9) does not change. This transaction does not affect net income, so Line (1) does not change. This transaction does not appear in the statement of cash flows but in a note to the financial statements.

c.  The journal entry to record this transaction is:

Bonds Payable .......................................................... 100,000
    Cash ..............................................................................                90,000
    Extraordinary Gain on Bond Retirement.............                                10,000

The Cash account decreases, so Line (9) decreases by $90,000. Retiring bonds is a financing activity, so Line (7) increases by $90,000. The extraordinary gain increases net income, so Line (1) increases by $10,000. Because this gain does not provide an operating source of cash, Line (3) increases by $10,000 to offset the gain and result in a zero net effect on cash flow from operations.

 d. The journal entry for this transaction is:

| | | |
|---|---:|---:|
| Bonds Payable | 100,000 | |
| Extraordinary Loss on Bond Retirement | 5,000 | |
|  Cash | | 105,000 |

The Cash account decreases, so Line (9) decreases by $105,000. Calling bonds is a financing activity, so Line (7) increases by $105,000. The extraordinary loss reduces net income, so Line (1) decreases by $5,000. Because this loss does not use an operating cash flow, Line (2) increases by $5,000 to offset the loss and result in a zero net effect on cash flow from operations.

 e. The journal entry to record this transaction is:

| | | |
|---|---:|---:|
| Interest Expense (= .06 × $90,000) | 5,400 | |
|  Cash (= .05 × $100,000) | | 5,000 |
|  Bonds Payable | | 400 |

The Cash account decreases by $5,000, so Line (9) decreases by $5,000. Net income decreases by $5,400 for interest expense, so Line (1) decreases by $5,400. Because the firm uses only $5,000 cash for this expense, Line (2) increases by $400 for the portion of the expense that does not use cash.

 f. The journal entry to record this transaction is:

| | | |
|---|---:|---:|
| Interest Expense (= .05 × $105,000) | 5,250 | |
| Bonds Payable | 750 | |
|  Cash (= .06 × $100,000) | | 6,000 |

The Cash account decreases by $6,000, so Line (9) decreases by $6,000. Net income decreases by $5,250, so Line (1) decreases by $5,250. Because the firm uses more cash than the amount of interest expense, Line (3) increases by $750. The total effect on cash flow from operations is $6,000 (= $5,250 + $750).

9.45    (Rhodes Company; preparing statement of cash flows.) A T-account work sheet for Rhodes Company appears after the statement of cash flows.

## RHODES COMPANY
### Statement of Cash Flows
### Year 2

Operations:

| | | |
|---|---|---|
| Net Income | $ 53,000 | |
| Addbacks and Additions: | | |
| Depreciation Expense | 48,000 | |
| Loss on Bond Retirement | 3,000 | |
| Bad Debt Expense | 9,000 | |
| Increase in Accounts Payable | 11,000 | |
| Subtractions: | | |
| Gain on Sale of Equipment | (4,900) | |
| Cash Used for Debt Service Exceeding Interest Expense | (5,000) | |
| Increase in Accounts Receivable | (15,900) | |
| Increase in Inventories | (12,000) | |
| Cash Flow from Operations | | $ 86,200 |
| Investing: | | |
| Sale of Property, Plant and Equipment | $ 19,900 | |
| Acquisition of Property, Plant and Equipment | (57,300) | |
| Cash Flow from Investing | | (37,400) |
| Financing: | | |
| Issue of Bonds | $ 50,000 | |
| Retirement of Bonds | (73,000) | |
| Dividends | (30,000) | |
| Cash Flow from Financing | | (53,000) |
| Change in Cash | | $ (4,200) |
| Cash, January 1, Year 2 | | 47,000 |
| Cash, December 31, Year 2 | | $ 42,800 |

## Supplementary Information

Rhodes Company issued $11,000 of common stock during Year 2 to acquire property, plant and equipment.

9.45 continued.

## Cash

| | | |
|---|---|---|
| √ 47,000 | | |

**Operations**

| | | | |
|---|---|---|---|
| (1) 53,000 | 4,900 | (5) | |
| (4) 48,000 | 5,000 | (9) | |
| (7) 3,000 | 15,900 | (12) | |
| (10) 9,000 | 12,000 | (13) | |
| (14) 11,000 | | | |

**Investing**

| | | |
|---|---|---|
| (5) 19,900 | 57,300 | (6) |

**Financing**

| | | |
|---|---|---|
| (8) 50,000 | 30,000 | (2) |
| | 73,000 | (7) |
| √ 42,800 | | |

| Accounts Receivable | | Allowance for Un-collectible Accounts | | Inventory | |
|---|---|---|---|---|---|
| √ 80,000 | | | 1,200 √ | √ 110,000 | |
| (12)15,900 | 8,900 (11) | (11) 8,900 | 9,000(10) | (13) 12,000 | |
| √ 87,000 | | | 1,300 √ | √ 122,000 | |

| Property, Plant and Equipment | | Accumulated Depreciation | | Accounts Payable | |
|---|---|---|---|---|---|
| √ 474,000 | | | 189,800 √ | | 70,000 √ |
| (3) 11,000 | 60,100 (5) | (5) 45,100 | 48,000 (4) | | 11,000 (14) |
| (6) 57,300 | | | | | |
| √ 482,200 | | | 192,700 √ | | 81,000 √ |

| Bonds Payable | | Common Stock | | Retained Earnings | |
|---|---|---|---|---|---|
| | 195,000 √ | | 100,000 √ | | 155,000 √ |
| (7) 70,000 | 50,000 (8) | | 11,000 (3) | (2) 30,000 | 53,000 (1) |
| (9) 5,000 | | | | | |
| | 170,000 √ | | 111,000 √ | | 178,000 √ |

# CHAPTER 10

## LIABILITIES: OFF-BALANCE-SHEET FINANCING, LEASES, DEFERRED INCOME TAXES, RETIREMENT BENEFITS, AND DERIVATIVES

*Questions, Exercises, Problems, and Cases: Answers and Solutions*

10.1    See the text or the glossary at the end of the book.

10.2    One premise underlying this statement is that the notes provide sufficient information to permit the analyst to make an informed judgment about the nature of the obligation or commitment and its associated risks. Current disclosures of off-balance-sheet commitments aggregate similar transactions, making an informed judgment about individual items difficult. Even if the disclosure permitted an informed judgment, the question arises as to whether information processing costs for analysts would decrease if firms actually recognized these items as liabilities. The counter argument to recognition of off-balance-sheet liabilities is that they differ in their risk characteristics relative to liabilities appearing on the books; thus disclosure in the notes is more appropriate than recognition in the balance sheet.

10.3    Using an executory contract to achieve off-balance-sheet financing results in the recognition of neither an asset (for example, leased assets) nor a liability (for example, lease liability) on the balance sheet. Using an asset sale with recourse results in a decrease in an asset (for example, accounts receivable) and an increase in cash. In both cases, no liability appears on the balance sheet.

10.4    The party with the risks and rewards of ownership effectively owns the asset, whatever the legal niceties. The asset should appear on the balance sheet of the owner. The capital lease criteria attempt to state unambiguously who has economic ownership.

10.5    The distinction depends upon which criteria of the lease made it a capital lease. The major difference is that at the end of a lease term the asset reverts to the lessor in a capital lease, whereas at the end of the installment payments, the asset belongs to the purchaser. The criteria for capitalizing a lease are such that the expected value of the asset when it reverts to the lessor is small, but misestimates can occur. In most other respects, capital leases and installment purchases are similar in economic substance.

10.6    The differences are minor. The lessee's asset is Leased Asset on the one hand and Actual Asset (Plant or Fixed Assets) on the other. The liability will have different titles. The effect on income and balance sheet totals is the same for both transactions.

10.7    Expenses are gone assets. The measure of expense over the life of a lease is the total outflow of cash to discharge the obligation. The accounting for leases, either operating or capital, does not change the total cash outflow, only the timing of the recognition of asset expirations.

10.8    Disagree. Operating Lease: Rent revenue for the lessor will equal rent expense for the lessee on an operating lease, but lessor also has depreciation expense on leased assets. Capital Lease: Interest revenue for the lessor should equal interest expense for the lessee on a capital lease. The lessor recognizes its cost to acquire or manufacture the leased asset as cost of goods sold under a capital lease. The lessor also recognizes revenue under a capital lease equal to the "selling price" of the lease asset on the date of signing the lease.

10.9    Deferred tax accounting matches against pre-tax book income each period the income taxes a firm has to pay currently plus (minus) the income taxes the firm expects to pay (save) in the future when revenues and expenses that appear in book income now appear in tax returns later.

10.10   This statement is incorrect. In order for deferred taxes to be a loan, there must be a receipt of cash or other goods or services at the inception of the loan and a disbursement of cash or other goods or services at the maturity date. The entries for a deferred tax liability are as follows:

**When Timing Differences Originate:**

Income Tax Expense.................................................    X
    Deferred Tax Liability.........................................        X

**When Timing Differences Reverse:**

Deferred Tax Liability..............................................    X
    Income Tax Expense...........................................        X

There are no cash or other asset flows involved and, therefore, no loan.

Another approach is to raise the question: How would cash flows have differed if a firm used the same methods of accounting for book as it used for tax? The response is that cash flows would have been the same even though deferred income taxes would have been eliminated. Thus, recognizing or not recognizing deferred taxes has no incremental effect on cash or other asset flows and, therefore, cannot represent a loan.

10.11   The Congress defines the manner in which firms calculate taxable income and income taxes payable. Corporations pay the income taxes each year that the income tax law legally requires them to pay. The amount shown for Deferred Tax Liability is not a liability. It may become a liability if the firm earns taxable income in the future. It represents the cumulative tax savings from using different methods of accounting for financial reporting and income tax purposes. The Congress and the FASB permit such differences in accounting methods because the objectives of income taxation and financial reporting differ. The income taxation system attempts to raise revenues in an equitable manner. Generally accepted accounting principles attempt to measure operating performance and financial position. If the Congress feels that it should not permit such differences, it should legislate either (1) that firms prepare their financial statements in conformance with the accounting methods used for tax purposes, or (2) that they compute taxable income in accordance with the accounting methods used for financial reporting purposes. Both approaches result in eliminating the Deferred Tax Liability account. Given the differences in objectives of the two reporting systems, it seems undesirable for Congress to take either of the actions indicated above. Congress should merely recognize that Deferred Tax Liability is not a liability but the result of accountants' attempts to obtain meaningful measures of operating performance over time.

10.12   Unlike Accounts Payable or Bonds, which "roll over" and new obligations replace them, the deferred tax liability does not arise from specific transactions. A firm computes taxes on operations as a whole, not on specific transactions. The analyst should attempt to ascertain when the firm is likely to pay the deferred taxes. Then the analyst should use the present value of those payments as the amount of the debt. If, as is likely, a stable or growing firm is never likely to pay the deferred taxes (for example, as with deferred taxes arising from depreciation charges for a growing firm), then the present value of the payments is zero, and the analyst should exclude the "liability" from the amount of debt. (This results in larger shareholders' equity.)

10.13   Deferred tax assets (liabilities) arise when a firm recognizes revenue (expense) earlier for tax purposes than book purposes or expenses (revenues) later for tax purposes than for book purposes. Deferred tax assets (liabilities) provide for lower (higher) taxable income in the future relative to book income and, therefore, future tax savings (costs).

10.14   The difference arises for two principal reasons: tax rate differences and permanent differences. The income tax rate on state, municipal and foreign income likely differs from the statutory U.S. tax rate. Also, firms recognize various revenues and expenses for book purposes that never appear (for example, interest on state and municipal bonds) or appear in smaller amounts (for example, dividends received from domestic subsidiaries) in taxable income.

10.15   The matching convention suggests that firms recognize as expenses each period all costs actually incurred currently or expected to be incurred in the future to generate the current period's revenues. Employees provide labor services each period in return for both current compensation (salary, health care benefits) and compensation deferred until retirement (pensions, health care benefits). The absence of deferred compensation arrangements would presumably lead employees to demand higher current compensation to permit them to fund their own retirement plans. Thus, firms must match current compensation and the present value of deferred compensation against the current period's revenues.

10.16   Laws require firms to contribute funds to an independent trustee to manage on behalf of employees. The employer cannot use these funds for its general corporate purposes. Firms must, however, report some underfunded pension obligations on the balance sheet as a liability.

10.17   One defines outputs (defined benefit) whereas the other defines inputs (defined contribution). Actuaries can design both to have the same expected costs with the same payment patterns by the company.
        Immediate funding for defined-contribution plans transfers all accounting problems subsequent to funding to the plan trustee. The defined-benefit plan could similarly transfer obligations to the pension fund by immediate cash payments, but the company would ultimately be responsible for making up any shortages caused by deviations of earnings or mortality from expectations.

10.18   Pension fund assets appear when a firm funds its pension plan faster than it expenses it. Pension fund liabilities appear when a firm expenses its pension plan faster than it funds it.

10.19   A derivative is a hedge when the firm holding the derivative bears a risk such that the change in the value of the derivative just offsets the change in the value of the firm as time passes.

        A derivative is not a hedge when changes in the fair value of the derivative do not offset other changes in firm value occurring at the same time.

10.20   A *fair-value hedge* is a hedge of an exposure to changes in the fair value of a recognized asset or liability or of an unrecognized firm commitment. A *cash-flow hedge* is a hedge of an exposure to variability in the cash flows of a recognized asset or liability, such as variable interest rates, or of a forecasted transaction, such as expected future foreign sales.

10.21   When the firm has a cash-flow hedge. Then the value of the firm stays the same, but no accounting asset nor liability changes in value to offset the change in the value of the derivative.

10.22 (Cypres Appliance Store; using accounts receivable to achieve off-balance sheet financing.)

a. (1) **January 2, Year 2**

| | | |
|---|---|---|
| Cash............................................................ | 89,286 | |
|     Bank Loan Payable..................................... | | 89,286 |
| To record bank loan. | | |

**December 31, Year 2**

| | | |
|---|---|---|
| Cash............................................................ | 100,000 | |
|     Accounts Receivable.................................... | | 100,000 |
| To record collections from customers. | | |

| | | |
|---|---|---|
| Interest Expense (= .12 × $89,286)................... | 10,714 | |
| Bank Loan Payable ........................................ | 89,286 | |
|     Cash ....................................................... | | 100,000 |
| To record interest expense on loan for Year 2 and repayment of the loan. | | |

(2)

| | | |
|---|---|---|
| Cash............................................................ | 89,286 | |
| Loss from Sale of Accounts Receivable........... | 10,714 | |
|     Accounts Receivable..................................... | | 100,000 |
| To record sale of accounts receivable; alternative title for the loss account is interest expense. | | |

b. Both transactions result in an expense of $10,714 for Year 2 for this financing. Both transactions result in an immediate increase in cash. Liabilities increase for the collateralized loan, whereas an asset decreases for the sale.

c. Cypres Appliance Store must attempt to shift credit and interest rate risk to the bank. The bank should have no rights to demand additional receivables if interest rates increase or uncollectible accounts appear. Likewise, Cypres Appliance Store should have no rights to buy back the accounts receivable if interest rates decline. The bank of course will not both lend on the receivables and purchase the receivables at the same price because it incurs different amounts of risk in each case.

10.23    (P. J. Lorimar Company; using inventory to achieve off-balance sheet financing.)

a.    (i)    **January 2, Year 5**

Cash.................................................................................. 300,000
    Bank Loan Payable............................................. 300,000
To record bank loan.

**December 31, Year 5**
Interest Expense (= .10 × $300,000)................ 30,000
    Bank Loan Payable............................................. 30,000
To record interest expense for Year 5.

**December 31, Year 6**
Cash.................................................................................. 363,000
    Sales Revenue...................................................... 363,000
To record sale of tobacco inventory.

Cost of Goods Sold............................................... 200,000
    Inventory................................................................ 200,000
To record cost of tobacco inventory sold.

Interest Expense (= .10 × $330,000)................ 33,000
Bank Loan Payable .............................................. 330,000
    Cash ........................................................................ 363,000
To record interest expense for Year 6 and
repayment of loan.

(ii)    **January 2, Year 5**
Cash.................................................................................. 300,000
    Sales Revenue...................................................... 300,000
To record "sale" of tobacco to bank.

Cost of Goods Sold............................................... 200,000
    Inventory................................................................ 200,000
To record cost of tobacco "sold".

b.    Both transactions result in a total of $100,000 income for the two years combined. The collateralized loan shows $163,000 gross profit from the sale in Year 6 and interest expense of $30,000 in Year 5 and $33,000 in Year 6. The "sale" results in $100,000 gross profit in Year 5. Cash increases by $300,000 in both transactions. Liabilities increase for the collateralized loan, whereas an asset decreases for the sale.

10.23 continued.

    c.   P. J. Lorimar Company must shift the risk of changes in storage costs for Year 5 and Year 6 and the selling price for the tobacco at the end of Year 6 to the bank. The firm should not guarantee a price or agree to cover insurance and other storage costs. Of course, the bank will not both lend on the inventory and "purchase" the inventory for $300,000 because it incurs different amounts of risk in each case.

10.24    (Boeing and American; applying the capital lease criteria.)

    a.   This lease is a capital lease because the lease period of 20 years exceeds 75 percent of the expected life of the aircraft. The lease does not meet any other capital lease criteria. The aircraft reverts to Boeing at the end of 20 years. The present value of the lease payments when discounted at 10 percent is $51.1 million ($6 million X 8.51356), which is less than $54 million (= 90 percent of the fair market value of $60 million).

    b.   This lease is a capital lease because the present value of the lease payments of $54.8 million (= $7.2 million X 7.60608) exceeds 90 percent of the $60 million fair market value of the aircraft.

    c.   The lease is not a capital lease. The present value of the required lease payments of $36.9 million (= $5.5 million X 6.71008) is less than $54 million (= 90 percent of the market value of the aircraft). The life of the lease is less than 75 percent of the expected useful life of the aircraft. The purchase option price coupled with the rental payments provides Boeing with a present value of all cash flows exceeding the usual sale price of the aircraft of $62.4 million [= ($5.5 million X 6.71008) + ($55 million X .46319)], so there does not appear to be a bargain purchase option.

    d.   This lease is not a capital lease. The present value of the minimum required lease payments is $50.9 million (= $6.2 million X 8.20141). The fee contingent on usage could be zero, so the calculations exclude it. The life of the lease is less than 75 percent of the useful life of the aircraft. The aircraft reverts to Boeing at the end of the lease period.

10.25    (FedUp Delivery Services; preparing lessee's journal entries for an operating and a capital lease.)

    a.   This lease is a capital lease because the present value of the lease payments of $22,581 (= $750 X 30.10751) exceeds 90 percent of the market value of the leased asset (.90 X $24,000 = $21,600). The life of the lease is less than 75 percent of the life of the leased property and the property reverts to GM at the end of the lease period, so the lease fails these criteria for a capital lease.

10.25 continued.

    b.  **Time of Signing Lease**
        No Entry.

        **End of Each Month**

| | | |
|---|---:|---:|
| Rent Expense | 750 | |
|    Cash | | 750 |
| To record monthly rental expense and payment. | | |

    c.  **Time of Signing Lease**

| | | |
|---|---:|---:|
| Leased Asset | 22,581 | |
|    Lease Liability | | 22,581 |
| To record capital lease. | | |

        **End of First Month**

| | | |
|---|---:|---:|
| Interest Expense (= .01 × $22,581) | 225.81 | |
| Lease Liability | 524.19 | |
|    Cash | | 750.00 |

To record interest expense and cash payment for first month; the book value of the lease liability is now $22,056.81 (= $22,581.00 − $524.19).

| | | |
|---|---:|---:|
| Depreciation Expense | 627.25 | |
|    Accumulated Depreciation | | 627.25 |

To record depreciation expense for the first month of $627.25 (= $22,581/36).

        **End of Second Month**

| | | |
|---|---:|---:|
| Interest Expense (= .01 × $22,056.81) | 220.57 | |
| Lease Liability | 529.43 | |
|    Cash | | 750.00 |

To record interest expense and cash payment for the second month.

| | | |
|---|---:|---:|
| Depreciation Expense | 627.25 | |
|    Accumulated Depreciation | | 627.25 |

To record depreciation expense for the second month.

**10.26** (Baldwin Products; preparing lessee's journal entries for an operating lease and a capital lease.)

a. This lease does not satisfy any of the criteria for a capital lease, so it is an operating lease. The leased asset reverts to the lessor at the end of the lease period. The life of the lease (3 years) is less than 75 percent of the expected useful life of the leased asset (5 years). The present value of the lease payments of $24,018 (= $10,000 × 2.40183) is less than 90 percent of the market value of the leased asset of $30,000.

b. **December 31, of Each Year**

| | | |
|---|---:|---:|
| Rent Expense | 10,000 | |
|     Cash | | 10,000 |
| To record annual rent expense and cash payment. | | |

c. **January 2, Year 6**

| | | |
|---|---:|---:|
| Leased Asset | 24,018 | |
|     Lease Liability | | 24,018 |
| To record capital lease. | | |

**December 31, Year 6**

| | | |
|---|---:|---:|
| Interest Expense (= .12 × $24,018) | 2,882 | |
| Lease Liability | 7,118 | |
|     Cash | | 10,000 |

To record interest expense and cash payment for Year 6. The book value of the lease liability is now $16,900 (= $24,018 − $7,118).

| | | |
|---|---:|---:|
| Depreciation Expense or Work-in-Process Inventory ($24,018/3) | 8,006 | |
|     Accumulated Depreciation | | 8,006 |
| To record depreciation expense for Year 6. | | |

**December 31, Year 7**

| | | |
|---|---:|---:|
| Interest Expense (= .12 × $16,900) | 2,028 | |
| Lease Liability | 7,972 | |
|     Cash | | 10,000 |

To record interest expense and cash payment for Year 7. The book value of the lease liability is now $8,928 (= $16,900 − $7,972).

| | | |
|---|---:|---:|
| Depreciation Expense or Work-in-Process Inventory | 8,006 | |
|     Accumulated Depreciation | | 8,006 |
| To record depreciation expense for Year 7. | | |

10.26 c. continued.

**December 31, Year 8**

| | | |
|---|---:|---:|
| Interest Expense (= .12 × $8,928) | 1,072 | |
| Lease Liability | 8,928 | |
|    Cash | | 10,000 |

To record interest expense and cash payment for Year 8. Interest expense does not precisely equal .12 × $8,928 due to rounding.

| | | |
|---|---:|---:|
| Depreciation Expense on Work-in-Process Inventory | 8,006 | |
|    Accumulated Depreciation | | 8,006 |

To record depreciation expense for Year 8.

d. 
| | |
|---|---:|
| Operating Lease Method: Rent Expense (= $10,000 × 3) | <u>$ 30,000</u> |
| Capital Lease Method: Interest Expense (= $2,882 + $2,028 + $1,072) | $ 5,982 |
| Depreciation (= $8,006 × 3) | <u>24,018</u> |
|    Total Expenses | <u>$ 30,000</u> |

10.27   (Sun Microsystems; preparing lessor's journal entries for an operating lease and a capital lease.)

a.   This lease is a capital lease. The life of the lease equals the expected useful life of the property. The present value of the lease payments of $12,000 [= $4,386.70 + ($4,386.70 × 1.73554)] equals the market value of the leased asset.

b.   **Beginning of Each Year**

| | | |
|---|---:|---:|
| Cash | 4,386.70 | |
|    Rental Fees Received in Advance | | 4,386.70 |

To record cash received in advance from lessee.

**End of Each Year**

| | | |
|---|---:|---:|
| Rental Fees Received in Advance | 4,386.70 | |
|    Rent Revenue | | 4,386.70 |

To record rent revenue for each year.

| | | |
|---|---:|---:|
| Depreciation Expense | 2,400.00 | |
|    Accumulated Depreciation | | 2,400.00 |

To record annual depreciation (= $7,200/3).

10.27 continued.

c. **January 2, Year 2**

| | | |
|---|---|---|
| Cash..................................................................... | 4,386.70 | |
| Lease Receivable (= $4,386.70 X 1.73554)............... | 7,613.30 | |
|    Sales Revenue................................................ | | 12,000.00 |

To record "sale" of work station..

| | | |
|---|---|---|
| Cost of Goods Sold.................................................. | 7,200.00 | |
|    Inventory....................................................... | | 7,200.00 |

To record cost of workstation "sold".

**December 31, Year 2**

| | | |
|---|---|---|
| Lease Receivable (= .10 X $7,613.30)........................ | 761.33 | |
|    Interest Revenue............................................ | | 761.33 |

To record interest revenue for Year 2.

**January 2, Year 3**

| | | |
|---|---|---|
| Cash..................................................................... | 4,386.70 | |
|    Lease Receivable............................................ | | 4,386.70 |

To record cash received at the beginning of
Year 3. The book value of the receivable is now
$3,987.93 (= $7,613.30 + $761.33 − $4,386.70).

**December 31, Year 3**

| | | |
|---|---|---|
| Lease Receivable (= .10 X $3,987.93)........................ | 398.77 | |
|    Interest Revenue............................................ | | 398.77 |

To record interest revenue for Year 3. Interest
revenue is slightly less than .10 X $3,987.93 due
to rounding of present value factors. The book
value of the receivable is now $4,386.70 (=
$3,987.93 + $398.77).

**January 2, Year 4**

| | | |
|---|---|---|
| Cash..................................................................... | 4,386.70 | |
|    Lease Receivable............................................ | | 4,386.70 |

To record cash received for Year 4.

10.28    (Ingersoll-Rand; preparing journal entries for income tax expense.)

a.   **Year 9**
Income Tax Expense ............................................... 67,400
Deferred Tax Liability............................................ 43,575
    Cash or Income Tax Payable................................             110,975

**Year 10**
Income Tax Expense ............................................... 90,000
Deferred Tax Liability............................................ 15,537
    Cash or Income Tax Payable................................             105,537

**Year 11**
Income Tax Expense ............................................... 118,800
    Deferred Tax Liability...........................................             14,185
    Cash or Income Tax Payable................................             104,615

b.   Taxable income exceeds book income for Year 9 and Year 10 but taxable income was less than book income for Year 11. Ingersoll-Rand probably reduced its expenditures on new depreciable assets during Year 9 and Year 10 so that depreciation expense for financial reporting exceeded depreciation deducted in computing taxable income. Ingersoll-Rand increased its capital expenditures during Year 11 so that depreciation deducted in computing taxable income exceeded depreciation expense recognized for financial reporting.

10.29    (L.A. Gear; preparing journal entries for income tax expense.)

a.   **Year 4**
Income Tax Expense ............................................... 34,364
Deferred Tax Asset ................................................ 3,555
    Cash or Income Tax Payable................................             37,919

**Year 5**
Income Tax Expense ............................................... 9,392
Deferred Tax Asset ................................................ 3,492
    Cash or Income Tax Payable................................             12,884

**Year 6**
Cash or Income Tax Receivable............................... 17,184
Deferred Tax Asset ................................................ 5,543
    Income Tax Expense (Credit)................................             22,727

b.   Book income and taxable income were both positive for Years 4 and 5. Taxable income exceeded book income. The deferred tax asset related to uncollectible accounts increased, suggesting an increased sales level for each year.

10.29 b. continued.

Book income and taxable income were both negative in Year 6. The loss for book purposes exceeded the loss for tax purposes. The increase in the deferred tax asset related to uncollectible accounts suggests increasing sales but decreasing profits on those sales.

10.30  (Sung Company; computations and journal entries for income taxes with both temporary and permanent differences.)

a.  **Year 1**

| | | |
|---|---:|---:|
| Income Tax Expense (.40 × $560,000) | 224,000 | |
| Deferred Tax Liability (.40 × $40,000) | 16,000 | |
|   Income Tax Payable—Current (.40 × $600,000) | | 240,000 |

**Year 2**

| | | |
|---|---:|---:|
| Income Tax Expense (.40 × $500,000) | 200,000 | |
|   Deferred Tax Liability (.40 × $50,000) | | 20,000 |
|   Income Tax Payable—Current (.40 × $450,000) | | 180,000 |

**Year 3**

| | | |
|---|---:|---:|
| Income Tax Expense (.40 × $620,000) | 248,000 | |
|   Deferred Tax Liability (.40 × $6,000) | | 24,000 |
|   Income Tax Payable—Current (.40 × $560,000) | | 224,000 |

b.  **Year 1**

| | | |
|---|---:|---:|
| Income Tax Expense [.40 × ($560,000 – $10,000)] | 220,000 | |
| Deferred Tax Liability (.40 × $50,000) | 20,000 | |
|   Income Tax Payable—Current (.40 × $600,000) | | 240,000 |

**Year 2**

| | | |
|---|---:|---:|
| Income Tax Expense [.40 × ($500,000 – $10,000)] | 196,000 | |
|   Deferred Tax Liability (.40 × $40,000) | | 16,000 |
|   Income Tax Payable—Current (.40 × $450,000) | | 180,000 |

**Year 3**

| | | |
|---|---:|---:|
| Income Tax Expense [.40 × ($620,000 – $10,000)] | 244,000 | |
|   Deferred Tax Liability (.40 × $50,000) | | 20,000 |
|   Income Tax Payable—Current (.40 × $560,000) | | 224,000 |

10.31 (Beneish Company; deriving permanent and temporary differences from financial statement disclosures.)

a.

| | Income Tax Expense | = | Income Taxes Currently Payable | + | Change in Deferred Tax Liability |
|---|---|---|---|---|---|
| | $78,000 | = | $24,000 | + | X |
| | X | = | $54,000 | | |

$$\text{Temporary Differences} = \text{Changes in Deferred Tax Liability}/.40$$

$$= \$54,000/.40$$

$$= \$135,000$$

Because income tax expense exceeds income taxes payable, book income exceeded taxable income.

b.

| | |
|---|---|
| Taxable Income: $24,000/.40 | $ 60,000 |
| Temporary Differences | 135,000 |
| Book Income before Taxes Excluding Permanent Differences | $195,000 |
| Permanent Differences (Plug) | 36,000 |
| Book Income before Taxes (Given) | $159,000 |

10.32    (Woodward Corporation; effect of temporary differences on income taxes.)

a.

|  | Year 1 | Year 2 | Year 3 | Year 4 |
|---|---|---|---|---|
| Other Pre-Tax Income .............. | $35,000 | $35,000 | $35,000 | $35,000 |
| Income before Depreciation from Machine.......................... | 25,000 | 25,000 | 25,000 | 25,000 |
| Depreciation Deduction: | | | | |
| .33 × $50,000........................... | (16,500) | | | |
| .44 × $50,000........................... | | (22,000) | | |
| .15 × $50,000........................... | | | (7,500) | |
| .08 × $50,000........................... | | | | (4,000) |
| Taxable Income | $43,500 | $38,000 | $52,500 | $56,000 |
| Tax Rate ................................. | .40 | .40 | .40 | .40 |
| Income Taxes Payable.............. | $17,400 | $15,200 | $21,000 | $22,400 |

b.

| **Financial Reporting** | Year 1 | Year 2 | Year 3 | Year 4 |
|---|---|---|---|---|
| Book Value, January 1 ............. | $50,000 | $37,500 | $25,000 | $ 12,500 |
| Depreciation Expense .............. | (12,500) | (12,500) | (12,500) | (12,500) |
| Book Value, December 31........ | $37,500 | $25,000 | $12,500 | $    -- |
| **Tax Reporting** | | | | |
| Tax Basis, January 1................ | $50,000 | $33,500 | $11,500 | $   4,000 |
| Depreciation Deduction............. | (16,500) | (22,000) | (7,500) | (4,000) |
| Tax Basis, December 31........... | $33,500 | $11,500 | $ 4,000 | $    -- |

c.

| **Financial Reporting** | Year 1 | Year 2 | Year 3 | Year 4 |
|---|---|---|---|---|
| Income before Depreciation...... | $60,000 | $60,000 | $60,000 | $ 60,000 |
| Depreciation Expense ($50,000/4)............................. | (12,500) | (12,500) | (12,500) | (12,500) |
| Pretax Income .......................... | $47,500 | $47,500 | $47,500 | $ 47,500 |
| Income Tax Expense at .40 ..... | $19,000 | $19,000 | $19,000 | $ 19,000 |

d.

| | Year 1 | Year 2 | Year 3 | Year 4 |
|---|---|---|---|---|
| Income Tax Payable (from Part a.)—Cr. ............................ | $17,400 | $ 15,200 | $ 21,000 | $22,400 |
| Change in Deferred Tax Liability (Plug): Cr. if Positive Dr. if Negative ......................... | 1,600 | 3,800 | (2,000) | (3,400) |
| Income Tax Expense—Dr. ........ | $19,000 | $ 19,000 | $ 19,000 | $19,000 |

10.32 d. continued.

**Year 1**

| | | |
|---|---|---|
| Income Tax Expense | 19,000 | |
|    Cash or Income Tax Payable | | 17,400 |
|    Deferred Tax Liability | | 1,600 |

**Year 2**

| | | |
|---|---|---|
| Income Tax Expense | 19,000 | |
|    Cash or Income Tax Payable | | 15,200 |
|    Deferred Tax Liability | | 3,800 |

**Year 3**

| | | |
|---|---|---|
| Income Tax Expense | 19,000 | |
| Deferred Tax Liability | 2,000 | |
|    Cash or Income Tax Payable | | 21,000 |

**Year 4**

| | | |
|---|---|---|
| Income Tax Expense | 19,000 | |
| Deferred Tax Liability | 3,400 | |
|    Cash or Income Tax Payable | | 22,400 |

10.33    (Lilly Company; reconstructing information about income taxes.)

## LILLY COMPANY
### Illustrations of Timing Differences and Permanent Differences

| | Financial Statements | Type of Difference | Income Tax Return |
|---|---|---|---|
| Operating Income Except Depreciation | $427,800 (6) | -- | $427,800 (4) |
| Depreciation | (322,800) (g) | Timing | (358,800) (3) |
| Municipal Bond Interest | 85,800 (5) | Permanent | -- |
| Taxable Income | -- | | $ 69,000 (2) |
| Pretax Income | $190,800 (g) | | |
| Income Taxes Payable at 40 Percent | | | $ 27,600 (g) |
| Income Tax Expense at 40 Percent of $105,000 = $427,800 − $322,800, Which Is Book Income Excluding Permanent Differences | (42,000) (g) | | |
| Net Income | $148,800 (1) | | |

10.33 continued.

Order and derivation of computations:
(g) Given.
(1) $148,800 = $190,800 – $42,000.
(2) $69,000 = $27,600/.40.
(3) Timing difference for depreciation is ($42,000 – $27,600)/.40 = $36,000. Because income taxes payable are less than income tax expense, we know that depreciation deducted on tax return exceeds depreciation expense on financial statements. Thus, the depreciation deduction on the tax return is $358,800 = $322,800 + $36,000.
(4) $427,800 = $358,800 + $69,000.
(5) Taxable income on financial statements is $105,000 = $42,000/.40. Total financial statement income before taxes, including permanent differences, is $190,800. Hence, permanent differences are $190,800 – $105,000 = $85,800.
(6) $190,800 + $322,800 – $85,800 = $427,800. See also (4), for check.

10.34   (Mascagni Company; interpreting hedging transaction.)

Fair-value hedge. Mascagni Company has an asset on the balance sheet whose change in market value it is hedging.

10.35   (DaimlerChrysler Corporation; interpreting derivatives and hedging disclosures.)

a.   The counterparty is the person who promises to pay DaimlerChrysler [DC] if the derivative entitles DC to receive funds. DC runs the risk that the counterparty who owes funds will not be able to pay. That is counterparty credit risk. DC minimizes such risk by dealing only with high quality counterparties.

b.   DC says it does not engage in such transactions in the third, italicized, sentence of the note. It apparently uses all derivatives for hedging activities.

c.   We cannot be sure, but it is likely that all hedges to deal with revenue variations are cash-flow hedges because revenues result from a series of future cash flows. If all revenues were committed to in advance by the purchaser, such as by paying all amounts in advance, then DC might engage in a fair-value hedge. Cost hedges could be either fair-value or cash-flow hedges, depending on the nature of the item hedged. Hedging a fixed purchase commitment is a fair-value hedge; hedging the cost of future labor services would be a cash-flow hedge.

d.   Ever since Chapter 2, we have seen that the recorded cost of an asset includes all costs of the hedging derivative instrument as part of the dollar cost of the asset being acquired when the purchase price is denominated in some other currency.

10.36   (Fixed Issue Company; journal entries for hedging transactions.)   (Dollar Amounts in Thousands)

a.   **January 1**

| | | |
|---|---:|---:|
| Cash.................................................................... | 10,000 | |
|    Bonds Payable............................................... | | 10,000 |

**June 30**

| | | |
|---|---:|---:|
| Interest Expense (1/2 × .09 × $10,000)..................... | 450 | |
|    Cash ............................................................. | | 450 |
| | | |
| Loss on Revaluation of Bonds................................. | 4,000 | |
|    Bonds Payable............................................... | | 4,000 |
| | | |
| Swap Contract (Asset) .......................................... | 3,800 | |
|    Gain on Revaluation of Swap Contract............... | | 3,800 |

**December 31**

| | | |
|---|---:|---:|
| Interest Expense (1/2 × .06 × $14,000)..................... | 420 | |
| Bonds Payable ...................................................... | 30 | |
|    Cash (1/2 × .09 × $10,000)................................ | | 450 |
| | | |
| Swap Contract (Asset) (1/2 × .06 × $3,800)............. | 114 | |
|    Interest Revenue............................................ | | 114 |
| | | |
| Cash [1/2 × (.09 − .06) × $10,000].............................. | 150 | |
|    Swap Contract (Asset)...................................... | | 150 |
| | | |
| Bonds Payable [$12,750 − ($10,000 + $4,000 − | | |
|   $30)] .................................................................. | 1,220 | |
|    Gain on Revaluation of Bonds........................... | | 1,220 |
| | | |
| Loss on Derivative Asset [$2,700 − ($3,800 + | | |
|   $114 − $150)] .................................................... | 1,064 | |
|    Swap Contract (Asset)...................................... | | 1,064 |

b.   Fair-value hedge.  Both the loss on the revaluation of the bond and the gain on the revaluation of the derivative asset appear in net income for the period.  Because the derivative is not a perfect hedge, the loss and the gain do not fully offset each other.  The hedge has been effective; in practice, we would not be surprised to see deviations of this magnitude in failure of the hedge to fully offset the gains and losses.

10.37   (Floating Issue Company; journal entries for hedging transactions.)   (Dollar Amounts in Thousands)

a.   **January 1**

| | | |
|---|---:|---:|
| Cash...................................................................... | 10,000 | |
|    Bonds Payable............................................... | | 10,000 |

10.37 a. continued.

**June 30**

| | | |
|---|---|---|
| Interest Expense (1/2 × .09 × $10,000)..................... | 450 | |
|     Cash......................................................................... | | 450 |
| | | |
| Other Comprehensive Income.................................. | 3,800 | |
|     Swap Contract (Liability)......................................... | | 3,800 |

**December 31**

| | | |
|---|---|---|
| Interest Expense (1/2 × .06 × $10,000)..................... | 300 | |
|     Cash......................................................................... | | 300 |
| | | |
| Other Comprehensive Income (1/2 × .06 × | | |
|     $3,800)..................................................................... | 114 | |
|         Swap Contract (Liability)................................ | | 114 |
| | | |
| Swap Contract (Liability) [1/2 × (.09 – .06) × | | |
|     $10,000].................................................................... | 150 | |
|         Cash.................................................................. | | 150 |
| | | |
| Interest Expense...................................................... | 150 | |
|     Other Comprehensive Income............................. | | 150 |
| | | |
| Swap Contract (Liability) [$2,700 – ($3,800 + | | |
|     $114 – $150)]......................................................... | 1,064 | |
|         Other Comprehensive Income......................... | | 1,064 |

b. Cash-flow hedge. One cannot tell from the data given how effective the hedge has been.

10.38 (Effects of leases on statement of cash flows.)

a. The journal entry to record this transaction is:

| | | |
|---|---|---|
| Depreciation Expense................................................ | 10,000 | |
|     Accumulated Depreciation ...................................... | | 10,000 |

Because this entry does not involve a debit or credit to the Cash account, Line (9) does not change. Depreciation expense reduces net income, so Line (1) decreases by $10,000. The recognition of depreciation expense does not affect cash, so Line (2) increases by $10,000.

b. The journal entry for this transaction is:

| | | |
|---|---|---|
| Cash.......................................................................... | 19,925 | |
|     Rent Revenue........................................................ | | 19,925 |

The debit to Cash results in an increase of $19,925 in Line (9). The credit to Rent Revenue increases Line (1), net income, by $19,925.

10.38 continued.

 c. The journal entry to record this transaction is:

| | | |
|---|---|---|
| Rent Expense............................................................ | 19,925 | |
|  Cash ................................................................. | | 19,925 |

The credit to Cash results in an decrease of $19,925 in Line (9). The debit to Rent Expense reduces Line (1), net income, by $19,925.

 d. The journal entry for this transaction is:

| | | |
|---|---|---|
| Leased Asset............................................................ | 100,000 | |
|  Lease Liability.................................................... | | 100,000 |

This transaction does not involve a change in cash, so Line (9) does not change. The entry does not affect net income, so Line (1) does not change. This transaction is an investing and financing activity that would not appear in the statement of cash flows but in a supplementary schedule or note to the financial statements.

 e. The journal entry to record this transaction is:

| | | |
|---|---|---|
| Interest Expense...................................................... | 15,000 | |
| Lease Liability ........................................................ | 4,925 | |
|  Cash ................................................................. | | 19,925 |

This entry results in a reduction in Cash, so Line (9) decreases by $19,925. Line (1) decreases by $15,000 for interest expense and Line (7) increases by $4,925 for the reduction in the lease liability. Thus, $15,000 of the reduction in cash appears in the operating section and $4,925 appears in the financing section of the statement of cash flows.

10.39 (Effects of income taxes on statement of cash flows.)

 a. The entry to record this event is:

| | | |
|---|---|---|
| Income Tax Expense (.4 X $200,000)........................ | 80,000 | |
|  Income Tax Payable (.4 X $150,000).................... | | 60,000 |
|  Deferred Tax Liability (.4 X $50,000)................... | | 20,000 |

This entry does not involve a change in Cash, so Line (9) does not change. The debit to income tax expense reduces Line (1), net income, by $80,000. Line (2) increases by $60,000 for the increases in a current operating liability. Line (2) also increases by $20,000 for the addback of an expense that does not use cash. Thus, the effect on cash flow from operations is zero.

10.39 continued.

 b. The journal entry for this event is:

  Income Tax Expense (.4 × $300,000)........................ 120,000
  Deferred Tax Asset (.4 × $40,000)............................ 16,000
   Cash (.4 × $340,000).............................................   136,000

  This entry reduces Cash, so Line (9) decreases by $136,000. The recognition of income tax expense reduces Line (1), net income, by $120,000. Line (3) increases by $16,000 for an expense that used more cash than the amount of the expense.

 c. The journal entry and explanation for this part are the same as in Part *b.* above. Line (1) decreases by $120,000, Line (3) increases by $16,000, and Line (9) decreases by $136,000.

 d. The journal entry is:.

  Cash........................................................................... 10,000
   Interest Revenue....................................................   10,000

  Interest on municipal bonds is nontaxable, so recognition of income taxes on the interest revenue is inappropriate (a permanent difference). The Cash account increases, so Line (9) increases by $10,000. The recognition of interest revenue increases Line (1), net income, by $10,000.

10.40 (Wal-Mart Stores; financial statement effects of operating and capital leases.)

 a. Interest Expense (= .11 × $1,694.2)...................... 186.4
  Lease Liability (Plug)............................................... 18.3
   Cash (Given)...........................................................   204.7

 b. Rent Expense............................................................ 249.3
   Cash .........................................................................   249.3

 c. **January 31, Year 9**
  Leased Asset............................................................. 1,586.5
   Lease Liability.........................................................   1,586.5
  To capitalize operating leases.

10.40 c. continued.

**January 31, Year 10**

| | | |
|---|---|---|
| Interest Expense (= .12 × $1,586.5) | 190.4 | |
| Lease Liability | 58.9 | |
|    Cash | | 249.3 |

To record interest expense and cash payment
on capitalized operating leases.

| | | |
|---|---|---|
| Depreciation Expense | 105.8 | |
|    Accumulated Depreciation | | 105.8 |

To record depreciation expense on capitalized
operating leases; $105.8 = $1,586.5/15.

10.41    (American Airlines; financial statement effect of operating and capital leases.)

(Amounts in Millions)

a.

| | |
|---|---|
| Capital Lease Liability, December 31, Year 10 | $ 2,233 |
| Interest Expense for Year 11 (= .08 × $2,233) | 179 |
| Cash Payment for Year 11 | (268) |
| New Leases Signed during Year 11 (Plug) | 259 |
| Capital Lease Liability, December 31, Year 11 | $ 2,403 |

b.

| | |
|---|---|
| Leasehold Asset, December 31, Year 10 | $ 1,716 |
| New Leases Capitalized during Year 11 (from Part a.) | 259 |
| Depreciation Expense for Year 11 (Plug) | (97) |
| Leasehold Asset, December 31, Year 11 | $ 1,878 |

c.  **December 31, Year 11**

| | | |
|---|---|---|
| Interest Expense | 179 | |
| Lease Liability | 89 | |
|    Cash | | 268 |

| | | |
|---|---|---|
| Depreciation Expense | 97 | |
|    Accumulated Depreciation | | 97 |

| | | |
|---|---|---|
| Leased Asset | 259 | |
|    Lease Liability | | 259 |

d.  **December 31, Year 11**

| | | |
|---|---|---|
| Rent Expense | 946 | |
|    Cash | | 946 |

10.41 continued.

    e.  **December 31, Year 10**

| | | |
|---|---:|---:|
| Leased Asset............................................................................. | 7,793 | |
|     Lease Liability.................................................................... | | 7,793 |

To capitalize operating leases as if they were
capital leases.

**December 31, Year 11**

| | | |
|---|---:|---:|
| Interest Expense (= .10 × $7,793)........................................ | 779 | |
| Lease Liability ...................................................................... | 167 | |
|     Cash .................................................................................... | | 946 |

To record interest expense and cash payment for
capitalized operating leases.

| | | |
|---|---:|---:|
| Depreciation Expense............................................................ | 354 | |
|     Accumulated Depreciation ............................................... | | 354 |

To record depreciation for Year 11; ($354 =
$7,793/22).

| | | |
|---|---:|---:|
| Leased Asset............................................................................. | 538 | |
|     Lease Liability.................................................................... | | 538 |

To record present value of new leases; $7,793 + X
− $167 = $8,164; X = $538.

10.42    (Carom Sports Collectibles Shop; comparison of borrow/buy with operating
and capital leases.)

    a.  $100,000/3.79079 = $26,379.725 = $26,380.

### Carom Sports Collectibles Shop Amortization Schedule

| Year | Start of Year Balance | Interest (10%) | Payment | Reduction | End of Year Balance |
|---|---:|---:|---:|---:|---:|
| 1 | $ 100,000 | $10,000 | $26,380 | $16,380 | $83,620 |
| 2 | 83,620 | 8,362 | 26,380 | 18,018 | 65,602 |
| 3 | 65,602 | 6,560 | 26,380 | 19,820 | 45,782 |
| 4 | 45,782 | 4,578 | 26,380 | 21,802 | 23,980 |
| 5 | 23,980 | 2,398 | 26,380 | 23,982 | (2) |

10.42 continued.

    b.  (1)  Asset—Computer System.
              Asset Contra—Accumulated Depreciation on Computer System.
              Liability—Bonds Payable and Interest Payable.

        (2)  None.

        (3)  Asset—Leased Computer System.
              Asset Contra—Accumulated Depreciation.
              Liability—Lease Liability.

    c.  $150,000 = $100,000 + (.10 \times \$100,000 \times 5)$.

    d.  (1)  Operating:  $131,900 = $26,380 \times 5$.
        (2)  Capital:    $131,900.

    e.  The method of accounting for a lease affects only the timing of expenses, not their total. Expenses under Plan (1) are larger because the firm borrows $100,000 for the entire 5 years, whereas under Plan (2) it pays the loan with part of each lease payment; with smaller average borrowing, interest expense is smaller.

    f.  (1)  $30,000 = $20,000 depreciation plus $10,000 bond interest.
        (2)  Operating-lease Method:    $26,380.
              Capital-lease Method:          $30,000 = $20,000 amortization +
                                                    $10,000 lease interest.

    g.  (1)  $30,000.
        (2)  Operating:  $26,380.
              Capital:     $22,400 (or $22,398) = $20,000 + $2,400.

10.42 g. continued.

## CAROM SPORTS COLLECTIBLES SHOP SUMMARY
### (Not Required)

|  | Year 1 | Year 2 | Year 3 | Year 4 | Year 5 | Total |
|---|---|---|---|---|---|---|
| **Plan 1** |  |  |  |  |  |  |
| Depreciation Expense | $20,000 | $20,000 | $20,000 | $20,000 | $20,000 | $100,000 |
| Interest Expense | 10,000 | 10,000 | 10,000 | 10,000 | 10,000 | 50,000 |
| Total | $30,000 | $30,000 | $30,000 | $30,000 | $30,000 | $150,000 |
| **Plan 2 (Operating)** |  |  |  |  |  |  |
| Lease Expense | $26,380 | $26,380 | $26,380 | $26,380 | $26,380 | $131,900 |
| **Plan 2 (Financing)** |  |  |  |  |  |  |
| Depreciation Expense | $20,000 | $20,000 | $20,000 | $20,000 | $20,000 | $100,000 |
| Interest Expense | 10,000 | 8,362 | 6,560 | 4,578 | 2,400* | 31,900 |
| Total | $30,000 | $28,362 | $26,560 | $24,578 | $22,400 | $131,900 |

*Plug to correct for rounding errors. By computations, this number is $2,398 = $26,380/1.10.

10.43   (IBM and Adair Corporation; accounting for lease by lessor and lessee.)

a.   **January 1, Year 11**

| | | |
|---|---|---|
| Cash | 10,000 | |
| Note Payable | | 10,000 |
| | | |
| Computer | 10,000 | |
| Cash | | 10,000 |

**December 31, Year 11**

| | | |
|---|---|---|
| Depreciation Expense | 3,333 | |
| Accumulated Depreciation | | 3,333 |
| | | |
| Interest Expense (.08 X $10,000) | 800 | |
| Note Payable (Plug) | 3,080 | |
| Cash ($10,000/2.57710) | | 3,880 |

**December 31, Year 12**

| | | |
|---|---|---|
| Depreciation Expense | 3,333 | |
| Accumulated Depreciation | | 3,333 |
| | | |
| Interest Expense [.08 X ($10,000 – $3,080)] | 554 | |
| Note Payable (Plug) | 3,326 | |
| Cash | | 3,880 |

10.43 continued.

b. **January 1, Year 11**
No entry.

**December 31, Year 11**

| | | |
|---|---|---|
| Rent Expense | 3,810 | |
| Cash | | 3,810 |

**December 31, Year 12**

| | | |
|---|---|---|
| Rent Expense | 3,810 | |
| Cash | | 3,810 |

c. **January 1, Year 11**

| | | |
|---|---|---|
| Leased Asset | 10,000 | |
| Lease Liability | | 10,000 |

**December 31, Year 11**

| | | |
|---|---|---|
| Depreciation Expense | 3,333 | |
| Accumulated Depreciation | | 3,333 |

| | | |
|---|---|---|
| Interest Expense (.07 X $10,000) | 700 | |
| Lease Liability (Plug) | 3,110 | |
| Cash ($10,000/2.62432) | | 3,810 |

**December 31, Year 12**

| | | |
|---|---|---|
| Depreciation Expense | 3,333 | |
| Accumulated Depreciation | | 3,333 |

| | | |
|---|---|---|
| Interest Expense [.07 X ($10,000 − $3,110)] | 482 | |
| Lease Liability (Plug) | 3,328 | |
| Cash | | 3,810 |

d. **January 1, Year 11**

| | | |
|---|---|---|
| Cash | 10,000 | |
| Sales Revenue | | 10,000 |

| | | |
|---|---|---|
| Cost of Goods Sold | 6,000 | |
| Inventory | | 6,000 |

e. **January 1, Year 11**

| | | |
|---|---|---|
| Computer Equipment | 6,000 | |
| Inventory | | 6,000 |

**December 31, Year 11**

| | | |
|---|---|---|
| Depreciation Expense | 2,000 | |
| Accumulated Depreciation | | 2,000 |

© 2003 Thomson Learning, Inc.

10.43 e. continued.

| | | |
|---|---|---|
| Cash | 3,810 | |
| Rent Revenue | | 3,810 |

**December 31, Year 12**

| | | |
|---|---|---|
| Depreciation Expense | 2,000 | |
| Accumulated Depreciation | | 2,000 |

| | | |
|---|---|---|
| Cash | 3,810 | |
| Rent Revenue | | 3,810 |

f. **January 1, Year 11**

| | | |
|---|---|---|
| Lease Receivable | 10,000 | |
| Sales Revenue | | 10,000 |

| | | |
|---|---|---|
| Cost of Goods Sold | 6,000 | |
| Inventory | | 6,000 |

**December 31, Year 11**

| | | |
|---|---|---|
| Cash | 3,810 | |
| Interest Revenue (see Part *c.*) | | 700 |
| Lease Receivable | | 3,110 |

**December 31, Year 12**

| | | |
|---|---|---|
| Cash | 3,810 | |
| Interest Revenue (see Part *c.*) | | 482 |
| Lease Receivable | | 3,328 |

g.

| Lessee | Year 11 | Year 12 | Year 13 | Total |
|---|---|---|---|---|
| **Borrow and Purchase** | | | | |
| Depreciation Expense.... | $ 3,333 | $ 3,333 | $ 3,334 | $ 10,000 |
| Interest Expense ............ | 800 | 554 | 286 | 1,640 |
| | $ 4,133 | $ 3,887 | $ 3,620 | $ 11,640 |
| | | | | |
| **Operating Lease** | | | | |
| Rent Expense ................. | $ 3,810 | $ 3,810 | $ 3,810 | $ 11,430 |
| | | | | |
| **Capital Lease** | | | | |
| Depreciation Expense.... | $ 3,333 | $ 3,333 | $ 3,334 | $ 10,000 |
| Interest Expense ............ | 700 | 482 | 248 | 1,430 |
| | $ 4,033 | $ 3,815 | $ 3,582 | $ 11,430 |

10.43 continued.

| h. **Lessor** | **Year 11** | **Year 12** | **Year 13** | **Total** |
|---|---|---|---|---|
| **Sale** | | | | |
| Sales Revenue.................. | $10,000 | $ -- | $ -- | $ 10,000 |
| Cost of Goods Sold .......... | (6,000) | -- | -- | (6,000) |
| | $ 4,000 | $ -- | $ -- | $ 4,000 |
| | | | | |
| **Operating Lease** | | | | |
| Rent Revenue.................. | $ 3,810 | $ 3,810 | $ 3,810 | $ 11,430 |
| Depreciation Expense.... | (2,000) | (2,000) | (2,000) | (6,000) |
| | $ 1,810 | $ 1,810 | $ 1,810 | $ 5,430 |
| | | | | |
| **Capital Lease** | | | | |
| Sales Revenue.................. | $10,000 | $ -- | $ -- | $ 10,000 |
| Cost of Goods Sold .......... | (6,000) | -- | -- | (6,000) |
| Interest Revenue............ | 700 | 482 | 248 | 1,430 |
| | $ 4,700 | $ 482 | $ 248 | $ 5,430 |

10.44    (U.S. Airlines; financial statement effects of capitalizing operating leases.)

| | **American** | **Delta** | **United** |
|---|---|---|---|
| a. $7,878/($7,878 + $3,380)........................ | 70.0% | | |
| $3,121/($3,121 + $1,827)....................... | | 63.1% | |
| $3,617/($3,617 − $267).......................... | | | 108.0% |
| | | | |
| b. ($7,878 + $8,164)/($7,878 + $8,164 + $3,380)............................................. | 82.6% | | |
| ($3,121 + $7,307)/($3,121 + $7,307 + $1,827)................................................ | | 85.1% | |
| ($3,617 + $10,645)/($3,617 + $10,645 − $267)................................................ | | | 101.9% |

c.    The airlines have high debt ratios without including operating leases. Inclusion of the operating leases in liabilities probably violates debt covenants of these airlines.

d.    The lease period probably runs for less than 75 percent of the useful life of their equipment or the lessor incurs the salvage value risk.

e.    The airlines often operate at a loss and are unable to take advantage of depreciation deductions. The airlines hope to obtain lower lease payments by allowing the lessor to claim the depreciation deductions for tax purposes.

10.45    (Deere & Company; interpreting income tax disclosures.)    (Amounts in Millions)

a.  **Year 10**

| | | |
|---|---|---|
| Income Tax Expense ..................................................... | 182 | |
| Deferred Tax Asset (= $82 – $77)............................. | 5 | |
|    Deferred Tax Liability (= $375 – $312)............... | | 63 |
|    Income Tax Payable or Cash................................. | | 124 |

b.  Book income before income taxes exceeded taxable income because income tax expense exceeds income taxes currently payable. Also, the deferred tax accounts on the balance sheet experienced a net credit change of $58 million (= $63 – $5) during Year 10, suggesting larger book income than taxable income.

c.  **Year 11**

| | | |
|---|---|---|
| Deferred Tax Asset (= $149 – $82)........................... | 67 | |
| Deferred Tax Liability (= $342 – $375)..................... | 33 | |
|    Income Tax Payable ............................................ | | 95 |
|    Income Tax Expense (Credit).............................. | | 5 |

d.  Book loss before income taxes was smaller than taxable income. Also, the deferred tax accounts on the balance sheet experienced a net debit change of $100 million (= $67 + $33) during Year 11, suggesting smaller book income (loss) than taxable income.

e.  The decline in book income before income taxes between Year 10 and Year 11 suggests the possibility of a slowdown in sales growth. Revenue recognized for tax purposes using the installment method exceeds revenue recognized at the time of sale for book purposes, resulting in a decrease in the deferred tax liability relating to installment sales. The increase in the deferred tax assets relating to uncollectible accounts and sales rebates and allowances suggest weak economic conditions, causing Deere to increase its provisions for these items for book purposes.

f.

| | |
|---|---|
| Change in Deferred Tax Liability Relating to Depreciable | |
|    Assets (= $215 – $208) ....................................................... | $ 7 |
| Income Tax Rate......................................................................... | ÷ .35 |
| Temporary Difference for Year 11............................................. | $ 20 |
| Book Depreciation...................................................................... | 209 |
| Tax Depreciation ....................................................................... | $ 229 |

10.46    (Sun Microsystems; interpreting income tax disclosures.)    (Amounts in Millions)

a.  **Year 5**

| | | |
|---|---|---|
| Income Tax Expense ............................................................ | 67 | |
| Deferred Tax Asset (= $150 – $142) ................................ | 8 | |
| Deferred Tax Liability (= $7 – $14) .................................. | 7 | |
|     Income Tax Payable or Cash (= $38 + $38 + $6) ........ | | 82 |

b.  Book income before income taxes was less than taxable income because there is a net debit change (= $8 + $7) in the deferred tax accounts on the balance sheet.

c.  **Year 6**

| | | |
|---|---|---|
| Income Tax Expense ............................................................ | 88 | |
| Deferred Tax Asset (= $174 – $150) ................................ | 24 | |
|     Deferred Tax Liability (= $27 – $7) ............................ | | 20 |
|     Income Tax Payable or Cash (= $28 + $60 + $4) ........ | | 92 |

d.  Book income before income taxes was less than taxable income because there is a net debit change (= $24 – $20) in the deferred tax accounts on the balance sheet.

e.  **Year 7**

| | | |
|---|---|---|
| Income Tax Expense ............................................................ | 167 | |
| Deferred Tax Asset (= $195 – $174) ................................ | 21 | |
| Deferred Tax Liability (= $25 – $27) ................................ | 2 | |
|     Income Tax Payable or Cash (= $123 + $57 + $10) ... | | 190 |

f.  Taxable income exceeds book income before income taxes.  The deferred tax accounts on the balance sheet experienced a net debit change (= $21 + $2) during Year 7.

g.  Sun probably decreased its capital expenditures during Year 7 because depreciation for book purposes exceeded depreciation for tax purposes (that is, the deferred tax liability relating to depreciation temporary differences decreased during Year 7).

10.47    (General Products Company; interpreting income tax disclosures.)

   a.   Book income was likely less than taxable income because the deferred
        tax accounts on the balance sheet experienced a net debit change
        during Year 3.

   b.   Book income was likely larger than taxable income because the
        deferred tax accounts on the balance sheet experienced a net credit
        change during Year 4.

   c.   The sales of products on account and under warranty plans increased
        continually during the three-year period. Estimated bad debt expense
        on each year's sales exceeded actual write-off of uncollectible accounts
        arising from the current and previous years' sales. Estimated
        warranty expense on products sold each year exceeded actual
        expenditures for warranties and products sold during the current and
        previous years.

   d.   Change in Deferred Tax Liability Relating to Temporary
            Depreciable Assets (= $213 – $155).....................................    $     58
        Income Tax Rate.........................................................................    ÷    .35
        Excess of Tax Depreciation Over Book Depreciation .............    $ 165.7

10.48 (Equilibrium Company; behavior of deferred income tax account when a firm acquires new assets every year.)

| Year | Units Acquired |
|---|---|
| 1 | 1 |
| 2 | 1 |
| 3 | 1 |
| 4 | 1 |
| 5 | 1 |
| 6 | 1 |
| 7 | 1 |

**TAX DEPRECIATION (ACRS)**

| | 1 | 2 | 3 | 4 | 5 | 6 | 7 |
|---|---|---|---|---|---|---|---|
| | $2,400 | $3,840 | $2,280 | $1,440 | $1,320 | $720 | $0 |
| | | 2,400 | 3,840 | 2,280 | 1,440 | 1,320 | 720 |
| | | | 2,400 | 3,840 | 2,280 | 1,440 | 1,320 |
| | | | | 2,400 | 3,840 | 2,280 | 1,440 |
| | | | | | 2,400 | 3,840 | 2,280 |
| | | | | | | 2,400 | 3,840 |
| | | | | | | | 2,400 |
| a. Annual Depreciation | $2,400 | $6,240 | $8,520 | $9,960 | $11,280 | $12,000 | $12,000 |
| b. Straight Line Depreciation = $2,000 per Machine per Year | 2,000 | 4,000 | 6,000 | 8,000 | 10,000 | 12,000 | 12,000 |
| c. Difference | $400 | $2,240 | $2,520 | $1,960 | $1,280 | $0 | $0 |
| d. Increase in Deferred Tax (40%) | $160 | $896 | $1,008 | $784 | $512 | $0 | $0 |
| e. Balance of Deferred Income Taxes | $160 | $1,056 | $2,064 | $2,848 | $3,360 | $3,360 | $3,360 |

f. The Deferred Income Taxes account balance will remain constant at $3,360 so long as the firm continues this replacement policy. If asset prices increase or physical assets increase, or both, the Deferred Tax Liability will continue to grow.

10.49    (Firm D; accounting for forward commodity contract.)

a.    Fair Value Hedge
      **October 31, Year 1**
      No entry.

      **December 31, Year 1**

| | | |
|---|---:|---:|
| Forward Commodity Contract (Asset) [10,000 × ($320 − $310)] | 100,000 | |
|     Gain on Revaluation of Forward Commodity Contract | | 100,000 |
| | | |
| Loss on Revaluation of Inventory [10,000 × ($320 − $310)] | 100,000 | |
|     Inventory | | 100,000 |

      **March 31, Year 2**

| | | |
|---|---:|---:|
| Forward Commodity Contract (Asset) [10,000 × ($310 − $270)] | 400,000 | |
|     Gain on Revaluation of Forward Commodity Contract | | 400,000 |
| | | |
| Loss on Revaluation of Inventory [10,000 × ($310 − $270)] | 400,000 | |
|     Inventory | | 400,000 |
| | | |
| Cash (10,000 × $270) | 2,700,000 | |
|     Sales Revenue | | 2,700,000 |
| | | |
| Cost of Goods Sold ($2,250,000 − $100,000 − $400,000) | 1,750,000 | |
|     Inventory | | 1,750,000 |
| | | |
| Cash [10,000 × ($320 − $270)] | 500,000 | |
|     Forward Commodity Contract | | 500,000 |

b.    Cash Flow Hedge
      **October 31, Year 1**
      No entry.

      **December 31, Year 1**

| | | |
|---|---:|---:|
| Forward Commodity Contract (Asset) [10,000 × ($320 − $310)] | 100,000 | |
|     Other Comprehensive Income | | 100,000 |
| | | |
| Other Comprehensive Income [10,000 × ($320 − $310)] | 100,000 | |
|     Inventory | | 100,000 |

10.49 b. continued.

**March 31, Year 2**

| | | |
|---|---:|---:|
| Forward Commodity Contract (Asset) [10,000 × ($310 − $270)].................................................................... | 400,000 | |
|     Other Comprehensive Income............................ | | 400,000 |
| | | |
| Other Comprehensive Income [10,000 × ($310 − $270)].................................................................... | 400,000 | |
|     Inventory......................................................... | | 400,000 |
| | | |
| Cash (10,000 × $270)................................................. | 2,700,000 | |
|     Sales Revenue................................................ | | 2,700,000 |
| | | |
| Cost of Goods Sold ($2,250,000 − $100,000 − $400,000)................................................................ | 1,750,000 | |
|     Inventory......................................................... | | 1,750,000 |
| | | |
| Cash [10,000 × ($320 − $270)]................................. | 500,000 | |
|     Forward Commodity Contract............................. | | 500,000 |

10.50    (Shiraz Company; attempts to achieve off-balance-sheet financing.)

[The chapter does not give sufficient information for the student to know the GAAP answers. The six items are designed to generate a lively discussion.]

**Transfer of Receivables with Recourse** *SFAS No. 77* (1983) sets out the following criteria to treat a transfer of receivables with recourse as a sale: (1) the seller (Shiraz) surrenders control of the future economic benefits and risks of the receivables, and (2) the purchaser of the receivables (Credit Company) cannot require the seller to repurchase the receivables except as set out in the original provision, and (3) the seller can estimate its obligation under the recourse provision.

Shiraz Company retains control of the future economic benefits. If interest rates decrease, Shiraz can borrow funds at the lower interest rate and repurchase the receivables. Because the receivables carry a fixed interest return, Shiraz enjoys the benefit of the difference between the fixed interest return on the receivables and the lower borrowing cost. If interest rates increase, Shiraz will not repurchase the receivables. Credit Company bears the risk of interest rate increases because of the fixed interest return on the receivables. The control of who benefits from interest rate changes and who bears the risk resides with Shiraz Company. Shiraz Company also bears credit risk in excess of the allowance. Thus, this transaction does not meet the first two criteria as a sale. Shiraz Company should report the transaction as a collateralized loan.

**Product Financing Arrangement** *SFAS No. 49* (1981) provides that firms recognize product financing arrangements as liabilities if (1) the arrangement requires the sponsoring firm (Shiraz) to purchase the inventory at specified prices and (2) the payments made to the other entity (Credit Company) cover all acquisition, holding, and financing costs.

Shiraz Company agrees to repurchase the inventory at a fixed price, thereby incurring the risk of changing prices. The purchase price formula includes a fixed interest rate, so Shiraz enjoys the benefits or incurs the risk of interest rate changes. Shiraz also controls the benefits and risk of changes in storage costs. Thus, Shiraz treats this product financing arrangement as a collateralized loan.

**Throughput Contract** *SFAS Statement No. 49* (1981) treats throughput contracts as executory contracts and does not require their recognition as a liability. Note, however, the similarity between a product financing arrangement (involving inventory) and a throughput contract (involving a service). Shiraz Company must pay specified amounts each period regardless of whether it uses the shipping services. The wording of the problem makes it unclear as to whether the initial contract specifies a selling price (railroad bears risk of operating cost increases) or whether the selling price is the railroad's current charges for shipping services each period (Shiraz bears risk of operating cost increases). It seems unlikely that the railroad would accept a fixed price for all ten years. Thus, it appears that Shiraz incurs a commitment to make highly probable future cash payments in amounts that cover the railroad's operating and financing costs. This transaction has the economic characteristics of a collateralized loan, even though GAAP permit treatment as an executory contract.

**Construction Joint Venture** The construction loan appears as a liability of the books of Chemical, the joint entity. Because Shiraz and Mission each own 50 percent of Chemical, neither company consolidates Chemical's financial statements with their own. (Chapter 11 discusses consolidated financial statements.) Thus, the loan will not appear on either Shiraz's or Mission's balance sheet by way of their accounting for their investment in Chemical.

GAAP treat the commitment to pay one-half of the operating and debt service costs as an executory contract, similar to the throughput contract. Even though the probability of making future cash payments is high, GAAP conclude that a liability does not arise until the firm receives future benefits from Chemical.

The only way that Shiraz will recognize a liability is if the debt guarantee gives rise to a loss contingency. If Mission defaults on its share of operating and debt service costs, the probability of Shiraz having to repay the loan increases sufficiently to warrant recognition of a liability. It is difficult to see the logic of GAAP in recognizing the full liability in this case while not recognizing one-half of the liability in situations described in the preceding paragraphs. In both cases, the probability of future cash outflows is high.

10.50 continued.

**Research and Development Partnership** *SFAS No. 68* (1982) requires firms to recognize financings related to research and development (R & D) as liabilities if (1) the sponsoring firm (Shiraz) must repay the financing regardless of the outcome of the R & D work, or (2) the sponsoring firm, even in the a absence of a loan guarantee, bears the risk of failure of the R & D effort.

Shiraz guarantees the bank loan in this case regardless of the outcome of the R & D effort and therefore must recognize a liability (satisfies first criterion above). It does not matter whether Shiraz has an option or an obligation to purchase the results of the R & D effort.

If Shiraz did not guarantee the bank loan, then the second criterion above determines whether Shiraz recognizes a liability. If Shiraz has the option to purchase the results of the R & D work, it does not bear the risk of failure and need not recognize a liability. If Shiraz has the obligation to purchase the results, it recognizes a liability for the probable amount payable. The problem does not make it clear whether the amount payable includes the unpaid balance of the loan or merely the value of the R & D work (which could be zero). It seems unlikely that the bank would lend funds for the R & D work without some commitment or obligation by Shiraz to repay the loan.

**Hotel Financing** Shiraz Company will recognize a liability for the hotel financing only if its debt guarantee satisfies the criteria for a loss contingency. It appears in this case that the probability of Shiraz having to make payments under the loan guarantee is low. The hotel is profitable and probably generating cash flows. In addition, the bank can sell the hotel in the event of loan default to satisfy the unpaid balance of the loan. Thus, Shiraz's loan guarantee is a third level of defense against loan default. If default does occur and the first two lines of defense prove inadequate to repay the loan in full, then Shiraz would recognize a liability for the unpaid portion.

# CHAPTER 11

## MARKETABLE SECURITIES AND INVESTMENTS

*Questions, Exercises, Problems, and Cases: Answers and Solutions*

11.1    See the text or the glossary at the end of the book.

11.2    Securities that a firm intends to sell within approximately one year of the date of the balance sheet appear as current assets. All other securities appear as noncurrent assets.

11.3    a.    Debt securities that a firm intends to hold to maturity (for example, to lock in the yield at acquisition for the full period to maturity) and has the ability to hold to maturity (for example, the firm has adequate liquid assets and borrowing capacity such that it need not sell the debt securities prior to maturity to obtain cash) appear as "debt held to maturity." All other debt securities appear in the "available for sale" category. The latter includes short-term investments in government debt securities that serve as a liquid investment of excess cash and short-and long-term investments in government and corporate debt securities that serve either as hedges of interest rate, exchange rate, or similar risks or as sources of cash at a later date to pay debt coming due.

   b.    The classification as "trading securities" implies a firm's active involvement in buying and selling securities for profit. The holding period of trading securities is typically measured in minutes or hours instead of days. The classification as "available for sale" implies less frequent trading and usually relates to an operating purpose other than profit alone (for example, to generate income while a firm has temporarily excess cash, to invest in a firm with potential new technologies). The holding period of securities available for sale is typically measured in days, months, or years.

   c.    Amortized acquisition cost equals the purchase price of debt securities plus or minus amortization of any difference between acquisition cost and maturity value. Amortized acquisition cost bears no necessary relation to the market value of the debt security during the periods subsequent to acquisition. The market value of a debt security depends on the risk characteristics of the issuer, the provisions of the debt security with respect to interest rate, term to maturity, and similar factors, and the general level of interest rates in the economy.

11.3 continued.

    d.   Unrealized holding gains and losses occur when the market value of a security changes while the firm holds the security. The unrealized holding gain or loss on trading securities appears in the income statement each period, whereas it appears in a separate shareholders' equity account each period for securities available for sale.

    e.   Realized gains and losses appear in the income statement when a firm sells a security. The realized gain or loss on trading securities equals the selling price minus the market value of the security on the most recent balance sheet. The realized gain or loss on securities available for sale equals the selling price minus the acquisition cost of the security.

11.4    Firms acquire trading securities primarily for their short-term profit potential. Including the unrealized holding gain or loss in income provides the financial statement user with relevant information for assessing the performance of the trading activity. Firms acquire securities available for sale to support an operating activity (for example, investment of temporarily excess cash) instead of primarily for their profit potential. Deferring recognition of any gain or loss until sale treats securities available for sale the same as inventories, equipment and other assets. Excluding the unrealized gain or loss from earnings also reduces earnings volatility.

11.5    The realized gain or loss for a security classified as available for sale equals the selling price minus the acquisition cost of the security. The realized gain or loss for a trading security equals the selling price minus the market value on the date of the most recent balance sheet. GAAP allocate all of the income from a security classified as available for sale to the period of sale, whereas GAAP allocate this same amount of income on a trading security to all periods between purchase and sale.

11.6    The required accounting does appear to contain a degree of inconsistency. One might explain this seeming inconsistency by arguing that the balance sheet and income statement serve different purposes. The balance sheet attempts to portray the resources of a firm and the claims on those users by creditors and owners. Market values for securities are more relevant than acquisition cost or lower-of-cost-or-market for assessing the adequacy of resources to satisfy claims. The income statement reports the results of operating performance. One might argue that operating performance from investing in marketable securities available for sale is not complete until the firm sells the securities. Another argument for excluding at least unrealized gains on marketable securities from earnings is that it achieves consistency with the delayed recognition of unrealized gains on inventories, equipment, and other assets.

11.7    a.    These accounts are both shareholders' equity accounts and reflect the change in the market value of securities since acquisition.

       b.    Dividend Revenue is an income statement account. It reflects the revenue recognized when a firm uses the market-value method. Equity in Earnings of Unconsolidated Affiliates is also an income statement account. It reflects the revenue recognized when a firm uses the equity method.

       c.    Equity in Earnings of Unconsolidated Affiliate is an income statement account. It reflects the revenue earned by a minority, active investor in an investee accounted for using the equity method. Minority Interest in Earnings of Consolidated Subsidiary is an account appearing on the consolidated income statement of a parent and its majority-owned, active investee. It represents the external, minority interest in the earnings of the investee.

       d.    Minority Interest in Earnings of Consolidated Subsidiary is an income statement account. It reflects the external, minority interest in the earnings of a majority-owned consolidated subsidiary. Minority Interest in Net Assets of Consolidated Subsidiary is a balance sheet account. It reflects the external, minority interest in the net assets of a consolidated subsidiary.

11.8    Dividends represent revenues under the market-value method and a return of capital under the equity method.

11.9    Under the equity method, the change each period in the net assets, or shareholders' equity, of the subsidiary appears on the one line, Investment in Subsidiary, on the balance sheet. When the parent consolidates the subsidiary, changes in the individual assets and liabilities that comprise the net asset change appear in the individual consolidated assets and liabilities. Likewise, under the equity method, the investor's interest in the investee's earnings appears in one line on the income statement, Equity in Earnings of Unconsolidated Subsidiary. When the parent consolidates the subsidiary, the individual revenues and expenses of the subsidiary appear in consolidated revenues and expenses.

11.10    If Company A owns less than, or equal to, 50 percent of Company B's voting stock, it is a minority investor in Company B. If Company A owns more than 50 percent of Company C, it is a majority investor in Company C. The entities holding the remainder of the voting stock of Company C are minority investors. Their minority interest appears on the consolidated balance sheet of Company A and Company C.

11.11    When the investor uses the equity method, total assets include the Investment in Subsidiary account. The investment account reflects the parent's interest in the *net* assets (assets minus liabilities) of the subsidiary. When the investor consolidates the subsidiary, total consoli-

11.11 continued.

dated assets include all of the subsidiary's assets. Consolidated liabilities include the liabilities of the subsidiary. Thus, total assets on a consolidated basis exceed total assets when the investor uses the equity method.

11.12    Buildings and equipment have a determinable useful life, whereas the expected useful life of goodwill is indefinite.

11.13    (Classifying securities.)

    a.  Securities available for sale; current asset.

    b.  Debt securities held to maturity; noncurrent asset.

    c.  Securities available for sale; current asset.

    d.  Securities available for sale; noncurrent asset.

    e.  Trading securities; current asset.

    f.  Securities available for sale; noncurrent asset (although a portion of these bonds might appear as a current asset).

11.14    (Vermont Company; journal entries to apply the market value method to short-term investments in securities.)

**8/21**

| | | |
|---|---|---|
| Marketable Securities | 45,000 | |
|    Cash | | 45,000 |

To record the cost of purchases in asset account:
(1,000 X $45) = $45,000.

**9/13**

No entry because September 13 is not the end of an accounting period.

**9/30**

| | | |
|---|---|---|
| Dividends Receivable | 500 | |
|    Dividend Revenue | | 500 |

To record declaration of dividend as revenue.

**10/25**

| | | |
|---|---|---|
| Cash | 500 | |
|    Dividends Receivable | | 500 |

To record receipt of dividend in cash.

11.14 continued.

**12/31**

| | | |
|---|---|---|
| Marketable Securities | 6,000 | |
|     Unrealized Holding Gain on Securities Available for Sale (SE/Comp Y) | | 6,000 |

To record increase in market price: 1,000 × ($51 – $45) = $6,000.

**1/20**

| | | |
|---|---|---|
| Cash (600 × $55) | 33,000 | |
|     Marketable Securities (600 × $45) | | 27,000 |
|     Realized Gain on Sale of Securities Available for Sale (IncSt) [600 × ($55 – $45)] | | 6,000 |

To record sale of 600 shares of Texas Instruments.

| | | |
|---|---|---|
| Unrealized Holding Gain on Securities Available for Sale (SE/Comp Y) [600 × ($51– $45)] | 3,600 | |
|     Marketable Securities | | 3,600 |

To eliminate changes previously recorded in the market value of Texas Instruments.

11.15 (Elson Corporation; journal entries to apply the market value method for short-term investments in securities.)

**10/15/Year 4**

| | | |
|---|---|---|
| Marketable Securities (Security A) | 28,000 | |
|     Cash | | 28,000 |

To record acquisition of shares of Security A.

**11/02/Year 4**

| | | |
|---|---|---|
| Marketable Securities (Security B) | 49,000 | |
|     Cash | | 49,000 |

To record acquisition of shares of Security B.

**12/31/Year 4**

| | | |
|---|---|---|
| Cash | 1,000 | |
|     Dividend Revenue | | 1,000 |

To record dividend received from Security B.

**12/31/Year 4**

| | | |
|---|---|---|
| Unrealized Holding Loss on Security A Available for Sale (SE/Comp Y) | 3,000 | |
|     Marketable Securities (Security A) | | 3,000 |

To record unrealized holding loss on Security A.

11.15 continued.

**12/31/Year 4**

| | | |
|---|---:|---:|
| Marketable Securities (Security B)............................ | 6,000 | |
|     Unrealized Holding Gain on Security B Available | | |
|       for Sale (SE/Comp Y)............................. | | 6,000 |
| To record unrealized holding gain on Security B. | | |

**2/10/Year 5**

| | | |
|---|---:|---:|
| Cash ......................................................................... | 24,000 | |
| Realized Loss on Sale of Securities Available for | | |
|     Sale ($24,000 – $28,000) (IncSt)............................. | 4,000 | |
|       Marketable Securities (Security A)...................... | | 28,000 |
| To record sale of Security A. | | |

| | | |
|---|---:|---:|
| Marketable Securities (Security A)............................... | 3,000 | |
|     Unrealized Holding Loss on Security A Available | | |
|       for Sale (SE/Comp Y)............................. | | 3,000 |
| To eliminate the effects of changes previously re- | | |
| corded in the market value of Security A. | | |

**12/31/Year 5**

| | | |
|---|---:|---:|
| Cash .......................................................................... | 1,200 | |
|     Dividend Revenue ................................................... | | 1,200 |
| To record dividend received from Security B. | | |

**12/31/Year 5**

| | | |
|---|---:|---:|
| Unrealized Holding Gain on Security B Available for | | |
|     Sale (SE/Comp Y)......................................... | 2,000 | |
|       Marketable Securities (Security B) ($53,000 – | | |
|       $55,000) ............................................. | | 2,000 |
| To revalue Security B to market value. | | |

**7/15/Year 6**

| | | |
|---|---:|---:|
| Cash .......................................................................... | 57,000 | |
|     Marketable Securities (Security B)........................ | | 49,000 |
|     Realized Gain on Sale of Securities Available for | | |
|       Sale ($57,000 – $49,000) (IncSt)......................... | | 8,000 |
| To record sale of Security B. | | |

| | | |
|---|---:|---:|
| Unrealized Holding Gain on Security B Available | | |
|     for Sale ($6,000 – $2,000) (SE/Comp Y) .................. | 4,000 | |
|       Marketable Securities (Security B)...................... | | 4,000 |
| To eliminate the effects of changes previously re- | | |
| corded in the market value of Security B. | | |

11.16   (Simmons Corporation; journal entries to apply the market value method to short-term investments in securities.)

**6/13/Year 6**

| | | |
|---|---|---|
| Marketable Securities (Security S) | 12,000 | |
| Marketable Securities (Security T) | 29,000 | |
| Marketable Securities (Security U) | 43,000 | |
|     Cash | | 84,000 |

To record acquisition of marketable equity securities as a temporary investment.

**10/11/Year 6**

| | | |
|---|---|---|
| Cash | 39,000 | |
| Realized Loss on Sale of Security U Available for Sale (IncSt) | 4,000 | |
|     Marketable Securities (Security U) | | 43,000 |

To record sale of Security U.

**12/31/Year 6**

| | | |
|---|---|---|
| Marketable Securities (Security S) ($13,500 – $12,000) | 1,500 | |
|     Unrealized Holding Gain on Security S Available for Sale (SE/Comp Y) | | 1,500 |

To revalue Security S to market value.

**12/31/Year 6**

| | | |
|---|---|---|
| Unrealized Holding Loss on Security T Available for Sale (SE/Comp Y) | 2,800 | |
|     Marketable Securities (Security T) ($26,200 – $29,000) | | 2,800 |

To revalue Security T to market value.

**12/31/Year 7**

| | | |
|---|---|---|
| Marketable Securities (Security S) ($15,200 – $13,500) | 1,700 | |
|     Unrealized Holding Gain on Security S Available for Sale (SE/Comp Y) | | 1,700 |

To revalue Security S to market value.

**12/31/Year 7**

| | | |
|---|---|---|
| Marketable Securities (Security T) ($31,700 – $26,200) | 5,500 | |
|     Unrealized Holding Loss on Security T Available for Sale (from 12/31/Year 6 Entry) (SE/Comp Y) | | 2,800 |
|     Unrealized Holding Gain on Security T Available for Sale (SE/Comp Y) | | 2,700 |

To revalue Security T to market value.

11.16 continued.

**2/15/Year 8**

| | | |
|---|---|---|
| Cash ............................................................................ | 14,900 | |
|     Marketable Securities (Security S) .......................... | | 12,000 |
|     Realized Gain on Sale of Security S Available for | | |
|         Sale ($14,900 – $12,000) (IncSt)......................... | | 2,900 |

To record sale of Security S.

| | | |
|---|---|---|
| Unrealized Holding Gain on Security S Available for | | |
|     Sale ($1,500 + $1,700) (SE/Comp Y)......................... | 3,200 | |
|         Marketable Securities (Security S) ...................... | | 3,200 |

To eliminate the effects of changes previously recorded in the market value of Security S.

**8/22/Year 8**

| | | |
|---|---|---|
| Cash ............................................................................ | 28,500 | |
| Realized Loss on Sale of Securities Available for | | |
|     Sale (Security T) ($28,500 – $29,000) (IncSt)......... | 500 | |
|         Marketable Securities (Security T) ...................... | | 29,000 |

To record sale of Security T.

| | | |
|---|---|---|
| Unrealized Holding Gain on Security T Available for | | |
|     Sale (SE/Comp Y)......................................................... | 2,700 | |
|         Marketable Securities (Security T) ...................... | | 2,700 |

To eliminate the effects of changes previously recorded in the market value of Security T.

11.17 (Fischer/Black Co.; working backwards from data on marketable securities transaction.)

a. $20,000 = $17,000 + $3,000.

b $17,000, the amount credited to Marketable Securities in the journal entry which the student might think of as $20,000 original cost, derived above, less $3,000 of Unrealized Holding Loss.

c. $5,000 loss from the debit for Realized Loss.

11.18 (Canning/Werther; working backwards from data on marketable securities transaction.)

a. $14,000 = $17,000 proceeds – $4,000 realized gain + $1,000 loss previously recognized because they are trading securities.

b. $13,000 = $17,000 proceeds – $4,000 realized gain which is selling price less original cost because they are securities available for sale.

11.19    (Reconstructing events from journal entries.)

   a.   The market value of a marketable security is $4,000 less than its book value and the firm increases the Unrealized Holding Loss account on the balance sheet.

   b.   A firm sells marketable securities for an amount that is $100 (= $1,200 − $1,300) less than was originally paid for them.

   c.   The market value of marketable securities is $750 more than its book value and the firm increases the Unrealized Holding Gain account on the balance sheet.

   d.   A firm sells marketable securities for an amount that is $100 (= $1,800 − $1,700) more than was originally paid for them.

11.20    (Apollo Corporation; amount of income recognized under various methods of accounting for investments.)

   a. and b.

      $3.0 million = .15 × $20 million.

   c.   $24 million = .30 × $80 million.

   d.   $24 million = .30 × $80 million. The firm need not amortize the $80 million [= $230 million − .30($500,000)] of goodwill

11.21    (Trusco; balance sheet and income effects of alternative methods of accounting for investments.)

| Part | Investment | Net Income |
|------|-----------|-----------|
| a. | $40 million | $2 million |
| b. | $39 million | $2 million |
| c. | $45 million | $2 million |
| d. | $129 million[a] | $15 million[b] |
| e. | $169 million[c] | $15 million[d] |

[a]$120 million + .30($50 million − $20 million) = $129 million.
[b].30 × $50 million = $15 million.
[c]$160 million + .30($50 million − $20 million) = $169 million.
[d].30 × $50 million = $15 million.

11.22    (Randle Corporation; journal entries to apply the market value method for long-term investments in securities.)

**April 10, Year 1**

| | | |
|---|---|---|
| Investment in Securities (M) .......................................... | 37,000 | |
|    Cash ................................................................. | | 37,000 |

11.22 continued.

**July 11, Year 1**

| | | |
|---|---|---|
| Investment in Securities (N)..................................................... | 31,000 | |
|    Cash ................................................................................. | | 31,000 |

**September 29, Year 1**

| | | |
|---|---|---|
| Investment in Securities (O)..................................................... | 94,000 | |
|    Cash ................................................................................. | | 94,000 |

**December 31, Year 1**

| | | |
|---|---|---|
| Cash ......................................................................................... | 7,900 | |
|    Dividend Revenue .......................................................... | | 7,900 |

**December 31, Year 1**

| | | |
|---|---|---|
| Unrealized Holding Loss on Investments in Securities | | |
|    (M)(SE/Comp Y)................................................................ | 2,000 | |
|      Investment in Securities (M)................................... | | 2,000 |

**December 31, Year 1**

| | | |
|---|---|---|
| Unrealized Holding Loss on Investment in Securities | | |
|    (O)(SE/Comp Y) ............................................................... | 7,000 | |
|      Investment in Securities (O) .................................... | | 7,000 |

**December 31, Year 1**

| | | |
|---|---|---|
| Investment in Securities (N)..................................................... | 7,000 | |
|    Unrealized Holding Gain on Investment in Secur- | | |
|      ities (SE/Comp Y)........................................................ | | 7,000 |

**October 15, Year 2**

| | | |
|---|---|---|
| Cash ......................................................................................... | 43,000 | |
|    Investment in Securities (M) ....................................... | | 37,000 |
|    Realized Gain on Sale of Investment in Securities | | |
|      (IncSt).......................................................................... | | 6,000 |

**October 31, Year 2 or December 31, Year 2**

| | | |
|---|---|---|
| Investment in Securities (M) ..................................................... | 2,000 | |
|    Unrealized Holding Loss on Investment in Secur- | | |
|      ities (SE/Comp Y) ...................................................... | | 2,000 |

**December 31, Year 2**

| | | |
|---|---|---|
| Cash ......................................................................................... | 5,600 | |
|    Dividend Revenue .......................................................... | | 5,600 |

**December 31, Year 2**

| | | |
|---|---|---|
| Investment in Securities (N)..................................................... | 7,000 | |
|    Unrealized Holding Gain on Investment in Secur- | | |
|      ities (N)(SE/Comp Y)................................................. | | 7,000 |

11.22 continued.

**December 31, Year 2**
Investment in Securities (O)........................................... 2,000
   Unrealized Holding Loss on Investment in Secur-
      ities (O)(SE/Comp Y).............................................                2,000

11.23    (Blake Company; journal entries to apply the market value method to long-term investments in securities.)

**July 2, Year 4**
Investment in Securities (G)........................................... 42,800
   Cash .....................................................................            42,800

**October 19, Year 4**
Investment in Securities (H)........................................... 29,600
   Cash .....................................................................            29,600

**October 29, Year 4**
Cash ........................................................................ 89,700
Realized Loss on Sale of Investments in Securities
   (IncSt)................................................................ 4,000
      Investment in Securities (F)..................................            93,700

**October 29, Year 4 or December 31, Year 4**
Investment in Securities (F)........................................... 2,500
   Unrealized Holding Loss on Investment in Secur-
      ities (F)(SE/Comp Y) ............................................            2,500

**December 31, Year 4**
Unrealized Holding Loss on Investment in Securities
   (G)(SE/Comp Y) ...................................................... 4,500
      Investment in Securities (G)..................................            4,500

**December 31, Year 4**
Investment in Securities (H)........................................... 2,000
   Unrealized Holding Gain on Investment in Secur-
      ities (H)(SE/Comp Y).............................................            2,000

**February 9, Year 5**
Investment in Securities (I) ........................................... 18,100
   Cash .....................................................................            18,100

**September 17, Year 5**
Cash ........................................................................ 32,300
   Investment in Securities (H)...................................            29,600
   Realized Gain on Sale of Investment in Securities
      (IncSt)................................................................            2,700

11.23 continued.

**September 17, Year 5 or December 31, Year 5**
Unrealized Holding Gain on Investment in Securities
    (H)(SE/Comp Y).............................................................. 2,000
        Investment in Securities (H)................................. 2,000

**December 31, Year 5**
Unrealized Holding Loss on Investment in Securities
    (G)(SE/Comp Y).............................................................. 1,400
        Investment in Securities (G)................................. 1,400

**December 31, Year 5**
Investment in Securities (I) ............................................ 2,600
    Unrealized Holding Gain on Investment in Secur-
        ities (I)(SE/Comp Y)............................................. 2,600

11.24    (Wood Corporation; journal entries to apply the equity method of accounting for investments in securities.)

**January 2**
Investment in Securities (Knox).................................... 350,000
Investment in Securities (Vachi) ................................... 196,000
Investment in Securities (Snow).................................... 100,000
    Cash ........................................................................ 646,000

**December 31**
Investment in Securities (Knox).................................... 35,000
Investment in Securities (Vachi) ................................... 12,000
    Investment in Securities (Snow)............................ 4,800
    Equity in Earnings of Affiliates............................. 42,200
$(.50 \times \$70,000) + (.30 \times \$40,000) - (.20 \times \$24,000) =$
$\$42,200.$

**December 31**
Cash ................................................................................... 19,800
    Investment in Securities (Knox)............................ 15,000
    Investment in Securities (Vachi) ........................... 4,800
$(.50 \times \$30,000) + (.30 \times \$16,000) = \$19,800.$

11.25    (Stebbins Corporation; journal entries to apply the equity method of accounting for investments in securities.)

a.  **January 1, Year 1**
    Investment in Securities (R).................................... 250,000
    Investment in Securities (S)..................................... 325,000
    Investment in Securities (T)..................................... 475,000
        Cash ................................................................... 1,050,000

11.25 a. continued.

**December 31, Year 1**

| | | |
|---|---|---|
| Investment in Securities (R)............................. | 50,000 | |
| Investment in Securities (S)............................. | 48,000 | |
|    Investment in Securities (T)......................... | | 75,000 |
|    Equity in Earnings of Affiliates................... | | 23,000 |

$(.25 \times \$200,000) + (.40 \times \$120,000) - (.50 \times \$150,000) = \$23,000.$

**December 31, Year 1**

| | | |
|---|---|---|
| Cash............................................................. | 63,250 | |
|    Investment in Securities (R)......................... | | 31,250 |
|    Investment in Securities (S)......................... | | 32,000 |

$(.25 \times \$125,000) + (.40 \times \$80,000) = \$63,250.$

**December 31, Year 1**

| | | |
|---|---|---|
| Depreciation Expense..................................... | 4,000 | |
|    Investment in Securities (R)......................... | | 4,000 |

The cost of the investment in Company R exceeds the book value of the net assets acquired by $50,000 [= $250,000 − (.25 × $800,000)]. Stebbins Corporation attributes $40,000 of the excess to buildings and must depreciate $4,000 (= $40,000/10) each year. The firm attributes the remaining excess to goodwill, which it need not depreciate.

The cost of the investment in Company S exceeds its book value by $25,000 [= $325,000 − (.40 × $750,000)]. Stebbins Corporation attributes this excess to goodwill. The acquisition cost of the investment in Security T equals the book value of the net assets acquired.

**December 31, Year 2**

| | | |
|---|---|---|
| Investment in Securities (R)............................. | 56,250 | |
| Investment in Securities (S)............................. | 30,000 | |
| Investment in Securities (T)............................. | 25,000 | |
|    Equity in Earnings of Affiliates................... | | 111,250 |

$(.25 \times \$225,000) + (.40 \times \$75,000) + (.50 \times \$50,000) = \$111,250.$

**December 31, Year 2**

| | | |
|---|---|---|
| Cash............................................................. | 64,500 | |
|    Investment in Securities (R)......................... | | 32,500 |
|    Investment in Securities (S)......................... | | 32,000 |

$(.25 \times \$130,000) + (.40 \times \$80,000).$

**December 31, Year 2**

| | | |
|---|---|---|
| Depreciation Expense..................................... | 4,000 | |
|    Investment in Securities (R)......................... | | 4,000 |

11.25 continued.

b.  Cash.............................................................................. 275,000
    Loss on Sale of Investments.................................. 9,500
       Investment in Securities (R)............................ 284,500
    $250,000 + $50,000 − $31,250 − $4,000 +
    $56,250 − $32,500 − $4,000 = $284,500.

11.26  (Mulherin Corporation; journal entries under various methods of accounting for investments.)

a.  **January 2**
    Investment in Hanson ............................................ 320,000
    Investment in Maloney........................................... 680,000
    Investment in Quinn................................................ 2,800,000
       Cash ................................................................... 3,800,000
    To record acquisition of investments.

    **December 31**
    Cash........................................................................ 6,000
       Dividend Revenue ............................................ 6,000
    To record dividend from Hanson: .15 × $40,000 =
    $6,000.

    **December 31**
    Unrealized Holding Loss on Investment in Secur-
       ities (SE/Comp Y)............................................. 15,000
          Investment in Hanson .................................. 15,000
    To apply the market value method to the invest-
    ment in Hanson.

    **December 31**
    Investment in Maloney............................................ 150,000
       Equity in Earnings of Maloney............................ 150,000
    To recognize share of Maloney's earnings; .30 ×
    $500,000 = $150,000.

    **December 31**
    Cash........................................................................ 54,000
       Investment in Maloney ..................................... 54,000
    To recognize share of Maloney's dividends; .30 ×
    $180,000 = $54,000.

    **December 31**
    Amortization Expense............................................. 8,000
       Investment in Maloney ..................................... 8,000
    To amortize excess acquisition cost for Maloney;
    $680,000 − (.30 × $2,000,000) = $80,000;
    $80,000/10 = $8,000.

11.26 a. continued.

**December 31**
Investment in Quinn................................................. 600,000
   Equity in Earnings of Quinn ..............................          600,000
To recognize share of Quinn's earnings.

**December 31**
Cash..................................................................... 310,000
   Investment in Quinn...........................................          310,000
To recognize share of Quinn's dividends.

b. Common Stock (Quinn)......................................... 200,000
   Additional Paid-in Capital (Quinn) ......................... 800,000
   Retained Earnings (Quinn)................................... 690,000
   Equity in Earnings of Quinn (Mulherin)................... 600,000
   Goodwill............................................................ 800,000
     Investment in Quinn (Mulherin)........................     3,090,000
   $2,800,000 + $600,000 − $310,000 = $3,090,000.

11.27 (CAR Corporation; consolidation policy and principal consolidation concepts.)

a. CAR Corporation should consolidate Alexandre du France Software Systems and R Credit Corporation or, under exceptional circumstances, use the market value method.

b. Charles Electronics....................................... (.75 × $120,000) = $  90,000
   Alexandre du France Software Systems..   (.80 × 60,000) =     48,000
   R Credit Corporation ................................. (.90 × 144,000) =   129,600
     Total Income from Subsidiaries............................... $267,600

c. Minority Interest shown under accounting assumed in problem:

Charles Electronics....................................... (.25 × $120,000) = $30,000
Alexandre du France Software Systems..          (None) =    --
R Credit Corporation ...................................          (None) =    --
                                                       $30,000

CAR Corporation subtracts the minority interest in computing net income.

11.27 continued.

d. Charles Electronics, no increase because already consolidated.

Alexandre du France Software Systems increase by 80 percent of net income less dividends:

$$.80 \times (\$96,000 - \$60,000) = \$28,800.$$

R Credit Corporation, no increase because equity method results in the same income statement effects as do consolidated statements. Net income of CAR Corporation would be:

$$\$1,228,800 = \$1,200,000 \text{ (as reported)} + \$28,800 \text{ (increase)}.$$

e. Minority Interest shown if CAR Corporation consolidated all companies:

| | | |
|---|---|---|
| Charles Electronics | (.25 X $120,000) = | $30,000 |
| Alexandre du France Software Systems.. | (.20 X 96,000) = | 19,200 |
| R Credit Corporation | (.10 X 144,000) = | 14,400 |
| | | $63,600 |

11.28 (Bush Corporation; equity method and consolidation elimination entries.) (Amounts in Millions.)

a.
| | | |
|---|---|---|
| Investment in Stock of Cheney Computer | 500 | |
|     Cash | | 500 |

To record acquisition of shares of common stock.

| | | |
|---|---|---|
| Investment in Stock of Cheney Computer | 100 | |
|     Equity in Earnings of Cheney Computer | | 100 |

To accrue Cheney Computer's earnings for the year.

| | | |
|---|---|---|
| Cash or Dividends Receivable | 30 | |
|     Investment in Stock of Cheney Computer | | 30 |

To recognize dividends received or receivable.

| | | |
|---|---|---|
| Amortization Expense | 8 | |
|     Investment in Stock of Cheney Computer | | 8 |

To amortize patent; $8 = (\$500 - \$420)/10$. Investment is now $562 = \$500 + \$100 - \$30 - \$8$.

11.28 continued.

b.
| | | |
|---|---|---|
| Common Stock | 300 | |
| Retained Earnings ($120 − $30) | 90 | |
| Equity in Earnings of Cheney Computer | 100 | |
| Patent | 72 | |
|     Investment in Stock of Cheney Computer | | 562 |

To eliminate investment account.

| | | |
|---|---|---|
| Accounts Payable | 3 | |
|     Accounts Receivable | | 3 |

To eliminate intercompany receivable and liability.

11.29 (Hanna Company; equity method and consolidation elimination entries.)

a.
| | | |
|---|---|---|
| Investment in Stock of Denver Company | 550,000 | |
|     Cash | | 550,000 |

To record acquisition of common stock.

| | | |
|---|---|---|
| Investment in Stock of Denver Company | 120,000 | |
|     Equity in Earnings of Denver Company | | 120,000 |

To accrue 100 percent share of Denver Company's earnings.

| | | |
|---|---|---|
| Cash or Dividends Receivable | 40,000 | |
|     Investment in Stock of Denver Company | | 40,000 |

To accrue dividends received or receivable.

b.
| | | |
|---|---|---|
| Common Stock | 200,000 | |
| Retained Earnings ($350 − $40) | 310,000 | |
| Equity in Earnings of Denver Company | 120,000 | |
|     Investment in Stock of Denver Company | | 630,000 |

To eliminate investment account; $630,000 = $550,000 + $120,000 − $40,000.

11.30 (Joyce Company and Vogel Company; equity method and consolidation work sheet entries.)

a. **Joyce Company's Books**

(1)
| | | |
|---|---|---|
| Investment in Stock of Vogel Company | 420,000 | |
|     Cash | | 420,000 |

To record acquisition of common stock.

(2)
| | | |
|---|---|---|
| Accounts Receivable | 29,000 | |
|     Sales Revenue | | 29,000 |

To record intercompany sales on account.

11.30 a. continued.

(2) Cost of Goods Sold............................................... 29,000
     Inventories.................................................... 29,000
    To record cost of intercompany sales.

(3) Advance to Vogel Company.............................. 6,000
     Cash............................................................ 6,000
    To record advance to Vogel Company.

(4) Cash.................................................................. 16,000
     Accounts Receivable.................................. 16,000
    To record collections on account from Vogel
    Company.

(5) Cash.................................................................. 4,000
     Advance to Vogel Company ........................ 4,000
    To record collection of advance from Vogel
    Company.

(6) Cash.................................................................. 20,000
     Investment in Stock of Vogel Company..... 20,000
    To record dividend from Vogel Company.

(7) Investment in Stock of Vogel Company.......... 30,000
     Equity in Earnings of Vogel Company ........ 30,000
    To accrue 100 percent share of Vogel Com-
    pany's net income.

(8) Amortization Expense...................................... 4,000
     Investment in Stock of Vogel Company..... 4,000
    To record amortization of patent; $4,000 =
    ($420,000 − $380,000)/10.

## Vogel Company's Books

(1) No entry.

(2) Inventories......................................................... 29,000
     Accounts Payable....................................... 29,000
    To record intercompany purchase of materi-
    als on account.

(3) Cash.................................................................. 6,000
     Advance from Joyce Company.................... 6,000
    To record advance from Joyce Company.

(4) Accounts Payable ............................................. 16,000
     Cash............................................................ 16,000
    To record payment for purchases on account.

11.30 a. continued.

    (5) Advance from Joyce Company .......................... 4,000
            Cash ................................................................... 4,000
        To record repayment of advance.

    (6) Retained Earnings............................................... 20,000
            Cash ................................................................... 20,000
        To record declaration and payment of divi-
        dend.

    (7) No entry.

b.  Common Stock ........................................................ 300,000
    Retained Earnings ($80,000 – $20,000).................... 60,000
    Equity in Earnings of Vogel Company...................... 30,000
    Patent...................................................................... 36,000
       Investment in Stock of Vogel Company.............. 426,000
    To eliminate investment account; $426,000 =
    $420,000 + $30,000 – $20,000 – $4,000.

    Accounts Payable ...................................................... 13,000
       Accounts Receivable............................................ 13,000
    To eliminate intercompany receivable and pay-
    able.

    Advance from Joyce Company ................................... 2,000
       Advance to Vogel Company ................................. 2,000
    To eliminate intercompany advance.

11.31  (Laesch Company; working backwards to consolidation relations.)

  a.  $80,000 = ($156,000 – $100,000)/.70.

  b.  72.7 percent = ($156,000 – $100,000)/$77,000.

  c.  $56,000 = ($156,000 – $100,000).

11.32  (Dealco Corporation; working backwards from consolidated income statements.) (Amounts in Millions.)

  a.  $56/$140 = 40 percent.

  b.  [.40 × (1 – .20) × $140] = $44.80.

  c.  [1 – ($42/$280)] = 1 – .15 = 85 percent.

11.33    (Alpha/Omega; working backwards from data which has eliminated intercompany transactions; requires Appendix 11.1.)

a.    $90,000 = $450,000 + $250,000 − $610,000.

b.    $30,000 is Omega's cost; $20,000 is Alpha's cost; $20,000 original cost to Alpha.

Markup on the goods sold from Alpha to Omega, which remain in Omega's inventory, is $10,000 (= $60,000 + $50,000 − $100,000).
    Because Alpha priced the goods with markup 50 percent over its costs, the cost to Alpha to produce goods with markup of $10,000 is $20,000 and the total sales price from Alpha to Omega is $30,000 (= $10,000 + $20,000).

11.34    (Homer/Tonga; working backwards from purchase data.)

a.    $1,070,000 = $90,000 + $980,000.

b.
| | |
|---|---:|
| Book Value of Total Assets (from Part *a.*) | $1,070,000 |
| Less Book Value of Current Assets | (210,000) |
| Less Book Value of Goodwill | 0 |
| Book Value of Depreciable Assets | $ 860,000 |

11.35    (Water Company and Soluble Company; financial statement effects of the purchase method.)

a.
| | | |
|---|---:|---:|
| Investment in Soluble Company | 280 | |
| Common Stock | | 280 |

b.
| | | |
|---|---:|---:|
| Common Stock | 50 | |
| Retained Earnings | 80 | |
| Property, Plant, and Equipment (Net) | 50 | |
| Goodwill | 100 | |
| Investment in Soluble Company | | 280 |

© 2003 Thomson Learning, Inc.

11.35 continued.

c.   (Amounts in Millions)

|  | Purchase Method |
|---|---|
| Assets: | |
|   Current Assets..................................................... | $ 350 |
|   Property, Plant and Equipment (Net)......................... | 650 |
|   Goodwill............................................................... | 100 |
|     Total Assets ................................................ | $ 1,100 |
| Equities: | |
|   Liabilities............................................................. | $ 570 |
|   Common Stock....................................................... | 380[a] |
|   Retained Earnings................................................. | 150 |
|     Total Equities.............................................. | $ 1,100 |

[a]$100 + $280 = $380.

d.

| | | |
|---|---|---|
| Investment in Soluble Company .............................. | 20 | |
|   Equity Earnings of Soluble Company .................. | | 20 |
| | | |
| Depreciation Expense ($50/5).................................... | 10 | |
|   Investment in Soluble Company........................... | | 10 |

e.   (Amounts in Millions)

|  | Purchase Method |
|---|---|
| Precombination Net Income............................................ | $ 80 |
| Additional Depreciation Expense: | |
|   $50/5................................................................. | (10) |
|     Revised Projected Net Income................................ | $ 70 |

f.

| | | |
|---|---|---|
| Common Stock ............................................................ | 50 | |
| Retained Earnings....................................................... | 80 | |
| Equity Earnings of Soluble Company........................ | 20 | |
| Property, Plant, and Equipment (Net)...................... | 40 | |
| Goodwill....................................................................... | 100 | |
|   Investment in Soluble Company........................... | | 290 |

11.36  (Bristol-Myers and Squibb; financial statement effects of the purchase method.)

a.  (Amounts in Millions)

| | Purchase Method |
|---|---|
| Assets, Except Goodwill........................................................ | $ 17,173[c] |
| Goodwill.............................................................................. | 2,569[d] |
|     Total Assets........................................................ | $ 19,742 |
| Liabilities........................................................................... | $ 3,325[b] |
| Shareholders' Equity.......................................................... | 16,417[a] |
|     Total Equities ..................................................... | $ 19,742 |

[a]$3,547 + $12,870 = $16,417.
[b]$1,643 + $1,682 = $3,325.
[c]$5,190 + $3,083 + $2,500 + $6,400 = $17,173.
[d]$12,870 − $1,401 − $2,500 − $6,400 = $2,569.

b.  (Amounts in Millions)

| | Purchase Method |
|---|---|
| Precombination Projected Consolidated Net Income...... | $ 1,748 |
| Building and Equipment Depreciation: | |
|     $2,500/10......................................................... | (250) |
| Patent Amortization: | |
|     $6,400/5 .......................................................... | (1,280) |
| Revised Projected Net Income............................................ | $ 218 |

11.37  (Effects on statement of cash flows.)

a.  The journal entry to record this transaction is as follows:

| | | |
|---|---|---|
| Marketable Securities............................................... | 59,700 | |
|     Cash ................................................................... | | 59,700 |

Because this entry involves a credit to the Cash account, Line (9) decreases by $59,700. The purchase of marketable securities is an Investing activity, so Line (5) increases by $59,700. Note that Line (5) carries a negative sign, so increasing it reduces cash.

b.  The journal entries to record this transaction are as follows:

| | | |
|---|---|---|
| Cash......................................................................... | 47,900 | |
|     Marketable Securities ............................................ | | 42,200 |
|     Realized Gain on Sale of Securities Available | | |
|         for Sale (IncSt)............................................... | | 5,700 |

|  |  |  |
|---|---|---|
| Unrealized Holding Gain on Securities Available for Sale (SE/Comp Y)........................................ | 1,800 | |
| Marketable Securities ($44,000 – $42,200)... | | 1,800 |

Because the first entry involves a debit to the Cash account, Line (9) increases by $47,900. The sale of marketable securities is an Investing activity, so Line (4) increases by $47,900. Because the realized gain is an income statement account, Line (1) increases by $5,700. We show all of the cash proceeds of sale ($47,900) on Line (4). We double count cash in the amount of the gain if we do not eliminate $5,700 from the Operations section of the statement of cash flows. Thus, Line (3) increases by $5,700 to offset the realized gain. The net effect of the entries on Line (1) and Line (3) is zero. The second entry does not involve an income statement account or the Cash account and therefore would not appear on the statement of cash flows.

c.  The journal entries to record this transaction are as follows:

|  |  |  |
|---|---|---|
| Cash............................................................. | 18,700 | |
| Realized Loss on Sale of Securities Available for Sale (IncSt)................................................... | 6,400 | |
| Marketable Securities...................................... | | 25,100 |
| | | |
| Marketable Securities ($25,100 – $19,600)............ | 5,500 | |
| Unrealized Holding Loss on Securities Available for Sale (SE/Comp Y)................................. | | 5,500 |

Because the first entry involves a debit to the Cash account, Line (9) increases by $18,700. The sale of marketable securities is an Investing activity, so Line (4) increases by $18,700. Because the realized loss is an income statement account, Line (1) decreases by $6,400. The loss used no cash so Line (2) shows an addback of $6,400. The second entry does not involve the Cash account, nor any income statement account, so it does not affect the statement of cash flows.

d.  The journal entry is as follows:

|  |  |  |
|---|---|---|
| Unrealized Holding Loss on Securities Available for Sale (SE/Comp Y)....................................... | 19,000 | |
| Marketable Securities ($220,500 – $201,500)....................................................... | | 19,000 |

This entry does not involve a debit or credit to the Cash account, so Line (9) is not affected. This entry also does not affect an income statement account (the Unrealized Holding Loss on Securities Available for Sale account is a shareholders' equity account), so Line (1) is not affected. Thus, this entry does not appear on the statement of cash flows.

11.37 continued.

e.  The journal entry is as follows:

| | | |
|---|---|---|
| Marketable Securities.............................................................. | 6,400 | |
|     Unrealized Holding Gain on Securities Available for Sale (SE/Comp Y)................................ | | 6,400 |

For the same reasons given in Part *d.* above, this entry does not appear on the statement of cash flows.

f.  The journal entry to record this transaction is:

| | | |
|---|---|---|
| Cash......................................................................................... | 7,000 | |
|     Dividend Revenue ..................................................... | | 7,000 |

The Cash account increases, so Line (9) increases by $7,000. Net income increases, so Line (1) increases by $7,000.

g.  The journal entry to record this event is:

| | | |
|---|---|---|
| Unrealized Holding Loss on Investment in Securities (SE/Comp Y)....................................................... | 2,000 | |
|     Investments in Securities...................................... | | 2,000 |

The Cash account does not change so there is no effect on Line (9). Net income does not change so there is no effect on Line (1). The firm would disclose this event in a supplementary schedule or note if the amount was material.

h.  The journal entry to record this transaction is:

| | | |
|---|---|---|
| Cash (.40 × $10,000)................................................. | 4,000 | |
| Investment in Affiliate [.40($25,000 – $10,000)]... | 6,000 | |
|     Equity in Earnings of Affiliate (.40 × $25,000)... | | 10,000 |

The Cash account increases in the amount of the dividend, so Line (9) increases $4,000. Net income on Line (1) increases by $10,000 for the equity in earnings. Because the firm recognizes more revenue ($10,000) than the cash received ($4,000), it must increase Line (3) by $6,000 to convert net income to cash flow from operations.

11.37 continued.

i.    The journal entry to record this event is:

Equity in Loss of Affiliate (.40 X $12,500)................    5,000
    Investment in Affiliate ...........................................        5,000

There is no effect on the Cash account so Line (9) does not change. Net income decreases for the share of the loss so Line (1) decreases by $5,000. Because the loss does not use cash, Line (2) increases by $5,000 when converting net income to cash flow from operations.

j.    The journal entry to record this event is:

Amortization Expense.................................................    2,000
    Investment in Affiliate ...........................................        2,000

There is no effect on the Cash account so Line (9) does not change. Net income on Line (1) decreases for amortization expense. Because the amortization expense does not reduce cash, Line (2) increases by $2,000 when converting net income to cash flow from operations.

11.38 (Effect of errors involving marketable securities and accounts receivable on financial statement polices.)

| | | Rate of Return on Assets | Debt Equity Ratio |
|---|---|---|---|
| a. | Unrealized Holding Loss on Securities Available for Sale (SE/Comp Y) ...... X | $\dfrac{NO}{O/S} = U/S$ | $\dfrac{NO}{O/S} = U/S$ |
| | Marketable Securities ......... X | | |
| b. | Investment in Securities ............ X | $\dfrac{NO}{U/S} = O/S$ | $\dfrac{NO}{U/S} = O/S$ |
| | Unrealized Holding Gain on Securities Available for Sale (SE/Comp Y) ....... X | | |
| c. | Cash ............ X | $\dfrac{U/S}{U/S} = U/S$ | $\dfrac{NO}{U/S} = O/S$ |
| | Dividend Revenue ....... X | | |
| d. | Cash ............ X | $\dfrac{O/S}{O/S} = O/S$ | $\dfrac{NO}{O/S} = U/S$ |
| | Investment Account ....... X | | |
| e. | Depreciation Expense ............ X | $\dfrac{O/S}{O/S} = O/S$ | $\dfrac{NO}{O/S} = U/S$ |
| | Investment Account ....... X | | |

*Note*: This problem asks only for the net effect of each error on the two financial ratios. The journal entries and the numerator and denominator effects appear to show the reason for the net effect.

11.39   (Effect of errors on financial statements.)

|     | Assets | Liabilities | Shareholders' Equity | Net Income |
| --- | --- | --- | --- | --- |
| a. | U/S | No | U/S | U/S |
| b. | O/S | No | O/S | No |
| c. | O/S | No | O/S | O/S |
| d. | O/S | No | O/S | O/S |
| e. | No | No | No | No |
| f. | O/S | O/S | No | No |
| g. | No | No | No | O/S |

11.40   (Dostal Corporation; journal entries and financial statement presentation of short-term securities available for sale.)

a.  **2/05/Year 1**

| | | |
| --- | --- | --- |
| Marketable Securities (Security A)............................ | 60,000 | |
| Cash ........................................................................ | | 60,000 |

**8/12/Year 1**

| | | |
| --- | --- | --- |
| Marketable Securities (Security B)........................... | 25,000 | |
| Cash ........................................................................ | | 25,000 |

**12/31/Year 1**

| | | |
| --- | --- | --- |
| Marketable Securities (Security A) ($66,000 – $60,000)................................................................... | 6,000 | |
| Unrealized Holding Gain on Security A Available for Sale (SE/Comp Y).................... | | 6,000 |
| Unrealized Holding Loss on Security B Available for Sale (SE/Comp Y)......................................... | 5,000 | |
| Marketable Securities (Security B) ($20,000 – $25,000)......................................................... | | 5,000 |

**1/22/Year 2**

| | | |
| --- | --- | --- |
| Marketable Securities (Security C)........................... | 82,000 | |
| Cash ........................................................................ | | 82,000 |

**2/25/Year 2**

| | | |
| --- | --- | --- |
| Marketable Securities (Security D)........................... | 42,000 | |
| Cash ........................................................................ | | 42,000 |

**3/25/Year 2**

| | | |
| --- | --- | --- |
| Marketable Securities (Security E)........................... | 75,000 | |
| Cash ........................................................................ | | 75,000 |

11.40 a. continued.

**6/05/Year 2**

| | | |
|---|---:|---:|
| Cash................................................................................ | 72,000 | |
|     Marketable Securities (Security A)...................... | | 60,000 |
|     Realized Gain on Sale of Securities Available | | |
|       for Sale (IncSt)......................................................... | | 12,000 |
| | | |
| Unrealized Holding Gain on Security A Available | | |
|     for Sale (SE/Comp Y)................................................. | 6,000 | |
|     Marketable Securities (Security A)................. | | 6,000 |

**6/05/Year 2**

| | | |
|---|---:|---:|
| Cash................................................................................ | 39,000 | |
| Realized Loss on Sale of Securities Available for | | |
|     Sale (IncSt)................................................................ | 3,000 | |
|     Marketable Securities (Security D)................. | | 42,000 |

**12/31/Year 2**

| | | |
|---|---:|---:|
| Marketable Securities (Security B) ($23,000 – | | |
|     $20,000)...................................................................... | 3,000 | |
|     Unrealized Holding Loss on Security B | | |
|       Available for Sale (SE/Comp Y).................... | | 3,000 |

**12/31/Year 2**

| | | |
|---|---:|---:|
| Unrealized Holding Loss on Security C Available | | |
|     for Sale (SE/Comp Y)................................................. | 3,000 | |
|     Marketable Securities (Security C) ($79,000 | | |
|       – $82,000).............................................................. | | 3,000 |

**12/31/Year 2**

| | | |
|---|---:|---:|
| Marketable Securities (Security E) ($80,000 – | | |
|     $75,000)...................................................................... | 5,000 | |
|     Unrealized Holding Gain on Security E | | |
|       Available for Sale (SE/Comp Y).................... | | 5,000 |

b. **Balance Sheet on December 31, Year 1**

| | |
|---|---:|
| Marketable Securities at Market Value................................... | $ 86,000 |
| Net Unrealized Holding Gain on Securities Available for | |
|     Sale ($6,000 – $5,000)......................................................... | $ 1,000 |

*Footnote*

Marketable Securities on December 31, Year 1 had an acquisition cost of $85,000 and a market value of $86,000. Gross unrealized gains total $6,000 and gross unrealized losses total $5,000.

11.40 continued.

   c.  **Balance Sheet on December 31, Year 2**

Marketable Securities at Market Value................................... $ 182,000
Net Unrealized Holding Loss on Securities Available for
    Sale........................................................................................ -0-

*Footnote*

Marketable Securities on December 31, Year 2 had an acquisition cost of $182,000 and a market value of $182,000. Gross unrealized gains total $5,000 and gross unrealized losses total $5,000. Proceeds from sales of marketable securities totaled $111,000 during Year 2. These sales resulted in gross realized gains of $12,000 and gross realized losses of $3,000. The net unrealized holding loss on securities available for sale changed as follows during Year 2:

Balance, December 31, Year 1 ............................................ $ 1,000 Cr.
Unrealized Holding Gain on Securities Sold ........................ (6,000) Dr.
Change in Net Unrealized Loss on Securities Held at
    Year End ($3,000 – $3,000 + $5,000)............................. 5,000 Cr.
Balance, December 31, Year 2 ............................................ $ --

11.41    (Rice Corporation; journal entries and financial statement presentation of long-term securities available for sale.)

   a.  **3/05/Year 1**

| | | |
|---|---|---|
| Investments in Securities (Security A)..................... | 40,000 | |
|     Cash ................................................................ | | 40,000 |

**5/12/Year 1**

| | | |
|---|---|---|
| Investments in Securities (Security B).................... | 80,000 | |
|     Cash ................................................................ | | 80,000 |

**12/31/Year 1**

| | | |
|---|---|---|
| Investments in Securities (Security A) | | |
|     ($45,000 – $40,000)............................................. | 5,000 | |
|       Unrealized Holding Gain on Security A | | |
|         Available for Sale (SE/Comp Y)................... | | 5,000 |

**12/31/Year 1**

| | | |
|---|---|---|
| Unrealized Holding Loss on Security B Available | | |
|     for Sale (SE/Comp Y)........................................... | 10,000 | |
|       Investments in Securities (Security B) | | |
|         ($70,000 – $80,000)....................................... | | 10,000 |

11.41 a. continued.

**3/22/Year 2**

| | | |
|---|---|---|
| Investments in Securities (Security C) | 32,000 | |
|   Cash | | 32,000 |

**5/25/Year 2**

| | | |
|---|---|---|
| Investments in Securities (Security D) | 17,000 | |
|   Cash | | 17,000 |

**5/25/Year 2**

| | | |
|---|---|---|
| Investments in Securities (Security E) | 63,000 | |
|   Cash | | 63,000 |

**10/05/Year 2**

| | | |
|---|---|---|
| Cash | 52,000 | |
|   Investments in Securities (Security A) | | 40,000 |
|   Realized Gain on Sale of Securities Available for Sale (IncSt) | | 12,000 |
| | | |
| Unrealized Holding Gain on Security A Available for Sale (SE/Comp Y) | 5,000 | |
|   Investments in Securities (Security A) | | 5,000 |

**10/05/Year 2**

| | | |
|---|---|---|
| Cash | 15,000 | |
| Realized Loss on Sale of Securities Available for Sale (IncSt) | 2,000 | |
|   Investments in Securities (Security D) | | 17,000 |

**12/31/Year 2**

| | | |
|---|---|---|
| Investments in Securities (Security B) ($83,000 − $70,000) | 13,000 | |
|   Unrealized Holding Loss on Security B Available for Sale (SE/Comp Y) | | 10,000 |
|   Unrealized Holding Gain on Security B Available for Sale (SE/Comp Y) | | 3,000 |

**12/31/Year 2**

| | | |
|---|---|---|
| Unrealized Holding Loss on Security C Available for Sale (SE/Comp Y) ($27,000 − $32,000) | 5,000 | |
|   Investments in Securities (Security C) | | 5,000 |

**12/31/Year 2**

| | | |
|---|---|---|
| Investments in Securities (Security E) ($67,000 − $63,000) | 4,000 | |
|   Unrealized Holding Gain on Security E Available for Sale (SE/Comp Y) | | 4,000 |

**11.41 continued.**

b. **Balance Sheet on December 31, Year 1**

Investments in Securities at Market Value............................ $ 115,000

Net Unrealized Holding Loss on Securities Available for
Sale ($5,000 – $10,000)......................................................... $ (5,000)

*Footnote*

Investments in Securities on December 31, Year 1 had an acquisition cost of $120,000 and a market value of $115,000. Gross unrealized gains total $5,000 and gross unrealized losses total $10,000.

c. **Balance Sheet on December 31, Year 2**

Investments in Securities at Market Value............................ $ 177,000

Net Unrealized Holding Gain on Securities Available for
Sale..................................................................................... $ 2,000

*Footnote*

Investments in Securities on December 31, Year 2 had an acquisition cost of $175,000 and a market value of $177,000. Gross unrealized gains total $7,000 (= $3,000 + $4,000) and gross unrealized losses total $5,000. Proceeds from sales of investments in securities totaled $67,000 during Year 2. These sales resulted in gross realized gains of $12,000 and gross realized losses of $2,000. The net unrealized holding loss on securities available for sale changed as follows during Year 2:

Balance, December 31, Year 1 ............................................. $ (5,000) Dr.
Unrealized Holding Gain on Securities Sold ....................... (5,000) Dr.
Change in Net Unrealized Loss on Securities Held at
Year End ($13,000 – $5,000 + $4,000)............................ 12,000 Cr.
Balance, December 31, Year 2 ............................................ $ 2,000 Cr.

11.42 (Zeff Corporation; reconstructing transactions involving short-term securities available for sale.)

| Cash | | Marketable Securities | |
|---|---|---|---|
| | | √ 187,000 | |
| (1) 14,000 | | | 10,000 (1) |
| | | (2) 1,000 | 3,000 (1) |
| | 20,000 (3) | (3) 20,000 | |
| | | √ 195,000 | |

11.42 continued.

| Net Unrealized Holding Gain on Securities Available for Sale | | Realized Gain on Sale of Securities Available for Sale | |
|---|---|---|---|
| | 12,000  √ | | |
| (1)        3,000 | | | 4,000 (1) |
| | 1,000 (2) | | |
| | 10,000  √ | | 4,000  √ |

    (1)  Sale of marketable securities during Year 2.
    (2)  Revaluation of marketable securities on December 31, Year 2.
    (3)  Purchase of marketable securities during Year 2.

11.43    (Sunshine Mining Company; analysis of financial statement disclosures for securities available for sale.) (Amounts in Thousands)

    a.  $10,267 loss = $11,418 − $21,685.

    b.  $2,649 gain = $8,807 − $6,158.

    c.  $12,459 = $21,685 − $6,158 − $3,068.

    d.  None.  The unrealized holding loss on current marketable securities of $2,466 (= $4,601 − $7,067) and the unrealized holding gain on noncurrent marketable securities of $2,649 (= $8,807 − $6,158) appear in the shareholders' equity section of the balance sheet.

11.44    (Callahan Corporation; effect of various methods of accounting for marketable equity securities.)

    a.  **Trading Securities**

| | Year 1 | Year 2 |
|---|---|---|
| Income Statement: | | |
| Dividend Revenue | $ 3,300 | $  2,200 |
| Unrealized Holding Gain (Loss): | | |
| ($54,000 − $55,000) | (1,000) | -- |
| ($15,000 − $14,000) | -- | 1,000 |
| Realized Holding Gain (Loss) ($14,500 + $26,000) − ($16,000 + $24,000) | -- | 500 |
| Total | $ 2,300 | $ 3,700 |
| Balance Sheet: | | |
| Current Assets: | | |
| Marketable Securities at Market Value | $54,000 | $ 15,000 |

11.44 continued.

b. **Securities Available for Sale (Current Asset)**

| | Year 1 | Year 2 |
|---|---|---|
| Income Statement: | | |
| Dividend Revenue | $ 3,300 | $ 2,200 |
| Realized Holding Gain (Loss): [$40,500 – | | |
| ($18,000 + $25,000)] | -- | (2,500) |
| Total | $ 3,300 | $ (300) |
| Balance Sheet: | | |
| Current Assets: | | |
| Marketable Securities at Market Value | $54,000 | $ 15,000 |
| Shareholders' Equity: | | |
| Net Unrealized Holding Gain (Loss) on Se- | | |
| curities Available for Sale (Comp Y): | | |
| ($54,000 – $55,000) | (1,000) | -- |
| ($15,000 – $12,000) | -- | 3,000 |

c. Same as Part *b.* except that the securities appear as Investments in Securities in the noncurrent assets section of the balance sheet.

d.

| | Trading Securities | Securities Available for Sale | |
|---|---|---|---|
| | | Current Assets | Noncurrent Assets |
| Year 1 | $ 2,300 | $ 3,300 | $ 3,300 |
| Year 2 | 3,700 | (300) | (300) |
| Total | $ 6,000 | $ 3,000 | $ 3,000 |

The unrealized gain on Security I of $3,000 (= $15,000 – $12,000) at the end of Year 2 appears in income if these securities are trading securities but in a separate shareholders' equity account if these securities are securities available for sale (either a current asset or a noncurrent asset). Total shareholders' equity is the same. Retained earnings (pretax) are $3,000 larger if these securities are trading securities and the unrealized holding gain account is $3,000 larger if these securities are classified as securities available for sale.

11.45 (Citibank; analysis of financial statement disclosures related to marketable securities.) (Amounts in Millions)

a.

| | | |
|---|---|---|
| Cash | 37,600 | |
| Realized Loss on Sale of Securities Available for Sale (IncSt) | 113 | |
| Realized Gain on Securities Available for Sale (IncSt) | | 443 |
| Marketable Securities | | 37,270[a] |

[a]$14,075 + $37,163 – $13,968 = $37,270.

11.45 a. continued.

| | | |
|---|---|---|
| Marketable Securities.......................................... | 262 | |
|     Unrealized Holding Loss on Securities Available for Sale ($37,270 − $37,008) (SE/Comp Y) ....................................................... | | 262 |

b. Balance, December 31, Year 10 ($957 − $510) ................. $ 447 Cr.
   Net Unrealized Holding Loss on Securities Sold (from Part a.)........................................................ 262 Cr.
   Increase in Net Unrealized Holding Gain on Securities Held on December 31, Year 11 (Plug)............................. <u>518</u> Cr.
   Balance, December 31, Year 11 ($1,445 − $218).............. <u>$ 1,227</u> Cr.

c. Interest and Dividend Revenue ........................................ $ 1,081
   Net Realized Gain on Securities Sold from Market Price Changes Occurring During Year 11: ($37,600 − $37,008)................................................. 592
   Net Unrealized Holding Gain on Securities Held on December 31, Year 11 (from Part b.) ............................. <u>518</u>
   Total Income ......................................................... <u>$ 2,191</u>

d. Citibank sold marketable securities during Year 11 which had net unrealized holding losses of $262 million as of December 31, Year 10. The sale of these securities at a gain suggests that market prices increased substantially ($592 million) during Year 11. The substantial increase in the net unrealized holding gain of $518 lends support to this conclusion about market price increases. Citibank could have increased its income still further by selecting securities for sale that had unrealized holding *gains* as of December 31, Year 10. If prices continued to increase on such securities during Year 11 prior to sale, the realized gain would have been even larger than the reported net realized gain of $330 million (= $443 − $113).

11.46 (Using contra and adjunct accounts for securities available for sale.)

a. **End of Year 1**

| | | |
|---|---|---|
| Current Asset Contra/Adjunct.................................... | 200 | |
|     Owners' Equity Contra/Adjunct (Unrealized Gains on Holdings of Securities Available for Sale) (Comp Y)............................................... | | 200 |

**End of Year 2**

| | | |
|---|---|---|
| Cash................................................................. | 120 | |
| Owners' Equity Contra/Adjunct (Unrealized Gains on Holdings of Securities Available for Sale) (Comp Y)............................................... | 350 | |
|     Marketable Securities..................................... | | 100 |
|     Realized Gain on Sale of Securities Available for Sale........................................................ | | 20 |
|     Marketable Securities Contra/Adjunct............ | | 350 |

11.46 continued.

b. One does not have to keep track of the individual holding gains and losses on each separate security. Rather, at the end of the period, one computes the market value of the securities on hand, their acquisition cost and subtracts the second from the first. If the number is positive, then that number represents a cumulative holding gain and will be the required debit balance in both the asset contra/adjunct account and in the owners' equity contra/adjunct account. (If the difference is negative, then the absolute value of the number will be the required credit balance in those accounts.) The adjusting entry then merely adjusts the existing balance in the account to the required balance. The student need keep track only of the original cost of the securities held as available for sale.

11.47 (Rockwell Corporation; journal entries and consolidation work sheet entries for various methods of accounting for intercorporate investments.)

a.

| | | |
|---|---|---|
| Investment in Stock of Company R...................... | 648,000 | |
| Cash ............................................................ | | 648,000 |
| To record acquisitions of shares of Company R. | | |

| | | |
|---|---|---|
| Cash and Dividends Receivable................................. | 48,000 | |
| Dividend Revenue ................................................ | | 48,000 |
| To record dividends received or receivable. | | |

| | | |
|---|---|---|
| Unrealized Holding Loss on Investment in Securities (SE/Comp Y)............................................. | 24,000 | |
| Investment in Stock of Company R................. | | 24,000 |
| To write down investment in stock of Company R account to market value; $24,000 = $648,000 − $624,000. | | |

b.

| | | |
|---|---|---|
| Investment in Stock of Company S.......................... | 2,040,000 | |
| Cash ............................................................ | | 2,040,000 |
| To record acquisitions of shares of Company S. | | |

| | | |
|---|---|---|
| Investment in Stock of Company S.......................... | 360,000 | |
| Equity in Earnings of Company S.......................... | | 360,000 |
| To accrue share of Company S's earnings; $360,000 = .30 × $1,200,000. | | |

| | | |
|---|---|---|
| Cash and Dividends Receivable................................. | 144,000 | |
| Investment in Stock of Company S .................... | | 144,000 |
| To record dividends received or receivable. | | |

11.47 continued.

c.  Investment in Stock of Company T.......................... 6,000,000
    Cash ........................................................................ 6,000,000
    To record acquisitions of shares of Company T.

    Investment in Stock of Company T.......................... 1,200,000
       Equity in Earnings of Company T........................ 1,200,000
    To accrue earnings of Company T; $1,200,000 =
    100% × $1,200,000.

    Cash and Dividends Receivable................................ 480,000
       Investment in Stock of Company T ..................... 480,000
    To record dividends received or receivable.

d.  Common Stock ........................................................... 2,400,000
    Retained Earnings ($3,600,000 – $480,000).......... 3,120,000
    Equity in Earnings of Company T ........................... 1,200,000
       Investment in Stock of Company T .................... 6,720,000
    To eliminate investment account on consolidation
    work sheet.

e.  Common Stock ........................................................... 2,400,000
    Retained Earnings ($3,600,000 + $1,200,000 –
      $480,000)................................................................ 4,320,000
        Investment in Stock of Company T ............... 6,720,000
    To eliminate investment account on consolidation
    work sheet.

f.  Investment in Stock of Company T.......................... 6,600,000
    Cash ........................................................................ 6,600,000
    To record acquisitions of shares of Company T.

    Investment in Stock of Company T.......................... 1,200,000
       Equity in Earnings of Company T........................ 1,200,000
    To accrue earnings of Company T.

    Cash and Dividends Receivable................................ 480,000
       Investment in Stock of Company T ..................... 480,000
    To record dividends received or receivable.

    Amortization Expense............................................... 60,000
       Investment in Stock of Company T ..................... 60,000
    To record amortization of patent; $60,000 =
    $300,000/5.

11.47 continued.

g. 

| | | |
|---|---|---|
| Common Stock | 2,400,000 | |
| Retained Earnings ($3,600,000 – $480,000) | 3,120,000 | |
| Equity in Earnings of Company T | 1,200,000 | |
| Patent ($300,000 – $60,000) | 240,000 | |
| Goodwill | 300,000 | |
|     Investment in Stock of Company T | | 7,260,000 |

To eliminate investment account on consolidation work sheet; $7,260,000 = $6,600,000 + $1,200,000 – $480,000 – $60,000.

11.48 (Peak Company and Valley Company; preparing a consolidation work sheet.)

a. See next page.

b. 

| | |
|---|---|
| Initial Investment | $ 70 |
| Plus Equity in Earnings of Valley | 10 |
| Minus Dividends Received from Valley | (4) |
| Minus Amortization of Patent ($20,000/10) | (2) |
| Book Value of Investment Account—End of Year | $ 74 |

c. 

| | | |
|---|---|---|
| Common Stock (Valley) | 5 | |
| Retained Earnings (Valley) | 41 | |
| Equity in Earnings of Valley Company (Peak) | 10 | |
| Patent (= $20,000 – 1/10 × $20,000) | 18 | |
|     Investment in Stock of Valley Company (Peak) | | 74 |

Initial Goodwill was $20,000 = $70,000 – $50,000.

11.48 continued.

a.

# PEAK COMPANY AND VALLEY COMPANY
## Consolidation Work Sheet
### (Amounts in Thousands)

| | Peak Company Debit | Peak Company Credit | Valley Company Debit | Valley Company Credit | Adjustments and Eliminations Debit | Adjustments and Eliminations Credit | Consolidated Debit | Consolidated Credit |
|---|---|---|---|---|---|---|---|---|
| Cash | $ 13 | | $ 6 | | | | $ 19 | |
| Accounts Receivable | 42 | | 20 | | | $ 8 (2) | 54 | |
| Investment in Stock of Valley Company | 56 | | -- | | | 56 (1) | -- | |
| Other Assets | 143 | | 85 | | | | 228 | |
| Cost of Goods Sold | 320 | | 90 | | | | 410 | |
| Selling and Administrative Expenses | 44 | | 20 | | | | 64 | |
| Income Tax Expense | 12 | | 5 | | | | 17 | |
| Accounts Payable | | $ 80 | | $ 25 | (2) $ 8 | | | $ 97 |
| Bonds Payable | | 50 | | 30 | | | | 80 |
| Common Stock | | 10 | | 5 | (1) 5 | | | 10 |
| Retained Earnings | | 80 | | 41 | (1) 41 | | | 80 |
| Sales Revenue | | 400 | | 125 | | | | 525 |
| Equity in Earnings | | 10 | | -- | (1) 10 | | | -- |
| Totals | $ 630 | $ 630 | $ 226 | $ 226 | $ 64 | $ 64 | $ 792 | $ 792 |

(1) To eliminate the investment account.
(2) To eliminate intercompany receivables and payables.

## 11.49 (Company P and Company S; preparing a consolidation work sheet.)

a.

**COMPANY P AND COMPANY S**
**Consolidation Work Sheet**
**(Amounts in Thousands)**

| | Company P Debit | Company P Credit | Company S Debit | Company S Credit | Adjustments and Eliminations Debit | Adjustments and Eliminations Credit | Consolidated Debit | Consolidated Credit |
|---|---|---|---|---|---|---|---|---|
| Receivables | $ 60 | | $ 40 | | | $ 12 (3) | $ 88 | |
| Investment in Stock of Company S | 272 | | -- | | | 272 (1) | -- | |
| Other Assets | 496 | | 352 | | | | 848 | |
| Cost of Goods Sold | 1,160 | | 496 | | | 40 (2) | 1,616 | |
| Other Expenses | 280 | | 112 | | | | 392 | |
| Accounts Payable | | $ 72 | | $ 48 | (3) $ 12 | | | $ 108 |
| Other Liabilities | | 88 | | 72 | | | | 160 |
| Common Stock | | 160 | | 80 | (1) 80 | | | 160 |
| Retained Earnings | | 316 | | 160 | (1) 160 | | | 316 |
| Sales Revenue | | 1,600 | | 640 | (2) 40 | | | 2,200 |
| Equity in Earnings of Company S | | 32 | | -- | (1) 32 | | | -- |
| Totals | $ 2,268 | $ 2,268 | $ 1,000 | $ 1,000 | $ 324 | $ 324 | $ 2,944 | $ 2,944 |

(1) Eliminate investment account.
(2) Eliminate intercompany sales.
(3) Eliminate intercompany receivables and payables.

11.49 continued.

b.

**COMPANY P AND COMPANY S**
**Consolidated Statement of Income**
**and Retained Earnings**
**For Year 2**

| | |
|---|---|
| Sales Revenue.................................................................................... | $ 2,200,000 |
| Expenses: | |
| Cost of Goods Sold ....................................................................... | $ 1,616,000 |
| Other Expenses............................................................................. | 392,000 |
| Total.................................................................................... | $ 2,008,000 |
| Net Income....................................................................................... | $ 192,000 |
| Less Dividends Declared ................................................................. | (40,000) |
| Increase in Retained Earnings for Year 2 ..................................... | $ 152,000 |
| Retained Earnings, December 31, Year 1 ...................................... | 356,000[a] |
| Retained Earnings, December 31, Year 2 ...................................... | $ 508,000 |

[a]$316,000 retained earnings on December 31, Year 2 + $40,000 dividend declared during year 2.

**COMPANY P AND COMPANY S**
**Consolidated Balance Sheet**
**December 31, Year 2**

Assets

| | |
|---|---|
| Receivables....................................................................................... | $ 88,000 |
| Other Assets .................................................................................... | 848,000 |
| Total............................................................................................ | $ 936,000 |

Equities

| | |
|---|---|
| Accounts Payable ............................................................................ | $ 108,000 |
| Other Liabilities.............................................................................. | 160,000 |
| Common Stock ................................................................................. | 160,000 |
| Retained Earnings........................................................................... | 508,000 |
| Total............................................................................................ | $ 936,000 |

**11.50** (Ely Company and Sims Company; preparing a consolidation work sheet.)

## ELY COMPANY AND SIMS COMPANY
### Consolidation Work Sheet
#### (Amounts in Thousands)

| | Ely Company Debit | Ely Company Credit | Sims Company Debit | Sims Company Credit | Adjustments and Eliminations Debit | Adjustments and Eliminations Credit | Consolidated Debit | Consolidated Credit |
|---|---|---|---|---|---|---|---|---|
| Cash......................... | $ 12,000 | | $ 5,000 | | | | $ 17,000 | |
| Accounts Receivable...... | 25,000 | | 15,000 | | | $ 7,500 (2) | 32,500 | |
| Investment in Sims Company Stock............. | 80,000 | | -- | | | 80,000 (1) | | |
| Other Assets................ | 85,000 | | 80,000 | | | | 165,000 | |
| Goodwill .................... | -- | | -- | | (1) $20,000 | | 20,000 | |
| Current Liabilities......... | | $ 45,000 | | $ 40,000 | (2) 7,500 | | | $ 77,500 |
| Common Stock............. | | 50,000 | | 10,000 | (1) 10,000 | | | 50,000 |
| Retained Earnings ........ | | 107,000 | | 50,000 | (1) 50,000 | | | 107,000 |
| Totals .................. | $202,000 | $202,000 | $100,000 | $100,000 | $87,500 | $87,500 | $234,500 | $234,500 |

(1) Eliminate investment account.
(2) Eliminate intercompany obligations.

11.51 (Company S and Company J; preparing a consolidation work sheet subsequent to year of acquisition.)

## COMPANY S AND COMPANY J
### Consolidation Work Sheet
### December 31, Year 2
### (Amounts in Thousands)

| | Company S Debit | Company S Credit | Company J Debit | Company J Credit | Adjustments and Eliminations Debit | Adjustments and Eliminations Credit | Consolidated Debit | Consolidated Credit |
|---|---|---|---|---|---|---|---|---|
| Cash | $ 36.00 | | $ 26.00 | | | | $ 62.00 | |
| Accounts and Notes Receivable | 180.00 | | 50.00 | | | $ 16.40 (2) | 213.60 | |
| Inventories | 440.00 | | 250.00 | | | | 690.00 | |
| Investment in Stock of Company J | 726.00 | | -- | | | 726.00 (1) | -- | |
| Plant Assets | 600.00 | | 424.00 | | | | 1,024.00 | |
| Accounts and Notes Payable | | $ 110.00 | | $ 59.00 | (2) $ 16.40 | | | $ 152.60 |
| Other Liabilities | | 286.00 | | 22.00 | | | | 308.00 |
| Common Stock | | 1,200.00 | | 500.00 | (1) 500.00 | | | 1,200.00 |
| Capital Contributed in Excess of Stated Value | | -- | | 100.00 | (1) 100.00 | | | |
| Retained Earnings | | 386.00 | | 69.00 | (1) 69.00 | | | 386.00 |
| Patent | | | | | (1) 57.00 | | 57.00 | |
| Totals | $1,982.00 | $1,982.00 | $ 750.00 | $ 750.00 | $ 742.40 | $ 742.40 | $2,046.60 | $2,046.60 |

(1) Eliminate investment account; all amounts given except plug for Patent.
(2) Eliminate intercompany obligations.

**11.52** (Hatfield Corporation and McCoy Corporation; effect of the purchase method on financial statements.)

a. **HATFIELD CORPORATION AND McCOY CORPORATION**
**Consolidated Balance Sheet**
**January 1, Year 8**

|  | Purchase Method |
|---|---|
| Assets at Historical Cost | $ 3,500 |
| Asset Revaluation | 400 |
| Goodwill | 200 |
| Total Assets | $ 4,100 |
| Liabilities | $ 1,500 |
| Common Stock ($1 Par) | 150[a] |
| Additional Paid-in Capital | 1,750[b] |
| Retained Earnings | 700 |
| Total Equities | $ 4,100 |

[a]$100,000 + (50,000 X $1) = $150,000.
[b]$400,000 + (50,000 X $27) = $1,750,000.

b. **HATFIELD CORPORATION AND McCOY CORPORATION**
**Consolidated Income Statement**
**First Year After Merger**

|  | Purchase Method |
|---|---|
| Sales | $ 14,000 |
| Other Revenues | 125 |
| Total Revenues | $ 14,125 |
| Expenses Except Income Taxes | (11,125) |
| Taxable Income | $ 3,000 |
| Tax Expense at 40% | (1,200) |
| Amortization of Increased Asset Costs | (80)[a] |
| Net Income | $ 1,720 |

[a]$400,000/5 = $80,000.

11.53   (Coke and Pepsi; effect of intercorporate investment policies on financial statements.)

a.   Coke as Reported:   [$1,364 + (1 − .34)($231)]/$9,280 = 16.3%.
     Coke's Bottlers:     [$290 + (1 − .34)($452)]/$11,110 = 5.3%.
     Coke and Bottlers
        Consolidated:     [$1,364 + (1 − .34)($231 + $452) +
                          .51($290)]/$18,675 = 10.5%.

     Pepsi as Reported:  [$1,091 + (1 − .34)($689)/$15,637 = 9.9%.

b.   Coke as Reported:   ($4,296 + $1,133)/$9,280 = 58.5%.
     Coke's Bottlers:     ($2,752 + $4,858)/$11,110 = 68.5%.
     Coke and Bottlers
        Consolidated:     ($7,048 + $5,991)/$18,675 = 69.8%.

     Pepsi as Reported:  ($3,264 + $7,469)/$15,637 = 68.6%.

c.   The rate of return on assets using reported amounts suggests that Coke is considerably more profitable than Pepsi. This measure of the rate of return on assets includes Coke's 49 percent interest in the earnings of its bottlers but does not include Coke's 49 percent interest in the assets of these bottlers. Coke's rate of return on assets with its bottlers consolidated includes 100 percent of the net income and assets of these bottlers. Thus, Coke appears only slightly more profitable than Pepsi during Year 11.

     Coke's liabilities to assets ratio is less than the corresponding ratio for its bottlers. On a comparable measurement basis with Pepsi, Coke has slightly more debt in its capital structure instead of approximately 14.7 percent less debt as indicated by the reported amounts [14.7% = (68.6% − 58.5%)/68.6%].

d.   Coke's intercorporate investment policy permits it to report higher profitability and lower debt ratios than if it held a sufficient ownership percentage to consolidate its bottlers. Coke's 49 percent ownership probably permits it to exert control over its bottlers because (1) the remaining 51 percent is widely-held by many individuals and institutions, and (2) Coke maintains exclusive contracts with its bottlers that tie their success to Coke's success. Thus, one might argue that consolidation reflects the economic reality of the relationship better than use of the equity method.

11.54  (Agee Electronics; preparing statement of cash flows.)  A T-account work sheet appears on the page following the statement of cash flows.

## AGEE ELECTRONICS
### Statement of Cash Flows
### For Year 5

| | |
|---|---:|
| **Operations:** | |
| Net Income | $ 320 |
| Depreciation Expense | 350 |
| Bad Debt Expense | 45 |
| Loss on Sale of Investments in Securities | 40 |
| Gain on Sale of Marketable Securities | (30) |
| Gain on Sale of Equipment | (40) |
| Decrease in Inventories | 50 |
| Increase in Other Current Liabilities | 110 |
| Increase in Accounts Receivable | (235) |
| Increase in Prepayments | (50) |
| Decrease in Accounts Payable | (30) |
| Cash Flow from Operations | $ 530 |
| **Investing:** | |
| Sale of Marketable Securities | $ 145 |
| Sale of Investments in Securities | 70 |
| Sale of Equipment | 80 |
| Acquisition of Marketable Securities | (125) |
| Acquisition of Property, Plant and Equipment | (480) |
| Cash Flow from Investing | $ (310) |
| **Financing:** | |
| Income in Bank Borrowing | $ 60 |
| Issue of Common Stock | 60 |
| Payment of Dividends | (285) |
| Cash Flow from Financing | $ (165) |
| Change in Cash | $ 55 |
| Cash, December 31, Year 4 | 130 |
| Cash, December 31, Year 5 | $ 185 |

11.54 continued.

### Cash

| | | | | | |
|---|---|---|---|---|---|
| √ | 130 | | | | |

#### Operations

| | | | | | |
|---|---|---|---|---|---|
| Net Income | (1) | 320 | 30 | (4) | Gain on Sale of Marketable Securities |
| Bad Debt Expense | (7) | 45 | | | |
| Loss on Investment in Securities | (8) | 40 | 40 | (11) | Gain on Sale of Equipment |
| Decrease in Inventories | (15) | 50 | 235 | (14) | Increase in Accounts Receivable |
| Depreciation | (19) | 350 | | | |
| Increase of Current Liabilities | (22) | 110 | 50 | (16) | Increase in Prepayments |
| | | | 30 | (20) | Decrease in Accounts Payable |

#### Investing

| | | | | | |
|---|---|---|---|---|---|
| | | | 125 | (13) | Purchase of Marketable Securities |
| Sale of Marketable Securities | (4) | 145 | | | |
| Sale of Investments | (8) | 70 | | | |
| Sale of Equipment | (11) | 80 | 480 | (18) | Purchase of PP&E |

#### Financing

| | | | | | |
|---|---|---|---|---|---|
| Bank Loan | (21) | 60 | 285 | (3) | Dividend Paid |
| Issue Common Stock | (23) | 60 | | | |
| √ | 185 | | | | |

| Marketable Securities | | Accounts Receivable | | Allowance for Uncollectible Accounts | |
|---|---|---|---|---|---|
| √ 270 | | √ 770 | | | 40 √ |
| | 115 (4) | | 35 (6) | (6) 35 | 45 (7) |
| (12) 15 | 5 (5) | (14) 235 | | | |
| (13) 125 | | | | | |
| √ 290 | | √ 970 | | | 50 √ |

11.54 continued.

| Inventories | | Prepayments | | Investments in Securities | |
|---|---|---|---|---|---|
| √ 620 | | √ 120 | | √ 460 | |
| | 50(15) | (16) 50 | | (9) 40 | 110 (8) |
| | | | | | 10(17) |
| √ 570 | | √ 170 | | √ 380 | |

| Property, Plant and Equipment | | Accumulated Depreciation | | Accounts Payable | |
|---|---|---|---|---|---|
| √ 2,840 | | | 1,210 √ | | 490 √ |
| (10) 140 | 150(11) | (11) 110 | | | |
| (18) 480 | | | 350(19) | (20) 30 | |
| √ 3,310 | | | 1,450 √ | | 460 √ |

| Bank Loans Payable | | Dividends Payable | | Other Current Liabilities | |
|---|---|---|---|---|---|
| | 820 √ | | 60 √ | | 90 √ |
| | 60(21) | (3) 285 | 305 (2) | | 110(22) |
| | 880 √ | | 80 √ | | 200 √ |

| Long-Term Debt | | Common Stock | | Additional Paid-In Capital | |
|---|---|---|---|---|---|
| | 510 √ | | 100 √ | | 460 √ |
| | 140(10) | | 50(23) | | 10(23) |
| | 650 √ | | 150 √ | | 470 √ |

| Unrealized Holding Gain—Marketable Securities | | Unrealized Holding Loss—Investment in Securities | | Retained Earnings | |
|---|---|---|---|---|---|
| | 40 √ | √ 120 | | | 1,510 √ |
| (5) 5 | | | 40 (9) | (2) 305 | 320 (1) |
| | 15(12) | (17) 10 | | | |
| | 50 √ | √ 90 | | | 1,525 √ |

11.55    (Cherry Corporation; preparing a statement of cash flows.)

a.

### Cash

| √ 287,000 | |
|---|---|

#### Operations

| (1) | 496,000 | 144,000 | (4) |
|---|---|---|---|
| (2) | 5,000 | 7,000 | (6) |
| (5) | 9,000 | 100,000 | (15) |
| (7) | 1,200 | 162,000 | (16) |
| (10) | 3,000 | 17,000 | (20) |
| (14) | 4,000 | | |
| (17) | 66,600 | | |
| (19) | 100,000 | | |

#### Investing

| (6) | 46,000 | 72,000 | (3) |
|---|---|---|---|
| (7) | 3,200 | 81,000 | (8) |
| | | 15,000 | (9) |
| | | 10,000 | (18) |

#### Financing

| (21) | 54,000 | 17,000 | (13) |
|---|---|---|---|
| √ | 450,000 | | |

| Accounts Receivable—Net | | | | Inventories | | |
|---|---|---|---|---|---|---|
| √ | 550,000 | | | √ | 298,000 | |
| (15) | 100,000 | 5,000 | (2) | (16) | 162,000 | |
| √ | 645,000 | | | √ | 460,000 | |

| Investments—Roy Co. | | | | Investments—Zuber Co. | | |
|---|---|---|---|---|---|---|
| √ | 39,000 | | | √ | 0 | |
| | | 39,000 | (6) | (3) | 111,300 | |
| | | | | (4) | 144,000 | 9,000 | (5) |
| √ | 0 | | | √ | 246,300 | |

| Plant Assets | | | | Accumulated Depreciation | | |
|---|---|---|---|---|---|---|
| √ | 381,000 | | | | | 144,000 | √ |
| (8) | 81,000 | 22,000 | (7) | (7) | 17,600 | 66,600 | (17) |
| (9) | 15,000 | | | | | | |
| √ | 455,000 | | | | | 193,000 | √ |

11.55 a. continued.

| | Patents (Net) | | | | Dividends Payable | |
|---|---|---|---|---|---|---|
| √ | 19,000 | | | | 0 | √ |
| (18) | 10,000 | 3,000 | (10) | | 181,000 | (12) |
| √ | 26,000 | | | | 181,000 | √ |

| | Accounts Payable | | | | Accrued Liabilities | |
|---|---|---|---|---|---|---|
| | | 70,000 | √ | | 41,800 | √ |
| | | 100,000 | (19) | (20) | 17,000 | |
| | | 170,000 | √ | | 24,800 | √ |

| | Long-Term Bonds Payable | | | | Common Stock | |
|---|---|---|---|---|---|---|
| | | 133,000 | √ | | 700,000 | √ |
| (13) | 17,000 | 4,000 | (14) | | 24,000 | (3) |
| | | 54,000 | (21) | | 28,000 | (11) |
| | | 174,000 | √ | | 752,000 | √ |

| | Additional Paid-in Capital—Common | | | | Preferred Stock | |
|---|---|---|---|---|---|---|
| | | 9,600 | √ | | 53,000 | √ |
| | | 4,800 | (3) | | 7,000 | (3) |
| | | 5,000 | (11) | | | |
| | | 20,000 | √ | | 60,000 | √ |

| | Additional Paid-in Capital—Preferred | | | | Retained Earnings | |
|---|---|---|---|---|---|---|
| | | 2,500 | √ | | 420,100 | √ |
| | | 3,500 | (3) | (11) | 33,600 | 496,000 | (1) |
| | | | | (12) | 181,000 | | |
| | | 6,000 | √ | | 701,500 | √ |

11.55 a. continued.

**Explanation of entries in work sheet (not required):**

(1) Net income of $496,000.

(2) Bad debt expense of $5,000.

(3) Issue of preferred shares totaling $10,500 (= 3,500 × $3), issue of common shares totaling $28,800 (= 2,400 × $12), and expenditure of $72,000 cash in the acquisition of 45 percent of Zuber, $111,300 = $10,500 + $28,800 + $72,000.

(4) Share of earnings of Zuber; $144,000 (= .45 × $320,000).

(5) Reduce investment for dividends declared by Zuber; $9,000 (= .45 × $20,000).

(6) Gain on sale of Roy; $7,000 (= $46,000 − $39,000).

(7) Loss on sale of plant; $1,200 (= $22,000 − $17,600 − $3,200).

(8) Acquire new plant for $81,000.

(9) Acquire new plant (major improvements) for $15,000; plug in Plant Assets account.

(10) Amortization of patents; $3,000.

(11) Stock dividend; .04 × 70,000 × $12 = $33,600.

(12) Dividends declared; $181,000 (= $145,000 + $36,000).

(13) Retire bonds at book value.

(14) Amortization of bond discount of $4,000 does not use cash.

(15) Plug for net increase in receivables.

(16) Plug for net increase in inventories.

(17) Plug for net increase in accumulated depreciation; an addback for expense not using cash.

(18) Acquire new patents (net) for $10,000; plug in Patents (Net) account.

(19) Plug for net increase in accounts payable.

(20) Plug for net decrease in accrued liabilities.

(21) Plug for issue of new bonds.

11.55 continued.

b.

**CHERRY CORPORATION**
**Statement of Cash Flows**
**For Year 6**

| | | |
|---|---:|---:|
| Operations: | | |
| Net Income | $496,000 | |
| Additions: | | |
| Bad Debt Expense | 5,000 | |
| Loss on Sale of Plant Asset | 1,200 | |
| Amortization of Patent | 3,000 | |
| Amortization of Discount | 4,000 | |
| Depreciation Expense | 66,600 | |
| Increase in Accounts Payable | 100,000 | |
| Subtractions: | | |
| Equity in Undistributed Earnings | (135,000) | |
| Gain on Sale of Investment | (7,000) | |
| Increase in Accounts Receivable | (100,000) | |
| Increase in Inventories | (162,000) | |
| Decrease in Accrued Liabilities | (17,000) | |
| Cash Flow from Operations | | $254,800 |
| Investing: | | |
| Sale of Investment in Roy Company | $ 46,000 | |
| Sale of Plant Asset | 3,200 | |
| Acquisition of Investment in Zuber Company | (72,000) | |
| Acquisition of Plant Assets | (81,000) | |
| Major Repairs to Plant Assets | (15,000) | |
| Acquisition of Patent | (10,000) | |
| Cash Flow from Investing | | (128,800) |
| Financing: | | |
| Issue of Bonds | $ 54,000 | |
| Redemption of Bonds | (17,000) | |
| Cash Flow from Financing | | 37,000 |
| Net Change in Cash | | $ 163,000 |
| Cash, January 1, Year 6 | | 287,000 |
| Cash, December 31, Year 6 | | $ 450,000 |

**Supplementary Information**
During Year 6 Cheery Corporation acquired 45 percent of the common stock of Zuber Company for $111,300, comprising $72,000 cash, $10,500 of preferred stock, and $28,800 of common stock.

**11.56** (Interaction of regulation and accounting rules for financial institutions, particularly banks.)

### Effects of Changing Market Value of Assets on a Bank's Activities
Bank Has Capital Ratio of 5 Percent

Step [1]: Market Value of Assets Increases, Also Increasing Owners' Equity
Step [2]: Bank Increases Lending to Maintain Capital (Leverage) Ratio at 5 Percent
Step [3]: Market Value of Original Bank Decreases, Decreasing Owners' Equity
Step [4]: Bank Decreases Lending to Maintain Captial (Leverage) Ratio at 5 Percent
Operating Income Excludes Gains and Losses in Market Value of Assets Held

**Balance Sheet**

*Original Bank, Before Market Value Changes*

| Assets | | Equities | | Partial Income Statement | | Rate of Return On: | |
|---|---|---|---|---|---|---|---|
| | | | | Revenues as % of Assets | | | |
| $1,000 | Original | Liabilities: Borrowings.............. | $950 | 7.0% | $70.0 | | |
| | | | | Interest Expense 5.5% | (52.3) | | |
| | | Owners' Equity: | | Operating Expense % of Assets | | | |
| | | Contributed Capital.. | 50 | 0.4% | (4.0) | | |
| | | Retained Earnings.... | 0 | | | | |
| | | Total Owners' Equity | $50 | Fixed costs......... | (1.0) | Assets.... | 1.3% |
| $1,000 | Totals | | $1,000 | Operating Income | $12.8 | Owners' Equity.. | 25.5% |

*Market Value of Assets Increases*   4.0%

| Assets | | Equities | | Partial Income Statement | | Rate of Return On: | |
|---|---|---|---|---|---|---|---|
| | | | | Revenues as % of Assets | | | |
| $1,000 | Original | Liabilities: Original Borrowings | $950 | 7.0% | $126.0 | | |
| [1] 40 | Market Value Increase | | | Interest Expense 5.5% | (94.1) | | |
| [2] 760 | New Lending | [2] New Borrowing........ | 760 | Operating Expense % of Assets | | | |
| | | Owners' Equity: | | 0.4% | (7.2) | | |
| | | Contributed Capital | 50 | Fixed costs......... | (1.0) | | |
| | | [1] Retained Earnings.... | 40 | | | | |
| | | Total Owners' Equity | $90 | | | Assets.... | 1.3% |
| $1,800 | Totals | | $1,800 | Operating Income | $23.8 | Owners' Equity.. | 26.4% |

*Market Value of Assets Decreases*   -4.0%

| Assets | | Equities | | Partial Income Statement | | Rate of Return On: | |
|---|---|---|---|---|---|---|---|
| | | | | Revenues as % of Assets | | | |
| $1,000 | Original | Liabilities: Original Borrowings | $950 | 7.0% | $14.00 | | |
| [3] (40) | Market Value Decline | | | Interest Expense 5.5% | ($10.45) | | |
| [4] (760) | Reduce Lending | [4] Reduce Borrowing.... | (760) | Operating Expense % of Assets | | | |
| | | Owners' Equity: | | 0.4% | ($0.80) | | |
| | | Contributed Capital | 50 | Fixed costs ........ | ($1.00) | | |
| | | [3] Retained Earnings.... | (40) | | | | |
| | | Total Owners' Equity | $10 | | | Assets ... | 0.9% |
| $200 | Totals | | $200 | Operating Income | $1.75 | Owners' Equity . | 17.5% |

# CHAPTER 12

## REPORTING EARNINGS, COMPREHENSIVE INCOME, AND SHAREHOLDERS' EQUITY

*Questions, Exercises, Problems, and Cases: Answers and Solutions*

12.1    See the text or the glossary at the end of the book.

12.2    The common shareholders would not likely receive an amount equal to the amounts in the common shareholders' equity accounts. The amounts in these accounts reflect acquisition cost valuations for assets. The firm might sell assets for more or less than their book values, with the common shareholders thereby receiving more or less than the amount in the common shareholders' equity accounts. Furthermore, the bankruptcy and liquidation process requires legal and other costs not now reflected on the balance sheet. The asset sales must generate sufficient cash to pay these costs before the common shareholders receive any residual cash.

12.3    Firms have issued securities in recent years (for example, convertible bonds and redeemable preferred stock) that have both debt and equity characteristics. A clear distinction between liabilities and shareholders' equity no longer exists. Firms might list various claims against a firm's assets in decreasing order of priority in the case of bankruptcy with no distinction between liabilities and shareholders' equity. Alternatively, firms might create a third category that includes securities with both debt and equity characteristics and include it between liabilities and shareholders' equity on the balance sheet.

12.4    The accounting for each of these transactions potentially involves transfers between contributed capital and retained earnings accounts and clouds the distinction between capital transactions and operating transactions. The market value method of accounting for stock options results in a reduction in net income and retained earnings and an increase in contributed capital. The accounting for stock dividends results in a reduction in retained earnings and an increased in contributed capital. The purchase of treasury stock represents a reduction in both contributed capital and accumulated earnings. The reissuance of treasury stock at a "loss" may result in a debit to both contributed capital and retained earnings. Thus, the Common Stock and Additional Paid-in Capital accounts do not reflect just capital transactions and Retained Earnings does not reflect just operating transactions.

12.5    The par value of preferred, rather than the amount contributed, serves as a basis for measuring the dividend rate and the amount of preference as to assets in event of liquidation. The par value of common stock may have legal significance in certain states, but it has no economic significance. Firms declare dividends based on the number of common shares outstanding, not on the par value of the common stock.

12.6    The three provisions provide different benefits and risks to the issuing firm and the investor and should sell at different prices. Callable preferred stock should sell for less than convertible preferred stock. The issuing firm gains benefits with an option to call, or repurchase, the preferred stock and must thereby accept a lower issue price. The investor gains benefits with an option to convert into capital stock and must pay a higher price. The mandatory redemption requirement makes the preferred stock more like debt than shareholders' equity. Its market price depends on market interest rates for similar maturity debt (versus the 4 percent yield on the preferred stock) and the rank-ordering priority of the preferred stock in bankruptcy.

12.7    The question addresses the tradeoff between relevance and reliability frequently encountered in accounting. Financial statement users desire information that helps them assess the economic value of firms. Information about the value of options is relevant information for this purpose. The measurement of the value of options is subject to varying degrees of subjectivity. Reliability decreases as subjectivity increases. Likewise, the usefulness of relevant information decreases as reliability decreases.

12.8    All three items permit their holder to acquire shares of common stock at a set price. Their values depend on the difference between the market price and the exercise price on the exercise date and the length of the exercise period. Firms grant stock options to employees, grant stock rights to current shareholders and either sell stock warrants on the open market or attach them to a debt or preferred stock issue. The issuance of stock options and stock rights does not result in an immediate cash inflow, whereas the issuance of a stock warrant usually does. Accountants credit a Stock Warrant account if the value of the stock warrant is objectively measurable. At the time of exercise of all these items, the accountant records the cash proceeds as a capital contribution.

12.9    The greater the volatility of the stock price, the larger is the potential excess of the market price over the exercise price on the exercise date and the greater the benefit to the employee. The longer the time between the grant date and the exercise date, the more time that elapses for the market price to increase. Offsetting the value of this increased benefit element is the longer time to realize the benefit, which reduces the present value of the option. Stock option valuation models discount the expected benefit element in a stock option to a present value. The larger the discount rate, the smaller is the present value of the benefit.

12.10   The theoretical rationale is matching expenses of employee compensation with the benefit received in the form of higher revenues from employees' services.

12.11   The response to this question requires tradeoffs between relevance and reliability. The market value method reflects the economic cost of stock options better than the APB Opinion 25 method. The latter method usually reports no expense for stock options. However, the market value method requires assumptions about the volatility of the stock, the expected time between the granting and exercise of options, and the discount rate. Management can make assumptions that can cause the cost of stock options to vary.

12.12   There are at least two issues here. First, the proposal gives management an opportunity to decide which income items are and are not likely to recur. Firms can manage earnings with their choice. Second, the proposal presumes that an analyst will not overlook certain income items that appear only in the statement of retained earnings. It also presumes that the firm will provide sufficient information about income items to judge for itself if it should be in earnings.

12.13   The FASB suggests that the distinction between performance-related (subject to significant influence by management) and non-performance-related (subject to external influences not controllable by management) items drives the exclusion. The real reason, however, we suspect, has to do with the volatility of some of the items of other comprehensive income. Including all holding gains and losses on securities held in earnings will cause reported earnings to fluctuate (in response to fluctuations in market prices) more than it would otherwise. Many, probably most, managers prefer to report stable earnings in contrast to fluctuating earnings. All else equal, the less risky the earnings stream—that is, the less volatile are reported earnings—the higher will be the market price of the firm's shares.

12.14   An error in previously-issued financial statements results from oversights or errors which the firm should not have made given reasonable diligence in accessing available information at the time. Accountants restate the previously-issued financial statements to correct the error. A change in an accounting estimate results from *new* information that suggests that the original estimate was inaccurate as judged *ex post*. Accountants adjust for changes in estimates during the current and future periods instead of restating previously-issued financial statements.

12.15   Yes. Earnings do not necessarily indicate the availability of idle cash funds for distribution. The corporation may have insufficient cash to meet maturing obligations, additional working capital requirements in connection with increasing accounts receivable and inventory replacement, replacements of equipment, or other such expenditures.

12.16   As the Retained Earnings account has grown, so has the firm's net assets. The firm has likely invested these assets in plant, not in cash and temporary marketable securities. The firm is unlikely to have cash in the amount of the increase in retained earnings available for paying dividends. If the firm had regularly declared stock dividends (to capitalize into the contributed capital accounts amounts permanently invested in plant assets), then the balance in the Retained Earnings account might better indicate the ability to pay cash dividends. But then, of course, the Retained Earnings account would have a smaller balance.

12.17   In the case of a cash dividend, the shareholder now holds the investment in two parts—cash and stock certificates. The sum of the cash and the book value of the stock after the dividend declaration equals the book value of the stock before the firm declared the dividend. It is common to speak of a cash dividend as income, but it is merely the conversion of a portion of the shareholder's investment into a different form. In a sense, the shareholder earns income on the investment when the corporation earns its income. Because of the realization test for income recognition in accounting, however, the shareholders do not recognize income (except under the equity method discussed in Chapter 11) until the firm distributes cash. A stock dividend does not even improve the marketability of the investment, although when a firm issues preferred shares to common shareholders or vice versa, shareholders may view the situation as similar to a cash dividend. The stock dividend capitalizes a portion of retained earnings.

12.18   The managers of a firm have knowledge of the plans and risks of the firm that external investors may not possess. Although laws prevent firms from taking advantage of this "inside information," inclusion of gains from treasury stock transactions in net income might motivate firms to buy and sell treasury stock to improve reported earnings. Excluding these gains from net income removes this incentive. Also, the accounting for the acquisition of treasury stock (that is, a reduction from total shareholders' equity) has the same effect on shareholders' equity as a retirement of the capital stock. The reissue of the treasury stock for more than its acquisition cost does not result in a gain any more than the issue of common stock for more than par value represents a gain.

12.19   Most firms acquire treasury stock with the intention of reissuing the stock upon the exercise of stock options or warrants or the conversion of debt or preferred stock into common stock. Thus, treasury stock typically does not remain as treasury stock for an extended period. The fallacy in this explanation is that firms destroy the stock certificates underlying shares purchased as treasury stock, the same as for retired stock, and issue new stock certificates to purchasers of the treasury stock, the same as for newly issued stock.

12.20   (Journal entries to record the issuance of capital stock.)

   a.   Cash (= 50,000 X $30)...................................... 1,500,000
            Common Stock (= 50,000 X $5)......................            250,000
            Additional Paid-in Capital (= 50,000 X $25)...         1,250,000

   b.   Cash (= 20,000 X $100).................................... 2,000,000
            Preferred Stock ...............................................         2,000,000

   c.   Patent (= 16,000 X $15)...................................    240,000
            Common Stock (= 16,000 X $10)..................            160,000
            Additional Paid-in Capital (= 16,000 X $5) .....             80,000

   d.   Convertible Preferred Stock.........................    400,000
            Common Stock (= 25,000 X $1)......................             25,000
            Additional Paid-in Capital (= $400,000 –
            $25,000)........................................................            375,000

   e.   Compensation Expense (= 5,000 X $12).............     60,000
            Common Stock (= 5,000 X $10)......................             50,000
            Additional Paid-in Capital (= 5,000 X $2)........             10,000

12.21   (Journal entries for the issuance of common stock.)

   a.   Inventory.......................................................    250,000
        Land ...............................................................    160,000
        Building..........................................................  1,200,000
        Equipment ......................................................    390,000
            Common Stock (= 40,000 X $15)....................            600,000
            Additional Paid-in Capital ...............................          1,400,000

   b.   Cash (= 10,000 X $50).....................................    500,000
            Redeemable Preferred Stock..........................            500,000

   c.   Cash (= 20,000 X $18)......................................    360,000
        Common Stock Warrants (= 20,000 X $2)........     40,000
            Common Stock (= 20,000 X $1)......................             20,000
            Additional Paid-in Capital ...............................            380,000

   d.   Preferred Stock (= 20,000 X $100) ..................... 2,000,000
            Common Stock (= 50,000 X $10)....................            500,000
            Additional Paid-in Capital ...............................          1,500,000

12.22   (Leonard Corporation; journal entries for employee stock options.)

   a.   **December 31, Year 3**
        Compensation Expense .................................     60,000
            Common Stock Options ..................................             60,000

12.22 a. continued.

**June 30, Year 5**

| | | |
|---|---|---|
| Cash (= 7,000 × $40)........................................ | 280,000 | |
| Common Stock Options [= (7,000/10,000) × $60,000]........................................ | 42,000 | |
|     Common Stock (= 7,000 × $10)...................... | | 70,000 |
|     Additional Paid-in Capital [= $42,000 + (7,000 × $30)]........................................ | | 252,000 |

**November 15, Year 6**

| | | |
|---|---|---|
| Cash (= 3,000 × $40)........................................ | 120,000 | |
| Common Stock Options [= (3,000/10,000) × $60,000]........................................ | 18,000 | |
|     Common Stock (= 3,000 × $10)...................... | | 30,000 |
|     Additional Paid-in Capital [= $18,000 + (3,000 × $30)]........................................ | | 108,000 |

b. **December 31, Year 3**
No entry.

**June 30, Year 5**

| | | |
|---|---|---|
| Cash (= 7,000 × $40)........................................ | 280,000 | |
|     Common Stock (= 7,000 × $10) ...................... | | 70,000 |
|     Additional Paid-in Capital (= 7,000 × $30).......... | | 210,000 |

**November 15, Year 6**

| | | |
|---|---|---|
| Cash (= 3,000 × $40)........................................ | 120,000 | |
|     Common Stock (= 3,000 × $10)...................... | | 30,000 |
|     Additional Paid-in Capital (= 3,000 × $30).......... | | 90,000 |

c. The market value method results in $60,000 less retained earnings and $60,000 more additional paid-in capital than the APB *Opinion 25* method, but total shareholders' equity increases by the cash received of $400,000 (= $280,000 + $120,000) in both cases.

12.23 (Watson Corporation; journal entries for employee stock options.)

a. **December 31, Year 6, Year 7, and Year 8**

| | | |
|---|---|---|
| Compensation Expense ............................................. | 25,000 | |
|     Common Stock Options ....................................... | | 25,000 |

**April 30, Year 9**

| | | |
|---|---|---|
| Cash (= 15,000 × $25)............................................. | 375,000 | |
| Common Stock Options [= (15,000/20,000) × $75,000]........................................ | 56,250 | |
|     Common Stock (= 15,000 × $10) ...................... | | 150,000 |
|     Additional Paid-in Capital [= $56,250 + (15,000 × $15)]........................................ | | 281,250 |

12.23 a. continued.

**September 15, Year 10**

| | | |
|---|---|---|
| Cash (= 5,000 × $25) | 125,000 | |
| Common Stock Options [= (5,000/20,000) × | | |
|    $75,000] | 18,750 | |
|       Common Stock (= 5,000 × $10) | | 50,000 |
|       Additional Paid-in Capital [= $18,750 + | | |
|         (5,000 × $15)] | | 93,750 |

b. **December 31, Year 6, Year 7, and Year 8**
No entry.

**April 30, Year 9**

| | | |
|---|---|---|
| Cash (= 15,000 × $25) | 375,000 | |
|    Common Stock (= 15,000 × $10) | | 150,000 |
|    Additional Paid-in Capital (= 15,000 × $15) | | 225,000 |

**September 15, Year 10**

| | | |
|---|---|---|
| Cash (= 5,000 × $25) | 125,000 | |
|    Common Stock (= 5,000 × $10) | | 50,000 |
|    Additional Paid-in Capital (= 5,000 × $15) | | 75,000 |

c. The market value method results in $75,000 less retained earnings and $75,000 more additional paid-in capital than the APB *Opinion 25* method, but total shareholders' equity increases by the cash received of $500,000 (= $375,000 + $125,000) in both cases.

12.24 (Haskins Corporation; journal entries for stock warrants.)

**February 26, Year 6**

| | | |
|---|---|---|
| Cash | 120,000 | |
|    Common Stock Warrants (= 40,000 × $3) | | 120,000 |

**June 6, Year 7**

| | | |
|---|---|---|
| Cash (= 30,000 × $40) | 1,200,000 | |
| Common Stock Warrants (= 30,000 × $3) | 90,000 | |
|    Common Stock (= 30,000 × $5) | | 150,000 |
|    Additional Paid-in Capital | | 1,140,000 |

**February 26, Year 8**

| | | |
|---|---|---|
| Common Stock Warrants (= 10,000 × $3) | 30,000 | |
|    Additional Paid-in Capital | | 30,000 |

12.25    (Higgins Corporation; journal entries for convertible bonds.)

a. **1/02/Year 1**

| | | |
|---|---|---|
| Cash .......................................................... | 1,000,000 | |
|    Convertible Bonds Payable ............................. | | 1,000,000 |

To record the issue of convertible bonds.

**1/02/Year 5**

| | | |
|---|---|---|
| Convertible Bonds Payable ................................ | 1,000,000 | |
|    Common Stock—$1 Par ................................... | | 40,000 |
|    Additional Paid-in Capital ............................... | | 960,000 |

To record conversion using book value of bonds.

b. **1/02/Year 1**

| | | |
|---|---|---|
| Cash .......................................................... | 1,000,000 | |
|    Convertible Bonds Payable ............................. | | 685,140.50 |
|    Additional Paid-in Capital ............................... | | 314,859.50 |

Issue of 10-percent semiannual coupon convertible bonds at a time when the firm could issue ordinary 10-percent bonds for $685,140.50 when the market interest rate is 15 percent compounded semiannually.

**Supporting Computations**

| | |
|---|---|
| $50,000 × 12.59441 ............................................................ | $ 629,720.50 |
| $1,000,000 × .05542 ............................................................ | 55,420.00 |
|    Issue Price ......................................................... | $ 685,140.50 |

Also, see Table 5 at the back of the book.

12.26    (Uncertainty Corporation; journal entries to correct errors and adjust for changes in estimates.)

a.

| | | |
|---|---|---|
| Retained Earnings ......................................... | 12,000 | |
|    Patent (or Accumulated Amortization) .............. | | 12,000 |

To correct error from neglecting to amortize patent during previous year.

b.

| | | |
|---|---|---|
| Accumulated Depreciation ............................... | 7,000 | |
|    Loss on Sale of Machine ......................................... | | 4,000 |
|    Gain on Sale of Machine ........................................ | | 3,000 |

To eliminate the balance in accumulated depreciation relating to the machine sold and convert a $4,000 loss on the sale to a $3,000 gain.

c.

| | | |
|---|---|---|
| Depreciation Expense .................................... | 50,000 | |
|    Accumulated Depreciation .................................... | | 50,000 |

Book value on January 1, Year 13 is $1,600,000 [= $2,400,000 − ($80,000 × 10)]. The revised annual depreciation is $50,000 (= $1,600,000/32).

12.26 continued.

    d.  Bad Debt Expense................................................. 10,000
         Allowance for Uncollectible Accounts ................ 10,000
       To adjust the balance in the allowance account
       to the amount needed to cover estimated un-
       collectibles.

12.27    (Journal entries for dividends.)

    a.  Retained Earnings........................................... 16,000
         Dividends Payable—Preferred Stock................... 16,000
       Dividend of $2.50 per share on 6,400 shares.

    b.  Dividends Payable—Preferred Stock ........................ 16,000
         Cash ............................................................... 16,000

    c.  Retained Earnings............................................... 250,000
         Common Stock................................................... 250,000

    d.  No entry.

12.28    (Watt Corporation; journal entries for dividends.)

    a.  **March 31, Year 6**
       Retained Earnings............................................. 10,000
         Dividends Payable ......... .............................. 10,000
       $10,000 = 20,000 × $.50.

    b.  **April 15, Year 6**
       Dividends Payable...................................... 10,000
         Cash ..................................................... 10,000

    c.  **June 30, Year 6**
       Retained Earnings (= 2,000 × $20)............................ 40,000
         Common Stock (= 2,000 × $15)............................ 30,000
         Additional Paid-in Capital ................................... 10,000

    d.  **September 30, Year 6**
       Retained Earnings............................................. 11,000
         Dividends Payable ............................................ 11,000
       $11,000 = 22,000 × $.50.

    e.  **October 15, Year 6**
       Dividends Payable............................................. 11,000
         Cash ............................................................... 11,000

    f.  **December 31, Year 6**
       Additional Paid-in Capital............................... 165,000
         Common Stock (= 11,000 × $15) ........................ 165,000

12.29    (Danos Corporation; journal entries for treasury stock transactions.)

a.   Treasury Stock................................................................ 480,000
        Cash (= 12,000 × $40)........................................................        480,000

b.   Cash (= 5,000 × $42)............................................. 210,000
        Treasury Stock (= 5,000 × $40)............................        200,000
        Additional Paid-in Capital.......................................        10,000

c.   Treasury Stock................................................................ 384,000
        Cash (= 8,000 × $48)........................................................        384,000

d.   Land................................................................................ 440,000
        Treasury Stock [= (7,000 × $40) + (3,000 ×
          $48)]........................................................................        424,000
        Additional Paid-in Capital.......................................        16,000

e.   Cash (= 5,000 × $46)............................................. 230,000
     Additional Paid-in Capital...................................... 10,000
        Treasury Stock (= 5,000 × $48)............................        240,000

12.30    (Melissa Corporation; journal entries for treasury stock transactions.)

a.   Treasury Stock................................................................ 120,000
        Cash (= 10,000 × $12).....................................................        120,000

b.   Bonds Payable................................................................ 72,000
        Treasury Stock (= 6,000 × $12)............................        72,000

c.   Treasury Stock................................................................ 300,000
        Cash (= 20,000 × $15).....................................................        300,000

d.   Land................................................................................ 540,000
        Treasury Stock [= (4,000 × $12) + (20,000 ×
          $15)]........................................................................        348,000
        Common Stock (= 6,000 × $5)..............................        30,000
        Additional Paid-in Capital.......................................        162,000

12.31    (Effects on statement of cash flows.)

a.   The journal entry to record this transaction is:

     Cash................................................................................ 200,000
        Common Stock................................................................        200,000

     The Cash account increases, so Line (9) increases by $200,000. Issuing common stock is a financing activity, so Line (6) increases by $200,000.

12.31 continued.

b. The journal entry to record this transaction is:

| | | |
|---|---|---|
| Common Stock | 50,000 | |
| Additional Paid-in Capital | 25,000 | |
| Cash | | 75,000 |

The Cash account decreases, so Line (9) decreases by $75,000. Repurchasing common stock is a financing activity, so Line (7) increases by $75,000.

c. The journal entry to record this transaction using the book value method is:

| | | |
|---|---|---|
| Convertible Bonds Payable | 100,000 | |
| Common Stock | | 10,000 |
| Additional Paid-in Capital | | 90,000 |

The journal entry to record this transaction under the market value method is:

| | | |
|---|---|---|
| Convertible Bonds Payable | 100,000 | |
| Loss on Conversion of Bonds | 140,000 | |
| Common Stock | | 10,000 |
| Additional Paid-in Capital | | 230,000 |

The Cash account does not change under either method of recording the transaction. The transaction does not appear on the statement of cash flows when the firm uses the book value method. When the firm uses the market value method, net income on Line (1) decreases for the loss. Line (2) increases to add back the loss to net income since it does not affect cash. The firm reports this financing transaction in a supplementary schedule or note.

d. The journal entry to record this transaction is:

| | | |
|---|---|---|
| Cash | 15,000 | |
| Additional Paid-in Capital | 5,000 | |
| Treasury Stock | | 20,000 |

The Cash account increases, so Line (9) increases by $15,000. Issuing treasury stock is a financing transaction, so Line (6) increases by $15,000.

12.31 continued.

e. The journal entry to record this transaction is:

| | | |
|---|---|---|
| Retained Earnings........................................................ | 300,000 | |
| Common Stock........................................................ | | 1,000 |
| Additional Paid-in Capital ...................................... | | 299,000 |

Because this transaction does not affect the Cash account, it does not appear in the statement of cash flows.

f. The journal entry to record this transaction is:

| | | |
|---|---|---|
| Retained Earnings........................................................ | 70,000 | |
| Dividends Payable .................................................. | | 70,000 |

Because this transaction does not affect the Cash account, it does not appear in the statement of cash flows.

g. The journal entry to record this transaction is:

| | | |
|---|---|---|
| Dividends Payable........................................................ | 70,000 | |
| Cash ....................................................................... | | 70,000 |

The Cash account decreases, so Line (9) decreases by $70,000. Paying dividends is a financing activity, so Line (8) increases by $70,000.

h. The journal entry to record this transaction is:

| | | |
|---|---|---|
| Cash........................................................................ | 20,000 | |
| Common Stock........................................................ | | 1,000 |
| Additional Paid-in Capital ...................................... | | 19,000 |

The Cash account increases, so Line (9) increases by $20,000. Issuing common stock under a stock rights plan is a financing activity, so Line (6) increases by $20,000.

12.32 (Wilson Supply Company; transactions to incorporate and run a business.)

a. **1/02**

| | | |
|---|---|---|
| Cash.......................................................................... | 9,000 | |
| Common Stock—$30 Stated Value...................... | | 9,000 |
| 300 shares X $30 = $9,000. | | |

b. **1/06**

| | | |
|---|---|---|
| Cash.......................................................................... | 60,000 | |
| Common Stock—$30 Stated Value...................... | | 60,000 |
| 2,000 shares X $30 = $60,000. | | |

12.32 continued.

   c.  **1/08**

| | | |
|---|---:|---:|
| Cash............................................................................... | 400,000 | |
|    Preferred Stock—Par............................................. | | 400,000 |

4,000 shares × $100 = $400,000.

   d.  **1/09**

No entry.

   e.  **1/12**

| | | |
|---|---:|---:|
| Inventories.................................................................. | 50,000 | |
| Land ............................................................................ | 80,000 | |
| Building....................................................................... | 210,000 | |
| Equipment .................................................................. | 120,000 | |
|    Preferred Stock—Par............................................. | | 100,000 |
|    Common Stock—$30 Stated Value...................... | | 360,000 |

   f.  **7/03**

| | | |
|---|---:|---:|
| Retained Earnings....................................................... | 20,000 | |
|    Dividends Payable on Preferred Stock ................ | | 20,000 |

$100 × (.08/2) × (4,000 + 1,000) shares = $20,000.

   g.  **7/05**

| | | |
|---|---:|---:|
| Cash............................................................................... | 825,000 | |
|    Common Stock—$30 Stated Value...................... | | 750,000 |
|    Additional Paid-in Capital .................................... | | 75,000 |

25,000 shares × $33 = $825,000.

   h.  **7/25**

| | | |
|---|---:|---:|
| Dividends Payable on Preferred Stock ...................... | 20,000 | |
|    Cash ........................................................................ | | 20,000 |

   i.  **10/02**

| | | |
|---|---:|---:|
| Retained Earnings....................................................... | 39,300 | |
|    Dividends Payable on Common Stock.................. | | 39,300 |

$1 × (300 + 2,000 + 12,000 + 25,000) shares = $39,300.

   j.  **10/25**

| | | |
|---|---:|---:|
| Dividends Payable on Common Stock ...................... | 39,300 | |
|    Cash ........................................................................ | | 39,300 |

12.33   (Hutchins Company; transactions to incorporate and run a business.)

a.   No formal entry is required.

b.   **July 8, Year 1**

| | | |
|---|---|---|
| Cash...................................................................... | 240,000 | |
|    Common Stock........................................... | | 240,000 |

6,000 shares issued at $40 per share.

c.   **July 9, Year 1**

| | | |
|---|---|---|
| Accounts Receivable ....................................... | 20,000 | |
| Inventories........................................................ | 30,000 | |
| Land .................................................................. | 40,000 | |
| Buildings........................................................... | 50,000 | |
| Equipment ........................................................ | 20,000 | |
|    Common Stock........................................... | | 160,000 |

4,000 shares issued at $40 per share.

d.   **July 13, Year 1**

| | | |
|---|---|---|
| Cash.................................................................. | 80,000 | |
|    Preferred Stock—Par................................. | | 80,000 |

e.   **Dec. 31, Year 1**

| | | |
|---|---|---|
| Income Summary .............................................. | 75,000 | |
|    Retained Earnings...................................... | | 75,000 |

f.   **Jan. 4, Year 2**

| | | |
|---|---|---|
| Retained Earnings............................................ | 31,600 | |
|    Dividends Payable on Preferred Stock ................. | | 1,600 |
|    Dividends Payable on Common Stock.................. | | 30,000 |

800 × $2 = $1,600; 10,000 × $3 = $30,000.

g.   **Feb. 1, Year 2**

| | | |
|---|---|---|
| Dividends Payable on Preferred Stock...................... | 1,600 | |
| Dividends Payable on Common Stock ...................... | 30,000 | |
|    Cash ............................................................. | | 31,600 |

h.   **July 2, Year 2**

| | | |
|---|---|---|
| Retained Earnings........................................... | 1,600 | |
|    Dividends Payable on Preferred Stock ................. | | 1,600 |

i.   **Aug. 1, Year 2**

| | | |
|---|---|---|
| Dividends Payable on Preferred Stock...................... | 1,600 | |
|    Cash ............................................................. | | 1,600 |

12.34   (Conrad Company; reconstructing transactions involving shareholders' equity.)

a.   $30,000 par value/$10 per share = 3,000 shares.

b.   $3,600/180 = $20 per share.

c.   300 − 180 = 120 shares.

d.   If the Additional Paid-in Capital is $15,720, then $15,000 [= 3,000 × ($15 − $10)] represents contributions in excess of par value on original issue of 3,000 shares. Then, $720 (= $15,720 − $15,000) represents the credit to Additional Paid-in Capital when it reissued the treasury shares.

    The $720 represents 120 shares reissued times the excess of reissue price over acquisition price:

$$120(\$X - \$20) = \$720, \text{ or } X = \$26.$$

The shares were reissued for $26 each.

e.   (1)   Cash (3,000 × $15).............................................. 45,000
            Common Stock ($10 Par Value)..................             30,000
            Additional Paid-in Capital ............................             15,000

    (2)   Treasury Shares......................................... 6,000
            Cash (300 × $20) ......................................             6,000

    (3)   Cash (120 × $26)....................................... 3,120
            Treasury Shares (120 × $20).......................             2,400
            Additional Paid-in Capital ............................             720

    (4)   Cash........................................................ 5,000
            Securities Available for Sale ......................             3,000
            Realized Gain on Sale of Securities Available for Sale (Income Statement)............             2,000

    (5)   Securities Available for Sale........................... 1,000
            Unrealized Holding Gain on Securities Available for Sale (Balance Sheet, Component of Other Comprehensive Income).......................................................             1,000

f.   Realized gain appears in Income (Earnings) Statement and the Unrealized Gain appears in Statement of Comprehensive Income or in reconciliation of Accumulated Other Comprehensive Income.

12.35 (Shea Company; reconstructing transactions involving shareholders' equity.)

a. $100,000 par value/$5 per share = 20,000 shares.

b. $33,600/1,200 = $28 per share.

c. 2,000 − 1,200 = 800 shares.

d. If the Additional Paid-in Capital is $509,600, then $500,000 [= 20,000 × ($30 − $5)] represents contributions in excess of par value on original issue of 20,000 shares. Then, $9,600 (= $509,600 − $500,000) represents the credit to Additional Paid-in Capital when it reissued the treasury shares.

The $9,600 represents 800 shares reissued times the excess of reissue price over acquisition price:

$$800(\$X − \$28) = \$9,600, \text{ or } X = \$40.$$

The shares were reissued for $40 each.

e. (1) Cash............................................................. 600,000
        Common Stock ($5 Par Value)..................... 100,000
        Additional Paid-in Capital ........................... 500,000

   (2) Treasury Shares.............................................. 56,000
        Cash ............................................................. 56,000

   (3) Cash............................................................. 32,000
        Treasury Shares.......................................... 22,400
        Additional Paid-in Capital ........................... 9,600
        800 × $40 = $32,000.

   (4) Cash............................................................. 12,000
        Realized Loss on Sale of Securities Available
           for Sale (Income Statement)......................... 2,000
              Securities Available for Sale..................... 14,000

   (5) Unrealized Holding Loss on Securities Avail-
        able for Sale (Balance Sheet, Component
        of Other Comprehensive Income)................ 7,000
              Securities Available for Sale..................... 7,000
        Write down securities from $25,000 to
        $18,000.

f. Realized Loss appears in Income (Earnings) Statement and the Unrealized Loss appears in Statement of Comprehensive Income or in reconciliation of Accumulated Other Comprehensive Income.

12.36   (Lowe Corporation; accounting for stock options.)

a.   Lowe Corporation recognizes no compensation expense under the APB *Opinion 25* method because the option price equals the market value of the stock on the date of the grant.

b.   **Year 1**:  zero compensation because all benefits occur after the granting of the stock option.

| | |
|---|---:|
| **Year 2:** .5(5,000 × $2.40) | $   6,000 |
| **Year 3:** [.5(5,000 × $2.40) + .5(6,000 × $3.00)] | 15,000 |
| **Year 4:** [.5(6,000 × $3.00) + .5(7,000 × $3.14)] | 19,990 |
| **Year 5:** [.5(7,000 × $3.14) + .5(8,000 × $3.25)] | 23,990 |
| **Year 6:** [.5(8,000 × $3.25) + .5(9,000 × $5.33)] | 36,985 |
| Total | $101,965 |

c.   The APB *Opinion 25* method results in $101,965 higher cumulative pre-tax earnings relative to the FASB *Statement 123* method as of December 31, Year 6.

d.   Total shareholders' equity will not differ between the two accounting methods.   Lowe Corporation increases the Common Stock Options account, a component of shareholders' equity, each year for the amount amortized.   Thus, retained earnings decreases by the same amount as contributed accounts increase, resulting in a zero net effect on total shareholders' equity.   This is the same effect on total shareholders' equity as the APB *Opinion 25* method.

12.37   (Jastern Company; accounting for detachable warrants.)

a.   The warrants reduced the amount borrowed, but not the interest rate. In reality, see Part *b.* below, the Company borrowed $855,812 at an interest rate of 12 percent per year and issued detachable warrants for $144,188.   One cannot ascertain whether or not this was a fair price for the option under the circumstances from the available data.

b.

| | |
|---|---:|
| Present Value of $80,000 in arrears for 5 years discounted at 12% is 3.60478 × $80,000 | $  288,382 |
| Present Value of $1,000,000 paid in 5 years discounted at 12% is .56743 × $1,000,000 | 567,430 |
| Present Value of loan repayments is | $ 855,812 |

The remaining $144,188 must be for the option.   Thus, the entry to reflect the economics of the situation is:

| | | |
|---|---:|---:|
| Cash | 1,000,000 | |
| Note Payable | | 855,812 |
| Additional Paid-in Capital | | 144,188 |

12.37 b. continued.

At each interest payment date, the entry is:

Interest Expense........................................................ 80,000 + X
   Cash........................................................................ 80,000
   Note Payable........................................................ X
Where X is the increase in interest expense to
recognize increase in book value of the note.

| End of Year | X = Increase in Note Payable[a] | Remaining Loan |
|---|---|---|
| 0 | -- | $ 855,812 |
| 1 | $22,697 | 878,509 |
| 2 | 25,421 | 903,930 |
| 3 | 28,472 | 932,402 |
| 4 | 31,888 | 964,290 |
| 5 | 35,710 | 1,000,000 |

[a] = $(.12 \times$ Amount in Last Column for Preceding Year$) - \$80,000$, except in Year 5 where it is the amount required to give $1,000,000 in last column.

c.  Cash............................................................................ 400,000
     Common Stock—$5 Par ...................................... 100,000
     Additional Paid-in Capital .................................. 300,000
  20,000 × $5 = $100,000.  20,000 × ($20 − $5) =
  $300,000.

d.  Yes. The firm could issue the same shares to other investors for $45 per share. This does not mean that shareholders were hurt by the entire transaction. They gambled with the lending-investor and "lost." If the option was fairly priced at $144,188, then all sides were treated fairly.

e.  During the life of the loan, disclosure of the amount of the options outstanding and their exercise price would enable the reader of financial statements to see the potential dilution of earnings overhanging the company.

12.38 (Alex Corporation; comprehensive review of accounting for shareholders' equity.)

a.

## BOOK VALUE PER SHARE
(Numerator is Total Book Value)

$$\frac{\$2,250,000}{50,000} = \$45.00 \text{ per share.}$$

$$\frac{\$2,250,000}{55,000} = \$40.91 \text{ per share.}$$

$$\frac{\$2,250,000}{100,000} = \$22.50 \text{ per share.}$$

$$\frac{\$2,125,000}{45,000} = \$47.22 \text{ per share.}$$

$$\frac{\$2,175,000}{45,000} = \$48.33 \text{ per share.}$$

$$\frac{\$2,300,000}{50,000} = \$46.00 \text{ per share.}$$

$$\frac{\$2,225,000}{50,000} = \$44.50 \text{ per share.}$$

$$\frac{\$2,200,000}{50,000} = \$44.00 \text{ per share.}$$

$$\frac{\$2,325,000}{55,000} = \$42.27 \text{ per share.}$$

$$\frac{\$2,500,000}{55,000} = \$45.45 \text{ per share.}$$

$$\frac{\$2,400,000}{60,000} = \$40.00 \text{ per share.}$$

$$\frac{\$2,400,000}{60,000} = \$40.00 \text{ per share.}$$

## JOURNAL ENTRY

b.

(1) Retained Earnings .......................... 150,000
    Common Stock (5,000 × $10) .......... 50,000
    Additional Paid-in Capital (5,000 × $20) . 100,000

(2) Common Stock ($10 Par Value) .......... 500,000
    Common Stock ($5 per Share) .......... 500,000

(3) Treasury Stock ........................... 125,000
    Cash (5,000 × $25) .................... 125,000

(4) Treasury Stock ........................... 75,000
    Cash (5,000 × $15) .................... 75,000

(5) Cash (5,000 × $35) ....................... 175,000
    Treasury Stock (5,000 × $25) .......... 125,000
    Additional Paid-in Capital ............ 50,000

(6) Cash (5,000 × $20) ....................... 100,000
    Additional Paid-in Capital ............ 25,000
    Treasury Stock (5,000 × $25) .......... 125,000

(7) Cash (5,000 × $15) ....................... 75,000
    Additional Paid-in Capital ............ 50,000
    Treasury Stock (5,000 × $25) .......... 125,000

(8) Cash (5,000 × $15) ....................... 75,000
    Common Stock (5,000 × $10) ........... 50,000
    Additional Paid-in Capital ............ 25,000

(9) Cash (5,000 × $50) ....................... 250,000
    Common Stock (5,000 × $10) ........... 50,000
    Additional Paid-in Capital ............ 200,000

(10) Bonds Payable ........................... 150,000
    Common Stock (10,000 × $10) .......... 100,000
    Additional Paid-in Capital ............ 50,000

(11) Bonds Payable ........................... 150,000
    Loss on Conversion of Bonds ........... 20,000
    Common Stock .......................... 100,000
    Additional Paid-in Capital ............ 70,000

12.38 continued.

c. (1) The acquisition of treasury shares, the declaration of dividends other than stock dividends, and the incurrence of a net loss reduce total book value.

(2) The issue of common shares for a price less than current book value per share (for example, under stock option plans), the acquisition of treasury shares for a price greater than current book value per share, and the sale or reissue of treasury shares at a price less than their acquisition cost (at a "loss") reduce book value per share.

12.39 (Neslin Company; reconstructing events affecting shareholders' equity.)

a. (1) Issue of 20,000 shares of common stock at $52 per share for cash or other assets.

(2) Acquisition of 4,000 shares of treasury stock for $55 per share.

(3) Reissue of 3,000 shares of treasury stock for $48 per share.

(4) Reissue of 1,000 shares of treasury stock for $60 per share.

(5) Net income of $2,400,000 closed to Retained Earnings.

(6) Securities available for sale on hand at year end have a market value of $1,050,000 greater than book value, but this represents a decline of $150,000 reported in Other Comprehensive Income.

(7) Dividends declared of $10 per share.

b. 
(1) 
| | | |
|---|---|---|
| Cash | 1,040,000 | |
| Common Stock | | 200,000 |
| Additional Paid-in Capital | | 840,000 |

(2) 
| | | |
|---|---|---|
| Treasury Stock | 220,000 | |
| Cash | | 220,000 |

(3) 
| | | |
|---|---|---|
| Cash | 144,000 | |
| Additional Paid-in Capital | 21,000 | |
| Treasury Stock | | 165,000 |

(4) 
| | | |
|---|---|---|
| Cash | 60,000 | |
| Treasury Stock | | 55,000 |
| Additional Paid-in Capital | | 5,000 |

(5) 
| | | |
|---|---|---|
| Income Summary | 2,400,000 | |
| Retained Earnings | | 2,400,000 |

12.39 b. continued.

(6) Unrealized Holding Gain on Holdings of
Securities Available for Sale ............... 150,000
    Securities Available for Sale ..........             150,000

(7) Retained Earnings ................................... 1,200,000
    Cash or Dividends Payable .................           1,200,000

12.40 (Wal-Mart Stores; journal entries for changes in shareholders' equity.)

(1) Income Summary ..................................... 1,291,024
    Retained Earnings ...............................           1,291,024

(2) Retained Earnings ................................. 158,889
    Dividends Payable or Cash .............................       158,889

(3) Cash ..................................................... 3,820
    Common Stock ..........................................           66
    Additional Paid-in Capital .............................       3,754

(4) Additional Paid-in Capital ..................................... 56,680
    Common Stock ........................................       56,680

(5) Investment in Securities ............................. 274,696
    Common Stock ........................................       1,037
    Additional Paid-in Capital .............................     273,659

(6) Treasury Stock ..................................... 25,826
    Cash .....................................................       25,826

(7) Unrealized Gains on Holdings of Securities
Available for Sale ............................... 57,086
    Securities Available for Sale ......................       57,086

12.41 (Wellington Company; journal entries for changes in shareholders' equity.)

(1) Income Summary ..................................... 210,500
    Retained Earnings ...............................       210,500

(2) Retained Earnings ................................. 120,000
    Cash or Dividends Payable .................       120,000

(3) Bonds Payable ................................. 70,000
    Common Stock ..........................................       6,270
    Additional Paid-in Capital .............................       63,730

12.41 continued.

| | | |
|---|---:|---:|
| (4) Cash...................................................................... | 950 | |
|     Common Stock................................................ | | 73 |
|     Additional Paid-in Capital .......................... | | 877 |
| | | |
| (5) Retained Earnings.............................................. | 62,810 | |
|     Common Stock................................................ | | 5,604 |
|     Additional Paid-in Capital .......................... | | 57,206 |
| | | |
| (6) Treasury Stock.................................................... | 48,600 | |
|     Cash ............................................................... | | 48,600 |
| | | |
| (7) Cash...................................................................... | 42,700 | |
|     Treasury Stock .............................................. | | 42,700 |
| | | |
| (8) Securities Available for Sale........................... | 44,400 | |
|     Unrealized Loss on Holdings of Securities | | |
|     Available for Sale .......................................... | | 44,400 |

12.42  (Baiman Corporation; preparing a statement of cash flows.)

a.

**Cash**

√ 45,000

**Operations**

| | | | | |
|---|---:|---:|---:|---|
| (1) | 48,000 | 15,000 | (9) |
| (4) | 28,000 | 20,000 | (10) |
| (5) | 4,000 | | |
| (6) | 3,000 | | |
| (12) | 1,000 | | |
| (14) | 7,000 | | |

**Investing**

| | | | |
|---|---:|---:|---|
| (5) | 8,000 | 45,000 | (11) |

**Financing**

| | | | |
|---|---:|---:|---|
| (8) | 12,000 | 39,000 | (2) |
| (13) | 4,000 | 25,000 | (16) |
| (15) | 38,000 | | |

√ 54,000

# 12.42 a. continued.

| Accounts Receivable—Net | | |
|---|---|---|
| √ | 160,000 | |
| (9) | 15,000 | |
| √ | 175,000 | |

| Inventory | | |
|---|---|---|
| √ | 115,000 | |
| (10) | 20,000 | |
| √ | 135,000 | |

**Property, Plant and Equipment**

| | | | |
|---|---|---|---|
| √ | 265,000 | | |
| (3) | 20,000 | 30,000 | (5) |
| (11) | 45,000 | | |
| √ | 300,000 | | |

**Accumulated Depreciation**

| | | | |
|---|---|---|---|
| | | 120,000 | √ |
| (5) | 18,000 | 28,000 | (4) |
| | | 130,000 | √ |

| Accounts Payable | | |
|---|---|---|
| | 105,000 | √ |
| | 1,000 | (12) |
| | 106,000 | √ |

| Dividends Payable | | |
|---|---|---|
| | 10,000 | √ |
| | 4,000 | (13) |
| | 14,000 | √ |

| Bonds Payable | | |
|---|---|---|
| | 90,000 | √ |
| | 3,000 | (6) |
| | 93,000 | √ |

| Convertible Bonds Payable | | |
|---|---|---|
| | | 50,000 | √ |
| (7) | 50,000 | | |
| | | -- | √ |

| Deferred Income Taxes | | |
|---|---|---|
| | 20,000 | √ |
| | 7,000 | (14) |
| | 27,000 | √ |

| Preferred Stock | | |
|---|---|---|
| | 60,000 | √ |
| | 60,000 | √ |

| Common Stock (Par) | | |
|---|---|---|
| | 25,000 | √ |
| | 4,000 | (3) |
| | 10,000 | (7) |
| | 8,000 | (15) |
| | 47,000 | √ |

| Additional Paid-in Capital | | |
|---|---|---|
| | 65,000 | √ |
| | 16,000 | (3) |
| | 40,000 | (7) |
| | 2,000 | (8) |
| | 30,000 | (15) |
| | 153,000 | √ |

| Retained Earnings | | |
|---|---|---|
| | | 55,000 | √ |
| (2) | 39,000 | 48,000 | (1) |
| | | 64,000 | √ |

| Treasury Stock | | |
|---|---|---|
| √ | 15,000 | | |
| (16) | 25,000 | 10,000 | (8) |
| √ | 30,000 | | |

b.

**BAIMAN CORPORATION**
**Statement of Cash Flows**
**For Year 2**

Operations:
Net Income ........................................................ $ 48,000
Addbacks and Additions:
Depreciation Expense............................. 28,000
Loss on Sale of Equipment...................... 4,000
Amortization of Bond Discount .............. 3,000
Increase in Accounts Payable................. 1,000
Increase in Deferred Income Tax
Liability...................................... 7,000
Subtractions:
(Increase) in Accounts Receivable ......... (15,000)
(Increase) in Inventories.......................... (20,000)
Cash Flow from Operations ............................. $ 56,000
Investing:
Acquisition of Property, Plant and
Equipment .......................................... $ (45,000)
Sale of Property, Plant and Equipment ..... 8,000
Cash Flow from Investing ................................ (37,000)
Financing:
Issue of Common Stock ............................ $ 38,000
Reissue of Treasury Stock......................... 12,000
Reacquisition of Common Stock.................. (25,000)
Dividends Paid ($39,000 – $4,000).............. (35,000)
Cash Flow from Financing................................ (10,000)
Net Change in Cash.......................................... $ 9,000
Cash, January 1, Year 2.................................... 45,000
Cash, December 31, Year 2................................ $ 54,000

**Supplementary Information**
1. Holders of convertible bonds with a book value of $50,000 exercised
   their option to convert their bonds into shares of common stock.

2. The firm issued common shares with a market value of $20,000 in
   the acquisition of a machine.

**12.43** (Merck & Co.; treasury shares and their effects on performance ratios.)

a.  Cash............................................................................ 714.1
      Treasury Stock ......................................................... 427.6
      Common Stock/Additional Paid-in Capital.......... 286.5

The common shares were issued at an option price of $49.28 per share [= $714.1/(.307 + 14.183)]. The treasury shares issued were purchased for $30.15 per share (= $427.6/14.183). The difference of $19.13 per share (= $49.28 − $30.15) was credited to Additional Paid-in Capital. The remaining credits to Common Stock and Additional Paid-in Capital were for the amounts received for the .307 common shares issued.

Treasury Stock......................................................... 2,572.8
  Cash ..................................................................... 2,572.8

These treasury shares were purchased for an average price of $93.75 per share (= $2,572.8/27.444).

b.

|  | **Year 3/Year 4** | **Year 4/Year 5** |
|---|---|---|
| Net Income: | | |
| [($3,870.5/$3,376.6) − 1]................ | +14.6% | |
| [($4,596.5/$3,870.5) − 1]................ | | +18.8% |
| | | |
| Earnings per Common Share: | | |
| [($3.20/$2.70) − 1].......................... | +18.5% | |
| [($3.83/$3.20) − 1]......... ............. | | +19.7% |

Earnings per share increases faster than net income because Merck reduces the number of shares outstanding each year by repurchasing shares of treasury stock.

c.

|  | **Year 3** | **Year 4** | **Year 5** |
|---|---|---|---|
| Book Value per Share: | | | |
| $11,735.7/(1,483.463 − 254.615).... | $9.55 | | |
| $11,970.5/(1,483.619 − 277.017).... | | $9.92 | |
| $12,613.5/(1,483.926 − 290.278).... | | | $10.57 |
| | | | |
| Percentage Change: | | | |
| [($9.92/$9.55) − 1].............................. | | +3.9% | |
| [($10.57/$9.92) − 1]........................... | | | +6.6% |

There are several reasons why book value per share increases more slowly than net income and earnings per share. First, dividends reduce shareholders' equity but not net income. Second, the repurchases of treasury shares reduce the numerator proportionally more than they reduce the denominator. The average repurchase price during Year 5 of $93.75 per share (see the answer to Part *a*.) had the effect of reducing

12.43 c. continued.

book value per share. Book value per share increased overall in Year 5 because of net income.

d.
|  | Year 3 | Year 4 | Year 5 |
|---|---|---|---|
| [$3,376.6/.5($11,139.0 + $11,735.7)].. | 29.5% | | |
| [$3,870.5/.5($11,735.7 + $11,970.5)].. | | 32.7% | |
| [$4,596.5/.5($11,970.5 + $12,613.5)].. | | | 37.4% |

e. No. Merck has purchased considerably more treasury shares than are needed for its stock option plans. Treasury shares do not receive dividends, so Merck does conserve cash. However, dividends have grown at approximately the same growth rate as net income. One purpose might have been to increase the return on common shareholders' equity. Cash generally earns a return of approximately 4 percent each year after taxes. By eliminating this low-yielding asset from the balance sheet, Merck's overall rate of return on common shareholders' equity increases. The market often interprets stock repurchases as a positive signal that management has inside information and thinks that the stock is undervalued. The positive signal results in an increase in the stock price. One can estimate the increase in market price by observing the average price at which Merck repurchased its shares each year:

Year 3: $1,570.9/33.377 = $47.07
Year 4: $2,493.3/38.384 = $64.96
Year 5: $2,572.8/27.444 = $93.75

Thus, the stock price doubled during the three-year period, whereas earnings increased by approximately 36 percent [= ($4,596.5/$3,376.6) − 1].

12.44 (Wendy's International; mandatorily redeemable preferred shares substitute for debt and help manage the debt/equity ratio.)

a. Wendy's prefers not to have even more debt on its Year 6 balance sheet than it already shows on its Year 5 balance sheet.

b. Wendy's consolidates Financial, so it eliminates in consolidation the intercompany debt issued by Wendy's to Financial and shows only Financial's issue to its purchasers outside the consolidated entity. Wendy's shows mandatorily redeemable preferred shares, sometimes called *mezzanine financing*, on its balance sheet, not debt. The name *mezzanine* results from the SEC's rule requiring the issuer to segregate such items from other components of shareholder's equity, midway between (on the mezzanine between) liabilities and other shareholders' equity.

12.44 continued.

<table>
<tr><td>c.</td><td colspan="2" align="center">**Year 6**</td><td align="center">**Year 5**</td></tr>
<tr><td>Treat<br>Preferred as<br>Shareholders'<br>Equity .......</td><td colspan="2">($207.8 + $253.9)/$1,781.4 = 25.9%</td><td>($295.9 + $346.6)/$1,509.2 = 42.6%</td></tr>
<tr><td>Treat<br>Preferred as<br>Debt ..........</td><td colspan="2">($207.8 + $253.9 + $200.0)/$1,781.4 = 37.1%</td><td>($295.9 + $346.6)/$1,509.2 = 42.6%</td></tr>
</table>

12.45    (Kellogg Company; analysis of non-recurring transactions; introduction to constructive liabilities.)

a.

| | Year 2 | Year 3 | Year 4 |
|---|---|---|---|
| Streamlining Charges ...... | 348.0 | 121.1 | 161.1 |
|   Liability for Stream-<br>    lining Costs ................ | 348.0 | 121.1 | 161.1 |

To record expense and
set up liability.

| | Year 2 | Year 3 | Year 4 |
|---|---|---|---|
| Liability for Streamlin-<br>  ing Costs ....................... | 254.0 | 160.8 | 163.5 |
|   Cash ............................ | 40.0 | 120.0 | 85.0 |
|   Other Assets<br>    Written Down or<br>    Written Off ............ | 214.0 | 40.8 | 78.5 |

To record cash spent to
discharge some of the
liability and to write off
assets already on hand,
now impaired or re-
moved.

One can combine these two entries as follows:

| | Year 2 | Year 3 | Year 4 |
|---|---|---|---|
| Streamlining Charges ...... | 348.0 | 121.1 | 161.1 |
| Liability for Stream-<br>  lining Costs .................... | | 39.7 | |
|   Liability for<br>  Streamlining<br>  Costs ..................... | 94.0 | | 2.4 |
|   Cash .......................... | 40.0 | 120.0 | 85.0 |
|   Other Assets<br>    Written Down or<br>    Written Off ........... | 214.0 | 40.8 | 78.5 |

12.45 continued.

b. Streamlining Charges ......      144.1

     Liability for Stream-
       lining Costs................             144.1

     To record expense and
     set up liability.

     Liability for Streamlin-
       ing Costs........................      23.0

       Streamlining
         Charges .................             23.0

Without the reversal, income for Year 3 would have been $23 smaller.

c. Without the reversal, income for Year 2 would have been $23 larger and income for Year 3 would have been $23 smaller. Income for the three years, as reported, and without the extra charge in Year 2, reversed in Year 3, are:

| | Year 4 | Year 3 | Year 2 |
|---|---|---|---|
| Net Earnings, as Reported............................ | $546.0 | $531.0 | $490.3 |
| Net Earnings, Without Need for Re-<br>versals........................................................ | $546.0 | $508.0 | $513.3 |

d. Kellogg reported smoothly growing earnings over the three-year period. Without the reversal, however, the pattern shows a dip from Year 2 to Year 3, before increasing in Year 4. Most analysts, all else equal, give higher valuations to firms reporting steadily rising income (such as Kellogg's actuals) than to yo-yo income (Kellogg with chargers and subsequent reversal). The ability to record charges, such as the retirement and severance costs where cash payments will be in the future and management has some discretion to affect the future amount, lowers the quality of earnings because it gives management the opportunity to manipulate income. Notice how a relative small reversal, $23 out of net income of about $500—an adjustment of less than 5 percent—gives a pattern of stable growth.

     Our colleagues who study non-recurring charges tell us that Kellogg discloses more extensively than most. In Kellogg's defense, then, we can say that if it had wanted to manipulate income and hide from the reader the fact that they had, then they could have given less detail than they did give. They need not have given so much detail, detail which allows the analyst to do the unscrambling that the actual disclosures allow us to do. Still, we would bet that Kellogg's management, in choosing the $23 amount for the reversal, had its eye on the income pattern that resulted.

12.45 continued.

e.  If firms are allowed or required to record constructive liabilities, then hard-to-audit judgments will enter the financial statements of a sort that will allow management to manipulate the timing of income recognition.

Kellogg's management surely has some discretion in timing, and probably in setting the number, of employee severances. It can use that discretion to alter incomes in small, but relatively powerful, ways. In the actual case of Kellogg, any reversal from Year 2 to Year 3 of about $3 [= ($513.3 − $508.0)/2] or more will result in removing the downward dip in income between Years 2 and 3 and replacing it with upward trend.

12.46  (Layton Ball Corporation; case introducing earnings-per-share calculations for a complex capital structure.)

a.  $\dfrac{\$9,500}{2,500} = \$3.80$ per share.

b.  1,000 options × $15 = $15,000 cash raised.

$\dfrac{\$15,000 \text{ new cash}}{\$25 \text{ per share}} = 600$ shares.

Total number of shares increases by 400 (= 1,000 − 600).

$\dfrac{\$9,500}{2,500 + 400} = \$3.276$ per share.

c.  2,000 warrants × $30 = $60,000 cash raised.

$\dfrac{\$60,000 \text{ new cash}}{\$25 \text{ per share}} = 2,400$ shares purchased.

Total number of shares decreases by 400 (= 2,000 − 2,400).

$\dfrac{\$9,500}{2,500 - 400} = \$4.524$ per share.

d.  Before taxes, each converted bond saves $41.66 2/3 in annual interest expense. After taxes, the savings in expense and increase in income is only $25 [= (1 − .40) × $41.66 2/3].

There are 100 bonds outstanding; each is convertible into 10 shares. Thus, the new earnings per share figure is:

$\dfrac{\$9,500 + \$25 \text{ savings per bond} \times 100 \text{ bonds}}{2,500 + 10 \text{ shares/bond} \times 100 \text{ bonds}} = \dfrac{\$12,000}{3,500 \text{ shares}} =$

$3.429 per share.

12.46 continued.

    e.   The warrants are antidilutive and should be ignored if we seek the maximum possible dilution of earnings per share.

$$\frac{\$9,500 + \$2,500 \text{ (Increase from interest savings)}}{2,500 + 1,000 \text{ (bond conversion)} + 400 \text{ (option exercise)}} = \frac{\$12,000}{3,900} =$$

        $3.077 per share.

    f.   Probably the *Wall Street Journal* should use the earnings per share that results in the maximum possible dilution. It should clearly ignore antidilutive securities. Do not conclude from the presentation in this problem that one can check the dilution characteristics of potentially dilutive securities one by one and know for sure which combination of assumed exercise and conversions lead to the minimum earnings per share figure. See S. Davidson and R. L. Weil, "A Shortcut in Computing Earnings per Share," *Journal of Accountancy*, December 1975, page 45.

12.47    (Case for discussion: value of stock options.)

The answer must be either *a.* or *b.* The cost per option cannot exceed one penny per share, for otherwise StartUp would merely buy the shares on the open market, rather than pay Goldman Sachs to relieve StartUp of the burden. The total cost of the options awarded to Bithead, then, cannot exceed $100 (= 10,000 shares × $.01 per share). We think the answer is likely to be in the range of $15–$40 for those shares, so we would answer *b.*

Within the last two decades, no subject has caused more controversy in accounting than the accounting for the cost of employee stock options. When it issued *SFAS No. 119* in 1995, FASB said that this issue threatened to end standard-setting in the private sector and that the debate had ceased to be rational.

Some firms, such as GE, grant to employees the right to buy a specified number of shares of the firm's stock at a fixed price, called the *exercise price*, usually the price on the day the firm awards the options to the employee, say $10 per share. The employee, typically, has several years to decide whether to exercise the option—that is, give up the option and cash in return for the shares. If the stock price rises above the exercise price, say to $18 per share, then the employee can give up the option and $10 in return for a share with current market value of $18.

Such options have value to employees who receive them and many companies, particularly the high-tech Silicon Valley companies, award such options as part of their compensation in hopes that the employer's shares will skyrocket in value, enriching the employee.

12.47 continued.

The accounting issue has been: how much should the employer firm, such as GE, charge to expense in the period when it awards an option to its employees. The FASB proposed a method for computing such amounts of expense and proposed requiring that firms report such amounts as expense. Some members of Congress pressured the FASB into not enacting its proposals.

William H. Scott, Jr. of Scientific Applications International Corporation of San Diego, has studied the costs to the issuing firm. He found that under a wide variety of conditions, the cost to the firm issuing an option exercisable at the market price on the date of grant is, for most firms, about 10–20 percent of the market value of the shares on the date of the grant. The cost to the firm of awarding the option can never exceed the market value of the share itself on the date of the award. This is true because the firm can always, on that day, go out into the market to buy a share for the current market price, building that share until the employee exercises the option.

At the height of the debate, chief financial officers (CFOs) from Silicon Valley lobbied against the FASB proposal. We believed that many of those CFOs did not understand the FASB proposal, nor its consequences. Consequently, at a private seminar on the subject at which one of us taught, we administered the question in the text to the Silicon Valley CFOs.

The Silicon Valley CFOs answered as follows: $a. = 3$, $b. =3$, $c. = 6$, $d. = 8$, $e. = 5$, and $f. = 1$. That is, only six of the 26 participating got the answer right, which means that 20 of the 26 got it wrong. In the discussion following, we pointed out that these officers should probably understand the cost of options better than they did before arguing so hard against the proposed accounting. It's no wonder that a CFO would dislike the proposed accounting for options which the CFO thinks cost $10,000 when they actually cost no more than $100. About 25 percent of the Silicon Valley CFOs had beliefs that much in error.

# CHAPTER 13

## STATEMENT OF CASH FLOWS: ANOTHER LOOK

*Problems and Cases: Answers and Solutions*

13.1    (Effects of transactions on statement of cash flows.)

a.    The journal entry to record this transaction is:

| | | |
|---|---|---|
| Retained Earnings........................................................ | 15,000 | |
|     Dividends Payable.................................................. | | 3,000 |
|     Cash........................................................................... | | 12,000 |

The credit to the Cash account reduces Line (9) by $12,000. Paying dividends is a financing activity so Line (8) increases by $12,000.

b.    The journal entry to record this transaction is:

| | | |
|---|---|---|
| Cash............................................................................... | 75,000 | |
|     Bank Loan Payable............................................... | | 75,000 |

The debit to the Cash account increases Line (9) by $75,000. Borrowing is a financing activity so Line (6) increases by $75,000.

c.    The journal entry to record this transaction is:

| | | |
|---|---|---|
| Cash............................................................................... | 20,000 | |
| Accumulated Depreciation......................................... | 35,000 | |
|     Machinery............................................................... | | 40,000 |
|     Gain on Sale of Machinery.................................. | | 15,000 |

The debit to the Cash account results in an increase in Line (9) of $20,000. Selling machinery is an investing activity so Line (4) increases by $20,000. The gain on the sale increases net income on Line (1) by $15,000. Because the full cash proceeds is an investing activity, Line (3) increases by $15,000 to subtract from net income a revenue that did not provide an operating source of cash.

13.1 continued.

d. The journal entry for this transaction is:

| | | |
|---|---:|---:|
| Rent Expense............................................................ | 28,000 | |
| Cash................................................................. | | 28,000 |

The credit to the Cash account reduces Line (9) by $28,000. The recognition of rent expense reduces net income on Line (1) by $28,000. Paying rent is an operating transaction so the accountant makes no adjustment to net income when computing cash flow from operations.

e. The journal entry to record this transaction is:

| | | |
|---|---:|---:|
| Marketable Securities............................................... | 39,000 | |
| Cash................................................................. | | 39,000 |

The credit to the Cash account reduces Line (9) by $39,000. Purchasing marketable securities is an investing transaction so Line (5) increases by $39,000.

f. The journal entry to record this transaction is:

| | | |
|---|---:|---:|
| Accumulated Depreciation......................................... | 14,000 | |
| Truck................................................................. | | 14,000 |

Because this transaction does not affect either the Cash account on Line (9) or net income on Line (1), it does not appear on the statement of cash flows.

g. The journal entry to record this event is:

| | | |
|---|---:|---:|
| Unrealized Holding Loss of Marketable Securities (SE/Comp Y)................................................. | 8,000 | |
| Marketable Securities......................................... | | 8,000 |

Because this entry does not affect either the Cash account on Line (9) or net income on Line (1), it does not appear on the statement of cash flows. The firm discloses in a supplementary schedule or note the write down of marketable equity securities totaling $8,000.

13.1 continued.

h. The journal entry to record this transaction is:

| | | |
|---|---|---|
| Interest Expense............................................................ | 15,000 | |
|     Bonds Payable ..................................................... | | 500 |
|     Cash...................................................................... | | 14,500 |

The credit to the Cash account results in a decrease in Line (9) of $14,500. The recognition of interest expense reduces net income on Line (1) by $15,000. Because the firm used only $14,500 of cash for this expense, Line (2) increases by $500 for the portion of the expense that did not use cash.

i. The journal entry for this event is:

| | | |
|---|---|---|
| Goodwill Impairment Loss......................................... | 22,000 | |
|     Goodwill................................................................ | | 22,000 |

This entry does not involve the Cash account so Line (9) does not change. The recognition of the impairment loss reduces net income on Line (1) by $22,000. Because this loss requires no cash outflow, Line (2) increases by $22,000 to convert net income to cash flow from operations.

j. The journal entry to record this transaction is:

| | | |
|---|---|---|
| Building........................................................................ | 400,000 | |
|     Note Payable........................................................ | | 360,000 |
|     Cash...................................................................... | | 40,000 |

The credit to the Cash account reduces Line (9) by $40,000. Acquiring a building is an investing transaction so Line (5) increases by $40,000. The firm discloses in a supplementary schedule or note the acquisition of a building by assuming a mortgage for $360,000.

k. The journal entry for this event is:

| | | |
|---|---|---|
| Bad Debt Expense....................................................... | 32,000 | |
|     Allowance for Uncollectible Accounts................ | | 32,000 |

This entry does not involve the Cash account so Line (9) does not change. The recognition of bad debt expense reduces net income on Line (1) by $32,000. Because this expense does not use cash, Line (2) increases by $32,000 to convert net income to cash flow from operations.

13.1 continued.

l.  The journal entry for this event is:

| | | |
|---|---|---|
| Allowance for Uncollectible Accounts..................... | 28,000 | |
|    Accounts Receivable ........................................... | | 28,000 |

This event does not affect the Cash account so Line (9) does not change. The event also does not affect net income so Line (1) does not change. Thus, the event would not normally appear in the statement of cash flows. An alternative acceptable answer is Line (2) increases by $28,000 and Line (3) increases by $28,000.

m.  The journal entry to record this transaction is:

| | | |
|---|---|---|
| Cash........................................................................... | 15,000 | |
|    Equity in Earnings of Affiliate ........................... | | 12,000 |
|    Investment in Securities ..................................... | | 3,000 |

The debit to the Cash account results in an increase in Line (9) of $15,000. The recognition of equity in earnings increases net income on Line (1) by $12,000. Because the firm received $3,000 more cash than its equity in earnings, Line (2) increases by $3,000 when converting net income to cash flow from operations. An alternative acceptable answer for the increase in Line (2) of $3,000 is that Line (2) increases by $15,000 for the dividend received and Line (3) increases by $15,000 to subtract the equity in earnings.

n.  The journal entries to record this transaction are:

| | | |
|---|---|---|
| Cash........................................................................... | 22,000 | |
| Realized Loss on Sale of Marketable Securities | | |
|    (IncSt)................................................................ | 3,000 | |
|       Marketable Securities....................................... | | 25,000 |
| | | |
| Marketable Securities............................................... | 2,000 | |
|    Unrealized Holding Loss on Marketable | | |
|       Securities (SE/Comp Y) ................................... | | 2,000 |

The debit to the Cash account results in an increase in Line (9) of $22,000. Selling marketable securities is an investing transaction so Line (4) increases by $22,000. The recognition of a realized loss on the sale reduces net income on Line (1) by $3,000. Because the loss does not use cash, the accountant increases Line (2) by $3,000 to add back the loss to net income when converting net income to cash flow from operations.

13.1 continued.

o. The journal entry to record this transaction is:

| | | |
|---|---|---|
| Preferred Stock | 10,000 | |
| Common Stock | | 2,000 |
| Additional Paid-in Capital | | 8,000 |

This transaction affects neither the Cash account [Line (9)] nor net income [Line (1)]. Thus, it would not appear on the statement of cash flows. The firm discloses in a supplementary schedule or note the conversion of preferred stock into common stock totaling $10,000.

p. The journal entry to record this transaction is:

| | | |
|---|---|---|
| Legal Expense | 5,000 | |
| Land | | 5,000 |

The transaction does not affect the Cash account so Line (9) does not change. The recognition of legal expense reduces net income on Line (1) by $5,000. Because this expense does not use cash, Line (2) increases by $5,000 to convert net income to cash flow from operations.

q. The journal entry for this transaction is:

| | | |
|---|---|---|
| Rental Fees Received in Advance | 8,000 | |
| Rent Revenue | | 8,000 |

This entry does not affect the Cash account so Line (9) does not change. The recognition of rent revenue increases net income on Line (1) by $8,000. Because this revenue does not increase cash during the current period, Line (3) increases by $8,000 to convert net income to cash flow from operations.

r. The journal entry to record this event is:

| | | |
|---|---|---|
| Long-Term Debt | 30,000 | |
| Current Portion of Long-Term Debt | | 30,000 |

This entry affects neither the Cash account [Line (9)] nor net income [Line (1)] and would therefore not appear on the statement of cash flows.

13.1 continued.

s. The journal entry to record this event is:

Contracts in Process ....................................................... 15,000
    Contract Revenue ................................................ 15,000

This entry does not affect the Cash account so Line (9) does not change. The recognition of contract revenue increases net income on Line (1) by $15,000. Because this revenue does not result in a change in cash, Line (3) increases by $15,000 to convert net income to cash flow from operations.

t. The journal entry to record this transaction is:

Land ............................................................................. 50,000
    Donated Capital (SE) .......................................... 50,000

This transaction affects neither the Cash account [Line (9)] nor net income [Line (1)] and therefore does not appear on the statement of cash flows. The firm discloses in a supplementary schedule or note the donation of land by a governmental agency totaling $50,000.

u. The journal entry to record this event is:

Unrealized Holding Loss on Investments in
    Securities (SE/Comp Y) ....................................... 8,000
        Investments in Securities ................................ 8,000

This transaction affects neither the Cash account [Line (9)] nor net income [Line (1)] so would not appear on the statement of cash flows. The firm discloses in a supplementary schedule or note the write down of marketable equity investments totaling $8,000.

v. The journal entry to record the recognition of depreciation is:

Inventories ................................................................. 60,000
    Accumulated Depreciation .................................. 60,000

The journal entry to record the sale of the inventory items is:

Cost of Goods Sold ...................................................... 60,000
    Inventories .......................................................... 60,000

These entries do not affect the Cash account so Line (9) does not change. The recognition of cost of goods sold containing depreciation reduces net income on Line (1) by $60,000. Because this expense does not use cash, Line (2) increases by $60,000 to convert net income to cash flow from operations.

13.1 continued.

w. The journal entry to record this transaction is:

Warranty Expense...................................................... 35,000
    Estimated Warranty Liability............................            35,000

This entry does not affect the Cash account so Line (9) does not change. The recognition of warranty expense reduces net income on Line (1) by $35,000. Because this expense does not use cash, Line (2) increases by $35,000 to convert net income to cash flow from operations.

x. The journal entry to record this transaction is:

Estimated Warranty Liability................................... 28,000
    Cash.........................................................................            28,000

The credit to the Cash account reduces Line (9) by $28,000. Using cash to service a warranty is an operating transaction. This entry does not affect net income on Line (1) this period. Thus, Line (3) increases by $28,000 to convert net income to cash flow from operations.

y. The journal entry to record this event is:

Income Tax Expense ................................................. 80,000
Deferred Tax Liability.............. ........................... 20,000
    Cash.........................................................................           100,000

The credit to the Cash account results in a reduction in Line (9) of $100,000. The recognition of income tax expense reduces net income on Line (1) by $80,000. Because the firm used more cash this period than the amount of income tax expense, Line (3) increases by $20,000 when converting net income to cash flow from operations.

z. The journal entry to record this event is:

Loss from Writedown of Inventories ........................ 18,000
    Inventories .............................................................           18,000

This entry does not affect the Cash account so Line (9) does not change. The recognition of the writedown reduces net income on Line (1) by $18,000. Because the writedown did not use cash, Line (2) increases by $18,000 to convert net income to cash flow from operations.

**13.2** (Effects of transactions on cash changes equation.)

a.

| | ΔC | = | ΔL | + | ΔSE | − | ΔN$C |
|---|---|---|---|---|---|---|---|
| Financing | −$12,000 | = | $3,000 | + | −$15,000 | − | $0 |

b.

| | ΔC | = | ΔL | + | ΔSE | − | ΔN$A |
|---|---|---|---|---|---|---|---|
| Financing | +$75,000 | = | $75,000 | + | $0 | − | $0 |

c.

| | ΔC | = | ΔL | + | ΔSE | − | ΔN$A |
|---|---|---|---|---|---|---|---|
| Operations | +$15,000 | = | $0 | + | +$15,000 | − | $0 |
| Investing | +$20,000 | = | $0 | + | $0 | − | $5,000 |
| Operations | −$15,000 | | | | | − | |
| Net | $20,000 | = | $0 | + | $15,000 | − | $5,000 |

d.

| | ΔC | = | ΔL | + | ΔSE | − | ΔNC$ |
|---|---|---|---|---|---|---|---|
| Operations | −$28,000 | = | $0 | + | −$28,000 | − | $0 |

e.

| | ΔC | = | ΔL | + | ΔSE | − | ΔN$A |
|---|---|---|---|---|---|---|---|
| Investing | −$39,000 | = | $0 | + | $0 | − | $39,000 |

f.

| | ΔC | = | ΔL | + | ΔSE | − | ΔN$A |
|---|---|---|---|---|---|---|---|
| | $0 | = | $0 | + | $0 | − | $14,000 |
| | | | | | | + | $14,000 |
| Net | $0 | = | $0 | + | $0 | + | $0 |

g.

| | ΔC | = | ΔL | + | ΔSE | − | ΔN$A |
|---|---|---|---|---|---|---|---|
| | $0 | = | $0 | + | −$8,000 | − | −$8,000 |

h.

| | ΔC | = | ΔL | + | ΔSE | − | ΔN$A |
|---|---|---|---|---|---|---|---|
| Operations | −$14,500 | = | $500 | + | −$15,000 | − | $0 |

i.

| | ΔC | = | ΔL | + | ΔSE | − | ΔN$A |
|---|---|---|---|---|---|---|---|
| Operations | −$22,000 | = | $0 | + | −$22,000 | − | $0 |
| Operations | +$22,000 | = | $0 | + | $0 | − | −$22,000 |
| Net | $0 | = | $0 | + | −$22,000 | − | −$22,000 |

j.

| | ΔC | = | ΔL | + | ΔSE | − | ΔN$A |
|---|---|---|---|---|---|---|---|
| Investing | −$40,000 | = | $360,000 | + | $0 | − | $400,000 |

k.

| | ΔC | = | ΔL | + | ΔSE | − | ΔN$A |
|---|---|---|---|---|---|---|---|
| Operations | −$32,000 | = | $0 | + | −$32,000 | − | $0 |
| Operations | +$32,000 | = | $0 | + | $0 | − | −$32,000 |
| Net | $0 | = | $0 | + | −$32,000 | − | −$32,000 |

l.

| | ΔC | = | ΔL | + | ΔSE | − | ΔN$A |
|---|---|---|---|---|---|---|---|
| | $0 | = | $0 | + | $0 | − | $28,000 |
| | | = | | | | + | $28,000 |
| Net | $0 | = | $0 | + | $0 | − | $0 |

13.2 continued.

m.

| | ΔC | = | ΔL | + | ΔSE | − | ΔN$A |
|---|---|---|---|---|---|---|---|
| Operations | $12,000 | = | $0 | + | $12,000 | − | $0 |
| Operations | $3,000 | = | $0 | + | $0 | − | −$3,000 |
| Net | $15,000 | = | $0 | + | $12,000 | − | −$3,000 |

n.

| | ΔC | = | ΔL | + | ΔSE | − | ΔN$A |
|---|---|---|---|---|---|---|---|
| Operations | −$3,000 | = | $0 | + | −$3,000 | − | $0 |
| Investing | +$22,000 | | | | | − | −$25,000 |
| Operations | +$3,000 | | | | | | |
| | $0 | = | $0 | + | $2,000 | − | $2,000 |
| Net | +$22,000 | = | $0 | + | −$1,000 | − | −$23,000 |

o.

| | ΔC | = | ΔL | + | ΔSE | − | ΔN$A |
|---|---|---|---|---|---|---|---|
| | $0 | = | $0 | + | $10,000 | − | $0 |
| | | | | | −$10,000 | − | |
| | $0 | = | $0 | + | $0 | − | $0 |

p.

| | ΔC | = | ΔL | + | ΔSE | − | ΔN$A |
|---|---|---|---|---|---|---|---|
| Operations | −$5,000 | = | $0 | + | −$5,000 | − | $0 |
| Operations | +$5,000 | = | $0 | + | $0 | − | −$5,000 |
| Net | $0 | = | $0 | + | −$5,000 | − | −$5,000 |

q.

| | ΔC | = | ΔL | + | ΔSE | − | ΔN$A |
|---|---|---|---|---|---|---|---|
| Operations | +$8,000 | = | $0 | + | $8,000 | − | $0 |
| Operations | −$8,000 | = | −$8,000 | + | $0 | − | $0 |
| Net | $0 | = | −$8,000 | + | $8,000 | − | $0 |

r.

| | ΔC | = | ΔL | + | ΔSE | − | ΔN$A |
|---|---|---|---|---|---|---|---|
| | $0 | = | $30,000 | + | $0 | − | $0 |
| | | = | −30,000 | | | | |
| Net | $0 | = | $0 | + | $0 | − | $0 |

s.

| | ΔC | = | ΔL | + | ΔSE | − | ΔN$A |
|---|---|---|---|---|---|---|---|
| Operations | +$15,000 | = | $0 | + | $15,000 | − | $0 |
| Operations | −$15,000 | = | $0 | + | $0 | − | $15,000 |
| Net | $0 | = | $0 | + | $15,000 | − | $15,000 |

t.

| | ΔC | = | ΔL | + | ΔSE | − | ΔN$A |
|---|---|---|---|---|---|---|---|
| | $0 | = | $0 | + | $50,000 | − | $50,000 |

u.

| | ΔC | = | ΔL | + | ΔSE | − | ΔN$A |
|---|---|---|---|---|---|---|---|
| | $0 | = | $0 | + | −$8,000 | − | −$8,000 |

v.

| | ΔC | = | ΔL | + | ΔSE | − | ΔN$A |
|---|---|---|---|---|---|---|---|
| Operations | −$60,000 | = | $0 | + | −$60,000 | − | $0 |
| Operations | +$60,000 | = | $0 | + | $0 | − | −$60,000 |
| Net | $0 | = | $0 | + | −$60,000 | − | −$60,000 |

13.2 continued.

w.

| | $\Delta C$ | = | $\Delta L$ | + | $\Delta SE$ | – | $\Delta N\$A$ |
|---|---|---|---|---|---|---|---|
| Operations | –$35,000 | = | $0 | + | –$35,000 | – | $0 |
| Operations | +$35,000 | = | $35,000 | + | $0 | – | $0 |
| Net | $0 | = | $35,000 | + | –$35,000 | – | $0 |

x.

| | $\Delta C$ | = | $\Delta L$ | + | $\Delta SE$ | – | $\Delta N\$A$ |
|---|---|---|---|---|---|---|---|
| Operations | –$28,000 | = | –$28,000 | + | $0 | – | $0 |

y.

| | $\Delta C$ | = | $\Delta L$ | + | $\Delta SE$ | – | $\Delta N\$A$ |
|---|---|---|---|---|---|---|---|
| Operations | –$80,000 | = | $0 | + | –$80,000 | – | $0 |
| Operations | –$20,000 | = | –$20,000 | + | $0 | – | $0 |
| Net | –$100,000 | = | –$20,000 | + | –$80,000 | – | $0 |

z.

| | $\Delta C$ | = | $\Delta L$ | + | $\Delta SE$ | – | $\Delta N\$A$ |
|---|---|---|---|---|---|---|---|
| Operations | –$18,000 | = | $0 | + | –$18,000 | – | $0 |
| Operations | +$18,000 | = | $0 | + | $0 | – | –$18,000 |
| Net | $0 | = | $0 | + | –$18,000 | – | –$18,000 |

13.3 (Alcoa; working backwards from statement of cash flows.)

(2) Cash (Operations—Depreciation Expense Add-back)............................................................ 664.0
  Accumulated Depreciation................................. 664.0

(3) Cash (Operations—Deferred Tax Addback)............ 82.0
  Deferred Income Tax Liability............................. 82.0

(4) Investment in Affiliates......................................... 47.1
  Cash (Operations—Equity in Undistributed
  Earnings Subtraction) ....................................... 47.1

(5) Cash (Investing—Sale of Marketable Secur-
&  ities)............................................................... 49.8
(11)  Cash (Operations—Gain on Sale of Mar-
   ketable Securities Subtraction)................... 20.8
  Marketable Securities .................................... 29.0

(6) Cash (Operations—Decrease in Accounts Re-
 ceivable)............................................................. 74.6
  Accounts Receivable ....................................... 74.6

(7) Inventories ............................................................. 198.9
  Cash (Operations—Increase in Inventories)...... 198.9

(8) Prepayments............................................................ 40.3
  Cash (Operations—Increase in Prepayments).. 40.3

13.3 continued.

(9) Cash (Operations—Increase in Accounts Payable) ................................................ 33.9

     Accounts Payable ............................................. 33.9

(10) Other Current Liabilities ................................. 110.8

     Cash (Operations—Decrease in Other Current Liabilities) ............................................. 110.8

(12) Marketable Securities.................................... 73.2

     Cash (Investing—Acquisition of Marketable Securities)............................................. 73.2

(13) Property, Plant and Equipment ...................... 875.7

     Cash (Investing—Acquisition of Property, Plant and Equipment) ............................. 875.7

(14) Investments in Securities ............................. 44.5

     Cash (Investing—Acquisition of Subsidiaries) ... 44.5

(15) Cash (Financing—Common Stock Issued to Employees) ................................................ 34.4

     Common Stock ................................................ 34.4

(16) Treasury Stock ............................................. 100.9

     Cash (Financing—Repurchase of Common Stock)........................................................ 100.9

(17) Retained Earnings........................................ 242.9

     Cash (Financing—Dividends Paid to Shareholders) ....................................................... 242.9

(18) Cash (Financing—Additions to Short-Term Borrowing).................................................... 127.6

     Notes Payable................................................. 127.6

(19) Cash (Financing—Additions to Long-Term Borrowing).................................................... 121.6

     Bonds Payable ............................................... 121.6

(20) Bonds Payable ............................................. 476.4

     Cash (Financing—Payments to Long-Term Borrowing).................................................... 476.4

(21) Property, Plant and Equipment ...................... 76.9

     Mortgage Payable........................................... 76.9

13.3 continued.

    (22)  Property, Plant and Equipment ............................. 98.2

             Capitalized Lease Obligation................................          98.2

    (23)  Convertible Bonds Payable................................... 47.8

             Common Stock.........................................................          47.8

13.4     (Ingersoll-Rand; working backwards from statement of cash flows.)

    (2)  Cash (Operations—Depreciation Expense Add-
         back)............................................................................ 179.4

          Accumulated Depreciation .............................         179.4

    (3)  Cash (Investing—Sale of Property, Plant, and
   &     Equipment.......................................................... 26.5

    (12)       Property, Plant and Equipment (Net)..............         22.9

            Cash (Operations—Gain on Sale
            Subtraction)...................................................           3.6

    (4)  Investment in Securities ....................................... 41.5

          Cash (Operations—Equity in Earnings
          Subtraction) .....................................................         41.5

    (5)  Cash (Operations—Deferred Taxes Addback)........ 15.1

          Deferred Income Taxes.......................................         15.1

    (6)  Cash (Operations—Decrease in Accounts Re-
         ceivable)...................................................................... 50.9

          Accounts Receivable .........................................         50.9

    (7)  Inventories ................................................................. 15.2

          Cash (Operations—Increase in Inventories)......         15.2

    (8)  Other Current Assets............................................... 33.1

          Cash (Operations—Increase in Other Cur-
          rent Assets).........................................................         33.1

    (9)  Accounts Payable....................................................... 37.9

          Cash (Operations—Decrease in Accounts
          Payable) ...............................................................         37.9

    (10)  Cash (Operations—Increase in Other Current
         Liabilities)................................................................... 19.2

          Other Current Liabilities ....................................         19.2

    (11)  Property, Plant and Equipment ............................ 211.7

         Cash (Investing—Acquisition of Property,
         Plant and Equipment) ......................................         211.7

13.4 continued.

| | | |
|---|---|---|
| (13) Marketable Securities..................................... | 4.6 | |
|     Cash (Investing—Acquisition of Marketable Securities)................................................ | | 4.6 |
| (14) Cash (Investing—Advances from Equity Companies)................................................ | 18.4 | |
|     Advances from Equity Companies................... | | 18.4 |
| (15) Short-Term Debt.......................................... | 81.5 | |
|     Cash (Financing—Repayment of Short-Term Debt)................................................ | | 81.5 |
| (16) Cash (Financing—Issue of Long-Term Debt).......... | 147.6 | |
|     Long-Term Debt Payable................................ | | 147.6 |
| (17) Long-Term Debt Payable ............................. | 129.7 | |
|     Cash (Financing—Repayment of Long-Term Debt)................................................ | | 129.7 |
| (18) Cash (Financing—Issue of Common Stock under Option Plan)..................................... | 47.9 | |
|     Common Stock, Additional Paid-in Capital..... | | 47.9 |
| (19) Cash (Financing—Sale of Treasury Stock) ............. | 59.3 | |
|     Treasury Stock, Additional Paid in Capital......... | | 59.3 |
| (20) Retained Earnings....................................... | 78.5 | |
|     Cash (Financing—Dividends Paid)...................... | | 78.5 |
| (21) Leasehold Asset........................................... | 147.9 | |
|     Capitalized Lease Obligation............................. | | 147.9 |
| (22) Preferred Stock.......................................... | 62.0 | |
|     Common Stock, Additional Paid-in Capital......... | | 62.0 |
| (23) Investments in Securities ........................... | 94.3 | |
|     Common Stock, Additional Paid-in Capital......... | | 94.3 |

13.5    See solution to Problem 8.42.

13.6    See solution to Problem 9.45.

13.7    See solution to Problem 11.54.

13.8    See solution to Problem 11.55.

13.9    See solution to Problem 12.42.

13.10    (Warren Corporation; preparing a statement of cash flows.)

a.

|  | Cash | | | |
|---|---|---|---|---|
| | √ 223,200 | | | |

**Operations**

| | | | | |
|---|---|---|---|---|
| Net Income | (5) 234,000 | | | |
| Loss on Sale of Machinery | (1b) 15,600 | | | |
| Amortize Patent | (2b) 5,040 | | | |
| Decrease in Accounts Receivable | (7) 18,000 | | | |
| Bad Debt Expense | (8) 2,400 | | | |
| Decrease in Inventories | (9) 66,000 | | | |
| Depreciation Expense | (11) 106,800 | | | |
| Amortize Leasehold Improvements | (12) 10,800 | | | |
| Increase in Accounts Payable | (13) 153,360 | | | |

**Investing**

| | | | | |
|---|---|---|---|---|
| Sale of Machinery | (1b) 57,600 | 463,200 (1a) | Acquisition of Machinery |
| | | 2,400 (2a) | Payment for Patent Defense |
| | | 180,000 (10) | Acquisition of Securities |

**Financing**

| | | | | |
|---|---|---|---|---|
| | | 13,200 (3) | Retirement of Preferred Stock |
| | | 60,000 (15) | Provision for Current Portion of Serial Bonds |

| | | | | |
|---|---|---|---|---|
| | √ 174,000 | | | |

13.10 a. continued.

| Accounts Receivable | | | Allowance for Un-<br>collectible Accounts | | | Inventory | | |
|---|---|---|---|---|---|---|---|---|
| √ 327,600 | | | | 20,400 √ | √ | 645,600 | | |
| | 3,600 (6) | (6) 3,600 | 2,400 (8) | | | | 66,000 (9) |
| | 18,000 (7) | | | | | | |
| √ 306,000 | | | | 19,200 √ | √ | 579,600 | | |

| Securities Held for<br>Plant Expansion | | Machinery and<br>Equipment (Cost) | | | Accumulated<br>Depreciation | | |
|---|---|---|---|---|---|---|---|
| √ -0- | | √ 776,400 | | | | 446,400 √ |
| (10) 180,000 | | (1a) 463,200 | 127,200 (1b) | (1b) 54,000 | 106,800 (11) |
| √ 180,000 | | √ 1,112,400 | | | | 499,200 √ |

| Leasehold<br>Improvements | | Allowance for<br>Amortization | | | Patents | | |
|---|---|---|---|---|---|---|---|
| √ 104,400 | | | 58,800 √ | √ | 36,000 | | |
| | | | 10,800 (12) | (2a) 2,400 | 5,040 (2b) |
| √ 104,400 | | | 69,600 √ | √ | 33,360 | | |

| Accounts Payable | | Dividends Payable | | | Bonds Payable<br>(Current) | | |
|---|---|---|---|---|---|---|---|
| | 126,000 √ | | -- √ | | | 60,000 √ |
| | 153,360 (13) | | 48,000 (4) | (15) 60,000 | 60,000 (14) |
| | 279,360 √ | | 48,000 √ | | | 60,000 √ |

| 6-Percent<br>Serial Bonds Payable | | Preferred Stock | | Common Stock | |
|---|---|---|---|---|---|
| | 360,000 √ | | 120,000 √ | | 600,000 √ |
| (14) 60,000 | | (3) 12,000 | | | |
| | 300,000 √ | | 108,000 √ | | 600,000 √ |

| Retained Earnings | |
|---|---|
| | 321,600 √ |
| (4) 48,000 | 234,000 (5) |
| (3) 1,200 | |
| | 506,400 √ |

13.10 continued.

b.

**WARREN CORPORATION**
**Statement of Cash Flows**
**For the Year Ending December 31, Year 5**

Operations:

| | | |
|---|---:|---:|
| Net Income | $234,000 | |
| Loss on Sale of Machinery | 15,600 | |
| Depreciation | 106,800 | |
| Amortization of Leasehold Improvements | 10,800 | |
| Amortization of Patents | 5,040 | |
| Bad Debt Expense | 2,400 | |
| Decrease in Accounts Receivable | 18,000 | |
| Decrease in Inventories | 66,000 | |
| Increase in Accounts Payable | 153,360 | |
| Cash Flow from Operations | | $612,000 |
| Investing: | | |
| Sale of Machinery | $ 57,600 | |
| Payment of Legal Fee for Patent Defense | (2,400) | |
| Acquisition of Securities for Plant Expansion | (180,000) | |
| Acquisition of Machinery | (463,200) | |
| Cash Flow from Investing | | (588,000) |
| Financing: | | |
| Retirement of Serial Bonds | $ (60,000) | |
| Retirement of Preferred Stock | (13,200) | |
| Cash Flow from Financing | | (73,200) |
| Net Change in Cash | | $ (49,200) |
| Cash, January 1, Year 5 | | 223,200 |
| Cash, December 31, Year 5 | | $174,000 |

**13.11** (Roth Company; preparing a statement of cash flows.)

a.

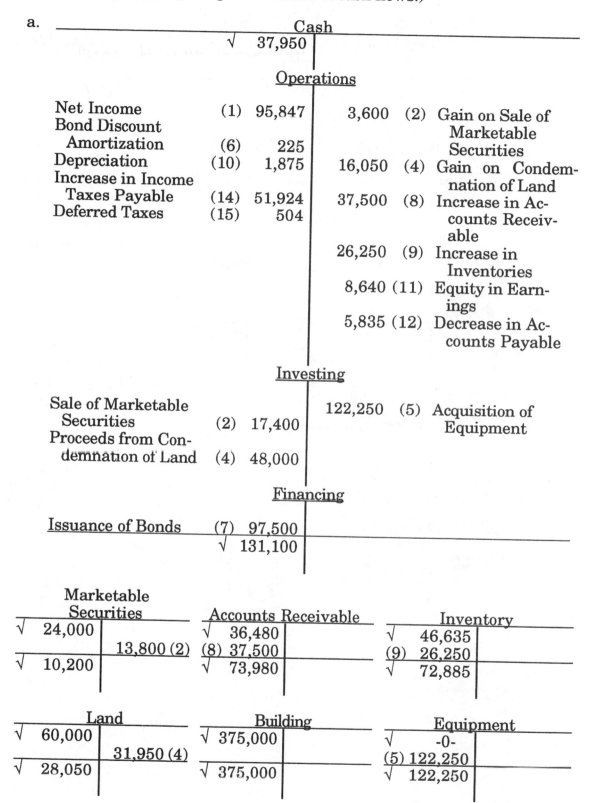

**Cash**

√ 37,950

**Operations**

| | | | | | |
|---|---|---|---|---|---|
| Net Income | (1) | 95,847 | 3,600 | (2) | Gain on Sale of Marketable Securities |
| Bond Discount Amortization | (6) | 225 | | | |
| Depreciation | (10) | 1,875 | 16,050 | (4) | Gain on Condemnation of Land |
| Increase in Income Taxes Payable | (14) | 51,924 | 37,500 | (8) | Increase in Accounts Receivable |
| Deferred Taxes | (15) | 504 | | | |
| | | | 26,250 | (9) | Increase in Inventories |
| | | | 8,640 | (11) | Equity in Earnings |
| | | | 5,835 | (12) | Decrease in Accounts Payable |

**Investing**

| | | | | | |
|---|---|---|---|---|---|
| Sale of Marketable Securities | (2) | 17,400 | 122,250 | (5) | Acquisition of Equipment |
| Proceeds from Condemnation of Land | (4) | 48,000 | | | |

**Financing**

| | | |
|---|---|---|
| Issuance of Bonds | (7) | 97,500 |
| | √ | 131,100 |

| Marketable Securities | | Accounts Receivable | | Inventory | |
|---|---|---|---|---|---|
| √ 24,000 | | √ 36,480 | | √ 46,635 | |
| | 13,800 (2) | (8) 37,500 | | (9) 26,250 | |
| √ 10,200 | | √ 73,980 | | √ 72,885 | |

| Land | | Building | | Equipment | |
|---|---|---|---|---|---|
| √ 60,000 | | √ 375,000 | | √ -0- | |
| | 31,950 (4) | | | (5) 122,250 | |
| √ 28,050 | | √ 375,000 | | √ 122,250 | |

## 13.11 a. continued.

| Accumulated Depreciation | |
|---|---|
| | 22,500 √ |
| | 1,875(10) |
| | 24,375 √ |

| Investment in 30-Percent Owned Co. | |
|---|---|
| √ 91,830 | |
| (11) 8,640 | |
| √ 100,470 | |

| Other Assets | |
|---|---|
| √ 22,650 | |
| √ 22,650 | |

| Accounts Payable | |
|---|---|
| | 31,830 √ |
| (12) 5,835 | |
| | 25,995 √ |

| Dividends Payable | |
|---|---|
| | -0- √ |
| | 12,000(13) |
| | 12,000 √ |

| Income Taxes Payable | |
|---|---|
| | -0- √ |
| | 51,924(14) |
| | 51,924 √ |

| Other Liabilities | |
|---|---|
| | 279,000 √ |
| | 279,000 √ |

| Bonds Payable | |
|---|---|
| | 71,550 √ |
| | 225 (6) |
| | 97,500 (7) |
| | 169,275 √ |

| Deferred Income Taxes | |
|---|---|
| | 765 √ |
| | 504(15) |
| | 1,269 √ |

| Preferred Stock | |
|---|---|
| | 45,000 √ |
| (3) 45,000 | |
| | -0- √ |

| Common Stock | |
|---|---|
| | 120,000 √ |
| | 45,000 (3) |
| | 165,000 √ |

| Unrealized Holding Loss on Marketable Securities | |
|---|---|
| √ 750 | |
| √ 750 | |

| Retained Earnings | |
|---|---|
| | 124,650 √ |
| (13)12,000 | 95,847 (1) |
| | 208,497 √ |

13.11 continued.

b.

**ROTH COMPANY**
**Statement of Cash Flows**
**For the Three Months Ended March 31, Year 7**

Operations:

| | | |
|---|---:|---:|
| Net Income | $ 95,847 | |
| Bond Discount Amortization | 225 | |
| Depreciation | 1,875 | |
| Deferred Income Taxes | 504 | |
| Increase in Income Taxes Payable | 51,924 | |
| Gain on Sale of Marketable Securities | (3,600) | |
| Gain on Condemnation of Land | (16,050) | |
| Equity in Earnings | (8,640) | |
| Increase in Accounts Receivable | (37,500) | |
| Increase in Inventories | (26,250) | |
| Decrease in Accounts Payable | (5,835) | |
| Cash Flow from Operations | | $ 52,500 |
| Investing: | | |
| Proceeds from Sale of Marketable Securities | $ 17,400 | |
| Proceeds from Condemnation of Land | 48,000 | |
| Acquisition of Equipment | (122,250) | |
| Cash Flow from Investing | | (56,850) |
| Financing: | | |
| Issue of Bonds | $ 97,500 | |
| Cash Flow from Financing | | 97,500 |
| Net Change in Cash | | $ 93,150 |
| Cash, January 1 Year 7 | | 37,950 |
| Cash, March 31, Year 7 | | $ 131,100 |

**Supplementary Information**

Holders of the firm's preferred stock converted shares with a book value of $45,000 into shares of common stock.

**13.12** (Biddle Corporation; preparing a statement of cash flows.)

a.

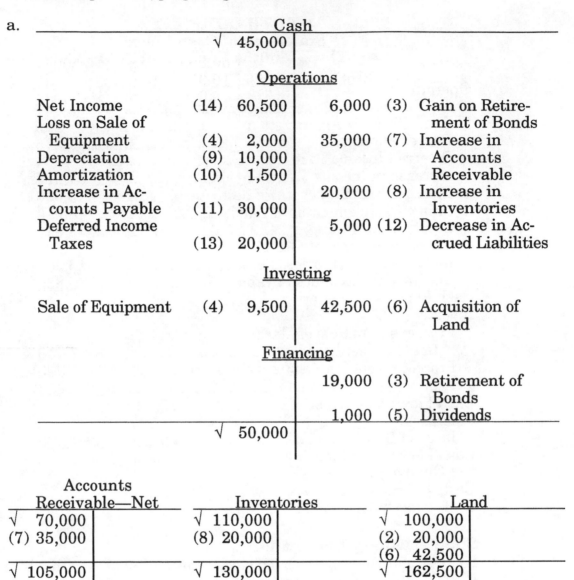

| Cash | | | | | |
|---|---|---|---|---|---|
| √ 45,000 | | | | | |

**Operations**

| Net Income | (14) | 60,500 | 6,000 | (3) | Gain on Retirement of Bonds |
| Loss on Sale of Equipment | (4) | 2,000 | 35,000 | (7) | Increase in Accounts Receivable |
| Depreciation | (9) | 10,000 | | | |
| Amortization | (10) | 1,500 | 20,000 | (8) | Increase in Inventories |
| Increase in Accounts Payable | (11) | 30,000 | 5,000 | (12) | Decrease in Accrued Liabilities |
| Deferred Income Taxes | (13) | 20,000 | | | |

**Investing**

| Sale of Equipment | (4) | 9,500 | 42,500 | (6) | Acquisition of Land |

**Financing**

| | | | 19,000 | (3) | Retirement of Bonds |
| | | | 1,000 | (5) | Dividends |
| | | √ 50,000 | | | |

| Accounts Receivable—Net | | Inventories | | Land | |
|---|---|---|---|---|---|
| √ 70,000 | | √ 110,000 | | √ 100,000 | |
| (7) 35,000 | | (8) 20,000 | | (2) 20,000 | |
| | | | | (6) 42,500 | |
| √ 105,000 | | √ 130,000 | | √ 162,500 | |

13.12 a. continued.

| Plant and Equipment | |
|---|---|
| √ 316,500 | |
| | 26,500 (4) |
| √ 290,000 | |

| Accumulated Depreciation | |
|---|---|
| | 50,000 √ |
| (4) 15,000 | 10,000 (9) |
| | 45,000 √ |

| Patents | |
|---|---|
| √ 16,500 | |
| | 1,500 (10) |
| √ 15,000 | |

| Accounts Payable | |
|---|---|
| | 100,000 √ |
| | 30,000 (11) |
| | 130,000 √ |

| Accrued Liabilities | |
|---|---|
| | 105,000 √ |
| (12) 5,000 | |
| | 100,000 √ |

| Deferred Income Taxes | |
|---|---|
| | 50,000 √ |
| | 20,000 (13) |
| | 70,000 √ |

| Long-term Bonds | |
|---|---|
| | 90,000 √ |
| (3) 25,000 | |
| | 65,000 √ |

| Common Stock | |
|---|---|
| | 105,000 √ |
| | 10,500 (1) |
| | 9,500 (2) |
| | 125,000 √ |

| Additional Paid-in Capital | |
|---|---|
| | 85,000 √ |
| | 21,000 (1) |
| | 10,500 (2) |
| | 116,500 √ |

| Retained Earnings | |
|---|---|
| | 73,000 √ |
| (1) 31,500 | 60,500 (14) |
| (5) 1,000 | |
| | 101,000 √ |

13.12 continued.

b.

**BIDDLE CORPORATION**
**Statement of Cash Flows**
**For the Year Ended December, Year 2**

| | | |
|---|---:|---:|
| Operations: | | |
| Net Income | $ 60,500 | |
| Loss on Sale of Equipment | 2,000 | |
| Depreciation | 10,000 | |
| Amortization | 1,500 | |
| Deferred Income Taxes | 20,000 | |
| Increase in Accounts Payable | 30,000 | |
| Gain on Retirement of Bonds | (6,000) | |
| Increase in Accounts Receivable | (35,000) | |
| Increase in Inventories | (20,000) | |
| Decrease in Accrued Liabilities | (5,000) | |
| Cash Flow from Operations | | $ 58,000 |
| Investing: | | |
| Sale of Equipment | $ 9,500 | |
| Acquisition of Land | (42,500) | |
| Cash Flow from Investing | | (33,000) |
| Financing: | | |
| Retirement of Bonds | $ (19,000) | |
| Dividends | (1,000) | |
| Cash Flow from Financing | | (20,000) |
| Net Change in Cash | | $ 5,000 |
| Cash, January 1, Year 2 | | 45,000 |
| Cash, December 31, Year 2 | | $ 50,000 |

**Supplementary Information**
During Year 2, Biddle Corporation issued common stock with a market value of $20,000 in the acquisition of land.

**13.13** (Plainview Corporation; preparing a statement of cash flows.)

a.

| Cash | | |
|---|---|---|
| √ 165,300 | | |

### Operations

| | | | | | |
|---|---|---:|---:|---|---|
| Net Income | (1) | 236,580 | 17,000 | (5) | Gain on Sale of |
| Loss from Fire | (6) | 35,000 | | | Marketable |
| Equity in Loss | (9) | 17,920 | | | Securities |
| Decrease in | | | 131,100 | (12) | Increase in |
| Accounts | | | | | Inventories |
| Receivable—Net | (11) | 59,000 | 1,400 | (13) | Increase in Pre- |
| Depreciation | (15) | 79,900 | | | payments |
| Increase in Ac- | | | 1,500 | (18) | Decrease in Ac- |
| counts Payable | (16) | 24,800 | | | crued Payables |
| Increase in Income | | | 500 | (20) | Deferred Taxes |
| Taxes Payable | (19) | 66,500 | | | |
| Loss on Retirement | | | | | |
| of Bonds | (21) | 5,000 | | | |

### Investing

| | | | | | |
|---|---|---:|---:|---|---|
| Sale of Marketable | | | 28,000 | (8) | Acquisition of |
| Securities | (5) | 127,000 | | | Machinery |
| Building Sold | (7) | 4,000 | 103,400 | (10) | Acquisition of |
| Bond Sinking Funds | | | | | Marketable |
| Utilized | (14) | 63,000 | | | Securities |

### Financing

| | | | | | |
|---|---|---:|---:|---|---|
| Sale of Treasury | | | 130,000 | (2) | Dividends |
| Stock | (3) | 6,000 | 145,000 | (17) | Payment of Note |
| Issuance of | | | | | Payable— |
| Debentures | (22) | 125,000 | | | Current |
| | | | 315,000 | (21) | Retirement of |
| | | | | | Bonds |
| √ 142,100 | | | | | |

## 13.13 a. continued.

| Marketable Securities | | |
|---|---|---|
| √ 129,200 | | |
| (10) 103,400 | 110,000 (5) | |
| √ 122,600 | | |

| Accounts Receivable—Net | | |
|---|---|---|
| √ 371,200 | | |
| | 59,000 (11) | |
| √ 312,200 | | |

| Inventories | | |
|---|---|---|
| √ 124,100 | | |
| (12) 131,100 | | |
| √ 255,200 | | |

| Prepayments | | |
|---|---|---|
| √ 22,000 | | |
| (13) 1,400 | | |
| √ 23,400 | | |

| Bond Sinking Fund | | |
|---|---|---|
| √ 63,000 | | |
| | 63,000 (14) | |
| √ -0- | | |

| Investment in Subsidiary | | |
|---|---|---|
| √ 152,000 | | |
| | 17,920 (9) | |
| √ 134,080 | | |

| Plant and Equipment—Net | | |
|---|---|---|
| √ 1,534,600 | | |
| (6) 65,000 | 100,000 (6) | |
| (8) 28,000 | 4,000 (7) | |
| | 79,900 (15) | |
| √ 1,443,700 | | |

| Accounts Payable | |
|---|---|
| | 213,300 √ |
| | 24,800 (16) |
| | 238,100 √ |

| Notes Payable—Current | |
|---|---|
| | 145,000 √ |
| (17) 145,000 | |
| | -0- √ |

| Accrued Payables | |
|---|---|
| | 18,000 √ |
| (18) 1,500 | |
| | 16,500 √ |

| Income Taxes Payable | |
|---|---|
| | 31,000 √ |
| | 66,500 (19) |
| | 97,500 √ |

| Deferred Income Taxes | |
|---|---|
| | 128,400 √ |
| (20) 500 | |
| | 127,900 √ |

| 6-Percent Mortgage Bonds | |
|---|---|
| | 310,000 √ |
| (21) 310,000 | |
| | -0- √ |

| 8-Percent Debentures | |
|---|---|
| | -0- √ |
| | 125,000 (22) |
| | 125,000 √ |

| Common Stock | |
|---|---|
| | 950,000 √ |
| | 83,500 (4) |
| | 1,033,500 √ |

| Additional Paid-in Capital | |
|---|---|
| | 51,000 √ |
| | 16,700 (4) |
| | 67,700 √ |

| Unrealized Holding Gain on Marketable Securities | |
|---|---|
| | 2,500 √ |
| | |
| | 2,500 √ |

| Retained Earnings | |
|---|---|
| | 755,700 √ |
| (2) 130,000 | 236,580 (1) |
| (3) 3,000 | |
| (4) 100,200 | |
| | 759,080 √ |

| Treasury Stock | |
|---|---|
| √ 43,500 | |
| | 9,000 (3) |
| √ 34,500 | |

13.13 continued.

b.

**PLAINVIEW CORPORATION**
**Statement of Cash Flows**
**For the Year Ended December, Year 5**

Operations:

| | | |
|---|---:|---:|
| Net Income ................................................................. | $236,580 | |
| Loss from Fire ............................................................ | 35,000 | |
| Equity in Loss of Subsidiary.................................... | 17,920 | |
| Depreciation.............................................................. | 79,900 | |
| Loss on Retirement of Bonds ................................. | 5,000 | |
| Gain on Sale of Marketable Securities.................... | (17,000) | |
| Deferred Income Taxes............................................. | (500) | |
| Decrease in Accounts Receivable—Net .................. | 59,000 | |
| Increase in Accounts Payable ................................. | 24,800 | |
| Increase in Income Taxes Payable .......................... | 66,500 | |
| Increase in Inventories............................................ | (131,100) | |
| Increase in Prepayments.......................................... | (1,400) | |
| Decrease in Accrued Payables................................. | (1,500) | |
| Cash Flow from Operations ..................................... | | $373,200 |
| Investing: | | |
| Marketable Securities Sold..................................... | $127,000 | |
| Building Sold.............................................................. | 4,000 | |
| Bond Sinking Funds Utilized.................................... | 63,000 | |
| Acquisition of Marketable Securities...................... | (103,400) | |
| Acquisition of Machinery......................................... | (28,000) | |
| Cash Flow from Investing ....................................... | | 62,600 |
| Financing: | | |
| Sale of Treasury Stock............................................. | $    6,000 | |
| Issue of Debentures ................................................. | 125,000 | |
| Dividends .................................................................. | (130,000) | |
| Retirement of Bonds ................................................ | (315,000) | |
| Payment of Short-Term Note.................................. | (145,000) | |
| Cash Flow from Financing....................................... | | (459,000) |
| Net Change in Cash.................................................. | | $ (23,200) |
| Cash, January 1, Year 5............................................ | | 165,300 |
| Cash, December 31, Year 5...................................... | | $142,100 |

**13.14** (UAL Corporation; preparing and interpreting the statement of cash flows.)

a. T-account work sheet for Year 9.

|  | **Cash** |  |  |
|---|---|---|---|
| √ | 1,087 |  |  |

|  | **Operations** |  |  |
|---|---|---|---|
| (1) | 324 | 106 | (4) |
| (3) | 517 | 147 | (7) |
| (11) | 56 | 39 | (8) |
| (15) | 42 | 67 | (9) |
| (17) | 12 | 49 | (16) |

|  | **Investing** |  |  |
|---|---|---|---|
| (4) | 1,199 | 1,568 | (2) |
| (10) | 40 | 957 | (6) |

|  | **Financing** |  |  |
|---|---|---|---|
| (12) | 325 | 110 | (13) |
| (18) | 4 | 98 | (19) |
| √ | 465 |  |  |

| **Marketable Securities** |  |  |
|---|---|---|
| √ | -- |  |
| (5) | 85 |  |
| (6) | 957 |  |
| √ | 1,042 |  |

| **Accounts Receivable** |  |  |
|---|---|---|
| √ | 741 |  |
| (7) | 147 |  |
| √ | 888 |  |

| **Inventories** |  |  |
|---|---|---|
| √ | 210 |  |
| (8) | 39 |  |
| √ | 249 |  |

| **Prepayments** |  |  |
|---|---|---|
| √ | 112 |  |
| (9) | 67 |  |
| √ | 179 |  |

| **Property, Plant and Equipment** |  |  |  |
|---|---|---|---|
| √ | 7,710 |  |  |
| (2) | 1,568 | 1,574 | (4) |
| √ | 7,704 |  |  |

| **Accumulated Depreciation** |  |  |  |
|---|---|---|---|
|  |  | 3,769 | √ |
| (4) | 481 | 517 | (3) |
|  |  | 3,805 | √ |

| **Other Assets** |  |  |  |
|---|---|---|---|
| √ | 610 |  |  |
|  |  | 40 | (10) |
| √ | 570 |  |  |

| **Accounts Payable** |  |  |
|---|---|---|
|  | 540 | √ |
|  | 56 | (11) |
|  | 596 | √ |

| **Short-Term Borrowing** |  |  |
|---|---|---|
|  | 121 | √ |
|  | 325 | (12) |
|  | 446 | √ |

**13.14 a. continued.**

| Current Portion Long-Term Debt | | |
|---|---|---|
| | 110 √ | |
| (13)  110 | 84 (14) | |
| | 84 √ | |

| Advances from Customers | |
|---|---|
| | 619 √ |
| | 42 (15) |
| | 661 √ |

| Other Current Liabilities | | |
|---|---|---|
| | | 1,485 √ |
| (16)  49 | | |
| | | 1,436 √ |

| Long-Term Debt | |
|---|---|
| | 1,418 √ |
| (14)  84 | |
| | 1,334 √ |

| Deferred Tax Liability | |
|---|---|
| | 352 √ |
| | 12 (17) |
| | 364 √ |

| Other Noncurrent Liabilities | |
|---|---|
| | 715 √ |
| | 4 (18) |
| | 719 √ |

| Common Stock | |
|---|---|
| | 119 √ |
| | 119 √ |

| Unrealized Holding Gain on Marketable Securities | |
|---|---|
| | -- √ |
| | 85 (5) |
| | 85 √ |

| Retained Earnings | |
|---|---|
| | 1,188 √ |
| | 324 (1) |
| | 1,512 √ |

| Treasury Stock | |
|---|---|
| √      14 | |
| (19)    98 | |
| √    112 | |

**Solutions**

13.14 a. continued.

a. T-account work sheet for Year 10.

Cash

| | | √ | 465 | | | |

Operations

| (1) | 101 | 286 | (4) |
|---|---|---|---|
| (3) | 560 | 25 | (7) |
| (15) | 182 | 74 | (8) |
| (16) | 390 | 30 | (9) |
| (18) | 4 | 44 | (11) |

Investing

| (4) | 1,697 | 2,821 | (2) |
|---|---|---|---|
| | | 17 | (6) |
| | | 35 | (10) |

Financing

| (12) | 1 | 84 | (13) |
|---|---|---|---|
| (17) | 230 | | |
| (19) | 2 | | |
| (20) | 5 | | |
| √ | 221 | | |

| Marketable Securities | | Accounts Receivable | | Inventories | |
|---|---|---|---|---|---|
| √ | 1,042 | √ | 888 | √ | 249 |
| (5) | 7 | (7) | 25 | (8) | 74 |
| (6) | 17 | | | | |
| √ | 1,066 | √ | 913 | √ | 323 |

| Prepayments | | Property, Plant and Equipment | | | Accumulated Depreciation | | |
|---|---|---|---|---|---|---|---|
| √ | 179 | √ | 7,704 | | | 3,805 | √ |
| (9) | 30 | (2) | 2,821 | 1,938 (4) | (4) 527 | 560 | (3) |
| √ | 209 | √ | 8,587 | | | 3,838 | √ |

13.14 a. continued.

| Other Assets | | | | Accounts Payable | | | | Short-Term Borrowing | | |
|---|---|---|---|---|---|---|---|---|---|---|
| √ | 570 | | | | | 596 | √ | | 446 | √ |
| (10) | 35 | | | (11) | 44 | | | | 1 | (12) |
| √ | 605 | | | | | 552 | √ | | 447 | √ |

| Current Portion Long-Term Debt | | | | Advances from Customers | | | | Other Current Liabilities | | |
|---|---|---|---|---|---|---|---|---|---|---|
| | | 84 | √ | | | 661 | √ | | 1,436 | √ |
| (13) | 84 | 89 | (14) | | | 182 | (15) | | 390 | (16) |
| | | 89 | √ | | | 843 | √ | | 1,826 | √ |

| Long-Term Debt | | | | Deferred Tax Liability | | | | Other Noncurrent Liabilities | | |
|---|---|---|---|---|---|---|---|---|---|---|
| | | 1,334 | √ | | | 364 | √ | | 719 | √ |
| (14) | 89 | 230 | (17) | | | 4 | (18) | | 2 | (19) |
| | | 1,475 | √ | | | 368 | √ | | 721 | √ |

| Common Stock | | | Additional Paid-in Capital | | | Unrealized Holding Gain on Marketable Securities | | |
|---|---|---|---|---|---|---|---|---|
| | 119 | √ | | 48 | √ | | 85 | √ |
| | 1 | (20) | | 4 | (20) | | 7 | (5) |
| | 120 | √ | | 52 | √ | | 92 | √ |

| Retained Earnings | | | Treasury Stock | | |
|---|---|---|---|---|---|
| | 1,512 | √ | √ | 112 | |
| | 101 | (1) | | | |
| | 1,613 | √ | √ | 112 | |

13.14 continued.

b.    **Comparative Statement of Cash Flows for UAL Corporation**
**(Amounts in Millions)**

| | Year 9 | Year 10 |
|---|---|---|
| Operations: | | |
| Net Income | $ 324 | $ 101 |
| Depreciation Expense | 517 | 560 |
| Deferred Income Taxes | 12 | 4 |
| Gain on Sale of Property, Plant and Equipment | (106) | (286) |
| (Increase) Decrease in Accounts Receivable | (147) | (25) |
| (Increase) Decrease in Inventories | (39) | (74) |
| (Increase) Decrease in Prepayments | (67) | (30) |
| Increase (Decrease) in Accounts Payable | 56 | (44) |
| Increase (Decrease) in Advances from Customers | 42 | 182 |
| Increase (Decrease) in Other Current Liabilities | (49) | 390 |
| Cash Flow from Operations | $ 543 | $ 778 |
| Investing: | | |
| Sale of Property, Plant and Equipment | $ 1,199 | $ 1,697 |
| Acquisition of Property, Plant and Equipment | (1,568) | (2,821) |
| Acquisition of Marketable Securities | (957) | (17) |
| (Increase) Decrease in Other Noncurrent Assets | 40 | (35) |
| Cash Flow from Investing | $(1,286) | $ (1,176) |
| Financing: | | |
| Increase in Short-Term Borrowing | $ 325 | $ 1 |
| Increase in Long-Term Borrowing | -- | 230 |
| Increase in Common Stock | -- | 5 |
| Decrease in Long-Term Borrowing | (110) | (84) |
| Acquisition of Treasury Stock | (98) | -- |
| Increase in Other Noncurrent Liabilities | 4 | 2 |
| Cash Flow from Financing | $ 121 | $ 154 |
| Net Change in Cash | $ (622) | $ (244) |
| Cash, January 1 | 1,087 | 465 |
| Cash, December 31 | $ 465 | $ 221 |

13.14 continued.

c.   During Year 9, cash flow from operations exceeded net income primarily because of the noncash expense for depreciation. Cash flows from operations and from the sale of property, plant and equipment were sufficient to finance capital expenditures. UAL Corporation used the excess cash flow as well as cash from additional short-term borrowing to repay long-term debt and reacquire treasury stock. It invested the remaining excess cash flow in short-term marketable securities. Although the balance in the cash account declined during Year 9, the combined balance in cash and marketable securities actually increased.

Net income declined in Year 10 relative to Year 9 but cash flow from operations increased. The increase occurred because UAL Corporation received increased cash advances from customers and stretched its other current liabilities. Cash flow from operations and from the sale of property, plant and equipment were insufficient to finance capital expenditures. UAL Corporation increased long-term borrowing and decreased the balance in its cash account to finance these capital expenditures.

One additional item to note for UAL Corporation is the significant turnover of aircraft each year. The airline sold older aircraft at a gain and replaced them with newer aircraft.

**13.15** (Irish Paper Company; preparing and interpreting the statement of cash flows.)

a. T-account work sheet for Year 9.

**Cash**

| | | |
|---|---|---|
| √ | 374 | |

**Operations**

| | | | | |
|---|---|---|---|---|
| (1) | 376 | 221 | (7) | |
| (6) | 306 | 31 | (8) | |
| (9) | 2 | 112 | (10) | |
| (12) | 54 | 59 | (11) | |
| (14) | 72 | 5 | (17) | |
| (18) | 87 | | | |

**Investing**

| | | | | |
|---|---|---|---|---|
| (7) | 5 | 92 | (3) | |
| (13) | 8 | 775 | (4) | |

**Financing**

| | | | | |
|---|---|---|---|---|
| (5) | 449 | 59 | (2) | |
| | | 129 | (16) | |
| | | 201 | (19) | |
| √ | 49 | | | |

| Accounts Receivable | | | Inventories | | | Prepayments | | |
|---|---|---|---|---|---|---|---|---|
| √ | 611 | | √ | 522 | | √ | 108 | |
| (10) | 112 | | (11) | 59 | | | | 54 (12) |
| √ | 723 | | √ | 581 | | √ | 54 | |

| Investments in Affiliates | | | Property, Plant and Equipment | | | Accumulated Depreciation | | |
|---|---|---|---|---|---|---|---|---|
| √ | 254 | | √ | 5,272 | | | | 2,160 √ |
| (3) | 92 | 2 (9) | (4) | 775 | 78 (7) | (7) | 74 | 306 (6) |
| (8) | 31 | | | | | | | |
| √ | 375 | | √ | 5,969 | | | | 2,392 √ |

| Other Assets | | | Accounts Payable | | | Current Portion Long-Term Debt | | |
|---|---|---|---|---|---|---|---|---|
| √ | 175 | | | | 920 √ | | | 129 √ |
| (7) | 220 | 8 (13) | | | 72 (14) | (16) | 129 | 221 (15) |
| √ | 387 | | | | 992 √ | | | 221 √ |

13.15 a. continued.

| Other Current Liabilities | | | Long-Term Debt | | | Deferred Income Taxes | | |
|---|---|---|---|---|---|---|---|---|
| | | 98 √ | | | 1,450 √ | | | 607 √ |
| (17) | 5 | | (15) | 221 | 449 (5) | | | 87 (18) |
| | | 93 √ | | | 1,678 √ | | | 694 √ |

| Common Stock | | | Retained Earnings | | | Treasury Stock | | |
|---|---|---|---|---|---|---|---|---|
| | | 629 √ | | | 1,331 √ √ | | 15 | |
| (19) | 201 | | (2) | 59 | 376 (1) | | | |
| | | 428 √ | | | 1,648 √ √ | | 15 | |

a. T-account work sheet for Year 10.

**Cash**

| | | |
|---|---|---|
| √ | 49 | |

**Operations**

| | | | | |
|---|---|---|---|---|
| (1) | 169 | | 19 | (8) |
| (7) | 346 | | 38 | (9) |
| (10) | 5 | | 106 | (11) |
| (14) | 186 | | 154 | (12) |
| | | | 10 | (17) |
| | | | 20 | (18) |

**Investing**

| | | | | |
|---|---|---|---|---|
| (3) | 86 | | 931 | (4) |
| (8) | 21 | | 78 | (13) |

**Financing**

| | | | | |
|---|---|---|---|---|
| (5) | 890 | | 59 | (2) |
| (19) | 4 | | 221 | (16) |
| √ | 114 | | | |

| Accounts Receivable | | | Inventories | | | Prepayments | | |
|---|---|---|---|---|---|---|---|---|
| √ | 723 | | √ | 581 | | √ | 54 | |
| (11) | 106 | | (12) | 154 | | | | |
| √ | 829 | | √ | 735 | | √ | 54 | |

13.15 a. continued.

| | Investments in Affiliates | | |
|---|---|---|---|
| √ | 375 | | |
| (9) | 38 | 86 | (3) |
| | | 5 | (10) |
| √ | 322 | | |

| | Property, Plant and Equipment | | |
|---|---|---|---|
| √ | 5,969 | | |
| (4) | 931 | 42 | (8) |
| (6) | 221 | | |
| √ | 7,079 | | |

| | Accumulated Depreciation | | |
|---|---|---|---|
| | | 2,392 | √ |
| (8) | 40 | 346 | (7) |
| | | 2,698 | √ |

| | Other Assets | |
|---|---|---|
| √ | 387 | |
| (13) | 78 | |
| √ | 465 | |

| Accounts Payable | | |
|---|---|---|
| | 992 | √ |
| | 186 | (14) |
| | 1,178 | √ |

| | Current Portion Long-Term Debt | | |
|---|---|---|---|
| | | 221 | √ |
| (16) | 221 | 334 | (15) |
| | | 334 | √ |

| | Other Current Liabilities | |
|---|---|---|
| | | 93 | √ |
| (17) | 10 | |
| | | 83 | √ |

| | Long-Term Debt | | |
|---|---|---|---|
| | | 1,678 | √ |
| (15) | 334 | 890 | (5) |
| | | 221 | (6) |
| | | 2,455 | √ |

| | Deferred Income Taxes | |
|---|---|---|
| | | 694 | √ |
| (18) | 26 | |
| | | 668 | √ |

| Common Stock | | |
|---|---|---|
| | 428 | √ |
| | 4 | (19) |
| | 432 | √ |

| | Retained Earnings | | |
|---|---|---|---|
| | | 1,648 | √ |
| (2) | 59 | 169 | (1) |
| | | 1,758 | √ |

| | Treasury Stock | |
|---|---|---|
| √ | 15 | |
| | | |
| √ | 15 | |

| | Other Current Liabilities | |
|---|---|---|
| | | 83 | √ |
| (17) | 45 | |
| | | 38 | √ |

| | Long-Term Debt | | |
|---|---|---|---|
| | | 2,455 | √ |
| (15) | 158 | 36 | (5) |
| | | 2,333 | √ |

| | Deferred Income Taxes | |
|---|---|---|
| | | 668 | √ |
| (18) | 7 | |
| | | 661 | √ |

13.15 a. continued.

| Common Stock | | Retained Earnings | | | Treasury Stock | |
|---|---|---|---|---|---|---|
| | 432 √ | | 1,758 √ | √ | 15 | |
| | 7 (19) | (1) 142 | | | | 1 (19) |
| | | (2) 59 | | | | |
| | 439 √ | | 1,557 √ | √ | 14 | |

b.

**IRISH PAPER COMPANY**
**Statement of Cash Flows**
**(Amounts in Millions)**

| | Year 9 | Year 10 | Year 11 |
|---|---|---|---|
| Operations: | | | |
| Net Income (Loss) | $ 376 | $ 169 | $ (142) |
| Depreciation Expense | 306 | 346 | 353 |
| Loss (Gain) on Sale of Property, Plant and Equipment | (221) | (19) | 34 |
| Equity in Undistributed Earnings of Affiliates | (29) | (33) | 2 |
| Increase (Decrease) in Deferred Income Taxes | 87 | (26) | (7) |
| (Increase) Decrease in Accounts Receivable | (112) | (106) | 159 |
| (Increase) Decrease in Inventories | (59) | (154) | 104 |
| (Increase) Decrease in Prepayments | 54 | -- | (2) |
| Increase (Decrease) in Accounts Payable | 72 | 186 | 136 |
| Increase (Decrease) in Other Current Liabilities | (5) | (10) | (45) |
| Cash Flow from Operations | $ 469 | $ 353 | $ 652 |
| Investing: | | | |
| Sale of Property, Plant and Equipment | $ 5 | $ 21 | $ 114 |
| Acquisition of Property, Plant and Equipment | (775) | (931) | (315) |
| (Increase) Decrease in Investments in Affiliates | (92) | 86 | (13) |
| (Increase) Decrease in Other Assets | 8 | (78) | (19) |
| Cash Flow from Investing | $(854) | $(902) | $ (233) |

13.15 b. continued.

| Financing: | | | |
|---|---|---|---|
| Issue of Long-Term Debt........................ | $ 449 | $ 890 | $ 36 |
| Sale of Common Stork or Treasury Stock................................................ | -- | 4 | 8 |
| Redemption of Long-Term Debt............. | (129) | (221) | (334) |
| Redemption of Common Stock Warrants..................................................... | (201) | -- | -- |
| Dividends ............................................. | (59) | (59) | (59) |
| Cash Flow from Financing......................... | $ 60 | $ 614 | $ (349) |
| Net Change in Cash.................................... | $(325) | $ 65 | $ 70 |
| Cash, January 1.......................................... | 374 | 49 | 114 |
| Cash, December 31..................................... | $ 49 | $ 114 | $ 184 |

**Supplementary Information**
During Year 10, Irish Paper Company assumed a mortgage payable of $221 million in the acquisition of property, plant and equipment.

c.   The pattern of cash flows for Year 9 is typical of a growing, capital-intensive firm.  Cash flow from operations exceeds net income because of the addback of depreciation expense.  Book income before taxes exceeds taxable income, resulting in a deferral of taxes payable. Accounts receivable and inventories increased to support the growth, while accounts payable increased to finance the increased inventories. Irish made significant capital expenditures during the year for which it had to rely in part on external debt financing.

The pattern of cash flows for Year 10 is similar to that for Year 9, again typical of a growing firm.  In this case, however, cash flow from operations declines relative to Year 9 because of reduced net income. The reduced net income occurs in part because of a smaller gain on sale of property, plant and equipment and in part because of larger depreciation and administrative expenses.  Irish financed its increased capital expenditures with additional long-term borrowing.

The pattern of cash flows for Year 11 is typical of a firm that stopped growing.  Sales and net income declined, the result of under-utilizing manufacturing capacity. Cash flow from operations increased, however, because Irish collected receivables and decreased its investment in inventories.  It also stretched its accounts payable. Cash flow from operations was more than sufficient to finance a reduced level of capital expenditures and repay long-term dept.

**13.16** (Breda Enterprises, Inc.; preparing a statement of cash flows.)

## BREDA ENTERPRISES, INC.
## Statement of Cash Flows
## For the Year Ended December 31, Year 6

| | | |
|---|---:|---:|
| Operations: | | |
| Net Income (1)................................................... | $ 90,000 | |
| Adjustments for Noncash Transactions: | | |
| Decrease in Merchandise Inventory (3)................... | 4,000 | |
| Increase in Accounts Payable (3)........................... | 12,000 | |
| Loss on Sale of Equipment (4)................................ | 13,000 | |
| Depreciation Expense (4)....................................... | 42,000 | |
| Amortization of Leasehold Asset (5)...................... | 5,000 | |
| Loss on Conversion of Bonds (8) ........................... | 15,000 | |
| Increase in Accounts Receivable (Net) (2) ............. | (10,600) | |
| Increase in Notes Receivable (2) ........................... | (15,000) | |
| Increase in Interest Receivable (2) [(.08 X $15,000) X (1/6)].................................... | (200) | |
| Decrease in Advances from Customers (2) ........... | (2,700) | |
| Realized Gain on Marketable Securities (7)........... | (4,600) | |
| Amortization of Bond Premium (8)........................ | (1,500) | |
| Cash Flow from Operations............................................. | | $ 146,400 |
| Investing: | | |
| Sale of Equipment (4).............................................. | $ 25,000 | |
| Sale of Marketable Securities (7)........................... | 9,100 | |
| Purchase of Equipment (4) ($31,000 + $38,000 − $26,000) ........................................................... | (43,000) | |
| Cash Flow from Investing............................................. | | (8,900) |
| Financing: | | |
| Reduction of Lease Liability (5)............................. | $ (2,400) | |
| Dividends (6)........................................................... | (24,000) | |
| Cash Flow from Financing ........................................... | | (26,400) |
| Change in Cash ............................................................... | | $ 111,100 |

13.17    (L.A. Gear; interpreting the statement of cash flows.)

a.  The rate of increase in net income suggests that L.A. Gear grew rapidly during the three-year period. Increased investments in accounts receivable and inventories used operating cash flow. Increases in supplier credit did not fully finance the increased working capital investments, resulting in negative cash flow from operations.

b.  During Year 7, L.A. Gear sold marketable securities and borrowed short term to finance the negative cash flow from operations. Accounts receivable and inventories convert into cash within one year, so short-term financing is appropriate. Selling marketable securities to help finance these working capital investments suggests that the revenue from these securities was less than the cost of additional short-term borrowing.

During Year 8, L.A. Gear relied on short-term borrowing to finance its working capital needs, matching the term structure of its financing with the term structure of its assets.

During Year 9, L.A. Gear issued additional common stock to finance its working capital needs. Several explanations for this switch in financing are possible. First, the proportion of debt in the capital structure may have reached a point after the borrowing in Year 8 that lenders considered the firm unduly risky, thereby raising the cost of additional borrowing. Second, L.A. Gear may have expected continuing rapid growth and wished to infuse a more permanent form of capital than short-term debt into the capital structure. Third, short-term borrowing rates might have increased significantly relative to long-term rates and L.A. Gear chose to access longer term sources of capital.

c.  L.A. Gear is growing rapidly, so that new capacity additions exceed depreciation recognized on existing capacity.

d.  L.A. Gear is not very capital intensive. The firm uses independent manufacturers in East Asia and markets its products through independent retailers. Thus, its property, plant and equipment serves primarily its administrative needs.

e.  L.A. Gear has few fixed assets that might serve as collateral for such borrowing. The principal collateral is short-term, so lenders likely prefer to extend short-term financing.

13.18 (Campbell Soup Company; interpreting the statement of cash flows.)

    a.   Campbell uses suppliers and other creditors to finance its working capital needs. Consumer foods is a mature industry in the United States, so Campbell's modest growth rate does not require large incremental investments in accounts receivable and inventories.

    b.   (1) Capital expenditures have declined slightly each year, suggesting little need to add productive capacity.

          (2) Depreciation expense is a growing percentage of acquisitions of property, plant and equipment, suggesting slower growth in manufacturing capacity.

          (3) Substantial trading in marketable securities each year. Mature, profitable firms tend to accumulate cash beyond their operating needs and invest in marketable securities until they need cash.

          (4) Acquisition of another business in Year 8. Firms in mature industries grow by acquiring other firms. Campbell financed this acquisition in part by selling marketable securities.

    c.   (1) Increases in long-term debt approximately equal repayments of long-term debt, particularly for Year 7 and Year 8. Mature firms tend to roll over debt as long as they remain in the no-growth phase.

          (2) Campbell repurchased a portion of its common stock with excess cash.

          (3) Dividends have grown in line with increases in net income and represent approximately a 37 percent payout rate relative to net income.

13.19 (Prime Contracting Services; interpreting the statement of cash flows.)

    a.   The firm reduced expenditures on fixed assets beginning in Year 7. It sold fixed assets in Year 9 and Year 10. The firm repaid debt under equipment loans and capital leases, probably because the firm sold or returned fixed assets that served as collateral for this debt. The increase in Other Current Liabilities indicates the heavier use of employees in providing services.

    b.   Net income declined between Year 6 and Year 8 as the firm attempted to build its new people-based service business. It collected accounts receivable from the previous asset-based service contracts. The continually increasing sales suggest that the firm collects receivables from its new people-based services more quickly than on its previous asset-based services contracts. Thus, the increase in accounts receiv-

13.19 b. continued.

able declined each year. The firm also stretched payments to employees, providing cash. Note that the increase in depreciation did not provide cash. The increased depreciation charge reduced net income and the addback merely offsets the reduction. The increased depreciation charge results from expenditures made on fixed assets in Year 6 and Year 7.

c. The people-based service business began to grow, leading to increasing net income. The firm also sold off fixed assets at a gain, increasing net income. The cash proceeds from sale of the fixed assets appear in the Investing section, not cash flow from operations. The firm experienced increased accounts receivable from this growing business in Year 9, which required cash. Additional increases in net income in Year 10 coupled with decreases in accounts receivable helped cash flow from operations in that year.

d. Net income has increased and long-term borrowing has decreased, reducing the firm's risk. Offsetting these changes, however, is a significant increase in short-term borrowing in Year 10.

13.20    (Cypress Corporation; interpreting the statement of cash flows.)

a. Although net income increased between Year 11 and Year 13, the firm increased accounts receivable and inventories to support this growth. It stretched its creditors somewhat to finance the buildup of accounts receivable and inventories, but not sufficiently to keep cash from operations from decreasing.

b. The principal factors causing cash flow from operations to increase in Year 14 is an increase in net income. Inventories decreased and the firm stretched its payable somewhat as well. The principal factors causing the increased cash flow from operations in Year 15 are increased and decreased accounts receivable.

c. The firm has repaid both short- and long-term debt, likely reducing its debt service payments. It invested excess cash in marketable securities. It also substantially increased its dividend. Even with these actions, cash on the balance sheet increased significantly, particularly in Year 15.

# CHAPTER 14

## SIGNIFICANCE AND IMPLICATIONS OF ALTERNATIVE ACCOUNTING PRINCIPLES

*Questions, Exercises, Problems, and Cases: Answers and Solutions*

14.1    See the text or the glossary at the end of the book.

14.2    This question emphasizes the dual dimensions of the standard-setting process that standard-setting bodies must reconcile. Such bodies need a conceptual foundation to guide their selection of accounting principles if the resulting financial statements are to have internal consistency and external usefulness over time. Such bodies cannot simply respond to various preparers and users on each issue addressed and hope to achieve the consistency and usefulness objectives stated above. Standard-setting bodies must recognize, however, the political nature of the standard-setting process and communicate on an on-going basis with its various constituencies. Such bodies may need to convince one or more constituencies of the desirability of a particular standard.

14.3    This question gets to the issue of uniformity versus flexibility in generally accepted accounting principles. One might argue that when the economic effects of a transaction on two firms are the same, the firms should use the same accounting method for the transaction. The firms should not have latitude to choose from among several alternative methods. On the other hand, when the economic effects of a transaction on two firms are different, the firms should have latitude to use different accounting methods. GAAP should not compel the firms to use the same method and inaccurately report the economic effects. In both cases, the economic effects should drive the *degree* of uniformity versus flexibility.

14.4    Because most firms select accounting methods for tax purposes that minimize the present value of income tax payments, this proposal would likely result in greater uniformity in financial statements. However, one might question the usefulness and meaningfulness of the resulting financial statements. The Congress sets income tax laws to accomplish certain governmental policies and not necessarily to measure accurately the economic effects of various transactions.

14.5    This question relates to the use of the cash basis versus the accrual basis of accounting. Chapter 3 discussed the deficiencies of the cash basis of accounting as a periodic measure of operating performance and the benefits of the accrual basis (more timely recognition of revenue, better matching of expenses with associated revenues). One of the "costs" of the accrual basis, however, is that it requires the allocation of revenues and expenses to periods of time. These allocations are the subject content of generally accepted accounting principles.

14.6    This statement is correct with respect to the *amount* of net income. Conservatism and profit maximizations relate to the *timing* of its recognition. Analysts use net income as a measure of the operating performance of a firm over time. The timing of income recognition affects the trend in earnings and thus the strategy a firm follows in selecting its accounting methods.

14.7    Net income over long time periods equals cash inflows minus cash outflows other than transactions with owners. Alternative accounting principles affect merely the timing of revenue and expense recognition. One accounting principle may report high revenues and expenses in early years and another accounting principle may report high revenues and expenses in later years. The first accounting principle produces higher (or lower) earnings in each of the early years as well as cumulatively. At some point, the second accounting principle produces higher (or lower) earnings in each year but the first method continues to report higher (or lower) cumulative earnings until earnings under the second accounting principle catch up.

14.8    Alternative accounting methods differentially affect the statement of cash flows. Cash flow differences generally occur when two firms use different methods of accounting on their tax returns. If the methods used by two firms on their tax returns are the same but on their financial statements are different, then their balance sheets and income statements will differ. Their statements of cash flows will differ under the indirect method only with respect to the adjustments made to convert net income to cash flow from operations. They will report identical amounts of cash flow from operations, however.

14.9    There are two responses to this question:

        1.  If the market reacts quickly and unbiasedly, then *someone* does the analysis. Sophisticated security analysts who trade continually in the markets likely perform the financial statement analysis.

        2.  There are settings outside of the organized securities markets where financial statement analysis is beneficial. These include banks lending to business customers, governments contemplating antitrust actions, labor unions considering negotiating strategy, and so on.

14.10    (Identifying generally accepted accounting principles.)

     a.   FIFO cost flow assumption.

     b.   Allowance method.

     c.   Equity method.

     d.   Capital lease method.

     e.   Weighted-average cost flow assumption.

     f.   Effective interest method.

     g.   Lower-of-cost-or-market valuation basis.

     h.   Direct write-off method.

     i.   Double-declining-balance method.

     j.   Market value method.

     k.   Percentage-of-completion method.

     l.   Allowance method.

     m.  LIFO cost flow assumption.

     n.   Operating lease method.

     o.   FIFO cost flow assumption.

     p.   Market value method.

     q.   Straight line method.

     r.   FIFO cost flow assumption.

     s.   Operating lease method.

     t.   LIFO cost flow assumption.

     u.   Capital lease method.

     v.   LIFO cost flow assumption.

14.11    (Identifying generally accepted accounting principles.)

  a.   Direct write-off method of accounting for uncollectible accounts.

       Write off of an uncollectible account.

  b.   Market value method of accounting for either marketable securities or long-term investments in securities.

       Receipt of a dividend in cash.

  c.   Market value method for marketable securities.

       Writedown of marketable securities to market value.

  d.   Equity method of accounting for long-term investments.

       Receipt of dividend from an investee.

  e.   Allowance method of accounting for uncollectible accounts.

       Recognition of expected loss from uncollectible accounts.

  f.   Operating method of accounting for leases by lessee.

       Payment of rent for rental services received this period.

  g.   Equity method of accounting for long-term investments.

       Accrual of investor's share of investee's earnings.

  h.   Allowance method of accounting for uncollectible accounts.

       Write off of an uncollectible account.

  i.   Lower-of-cost-or-market valuation basis for inventories.    In most cases, the debit entry is made to cost of goods sold.

       Write down of inventories to market value.

  j.   Capital lease method of accounting for long-term leases by lessee.

       Payment of cash for interest and for reduction in principal of lease liability.

14.12   (Identifying generally accepted accounting principles.)

    a.  Lower-of-cost-or-market method.

    b.  LIFO.

    c.  FIFO.

    d.  Market value method.

    e.  Equity method.

    f.  Sum-of-the-years' digits.

    g.  Sum-of-the-years' digits.   Conservatism is defined in terms of *cumulative* reported earnings rather than earnings for a single year.

    h.  Capital lease method.

    i.  Capital lease method.

14.13   (West Company and East Company; impact of capitalizing and amortizing versus expensing when incurred.)

**a. and b.**  See following two pages.

    c.  When R & D costs are constant each year, the largest difference in R & D expense occurs in the first year. For Year 5 and thereafter, R & D expense is the same whether the firm expenses the costs when incurred or capitalizes and then amortizes them over five years. The amount shown on the balance sheet as Deferred R &D Costs increases each year for four years when the firm uses the deferral method but stabilizes beginning in Year 5. The cumulative earnings are $200 million greater under the deferral than the immediate expense procedure as long as R & D costs remain at $100 million per year.

        When R & D costs increase each year, the effects are different. R & D expense under the immediate expensing procedure continues to be larger than under the deferral method. Likewise, the amount shown on the balance sheet each year as Deferred R & D Costs continues to increase each year. The larger is the increase in R & D costs each year, the larger will be the difference in R & D expense and deferred R & D costs between the immediate expensing and deferral methods.

14.13 continued.

(Amounts in Millions)

a.

|  | Year | | | | | |
|---|---|---|---|---|---|---|
|  | 1 | 2 | 3 | 4 | 5 | 6 |
| **R & D Expense** | | | | | | |
| West Company | $100 | $100 | $100 | $100 | $100 | $100 |
| East Company: | | | | | | |
| Year 1 Costs | $ 20 | $ 20 | $ 20 | $ 20 | $ 20 | $ 20 |
| Year 2 Costs | | 20 | 20 | 20 | 20 | 20 |
| Year 3 Costs | | | 20 | 20 | 20 | 20 |
| Year 4 Costs | | | | 20 | 20 | 20 |
| Year 5 Costs | | | | | 20 | 20 |
| Year 6 Costs | | | | | | 20 |
| Total Expense | $ 20 | $ 40 | $ 60 | $ 80 | $100 | $100 |
| | | | | | | |
| **Deferred R & D Costs** | | | | | | |
| West Company | $ 0 | $ 0 | $ 0 | $ 0 | $ 0 | $ 0 |
| East Company: | | | | | | |
| Year 1 Costs | $ 80 | $ 60 | $ 40 | $ 20 | $ 20 | $ 20 |
| Year 2 Costs | | 80 | 60 | 40 | 40 | 40 |
| Year 3 Costs | | | 80 | 60 | 60 | 60 |
| Year 4 Costs | | | | 80 | 80 | 80 |
| Year 5 Costs | | | | | | |
| Year 6 Costs | | | | | | |
| Total Deferred Costs | $ 80 | $140 | $180 | $200 | $200 | $200 |

14.13 continued.

b.

| | | | Year | | | |
|---|---|---|---|---|---|---|
| | 1 | 2 | 3 | 4 | 5 | 6 |
| **R & D Expense** | | | | | | |
| West Company | $100 | $120 | $140 | $160 | $180 | $200 |
| East Company: | | | | | | |
| Year 1 Costs | $ 20 | $ 20 | $ 20 | $ 20 | $ 20 | |
| Year 2 Costs | | 24 | 24 | 24 | 24 | $ 24 |
| Year 3 Costs | | | 28 | 28 | 28 | 28 |
| Year 4 Costs | | | | 32 | 32 | 32 |
| Year 5 Costs | | | | | 36 | 36 |
| Year 6 Costs | | | | | | 40 |
| Total Expense | $ 20 | $ 44 | $ 72 | $104 | $140 | $160 |
| | | | | | | |
| **Deferred R & D Costs** | | | | | | |
| West Company | $ 0 | $ 0 | $ 0 | $ 0 | $ 0 | $ 0 |
| East Company: | | | | | | |
| Year 1 Costs | $ 80 | $ 60 | $ 40 | $ 20 | | |
| Year 2 Costs | | 96 | 72 | 48 | $ 24 | |
| Year 3 Costs | | | 112 | 84 | 56 | $ 28 |
| Year 4 Costs | | | | 128 | 96 | 64 |
| Year 5 Costs | | | | | 144 | 108 |
| Year 6 Costs | | | | | | 160 |
| Total Deferred Costs | $ 80 | $ 156 | $ 224 | $ 280 | $ 320 | $ 360 |

14.14 (Humble Company and Huff Company; impact of alternative accounting principles on two firms.)

a.

**Comparative Income Statements**
**For the Year Ending December 31, Year 1**

| | Humble Company | | Huff Company | |
|---|---|---|---|---|
| | Financial Statement | Tax Return | Financial Statement | Tax Return |
| Sales Revenue | $2,700,000 | $2,700,000 | $2,700,000 | $2,700,000 |
| Expenses: | | | | |
| Cost of Goods Sold | $1,239,000[a] | $1,239,000[a] | $1,221,000[b] | $1,221,000[b] |
| Depreciation on Equipment | 500,000[c] | 293,700 | 275,000 | 293,700 |
| Sales Promotion | 375,000 | 375,000 | 93,750 | 375,000 |
| Selling, General and Administrative | 150,000 | 150,000 | 150,000 | 150,000 |
| Expenses before Income Taxes | $2,264,000 | $2,057,700 | $1,739,750 | $2,039,700 |
| Net Income before Income Taxes | $ 436,000 | $ 642,300 | $ 960,250 | $ 660,300 |
| Income Tax Expense | 130,800[d] | | 288,075[d] | |
| Net Income | $ 305,200 | | $ 672,175 | |

[a]$[\$1,641,000 - (30,000 \times \$8.00) + (20,000 \times \$8.10)] = \$1,239,000.$
[b]$\$1,641,000 - (50,000 \times \$8.40) = \$1,221,000.$
[c]$10/55 \times \$2,750,000 = \$500,000.$

[d]**Computation of Income Tax Expense**
Income Taxes Payable—Current:

| | | |
|---|---|---|
| Humble Company: .30 × $642,300 | $ 192,690 | $ 198,090 |
| Huff Company: .30 × $660,300 | | |
| Credits (Debits) to Deferred Income Taxes: | | |
| Humble Company: Dr. .30($293,700 – $500,000) | (61,890) | |
| Huff Company: Cr. .30[($293,700 – $275,000) + ($375,000 – $93,750)] | | 89,985 |
| Total Income Tax Expense | $ 130,800 | $ 288,075 |

14.14 continued.

b.

### Comparative Balance Sheet
### December 31, Year 1

|  | Humble Company | Huff Company |
|---|---|---|
| *Assets* | | |
| Cash | $ 639,848 | $ 635,528 |
| Accounts Receivable | 1,300,000 | 1,300,000 |
| Merchandise Inventory | 402,000 | 420,000 |
| Equipment (at Acquisition Cost) | 2,750,000 | 2,750,000 |
| Less Accumulated Depreciation | (500,000) | (275,000) |
| Deferred Sales Promotion Costs | -- | 281,250 |
| Deferred Tax Asset | 61,890 | -- |
| Total Assets | $4,653,738 | $5,111,778 |
| *Equities* | | |
| Accounts Payable | $ 310,000 | $ 310,000 |
| Income Taxes Payable | 38,538 | 39,618 |
| Deferred Tax Liability | -- | 89,985 |
| Common Shares | 500,000 | 500,000 |
| Additional Paid-in Capital | 3,500,000 | 3,500,000 |
| Retained Earnings | 305,200 | 672,175 |
| Total Equity | $4,653,738 | $5,111,778 |

14.14 continued.

c.

## Comparative Statement of Cash Flows
### For the Year Ended December 31, Year 1

| | Humble Company | Huff Company |
|---|---|---|
| Operations: | | |
| Net Income | $ 305,200 | $ 672,175 |
| Depreciation Expense | 500,000 | 275,000 |
| Portion of Income Tax Expense Not Currently Payable | -- | 89,985 |
| Increase in Accounts Payable | 310,000 | 310,000 |
| Increase in Income Tax Payable | 38,538 | 39,618 |
| Excess of Cash Used for Sales Promotion over Amount Recognized as Expense | -- | (281,250) |
| Excess of Income Tax Paid over Income Tax Expense | (61,890) | -- |
| Increase in Accounts Receivable | (1,300,000) | (1,300,000) |
| Increase in Merchandise Inventories | (402,000) | (420,000) |
| Cash Flow from Operations | $ (610,152) | $ (614,472) |
| Investing: | | |
| Acquisition of Equipment | (2,750,000) | (2,750,000) |
| Financing: | | |
| Issue of Common Stock | 4,000,000 | 4,000,000 |
| Net Change in Cash | $ 639,848 | $ 635,528 |
| Cash, January 1 | 0 | 0 |
| Cash, December 31 | $ 639,848 | $ 635,528 |

d.

| | |
|---|---|
| Cash on December 31, Year 1: Humble Company | $ 639,848 |
| Additional Income Taxes Currently Payable by Huff Company: $198,090 − $192,690 | (5,400) |
| Portion of Additional Income Taxes Not Yet Paid: $39,618 − $38,538 | 1,080 |
| Cash on December 31, Year 1: Huff Company | $ 635,528 |

14.15   (Brown Corporation; impact of two sets of alternative accounting principles on net income and cash flows.)

a.

**BROWN CORPORATION**
**Income Statements Under Alternative Principles**
**For the Year Ending December 31, Year 1**

| | Set A | | Set B | |
|---|---|---|---|---|
| | Financial Statement | Tax Return | Financial Statement | Tax Return |
| Sales Revenue | $504,000 | $504,000 | $504,000 | $504,000 |
| Expenses: | | | | |
| Cost of Goods Sold | $335,250 [1] | $335,250 [1] | $315,750 [2] | $315,750 [2] |
| Depreciation on Equipment | 22,500 [3] | 16,073 | 11,250 [4] | 16,073 |
| Training | 37,500 | 37,500 | 7,500 | 37,500 |
| Selling, General and Administrative | 60,000 | 60,000 | 60,000 | 60,000 |
| Expenses before Income Taxes | $455,250 | $448,823 | $394,500 | $429,323 |
| Net Income before Income Taxes | $ 48,750 | $ 55,177 | $109,500 | $ 74,677 |
| Income Tax Expense—Current | 16,553 [5] | | 22,403 [7] | |
| Income Tax Expense—Deferred | (1,928)[6] | | 10,447 [8] | |
| Net Income | $ 34,125 | | $ 76,650 | |

[1](37,500 × $2.40) + (15,000 × $2.20) + (22,500 × $2.10) + (82,500 × $2.00) = $335,250.
[2](150,000 × $2.00) + (7,500 × $2.10) = $315,750.
[3].20 × $112,500 = $22,500.
[4]$112,500/10 = $11,250.
[5].30 × $55,177 = $16,553.
[6].30 × ($16,073 − $22,500) = −$1,928.
[7].30 × $74,677 = $22,403.
[8].30($16,073 − $11,250) + .30($37,500 − $7,500) = $1,447 + $9,000 = $10,447.

14.15 continued.

b.

**BROWN CORPORATION**
**Cash Flow from Operations**
**For Year 1**

| | Set A | Set B |
|---|---|---|
| Net Income | $ 34,125 | $ 76,650 |
| Additions: | | |
| Depreciation Expense | 22,500 | 11,250 |
| Excess of Income Tax Expense over Amount Currently Payable | -- | 10,447 |
| Increase in Accounts Payable | 30,200 | 30,200 |
| Increase in Income Taxes Payable | 4,138 | 5,601 |
| Subtractions: | | |
| Excess of Cash Used for Training over Amount Reported as an Expense | -- | (30,000) |
| Excess of Income Taxes Currently Payable over Income Tax Expense | (1,928) | -- |
| Increase in Accounts Receivable | (120,000) | (120,000) |
| Increase in Merchandise Inventories | (135,000) | (154,500) |
| Cash Used for Operations | $ (165,965) | $ (170,352) |

c.

| | |
|---|---|
| Cash Flow from Operations, Set A | $ (165,965) |
| Additional Income Taxes Currently Payable Under Set B:  $22,403 – $16,553 | (5,850) |
| Portion of Additional Income Taxes Not Yet Paid: $5,601 – $4,138 | 1,463 |
| Cash Flow from Operations, Set B | $ (170,352) |

14.16  (Chicago Corporation; comprehensive review problem.)

a.

| | |
|---|---|
| Balance, January 1, Year 2 | $ 100,000 |
| Provision for Year 2 | 120,000 |
| Less Balance, December 31, Year 2 | (160,000) |
| Write-offs during Year 2 | $ 60,000 |

b.

| | LIFO | FIFO |
|---|---|---|
| Beginning Inventory | $ 1,500,000 | $ 1,800,000 |
| Purchases | 5,300,000 | 5,300,000 |
| Available for Sale | $ 6,800,000 | $ 7,100,000 |
| Less Ending Inventory | (1,800,000) | (1,700,000) |
| Cost of Goods Sold | $ 5,000,000 | $ 5,400,000 |
| Net Sales | $13,920,000 | $ 13,920,000 |
| Less Cost of Goods Sold | (5,000,000) | (5,400,000) |
| Gross Profit | $ 8,920,000 | $ 8,520,000 |

**14.16 continued.**

c. The quantity of inventory increased because the LIFO ending inventory is larger than the LIFO beginning inventory. The acquisition costs of the inventory items decreased because the FIFO ending inventory is less than the FIFO beginning inventory despite an increase in quantity during the year.

d. None of the companies declared dividends during Year 2 because the changes (increases) in the investment accounts equal the amounts recognized as Chicago Corporation's equity in the earnings of these companies.

e.
| | | |
|---|---:|---:|
| Investment in Chicago Finance Corporation | 1,800,000 | |
| Investment in Rosenwald Company | 125,000 | |
| Investment in Hutchinson Company | 75,000 | |
|     Equity in Earnings of Chicago Finance Corporation | | 1,800,000 |
|     Equity in Earnings of Rosenwald Company | | 125,000 |
|     Equity in Earnings of Hutchinson Company | | 75,000 |

f. Year 1: $4,000,000 \times 2/40 = \$200,000$.
Year 2: $(\$4,000,000 - \$200,000) \times 2/40 = \$190,000$.

g.
| | | |
|---|---:|---:|
| Cash | 400,000 | |
| Accumulated Depreciation | 800,000 | |
|     Machinery and Equipment | | 1,000,000 |
|     Gain on Sale of Machinery and Equipment | | 200,000 |

h.
| | | |
|---|---:|---:|
| Interest Expense | 288,000 | |
|     Bonds Payable (= $3,648,000 - \$3,600,000$) | | 48,000 |
|     Cash (= $.06 \times \$4,000,000$) | | 240,000 |

i. Effective interest rate $\times \$3,600,000 = \$288,000$. The effective interest rate = 8 percent. Chicago Corporation issued these bonds for less than their face value because the coupon rate of 6 percent is less than the market interest rate at the time of issue of 8 percent.

j. Difference between book and taxable depreciation = $\$150,000/.30 = \$500,000$.

Because the Deferred Tax Liability account increased, tax depreciation must be $500,000 larger than depreciation for financial reporting.

14.16 continued.

k. Cash.......................................................................... 1,000,000
    Treasury Shares........................................................             400,000
    Additional Paid-in Capital........................................             600,000

l. Acquisition Cost........................................................ $1,250,000
    Less Book Value.......................................................   (750,000)
    Accumulated Amortization....................................... $   500,000

      Because the patent is being amortized at the rate of $125,000 per year, the patent was acquired four years before the balance sheet date (= $500,000/$125,000).

m. If Chicago Corporation owns less than 20 percent of the common stock of Hutchinson Company, it must use the market-value method. Chicago Corporation would show the Investment in Hutchinson account at its market value of $125,000 (= $100,000 + $25,000) and show a $25,000 amount in the Unrealized Holding Gain on Investment in Securities account in Accumulated Other Comprehensive Income in the shareholders' equity section of the balance sheet. Hutchinson Company did not declare dividends during the year. Thus, net income of Chicago Corporation would decrease by the $75,000 equity in Hutchinson Company's earnings during Year 2 recognized under the equity method. Consolidated retained earnings would, therefore, be $75,000 less than as now stated. In the statement of cash flows, there would be $75,000 smaller net income and no subtraction of $75,000 for the equity in earnings of Hutchinson Company.

n. Capitalized Lease Obligation ($1,100,000 –
    $1,020,000)............................................................    80,000
    Interest Expense......................................................    90,000
        Cash..................................................................             170,000

    Amortization of Leased Property Rights.................   150,000
        Accumulated Amortization..............................             150,000
    Total expense would be $240,000 (= $90,000 + $150,000).

o. The income statement would show a $200,000 loss from the price decline, and retained earnings would be $200,000 less than as shown. The Inventories account would be shown at $1,600,000 instead of $1,800,000. There would be an addback for the loss on the statement of cash flows because the loss did not use cash.

14.16 continued.

p.  Basic earnings per share $= \dfrac{\$4,400,000 - \$120,000}{1,600,000} = \$2.675.$

Fully diluted earnings per share $= \dfrac{\$4,400,000}{1,600,000 + ?} = \$2.20.$

The number of common shares that would be issued is 400,000.

q.

| | Cash | |
|---|---|---|
| √ | 200,000 | |

| | Operations | |
|---|---|---|
| (1) 4,400,000 | 100,000 | (3) |
| (11) 1,000,000 | 300,000 | (4) |
| (12) 125,000 | 1,800,000 | (5) |
| (13) 150,000 | 125,000 | (6) |
| (15) 60,000 | 75,000 | (7) |
| (16) 130,000 | 200,000 | (9) |
| (17) 50,000 | 20,000 | (14) |
| (18) 260,000 | | |
| (19) 48,000 | | |
| (22) 170,000 | | |

| | Investing | |
|---|---|---|
| (9) 400,000 | 100,000 | (8) |
| | 1,700,000 | (10) |

| | Financing | |
|---|---|---|
| (23) 1,000,000 | 2,200,000 | (2) |
| | 968,000 | (20) |
| | 80,000 | (21) |
| √ 325,000 | | |

| | Accounts Receivable | |
|---|---|---|
| √ | 500,000 | |
| (3) | 100,000 | |
| √ | 600,000 | |

| | Merchandise Inventory | |
|---|---|---|
| √ | 1,500,000 | |
| (4) | 300,000 | |
| √ | 1,800,000 | |

14.16 q. continued.

| Prepayments | | | Investment in Chicago Finance Corp. | | |
|---|---|---|---|---|---|
| √ | 200,000 | | √ | 2,200,000 | |
| | | | (5) | 1,800,000 | |
| √ | 200,000 | | √ | 4,000,000 | |

| Investment in Rosenwald Corp. | | | Investment in Hutchinson Corp. | | |
|---|---|---|---|---|---|
| √ | 900,000 | | √ | 100,000 | |
| (6) | 125,000 | | (7) | 75,000 | |
| √ | 1,025,000 | | √ | 175,000 | |

| Land | | | Building | | |
|---|---|---|---|---|---|
| √ | 400,000 | | √ | 4,000,000 | |
| (8) | 100,000 | | | | |
| √ | 500,000 | | √ | 4,000,000 | |

| Machinery and Equipment | | | Property Rights Under Lease | | |
|---|---|---|---|---|---|
| √ | 7,300,000 | | √ | 1,500,000 | |
| (10) | 1,700,000 | 1,000,000 (9) | | | |
| √ | 8,000,000 | | √ | 1,500,000 | |

| Accumulated Depreciation and Amortization | | | Patent | | |
|---|---|---|---|---|---|
| | | 3,800,000 √ | √ | 875,000 | |
| (9) | 800,000 | 1,000,000 (11) | | | 125,000 (12) |
| | | 4,000,000 √ | √ | 750,000 | |

| Goodwill | | | Accounts Payable | | |
|---|---|---|---|---|---|
| √ | 1,125,000 | | | | 400,000 √ |
| | | | | | 150,000 (13) |
| √ | 1,125,000 | | | | 550,000 √ |

| Advances from Customers | | | Salaries Payable | | |
|---|---|---|---|---|---|
| | | 660,000 √ | | | 240,000 √ |
| (14) | 20,000 | | | | 60,000 (15) |
| | | 640,000 √ | | | 300,000 √ |

14.16 q. continued.

| Income Taxes Payable | | |
|---|---|---|
| | 300,000 | √ |
| | 130,000 | (16) |
| | 430,000 | √ |

| Rent Received in Advance | | |
|---|---|---|
| | 0 | √ |
| | 50,000 | (17) |
| | 50,000 | √ |

| Other Current Liabilities | | |
|---|---|---|
| | 200,000 | √ |
| | 260,000 | (18) |
| | 460,000 | √ |

| Bonds Payable | | |
|---|---|---|
| | 3,600,000 | √ |
| | 48,000 | (19)) |
| | 3,648,000 | √ |

Equipment

| Mortgage Payable | | | |
|---|---|---|---|
| | | 1,300,000 | √ |
| (20) | 968,000 | | |
| | | 332,000 | √ |

| Capitalized Lease Obligation | | | |
|---|---|---|---|
| | | 1,100,000 | √ |
| (21) | 80,000 | | |
| | | 1,020,000 | √ |

| Deferred Tax Liability | | |
|---|---|---|
| | 1,400,000 | √ |
| | 170,000 | (22) |
| | 1,570,000 | √ |

| Convertible Preferred Stock | | |
|---|---|---|
| | 2,000,000 | √ |
| | | |
| | 2,000,000 | √ |

| Common Stock | | |
|---|---|---|
| | 2,000,000 | √ |
| | | |
| | 2,000,000 | √ |

| Additional Paid-in Capital | | |
|---|---|---|
| | 2,400,000 | √ |
| | 600,000 | (23) |
| | 3,000,000 | √ |

| Retained Earnings | | | |
|---|---|---|---|
| | | 2,800,000 | √ |
| (2) | 2,200,000 | 4,400,000 | (1) |
| | | 5,000,000 | √ |

| Treasury Stock | | | |
|---|---|---|---|
| √ | 1,400,000 | | |
| | | 400,000 | (23) |
| √ | 1,000,000 | | |

r. The total shareholders' equity of Chicago Corporation is not an accurate measure of the value or worth of the firm for the following reasons.

(1) The balance sheet does not include such resources of the firm as superior managerial expertise, a well-trained labor force, or goodwill.

14.16 r. continued.

    (2) The balance sheet shows assets at acquisition cost (net of accumulated depreciation or amortization in some instances). These amounts will likely differ from the current replacement costs or net realizable value of these assets.

    (3) The total liabilities of Chicago Corporation do not include uncapitalized long-term operating leases. The liabilities do include Deferred Tax Liability. However, if the firm continues to grow, it is questionable whether Chicago Corporation will have to pay these taxes.

    (4) Chicago Corporation reports the long-term debt at the present value of the future cash flows discounted at the market rate on the date of issue. The current market values of these obligations may differ significantly from their book values.

s.(1) *For Narrowing:*

    (1) Lead to better interfirm and interperiod comparisons of financial statement data.

    (2) Make financial statements easier to understand, because the reader will not need to be familiar with as many accounting methods.

    (3) Reduces opportunities for management to manipulate earnings by selecting or changing accounting principles.

s.(2) *For Continuing Present System:*

    (1) Management should have the flexibility to select the methods that most fairly reflect the firm's financial position and results of operations. A narrowing of acceptable methods may result in some firms showing less fairly their financial position and results of operations.

    (2) Investors may see through the effects of using different accounting methods, as suggested by efficient markets theory and as supported by empirical research, which suggests additional disclosures rather than greater uniformity.

    (3) Because the specification of accounting principles is a political process, standard-setting bodies would probably encounter difficulties obtaining consensus on which currently acceptable methods to eliminate.

**14.17** (Tuck Corporation; comprehensive review problem.)

a.
| | | |
|---|---|---:|
| Balance in Marketable Equity Securities on December 31, Year 21 | | $ 125,000 |
| Less Cost of Marketable Equity Securities Sold | | (35,000) |
| Plus Decrease in Unrealized Holding Loss on Marketable Securities | | 4,000 |
| Plus Cost of Marketable Equity Securities Purchased | | ? |
| Balance in Marketable Equity Securities on December 31, Year 22 | | $ 141,000 |

The cost of marketable equity securities purchased is $47,000.

b.
| | |
|---|---:|
| Cost of Marketable Equity Securities Sold | $ 35,000 |
| Less Loss on Sale of Marketable Equity Securities | (8,000) |
| Sales Proceeds | $ 27,000 |

c.
| | |
|---|---:|
| Balance in Allowance Account on December 31, Year 21 | $ 128,800 |
| Plus Provision for Estimated Uncollectible Accounts | ? |
| Less Write-offs of Specific Customers' Accounts | (63,000) |
| Balance in Allowance Account on December 31, Year 22 | $ 210,400 |

The provision for estimated uncollectibles is $144,600.

d.

| | LIFO | Difference | FIFO |
|---|---:|---:|---:|
| Beginning Inventory | $1,257,261 | $ 430,000 | $1,687,261 |
| Purchases | 2,848,054 | -- | 2,848,054 |
| Available | $4,105,315 | $ 430,000 | $4,535,315 |
| Less Ending Inventory | (1,525,315) | (410,000) | (1,935,315) |
| Cost of Goods Sold | $2,580,000 | $ 20,000 | $2,600,000 |

e.
| | | |
|---|---:|---:|
| Unrealized Holding Loss on Investments in Securities (SE/Comp Y) | 5,000 | |
| Investments in Securities | | 5,000 |

To recognize unrealized holding loss on investments in securities.

f. Dividend revenue of $8,000. The unrealized loss of $5,000 (see Part *e.*) is not included in the calculation of net income for Year 22.

14.17 continued.

g.  Investment in Davis Corporation............................. 87,000
    Equity in Earnings of Unconsolidated
        Affiliates ......................................................... 87,000
    To recognize share of Davis Corporation's earn-
    ings in Year 22; .40 × $217,500 = $87,000.

    Cash......................................................................... 24,000
        Investment in Davis Corporation....................... 24,000
    To recognize dividend received from Davis Corpo-
    ration; .40 × $60,000 = $24,000.

    Investment in Davis Corporation............................. 20,000
     Cash ...................................................................... 20,000
    To record additional investment in Davis
    Corporation.

h.  Cash......................................................................... 7,000
    Accumulated Depreciation....................................... 19,000
        Equipment ........................................................... 23,000
        Gain on Sale of Equipment................................. 3,000

i.  Present Value of Lease Payment Due at Signing at Janu-
    ary 2, Year 10......................................................... $  10,000
    Present Value of Nineteen Lease Payments Due on Janu-
    ary 2 of Each Subsequent Year at 8 Percent; $10,000
    × 9.6036.................................................................... <u>96,036</u>
    Total.......................................................................... <u>$ 106,036</u>

j.  Balance in Rental Fees Received in Advance on December
    31, Year 21.............................................................. $  46,000
    Plus Cash Received for Rentals during Year 22...................... ?
    Less Rental Fees Earned during Year 22................................ <u>(240,000)</u>
    Balance in Rental Fees Received in Advance on December
    31, Year 22.............................................................. <u>$  58,000</u>

    Cash received during Year 22 totaled $252,000.

k.  Balance in Estimated Warranty Liability on December
    31, Year 21.............................................................. $75,200
    Plus Estimated Warranty Cost Provision for Year 22........... 46,800
    Less Cost of Actual Warranty Services................................. <u>(?)</u>
    Balance in Estimated Warranty Liability on December
    31, Year 22.............................................................. <u>$78,600</u>

    Warranty costs incurred during Year 22 totaled $43,400.

14.17 continued.

l. First 6 Months:  .025 × $1,104,650.00.............................. $27,616.25
   Second 6 Months:  .025 × $1,102,266.25a ....................... 27,556.66
      Total Interest Expense........................................ $55,172.91

a$1,104,650.00 − ($30,000.00 − $27,616.25) = $1,102,266.25.

m. Interest Expense................................................ 20,996
   Mortgage Payable ............................................. 19,004
      Cash....................................................... 40,000
   To record mortgage interest and principal pay-
   ment; $20,996 = .07 × ($262,564 + 37,383).

n. Present Value of Payment on January 1, Year 23..................... $10,000
   Present Value of Seven Remaining Lease Payments
      ($10,000 × 5.20637)........................................ 52,064
         Total.................................................. $62,064

o. Capitalized Lease Obligation, December 31, Year 21................ $62,064
   Lease Payment on January 1, Year 23............................. (10,000)
   Interest Expense for Year 22 (.08 × $52,064)................... 4,165
      Total ($10,000 + $46,229)................................. $56,229

p. Income Tax Expense ........................................... 150,000
      Income Tax Payable......................................... 135,000
      Deferred Tax Liability ($145,000   $130,000). 15,000

q. Income Tax Payable—Current, December 31, Year 21.......... $140,000
   Provision for Current Taxes Payable (See Part p.)................. 135,000
   Less Cash Payments Made during Year 21........................... (?)
   Income Tax Payable—Current, December 31, Year 22.......... $160,000

Cash payments for income taxes during Year 21 were $115,000.

r. $\dfrac{\text{Deferred Tax Expense Relating to Depreciation}}{\text{Income Tax Rate}} = \dfrac{\$12,000}{.30} = \$40,000.$

s. Convertible Preferred Stock (5,000 × $100)........... 500,000
      Common Stock (25,000 × $10)......................... 250,000
      Additional Paid-in Capital........................... 250,000
   To record conversion of preferred into common
   stock.

14-21

14.17 continued.

t.  Treasury Stock................................................................ 8,800
        Cash...................................................................... 8,800
    To record purchases of treasury stock.

    Cash................................................................................ 25,200
        Treasury Stock....................................................... 21,600[a]
        Additional Paid-in Capital...................................... 3,600[b]
    To record the sale of treasury stock.

    [a]1,800 shares X $12 = $21,600.

    [b]Additional Paid-in Capital on December 31, Year 21............. $ 130,000
    Plus Amount Arising from Conversion of Preferred
        Stock................................................................................... 250,000
    Plus Amount Arising from Issue of Common Stock............. 200,000
    Plus Amount Arising from Sale of Treasury Stock............... ?
    Additional Paid-in Capital on December 31, Year 22............ $ 583,600

    The additional paid-in capital arising from the treasury stock sales is $3,600.

14.17 continued.

u.

Cash

| | | | | |
|---|---|---|---|---|
| √ | 240,000 | | | |

Operations

| | | | | |
|---|---|---|---|---|
| (1) | 300,000 | 87,000 | (7) |
| (3) | 8,000 | 15,000 | (10) |
| (8) | 24,000 | 3,000 | (11) |
| (13) | 56,000 | 4,827 | (14) |
| (16) | 2,911 | 78,400 | (24) |
| (19) | 15,000 | 268,054 | (25) |
| (28) | 57,600 | 4,000 | (26) |
| (29) | 12,000 | | |
| (30) | 3,400 | | |
| (31) | 500 | | |
| (33) | 20,000 | | |

Investing

| | | | | |
|---|---|---|---|---|
| (3) | 27,000 | 47,000 | (5) |
| (11) | 7,000 | 20,000 | (9) |
| | | 1,373,600 | (12) |

Financing

| | | | | |
|---|---|---|---|---|
| (15) | 828,409 | 119,500 | (2) |
| (21) | 600,000 | 19,004 | (17) |
| (22) | 25,200 | 5,835 | (18) |
| (27) | 100,000 | 8,800 | (23) |
| (32) | 5,000 | | |
| √ | 278,000 | | |

| Marketable Securities—Net | | | | Accounts Receivable—Net | | |
|---|---|---|---|---|---|---|
| √ | 125,000 | | | √ | 1,431,200 | |
| | | 35,000 | (3) | (24) | 78,400 | |
| (4) | 4,000 | | | | | |
| (5) | 47,000 | | | | | |
| √ | 141,000 | | | √ | 1,509,600 | |

14-23

**14.17 u. continued.**

| Inventories | | | |
|---|---|---|---|
| √ | 1,257,261 | | |
| (25) | 268,054 | | |
| √ | 1,525,315 | | |

| Prepayments | | | |
|---|---|---|---|
| √ | 28,000 | | |
| (26) | 4,000 | | |
| √ | 32,000 | | |

| Investment in Thayer—Net | | | |
|---|---|---|---|
| √ | 92,000 | | |
| | | 5,000 | (6) |
| √ | 87,000 | | |

| Investment in Hitchcock | | | |
|---|---|---|---|
| √ | 120,000 | | |
| (10) | 15,000 | | |
| √ | 135,000 | | |

| Investment in Davis | | | |
|---|---|---|---|
| √ | 215,000 | | |
| (7) | 87,000 | | |
| (9) | 20,000 | 24,000 | (8) |
| √ | 298,000 | | |

| Land | | |
|---|---|---|
| √ | 82,000 | |
| | | |
| √ | 82,000 | |

| Building | | |
|---|---|---|
| √ | 843,000 | |
| √ | 843,000 | |

| Equipment | | | |
|---|---|---|---|
| √ | 497,818 | | |
| (12) | 1,373,600 | 23,000 | (11) |
| √ | 1,848,418 | | |

| Leasehold | | |
|---|---|---|
| √ | 98,182 | |
| √ | 98,182 | |

| Accumulated Depreciation and Amortization | | | |
|---|---|---|---|
| | | 376,000 | √ |
| (11) | 19,000 | 56,000 | (13) |
| | | 413,000 | √ |

| Goodwill—Net | | |
|---|---|---|
| √ | 36,000 | |
| √ | 36,000 | |

| Notes Payable | | | |
|---|---|---|---|
| | | 100,000 | √ |
| | | 100,000 | (27) |
| | | 200,000 | √ |

| Accounts Payable | | | |
|---|---|---|---|
| | | 666,100 | √ |
| | | 57,600 | (28) |
| | | 723,700 | √ |

| Rental Fees Received in Advance | | | |
|---|---|---|---|
| | | 46,000 | √ |
| | | 12,000 | (29) |
| | | 58,000 | √ |

14.17 u. continued.

| Estimated Warranty Liability | | |
|---|---|---|
| | 75,200 | √ |
| | 3,400 | (30) |
| | 78,600 | √ |

| Interest Payable on Notes | | |
|---|---|---|
| | 1,500 | √ |
| | 500 | (31) |
| | 2,000 | √ |

| Dividends Payable | | |
|---|---|---|
| | 25,000 | √ |
| | 5,000 | (32) |
| | 30,000 | √ |

| Income Taxes Payable—Current | | |
|---|---|---|
| | 140,000 | √ |
| | 20,000 | (33) |
| | 160,000 | √ |

| Bonds Payable | | | | |
|---|---|---|---|---|
| | | 1,104,650 | √ | |
| (14) | 4,827 | 828,409 | (15) | |
| | | 2,911 | (16) | |
| | | 1,931,143 | √ | |

| Mortgage Payable | | | |
|---|---|---|---|
| | | 299,947 | √ |
| (17) | 19,004 | | |
| | | 280,943 | √ |

| Capitalized Lease Obligation | | | |
|---|---|---|---|
| | | 62,064 | √ |
| (18) | 5,835 | | |
| | | 56,229 | √ |

| Deferred Tax Liability | | |
|---|---|---|
| | 130,000 | √ |
| | 15,000 | (19) |
| | 145,000 | √ |

| Convertible Preferred Stock | | | |
|---|---|---|---|
| | | 700,000 | √ |
| (20) | 500,000 | | |
| | | 200,000 | √ |

| Common Stock | | |
|---|---|---|
| | 1,000,000 | √ |
| | 250,000 | (20) |
| | 400,000 | (21) |
| | 1,650,000 | √ |

| Additional Paid-in Capital | | |
|---|---|---|
| | 130,000 | √ |
| | 250,000 | (20) |
| | 200,000 | (21) |
| | 3,600 | (22) |
| | 583,600 | √ |

| Unrealized Holding Loss on Marketable Securities | | | |
|---|---|---|---|
| √ | 25,000 | | |
| | | 4,000 | (4) |
| √ | 21,000 | | |

## 14.17 u. continued.

| Unrealized Holding Loss on Investment in Securities | | | | Retained Earnings | | |
|---|---|---|---|---|---|---|
| √ | 16,000 | | | | 277,000 | √ |
| (6) | 5,000 | | (2) | 119,500 | 300,000 | (1) |
| √ | 21,000 | | | | 457,500 | √ |

| Treasury Stock | | | | |
|---|---|---|---|---|
| √ | 27,000 | | | |
| (23) | 8,800 | 21,600 | (22) | |
| √ | 14,200 | | | |

### References to T-Account Entries

(1) Net Income.
(2) Dividends declared by Tuck Corporation.
(3) Sale of marketable securities.
(4) Recovery of unrealized holding loss on marketable securities.
(5) Purchase of marketable securities.
(6) Write down of investment in Thayer Corporation to market value.
(7) Tuck's share of Davis Corporation's earnings.
(8) Tuck's share of Davis Corporation's dividends.
(9) Additional investment in Davis Corporation.
(10) Tuck's share of Hitchcock's earnings ($102,000 – $87,000).
(11) Sale of equipment at a gain.
(12) Acquisition of equipment.
(13) Depreciation expenses.
(14) Interest on 6-percent bonds.
(15) Issue of 8-percent bonds.
(16) Interest on 8-percent bonds.
(17) Payment of principal on mortgage.
(18) Payment of principal on lease obligation ($10,000 – $4,165).
(19) Deferred tax liability.
(20) Conversion of preferred stock.
(21) Issue of common stock.
(22) Sale of treasury stock.
(23) Purchase of treasury stock.
(24) Increase in accounts receivable.
(25) Increase in inventories.
(26) Increase in prepayments.
(27) Increase in notes payable.
(28) Increase in accounts payable.
(29) Increase in rental fees received in advance.
(30) Increase in estimated warranty liability.
(31) Increase in interest payable.
(32) Increase in dividends payable.
(33) Increase in income taxes payable—current.

14.18　(Champion Clothiers, Inc.; selecting accounting methods.)

The objectives of the case are as follows:

1.　To illustrate the impact of alternative accounting methods on the financial statements.

2.　To illustrate the wide array of avenues open to a firm to manage reported earnings.

3.　To consider the arguments for and against managing earnings.

**Techniques for Managing Earnings**

The techniques for managing earnings fall into three categories: (1) selection of accounting methods (LIFO versus FIFO, accelerated versus straight-line depreciation), (2) application of accounting methods (nature of LIFO pools, depreciable lives of plant assets, amortization period on pension obligation), and (3) timing of asset acquisitions and dispositions (maintenance and advertising, sale of marketable securities and land).

　　*LIFO versus FIFO.* Remaining on LIFO is probably the best choice here because of the potential tax savings. Most firms now use LIFO for financial reporting as well, so that lack of comparability with one's competitors is not an issue. As discussed later, a number of research studies have shown that investors look through the accounting numbers to the underlying economics of accounting choices. Evidence indicates that the stock market penalizes firms that select FIFO in order to report higher earnings (at the expense of paying more taxes). There are sufficient disclosures in the annual report to convert a LIFO firm to a FIFO basis if an analyst feels it is a more appropriate cost flow assumption. Thus, a firm can realize the tax benefits of LIFO and disclose sufficient information so that the analyst can compute FIFO earnings.

　　*Nature of LIFO Pools.* It is obvious that broader pools are preferable for tax purposes in order to minimize the probability of dipping into an old, lower priced layer. The consistency requirement between tax and financial reporting for LIFO dictates remaining with broader pools for financial reporting as well. If a firm practices earnings management, it is preferable to use avenues that do not have negative economic consequences.

　　*Depreciable Lives and Depreciation Method.* Unlike LIFO, there is no consistency requirement between tax and financial reporting with respect to depreciation. Thus, a firm must choose on other grounds. A firm might use economic reality as the criterion. On this basis, the depreciable life would be the economic life of the assets. The depreciation method selected would be one that mirrored the economic decline in the usefulness of the assets. Unfortunately, the firm cannot observe or predict either of these items very accurately. The choice comes down to whether the firm wishes

14.18 continued.

to portray a conservative or a nonconservative image to investors. The vast majority of publicly-held firms takes the nonconservative position and writes off depreciable assets over their estimated economic lives using the straight-line method. This is the position we would take.

*Amortization Period for Pension Obligation.* There is no necessity that the firm fund the pension obligation over the same period that it amortizes it to expense. Assuming that the economics (funding) will not change, we would opt for the longer amortization period to increase earnings.

*Delay of Maintenance Expenditures.* The firm can take this action to improve earnings in the short run, but it catches up later. Delaying the expenditure until 2004 will depress 2004 earnings. Delaying the maintenance indefinitely could affect the operational efficiency of the assets involved. We would tend not to use this avenue if other options were available to obtain the desired earnings per share.

*Delay of Advertising Expenditures.* The desired timing of the advertising campaign should be the deciding factor here. Because the post-Christmas timing seems set, we would not argue for delaying it. We might approach the firm's auditor about the possibility of capitalizing the advertising expenditure in 2003 and writing it off as an expense in 2004, the year of expected benefit. Auditors are reluctant to do this on intangibles such as advertising, but it is worth a try. The problem with this, however, is that this treatment of the expenditure negatively affects 2004 earnings.

*Sale of Marketable Securities.* The securities were probably purchased as a temporary investment of excess cash. If the firm could invest the sales proceeds in another investment alternative with equivalent returns and risk after considering transaction costs, we might use this avenue for propping up earnings for 2003. However, if the firm held the marketable securities for longer term purposes and viewed them as a desirable long-term investment, we would not likely sell them.

*Sale of Land.* As long as the firm still viewed the parcels as attractive locations for future stores, we would not sell them at this time.

The president of Champion is concerned with the *trend* in earnings per share. Several of the choices require retroactive restatements of prior years' earnings per share (LIFO versus FIFO, accelerated versus straight-line depreciation, purchase versus pooling of interests). These restatements affect the trend line of the desired level of earnings per share for 2003.

Assuming that the firm changes its depreciable life, depreciation method, corporate acquisition method, and pension obligation amortization period, earnings per share for 2000 through 2003 would be as follows:

14.18 continued.

| | 2000 | 2001 | 2002 | 2003 |
|---|---|---|---|---|
| As Reported or Expected................. | $ 1.20 | $ 1.38 | $ 1.60 | $ 1.65 |
| Depreciable Lives ........................... | -- | -- | -- | + .04 |
| Depreciation Method........................ | + .05 | + .06 | + .07 | + .08 |
| Pension Amortization Period......... | -- | -- | -- | + .05 |
| Revised ........................................... | $ 1.25 | $ 1.44 | $ 1.67 | $ 1.82 |

Earnings per share increased approximately 16 percent per year between 2000 and 2001. Maintaining this growth rate requires 2003 earnings per share to be approximately $1.94. We would be inclined to get some of the additional twelve cents per share needed from the sale of marketable securities as long as there were no negative economic consequences of doing so. We would probably stop at this point and report earnings per share of $1.84. Using other avenues would probably have negative economic consequences.

## Arguments For and Against Managing Earnings

The arguments for and against managing earnings vary both as to their underlying logic and to the evidence that is brought to bear in support of the position. The section presents the arguments in as unbiased a manner as possible so that readers can make up their own minds.

*Capital Market Efficiency.* The major argument against managing earnings is that capital markets are efficient, in the sense that market prices adjust quickly and in an unbiased manner to publicly available information, and that earnings management is therefore a waste of valuable managerial time. An expanding number of theoretical and empirical studies have provided support for the efficiency of capital markets. For example, several studies have examined the effects of changes in accounting methods on stock prices. Researchers have shown that changes in accounting methods that have no real or economic effects (that is, those that do not affect cash flows) have little affect on stock prices. Using information from the financial statements and notes, the stock market at the aggregate level distinguishes changes with real effects from those that do not have real effects and reacts accordingly.

Proponents of earnings management acknowledge this recent work but counter with three observations. First, all of the empirical work on market efficiency has looked at the aggregate market (for example, all stocks traded on the New York Stock Exchange). There are numerous examples of cases where the market priced the securities of particular firms at a particular point in time inefficiently. Proponents of this view point to examples where the market prices of particular firms' shares decreased dramatically after the effects of using specific accounting procedures were carefully analyzed and reported in the financial press.

14.18 continued.

Second, the empirical work on market efficiency has focused for the most part on publicly-available information. There is little or no evidence to suggest that the market is able to access "inside" or nonpublic information. Information about the effects of changes in accounting methods is available in the financial statements and notes and has been studied empirically. However, information about management's efforts to manage the timing of asset acquisitions or dispositions is usually not disclosed separately and consequently has not been adequately studied.

Third, proponents of earnings management note that most of the empirical work on capital market efficiency has focused on equity securities traded on the New York Stock Exchange. Researchers have not tested adequately the efficiency of other capital markets (for example, the over-the-counter-market as well as short-term credit and long-term debt markets).

Proponents of earnings management would conclude that capital markets are not necessarily perfectly efficient in all cases. If by managing earnings the firm can take advantage of these inefficiencies and obtain capital at a lower cost than if earnings management were not practiced, then the shareholders of the firm are better off.

Opponents of earnings management might accept the notion that some degree of inefficiency exists in capital markets. They would then argue, though, that capital resources get allocated in a less than socially-optimal way if, because of earnings management, certain firms receive more resources than would otherwise be the case.

*Management Incentives and Survival.* Because over long enough time periods net income equals cash inflows minus cash outflows from operating and investing activities, some corporate managers acknowledge that earnings management is not particularly beneficial in the long run. They point out, however, that the long run is made up of a series of short-run periods in which shareholders' make decisions to retain or to fire management. Shareholders, they would argue, do not want to see wide, unexpected fluctuations in earnings from year to year. Earnings management is necessary to smooth out these fluctuations and create the impression that management has operations under control. Corporate managers also observe that all firms practice earnings management and that management's survival dictates that they do so to maintain the firm's position relative to other firms. They further point out that researchers have not yet provided sufficient and convincing evidence for not managing earnings. Opponents of earnings management, primarily academic researchers, point to an expanding number of studies that call into question the perceived benefits of earnings management. Whether the two viewpoints are ultimately reconcilable depends on the results of continuing research on the relation between accounting numbers and stock prices.

**14.19** (Petite-Mart, Inc.; identifying quality of earnings issues.)

a. Schedule 14.1 of this solution manual presents a common-size income statement for Petite-Mart, Inc. for fiscal Year 6, Year 7, and Year 8 based on its reported amounts. The discussion that follows suggests possible quality of earnings issues.

**Cost of Goods Sold**—LIFO matches current costs against revenues as long as a firm does not dip into LIFO layers. LIFO, therefore, provides a better indication of the ongoing profitability of a firm than FIFO. FIFO includes varying amounts of holding gains and losses depending on the rate of changes in acquisition costs each period. Petite-Mart, Inc., however, dipped into LIFO layers during fiscal Year 8 and, thereby reduced its cost of goods sold by $916 million. Sales declined between fiscal Year 7 and fiscal Year 8, so unexpected demand would not seem to explain the LIFO liquidation. The cost of goods sold to sales percentage increased slightly during the previous two years. Perhaps still further expected increases in this percentage led management to intentionally delay replacing inventory items, thereby, boosting net income. Without the LIFO liquidation, cost of goods sold would have been $35,176 million (= $34,260 million + $916 million) and the cost of goods sold to sales percentage would have been 70.0 percent (= $35,176 million/$50,234 million).

**Depreciation Expense**—The increase in depreciable lives for equipment from five to eight years decreased depreciation expense by $1,583 million. The equipment in a retail clothing store likely includes display counters, computers, and security devices. The desire of clothing retailers to maintain attractive stores would seem to suggest that an eight-year life for display counters is somewhat long. Changes in technologies would likely lead to obsolescence of computers and security devices prior to eight years. Thus, the change in depreciable life appears driven by a desire to increase earnings. Expenditures on equipment increased more rapidly than sales during the three-year period. Depreciation expense as a percentage of sales increased significantly between fiscal Year 6 and fiscal Year 7. Perhaps management anticipated still further increases in this expense percentage in future years and desired to dampen its effect. If the company had continued to use a five-year depreciable like, depreciation expense would have been $4,995 million (= $3,412 million + $1,583 million).

Another issue regarding depreciation is the company's policy of continuing to depreciate the building over 20 years after learning of the health and safety regulations. One must at least wonder whether a shorter life is more appropriate. The company may, however, have adequately dealt with the issue by recognizing the asset impairment loss.

14.19 a. continued.

**Advertising Expense**—Advertising expense as a percentage of sales decreased from 4.1 percent in fiscal Year 7 to 3.7 percent in fiscal Year 8. Given the decreased sales, one must wonder why the firm did not at least maintain the percentage, if not the amount, of spending. The advertising expense percentage was approximately 4 percent in fiscal Year 6 and fiscal Year 7, which appears to be the more recurring level.

**Uncollectible Accounts and Sales Returns**—This expense as a percentage of sales was approximately 2 percent during fiscal Year 6 and fiscal Year 7 and then dropped to 1.4 percent in fiscal Year 8. An analysis of the allowance accounts reveals the following:

### Allowance for Uncollectible Accounts and Sales Returns

|  | Year 6 | Year 7 | Year 8 |
|---|---|---|---|
| Balance, Beginning of Fiscal Year......... | $ 1,438 | $ 1,785 | $ 2,010 |
| Plus Provision for Year........................... | 994 | 1,010 | 703 |
| Less Write-Offs and Sales Returns...... | (647) | (785) | (954) |
| Balance, End of Fiscal Year................... | $ 1,785 | $ 2,010 | $ 1,759 |

Actual write-offs and sales returns increased during the three-year period. The provision for fiscal Year 6 and fiscal Year 7 exceeded the write-offs and returns as one would expect. One view is that management intentionally reduced the provision in Year 8 to boost earnings. An alternative view is that such a reduction is warranted because the balance in the allowance account is too large. Consider the following analysis:

### Accounts Receivable

| January 31: | Year 5 | Year 6 | Year 7 | Year 8 |
|---|---|---|---|---|
| Accounts Receivable (Net)........... | $ 8,000 | $ 8,560 | $ 9,159 | $ 8,782 |
| Plus Balance in Allowance Account................................. | 1,438 | 1,785 | 2,010 | 1,759 |
| Accounts Receivable (Gross)....... | $ 9,438 | $ 10,345 | $ 11,169 | $ 10,541 |
| Balance in Allowance Account as a Percentage of Gross Accounts Receivable...................... | 15.2% | 17.3% | 18.0% | 16.7% |

There is some evidence here that a reduction in the provision might be appropriate.

**Asset Impairment Charge**—The *need* for recognizing an asset impairment charge arose from new regulations and, therefore, was not under the control of management. The *timing* of recognition was, however, under management's control. Operating income as a percen-

14.19 a. continued.

tage of sales would be 9.3 percent (= 4.6% + 4.7%) without the impairment loss. Thus, operating profitability declined between fiscal Year 6 and fiscal Year 7. Management might have attempted to get analysts to take their eye off the reasons for the decline in the operating income percentage without the restructuring charge by posting the large impairment loss. The charge is clearly nonrecurring. The analyst should, therefore, eliminate it and its tax effect when assessing ongoing profitability.

**Gain on Sale of Land**—The gain on the sale of land is likewise nonrecurring and in this case, peripheral to the firm's principal business activities. The analyst should eliminate it when assessing profitability. Given the other means used by the firm to increase earnings in fiscal Year 8 one wonders whether the sale of the land at a gain was motivated by valid business reasons instead of propping up earnings.

**Capitalized Interest Costs**—GAAP requires firms to capitalize interest cost during the construction period of self-constructed assets. It seems unlikely that the firm would have spent $1,840 million on new construction to enable it to capitalize $147 million of interest costs. Thus, this action does not appear motivated by earnings management.

b. Schedule 14.2 of this solution manual presents revised income statements in both dollar amounts and common-size percentages for fiscal Year 6, Year 7, and Year 8. We make adjustment for the LIFO liquidation, change in depreciable lives of equipment, advertising expense, uncollectible accounts and sales returns provision, asset impairment charge, and gain on sale of land.

c. Petite-Mart, Inc. shows a clear pattern of declining profitability. The deterioration occurs primarily because of increases in the cost of goods sold and depreciation expense percentages. Given the fashion orientation of its product line, one wonders about product obsolescence and failure to adapt to new fashion trends. The increased depreciation percentage results primarily from rapid increases in equipment. Perhaps the firm invested in new computer equipment for customer checkout and inventory control reasons. Such technologies are essential for remaining competitive in today's retailing environment.

14.19 a. continued.

**Schedule 14.1**
**COMMON-SIZE INCOME STATEMENT FOR PETITE-MART, INC.**

| | Year 6 | Year 7 | Year 8 |
|---|---|---|---|
| Sales | 100.0% | 100.0% | 100.0% |
| Cost of Goods Sold | (68.0) | (68.1) | (68.2) |
| Depreciation Expense | (6.5) | (7.9) | (6.8) |
| Selling and Administrative: | | | |
|    Advertising Expense | (4.0) | (4.1) | (3.7) |
|    Bad Debt and Sales Returns Expense | (2.0) | (1.9) | (1.4) |
|    Other Selling and Administrative | (9.0) | (8.7) | (9.4) |
| Asset Impairment Charge | -- | (4.7) | -- |
| Operating Income | 10.5% | 4.6% | 10.5% |
| Gain on Sale of Land | -- | -- | 1.4 |
| Interest Expense | (2.4) | (2.2) | (2.1) |
| Income before Income Taxes | 8.1% | 2.4% | 9.8% |
| Income Tax Expense | (2.8) | (.8) | (3.3) |
| Net Income | 5.3% | 1.6% | 6.5% |

14.19 b. continued.

## Schedule 14.2
## REVISED INCOME STATEMENTS FOR PETITE-MART, INC.

| | Year 6 | | Year 7 | | Year 8 | |
|---|---|---|---|---|---|---|
| Sales ................... | $49,680 | 100.0% | $53,158 | 100.0% | $50,234 | 100.0% |
| Cost of Goods Sold ................. | (33,782) | (68.0) | (36,200) | (68.1) | (35,176)[a] | (70.0) |
| Depreciation Expense .......... | (3,235) | (6.5) | (4,167) | (7.9) | (4,995)[b] | (10.0) |
| Selling and Administrative: | | | | | | |
| Advertising...... | (1,987) | (4.0) | (2,179) | (4.1) | (2,060)[c] | (4.1) |
| Bad Debt and Sales Returns ........... | (994) | (2.0) | (1,010) | (1.9) | (954)[d] | (1.9) |
| Other Selling and Administrative....... | (4,472) | (9.0) | (4,625) | (8.7) | (4,723) | (9.4) |
| Operating Income................. | $ 5,210 | 10.5% | $ 4,977 | 9.3% | $ 2,326 | 4.6% |
| Interest Expense............... | (1,172) | (2.4) | (1,187) | (2.2) | (1,042) | (2.1) |
| Income before Income Tax ..... | $ 4,038 | 8.1% | $ 3,790 | 7.1% | $ 1,284 | 2.5% |
| Income Tax Expense................ | (1,373) | (2.8) | (1,289)[e] | (2.4) | (437)[f] | (.8) |
| Net Income.......... | $ 2,665 | 5.3% | $ 2,501 | 4.7% | $ 847 | 1.7% |

[a]$34,260 + $916 = $35,176.

[b]$3,412 + $1,583 = $4,995.

[c].041 × $50,234 = $2,060.

[d].019 × $50,234 = $954.

[e].34 × $3,790 = $1,289.

[f].34 × $1,284 = $437.

# APPENDIX

## COMPOUND INTEREST: CONCEPTS AND APPLICATIONS

*Questions, Exercises, Problems, and Cases: Answers and Solutions*

A.1    See the text or the glossary at the end of the book.

A.2    Rent paid or received for the use of the asset, cash.

A.3    In simple interest, only the principal sum earns interest. In compound interest, interest is earned on the principal plus amounts of interest not paid or withdrawn.

A.4    There is no difference; these items refer to the same thing.

A.5    The timing of the first payment for an annuity due is *now* (at the beginning of the first period) while that for an ordinary annuity is at the *end* of the first period. The future value of an annuity due is computed as of one year after the final payment, but for an ordinary annuity is computed as of the time of the last payment.

A.6    The discount rate that sets the net present value of a stream of payments equal to zero is the implicit rate for that stream.

(1) Guess a rate.

(2) Compute the net present values of the cash flows using the current guess.

(3) If the net present value in (2) is less than zero, then increase the rate guessed and go to Step (2).

(4) If the net present value in (2) is greater than zero, then reduce the rate guessed and go to Step (2).

(5) Otherwise, the current guess is the implicit rate of return.

The process will converge to the right answer only if one is systematic with the guesses, narrowing the range successively.

A.7     Present values increase when interest rates decrease and present values decrease when interest rates increase.

A.8     6 percent. The present value will be larger the smaller the discount rate.

A.9     (Effective interest rates.)

   a.   12 percent per period; 5 periods.

   b.   6 percent per period; 10 periods.

   c.   3 percent per period; 20 periods.

   d.   1 percent per period; 60 periods.

A.10    a.   $100 × 1.21665 = $121.67.

   b.   $500 × 1.34587 = $672.94.

   c.   $200 × 1.26899 = $253.80.

   d.   $2,500 × (1.74102 × 1.74102) = $7,577.88

            $(1.02)^{56} = (1.02)^{28} × (1.02)^{28}$.

   e.   $600 × 1.43077 = $858.46.

A.11    a.   $100 × .30832 = $30.83.

   b.   $250 × .53063 = $132.66.

   c.   $1,000 × .78757 = $787.57.

A.12    a.   $100 × 14.23683 = $1,423.68.

   b.   $850 × 9.89747 = $8,412.85.

   c.   $400 × 49.96758 = $19,987.03.

A.13    a.   €5,000 × 3.20714 × 1.06 = €16,998.

   b.   €5,000 × 10.06266 × 1.25971 = €63,380.

A.14    a.   €150,000 × .62741 = €94,112.

   b.   €150,000 × .54027 = €81,041.

A.15    a.  $4,000 × 6.97532 = $27,901.

        b.  $4,000 × 7.33593 = $29,344.

A.16    a.  ¥45,000,000/10.63663 = ¥4.23 million.

        b.  ¥45,000,000/12.29969 = ¥3.66 million.

A.17    a.  €90,000 × 14.20679 × 1.05 = €90,000 × (15.91713 − 1.0) = €1,342,542.

        b.  €90,000 × 18.53117 × 1.10 = €90,000 × (21.38428 − 1.0) = €1,834,585.

A.18    a.  £145,000/4.62288 = £31,366.

        b.  £145,000/4.11141 = £35,268.

A.19    a.  (10)  $100 × T(1, 5, 4).

             (11)  $100 × T(2, 30, 4).

             (12)  $100 × T(3, 13, 1.5).

             (13)  DM5,000 × T(1, 20, 6) × T(1, 1, 6) =
                   DM5,000 × T(1, 20, 6) × 1.06 =
                   DM5,000 × T(1, 21, 6)—but this is not in the tables.

             (14)  Fr150,000 × T(2, 8, 6).

        b.  (15)  $4,000 × T(3, 6, 8).

             (16)  ¥45,000,000/T(3, 8, 12).

             (17)  90,000 lira × T(3, 11, 10) × 1.10 =
                   90,000 lira × T(3, 11, 10) × T(1, 1, 10).

             (18)  £145,000/T(4, 6, 12).

        c.  Asking questions about compound interest calculations on examinations presents a difficult logistical problem to teachers. They may want the students to use compound interest tables, but not wish to incur the costs of reproducing them in sufficient numbers for each student to have a copy. They may not wish to give an open book test. This device is useful for posing test questions about compound interest. The device is based on the fact that teachers of accounting are not particularly interested in testing their students' ability to do arithmetic. Teachers want to be sure that students know how to use the tables and calculating devices efficiently in combination. Such a combination suggests that the human do the thinking and the calculator do the multiplications and divisions.

A.20    a.  $1,000(1.00 + .94340) + $2,000(4.21236 − .94340) + $2,500(6.80169 − 4.21236) = $14,955.

        b.  $1,000(1.00 + .92593) + $2,000(3.99271 − .92593) + $2,500(6.24689 − 3.99271) = $13,695.

        c.  $1,000(1.00 + .90909) + $2,000(3.79079 − .90909) + $2,500(5.75902 − 3.79079) = $12,593.

A.21    a.  $3,000 + ($3,000/.06) = $53,000.

        b.  $3,000 + ($3,000/.08) = $40,500.

A.22    a.  $3,000/(.06 − .02) = $75,000.

        b.  $3,000/(.08 − .02) = $50,000.

        c.  [$3,000/(.06) − .02)] × .79209 = $59,406.75.

        d.  [$3,000/(.08 − .02)] × .73503 = $36,751.50.

A.23    a.  $60,000 + ($60,000/.1664) = $420,577.  $(1.08)^2 − 1 = .1664$.

        b.  $60,000 + ($60,000/.2544) = $295,850.  $(1.12)^2 − 1 = .2544$.

A.24    7.00 percent.  Note that $100,000/$55,307 = 1.80809.  See Table 4, 2-period row and observe 1.80809 in the 7-percent column.

A.25    12 percent = $($140,493/$100,000)^{1/3} − 1$.

A.26    a.  16 percent = $($67,280/$50,000)^{1/2} − 1$.

        b.

| Year (1) | Book Value Start of Year (2) | Interest for Year = (2) × .16 (3) | Amount (Reducing) Increasing Book Value (4) | Book Value End of Year = (2) + (3) + (4) (5) |
|---|---|---|---|---|
| 1 | $ 50,000 | $ 8,000 |  | $ 58,000 |
| 2 | 58,000 | 9,280 | $ (67,280) | -0- |

A.27  (Berman Company; find implicit interest rate; construct amortization schedule.)

a.  14.0 percent.

$$\text{Let } x = \frac{\$8,000}{(1+r)} + \frac{\$8,000}{(1+r)^2} + \frac{\$8,000}{(1+r)^3} + \frac{\$100,000}{(1+r)^3} = \$86,000$$

If $r = 14.0$ percent, then $x = \$18,573 + \$67,497 - \$86,000 = \$70$.

If $r = 14.1$ percent, then $x = \$18,542 + \$67,320 - \$86,000 = \$138$.

b.

| Year (1) | Book Value Start of Year (2) | Interest for Year = (2) X .14 (3) | Payment End of Year (Given) (4) | Amount (Reducing) Increasing Book Value = (3) − (4) (5) | Book Value End of Year = (2) + (5) (6) |
|---|---|---|---|---|---|
| 1 | $ 86,000 | $ 12,040 | $ 8,000 | $  4,040 | $ 90,040 |
| 2 | 90,040 | 12,605 | 8,000 | 4,605 | 94,645 |
| 3 | 94,645 | 13,250* | 108,000 | (94,750) | (105) |
| OR 3 | 94,645 | 13,355* | 108,000 | (94,645) | -0- |

*Interest would actually be recorded at $13,355 (= $108,000 − $94,645) so that the book value of the note reduces to zero at its maturity.

A.28  a.  Terms of sale of 2/10, net/30 on a $100 gross invoice price, for example, mean that the interest rate is 2/98 for a 20-day period, because if the discount is not taken, a charge of $2 is levied for the use of $98.  The $98 is used for 20 days (= 30 − 10), so the number of compounding periods in a year is 365/20 = 18.25. The expression for the exact rate of interest implied by 2/10, net 30 is $(1 + 2/98)^{(365/20)} - 1 = 1.020408^{18.25} - 1 = 44.59\%$.

b.  Table 1 can be used.  Use the 2-percent column and the 18-period row to see that the rate implied by 2/10, net 30 must be at least 42.825 percent (= 1.42825 − 1).

A.29  (Present value of a perpetuity).

$30,000 + ($10,000/.01) = $1,030,000.

A.30  Present value of future proceeds = .72845($35,000) + C = $35,000; where C represents the present value of the foregone interest payments.  Table 2, 16-period row, 2-percent column = .72845.

C = $35,000 − $25,495.75 = $9,504.25.

A.31   a.  Will: $24,000 + $24,000(3.31213) = $103,488.72 (Preferred).

Dower Option: $300,000/3 = $100,000.

b.  Will: $24,000 + $24,000(3.03735) = $96,896.40.

Dower Option: $300,000/3 = $100,000 (Preferred).

A.32   Present value of deposit = $3.00.

Present value of $3.00, recorded 20 periods, have discounted at .50 percent per period = $3.00 × .90506 = $2.72.

Loss of $.28 (= $3.00 − $2.72) in foregone interest vs. Loss of $1.20 in price.

Net advantage of returnables is $.92.

A.33   $1.00(1.00 + .92456 + .85480 + .79051 + .73069) = $1.00 × 4.30036 = $4.30.

$4.30 − $3.50 = $.80.

A.34   $600/12 = $50 saved per month.        $2,000/$50 = 40.0.

Present value of annuity of 1 discounted at 1 percent for 50 periods = 39.19612.

The present value of the annuity is $40 when the annuity lasts between 51 and 52 weeks. Dean Foods will recoup its investment in about one year.

A.35   a.  $ 3,000,000 × 7.46944 = $ 22,408,320.

b.  $ 3,000,000 × 7.36578 = $ 22,097,340
           500,000 × 1.69005 = ___845,025
                                 $ 22,942,365

c.  $ 2,000,000 × 7.36578 = $ 14,731,560
         1,000,000 × 2.40183 =   2,401,830
           500,000 × 1.69005 = ___845,025
                                 $ 17,978,415

d.  $17,978,410 × .20     = $   3,595,682.

**A.36** (Friendly Loan Company; find implicit interest rate; truth-in lending laws reduce the type of deception suggested by this problem.)

The effective interest rate is 19.86 percent and must be found by trial and error. The time line for this problem is:

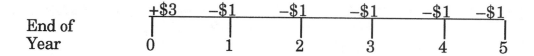

| | +$6,000 | −$2,000 | −$2,000 | −$2,000 | −$2,000 | −$2,000 |
End of
Year

| | 0 | 1 | 2 | 3 | 4 | 5 |

which is equivalent, at least in terms of the implied interest rate, to:

| | +$3 | −$1 | −$1 | −$1 | −$1 | −$1 |
End of
Year

| | 0 | 1 | 2 | 3 | 4 | 5 |

Scanning Table 4, 5-period column, one finds the factor 2.99061, which is approximately 3.00, in the 20-percent column, so one can easily see that the implied interest rate is about 20 percent per year.

**A.37** (Black & Decker Company; derive net present value/cash flows for decision to dispose of asset.)

$40,698. The $100,000 is gone and an economic loss of $50,000 was suffered because of the bad purchase. The issue now is do we want to swap a larger current tax loss and smaller future depreciation charges for no tax loss now and larger future depreciation charges.

The new machine will lead to depreciation charges lower by $10,000 per year than the "old" machine and, hence, income taxes larger by $4,000. The present value of the larger taxes is $4,000 × 3.60478 (Table 4, 12 percent, 5 periods). Let S denote the proceeds from selling the old machine. The new current "outlay" to acquire the new machine is $50,000 − S − .40($100,000 − S) or $10,000 − .60S, so that for the new machine to be worthwhile:

$$\$10,000 - .60S < -\$14,419$$

OR

$$.6S > \$24,419$$

OR

$$S > \$40,698.$$

A.38    (Lynch Company/Bages Company; computation of present value of cash flows; untaxed acquisition, no change in tax basis of assets.)

a.   $440,000 = $390,000 + $50,000 = $700,000 − $260,000.

b.   $3,745,966 = $440,000 × 8.51356; see Table 4, 20-period column, 10-percent row.

A.39    (Lynch Company/Bages Company; computation of present value of cash flows; taxable acquisition, changing tax basis of assets.)

$4,258,199. If the merger is taxable, then the value of the firm V satisfies:

$$
\begin{aligned}
(1) \qquad V &= 8.51356 \times [\$700{,}000 - .40(\$700{,}000 - V/20)] \\
V &= \$5{,}959{,}492 - \$2{,}383{,}797 + .17027V, \text{ or} \\
.83972V &= \$3{,}575{,}695, \text{ so} \\
V &= \$4{,}258{,}199.
\end{aligned}
$$

To understand (1), observe that:

$$
\begin{aligned}
V &= \text{Value of firm} \\
V/20 &= \text{New depreciation charge} \\
\$700{,}000 - V/20 &= \text{New taxable income} \\
.40(\$700{,}000 - V/20) &= \text{New income tax payable, so} \\
\$700{,}000 - .40(\$700{,}000 - V/20) &= \text{New aftertax cash flow to be capitalized at 10 percent for 20 years using present value factor 8.51356.}
\end{aligned}
$$

A.40 (Ragazze; analysis of benefits of acquisition of long-term assets.)

a. $270,831.

| Dec. 31 Year | Cash Inflows | | Cash Outflows | | Total | Present Values at 12% | |
|---|---|---|---|---|---|---|---|
| | Operating Receipts (1) | Salvage (2) | Maintenance (3) | Test Runs (4) | (1) + (2) − (3) − (4) (5) | Factor (6) | Cash Flow (7) |
| 0 | | | | | | | |
| 1 | | | | $ 20,000 | $ (20,000) | 0.89286 | $ (17,857) |
| 2 | $ 130,000 | | $ 60,000 | | 70,000 | 0.79719 | 55,804 |
| 3 | 130,000 | | 60,000 | | 70,000 | 0.71178 | 49,825 |
| 4 | 130,000 | | 60,000 | | 70,000 | 0.63552 | 44,486 |
| 5 | 130,000 | | 60,000 | | 70,000 | 0.56743 | 39,720 |
| 6 | 130,000 | | 100,000 | | 30,000 | 0.50663 | 15,199 |
| 7 | 130,000 | | 100,000 | | 30,000 | 0.45235 | 13,570 |
| 8 | 130,000 | | 100,000 | | 30,000 | 0.40388 | 12,116 |
| 9 | 130,000 | $ 30,000 | | | 160,000 | 0.36061 | 57,698 |
| | | | | | | | $ 270,831 |

(7) = (5) × (6).

b. $78,868 = $250,000/3.16987.

A.41    (Valuation of intangibles with perpetuity formulas.)

a.  $50 million = $4 million/.08.

b.  Increase.

c.  $66 2/3 million = $4 million/(.08 − .02).

d.  Increase.

e.  Decrease.

A.42    See following page.

A.43    (Horrigan Corporation; Perpetuity Growth Model Derivation of Results to Appendix to Chapter 5.)  (Dollar Amounts in Millions)

| End of Year | Present Value Factor for End of Year 4 [Table 2] | Excess Cash to Owners [Column 5 on Page 290] | | Present Value Dollars for End of Year 4 [Column 6 on Page 290] |
|---|---|---|---|---|
| 4 | 1.00000 | | | |
| 5 | 0.83333 | $    7.0 | | $        5.8 |
| 6 | 0.69444 | 24.0 | | 16.7 |
| 7 | 0.57870 | 55.0 | | 31.8 |
| 8 | 0.48225 | 109.0 | | 52.5 |
| 9 | 0.40188 | 204.0 | | 82.0 |
| 9 | 0.40188 | 2,856.0 | = 1.12 x $204/(.20 − .12)..... | 1,147.8 |
| | | | Sum of above......................... | $   1,336.6 |
| | | | Shares Outstanding ............ | 16.0 |
| | | | Present Value per Share.... | $      83.54 |

At the end of Year 9, the present value of a stream of $204 received in arrears, growing at 12 percent per year, with first cash flow equal to $204 x 1.12 = $228.48 is:

$$1.12 \text{ x } \$204/(.20 − .12) = \$228.48/.08 = \$2,856.0.$$

The calculations then reduce that $2,856.0 to present value at the end of Year 4.

A.42 (Gulf Coast Manufacturing; choosing between investment alternatives.)

## Basic Data Repeated from Problem

| | Lexus | Mercedes-Benz |
|---|---|---|
| Initial Cost at the Start of Year 1 | $ 60,000 | $45,000 |
| Initial Cost at the Start of Year 4 | | 48,000 |
| Trade-in Value | | |
| End of Year 3 | | 23,000 |
| End of Year 6 [Note A] | 16,000 | 24,500 |
| Estimated Annual Cash Operating Costs, Except Major Servicing | 4,000 | 4,500 |
| Estimated Cash Cost of Major Servicing | | |
| End of Year 4 | 6,500 | |
| End of Year 2 and End of Year 5 | | 2,500 |

Note A:
At this time Lexus is 6 years old; second Mercedes-Benz is 3 years old.

## Present Value Computations

| | Factor | Source [B] | Lexus | Mercedes-Benz |
|---|---|---|---|---|
| Initial Cost at the Start of Year 1 | 1.00000 | | $ 60,000 | $ 45,000 |
| Initial Cost at the Start of Year 4 | 0.75131 | T[2,3,.10] | | 36,063 |
| Trade-in Value | | | | |
| End of Year 3 | 0.75131 | T[2,3,.10] | | (17,280) |
| End of Year 6 [Note A] | 0.56447 | T[2,6,.10] | (9,032) | (13,830) |
| Estimated Annual Cash Operating Costs, Except Major Servicing | 4.35526 | T[4,6,.10] | 17,421 | 19,599 |
| Estimated Cash Cost of Major Servicing | | | | |
| End of Year 4 | 0.68301 | T[2,4,.10] | 4,440 | |
| End of Year 2 and End of Year 5 | 0.82645 | T[2,2,.10] | | 2,066 |
| | 0.62092 | T[2,5,.10] | | 1,552 |
| Sum of Present Values of All Costs | | | $ 72,829 | $ 73,170 |

[B]T[i,j,r] means Table i (= Table 2 or Table 4) from the back of the book, row j, interest rate r.

a. Strategy L, buying one Lexus has lower present value of costs, but the difference is so small that we'd encourage the CEO to go with his whim, whatever it may be. Also, the relatively new theory of real options will likely prefer Strategy M because it gives the owner more choices at the end of the third year.

b. Depreciation plays no role, so long as we ignore income taxes. Only cash flows matter.